Ross, John; Ross, James Clark

Narrative of a second voyage

in search of a north-west passage

Ross, John; Ross, James Clark

Narrative of a second voyage

in search of a north-west passage

Inktank publishing, 2018

www.inktank-publishing.com

ISBN/EAN: 9783747750995

APPENDIX

TO THE

NARRATIVE

OF A

SECOND VOYAGE IN SEARCH

OF A

NORTH-WEST PASSAGE,

AND OF A

RESIDENCE IN THE ARCTIC REGIONS

DURING THE YEARS 1829, 1830, 1831, 1832, 1833.

BY

SIR JOHN ROSS, *C.B.*, *K.S.A.*, *K.C.S.* &c. &c.

CAPTAIN IN THE ROYAL NAVY.

INCLUDING THE REPORTS OF

COMMANDER, NOW CAPTAIN, JAMES CLARK ROSS, *R.N.*, *F.R.S.*, *F.L.S.*, &c.

AND

The Discovery of the Northern Magnetic Pole.

LONDON:

A. W. WEBSTER, 156, REGENT STREET.

1835.

CONTENTS.

LIST OF PLATES FOR THE APPENDIX.

PREFACE.

The narrative of my late voyage in search of a north-west passage, having been increased in its length far beyond my expectations, it became necessary to reserve for the Appendix every thing which did not actually belong to the work itself. I have to regret, therefore, that matter of much importance to myself has consequently been postponed; among which I may mention the two following letters, which having been already published in the newspapers, for the purpose of showing to the public that I was not ungrateful for the sympathy so universally manifested towards me and my companions.

I had, indeed, deemed them an unnecessary addition to the narrative itself, but certainly not without the intention of again gratifying my feelings by publishing them, and some others, a second time, in justice to myself and to those whose humane endeavours cannot be too often or too fully acknowledged.

A

To the Committee for the Management of the Affairs of Captain Back's Expedition.

Portland Hotel, London, October 26, 1833.

GENTLEMEN,

Of the many circumstances of high gratification which have welcomed the delivery of myself and companions from four years' severe suffering, there is nothing (next after a deep sense of the merciful Providence wherewith we have been surrounded in such great perils) which has excited in me so strong a feeling of gratitude, as the humane and generous sympathy of a number of persons who, at the chance of being instrumental in our preservation, contributed, with the assistance of his Majesty's government, a sum, ample for the purpose of paying the expense of an expedition, which was so promptly and with so much judgment put in motion by your committee, and so wisely confided to the guidance of Captain Back, whose known intelligence and intrepidity gave the committee a certainty that all would be done which a sagacious mind and unflinching perseverance could accomplish.

It is my wish and duty to make the earliest acknowledgment, of this instance of wide-extended compassion towards us, and I venture to rely on the favour of the committee, to receive with allowance, this imperfect expression of my feelings towards them, to his Majesty's government, to the contributors to the undertaking, and to the Hudson's Bay Company, for efforts which might have proved, as designed, the means of snatching myself and my faithful companions from the further sufferings which, almost to the last moment, we seemed doomed to encounter.

I have the honour to be,

Gentlemen,

Your very humble and grateful servant,

JOHN ROSS, Capt. R.N.

Arctic Land Expedition.—Answer.

21, Regent Street, October 22, 1833.

Sir,

I have the honour to acknowledge the receipt of your letter dated the 20th inst. addressed to the Committee for managing the Arctic Land Expedition, and returning your thanks to its members, to the Hudson's Bay Company, and to all the Subscribers towards the equipment of that expedition, for the exertions made by them in hopes of rescuing you and your brave companions from your perilous situation.

In reply, I beg, in the name of the committee and of all the subscribers, to offer you our warmest congratulations on your safe return; and although the main object of Captain Back's expedition is thus attained without his assistance, yet we feel much gratified that it should have gone, inasmuch as it proves to all future adventurers in a like career, that their country will not be unmindful of them; while, on the other hand, your return also

A 2

shows that no situation should be considered too desperate to be beyond the reach of a similar exertion.

I have the honour to be,

Sir,

Your most obedient servant,

CHARLES OGLE, Chairman.

To Captain John Ross, Royal Navy.

The above correspondence requires no comment, as they must fully convey to the public the feelings of both parties. I have now to introduce the two following letters, which were originally intended to precede the narrative, but which were omitted for reasons already mentioned.

Victory Discovery Ship, Union Dock,
London, March 28, 1829.

Sir,

I request you will have the goodness to submit to the Lords Commissioners of the Admiralty, that I am about to undertake a voyage of discovery at the entire cost of myself and others, and in event of complete success in the discovery of a north-west passage, and subsequently falling in with his Majesty's ships of war, or those belonging to foreign nations, it may be proper and necessary that I should have on board a document to prove that my vessel is navigated, and my expedition undertaken with the approbation and good wishes of the Lords Commissioners of the Admiralty, and feeling assured of their Lordships' encouragement and protection.

I have the honour to remain,

Sir,

Your most obedient servant,

JOHN ROSS, Capt. R.N.

To the Right Hon. J. W. Croker, &c. &c. &c.

Answer.

Admiralty Office, March 23, 1829.

Sir,

Having laid before my Lords Commissioners of the Admiralty your letter of this day's date, stating that you are about to undertake a voyage of discovery at the entire cost of yourself and others, and in the event of complete success in the discovery of a north-west passage, and subsequently falling in with his Majesty's ships of war or others belonging to foreign states, it would be desirable that you should possess a document to prove that your vessel is navigated, and your expedition undertaken, with the approbation and good wishes of their Lordships, I have it in command to express their Lordship's approbation and good wishes relative to the expedition in question, and also their authority to you to state the same.

I am, Sir,

Your obedient servant,

J. W. CROKER.

To Captain Ross, R.N.
Victory Discovery Ship, Union Dock.

The next article, which I trust will be read with interest, is an additional Sketch of the Esquimaux, whom we discovered in Boothia Felix, and whom we named Boothians. This is given as an introduction to the biography of the most remarkable, whose portraits are given to represent both their colour, features, and costume, and, I may add, of the inhabitants of the most remote corner of the globe: added to which are a vocabulary and dialogues in the Esquimaux, Danish, and English languages, carefully corrected by my friend, Mr. Kijer, according to the works of Fabricius. The reports on Chronometers, which follow, will be perused with attention by every practical navigator, as well as the reports on the various instruments which accompanied the expedition.

My new theory of the Aurora is respectfully submitted to the public, as the result of a long series of observations carefully made under very advantageous circumstances, in Scotland, as well as during my late residence of four winters in the Arctic Regions, and have been read at the British Association in Dublin.

The Natural History has been compiled by Commander (now Captain) James Clark Ross, whose acquirements in that branch of science are well known and acknowledged; and it will there be found manifest that something has been done which must interest the naturalist.

I have preferred giving my own observations on the Diurnal Variation and Dip of the Magnetic Needle, to those of Commander Ross, understanding that his will appear elsewhere. The Geology is somewhat defective, from the impossibility of bringing home specimens from the most interesting places; but the Meteorological Tables, which have been kept according to the plan suggested by Captain Beaufort, are submitted to the public as the most complete of the kind ever published.

The Surgeon's Report, and the Analyses of several Fluids, and the State of the Provisions which we found, require no comment. These, with the Philosophical Observations, will be read with interest.

In the Tables of Latitude and Longitude of places on the newly-discovered coast, I have given in *italics* the names which the natives gave them, for which there was not room in the chart, and which will effectually correct the discrepances and omissions, which have been noticed by the subscribers, but which was occasioned by my unavoidable absence, and by my not being in possession of Commander Ross's narrative until long after the chart was printed and approved of by his Majesty; to whom it was submitted by Commander Ross and myself, on our arrival, with *no names affixed.*

I ought also to observe that Sir Felix Booth, with whose

permission it was thus submitted, had, as the owner of the ship, the just and exclusive right of giving names to every place. In justice to the crew, I have added a short Biographical Sketch of each; and I have concluded this work by giving a List of my generous Subscribers, with my most grateful thanks.

NIMNA HIMNA

SKETCH

OF THE

ESQUIMAUX FOUND IN THE TERRITORY OF BOOTHIA FELIX.

AS it has appeared to many of my readers, that the account I have given of the natives of Boothia in the Narrative of my Voyage was more limited than it ought, or would have been, had circumstances permitted—and that correct portraits displaying their features and dress—which I could not afford to give at greater length in the narrative would be acceptable in this portion of the work, I have commenced it, in the first place with a general sketch, and secondly with the individual description and history to accompany and explain each of the drawings.

I need not dwell much on their manners and customs, nor enter into any great details respecting their arts and inventions; since I could add little to what is already well known, and need not repeat what can be found in many books. As to their personal appearance, including, with their stature, forms,

B

and physiognomy, their dresses, it so accurately resembles that of the other tribes of Esquimaux so often described, that I may almost pass it over, while referring to the different plates in this volume, and their accompanying explanations.

I had abundant reason, in the first place, to believe that the natives of this spot, uniting with these a few with whom we had but a temporary and slender communication, were entirely unacquainted with Europeans: while the nearest approach to any knowledge of them was, to have conversed with some one who had conversed with a third person who had seen them at Igloolik, and, possibly, elsewhere. Nor was this contradicted by their possession of a few European knives. Of these, they had indeed but three; nor did those on which the maker's mark could be traced, permit our believing that they had been obtained from Sir Edward Parry. In reality, they admitted themselves to have possessed those for a "very long time," while unable to explain whence they had been obtained; so that no conclusions of any kind could be drawn from this circumstance.

Thus ignorant of civilized society, they were equally unacquainted with the warlike tribes of America; whether those of their own race, or the races which are included under the general term Indians. The peculiar insulation of the tract to which they confine themselves, is not only the cause of this, but is likely to operate henceforward, without interruption. While that tract is sufficient to give room for their summer and winter migrations, it supplies all their wants, and therefore leaves them no temptation to wander eastward, where they might possibly hereafter come into contact with Europeans: while the nature of the country surrounding the isthmus which divides them from the larger mass of the continent of America, together with that of the country which must be traversed to reach this, as effectually precludes the visits of the Indians and the western Esquimaux, as it checks any desire on their parts to roam beyond their present limits.

Excepting, therefore, the people whom I found in 1818, and whom I termed Arctic Highlanders, the natives of this spot form the narrowest and most insulated tribe of men that has yet been discovered by navigators: a fact which gives interest to whatever their characters may present. Here, if any where, we ought therefore to find how the human mind is developed under the narrowest education, in what manner the "light of nature" as it is termed, operates on the moral character and conduct, and how far human reason can proceed, under the smallest possible quantity of materials to act on, and under a very narrow range of application. If also there are peculiarities of character, whether for good or evil, the moralist and metaphysician may here speculate on what belongs to the original mental constitution of these people, and what is derived from their narrow and limited intercourse with their own species, in a society so restricted in numbers, and so incapable of changing customs or altering habits, where there is nothing beyond themselves to see, and no one to imitate.

Whatever species of purity this may imply, the vices which they possess must, like their virtues, be those that originate among themselves: the natural produce of the human passions, acting where there is no control from religion, from the belief of an omnipotent Creator and Governor; and where checked, subject to none but those checks which the mutual convenience of the society renders necessary. It is at least certain that they had never possessed the opportunity of acquiring the vices of civilization when we first knew them; but I cannot confidently affirm that they learned no evil from us.

If the fondness of the Esquimaux race for their children has been noted by those who have preceded us in these regions, it is a portion of their character which has been amply confirmed by our own observations on the present tribe. The testimonies of this never failed; nor could they be flattered and gratified more than by the attentions and caresses bestowed by us on their offspring. It equally confirms prior observations to say, that we never saw any chastisement administered, nor ever witnessed even harsh language to them; while, in return, the children are affectionate, attached, and obedient. To say more on this subject would indeed be but to repeat what has already been noticed by Captain Lyon, in many instances, in his account of other tribes.

But there was one material point in which I must differ from my predecessors: though indeed I cannot call this differing, since each of us can but note what he has seen. It only follows, that from some cause, which neither I, nor they, I imagine, can assign, the people of this district differ in a very material point of character from those with whom they were so well acquainted; as the superiority, in a very high degree, lies with those whose feelings and practices we had occasion to study. The facts, on both sides, were noted; and though I should not make the deductions myself, they could be made by any reader.

It cannot be forgotten, by those who have interested themselves in the history of the people of Igloolik, that the aged parent was neglected, and that the helpless or widowed females in particular, were not simply suffered to starve, but robbed of their little property. We had not the means of studying a very numerous tribe, and, of course, many facts could not have come under our notice; but, such as they were, they could not have been exceptions, since they seemed consistent with the whole feelings and course of the community, and may, therefore, be safely taken as instances of general character and practice. Not to name mere instances, we found the aged Illiktu drawn on a sledge by his companions, when the old man above alluded to was suffered to walk as he best could; as was equally the case with Tulluahiu, whom we supplied with a wooden leg to replace his loss. If the ancient wife of the former was as well clothed and fed as any of the rest of the tribe, it was more remarkable to find two old and destitute females in the same good condition, and as well taken care of in every manner as if they were still of use.

If this feature of their character removes from these people that charge of most disgusting selfishness and inhumanity which rests with so much justice on those of Igloolik, according to the published accounts, I need but notice, that there exists here the same custom of adoption as in that tribe, with the same consequences and practices, on both sides. If there was aught of difference, in any respect, it did not fall under our cognizance.

I do not know that there were any differences between the state of the connubial relations and practices in this place and at Igloolik, or wherever else these have been remarked; while there has been a little obscurity in some of the accounts of this subject. It is my business, at any rate, to relate what came to our knowledge.

A state of celibacy is unknown: the mere supposition of such a condition is treated as a chimera, nor did they know how to believe that any of us could be without wives. Every woman therefore finds a husband, as every man procures a wife: but, often, inevitably, under a system of polygamy; since the sexes cannot always be equal in numbers. The rule also appears to be, if it be not rather a natural arrangement than a law, that the most expert hunters obtain the superfluous women, as best able to maintain them; though we did not know of any instance of a man possessing more than two wives; of which the first, or eldest, is the senior in command and respect. In the same way, it is the strongest or most useful woman who most readily obtains a second husband: while, under either mode of this polygamy, or, possibly, only bigamy, the most perfect harmony seems always to subsist among the parties. If, never witnessing any angry word between husband and wife, and seeing each for ever treating the other with indulgence and frankness, we were willing to conclude that these people had attained that perfection of domestic happiness which is so rarely found any where, it is a conclusion, I fear, that reflection would not justify, and that a more intimate experience perhaps would not have confirmed.

The forms of matrimony seemed here not to differ from what has been observed in other tribes of the Esquimaux, excepting that the young female must make her choice as soon as she is marriageable—but, the contract, such as it is, is settled between the parents for their children, and often at a very early age: the time of marriage seems to be about the age of fifteen; and there is no other form but that of the female going to the hut of her destined husband.

I believe that the practice of repudiation and change, whether of husbands or wives, has been found in all the Esquimaux who have come under the notice of navigators. Be that as it may, it is the custom in this district, though it was not easy to trace the extent to which it is carried. How far it may depend on satiety or disagreement, we could not discover, or on the desire of change, or on more improper feelings, on either side: but where the morals and the feelings are both so extremely lax on this subject as we found them, it would be an idle and silly defence of this or any other mode of the savage condition, to suppose that vice, or what at least we must consider such, was a frequent source of this practice. It has been the custom, on one side, to overrate the virtues of savage nations, and, on the other, to exaggerate their vices. These things must be left to the novelist, and to the navigator who desires to emulate him, for the sake of producing an effect; to the false philanthropist and the lover of paradox; and to him whose temper may have been soured by such collision, or who may have commenced with a prejudice distorting all that he saw. But the passions of our nature will strive to break forth, under all the restraints that society and religion can impose; and how should they not actually reign, where there is neither to check their operation, where there is nothing to say, This is wrong; still more, where there is no inconvenience contemplated, to balance that which is gratifying, and may also be convenient?

But if there is no vice where there are no religion and no moral law to say, This is disobedience to God, and where custom and admission say that no injury is committed against our fellow-creatures, then is there also no vice in that want of chastity which is as remarkable here as it has been found among all the scattered tribes of the Esquimaux on the American shores. Who is there among the moralists to settle this question? Be it determined as it may, that "moral sense" on this subject, which is so generally diffused, is here deficient; since it is grossly unjust to attribute to selfishness alone, the respect entertained for chastity in the female sex; in whatever manner the value of this in the other is judged of. The Esquimaux of Igloolik, at least, are proved to be in the last degree selfish: yet the virtue in question is held, by them, in no repute.

We at least must speak as we, under civilization, feel. The conduct of the present people, as of all the rest of this race, is not more pure than that of the brute beasts: it is far less so than that of the pairing animals. But I need not dwell on a disgusting and improper subject: it has been told once; and it must suffice that it has been once told.

If I have already noticed the custom of adoption, I need not dwell on it: the reasons are the expected services from the subsidiary child: and the new attachment, on both sides, is equal to that between the natural parent and progeny. Thus also it is, that the widow with children, most especially if those are boys, becomes a prize, be her age what it may compared to that of the suitor; since these become equally the property of the husband and bound to support both.

Respecting their treatment of dead relations, or of the dead in general, we had a good opportunity of judging; as two deaths occurred within our experience. Illictu, the old man, was long left in the hut where he died, and would have been devoured by foxes and bears, had we not interred his remains. The incision found in his abdomen was unquestionably made after death: but we never learned its purpose, and could not conjecture whether it was a superstitious practice. The boy who had been killed by a stone was not found, and we were ignorant what became of him. But as we observed many graves in different places, it is evident that those who formerly inhabited this country conformed, in this, to those of other tribes. On his death, there was an appearance of much despair, ending in anger directed toward us: but we had reason to understand that their lamentations for death, though severe, were soon over, nor could we hear of any ceremonies used on this occasion or on that of a funeral.

C

That these people are as egregiously conceited as all other savage tribes, can be no matter of surprise, when it is the character, not of nations alone, but of individuals, to be conceited in proportion to their ignorance. The land which they inhabit was, of course, the best of all possible lands; and it was equally matter of course, that those who had been born at one spot should extol its superiority over every other in the same district. But this is the attachment to home: it is what no sound moralist should blame, notwithstanding its occasional inconveniences, political or otherwise; since it is that source of happiness and contentment which has been beneficently given to all mankind, in whatever situation necessity or expediency has placed them. We were quite content, ourselves, that they should prefer a covering of snow to the green face of nature, and should make themselves happy with blubber, oil, and sleep; nor indeed would it be easy to dispute most of those points with them, when they could travel easier than we, could house themselves with a hundredth part of the labour, could find delights where we experienced only suffering, could outdo us in killing the seal, could regale on abundant food where we should starve because we could not endure it, and found ours as nauseous to them as theirs was to us.

That they have never known war, it is perhaps superfluous to state, but it was interesting to discover in what light they considered the crime of murder, to which some punishment has been assigned by every people, in whatever condition. We could only, however, hear of one instance on record; where, in a quarrel about the division of a reindeer, one of the disputants had stabbed the other. What we could understand was, that the murderer's punishment consisted in being banished to perpetual solitude, or shunned by every individual of the tribe; insomuch that even his sight was avoided by those who might inadvertently meet him. When asked why his life was not taken in return, it was replied that this would be to make themselves equally bad, that the loss of his life would not restore the other; and that he who should commit such an act would be held equally guilty. To these arguments, I imagine, no reply could easily be made, where there was no positive law to quote, within the compass of their understanding: but it would not be easy to deny that they carried in them an air of reflection and of humanity not undeserving of praise.

It could not be conjectured that any one of the tribe possessed authority over the rest, that there was any one in the nature of a patriarch, where there was no chief. If superior age or talents commanded any respect, neither of these appeared to possess any influence. There seemed not the slightest approach, even to that insensible government, which, generally, in some manner, acts so as to unite a tribe in one common pursuit, or to combine them in a single society, so that the conduct of the whole, in their migrations and occupations, is similar and simultaneous. Here, every family decamped and travelled as its own views or caprices dictated; all being as independent as they seemed, since each could soon construct its own habitation without the aid of others, and proceed to procure its own sustenance without the help of society.

The selfishness of this race, as known to Sir Edward Parry, cannot be more strongly marked than he has done it in his description of his intercourse with them. It admits of no dispute: yet such was not the character of the present tribe. I have already said that they paid as much attention to the aged and destitute as could have been done by any civilized people: and we had opportunities of observing, that so far from seeking the exclusive gratification of their own hunger or appetites, (the ever ready and most marked test of animal selfishness,) they were always ready to divide their provisions, even where they had not enough for the next day, with those who were in want.

The striking and most repulsive want of gratitude in those who came under the cognizance of that observer, was certainly not evinced by the present tribe. So far from this, our experience led us to assign them a character the very reverse: though the virtue of gratitude, if it be practically esteemed a virtue, as men may safely doubt, is not so very abounding or so much cultivated, even under civilization and the lights of morals and religion, as to have led to any great censure of these people had they been without it. If those against whom the charge of ingratitude has been, and with unquestionable justice, brought, are what men ought not to be, there is that to be recollected, which, though not an exculpation, forms a solution of an imagined difficulty, which has possibly been overlooked: in civilized society, it is acknowledged and admitted that ingratitude is a vice: but it is a profitable or an advantageous one, and, while practised as such, it becomes necessary to conceal or suppress, as far as that is possible, the open and shameless display. The "children of nature," as they are, customarily, though very idly termed, go direct to the mark which others reach in a more circuitous and hidden manner: there is no check, from opinion, or usage, or morality: it is a convenient or profitable usage, and the shortest road to the desired end is taken. Where the extreme of self-love forms the basis of a character, whether it be that of a whole tribe at Igloolik, or of an individual in England, ingratitude becomes an affair of course: it is a portion of the same virtue, where it is the custom to consider selfishness as the most needful of those, and thus, under such a code of brute morality, the most laudable.

Be the fact as it may, however, as far as these general views are concerned, we must have been egregiously deceived, or, possibly, have contributed to our own deception, if the tribe of our acquaintance, here, did not display as much gratitude as could have been expected any where, if they did not impress us with the conviction that this formed a portion of a character which appeared in general so amiable, or, at the very least, so unexceptionable.

It is not only, that, far exceeding the usual short and dry form of thanks, so general among this race, they seemed truly sensible of the favours conferred; but the impression was found to remain. The thanks were renewed long after the services had been rendered, and when, according to the common course of things, these should have been forgotten; while they were often accompanied by a free gift of some kind. It is but a part of the same character, that they were ever ready to confess a fault, and to make reparation, as they best could, either by apology, or restoration, or services; while ever seeming uneasy till they were forgiven and restored to favour.

I may indulge in relating one petty history, by which this part of their character will be better illustrated than by any general statements, and I have no right to consider it the exception, rather than the rule, where no similar opportunity offered; since it seemed to be consistent with their general character; and in other points than this.

It had been settled, early in the spring, that Ooblooria and Awack, the son and nephew of Ikmallik, should provide themselves with a sledge, dogs, and provisions, and accompany Commander Ross, who was to furnish his own supplies and carriage, and to proceed to Neitchillee, about fifty miles off, under their guidance. They accordingly came, at the appointed time, which was fixed by counting on the fingers, and by drawing on the snow the appearance which the moon would then present; the stipulated quota of provisions being for five days.

On arriving, however, they found that four families, including some relations, were hutted near the ship, and had been unsuccessful in their hunting; on which they unpacked their sledges, and gave up so much of their stores as only to leave themselves enough for two days. This was barely sufficient to carry them on to Neitchillee, yet not enough to maintain them during their return; but they had expected to find a deposit of fish at that place. Unluckily, a storm of snow detained the whole party; and, in the calculated time, the provisions of the guides were exhausted. The needful supply was therefore given them from our own stores, which they promised to replace on their arrival at Neitchillee.

Here, however, when they at length arrived, their deposits could not be found, from the mass of snow by which they had been overwhelmed; in consequence of which they were again supplied with food enough to enable them to return to the ship. Here they related all that had been done for them, with the strongest expressions of gratitude; adding that their parents would come and thank Commander Ross, when he returned, for the kindness which he had shown. This was done on the next day, by our furnishing the means of that journey after we had accommodated them on board for the night; when the father and mother arrived with a present of seal-skins of the best quality, and an offer to make them up into the water-proof boots for which they were intended; while they seemed exceedingly pleased that we accepted them without offering any remuneration. In a few days they returned with the manufactured articles; nor did their gratitude end even then, since it was often expressed afterwards, and, even at the distance of four months, with a promise of a similar pair when the ship should arrive at Neitchillee.

If the Esquimaux race has often been noted for cheerfulness and good temper, we found that confirmed here. Under the latter quality, if kind in their domestic relations, as I formerly noticed, so were they to their dogs; unlike to many of their fraternity, who have been noticed for their ill-treatment of these useful animals.

That these dogs were in bad training, was a natural consequence. Their cheerfulness was often vivacity, so that we might consider them a lighthearted people; and they seemed to possess great command of temper. The only show of resentment for what was thought an offence, was silence, after which they commonly left us and returned to their homes.

The thievish propensities of savage nations are familiar: there is not a voyager's narrative which does not dwell on them; and such excuses or defences have been made as these narrators could best contrive. I need not repeat the satirical defence which asks, what civilized Europeans, under equal temptations, and no restraints from divine or human laws, would act in a different manner. It seems a very simple question after all. Here, at least, whatever it may be elsewhere, there is no written divine law against theft, nor does there appear to be any moral sense which says that it is, abstractedly, and universally, wrong. Human laws there are none; and there can therefore be no check but that of the inconvenience: as some modern pedants write, they are governed by the principle of utility. But while there is much convenience in acquiring the coveted property, there is no counterbalancing evil: the society suffers nothing, while many or all may gain. The case of a wreck on our own shores is not essentially different: the resemblance to an enemy's town subjected to plunder is still more perfect. The thefts of savages are a warfare on property which seems placed in their power; it has been open warfare and bloodshed whenever they have dared; and when too feeble, it is such plunder as is attainable, without hazard, and by whatever dexterity. That such is the principle by which they are guided in this case of theft, seems indeed fully proved by the fact that they do not rob each other; the evil in such a case would be felt and remedied.

The reasoning of these Esquimaux, however, seemed of a different nature, and of a more "liberal" character: it has often been used in far other lands, and has been considerably acceptable to the multitude, before the days of Wat Tyler and since; as it is a rule of action for him who pilfers a book from a library or a rare shell from a cabinet. Not only are the sea and the land, with the animals which they bear, the common property of those who want them, but the same is true of every thing which can be found on the face of the earth. It is the want alone, therefore, with the power of using, which constitutes the right to possession: but it is a corollary from the general argument, which might not be so acceptable to those who use it among ourselves, under which they restore the stolen article when they find the original owner to be in want of it.

In this manner did they practically conduct themselves toward us. No secret was made of the theft among themselves, so that the knowledge soon came to the owner, to whom the stolen article was returned on demanding it. Nor were the accusation, and the term thief, more than a matter of merriment: though after we had taken some trouble to explain to them that to steal was "bad," very few instances of a similar nature occurred. In one case, the husband, aware of his wife's propensities, always brought back what she had taken away.

The extremely envious disposition of some of the Esquimaux has

D

been noticed, among their other faults. I must not be quite sure that we were not inclined to see every thing here in the most favourable light: but while admitting that every man wished to possess, by purchase, whatever his neighbour had obtained, we did not observe any workings of that bad passion in this desire.

We did not observe any propensity to falsehood, or disposition to deceive; and, on every occasion, there seemed a desire to communicate all the information in their power, while, as far as we examined, this also proved correct. It was on the same principle, that we could always trust their promises; there was the "point of honour" engaged; and on the only occasion on which they broke one, in not keeping an appointment as guides, they long after accused themselves of "being very bad" for not giving notice; though, to have done so, would have been to lose a day of their hunting when they were without provisions.

Such is the little we could discover or infer respecting the moral character of these people. It ought not to be an unexpected one, considering the mild dispositions of this race in general, and the circumstances in which they are placed in this narrow community and district. May I not say that it is a good one, and that the man of these lands may be considered a "virtuous savage?" May I ask where are the civilized communities in which there is a more favourable balance of the vices and virtues? since it is thus, and not by the varied action of either, that this question must be judged. This at least I may say, that the all-wise and beneficent Creator has not neglected this race, and that in giving them the means of animal happiness united to the desires which prefer those means to all others, he has also, in his own way, instilled into them such principles as tend to preserve their moral happiness and order: while it is not for man to say in what manner he will hereafter judge those who have obeyed the impulses to good, and those who have indulged the propensities to evil.

But, of Him, they have no knowledge: in this they resemble all their unconverted brethren of the same great tribe; while I need not repeat the remarks so often made on this subject. Like others, we found nothing that even approximated to this wide-spread piece of knowledge; and could only conclude that their opinions respecting a future state coincided with those which prevail among the Esquimaux at large. If they were influenced by any superstitions which have a reference to a Providence or a future life, we did not discover them: and though possessing an angekok, like all the others, he did not seem to be treated with much deference or any respect.

We discovered in them a strong propensity to imitation and to mimicry: a property which they converted to immediate use, in learning to feed themselves in the same manner as we did, and with the same utensils; and under which also they sometimes amused themselves in aping our gait and manners: above all, in the English custom of uselessly walking up and down under the notion of exercise: a practice which they could as little comprehend as the Orientals, to whom it is so often a subject of wonder.

This principle extended also to drawing, in which, even with our pencils, they were speedily proficients: while further rendering this talent very useful to us, in delineating the geography of the country; as has been found equally common in the other tribes of

D 2

these people. All their geographical knowledge seemed very accurate; and, to every river, hill, bay, or lake, there was a name: while it seemed to give them great pleasure to be able to communicate this information.

Notwithstanding the vanity which made them prefer whatever was there own, despising, or affecting to despise, even our guns, in comparison with their own weapons, they were very desirous to know the name and use of every thing; nor had we any difficulty in making them comprehend the latter, in spite of our ignorance of their language. I must, in reality, consider them as an acute-minded people, who would be ready, after a little while, to receive instruction, and probably to adopt some inventions, and customs also, as far as these could be admissible under the circumstances in which they are placed.

Of their intellectual faculties, beyond these points, it is difficult to form any judgment, so limited is the scope for the exertion of those; nor can I refer to aught more than their dexterity in hunting, and the practice of those useful arts which I shall immediately notice. But they are an energetic and active people; and though given to great excess in eating, like all others of their race, never appearing to give way to pure indolence, even when well fed. On the contrary, they seemed always busied in something, even when at home: as some of us were inclined to think that much of their eating arose rather from the necessity of doing something than from appetite.

In procuring their food, they seemed also more provident and systematic than the Esquimaux have generally been found.

Nothing can be more regular and orderly than their migrations from one place to another, in pursuit of the different kinds of game; while their system of storing up provisions, and oil for fuel, in different places, to meet future wants, seemed as perfect as possible. These are prepared in advance, at the several stations where the musk ox, the reindeer, and the seal are to be hunted; and thus they can undertake their furthest migrations with the most perfect security.

No one expects to hear that they are a more cleanly people than their fraternity elsewhere, and I need not repeat the disgusting details. Man is permitted to be more dirty than the beasts, and he is certainly not slow in taking advantage of this privilege wherever he dares. But, here there is really some excuse, and the people were not unwilling to be clean. They cannot well avoid contamination from the oil which they use as food and fuel; as, in a confined hut, where every thing must be dried at the flame of the lamp, the effects of smoke are equally inevitable. But the excuse, above all, is the want of water: and it has been resorted to as an excuse for similar neglect where it is not the rare and expensive article which it is here. The expenditure of fuel required to thaw what they drink is very great, as the quantity of water which they thus consume is enormous; very often they cannot procure enough, or suffer severely from thirst should their oil be expended: so that we need not be surprised if they do not wash themselves in winter: while the habit of ten months in every year of life can scarcely be broken through in the two short ones during which water can be procured.

Yet they wash their faces at least, by using a piece of wetted bear-skin as a towel; while they were well pleased to be put into good order on board, even to the act of combing and cutting their hair, and the loss of their beards under the barber's hands. The hair of the men is indeed kept quite short, being an evident improvement of their appearance as compared with the long-haired tribes, as well as a decided peculiarity: it is the women alone who wear it long, and tied into two bundles, or long cues, hanging over the two shoulders.

They seem little addicted to ornaments, and were very indifferent to our beads; it was on the children almost solely that these were placed: while their own consisting of fringes of skin, teeth, and other things, were similar to those which have often been described.

Their dresses being shown in plates and described in the explanations, I may omit any notice of those, as of many other matters. As elsewhere, the outer dress is always taken off and cleared of snow on entering the huts, altering their appearance in such a manner that they can scarcely be recognised. The snow sofas on which they sleep have no covering of branches, as is common elsewhere: the first layer is that of seal-skins, above which are deer-skins with the hair uppermost, being the sheet or blanket; while a similar skin forms the coverlet. In what manner they sleep, I need not repeat: and the beds are not cold, except in very severe weather, though the temperature of the walls cannot be above the freezing point. The lamp is ever burning; since it is the fire for cooking when not required as light.

Their snow huts have been so particularly described that it is superfluous to speak of them again: while I have also noticed their method of proceeding with the construction in the course of the preceding journal. I need only name what has not yet been mentioned, namely, their method of procuring the ice window, which, in this country, is not to be found on the surface of a pond. For this purpose, a seal-skin is laid on the snow, so managed at the edges that it may contain two inches of water in depth, procured by thawing snow before the lamp. This is immediately frozen into a transparent plate: and such, I presume, is esteemed the value of the fuel used for this purpose, that these windows are always removed and carried with them in their migrations. It is already equally known, that when the roofs of the snow huts begin to melt under the influence of the sun, they are removed, and a covering of skins substituted, as the summer tents consist of skins raised into a conical form by means of a central pole, from which lines are extended, and surrounded at the base by circles of stones.

The walrus does not frequent these straits: and whether it is that the whale is rare or not, we could not understand that they ever took any, and many had never seen one. The seal, the musk ox, the reindeer, the fox, and the hare, form their quadruped game: they kill but few grouse, which, being considered delicacies, are reserved for the women and children; but their supplies of fish seem to be very considerable. This last is eaten raw, if often half dried: the flesh of animals seems acceptable in any way, but it is always cooked, if possible, apparently for the sake of the oil soup.

In the method of taking these several animals, there is nothing which has not been often described. The reindeer are generally shot by arrows, in the water, as is usual elsewhere; and, in their canoes, there is nothing to notice, if I except their manner of ferrying the women and children, by stuffing the latter within the skin of the boat, and making the former lie flat behind her husband; in a rather dangerous position, when the least movement would upset the whole crew.

Under the great scarcity of wood here, since very little is ever drifted on these shores, and in the want of the walrus and the whale, they are almost limited to the use of the reindeer's horn in the making of their spears and other weapons; but these so nearly resemble those noticed by Crantz and others, that I need not describe them, unless indeed the fish-spear be not different from any of which I have read. The shaft of this, seven or eight feet long, is made of wood, if that can be procured; if not, of horn; and is furnished at the end with three points, so as to resemble a trident, of which, the central one is plain, and the two outer barbed, as may be seen by one of the plates.

This want of materials compels them also to adopt a method of constructing their sledges, which differs very materially from all others hitherto described. A number of salmon are packed together into a cylinder about seven feet long, and wrapped up in the skins taken from the canoes, which cease to be of use when the frost is arrived. Being then well corded with thongs, two of these cylinders are pressed into the shape of the runners, and, having been left to freeze, are secured by cross bars made of the legs of the deer or musk ox, so as to form the bottom of the sledge. This being done, the bottom of the runner is covered with a mixture of mossy earth and water, which soon freezes, to the depth of two inches; after which comes the final process of plating the surface, that it may run smoothly over the snow. The operator takes some water in his mouth, and, when somewhat mixed with saliva, it is deposited on a bear-skin which is then rubbed over the runner, as by a brush, gradually, till a coating of half an inch thick is produced, when the work is finished; the ice produced in this manner having an unusual degree of tenacity, and being also more slippery than the ordinary material.

These carriages travelled much more lightly than our own, which were shod with iron; but as they cease to be of use as soon as the thermometer reaches the freezing point, they are taken to pieces; the fish being eaten, and the skins converted into bags, while the bones are reserved for the dogs. In the preceding journal I have noticed the sledges made of ice.

In their miserable singing there is nothing which has not often been described; and this is equally true of their dances, or rather dance, which seems intended to imitate the motions of a bear.

E

On Stone by J. Brandard, from the original Drawing by Captain Ross

ALICTU AND KANGUAGIU.

ALICTU AND KANGUAGIU.

Alictu and his wife are represented as clothed in seal-skins over deer-skins, and a staff of bone in the hand of the former. This individual was about seventy years of age, infirm, and bent so that his stature did not exceed five feet; he was remarkable for being the person selected as a sacrifice on the first day of our communication, being placed on a sledge about ten paces in front of the column consisting of thirty men, three deep, who being armed with knives were waiting in breathless anxiety to behold the manner in which their aged companion would be treated, and on which depended their conduct towards us. He remained on the sledge with his arms folded, and with a countenance perfectly resigned to his fate, until Commander Ross approached and caressed him; even then he seemed to doubt that he was not destined to be the first to receive the poniard; and it was not until unequivocal proofs of friendship were interchanged with the whole party that he appeared satisfied his last moments had not arrived. He was much pleased to have his sledge drawn to the ship by myself and the sailors, and he was one of those first brought on board to see the wonders of the interior. He never visited the ship after the first day, and his death was announced to us on the second of March by an old woman and his eldest son Tiagashu, who took particular care of him, and who abundantly shed tears on acquainting us of his demise. He had four sons who all paid him great attention, and he lived to see his great-grand-children. He left a widow about ten years younger than himself. On examining his corpse a large but not deep incision was found in the abdomen evidently made long after his death, and probably to prove that he was really dead. The whole of the party left the snow huts at North Hendon, where he died, on the following day, leaving a small piece of wood on the top of the hut, and, after the party had gone out of our reach, his remains were interred by us to prevent its being devoured by foxes. Before leaving Felix Harbour the surgeon procured the skull, which I intended for the Phrenological Society, but which was one of the many valuable specimens of natural history which was of necessity left behind when we abandoned the ship at Victoria Harbour—his eyes were black and very small; his hair, of which I have preserved a specimen, was grey approaching to white, when he died he was corpulent, and seemed to have no disease but old age.

Kanguagin, his widow, was afterwards found in possession of Poweytak, whose kindness to her, although helpless from infirmity and old age, will appear hereafter. She was certainly above sixty, about the middle size, and rather corpulent, her hair was grey and her face much wrinkled as well as tatooed. She was triply clothed in reindeer-skins, and was never seen out of the hut within which she is represented to be sitting, excepting when the family were removing to another station.

On Stone by J. Brandard from the original Drawing by Captain Ross

KAWALUA. TIAGASHU. ADLURAK.

Printed by Graf & Soret

KAWALUA, TIAGASHU, AND ADLURAK.

Tiagashu was the eldest son of Alictu, and who took particular care of his father; he was five feet six inches and five-eighths high, slender and weaker than the rest, his eyes were very small, and he appeared to be of a mild disposition. He was extremely industrious, and anxious to support his family, which consisted of a wife, three children of his own, and one of hers by a former husband, besides his father: he was not very successful. In May, 1830, he was reduced to absolute starvation, when he was assisted by Ikmallik's party as long as they could, but afterwards by us, for which he was very grateful, but never had it in his power to make a return. He shed tears on his father's death, and seemed anxious that we should refrain from going to the hut where he was left.

Adlurak, his wife, was one of the best looking; she was remarkable for having large eyes, while those of her husband were very small, and she was perfectly aware of the peculiarity she possessed. She was of a lively disposition and was proud of having four children, two of which were still at the breast; for some time she was a daily visiter, and was one of the most honest.

Kawalua was about sixteen years of age, five feet seven inches high, and well made; he had neither father nor mother, but being nephew to Ikmallik, was an inmate with his family. This lad was one of the most inquisitive, and soon became a favourite with us all:

I therefore fixed on him to remain on board, with the intention of teaching him to read; and having on board an Esquimaux bible and the grammar published by Fabricius, I had hoped to make him useful. For this purpose he remained on board, and I began to teach him his letters; but on the second day he came to me and said, that Aglugga had told him that he was not to stay any longer, and nothing could persuade him to remain. My good intentions were therefore completely frustrated, which I had subsequently great reasons to regret. On the second year we met with him several times, and he was always rejoiced to meet us, enumerating at each interview the presents he had received.

On Stone by J Brandard from the original Drawing by Captain Ross

ILLICTU. OOTOOGIA.

ILLICTU AND OTOOGIU.

ARE represented standing at the pool of Shagavoke, where both salmon and reindeer are killed in the autumn; the piles of stones are erected by the natives, for the purpose of preventing the reindeer from passing along the shore when they wish to drive them into the pool. A man or a dog being sent among them make all to appear moving, which alarms the animals and causes them to take the water; where they are attacked and killed by men in canoes.

Otoogiu was five feet three inches and five-eighths high, inclining to corpulency, his face broad; he was always clad in deer-skin jacket and seal-skin trousers. He was called an angekok or conjuror, but no one had any faith in his predictions, which were always a subject of merriment. He was among the first to show a disposition to possess himself of what he saw, and his taking out of my cabin the magnifying lens, which he is represented to be holding in his right hand, gave us a good opportunity of convincing him and his companions of the danger of meddling with what belonged to us—as related in the Narrative. His wife's name was Kuauga, who had two children; she was five feet three inches and a quarter high and rather good looking.

Illictu, the son of Kunana was a very fine lad about fifteen years of age, five feet six inches high. He was one who accompanied Commander Ross on his expedition to the north. When two musk oxen were killed on this occasion, he demonstrated that he was very fond of fresh beef, and that he could eat without being satiated for one whole day. We found him on the following year with his father near Cape Lawrence, and very much improved. He had been successful in hunting both reindeer and seals, and supplied me with skins and oil for fuel on the journey in which the Magnetic Pole was discovered.

Otoogin is represented with the magnifying lens which he had stolen in one hand, and a knife made of bone in the other. Illictu has in one hand a rod made of reindeer's horn, used for probing the depth of the snow, and in the other a fish-hook made of bone, which I purchased of him, and which now is in my possession. When we met him at Padliak, on the following year, he supplied us with about fifteen pounds of excellent venison, for which he was well rewarded. On seeing the surgeon with a swelled face, he ran suddenly to him, blew in his face, and hit him a pat on the face, which we understood afterwards, was a cure for every complaint; and as the surgeon very soon got well after that ceremony, his recovery was entirely attributed to that charm. At that moment he had suspended to his neck a small phial containing an emulsion which the surgeon had given to him six months before, which instead of taking inwardly, as intended, was hung to his neck as a charm.

[illegible] by [illegible] from the original Drawing by Captain [illegible]

KUNANA.

KUNANA.

This native, both in features and character, differed considerably from the rest; he measured five feet eight inches and five-eighths, was of a robust and healthy appearance; his forehead appeared lower than it really was, from his eyebrows being very much arched; he was the most successful of all the hunters, particularly in killing bears, and he was constantly clad in bear-skins. Illictu, before mentioned, was his son by a first wife, which he had probably *spared* to a friend. By his second wife, which we saw at Cape Lawrence, he had two young children. His hut was almost entirely covered with snow at that time, but he had a large store of seal-oil, reindeer flesh, and salmon, buried under the snow, also skins of every kind; and from him I bought a very large deer-skin, which was my bed during my fatiguing journey from Victoria harbour to Fury beach, and is now in possession of Sir Felix Booth. He informed us that Kablala (a woman who had a club foot, and who was highly respected by all on that account) had been with him, and had departed only a few days before with Tulooah, her husband. Kunana was one of those who gave us many supplies, consequently he was well stored with knives, spear-heads, hooks, &c., which he had received in exchange. On my return from Artists' bay, he convoyed us several miles, pointing out the names of the various capes, rivers, and stations, which we passed, and

F

and kindly directed us to the best route to Cape Isabella and Padliak. His wife Nangiak seldom came to the ship, and never without her husband. As they were the most successful, they were never in want, nor were they at all covetous or inclined to pilfer. Her stature was four feet nine inches and one-eighth, her complexion like that of her husband, lighter than the others, and her appearance healthy. She had two young children besides Illictu, and the family were always thankful for what was given them.

HIBLUNA.

(Owhee.)

Hibluna was remarkable for being the plainest-looking woman in the whole tribe, and also for being the most lively; when a present was made to her of any useful article, such as a tin preserved meat case, her joy knew no bounds. Above, she is represented in one of her ecstasies on receiving a woman's knife which she holds in her right hand, and in her left a bone knife, while she is jumping up and exclaiming, *Owhee! Owhee!* by which name she was soon known to the sailors. On this occasion, she had brought us a fine piece of a musk ox in a frozen state, and which we found to be most excellent food. She was one of our daily visitors, having with her an infant which she used to produce quite naked, even when the thermometer was 43° below zero of Fahrenheit. Her height was five feet three inches and a quarter, was near forty years of age, and extremely dirty and badly clothed; her face was broad, her nose flat, and the want of her fore teeth, added to her unseemly appearance; her husband's name was Kunana (2d), and she had two young children; however she was so good humoured and merry that she was a favourite among the sailors.

Eringahrin, Hibluna's sister, was so extremely like her, that when they were apart it was difficult to discern which was which; but when together it was more easy, as the former was only four

F 2

feet ten inches high. She had also lost her front teeth, and in habit and appearance was equally disgusting. Her husband's name was Ootoonina, who being as ill-looking as herself was an excellent match. They were both our guides and companions during our journey in 1831 across the lakes to the western sea. She was also of a lively disposition, and the sailors, who could not pronounce her name, christened her *Nancy*, to which she answered with perfect readiness; and was likewise a favourite with the sailors. Her husband was a very successful fisherman, and they had always plenty; but she seemed to be a very bad housekeeper, and was not so industrious as the rest, and was never neatly dressed or clean. One of her children was at the breast, and the other was about five years old, which in the summer ran about naked.

On Stone by ... Brandard from the Original Drawing by Captain Ross.

MANELLIA ADELIK

MANELLIA AND ADELIK.

MANELLIA was the wife of Nullungiak, and one of the prettiest of the females; her stature was only four feet seven inches and a half; her features were small and regular, and her hands and feet were in proportion, very little; and she was, notwithstanding her dirtiness, rather interesting. She is represented in the plate with a child on her back, which was born at North Hendon, but which died on the following year. Her manner was much milder than the rest, nor did she appear to covet what she saw.

Adelik is an old woman who was a daily visitor to the ship. She appeared to observe with great attention every occurrence which took place, also to mimic or imitate people's actions. She is represented in the plate ludicrously imitating one of the officers who used to walk up and down near the ship's side for exercise, of which she could not see the utility. The staff in her hand is one of the spears with which seals are killed. She appeared about fifty-five years of age, and being rather bent was only about four feet seven inches in stature. She was supported by her children, and she was daily employed gleaning at the place where sweepings had been previously deposited on the ice at a little distance from the ship. Her face was much weather-beaten, and had in it the delineation of care and anxiety. She was never detected in dishonest practices.

Manellia and her husband returned to North Hendon in the following or second summer, where there infant died, soon after which they departed and took up their station at Padliak, where we found them living on *erkalook,* a small sea fish, which has been already described.

tone by C Bradford from the Original Drawing by Captain Ross

POYETTAK, KAKIKAGIU, AND AKNALUA.

Kakikagiu is represented standing between her two husbands. She was a native of Akullee, and by far the most robust woman we met with; her stature was five feet three inches and a quarter; her face was broad, her eyes, nose, and mouth small, as also her hands and feet, in proportion to her figure which was completely *en bon point;* her favourite husband was Aknalua, who was decidedly better looking than Poyettak, accordingly the latter was sent out to hunt and procure food whilst the other remained at home, and it was rather surprising to see how cheerfully he would obey from time to time this, which appeared to us, unfair command, of a capricious or partial wife, and bring home the fruits of his labours to be equally divided! On one of these occasions, Poyettak was sent to guide Commander Ross to the Umingmak (musk ox) mountains, and was absent a whole week. It was this woman who had obtained some knowledge of the ships under Sir Edward Parry, and by whose advice the party advanced to communicate with us; when Poweytag had lost his adopted child, the fury of the old man was appeased by her interference, and she was one of the most useful and intelligent in giving us information about the coast, rivers, stations, &c. Latterly she was not very honest, and Aknalua made her return a carpenter's rule which she had taken and concealed. She was about twenty-five years of age.

Poyettak was about twenty-eight years of age, he measured five feet four inches and five-eighths; his complexion was darker than that of Aknalua, and his features not so pleasing, though small in proportion; he was however a successful hunter, and very active.

Aknalua was about twenty-six years of age, measured five feet eight inches, was strong and well made; his complexion was not so dark as many of them, and his features were very pleasing; he seemed to have a very good temper, and often came to the ship, but never was accused of taking any thing away. Being his wife's favourite, he generally came to the ship with her, and was neither covetous nor dishonest.

We did not see this family after the first year.

by Brandard from the original Drawing by Captain [illegible]

KEMIG

KEMIG.

This young woman, who was the most corpulent of the whole tribe, is represented as sitting on the bed within a snow hut, to have the tatooing delineated; this consisted of three lines horizontally across each cheek, and three vertically across the chin, a double line round the neck and breast above the shoulder, another below the shoulder, and a third above the elbow; between each of these lines, which encircled the arms and parallel to each other, there were ornamental devices, but without any meaning; and all the women were tatooed exactly in the same way. She was five feet four inches and a quarter high, and was about twenty-five years of age. Her husband's name was Konag, who was also young, but they had no children, which is considered a great reproach to both parties. They went to the western sea in the summer of 1830, but returned in 1831 to us at Sheriff's harbour, at which time she had become much more corpulent, and was still without a family. Her skin was a dirty copper colour, her face was broad, her brow very low, her eyes, nose, and mouth small, and her cheeks very red. She seemed very indolent, as well as her husband; and, at one time, they were so unsuccessful that we had to relieve their wants to keep them from starving. Her mother, whose name was Nimna Himna, but nicknamed by the sailors, Old Greedy, as well as herself, was a constant visitor to the ship,

G

and generally carried off something which she had picked up. On one occasion, when coming up the ladder, she was tumbled off by the surgeon, and falling on her back, pretended to faint; from which, although all the doctor could do could not recover her, she was restored by the offer of an empty tin case, which had contained preserved meat: a stratagem which she subsequently tried more than once without success. She was about sixty years of age, five feet two inches high, extremely ill-looking, and decidedly the most disgusting of the whole tribe.

On Stone by [illegible] Standard from the [illegible]riginal [illegible]rawing by Captain Ross

KANAYOKE.

KANAYOKE.

KANAYOKE came to the ship at Felix harbour, in the spring of 1830; he had wintered at Padliak, and, having crossed the isthmus, joined a party about six miles to the northward, one of whom guided him to us. It appeared that he was the father of Poyetta, by Kanguagin, Alictu's widow, now the wife of his brother, Poweytag. He was about sixty-five years of age, was five feet eight inches high, and remarkable for being darker in colour than any of the rest. It appears that he lived to the westward, and had communication with a tribe in that direction where the females were most numerous; and when a wife was wanted for some of his own party, he transferred to him his own wife, and went for another to himself, a friendly service which we understood he had performed no less than five times; and he had now brought his sixth spouse, by whom he had three young children, to visit three of his former wives, and we witnessed the whole party living together in perfect harmony! The advantages of this, as far as he was concerned, were obvious; for in each of the five different families he had a son or two, so that in his old age he might, according to custom, claim support from all or any of them, or from the most successful in hunting, as he was entitled to the share of a father. He brought several good specimens of natural history, for which he was well rewarded, and he gave us some valuable information

G 2

respecting the western sea and the nature of the country to the westward. He also informed us, that Kablala, who had a club-foot, and her husband, were to be at Padliak, and that we should see them next year. On the second visit, he brought his present wife and children to see us, whose description will occupy the next page.

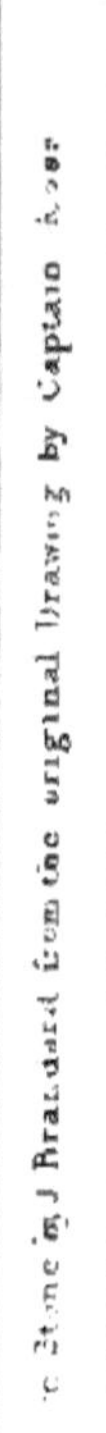

On Stone by J Brandard from the original Drawing by Captain Ross

OOBLOORIA   PANINGAYUKE.   AMINGO   NULLINGIAK

OOBLOORIA, PANINGAVOKE, AMINGO, AND NULLINGIAK.

Amingo, the sixth wife of Kanayoke, is represented sitting at the table in the cabin of the Victory, between her two children, and an infant on her shoulder whose name was Aknallua. She was extremely well clothed in deer-skins, and so were her children, of whom the parents were very fond. Her complexion was much lighter and paler than the other females, and her behaviour very modest and unassuming. She sat at the table, and viewed the pictures that were set before her with great delight, pointing out to her children every thing she thought wonderful, as soon as it had been explained to herself. Her children were also very pretty, the eldest about four years old, the next two and a half, and the youngest about six months. After remaining some time, she returned to the huts, about six miles off, and we had not an opportunity of seeing her again. We understood that the whole family had gone off, with that of Kablala, to the westward.

Ooblooria, who is represented standing with a whip in one hand and a coil of line in the other, came with them. He was the eldest son of Ikmallik and Apelaglin, about seventeen years of age; his stature was five feet two inches and three-quarters, stout made; his dress, on this occasion, was rather ornamental as well as useful, having above his deer-skin jacket, a tippet made of the belly part of the deer-skin, which being white, had a very pretty, as well as comfortable appearance; he was one of the guides which Commander Ross had on his first journey to Neitchillee and Padliak, on which occasion his provisions ran short, and his gratitude, as well as that of his parents, has been dwelt upon already in the Narrative. He was a fine active and intelligent lad, and was, consequently, a great favourite with us. He was married to Shullanina, Tulluahiu's daughter, and his own cousin, his mother, Apellagliu, being Tulluahiu's sister. We had no reason to doubt that he was strictly honest, as also the whole family, who were certainly, and very deservedly, the favourites; and as they showed no disposition even to covet, they were always presented with more of what was useful to them than the rest.

On Stone by J Brandard from the original Drawing by Captain Ross

KONYAROKLICK. NEWEETIOKE.

OR BALD HEAD.

Printed by Graf & Soret

NEWEETIOKE AND KONYAROKLIK.

NEWEETIOKE was brother to Ikmallik, and certainly the tallest of the Boothians, being five feet ten inches high, but he had been described to us much taller before he came to us the second year at Sheriff's harbour; but when he stood up beside Mr. Abernethy, who was six feet two inches, he looked so much shorter that his brother was quite astonished. He is dressed in a bear-skin jacket with deer-skin sleeves, and his trousers were bear-skin. He had, of course, been told all about us before he came, and his brother having received a great many things, he was led to expect the same; he had, however, very little to give in exchange, and consequently was disappointed, and when nothing else would do he fell on an ingenious stratagem to obtain a piece of wood which he had fixed his mind upon. Having consulted his companions, it was agreed that they were to show us their method of killing seals, accordingly one personated a seal lying on the ice, now and then pretending to sleep, and sometimes holding up his head as if to look around; while the others, watching his motions, gradually approach by creeping on their bellies, with a spear. Neweetioke, while this farce was going on, and supposing that our attention was entirely engrossed with it, slipped away, and having got the piece of wood, placed it along his spear, and on each end put over a boot, as if to carry them for the purpose of drying them by suspending them across his shoulders; but he did not escape the vigilance of our look-out men, who caught him in the act, which was fatal to his obtaining any thing he wanted, and had he not been Ikmallik's brother, he would have been sent off in disgrace. He had a wife and two children, the eldest of which was one of the performers in the stratagem. The detection, however, caused a hearty laugh. Although his forehead was low, his features were larger than most of them, and he appeared to be about forty-five years of age.

Konyaroklik (or Bald-head) came at the same time with Neweetioke, and had one son, called Ulla, of whom he was very proud; he was still more so of his *bald head*, which was unique here, being the only instance we saw of it. He was five feet six inches high, about fifty years of age, and rather good-looking. He brought us some skins, for which he was liberally paid, and was delighted when he saw his portrait, which I made of him. His costume was a dark deer-skin jacket and bear-skin trousers.

DLIA AWITIGIN. PAL RAK

UDLIA, AWTIGIN, AND PALURAK.

Awtigin is represented in the engraving standing between his two wives. This family came to us at Sheriff's harbour in the spring of 1831, having learnt of our position from our former friends. His jacket is of reindeer-skin, as also those of his wives; his trousers are of bear-skin, and his wives' seal-skin, as also their boots. They had several good skins to dispose of, and left us well pleased with what they had in exchange. It appeared that he had first taken Udlia for a wife, and, in consequence of her having no child, he took Palurak in addition, by whom he has a son; notwithstanding this, the two wives appeared on perfect good terms with each other, and were equally beloved (if I may so call it) by their husband. Awtigin was five feet six inches high, stout made, but had rather a stupid look. He was very desirous to possess many things which he saw, but was not detected in pilfering.

Udlia was five feet one inch and a half high, and rather delicately made; she could not be above twenty-five years of age, while her copartner was two inches shorter, and about two years younger. The child's name was Karuktachiu, and was about two years old. These females were delighted with the presents which we gave them, and showed no disposition to covet or to steal. After remaining with us about a week they departed to fish on one of the lakes.

H

Like the rest, they promised to return, but our departure would disappoint them, as we left Sheriff's harbour in the August following.

SHULLANINA, TULLUAHIU, AND TIRIKSHIU.

TULLUAHIU, his wife Tirikshiu, and his daughter Shullanina, being the most remarkable family we met with; a plate of them has been given in the book, and their names are so often introduced that little of their history remains to be told. The former, whose name signifies a young raven, was about forty years of age, he measured five feet eight inches, and was rather more corpulent than the rest, probably from being unable to take exercise; his features and costume are well represented, as also those of his wife and daughter. When we approached them on the first day of communication, Tulluahiu was stationed in the middle of the column, standing on one leg, and supported between Ikmallik and another, and was armed with a long knife, which he kept behind his back until peace was established. He was one of the first we had on board, and was remarkable for imitating every thing he saw done. It has been already mentioned that the wooden leg which we gave him was the means of establishing friendship between us, and he was always grateful for that signal service which we rendered to him. He was never detected stealing, but his wife was not so honest, and when she did succeed in carrying any thing away, her husband always made her bring it back. In the plate she is represented concealing a piece of wood, in which she was detected. She was sister to Ikmallik, and being five feet five inches and a quarter high, was one of the tallest of the women; her name signified an ermine, and she was about thirty-eight years of age. Shullanina, her daughter, was the eldest of three children; she was decidedly the prettiest girl and had the best figure; her cheeks were rosy, and, when washed with soap and water, she looked very well, and appeared to have every amiable quality. The proof she gave of her obedience, by consenting to be exchanged for a wooden leg, has already been dwelt upon in the Narrative, as well as her subsequent marriage with her cousin Oblooria, Ikmallik's son. After which I met with the whole family at Lindsay river. At Sheriff's harbour, a very short time after, they paid us a visit. Tulluahiu had damaged the trunk part of his wooden leg; this was repaired by bands of copper, and several spare legs given to him before we parted for the last time, and which excited new demonstrations of their gratitude and regard.

IKMALLIK AND APELLAGLIU.

IKMALLIK, and his wife Apellagliu, were certainly the best of the whole of the natives, and they seemed most respected by the rest. They are represented in the Narrative as drawing a map of the country; and, from the information which he likewise gave us, he obtained the name of the "Hydrographer," and we always found what he, or his son Ooblooria, told us to be correct. They brought us every thing they could procure, leaving it entirely to us what they were to have in exchange, and were always contented with whatever was given to them; by this kind of conduct they gained our confidence and esteem, and in the end they got best rewarded. They were extremely attached to their children, and for any kindness shown to them their gratitude knew no bounds. The mutual desire to oblige each other, and every one else, was at once manifest and delightful. Ikmallik was the first who remained a whole night and slept on board, having been employed by me in building my magnetic observatory of snow, which he did cheerfully and extremely well. His youngest child, about two years old, was called Camuka, and was very pretty; she was clothed in skins so as to resemble a ball, and was often entertained with prints in the cabin. Besides their own three children, two of which were at the breast, they had supported two nephews who had lost their parents; one of which, Awack, had now grown up, and was the companion and friend of Ooblooria; he was one of the most active and expert hunters, as well as the most successful of the whole, and was one of Commander Ross's guides on the first journey. I met with him afterwards in Thoms bay, and he was the means of our discovering the great Salmon (Lord Lindsay) river.

Apellaglin was five feet three inches and a half high, rather corpulent, and by no means good looking; she was sister to Tullnahin, in whose features there was a family resemblance, and was about thirty-six years of age. Awack was about twenty-two, had a very pleasing countenance, and was five feet eight inches high.

Ikmallik had another brother, besides Neweetioke, who was named Atayaraktak, who was an active young man, about thirty, and five feet eight inches and a half high; his wife was a very delicate person, and they had two children. It was this man and Ookurahin who first conducted me to Neitchillee, while Commander Ross was on a journey to the westward. Ookurachin was also a nephew to Ikmallik, but lived with his mother Alurak.

AJOUA, AUOWAHRIU, AND NAQUASSIAK.

AJOUA was an old woman, the mother of Tulluahiu and Auowahriu, who was very much bent, and could not walk without the aid of a staff; she was very covetous, and asked for almost every thing she saw; at length I proposed that she should carry off the ship on her back, which had the appearance of being bent for receiving a burden, at which her sons were much amused; we received, however, from her a curious piece of wood which had been given to her by Cablala, and would have been a passport if we had succeeded in getting to the westward. This curiosity I have still in my possession: of course she was well rewarded for it; but she always put us in mind that her parting with it was a great favour. Auowahriu was her second son, and was also a cripple from accident; he had been a very powerful man and an excellent hunter, and was remarkable for the nice order in which he kept his spears, bows, and arrows. He was very dexterous at killing salmon, and in the management of a canoe; we met with him for the last time at the salmon fishery, at the mouth of Lindsay river. He had three children who had lost their mother. Naquassiak, the eldest, was about sixteen years of age, very tall and thin, but not very active; when he went to show Commander Ross the way to Shagavoke, he was detected in telling a falsehood, and thereby obtained the nickname of *Shaglo,* which signifies a lie; but he never was offended at this appellation, which indeed was a source of merriment whenever it was mentioned. The other two children were infants; but when Tiagashu died, his widow Alurak became the wife of Anowahriu, and took charge of the children. This family were not covetous nor inclined to pilfer, and were therefore always in favour.

NOYENNAK AND IBLUSHE, TIKATAGIU.

These young men were brothers of Tiagashu, Poyettak, and Aknallua, by the same mother, but by a different father. Noyennak was about twenty-five years of age, five feet four inches and three-eighths high; his complexion was lighter and more sallow than his brothers, and he seemed very quiet and inoffensive; he contributed to the support of his aged mother, and when his father Alictu died he was much grieved. Iblushe, his brother, was about thirty years of age, five feet five inches and three-quarters high, and also of a light sallow complexion. He was remarkable for wearing ornaments of foxes' teeth hung round his forehead, and at each temple a bear's tooth; his countenance bespoke extreme good-nature, which we found completely verified. We understood that this family suffered considerably for want of food after they left us, and we did not meet them again on the second year.

Tikatagiu was one of those who did not come to us until late in the first season. He was a very fine young man, about twenty-six years of age, and measured five feet nine inches. His wife, whose name was Kuria, was a very shy delicate woman, and had one infant named Karuktachiu. He was an excellent hunter, and had a very superior dog, of which he was very fond, and could not be bribed to part with him. He came and built a snow hut very near to the ship, and remained until he had exchanged skins and other articles which he could spare, for wood and iron. I met him some time afterwards at Neitchillee, and obtained a supply of fish, which were then in great plenty.

MILLUCTU, TOPAKA, AWACK (1), AND ALLINACHRIU.

Milluctu was one of those who was very much at the ship, and was rather inclined to possess himself of what he saw, and was particularly jealous of any one receiving more than himself; when he perceived the quantity of wood which composed Tullnahiu's wooden leg, he complained that he could not walk on his right leg, and begged that he also might have a wooden one: when he was told that of course his leg, like that of Tullnahiu, must be taken off, he said he had not time, or that it was not convenient now, and promised he would come to-morrow; but when he came he said that *his leg was better*. On another occasion when Ikmallik was rewarded with a tin meat-case, for dancing like a bear, in a ring formed by the women, he began also to exhibit; but his performance was so much inferior to his predecessor, that he only excited laughter; but seeing that he w s very much disappointed, I gave him a tin case also, which turned the laugh on his side. He was about twenty-five years of age, five feet four inches high, and well made. He had a wife and two children; and his mother, an old woman named Topaka lived with him. This old lady was the first who committed a theft, by stealing a pair of brass snuffers, which was, however, found out by the rest, and immediately returned. She was one of those who gleaned daily on the dunghill. Awack (1) was a man about forty-five years of age, five feet three

I 2

inches and three quarters high; he was very quiet and industrious, and exchanged a great many articles with us honestly. His wife's name was Allenachriu, about his own age, they had a boy named Illiklaptuain and a girl called Beaktakhilla, the former six and the latter seven and a half years old. We met them afterwards in Padliak, in possession of plenty of fish, with which they supplied us; and the lady politely convoyed us several miles on our way home. We did not see them during the last two years.

As the rest of the natives have nothing remarkab'e or peculiar to them, I shall only mention a few of their names, &c.

Aunai, an old woman, sixty years of age, five feet three inches and a quarter high.—Anatiu, an old woman, sixty-four years of age, four feet ten inches and seven-eighths high.—Strowok, an old woman, fifty-five years of age, five feet two inches and a half high.—Ugluta, an old woman, fifty years of age, five feet high.—Sheppung, a child, five years of age.—Karaksachiu, a child, six years of age.—Nangiak, a woman, forty years of age, four feet nine inches and a half high.

The above will be sufficient to show that the Boothians are generally below the middle size. The first party we met with consisted of ninety-nine souls, viz., thirty-three men, twenty-five of whom had wives; twelve old men and women, and twenty-nine children. We afterwards met with about sixty more, so that the country is but thinly peopled, the whole population amounting to no more than a hundred and sixty souls. Upon the whole, in the unqualified state of nature in which they were found, they were the happiest of human beings, on whom Providence has kindly and bountifully bestowed every necessary gift, if not every blessing.

VOCABULARY

OF THE

ENGLISH, DANISH, AND ESQUIMAUX LANGUAGES.

PREFACE.

In compiling the following vocabulary and dialogues I have adhered to the method of spelling the words which was published by Fabricius, both in the shape of a Grammar and a Dictionary; the last edition of which was printed at Copenhagen in 1804, and to which I refer my readers for any further explanation than I have thought necessary to give.

The pronunciation of the vowels, both in the Danish and Esquimaux language is as follows:

A	sounds as	A	in	War.
E	. .	E	.	Cellar.
I	. .	I	.	Line.
O	.	O		Block.
U		U	.	Full.
Oa . .		O		Load.
Ou .	.	Oo .	.	Rood.
Ej . . .	. . .	Y .	.	Fly.
Aj . . .	. . .	I	.	I.

The consonants are the same as in the English language, with the following exceptions:

G sounds as G in Gay.
J . . . Y . . Yesterday.

L and R, in the Esquimaux language, never begin a word, excepting in *lu* (and), which, however, is often a definite termination. Neither does H begin any but a proper name.

In the whole narrative I have adhered to the above pronunciation, which to me was perfectly easy, from being acquainted with the Swedish and Danish languages, and which is, indeed, the best method as being the least complicated; but it will be observed that Commander Ross has not followed this plan, and therefore in reading his narrative this must not be attended to.

N.B.—This Vocabulary is extended, that it may be found useful to those who navigate Davis's straits and Baffin's bay, as well as to future Voyages of Discovery.

VOCABULARY

OF THE

ENGLISH, DANISH, AND ESQUIMAUX LANGUAGES.

ENGLISH.	DANISH.	ESQUIMAUX.
Abate	Aftage	Miklinek.
Able (I am)	Jeg er istand	Piginnavonga.
Abode	Opholdsted	Inne.
Accuse	Beskylde	Passiklernek.
Ache	Smerte	Anniaut.
Admonish	Formane	Okaukriksaïnek.
Adorn	Pryde	Arsoaïnek.
Advance	Komme frem	Sœrbsarnek.
Advantage	Fordeel	Ajungikot.
Affirm	Sige ja	Angernek.
Afraid (he is)	Han er bange	Erksiok.
After him or it	Efter ham	Kingorna.
Again	Igjen	Ama.
Air	Luft	Silla.
Ale	Ol	Imiak.
Alien	Fremmed	Tekkornartak.
Alone	Alene	Kissime.
Also	Ogsaa	Ama.
Although	Endskyöndt	Nauk, v. umni.
Altitude	Höyde	Portursusek.
Always	Allevegne	Tamatigut.
Amiable	Elskværdig	Assanartok.
Anchor	Anker	Kisak.
Ancient	Gammel	Utokak.
Angry (he is)	Han er vred	Kamakpok.
Answer	Svar	Akke.
Answer (to)	At svare	Akkinek.
Ant	Myre	Myre (Prov. 6,6).
Anxiety	Frygt	Erkse.
Any of them	Nogle	Illejt or illejsa.
Apple	Æble	Paurnarsoak.
Apprentice	Lærling	Ajokœrsugak.
Approach	Nærme sig	Padlinguek.
Approves (he) it	Han billiger det	Illuarà.
Arm	Arm	Tellek.
Arm (right)	Höyre Arm	Tellerpik.

ENGLISH.	DANISH.	ESQUIMAUX.
Armour	Vaaben	Sekkut.
Arrive	Komme	Tikinek.
Arrow	Piil	Karsok.
Ashes	Aske	Arsæt.
Ass	Asen	Siutitok (N.B.)
Assassin	Morder	Innuærsok
Assist	Hjelpe	Ikioïnek.
Attachment	Kjerlighed	Assennirsusek.
Attendant (his)	Hans Ledsager	Ajpa, v. ajpet.
Aunt	Faster	Aja.
Austral	Sydlig	Kauangarnitsok.
Autumn	Höst	Okiak.
Auk (little)	Söekonge	Akpalliârsuk.
Awakes (he)	Han vaagner	Iterpok.
Awake (he is)	Han er vaagen	Pigarpok, v. erkomavok.
Baby	Barn	Nalungiak.
Bachelor	Pebersvend	Nukakpiak.
Back (of a man)	Ryg	Tunno.
Bad	Ond	Ajortok.
Bag	Pose	Pók.
Ball	Bold	Arksak.
Base	Slet	Isumaluktok.
Bay	Bugt	Kangerdluk.
Beard	Skjæg	Umik.
Beats (he) me	Han slaaer mig	Unatarpanga
Beauty	Skjönhed	Pinnersusek.
Bee	Bie	Egytsak.
Beer	Öl	Imiak.
Before	För	Siorna.
Beg	Bede	Krenunek.
Beggar	Betler	Krenursok.
Behaviour	Opförsel	Kannong — illiorsusek.
Belief	Troe	Opèrnek.
Believe	Troe	Opèrnek.

K

ENGLISH.	DANISH.	ESQUIMAUX.
Belly of a man / Belly of a fish	Bug	Nærsæt.
Bible	Bibel	Bibelit.
Big (large)	Tyk	Silliktok.
Big with young	Frugtsommelig	Nartursok.
Billow	Bölge	Mallik.
Bird	Fugl	Tingmiak.
Bitch (large)	Tæve	Kremmersoak arnak.
Bitch with young	Tæve med Hvalpe	Sardliak.
Black	Sort	Kernektok.
Blankets	Lagener	Tungit.
Bleed	Aarelade	Auærsinek.
Bless	Velsigne	Pidluarkorsinek.
Bliss	Velsignelse	Pidluarkorsut.
Blood	Blod	Auk.
Blow	Blæse	Annordlernek.
Blue	Blaae	Tungiortok.
Boast	Bryste sig	Makkittauek.
Body	Legem	Timme.
Boil	Kaage	Iganek.
Bone	Been	Saurnek.
Bone (back)	Rygbeen	Kremertlok.
Bounty	Godhed	Isumagiksusek.
Box	Æske	Mattursartok.
Bow	Bue	Pissikse.
Brain	Hjerne	Karisak.
Brandy	Brændevin	Sillakaugitsok.
Bread	Bröd	Tiniursak.
Break	Briste	Asserornek.
Breast (woman's)	Bryst	Ivienge.
Breeches	Buxer	Kardleet.
Breeches (of women)	Buxer	Serkinek.
Bride	Brud	Nullicksak.
Broad	Bred	Silliktok.
Brook	Elv	Kôk v. kôrsoak v. kogejtsiak.
Buoy (sealskin)	Blære	Auatak.
Burden	Byrde	Nangmaut.
Burial	Begravelse	Illinek.
Burn	Brænde	Ikinek.
Button	Knap	Attesingoak.
Butterfly	Flue	Niviugak.
Buy	Kjöbe	Pissiniarnek.

ENGLISH.	DANISH.	ESQUIMAUX.
Cabin	Kahyt	Nalekkaminua.
Cable	Toug	Aklunaursak.
Cape, or hood	Hue, Hætte	Nesak.
Calf of a reindeer	Rhenskalv	Norrak.
Call	Kalde	Kakorsinek.
Calling	Kald	Kakorsut.
Calm (it is)	Det er stille	Kaïtsungavok.
Candle	Lys	Nennerout.
Candlestick	Lysestage	Nenneroursivik.
Canoe	Kajak	Kajak.
Cape, head of a land	Forbjerg	Nouk.
Captain	Captain	Nalegak.
Cash	Kasse	Iklerfik.
Cautious	Forsigtig	Missiksortok.
Cave	Hule	Itersak.
Cease	Ophöre	Sorarnek.
Certainly	Visselig	Illomut.
Chace of reindeer	Rhensjagt	Auarnek.
Chair	Stol	Ivksiavik.
Chalk	Kride	Aglaut.
Chamber	Kammer	Iuningoak.
Changes (it)	Det forandres	Adlangorpok.
Channel	Sund	Ikkerasak.
Charcoal	Steenkul	Aumarsoït
Chaste	Kydsk	Petejuïtsok.
Cheap	Let kjöbs	Akkikitsok.
Cheerful (he is)	Han er glad	Nuennarpok.
Cheese	Ost	Imuk.
Chew	Tygge	Tamoarnek.
Chicken	Kylling	Piârak.
Child	Barn	Merak.
Chimney	Skorsteen	Pÿorfik.
Choose (do you)	Vil du	Piomavit ? pisavit ?
Christmas	Juul	Jule.
Church	Kirke	Okallukfik.
Circle	Passer	Angmaloriksaut.
Citizen	Borger	Iglorperksoarmio
City	Stad	Iglorperksoit.
Civil	Höflig	Innuksiarnersok.
Claw	Kloe	Kukkik.
Clean (it is)	Det er reent	Sellisimavok.
Clock	Klokke	Nællunærkotak.
Cloth	Klæde	Annoraksak.

ENGLISH.	DANISH.	ESQUIMAUX.	ENGLISH.	DANISH.	ESQUIMAUX.
Clothes	Klæder	Annorarsæt.	Cruel	Grusom	Nakitejtsok.
Cloud	Skÿe	Nuïak.	Cruelty	Grusomhed	Nakitejtsusek.
Coach, a sledge with wheels	Vogn	Kamutik ark-sakaursuglik.	Cruise	Krÿdse	Arksornek.
			Crash	Knuse	Serkomitsinek.
Coal, charcoal	Steenkul	Aumarsoit.	Cry	Raabe	Torklularnek.
Coast	Kyst	Siksak.	Cup, teacup	Thekop	Thètortik.
Coat	Kjole	Annorak.	Cure, medicine	Cuur	Nekkursaut.
Coin, money	Penge	Anningaursæt.	Curtain of a tent	Forhæng	Umik.
Cold	Kulde	Isse.	Custom	Vane	Illerkok.
Cold (get a)	Forkjöles	Nuangnek.	Cuts (he) it	Han skjærevdetaf	K'ppiva.
Colours (a painter's)	Farver	Kallipautit.	Daily, every day	Daglig	Udlut aungud-lugit.
Comb	Kam	Illejautit, v. komangniutit.	Damage of a ship	Læk, Skade	Asseroruek.
			Damp	Damp	Pÿok.
Comes, he	Han kommer	Aggerpok.	Danger	Fare	Nauværsusek.
Company	Selskab	Illegeengnek.	Dares, he	Han vover	Sapèpok.
Compass	Compas	Pyorsiut.	Dark	Mörk	Tartok.
Compassion	Medlidenhed	Nakinnirsusek.	Dawning	At det dages	Kaulemek.
Conceal	Skjule	Irsertoïnek.	Day	Dag	Udluk.
Conduct	Opförsel	Kannong—illi-orsusek.	Dead	Död	Tokorsok.
			Deaf	Döv	Tussilartok.
Confidence	Tillid	Tette.	Deal (to)	Dele	Augoaïnek.
Conjurer	Hexemester	Angekok.	Deal (a) of it	Deel	Illa.
Conscience	Samvittighed	Isuma.	Dear	Kjær	Assarsak.
Consume	Fortæres	Nunguneng.	Death	Död	Toko.
Copper	Kobber	Kangusak auk padlartok.	Debt	Gjeld	Akketsugak.
			Deceit, lie	Bedragerie	Seglo.
Corn to make groats of	Korn	Suaursecksæt.	Deceives (he) me	Han narrer mig	Seglokrittar-pànga.
Corn to make beer of		Imiecksæt.	Decent	Sömmelig	Kursegunartok.
			Deck of a ship	Dæk	Kâ.
Corn to make bread of		Timiursecksæt.	Decree, law	Beslutning	Pekkorsut.
			Deep	Dyb	Itirsok.
Corner	Hjörne	Tekerkok.	Deer (rein)	Rhensdyr	Tukto.
Cost	Betaling	Akke.	Defect, want	Mangel	Ajorsaut.
Count, number	Tal	Kissitse.	Defence	Beskyttelse	Igdlersout.
Counting	Tælle	Kissitsinek.	Defend	Beskytte	Igdlersoïnek.
Cow	Koe	Umingmák.	Defray, pay	Betale	Akkillernek.
Cowpock	Kokoppe	Koppe (Danish).	Defy	Trodse	Pilfereenek.
Creator	Skaber	Pingortitsirsok.	Delays (he) it	Han opsætter det	Kakugorpa.
Creatures	Skabninger	Pingortitæt.	Delight	Være glad	Nuennàrnek.
Creep	Krybe	Kajeksoarnek.	Deliver, save	Frelse	Annaursinek.
Crew	Mandskab	Kivgæt.	Demand	Bön	Krenut.
Crowd of men	Folkeskare	Innuerksoit.	Demand	Bede	Krenunek.

ENGLISH.	DANISH.	ESQUIMAUX.
Deny	Nægte	Nâggarnek.
Depth	Dybde	Itirsusek.
Desert	Örken	Innukajuïtsok.
Descend	Nedstige	Akkarnek.
Design	Hensigt	Piomarsak.
Desire	Önske	Kiksaut.
Destroy	Odelægge	Piörngærutitsinek.
Detains (he) it	Han opholder det	Innerterpa.
Detects (he) it	Han aabenbarer det	Nællunejarpa.
Detests (he) it	Han afskyer det	Kringara, v. umiga
Devotion	Gudsfrygt	Naleugnek Gudimut.
Dew	Dug	Isugutanek.
Dice, cards	Tærninger Kort	Innukkæt.
Direct	Styre	Tessioïnek.
Dirt	Skarn	Ippek — plur. ervkit.
Disease	Sygdom	Nappaut.
Distance	Afstand	Ungesiksusek.
Distant	Fjern	Ungesiksok, v. anasiksok.
Distress	Nöd	Pidluejtsusek.
Dives (it) — a bird, a seal, or animal	Dykker	Aglorpok. Akkarpok.
Dog	Hund	Kremmek.
Door	Dör	Isertarfik.
Down (Eider duck)	Duun	Uvlut.
Draught	Drik	Imigeksak.
Draw	Male	Aglengnek, v. arsillinek.
Dreadful	Skrækkelig	Erksinartok.
Dream	Dröm	Sinektugak.
Dress	Dragt	Attirsæt.
Drink	Drikke	Imernek.
Drum	Tromme	Krillaut.
Dry	Tör	Pennertok.
Duck (Eider)	Edderfugl	Mitek.
Duck (king)	Spidsbergens E.	Kringalik, v. arnauiartak.
Dust	Stöv	Pyoalâk.

ENGLISH.	DANISH.	ESQUIMAUX.
Duty	Pligt	Pirseksak.
Dwell	Boe	Innekarnek.
Dye (to)	Farve	Kallipanguek.
Each	Enhver	Nungudlune.
Ear	Öre	Siut.
Early in the morning	Tidlig	Udlârallangoak.
Earn	Höste	Kattersoinek.
Earnest	Alvorlig	Illungersortok.
Earth	Jord	Nuna, v. Irbsok.
Earthenware	Leerkar	Marræt.
Easy, not difficult	Let	Ajornangitsok.
Eat	Spise	Nerrinek.
Eclipse	Formörkelse	Târsinek.
Eel	Aal	Nimeriak.
Elbow	Albue	Ikusik.
Eloquent, agreeable to hear	Veltalende	Tussarominartok.
Embark	Gaae ombord	Ikarnek.
Emetic	Brækmiddel	Meriarsaut.
Eminence of land	Höyde	Kingiksusek.
Emperor	Kejser	Kejsere (Danish).
Empty	Tom	Immakangitsok.
End	Ende	Naggate, v. iso.
Endless, eternal	Uendelig	Isukangitsok.
Ensign, flag	Flag	Aukpadlartok; propr. the red.
Enter	Gaae ind	Isernek.
Entry of a hut	Indgang	Pâk.
Evade	Undslippe	Annigoïnek.
Even	Endog	Aglæt.
Evening	Aften	Unnuk.
Event	Hændelse	Nellautsartugak.
Evil	Ond	Ajortok.
Exalted	Ophöyet	Kotsiksok.
Excels (he)	Han overgaaer	Sualungnerrovok
Exchange	Bytte	Taursinek.
Excite	Opmuntre	Kajumiksaïnek.
Excuse	Undskylde	Paitsisiksarsiornek.
Exert	Anstrenge sig	Åksorornek.
Exorbitant	Ubillig	Sualuktok.
Expect	Forvente	Nerigungnek.
Expectation	Farventning	Nerigut.

ENGLISH.	DANISH.	ESQUIMAUX.
Explains (he) it	Han forklarer det	Sukuïarpa.
Exposes (he) it	Han aabenbarer det	Nuellunejarpa.
Express, post	Expres	Paurtok.
Extends (he) it	Han udstrækker det	Tessipa.
Extinguishes, a light	Udslukkes	Kammipok.
Extremely	Overmaade	Aksut, v. aksursoak.
Extricates (he) it	Han udreder det	Illejarpa.
Eye	Oye	Irse.
Eyebrow	Oyenbryn	Kablo.
Eyelid	Öyelaag	Irsib mattua.
Face	Ansigt	Kenak.
Fact	Gjerningssag	Sulliak.
Fades (it), dies	Visner	Tokovok.
Fagot, flute, pipe	Trompet	Kardlortaut.
Faint	Besvime	Ounarsinek.
Fair, *adj.*	Smuk	Pinnersok.
Faith	Troe	Operneck.
Faithful	Trofast	Aulajangersok.
Fall (to)	Falde	Ordlonek, nakkarnek, nivernek, tammarnek.
False	Falsk	Opernangitsok.
Famine, hunger	Hunger	Kangnek.
Famine	Hungersnöd	Pertluk.
Famous	Bekjendt	Tytsinrsok.
Far (it is)	Det er langt borte	Ungesikpok, aunsikpok.
Farmer	Bonde	Naursoriksaïrsok.
Farther, again	Videre	Ama, amalo.
Fat	Feed	Puellarsok.
Father	Fader	Atatak.
Fathom	Favn	Issagak.
Fault	Fejl	Tammartanzek.
Fear	Frygt	Erkse (Ross voyage, erkshe).
Feather	Fjer	Merkok.
Fee	Belönning	Akke.
Fees (he)	Betaler	Akkiok.
Feels (he) it	Föler	Saiipa.
Feeling	Fölelse	Missigirsak.

ENGLISH.	DANISH.	ESQUIMAUX.
Fellow	Cammerad	Ajpak.
Ferryman	Færgemand	Ikaursirsok.
Fertile	Frugtbar	Naursoriksok.
Fetches (he) it	Henter	Aïä.
Fetters	Lænker	Kallimnerit.
Few	Faa	Ikitut.
Fickle	Ubestandig	Aulæjarsok.
Field	Mark	Narksak.
Fœtus (of a seal)		Iblau.
Fight (they)	Slaaes	Panikpuk.
Fight (a)	Slagsmaal	Paningnek.
Fills (he) it	Fylder	Imerpa.
Fin of a seal	Lalle	Tellerrok.
Final	Endelig	Kingurdlek.
Fine (pretty)	Smuk	Pinnersok.
Finger	Finger	Aksak.
Finishes (he) it	Ender	Naggaserpa.
Fire	Ild	Ingnek.
Fireside	Vramin	Kirsseksout.
Fish	Fisk	Aulisægak.
Fish-hook	Fiskekrog	Karasursak—karssursak.
Fit	Tjenlig	Ajungitsok.
Fix (to) any thing	Gjöre fast	Aulæjangersaïnek.
Flames (it)	Luer	Ikuellavok.
Flannel, or wadmal	Flanel, wadmel	Annoraksak merkolik.
Flaps (the bird)	Feagrer	Isarkellavok.
Flat	Fead	Manitsok.
Flea	Loppe	Piksiksak.
Flesh	Kjöd	Nekkre.
Flexible	Böyelig	Kretuktok.
Flight	Flugt	Kremaniarnek.
Flings (he) it	Kaster	Egipa.
Floats (it)	Flot (er)	Puktavok.
Flogs (he) him	Pidsker	Orpikpa.
Flood, high water	Flod	Ulle (river kok).
Floor	Gulv	Nettek.
Flour	Meel	Kajursæt.
Flows (the river)	Flyder	Kokpok.
Flower	Blomst	Naursok.
Flag (a)	Flue	Niviugak.
Fog	Taage	Pÿok.
Fold (on clothes)	Fold	Koglungnek.

ENGLISH.	DANISH.	ESQUIMAUX.
Follows (he) him	Fölger	Mallikpa.
Folly	Daarskab	Siunekangitsusek
Food	Föde	Nerrirseksak.
Fool	Nar	Mitartok.
Foot	Fod	Isikkæt (plur. of isigak, a toe).
Forbids (he) it	Forbyder	Pekkongila.
Forehead	Forhoved	Kauk.
Foreigner	Fremmed	Tekkornartak.
Forfeits (he) it	Forspilder	Tammarpa.
Forge (a)	Smedde	Saffiorfik.
Fork	Gaffel	Ajeksautik.
Forgets (he)	Glemmer	Puiorpok.
Forgives (he) it	Tilgiver	Isumakærpa.
Fortunate	Lykkelig	Pidluartok.
Foul	Smudsig	Minguktok.
Foundation	Grundvold	Tungavik.
Fountain	Kilde	Puilarsok.
Fowl	Fugl	Tingmiak.
Fox	Ræv	Terienniak.
Frame	Ramme	Innerfik.
Fraternity	Broderskab	Kattænguti-geengnek.
Fraud	List	Pekkosersout.
Free	Frie	Kivgaungitsok.
Freezes (it)	(Det) fryser	Issekau.
Frequent (to)	Besöge tit	Tikerarajungnek.
Frequenter (a)	Besöger	Tikiukajuktok.
Fresh, not salt	Fersk	Tarajorningitsok (R. v. tariornityoke.*
Friend	Ven	Ikingut.
Friendship	Venskab	Ikingutigeeng-nek.
Fright	Frygt	Erkse.
From (the fox)	Fra	Terienniamit, from: mit
Frugal	Tarvelig	Ibleruktok (N.B.)
Fruit	Frugt	Paurnæt.
Fry	Rogn	Suak.
Fries (he) it	Steger	Syeppa.
Fryingpan	Stegepande	Syetsivik.
Fulfils (he) it	Opfylder	Erkorpa.
Fully, he fulfils it fully	Fuldkommen	Erkordluïnarpa, luïnarpok: fully

ENGLISH.	DANISH.	ESQUIMAUX.
Fume	Rög	Issek.
Fun (to)	Bedrage	Seglokrittaïnek.
Furious	Rasende	Sekkunersok.
Furnace	Ovn	Kirsarsout.
Furnish	Meddele	Tunnirsinek.
Fur	Foder	Illupak.
Further!	Videre!	Ama!
Furthers (he) him	Hjelper	Ikiorpa.
Future	Tilkommende	Pirsuksak.
Gains (he) at play	Vinder	Immiarsiok (NB)
Gale (it is a)	Storm	Annordlersor-sovok
Gall	Galde	Sungak.
Game, seal, deer, &c.	Vildt	Nekke.
Game, birds	Vildt	Tingmirsæt.
Garden	Have	Nautjevik.
Garment	Klædning	Annorarsæt.
Garrison, soldiers	Guarnison	Sekkutout.
Garter	Hosebaand	Navlokot.
Gather	Samle	Kattersöinek.
Gay	Glad	Nuennartok.
Generous (he is)	Höimodig	Ajungilak.
Gently	Sagte	Kigejtsomik.
German, at Baal's River	Tydsker	Nourdlek.
Ghost	Aand	Annersak.
Holy Ghost	Helligaand	Annersak illu-artok.
Giddy	Svimmel	Uirpsartok.
Gift	Gave	Tunnirsut.
Gilt	Forgyldt.	Erdlingnarto-nik kajortomik kallipautilik.
Gilt, *subst.*	Forgyldning	Kallipaun erd-lingnartok.
Ginger	Ingefær	Kassillitsok.
Girdle	Belte	Kreterrut.
Girl	Pige	Niviarsiak.
Gives (he) him	Giver	Tunnia.
Glass	Glas	Imertarfik.
Glazes (he) it	Glaserer	Krebleriksarpa.
Gloomy of face	Mörk	Aunuktok.
Glory	Ære	Ussornarsusek.
Gloss	Glands	Kreblersusek.

* Tarajornityoke, tarajornitsok—salt. Not salt, tarajorningitsok.

ENGLISH.	DANISH.	ESQUIMAUX.
Glove	Handske	Aket (a pair, aketik).
Glue	Liim	Nepiniko.
Gnat (mosquito)	Myg	Ipernak.
Goal, border	Maal	Kiglik.
God	Gud	Gude (Dan.)
Gold	Guld	Gulde (Dan.) kangusak erdlingnartok. aukpadlartok.
Good	God	Ajungitsok.
Goods	Gods	Pekkotit.
Goose	Gaas	Nerdlek.
Gooseberry	Stikkelsbær	Paurnæt.
Gospel	Evangelium	Evangeliume (Dan.)
Gout	Værk	Auæluk.
Gown	Kjole	Annorak.
Grace	Naade	Sajma.
Grain	Korn	Timiurseksak.
Grape	Drue	Paurnak vinik-salik.
Grass	Græs	Ivik.
Grater	Rivejern	Aksaligutit.
Grave (a)	Grav	Illivek.
Gravel	Grovt sand	Siorarsoït.
Gray hair	Graae Haar	Kæk.
Greases (he) it	Smörer	Orksorpa.
Great	Stor	Angirsok.
Greedy	Graadig	Nerriaursok.
Green	Grön	Sungarpalluktok.
Greenland	Grönland	Innuit nunæt (Men's land).
Grey haired	Graahærdet	Kærsuktok.
Grief	Græmmelse	Isumalungnek.
Grieves (he)	Græmmer sig	Isumalukpok.
Groan	Stönne	Nimarnek.
Groin	Lyske	Akkullak (N.B.)
Growls (the dog)	Knurrer	Katimarpok.
Grumble	Knurren	Okallorulungnek
Grows (the plant)	Groer	Naulerpok.
Gruel	Havresuppe	Nivgursæt (N.B.)
Guard	Vagt	Pigartok.
Guess (to)	Gjette	Erkoiniarnek.
Guest	Gjest	Tikerak.

ENGLISH.	DANISH.	ESQUIMAUX.
Guides (he) him	Leder	Tessiorpa.
Guilt	Bröde	Ajortuliiak.
Guilty	Skyldig	Pitlægeksak.
Guitar	Guitarre	Syænnek, v. kukkilligut.
Gum in the ears	Gummi	Siksik.
Gums of a man	Gummer	Kigutit næggoviæt (N.B.)
Gun	Flint	Aulejt.
Gunpowder	Krudt	Paursæt.
Habit	Vane	Illerkok.
Hail, from heaven, frozen rain	Hagl	Natakornak.
Hair (of the head)	Hovedhaar	Nytsæt.
Hair (of an animal)	Haar	Merkut.
Hall	Sal	Innersoak.
Ham	Hasen	Navlo.
Hand	Haand	Aksæt.
Handkerchief	Lommeklæde	Kakkiksaut.
Handle (a)	Skaft	Epo.
Handsome	Smuk	Pinnersok.
Handspike	Bærestang	Ersut.
Hangs (he) him	Hænger	Kremipa.
Happen	Træffe sig	Nellautsartornek.
It happened	Det hændte sig	Nellautsartorpok, v. pisimavok.
I happened *		
Happy	Salig	Pidliuartok.
Happiness	Salighed	Pidluarsusek.
Harbour, for a boat, for a ship	Havn	Umiajtsiallivik. kisarfik.
Hard	Haard	Mangertok.
Hardens (it)	Forhærdes	Mangertipok.
Hardship	Besværlighed	Ajornartout.
Hare	Hare	Ukalek.
Harms (he) him	Fornærmer	Innarlerpa.
Harness	Sele	Anno.
Harrow	Harve	Erkriternrsoit (N.B.)
Harvest	Höst	Okiak.
Haste (to)	Haste	Tuoviornek.
Hat	Hat	Kangursak.

* Happen, it happens, I happened, must be translated by sunnaufa, *just*, unawares.

ENGLISH.	DANISH.	ESQUIMAUX.
Hates (he) him	Hader	Umiga.
Haughty	Trodsig	Pitsereetsok.
Hay	Höe	Ivik.
Hazy	Taaget	Pyolik.
Head	Hoved	Niakok.
Headach	Hovedpine	Niakordlunguek.
Heal	Læge	Kaïtsorsaïnek.
Health	Sundhed	Nekkorneck.
To thy good health	Din Sundhed	Innudluarkudlutit, your: luse
Heap	Hob	Koë.
Hear	Höre	Tussarnek.
Hearken	Lytte	Siumiksarnek.
Heart	Hjerte	Umat.
Hearty, from heart	Hjertelig	Umanit.
Heat	Varme	Kiek.
Heave something	Kaste	Egitsinek.
Heaven	Himmel	Krillak.
Heavy	Tung	Okemejtsok.
Hedge (a)	Indhegning	Ungælok.
Heedless	Tankelös	Isumakangitsok.
Heel	Hæl	Kimik.
Height	Höide	Portursusek.
Heir	Arving	Kingorngursirsok
Helm	Roer	Akout.
Helps (he) him	Hjelper	Ikiorpa.
Hem!	Aah!	Ijah!
Hen	Höne	Tukingarsolik.
Hence	Herfra	Manga.
Herb	Urt	Naursok.
Here	Her	Mane.
Hide	Dölge	Angiornek.
Hide	Hud	Amek.
High	Höi	Kotsiksok.
Hinders (he) it	Hindrer	Innerterpa.
High, tall	Höi	Portursok.
Hints (he) at it	Underretter	Nællunærpa.
Hire	Hyre	Kivgartout.
Hoarse	Grovmælet	Katitók.
Hog	Sviin	Poleke.
Hoists (he) it	Hejser	Amorpa.
Holds (he) it	Holder	Tigua.
Hole of a fox	Hul	Sisse.
Holy	Hellig	Illuartok.

ENGLISH.	DANISH.	ESQUIMAUX.
Home, house	Hjem	Iglo (land, nuna)
At home	Hjemme	Iglomiue (nunamine).
Honest	Skikkelig	Isumagiksok.
Hoof	Hov	Kukkik.
Hook in a boat	Hage	Niksik.
Hoop for a ton	Baand	Sokartak.
Hope (to)	Haabe	Nerigunguek.
Hops	Humle	Sungarnitsok (N.B.)
Horse	Hest	Hestersoak (Dan.)
Hot	Heed	Ounartok.
Hour	Time	Nællunækotam akkunera.
House	Huus	Iglo.
Hugs (he) him	Omfavner	Erkripa.
Hulls (it)	Driver	Savikpok.
Humble	Ydmyg	Kannilartok.
Hungry	Hungrig	Pertlilersok.
Hunt (Reind.)	Jage	Auarnek.
Hurricane	Orkan	Annorasuak.
Hurry (to)	Ile	Arinek.
Hurts (he) it	Beskadiger	Asserorpa.
Husband	Mand	Uvek.
Hushes (the seal)	Er stille	Terdlikpok.
Hut	Hytte	Iglo, v. iglungoak.
He is in the hut	Han er i Hytten	Iglomepok, v. iglungoamepok
Huzza	Hurra	Hurra (Dan.)
Hymn	Psalme	Tuksiaut.
Ice (of salt water)	Iis	Sikko.
Ice (of freshwater)		Sermek.
Iceberg	Iisfjeld	Illuliak.
Idle	Ledig	Sullicksakangitsok.
Idol	Afgud	Gudepiluk.
If it hushes	Hvis den er st.	Terdlikpet (see Hush).
Ignorance	Uvidenhed	Nællursusek.
Ill	Ond	Ajortok.
Illegal	Ulovlig	Innertigak.
Illness	Upasselighed	Ikpigosungnek.
Image	Billede	Arsilliak.

ENGLISH.	DANISH.	ESQUIMAUX.
Imitates (he) him	Efterligner	Arsiginiarpa.
Immense	Umaadelig	Kiglikangitsok.
Immortal	Udödelig	Tokuksaungitsok.
Immovable	Urokkelig	Aulæjangitsok.
Imparts (he) him	Meddeler	Illalerpa.
Impartial	Upartisk	Nellinginarsiortok.
Impatience	Utaalmodighed	Erinnitsengnek.
Impediment	Hindring	Akkornot.
Imperfect	Ufuldkommen	Namaglnangitsok.
Impertinence	Uforskammenhed	Kangusuïtsusek.
Impiety	Ugudelighed	Ajortullioromatounek.
Importance	Vigtighed	Ange.
Imposition	Beskyldning	Passiklint (N.B.)
Improbable	Usandsynlig	Opernangitsok.
Improper	Upassende	Arksoarnartok.
Improve	Forbedres	Illuarsarnek.
Imprudence	Uforstand	Sillakangitsusek.
Impure	Ureen	Minguktok.
Inch	Tomme	Kudlo.
Incision	Indsnit	Kidlek.
Increase	Foröges	Agdliartornek.
Incredible	Utrolig	Operirseksaungitsok.
Incurable	Incurabel	Mammisuïtsok.
Indeed	Virkelig	Illomut.
Indisposed	Upasselig	Ikpigosuktok.
Induces (he) him	Bevæger	Kajungersipa.
Inexhaustible	Uudtömmelig	Nunguksaungitsok.
Infamous	Berygtet	Tytsionerdluktok (N.B.)
Infant	Barn	Nalóngiak.
Infection	Smitte	Ajtsornartok.
Infinite	Uendelig	Isukangitsok.
Infirm	Svag	Nukangatsok.
Inflexible	Uböjelig	Perkrêtsok.
Infuses (he) it	Indgyder	Koïa.
Ingenious	Sindrig	Isumatòk.

ENGLISH.	DANISH.	ESQUIMAUX.
Ingrafts (he) it	Indpoder	Ikursorpa.
Ingrave	Indgrave	Aglengnek (NB.)
Inhabitant	Indbygger	Innuk.
Ink	Blæk	Blikke (Dan.)
Inkhorn	Blækhorn	Blikkillivik.
Inlet	Fjord	Kangek.
Inmost	Inderst	Illupak.
Inn	Værtshuus	Siniktarfik.
Innocent	Uskyldig	Pitlægeksaungitsok.
Inquire	Undersöge	Kiglisioïnek.
Inquisitor	En Undersöger	Kiglisioïrsok.
Insensible	Ufölsom	Missigirsakangitsok.
Insertion	Tilsætning	Illaursak.
Insolent	Uforskammet.	Kangusuïtsok.
Instantly	Strax	Erngeinak.
Instead of me	Istedetfor mig	Simnerdlunga (a verb).
Instrument	Instrument	Sennet.
Insult	Forhaane	Miteklernek.
Intend	Have i Sinde	Piomanek.
Intention	Hensigt	Piomursak.
Interior of it	Det Indvendige	Illua.
Internal (in it)	Indvortes	Illuanetok.
Interpret	Fortolke	Sukuïaïnek.
Inters (he) it	Han begraver det	Illia.
Interrupts (he) it	Afbryder(han)det	Sorarupa.
Interval	Mellemrum	Akkunek.
Interview	Sammenkómst	Nellaunek.
Intimates (he) it	Tilkjendegiver	Nællunærpa.
Intimidate	Forskrække	Erksisaïnek.
Intire	Heel	Illuïtsok.
Intirely	Oprigtigen	Pekkoserdlungitsomik.
Into dust	Til Stöv	Pyoala-mut*
Intreats (he) him	Bönfalde	Manigorpa.
Intrenchment	Forskandsning	Saliakot.
Invents (he)	Opdager	Nerpsarpok.
Iron	Jern	Savik.
Irresistible	Uimodstaaelig	Arktornartok.
Irritates (he) him	Opirre	Ningeksarpa.
Island	Öe	Krikertak.

* Mut is "into;" every *preposition* is affixed to the end of its noun.

L

ENGLISH.	DANISH.	ESQUIMAUX.	ENGLISH.	DANISH.	ESQUIMAUX.
Itch	Klöe	Ungilek.	Kitchen	Kjökken	Pak, v. pangoak, v. parsoak.
Item	Item	Ama.			
Ivory of a walrus	Elefenbeen	Tugak.	Kitten of a hare	Killing	Ukalèrak, kitten èrak.
Jacket	Tröie	Torojo (Dan.)	Knapsack	Randsel	Pok.
Jaw	Kjæbe	Aglerok.	Kneepan	Knæskal	Serkoak.
Jawbone	Kjæbebeen	Aglerok.	Knife	Kniv	Savik.
Jest, lie	Spög	Seglo.	Knit (a)	Strikket Töi	Tessitsuarsok.
Just now	Just nu	Tersa tava.	Knock	Banke	Kassuktoïnek.
Jewel	Juveel	Ujarak erdlingnartok.	Knot	Knude	Krelernek.
			Knows (he) him	Kjender	Ilirsara.
Joins (he) them	Forener	Kattitipej.	Knowledge	Kundskab	Ilisimarsusek.
Joiner	Snedker	Sennarsok.	Knuckle	Knokkel	Napparsortak.
Jokes (he) upon him	Narrer	Seglokrittarpa.	Labour	Arbejde	Sulliornek.
			Lace	Snor	Aklunaursak.
Jolly	Glad	Nuennartok.	Lad	Dreng	Nukakpiarak.
Journey	Rejse	Iugerdlanek.	Ladder	Stige	Majoartarfik.
Joy	Glæde	Tipejtsungnek.	Ladle	Sköv	Alluksaursoak.
Judge (a)	Dommer	Erkartoursirsok.	Lady, woman	Dame	Arnak.
Judgment	Dom	Erkartout.	Lake	Söe	Tessek (large tessersoak, sm. tessingoak.
Jug	Dunk	Marrak.			
Juice of fruits	Saft	Tungo.			
Jump (to)	Springe	Pissingnek.	Lame (he is)	Lam	Sefeepok.
Justice	Retfærdighed	Akkinnersidluarsimarsusek.	Lamp	Lampe	Kodlek.
			Land	Land	Nuna.
Justly	Retfærdigen	Illuartomik.	Lane	Gyde	Akkosiningoak.
Just so	Just saaledes	Tajma!	Language	Sprog	Okauzit (proprie words).
Knee	Knæ	Serkok.			
Keel	Kjöl	Kyek.	Lanthorn	Lygte	Nenneroarfik.
Keen	Skarp.	Kenariksok.	Laps (he) it	Svöber	Imupa.
Keeps (he) it	Beholder	Torkorpa.	Larboard *		
Kernel	Kjerne	Saurnek.	Lards (he) it	Spækker	Orksorpa.
Kettle	Kjedel	Ounavik.	Larder, storehouse	Proviantbod	Augoarfik.
Key	Nögle	Makpersaut.			
Kicks (he) it	Sparker	Tukerpa.	Large	Stor	Angirsok.
Kidney	Nyre	Tarto.	Lashes (he) him	Pidsker	Ipperartorpa.
Kills (he) it	Dræber	Tokopa.	Late (it is)	Sildig	Unnukpok.
Kind	Artig	Innuksiarnersok.	Laugh	Lee	Iglarnek.
			Law	Lov	Inneizisit.
Kindness	Artighed	Innuksiarnersusek.	Lawful (it is)	Lovligt	Inneizisit pekkoæt.
King	Konge	Konge (Dan.)	Lazy	Lad	Erkræjasuktok.
Kiss	Kys	Kunik.	Leaches (he) it	Sönderskjærer	Pillekpa.

* The translation hereof is determined by the position of the ship.

ENGLISH.	DANISH.	ESQUIMAUX.	ENGLISH.	DANISH.	ESQUIMAUX.
Leads (he) him	Leder	Tessiorpa.	Lining (inside)	Det Indvendige	Illo.
Leaf	Blad	Pillo.	Lie	Lögn	Seglo.
Leakage	Lækkage	Angmarnek (N.B.)	Lion	Löve	Löve (Dan.)
			Lip	Læbe	Kardlo.
Leaky (it is)	Læk	Angmarpok (N.B.)*	Liquid	Flydende	Puilarsok.
Lean	Mager	Selluktok.	List of contents in a book	Register	Nællunœrut.
Leans on (he) it	Læner sig	Egarfiga.	Listen	Lytte	Siumiksatnek.
Learns (he) it	Lærer	Ilipa.	Little	Liden	Mikirsok.
Least, *adj.*	Mindst	Mingnek.	Live	Leve	Innunek.
Leather	Læder	Amek.	Liver	Lever	Tingo.
Leaves (he) it	Forlader	Kremekpa.	Load	Byrde	Nangmœgak.
Leaves (it)	Ophörer	Sorarpok.	Lock	Laas	Parnœrsaut.
Lee	Læe	Orkoak.	Lodging	Logis	Inne.
Left side	Venstre side	Saumiæt tunga.	Lofty	Höy	Kingiktok.
Left hand	Venstre haand	Saumik.	Loin	Lænd	Kretek.
Leg	Been	Nio.	Look	See	Tekkonek.
Legal	Lovlig	Innertersiman-gitsok.	Loose (it is)	Lös	Pœrpok.
			Loss	Tab	Tammarnek.
Leisure (he is at)	Ledighed	Sullicksakan-gilak.	Loud	Lydelig	Nipitôk.
			Love	Kjerlighed	Assenuirsusek.
Lends	Laaner ud	Attartortitsiok.	Lovely	Elskelig.	Assanartok.
Length	Længde	Tekkirsusek.	Lover	Elsker	Assarse.
Less	Mindre	Mingnerrursok.	Louse	Luus	Komak.
Lessens (it)	Formindskes	Mikliok.	Lousy (he is)	Luset (han er)	Komakpok.
Lesson of a pupil	Leetie	Iliniægeksak.	Low	Lav	Pukitsok.
Letter	Brev	Aglegak.	Luncheon	Et Stykke Mad	Nerriarut.
Level land	Jevn	Manitsok.	Lungs	Lunge	Puak.
Liberty	Frihed	Kivgaungitsusek.	Lustre	Glimmer	Kreblersusek.
Licks (he) it	Slikker	Allukpa.	Life	Liv	Innunek.
Life	Liv	Innunek.	Mad	Gal	Peblerortok.
Lifts (he) it	Löfter	Kivikpa.	Maid	Möe	Niviarsiak.
Light, *adj.*	Lys	Kaumarsok	Mails (he) it	Beklæder	Kadlerpa.
Light, *subst.*	Lys	Kau,v. nennerout	Makes (he)	Gjör	Piok.
Light	Let	Okêtsok.	Mall, hammer	Hammer	Kautak.
Lightens (he) it	Oplyser	Kaumarsarpa.	Malt	Malt	Imicksak.
Lightens (he) it	Letter	Okêdlia.	Man	Menneske	Innuk.
Lightning	Lyn	Ingnaglegiak.	Man	Mand	Angut.
Like (it is) to it	Lig	Arsiga.	Man of war	Orlogsskib	Sekkutout.
Likeness	Lighed	Arsigeeksusek.	Manly	Mandig	Angutauserdlune
Limb	Lem	Aunæt.	Manner	Maade	Ilerkok.
Limp (to)	Halte	Sefeenek.	Manure (to)	Gjöde	Orksoïnek.
Line (whale)	Line	Allek.	Many	Mange	Kapseet.

* Better perhaps "uvsingilak."

ENGLISH.	DANISH.	ESQUIMAUX.	ENGLISH.	DANISH.	ESQUIMAUX.
Map	Kort	Arsilliak (N.B.)	Misfortune	Ulykke	Pertlout.
Mark	Mærke	Nællunaerkot.	Misleads (he) him	Forförer	Asserorpa.
Market	Torv	Pissiniarfik(NB.)	Miss	Vildfarelse	Tammartauzek.
Marriage	Bryllup	Katternavik.	Mistake	Tage fejl	Tammardlungnek.
Marrow	Marv	Patek.	Mistress, wife	Madame	Nulliak.
Marsh	Mose	Pinguït.	Misty, foggy (it is)	Taaget (det er)	Pyolirksovok.
Match	Lige	Nelle.	Mixes (he) it	Blander	Akupa.
Matches (he) him	Er lige med	Nedlerpà.	Mocks (he)	Spotter	Miteklerpok.
Mate	Styrmand	Akkutok.	Moist	Fugtig	Isugutarsok.
Mathematics	Mathematik	Kissitsinek.	Moment (in a)	I Öyeblikket	Tersugo.
Matrimony	Ægteskab	Nulliareengnek.	Money	Penge	Anningaursæt.
Matter (what is the)?	Hvad vil du?	Syssavit?	Month and moon	Maaned, Maane	Kaumæt.
Mature	Moden	Enersimarsok.	Moon (it is full)	Det er fuld Maane	Anningat imiksiok.*
Maxim (doctrina)	Grundsætning	Ajokærsut.	Morning	Morgen	Udlak.
Meadow	Eng	Pinguït.	Mortar	Morter	Asserorterivik.
Meal	Meel	Kajursæt.	Moss (lich isl.)	Moos	Orksursak.
Mean	Ringe	Nikkanartok.	Mother	Moder	Ananak.
Means	Middelstand	Akkudlek.	Motion	Bevægelse	Aulanek.
Means	Middel	Pirsut.	Mould	Skimmel	Okok.
Measles of a skin	Narv	Ekarte.	Mountain	Fjeld	Kakkak.
Measure	Maal	Oktout.	Mouth	Mund	Kanek.
Meat	Kjöd	Nekkriksak.	Moves (it)	Bevæges	Aulavok.
Mediator	Midler	Sajmarsaïrsok.	Mud	Mudder	Mauvak.
Medium, v. means			Multitude	Mængde	Amerdlarsusek.
Meet	Mödes	Nellaunek.	Murder	Mord	Innuærnek.
Member of it	Lem	Illa.	Musters (he) it	Mönstre	Tekkotipa.
Memory	Hukommelse	Erkaïrsut.	Mustard	Senep	Senepe (Dan.)
Mends (it)	Forbedres	Ajorungnærpok.	Mutiny	Oprör	Pikititsinek.
Mentions (he) it	Omtale	Okautiga.	Mutton	Faarekjöd	Saua.
Mercy	Barmhjertighed	Nakinningnek.	Mystery	Mysterium	Nællunartok.
Merit	Fortjeneste	Piksak.	Nail, iron or copper	Nagle	Kikiek.
Merry	Moersom	Tivsinartok.	Nail of fingers or toes	Nægl	Kukkik.
Message	Budskab	Okalluktout.	Naked	Nögen	Tamakangitsok.
Midwife	Jordemoder	Ernisuksiortok.	Name	Navn	Attek.
Mile	Miil	Mile (Dan.)	What is thy name?	Hvad hedder du?	Kannong, attekarpit?
Milk	Melk	Imuk; of a woman, amamak.	Namely	Nemlig	Imejtok.
Mill	Mölle	Asserorterivik.	Naps of cloth	Luug	Merkut, plural of merkok.
Mind	Sind	Isuma.			
Minor	Mindre	Mingnerrursok.			
Mischief	Fortred	Nagliut.			
Misery	Elendighed	Pidluejtsusek.			

* It is new moon ("Nye Maane") "ussiok;" it is first quarter ("Förste Quarteer") "anningat igdlokarpok;" it is last quarter ("sidste Quarteer") "anningat igdloærupok."

ENGLISH.	DANISH.	ESQUIMAUX.
Narrow	Smal	Amitsok (Ross voy. amityoke).
Nasty	Skiden	Ippertok.
Naughty	Unyts	Suksaungitsok.
Navel of a child	Navle	Kallisek.
Navy	Marine	Umiarsoarperksoït.
Near	Nær	Kannitok.
Neat	Net	Kurseguunartok.
Necessity (it is a)	Nödvendighed	Pirsariakarpok.
Neck, lat. collum	Hals	Kongæsek.
Neckcloth	Halsklæde	Kongæserut.
Need (to)	Trænge	Ajorsarnek.
Needle	Synaal	Merkut, plural merkutit.
Neglects (he) it	Forsömmer	Assiginnarpa.
Neighbour, fellow man	Næste	Innukate.
Nests of birds	Reder	Innit.
Never (he comes)	Aldrig (han kommer)	Pinauviœngilak (piok, he comes; nauviœngilak, never).
New	Nye	Nutak.
Next to it (it is)	Næst ved (det er)	Senniauepok.
Nibble	Bide	Nerritsiarnek.
Nice (he is)	Vanskelig	Ajornakau.
Nickname	Ögenavn	Ajtseraut.
Night	Nat	Unnuak.
Nods (he)	Nikker	Sikkikpok.
Noise	Tummel	Perpallungnek.
Noon	Middag	Udlub kerka.
Nose	Næse	Kringak.
Nostril	Næsebor	Kringak.
Nothing (it is)	Intet (det er)	Sungilak.
Notion	Mening	Isuma.
Novelty	Nyhed	Nutaursusek.
Now	Nu	Mana.
Number	Tal	Kissitsit.
Numberless	Utallig	Kissiksaungitsok
Nurses (she) it	Ammer	Milluktipa
Wet nurse	Amme	Milluktitsirsok
Nutmeg	Muskatnöd	Kassilitsok.
Nutriment	Föde	Nerrirseksak, v. innutiksak.
North wind	Nordenvind	Anangnak.
Oak (a log of)	Eeg	Kressuk mangertok.
Oar	Aare	Eput.
Obedient	Lydig	Nalektok.
Obeys (he)	Lyder	Nalekpok.
Oblong	Aflang	Angmalungajektok (N.B.)
Obstacle	Hindring	Akkornot.
Obstinate	Halstarrig	Perkrêtsok.
Obstruction (he has)	Forstoppelse	Tettuiok (a sickness).
Obtains (he) it	Erholder	Angumera.
Obvious (it is)	Tydelig	Nællunangilak.
Occupies (he) it	Besidder	Piga.
Occurs (he) him	Möder	Nellaupa.
Odd	Besynderlig	Tupingnartok.
Offence	Forbrydelse	Pinerdlugak.
Offends (he) him	Fornærmer	Ningeksarpa.
Office of the church	Tjeneste	Nalegiarnek.
Often	Ofte	Kapseennik.
Oil	Olie	Olie (Dan.)
Ointment	Salve	Tennirsut.
Old	Gammel	(Man) utokak; (thing) nutaungitsok.
Omits (he) it	Undlader	Pingila.
Once	Engang	Kanga.
Only, *adj.*	Alene	Kissime.
Open (it is)	Aaben	Angmarpok.
Opiate	Opiat	Siniksaut (N.B.)
Oppresses (he) him	Undertrykker	Kunnutipa.
Opulent	Formuende	Pekkentilirksoak.
Orders (he) it	Ordner	Arkriksorpa.
Ore	Ærts	Kangusak.
Oriental	Orientalsk	Pauangarnitsak
Origin	Begyndelse	Naggovik.
Ornament	Prydelse	Arsut.
Ostentation	Pralerie	Ussorsitsaut.
Otherwise	Anderledes	Adlamik.
Oven	Ovn	Kirkseksout.
Over it	Ovenpaa	Kane.

ENGLISH.	DANISH.	ESQUIMAUX.	ENGLISH.	DANISH.	ESQUIMAUX.
Out (it is)	Ude	Sillamepok.	Peasant	Bonde	Naursoriksaïrsok.
Outlet	Aflöb	Akkut.	Peel	Skal	Kallipak.
Outside	Ydersiden	Kallek.	Pen	Pen	Aglaut.
Owe	Skylde	Akkeetsornek.	Penetrates (it) it	Gjennemtrænger	Kiblikpa.
Owl	Ugle	Opik.	Pensive	Tankefuld	Isumatok.
Own (to)	Bekjende	Nællunærnek.	People	Folk	Innuïejt.
Owner (its)	Ejer	Innua (prop. its man).	Pepper	Peber	Kassilitsok.
Ox	Oxe	Umingmak.	Perfect (it is)	Fuldkommen	Namaksiok.
Pace	Skridt	Abloriak.	Performs (he) it	Fuldförer	Namaksia.
Pack	Byldt	Ersugak.	Perhaps	Maaskee	It is perhaps perfect, namaksinerpok.*
Paddle, of a canoe, of a boat	Aare	Paurtik, eput.	Peril	Fare	Nauvirnartok.
Padlock	Hængelaas	Parnœrsaut.	Perish in a canoe	Omkomme	Kajaunek.
Page in a book	Side	Kopernek.	Perish in a women boat		Umionek.
Pail	Spand	Kattak.	Permits (he) it	Tillader	Akkoera.
Pain	Pine	Annernartok.	Perpetual	Bestandig	Naksaungitsok.
Paints (he)	Afmaler	Arsilliok.	Personal, self	Selv	Nangminek.
Paint (a)	Malerie	Arsilliak.	Persuades (he) him	Overtaler	Kajumiksarpa.
Pair (to)	Parres	Nulliarnek.	Pert	Munter	Krêlarsok.
Palate	Gane	Krillak.	Peruses (he) it	Gjennemlæser	Attuarkriksarpa.
Pale	Bleg	Asingarsok.	Pestle	Stöder	Asserorterut.
Palpable	Fölelig	Mallungnartok.	Pew	Kirkestol	Ivksiavik.
Pan (frying)	Stegepande	Syetsivik.	Phrase	Phrase	Okauzek.
Pane	Rude	Igalaksak.	Picks (the bird)	Pikker	Ikkuksiok.
Paper	Papiir	Papire (Dan.) erruktoriursæt.	Pickles (he) it	Salter	Tarajorpa.
Parcel	Pakke	Imutak.	Picture	Malerie	Arsilliak.
Parchment	Pergament	Unnek.	Piece	Stykke	Asserkoko.
Parsley	Petersillie	Naursut, nautjeæt.	Piety	Gudsfrygt	Nalengnek Gudimut.
Parsnip	Pastinak		Pig	Griis	Polekerak (N.B.)
Part (to)	Adskilles	Auïngnek.	Pigeon	Due	Due (Dan.)
Pass	Gane	Ingerdlanek.	Pike of a soldier	Spyd	Sekko.
Path	Stie	Akkosiningoak.	Pillow	Hovedpude	Akit, v. akisingoak.
Patience	Taalmodighed	Illelarnek.	Pilot	Lods	Ilisimarsok (N.B.)
Paw	Kloe	Kukkik.	Pin	Naal	Kukkilit.
Pays (he) it	Betaler	Akkillerpa.	Pincers	Tang	Pyssugutik.
Pay	Betaling	Akkiksak.	Pinches (he) him	Kniber	Pyssukpa.
Pea	Ært	Ærte (Dan.)	Pines (he)	Tæres	Uïngærupok.
Peace	Fred	Erkriksinek.			
Pear, apple	Pære, Æble	Paurnarsoak.			
Perches (the bird)	Sætter sig	Mipok.			

* Perhaps, "nerpok."

ENGLISH.	DANISH.	ESQUIMAUX.
Pious	Gudfrytig	Gudimut nalektok.
Pipe for smoking	Pibe	Pyortaut.
Pit	Hul	Itersak.
Pitch (to)	Styrte	Ordlonek.
Pitcher	Leerkrukke	Marrak.
Pity	Medlidenhed	Nakinnirsusek.
Place	Plads	Inne.
Plain	Slette	Narksak.
Plains (he) it	Jevner	Manniksarpa.
Plank	Planke	Segliligarsoak.
Plants (he) it	Planter	Ikursorpa.
Plate	Plade	Singartugak.
Play (to) with cards	Spille	Innuarnek.
Pleasant	Fornöyelig	Nuennersok.
Pleases (it) him	Behager	Nuennera.
If thou please	Em du behager	Pionaguit.
Pleasure	Fornöyelse	Tipejtsut.
Plenty	Mængde	Köe.
Plows (he) it	Plöyer	Kreporkarpa.
Plum, pear, &c.	Blomme, pære	Paurnarsoak.
Point of land	Næs	Nouk.
Poison	Gift	Tokonartok.
Polite	Höflig	Innuksiarnersok.
Pomatum	Pomade	Tennirsut.
Pond	Park	Tessingoak.
Poop of a ship	Bagstavn	Akko.
Poor	Fattig	Peetsok.
Pork	Flesk	Poleke.
Port	Port	Isertarsirksoak.
Postpones (he) it	Öpsætter	Kakugorpa.
Pot	Potte	Iga.
Potatoes	Vrartoller	Nautjeet.
Pound	Pund	Urssersaut.
Pours (he) it	Udgyder	Kona.
Powder	Krudt	Paursaut.
Power	Magt	Pirsaut.
Practice	Vane	Illerkok.
Prate	Prat	Okallektarnek.
Pray	Bede	Tuksiarnek.
Prayer	Bön	Tuksiaut.
Prayer-book	Bönnebog	Tuksiautit (plur. of tuksiaut).
Preach	Præke	Okallungnek.

ENGLISH.	DANISH.	ESQUIMAUX.
Precipice	Bratning	Innak.
Preface	Fortale	Siulerkot.
Prefers (he) it	Foretrokke	Ajunginerrotipa.
Prepare one's self	Lave sig til	Pilersarnek.
Present (to)	Forære	Tunnirsinek.
Present (a)	Foræring	Tunnirsut.
Present (to give a)	Forære	Tunnirsinek.
Presently	Strax	Erngeinak.
Preserves	Syltetöy	Torkugak (N.B.)
Press	Presse	Nakkrittaut.
Plover, bird	Brokfugl	Kajordlek.
Presume	Formode	Isumakaraek.
Pretence	Paaskud	Pajtsisiksak.
Pretend	Foregive	Pajtsisiksarsiornek.
Pretension	Fordring	Pekkorsinek.
Prevalent (it is)	Overlegen	Sualukpok.
Prevents (it)	Forekommer	Akkornotavok.
Price	Priis	Akke.
Pride	Stolthed	Makkittarsusek.
Prince	Prinds	Rongim ernera, v. erkardlia.
Prints (he) it	Trykker	Nakkrittarpa.
Princess	Prindsesse	Rongib panna, v. erkardlia.
Prison	Fængsel	Parnaersortik.
Privy, a house	Privet	Anatartik.
Prize	Priis	Akke.
Produces (he) it	Fremstiller	Nuisipa.
Produce	Frugt	Kinguniksak.
Progress	Fremskridt	Agdliartornek.
Promise	Lövte	Unnersugak.
Promotes (he) it	Fremhjelper	Ikiorpa.
Proof	Pröve	Okattarut.
Property	Eyendom	Pigirsak.
Propriety	Egenskab	Kamong esusek
Prosperity	Held	Pidluarnek.
Protection	Beskyttelse	Igdlersornek.
Proud	Stolt	Makkittarsok.
Provokes (he) him	Fortörne	Ningeksarpa.
Prunes	Blommer	Paurnaet.
Publican	Tolder	Tunnirsutunnik kattersorsok.
Puff	Er opblæst	Pudlekpok.
Pull in a boat	Roe.	Epunek.

ENGLISH.	DANISH.	ESQUIMAUX.	ENGLISH.	DANISH.	ESQUIMAUX.
Pulpit	Prækestoel	Okalluktarfik.	Raw (it is)	Raa	Ajpavok.
Pump	Pompe	Miluartok.	Rays (the sun)	Straaler	Nuersorpok.
Punish	Straffe	Pitlarnek.	Razor	Rageknív	Ungiaut.
Purchase	Kjöbe	Pissiniarnek.	Reach it (Lat. cedo !)	Ræk hid !	Kaïrsuk !
Pure	Reen	Erröitok.			
Purpose	Forsæt	Piomarsak.	Reads (he)	Læser	Attuarpok.
Purses (he) it	Renser	Ervkrejarpa.	Ready (it is)	Færdig	Piarærpok.
Pursues (he) him	Forfölger	Mallersorpa.	Reason	Fornuft	Silla.
Push (to)	Anstrænge	Aksorornek.	Receives (he) it	Modtager	Pia.
Put	Lægge	Illirsinek.	Recently	Nyligen	Tersa tava.
Putrid	Raaden	Mikiak.	Reckon	Regne	Kissitsinek.
Puzzles (it) him	Bemöyer	Erdlokotipa.	Reckoning	Regning	Kissitsisit.
Quality	Beskaffenhed	Kannoug-esusek.	Recollects (he) it	Erindrer	Erkaïa.
Quantity	Störrelse	Angirsusek.	Recovery	Helbredelse	Piungnærsusek.
Quarrel	Uenighed	Akkerareengnek.	Recreation	Fornöjelse	Nuennârut.
Quay, beach	Strand	Siksak.	Rectifies (he) it	Berigtiger	Illuarsarpa.
Queen	Dronning	Kongib nullia.	Red	Röd	Aukpadlartok.
Quenches fire	Slukkes	Kummipok.	Redeemer	Forlöser	Annaursirsok.
Question	Spörgsmaal	Apersut.	Redemption	Forlösning	Annaut.
Quick	Hurtig	Akunit !	Redresses (he) it	Retter	Ajunginerrotipa.
Quiet (to be)	Tie stille	Nipangernek.	Reef	Rif	Ikkatok.
Quires (he)	Synger i choret	Akpipok.	Refreshes (he) him	Vederqvæger	Nekkursektipa.
Quits (he) him	Forlader	Kremekpa.			
Quiver	Pilekogger	Karksut pogæt.	Refreshment	Vederqvægelse	Nekkursaut.
Race	Slægt	Kingueksæt.	Refuge	Tilflugt	Kremaviksak.
Radish	Rædike	Nautjeak.	Refuses, says no	Afslaae	Naggarpok.
Black Radish	Sort Rædike		Regards (he) it not	Ikke agte	Suksaringila.
Rag	Pjalt	Annoraminek.			
Rage	Raserie	Sekkunek.	Rejects (he) him	Forstöder	Ajektorpa.
Rails (he) it	Omgiver	Ungalorpa.	Reigns (he)	Hersker	Nalegavok.
Rain	Regn	Sielluk.	Relates (he) it	Beretter	Okautiga.
Rainbow	Regnbue	Krillaungursak v. nerigursak.	Relation	Slægtskab	Erkardlereeng-nek.
Rainy (the weather is)	Regnveir	Siedleïnarpok.	Relief	Tröst	Sungersout.
			Relishes (he) it	Finder Smag i	Mammara.
Rank	Stinkende	Tipitôk.	Relics (he) on it	Stoler paa	Tunnara.
Rapid (the stream is)	Der er stærk Ström	Sarfarkau.	Remain	Rest	Siunek.
			Remark	Anmærkning	Narkrigut.
Rascal	Skurk	Isumaluktopi-lurksoak.	Remedy, medicine	Remedium	Nekkursaut.
Rash	Ubesindig	Sillærutok.	Remembers (he)	Erindrer	Erkaïok.
Rate (of high)	Dyre	Akkissok.	Remote	Fjern	Ungesiksok.
Ratifies (he) it	Stadfæster	Narkriksorpa.	Removes (he) it	Bortbringer	Noukpa.
Ravages (he) it	Odelægger	Piorngærutipa.	Renew	Fornye	Nutangortitsinek
Rave	Være gal	Peblerornek.	Repairs (he) it	Reparerer	Illuarsarpa.

ENGLISH.	DANISH.	ESQUIMAUX.
Repeats (he) it	Gjentager	Utertarpa.
Repents (he)	Fortryder	Perkriksimiok.
Report	Beretning	Unniut.
Reposes (he)	Ligger	Innarpok.
Represents (he) it	Forestiller	Nællunejarpa.
Reproach	Bebrejdelse	Arksoardliut.
Request	Bön	Krenut.
Rescues (he) him	Befrier	Annigortipa.
Resembles (it) him	Ligner	Arsiga.
Resides (he) at Iglolik	Boer	Iglolik nunaga.
Resigns (he) it	Opgive	Ipperarpa, v. kremekpa.
Resists (he) it	Modstaaer	Akkerartorpa.
Resolves (he)	Beslutter	Piomavok.
Rests (he)	Hviler	Kassuærsarpok.
Restore	Give tilbage	Utertitsinek.
Retains (he) it	Beholder	Illumioga.
Returns (he)	Vender tilbage	Uterpok, v angerdlarpok.
Revelation of St. John	Aabenbaring	Tekkordlogak.
Revenge	Hævne	Akkiniarnek.
Reviews (he) it	Gjennemseer	Missilingniarpa.
Revokes (he) it	Tilbagekalder	Utertipa.
Reward	Belönning	Akke.
Rib	Ribbeen	Tullimak.
Rich	Riig	Pissók.
Rid	Befrie	Annigoutitsinek.
Rides (the ship)	Ankrer	Kisarput.
Rises (the tide)	Vandet voxer	Ullilerpok.
Rigs (he) him	Pudser	Arsorpa.
Right	Ret	Illuartok.
Right	Ret	Pirseksak.
Right hand	Höyre haand	Tellerpik.
Ring of the ear	Örenring	Siunio.
Ring of the finger	Fingerring	Aksanio.
Ripe	Moden	Enersimarsok.
Rise, get up	Rejse sig	Makkinek.
River	Flod	Kok.
Road	Vey	Akkosinek.
Roasted	Stegt	Syettak.
Robs (he) him	Plyndrer	Pejarpa.

ENGLISH.	DANISH.	ESQUIMAUX.
Rock, in the sea	Skjær	Ikkardlok.
Rock, on shore	Fjeld	Kakkak.
Rod	Riis	Orpik.
Rogue	Kjeltring	Innupiluk.
Roof	Tag	Auvek.
Room	Værelse	Inne.
Root	Rod	Tungavik.
Rope	Toug	Aklunaursak.
Rough	Ujevn	Maneetsok.
Round it	Omkring	Auatagut.
Roe, of fish	Rogn	Suak.
Rubs (he)	Gnider	Aggiaïok.
Rudder	Roer	Akkout.
Rude (a) man	Uvidende	Nællursok.
Rue (to)	Angre	Perkriksiminek.
Rug	Uldent Töy	Merkolik.
Ruin (to)	Ödelægge	Piorngærutitsinek.
Rule (to)	Regjere	Nalegaunek.
Ruff, for the neck	Krave	Saliakot, v. kongæserut.
Rum	Rum	Sillakangitsok ankpadlartok.
Rumours (he) it	Udspreder	Tytsiotipa.
Runs (he)	Löber	Akpapok.
Rust	Rust	Mangertornek.
Sabre	Sabel	Pænna.
Sack	Sæk	Pok.
Safe	Sikker	Nauviænangitsok
Sail	Seil	Tingerdlaut.
Sailor	Matros	Kivgak.
Salmon	Lax	Ekalluk.
Salt	Salt	Tarajok (adject. tarajornitsok).
Salutation	Hilsen	Innudluarkorsinek
Salute	Salut	
Salvation	Frelse	Annaursinek.
Sample	Pröve	Missiligut.
Sand	Sand	Siorak.
Sands	Sandörkener	Innuïlak.
Sauce	Sauce	Missugutiksak.
Saucy	Næsviis	Innuksisimangitsok.
Saviour	Frelser	Annaursirsok.
Saw	Saug	Pillektout.

ENGLISH.	DANISH.	ESQUIMAUX.
Says (he)	Siger	Okarpok.
Scale	Vægt	Urssersaut.
Scales, on fish	Skjæl	Taptaursæt.
Scanty	Knap	Erdliktok.
Scar	Ar	Krelerok.
Scarce	Sjelden	Erdlingnartok.
School	Skole	Iliniarfik.
Schoolfellow	Skolekammerat	Iliniarkate.
Science	Videnskab	Ilisimanartok.
Scissors	Sax	Krejutik.
Scolds (he) at him	Skjænder paa	Nauværpa.
Score, 20	En snees	Innuk (a man's 10 fingers and 10 toes).
Scorns (he) it	Bespotter	Mitekpa.
Scorn	Spot	Miteklerneck.
Scrapes (he) it	Skraber	Killiorpa.
Scratches (he)	Kradser	Kukkillektorpok.
Scream,	Skrige	Niblernek.
Screens (he) it	Bedække	Perorpa, v. mattorpa.
Screw	Skrue	Skrue (Dan.)
Scripture	Skriften	Aglekkæt.
Scurvy	Skjörbug	Auæluk.
Sea	Hav	Imak.
Seafaring man	Söefarende	Imarsiortok.
Sealingwax	Lak	Nakrirsut.
Seam (a)	Söm	Killuk.
Searches (he)	Söger	Ujardlerpok.
Season (summer)	Sommer	Aursak.
Seat	Sæde	Ivksiavik.
Secret	Hemmelig	Angiortok.
Secure (he) is	Sikker	Erkrikpok.
Seduces (he) him	Forförer	Ajokærsornerdlukpa.
Sees (he)	Seer	Tekkovok.
Seed	Sæd	Kinguniksak.
Seeks (he) it	Söger	Ujarpa.
Seems (he)	Synes	He seems to see, Tekkokokau.
Seizes (he) him	Griber	Tigua.
Seldom	Sjelden	Kakutigut.
Selects (he) it	Vælger	Krennerpa.
Sells (he) it	Sælger	Tunnia.

ENGLISH.	DANISH.	ESQUIMAUX.
Sennight	Uge	Sabbatik akkuneræk.
Sense	Fölelse	Missigirsusek.
Sentence	Dom	Erkartout.
Separates (he) it	Adskiller	Auïkpa.
Serious	Alvorlig	Illungersortok.
Sermon	Prædiken	Okalluzek.
Serpent	Slange	Pullateriársuk.
Servant	Tjener	Kivgak.
Sets sail (he)	Sætter Sejl til	Tiksiuserpok.
Sets (the sun)	Solen gaaer ned	Sekkrinek tarrilerpok.
Settle	Blive staaende	Aulajungnærnek.
Sew	Sye	Mersornek.
Shabby cloth	Forreven	Alliksimarsok.
Shade	Skygge	Tarrak.
Shakes (he) it	Ryster	Aulaterpa.
Shame	Skam	Kangusungnek.
Shape	Skikkelse	Arse.
Share of it	Deel	Illa.
Sharp (it is)	Skarp	Ipikpok.
Shave	Rage	Ungiarnek.
Sheath	Skede	Inne.
Sheds (he) it	Udgyder	Koïa.
Sheep	Faar	Saua.
Sheet of a table	Dug	Saliakot.
Shelters (he) him	Beskytter	Igdlersorpa.
Shews (he) it	Viser	Niptarpa.
Shield	Skjold	Erkornauværkot.
Shifts (he) from a place	Flytter	Noukpok.
Shines (it)	Skinner	Krebblerikpok.
Ship	Skib	Umiarsoït.
Shirt	Skjorte	Illudlek.
Shoar (shore)	Strand	Siksak.
Shock (to)	Stöde	Aponek.
Shoes	Skoe	Atteraursæk.
Shoots (he)	Skyder	Egipok.
Shop	Krambod	Niuvertarlik.
Short	Kort	Naïtsuk.
Shoulder	Skulder	Tue.
Shudders (he)	Skjælver	Olikpok
Shuns (he) it	Skyer	Ingalekpa.
Sheet of paper	Ark	Erruktoriursak.
Shy	Sky	Nyoartok.

ENGLISH.	DANISH.	ESQUIMAUX.	ENGLISH.	DANISH.	ESQUIMAUX.
Sick	Syg	Napparsimarsok.	Smooth water	Smult	Kaitsungarsok.
Side (its)	Side	Sennia.	Snare	Snare	Nigak.
Sieve (a)	Sold	Nakkalaterut.	Snatches (he) it	Snapper	Kalluva.
Sign	Tegn	Nællunærkot.	Sneezes (he)	Nyser	Tangajorpok.
Silent (he is)	Tier	Nipangerpok.	Snores (he)	Snorker	Kangoïok.
Silk (adject.)	Silke	Satok.	Snow	Snee	Aput
Silver	Sölv	Sölve (Dan.) kangusak erdlingnartok kakortok.	Snuff	Snuustobak	Sunnorse
			Soap	Sæbe	Kakorsaut.
			Soft	Blöd	Akitsok.
			Soil	Smuds	Mingo.
Sin (to)	Synde	Ajortulliornek (a sin, ajorte).	Soldier	Soldat	Sekkutok, v. sorsuktuksak.
Since (hereafter)	Siden	Kingorna.	Sometimes	Undertiden	Illane.
Sincere	Oprigtig	Illungersortok.	Son	Sön	Ernek, v. niarnak.
Sinew	Sene	Yalo.			
Sings (he)	Synger	Ivngerpok.	Song	Sang	Ivngerut.
Sink	Synke	Ajtsingnek.	Sooths (he)	Smigrer	Kujarmavok.
Sister, or brother	Söster	Kattængut.	Sore	Byld	Ajoak.
Sits (he)	Sidder	Ivksiavok, v. ingipok.	Sorrow	Sorg	Alliejsut.
			Sorry	Bedrövet	Alliejsuktok.
Situation	Beliggenhed	Sumesusek.	Soul	Sjæl	Tarnek.
Skates (snow)	Skier	Sissorautik.	Sound (noise)	Lyd	Perpallunguek.
Skate	Sköjte	Sardlirsaut.	Sound (it has good)	Lyder godt	Nipigikpok.
Sketch	Skizze	Arsilliak.			
Skill	Dygtighed	Piukursusek.	Sound (it has a bad)	Lyder ilde	Nipilukpok.
Skin	Skind	Amek.			
Sky	Himmel	Krillak.	Sour	Suur	Sernartok.
Sledge	Slæde	Kamutik.	Sows (he) it	Saaer	Siammartipa.
Sleeps (he)	Sover	Sinikpok.	Spade	Spade	Tuggaut.
Sleepy (he is)	Sövnig	Uernarpok.	Spares (he) it	Sparer	Iblera.
Sleeve	Ærme	Ak.	Sparks (it)	Gnistrer	Ikuellekpok.
Slices (he)	Gjör tynd	Seglileriok.	Sparrow, Emb. niv.	Spurv	Kopanauarsuk.
Slides (he)	Glider	Sissorarpok.			
Slight	Tynd	Satok.	Speaks (he)	Taler	Okallukpok.
Slops (he) it	Spilder paa	Koïa.	Spectacles	Briller	Irsaursæk.
Slope	Skak	Kurksangarsok.	Speech	Tale	Okalluzek.
Slow (he is)	Langsom	Kigeipok.	Speeds (he)	Iler	Tuoviorpok.
Slumbers (he)	Slumrer	Siniorarpok.	Spells (he)	Bogstaverer	Taiorpok.
Small	Liden	Mikirsok.	Spice	Kryderie	Kassillitsok.
Smart	Smertefuld	Annernartok.	Spirit (brandy)	Spiritus	Sillakangitsok.
Smell	Lugt	Tipe (its smell, tivka).	Splendour	Glands	Krebleriksusek.
			Splits (it)	Splitter	Kopivok.
Smiles (he)	Smiler	Kongojukpok.	Spoils (he) it	Spolerer	Asserorpa.
Smith	Smed	Saffiortok.	Sport, as a child	Lege	Pingoarnek.
Smokes (he)	Ryger	Pyortarpok.	Spot	Plet	Inne.

ENGLISH.	DANISH.	ESQUIMAUX.	ENGLISH.	DANISH.	ESQUIMAUX.
Spout	Rende	Illulinek.			Kapput (where is thy st. kapputet nau ?)
Spreads (it)	Spredes	Siammarpok.	Sting of insects	Braad	
Spring	Foraar	Upernak.			
Springtide (at)	Spring	Sarfariksimet, v. pet.	Stirs (he) him up	Opmuntrer	Kajumiksarpa.
			Stitch, a disease	Sting	Kapportitsiuek.
Springtide (it is)		Sarfariksiok.	Stocks (he) it	Forvarer	Torkorpa.
Springtide (it is not)		Kingoartalerpok.	Stomach	Mave	Nak.
			Stone	Steen	Ujarak.
Springle	Snare	Nigak.	Stoops (he)	Bukker sig	Pupok.
Spunge	Svamp	Ermigut.	Stop	Standse	Uningnek.
Spurs, of a sledge	Opstandere	Napparirsæk.	Store	Forraad	Koë.
Spies (he) it	Undersöger	Kiglisiorpa.	Storm	Storm	Annorasuak.
Square	Fiirkantet	Koaksuktok.	Story	Historie	Okalluktuak.
Squeeze	Trykke	Nimnernek.	Stout	Stærk	Nekkortok.
Stable	Stald	Nerssutin innæt.	Straight	Lige	Nardlursok.
Stair	Trappe	Majoartarfik.	Strains (he)	Anstrænger sig	Aksororpok.
Upstairs	Oppe	Kalliænne.	Strange	Besynderlig	Tupingnartok.
Downstairs	Nede	Sammane.	Stranger	Fremmed	Tekkornartak.
Stalk	Stilk	Næggovik.	Strap, belonging to the bladder of a canoe	Kobberem	Aklunak.
Stamp	Stampe	Tukarnek.			
Star	Stjerne	Udloriak (N.B.)			
Starch	Stivelse	Kreratakot.	Stream	Ström	Sarfak.
Start	Forbauses	Annilarnek.	Strength	Styrke	Nuke, v. tengek.
Starve	Lide Nöd	Pertlungnek.	Stretches (he) it	Udstrækker	Isuïpa.
State	Tilstand	Kannong-esusek.	Strikes (he) him	Slaaer	Unatarpa.
States, lands	Stater	Nunæt.	String	Snor	Aklunaursak.
Statues, of men	Statuer	Innursæt.	String (shoe)	Skoetvinde	Singek.
Staves	Staver	Nappariaursæt, N.B.	Strips (he) him	Afklæder	Mattarpa.
			Strong	Stærk	Pikkunartok.
Stay (to)	Blive	Uningnek.	Struggle (they)	Strides	Panikput.
Steady	Stadig	Aulæjangersok.	Stupid	Dum	Sillakardluangitsok.
Steal (to)	Stjæle	Tiglingnek (he st. tiglikpok; thou st. tiglikpotit).	Subdues (he) him	Undertvinger	Kunnutipa.
			Subject	Undersaat	Nalekte
			Subsist, live	Ernære sig	Innunek.
Steam	Damp	Isseriak.	Succeeds (it)	Fölger	Tugliovok.
Steel	Staal	Sissek.	Success	Lykke	Pidluarnek.
Steep	Brat	Imnarsok.	Succours (he) him	Hjelper	Ikiorpa.
Steers (he)	Styrer	Akkopok.	Sucks (the child)	Dier	Millukpok.
Step (a)	Trin	Abloriak.	Sues (he) for it	Söger om	Krenutiga.
Stern of a ship	Spejl	Akko.	Suffers (he)	Lider	Anniarpok.
Stews (he)	Stuver, koger	Outsiok.	Sufficient	Tilstrækkelig	Namaktok.
Sticks (he) him	Gjennemborer	Kappiva.			
Stiff (it is)	Stiv	Kreratavok.	Sugar	Sukker	Sukko (Dan.) tungosungnitsok.
Still	Endnu	Sulle.			

ENGLISH.	DANISH.	ESQUIMAUX.
Summer	Sommer	Aursak.
Sun	Sol	Sekkinek.
Sun (the) rises	Staaer op	Nuïlerpok.
Sun (the) sets	Gaaer ned	Tarrilerpok.
Sure (to be)	Sikkert	Illomut.
Surgeon	Doctor	Nekkursaïrsok.
Surrounds (he) it	Omringer	Ungalorpa.
Surveys (he) it	Beseer det	Krennerpa, v. tagusarpa.
Suspect	Mistænkt	Passirsak.
Swallows (he) it	Svælger det	Eià.
Sweats (he)	Sveder	Kiegukpok.
Sweeps (he) it	Fejer det	Sengiarpa.
Swift of foot	Let	Okrillarsok.
Swims (he)	Svömmer	Nellokpok.
Swings (he) it	Svinger det	Aulapa
Swoons (he)	Besvimer	Ounarsiok.
Sword	Sværd	Pænna.
Symptom	Symtom	Nællunærkot.
Syrup	Sirup	Tungasunguitsok
Table	Bord	Nekkrivik.
Tail, of a dog	Hale	Pamiok (not of a bird).
Takes (he) it	Tager det	Tigua.
Talk	Tale	Okallungnek.
Tall	Höy	Tekkirsok.
Tallow	Talg	Tonno.
Tame	Tam	Nyoïtsok.
Tankard	Kruus	Imertarbik.
Tar	Tjære	Uvserut.
Tarry	Nöle	Mullunek.
Task	Dagværk	Sullicksak.
Tastes (he) it	Smager det	Ursserpa.
Taylor	Skræder	Mersortok.
Tea	Thee	The (Dan).
Teaches (he) him	Underviser ham	Ajokærsorpa.
Tear	Taare	Kodhlinek.
Teases (he) him	Driller ham	Innukotiga.
Telescope	Kikkert	Kernut.
Tell	Sige	Okarnek.
Tempest (it is)	Er Storm	Annordlersorsovok.
Tends (he) him	Betjener ham	Kivgartoupa.
Tender, servant	Tjener	Kivgak.
Tent	Telt	Topek.
Terrible	Frygtelig	Erksinartok.
Test	Pröve	Missiligut.
Testify	Bevidne	Unnipkarnek.
Thanks	Tak	Kujanak.
Thaws (it)	Töer	Issengiarpok.
Thick	Tyk	Irvsortok.
Thief	Tyv	Tigliktok.
Thigh	Laar	Ukpat.
Thimble	Fingerböl	Tikek.
Thing	Ting	Pik.
Thin	Tynd	Sâtok.
Think	Tænke	Erkarsarnek.
Thirst	Törst	Imerosungnek.
Thirsty	Törstig	Imerosuktok.
Thistle	Tidsel	Kenariksok.
Thorn	Torn	Kakkidlarnek-otaursak.
Thought	Tanke	Erkarsaut.
Thrashes the ox	Tærsker	Tukarpok.
Thread	Traad	Yaluksak.
Threatens (he) him	Truer ham	Syorasarpa.
Thrives (a plant)	Vozer	Nauvok.
Throat	Strube det	Torkluk.
Throws (he) it	Kaster	Nellukpa.
Thumb	Tommelfinger	Kudlo.
Thunder	Torden	Iktolarnek.
Tick (to)	Borge	Akkeetsornek.
Tide (the) rises	Vandet vozer	Ullilerpok.
Tide (the) falls	Vandet falder	Tinnilerpok.
Tie	Baand	Krelerut.
Tight	Tæt	Sukangarsok.
Till (a)	Skuffe	Amursariak.
Time (day)	Tid, v. Dag	Udlok.
Tin	Tin	Akkertlursak.
Tinder	Tönder	Arksaligak.
Tinder-box	Fyrtönde	Ikitsiniut.
Tires (it) him	Plager ham	Erdlokopa.
Tiresome	Kjedelig	Erdlokrinartok.
Toe	Taae	Isigak.
Toil (to)	Slæbe	Aksorornek.
Tolerable	Taalelig	Arktornangitsok.
Tomb	Grav	Illivek.
Tongs	Tang	Pyssugut.
Tools	Töy	Sennetit.

ENGLISH.	DANISH.	ESQUIMAUX.
Tooth	Tand	Kigut.
Torch	Kirkelys	Nenneroursoak.
Torment	Pine	Anniaut.
Touches (he) it	Berörer det	Aktorpa.
Tows (he)	Bogserer	Kallipok.
Towards the tree	Mod Træet	Orpingmut (towards, mut).
Tower	Taarn	Kakkalliak.
Town	Bye	Iglorperksoït.
Traces (he) him	Fölger ham	Mallikpa.
Trade	Handle	Pissiniarnek.
Trains (he) them—dogs	Över dem	Suugiursarpej.
Train, of a bird	Hale Fugle	Pavkit.
Train oil	Tran Stiert	Orksok.
Transfers (he) it	Bringer det	Neksarpa.
Translates (he) it	Oversætter det	Nukterpa.
Transmits (he) it	Oversender det	Neksiupa.
Trap (fox)	Fælde	Pudlek.
Travels (he)	Rejser	Ingerdlavok.
Travellers	Rejsende	Ingerdlarsok.
Treacles (he) it	Troder paa	Tungmarpa.
Treason	Forræderie	Kiglout.
Treasure	Skat	Akkiksaut.
Treats (he) him	Beværter En	Nerdlerpa.
Tree	Træ	Orpik.
Trespasses (he)	Fejler	Kiglornuvok.
Trial	Fristelse	Urssernartok.
Tricks (he) him	Bedrager ham	Seglokrittarpa.
Trifle	Smaating	Piungitsok.
Triples (he) it	Tredobbler	Pingaseriarpa.
Trot	Trav	Pangalingnek.
Trouble	Besværlighed	Erdlokirsut.
True (he is)	Sandrue (er)	Seglungilak.
Truth	Sandhed	Seglungitsusek.
Tries (he) it	Pröver det	Ursserpa.
Tub	Kar	Erkorsivik.
Tumour	Svulst	Pudlengnek.
Tune, of a hymn	Melodie	Erinak.
Turn	Vende sig	Kavinek.
Turns (he) it	Drejer det	Kavitipa.
Turner	Drejer (en)	Kavititsirsok.
Turnip Turnip (Swed.)	Roe	Nautseïak.
Twilight (it is)	Tusmörke (er)	Tarsarpok

ENGLISH.	DANISH.	ESQUIMAUX.
Twins	Tvillinger	Mardlulliæk.
Twist	Fletning	Perdlak.
Type	Sindbilled	Arssersout.
Ugly	Hæslig	Pinnêtsok.
Ultimately	Tilsidst	Kesa.
Umbrella	Skjærm	Ulle.
Unaccountable	Uforklarlig	Nællunejcksaungitsok.
Unaffected	Ubevæget	Kibligunekkaugitsok.
Unanimous	Samdrægtige	Illegeeglutik.
Unavoidable	Uundgaaelig	Ingalcksaungitsok (N.B.)
Unbecoming	Usömmelig	Innardluktok.
Unburdens it	Aflæsses	Ussærpok (a sledge).
Unbuttons (he) it	Opknapper den	Attesærpa.
Uncertain	Uvis	Opernangitsok.
Uncivil	Uhölflig	Innuksiarnêtsok.
Uncle, father's brother	Onkel	Aka.
Undeniable	Unægtelig	Missicksaungitsok (N.B.)
Underneath it	Underneden	Attane.
Understands (he)	Forstaaer	Sinnekarpok.
Understanding	Forstand	Silla.
Undertakes (he) it	Forsöger det	Ursserpà.
Underwrite	Skrive under	Attane aglengnek (N.B.)
Underwriter	Underskrevne	Attane aglegaursok.
Undone (I am)	Ödelagt	Næglingnakaunga.
Undress	Afklæde	Mattarnek.
Undressed	Afklædt	Mattarsimarsok.
Uneasy (he is)	Urolig	Kollarpok.
Unequal things	Ulige	Arsigeensitsut.
Uneven ground	Ujevn	Mancetsok.
Unexpectedly	Pludselig	Tersangaïnak.
Unfair	Uredelig	Pekkoserdluktok
Unfit	Unÿttigt	Attungitsok.
Unfolds (he) it	Udbreder det	Issaëkpà.
Unfortunate	Uheldig	Pidluangitsok.
Ungrateful	Utaknemmelig	Kujasuitsok.
Uniform things	Eensformige	Arsigeeksut.

ENGLISH.	DANISH.	ESQUIMAUX.
Union	Foreening	Illegeeugnek.
Unknown	Ukjendt	Ilirsaringitsak.
Unlawful	Ulovlig	Innertigak.
Unlimited	Ubegrændset	Kiglikangitsok.
Unlucky	Ulykkelig	Pidluejtsok.
Unnecessary	Unödvendig	Pirsariakangitsok.
Unpaid	Ubetalt	Akkeetsugak.
Unpleasant	Ufornöyelig	Tipejtsungnangitsok.
Unreasonable	Ufornuftig	Sillakangitsok.
Unreserved	Aabenhjertig	Pekkoserdlungitsok.
Unruly	Uregjerlig	Utercetsok.
Unseen	Usynlig	Tekkuksaungitsok.
Unsettled	Ubestandig	Aulæjarsok.
Unshaken	Urokkelig	Aulæjangersok.
Unsteady	Ustadig	Aulæjarsok.
Unthought	Upaatænkt	Erkarsautigirsaungitsok.
Until I die	Til min död	Tokytserdlunga.
Until we return	Til vi komme igjen	Utilerserdluta.
Untruth	Usandsed	Seglo.
Unusual	Usædvanlig	Attortangitsok.
Unwieldy	Tung	Oketsok.
Upright	Retskaffen	Illuartok.
Urges (he) him	Tilskynder	Okaukriksarpa.
Urn	Urne	Marrak.
Use	Skik	Illerkok.
Useful	Nyttig	Attortok.
Usual	Sædvardig	Attortartok.
Utter (in the sea)	Yderst	Anasiksok.
Vain	Forfængelig	Piungitsok.
Vain (in)	Forjæves	Imaglaet.
Valet	Tjener	Kivgak.
Valley	Dal	Korok.
Value	Værd	Akke.
Vanity	Forfængelighed	Piungitsusek.
Vapour	Dunst	Pyok.
Various	Forskjellige	Arsigeengitsut.
Vary	Forandre	Adlangortitsinek.

ENGLISH.	DANISH.	ESQUIMAUX.
Vault	Seiret, Locum	Anartarbik.
Vegetables	Grönsager	Nautsciæt.
Veil	Slöer	Talut.
Vein	Aare	Takkak.
Venal things	Falbuden	Nuisitak.
Ventures (he)	Vover	Sapépok.
Verbal (with words)	Med Ord	Okauzinnik.
Verdict	Kjendelse	Unnipkârut.
Verse	Vers	Verse (Dan.)
Very	Meget	Aksut.
Vessel (whale boat)	Fartöy	Umiajtsiak.
Vexes (he) him	Plager ham	Nagleïa.
Vice	Last	Ajortulliorornatounek.
Victim	Offer	Tunnirsut tokoteksak.
Victory	Sejer	Ajugaunek.
Vie, at pulling (see pull)	Kappes	Epukaniunek (kaniunek is vie).
Views (he) it	Beseer det	Tekkordlorpa.
Vigour	Kraft	Nuke.
Vinegar	Viinædike	Sernartok.
Violates (he) it —a promise	Krænker ham	Unniorkotipa.
Violence	Voldsomhed	Angutausersounek.
Virtue	Dyd	Ajungitsusek.*
Virtuous	Dydig	Ajungitsok.
Visible	Synlig	Tekkuksaursok.
Voice	Stemme	Nipe.
Vomit	Spye	Meriarnek.
Vow	Löfte	Unnersugak.
Voyage	Rejse	Ingerdlanek.
Vulnerates (he) him	Saarer ham	Ikkilerpa.
Wade	Vade	Nellorarnek.
Wafer	Vaffel	Igalaursak. N.B.
Waft	Flyde	Puktanek.
Wages	Hyre	Kivgartout.
Waggon	Vogn	Arksakaursolik.

* Ajungilak, the primitive of these words signifies, he, she, it is good, or fit; a word for *moral goodness* is wanting in the Esquimaux language.

ENGLISH.	DANISH.	ESQUIMAUX.	ENGLISH.	DANISH.	ESQUIMAUX.
Wainscot	Vognskud	Segliligak mangertok, N.B.	Week	Uge	Sabbatikakkunerok, v. Udlut arbanek—mardluk.
Waist	Midie	Kretek.			
Waistcoat	Vest	Akangitsok.			
Waits (he) him	Venter	Utakkria.	Weep	Græde	Krianek.
Wakes	Vaager	Erkomavok.	Weighs (he) it	Vejer	Urssersarpa.
Wakens (he)	Vaagner	Iterpok.	Weight	Vægt	Urssersaut.
Wakens (he) him	Vækker	Itersarpa.	Well	Vel	Ajungitsomik.
Walk (to)	Spadsere	Pissungnek.	Wet	Vaad	Kausersok.
Wall	Væg	Karmak.	Wheat	Hvede	Hvede (Dan.)
Wander	Vandre	Ingerdlanek.	Wheel	Hjul	Arksakaursok.
Want (a)	Mangel	Ajorsaut.	Whelp of a dog	Hvalp	Kremmêrak.
War	Krig	Sekkuautik.	Wherefore	Hvofor	Saag?
Warbles (it)	Bæver	Aulavok.	Whets (he) it	Hvæsser den	Ipiksarpa.
Warehouse	Proviantbod	Augoarbik.	While he weeps	Medens, lat. dum	Kriamet.*
Warmth	Varme	Kiek.	Whip	Pidsk	Ipperautak.
Warns (he) him	Advarer ham	Syorasarpa.	Whiskers (beard)	Bakkenbart	Umik.
Warrants (he) it	Bekræfter det	Narkriksorpa.	Whisper	Hviske	Issirvsornek.
Wasp	Vespe	Egytsarsoak.	Whistle	Flöyte	Uingiarnek.
Wastes it	Forgaaer	Nungulerpok.	White	Hvid	Kakortok.
Watches (he)	Vaager	Pigarpok.	Whitsuntide	Pindsetid	Pintse (Dan.)
Watch	Uhr	Nællunærkotak.	Whole	Heel	Illuïtsok.
Watchmaker	Uhrmager	Nællunærkutsiortok.	Wholesome	Sund	Perkriksaïrsok.
Water (fresh)	Vand	Imek.	Wicked	Ryggeslös	Ajortullioromatôk.
Waterman	Færgemand	Ikaursirsok.	Wide	Viid	Nerotok.
Wave	Vove, v. Bölge	Mallik.	Widens it	(Det) bliver viidt	Nerotungorpok.
Wavers	Vakler	Aulavok.	Widow	Enke	Uiglarnek.
Waxes (it)	Voxer	Agdliartorpok.	Widower	Enkemand	Nullærnek.
Way	Vej	Akkosinek.	Width	Vide	Nerotoursusek.
Weak	Svag	Sengêtsok.	Wife	Kone	Nulliak.
Weakens (he)	Svækkes	Ajulerpok.	Wild	Vild	Nyoartok.
Weakness	Svaghed	Ajulersusek.	Wilderness	Örken	Innukajuitsok.
Wealth	Rigdom	Pekkouterperksoït.	Wile	List	Pekkoserdlungnek.
Wealthy	Riig	Pekkoutilik.	Will (I)	Jeg vil	Piomavonga.
Wears it	Opslides	Asseroriartorpok.	Wills (he)	Vil	Piomavok.
Weary	Træt	Kassursok.	Wind	Vind	Annorè.
Weather	Vejr	Silla.	Window	Vindue	Igalak.
Weaves (he)	Væver	Ikartiteriok.	Wine	Viin	Vine (Dan.)
Wedding	Bryllup	Nulliartarnek.	Wink	Vinke	Isingmiksaïnek.
Wedges (he) it	Klöver	Kopiva.	Winter	Vinter	Okiok.
Wedlock	Ægteskab	Nulliareengnek.	Wipes (he) it	Aftörrer	Allerterpa.

* While is translated by a mood of the verb whereto it belongs.

ENGLISH.	DANISH.	ESQUIMAUX.	ENGLISH.	DANISH.	ESQUIMAUX.
Wise	Viis	Hisimarsok.	Wretch	Stakkel	Innukuluk.
Wish	Önske	Kiksarnek.	Wretched	Elendig	Nagliuktok.
Wit	Forstand	Silla.	Wrinkle	Rynke	Erkrinek.
Withdraws (he)	Gaaer bort	Audlarpok.	Wrist	Haandled	Arksaut.
Withers it	Visner	Tokolerpok.	Writ	Skrift	Aglegak.
Witness	Vidne	Narkrikse.	Writes (he)	Skriver	Aglekpok.
Wolf	Ulv	Amarok.	Writing-desk	Skrivepult	Aglektarbik.
Woman	Quinde	Arnak.	Wrong	Feil	Kiglok.
Wonders (he)	Forundres	Tupigosukpok.	Wrong (I am)	Jeg feiler	Kiglornuvonga, v. seglovonga.
Wonderful	Forunderlig	Tupingnartok.	Wrong (thou art)	Du feiler	Kiglornavotit, v. seglovotit.
Wood	Træ	Kressuk.	Wronged	Fornærmet	Innardligak.
Wool	Uld	Merkut.	Wry	Krum	Pekkingarsok.
Word	Ord	Okauzek.	Yard	Alen	Urssersaut.
Works (he)	Arbeider	Sulliok.	Yarn	Garn	Yalursær.
Work	Arbeid	Sulliak.	Yawns (he)	Gaber	Aitsarpok.
World	Verden	Sillarsoak.	Year	Aar	Okiok.
Worm	Orm	Kopertlok.	Yelk	Æggeblomme	Tingursak.
Worn	Forslidt	Attanetængo-akangitsok.	Yellow	Guul	Sungârpalluktok.
Worship (at church)	Gudsdyrkelse	Nalegiarnek.	Yet	Endnu	Sulle.
Worsted stockings	Strömper	Allersik.	Yields (he)	Giverester	Kunnuvok.
Worth	Værd	Akke.	Yoke	Aag	Nangmaut.
Wound	Saar	Ikke.	Young	Ung	Innusuktok.
Wrecks the ship	Forliser	Asserorput.	Youth (a)	Ungt menneske	Innusuk.
Wraps (he) it	Svöber	Imupa.	Zealous (he is)	Nidkiær	Kemakpok.
Wreaths	Fletter	Perdlaïok.	Zone	Belte	Kreterrut.

N

THE NATIVE POPULATION OF GREENLAND.

	THE SETTLEMENTS.	Baptized.	Unbaptized.	MEN.					WOMEN.					Total of both Sexes.	NOTES.
				Married.	Widowers.	Unmarried.		Total.	Married.	Widows.	Unmarried.		Total.		
						beyond 12 years.	below 12 years.				beyond 12 years.	below 12 years.			
a	Julianeshaab (Greenl. Krakortok).....	1059	3	131	26	145	107	469	137	63	187	206	593	1062	Besides two Moravian Missions.
b	Arsut, Rilenlenk, and Upernivik.....			31	16	87	114	298	91	35	62	120	308	606	Here is no Settlement and no Mission.
b	Frederikshaab (Gr. Pamiut)			67	16	79	95	257	69	37	101	104	311	568	Here is no Mission of the Moravians.
b	Fiskenæsset (Gr. Krikertarsoejtsiak)...	58		10		5	11	26	10	1	6	15	32	58	Here is one Mission of the Moravians.
b	Godthaab (Baal's River, Gr. Nouk)...	301		45	3	26	61	135	47	21	50	48	166	301	Besides the Moravian Mission, Neu Herrnhut.
c	Sukkertop (Gr. Mannètsok)	449		68	2	47	96	213	71	21	62	82	236	449	
c	Holsteinborg (the dist. Gr. Amertlok)	552		80	13	66	100	259	83	28	88	94	293	552	
d	Egedesminde (Gr. Ausieit)	390	1	56	13	46	79	184	62	26	47	72	207	391	
d	Hunde Eiland (Dog's Island)	97		17	4	13	14	48	19	3	8	19	49	97	
d	Christianshaab............................	108		16	1	11	22	50	19	4	14	21	58	108	
d	Claushavn	230		45	7	14	41	107	49	7	22	45	123	230	
d	Jacobshavn................................	276		48	11	27	75	131	54	17	20	54	145	276	
d	Kronprindsens Eyland (Whale Island)	57	1	7	2	6	11	26	7	3	11	11	32	58	
d	Godhavn (Leifly)........................	154		21	2	19	38	80	23	7	20	24	74	154	
e	Ritenbenk	261	3	48	7	25	46	126	48	10	32	48	138	264	
e	Umanak (Women's Island?)........	500	5	78	12	79	86	255	84	24	49	93	250	505	
		4492	13	768	135	695	1056	2664	873	307	779	1056	3015	5679	

The Missionaries of the Established Church reside at Julianeshaab, Godthaab, Holsteinborg, Egedesminde, Umanak, and Upernivik; their districts are noted with letters as their residence.
The difference between married men and married women arises from some of the latter being married to Danes.

Note.—The MORAVIAN MISSIONS at Julianeshaab district, 494 men, and 536 women.
at Fiskenæsset ditto 153 do. and 214 do.
at Godthaab ditto 156 do. and 214 do.

Total...... 733 men 964 women. Total of both sexes, 1697
which have not been included in the previous register.

DIALOGUES

IN THE

ENGLISH, DANISH, AND ESQUIMAUX LANGUAGES.

DIALOGUES, &c.

ENGLISH.	DANISH.	ESQUIMAUX.
RELATING TO COASTS, LAND, &c.		
Have you seen the land?	Har Du seet Land?	Nuna tekkogalloarpiuk?
How far is the land?	Hvor langt er Landet borte?	Nuna kannong ungesiksiga?
How near is the laud?	Hvor nær er Landet?	Nuna kannok kannitiga?
In what direction is the land?	Hvor er Landet?	Nuna nau?
Point to the land.	Peeg paa Landet.	Nuna tikoardlugo.
Where is the water?	Hvor er Vandet?	Imak nau?
Point to the water.	Peeg paa Vandet.	Imak tikoardlugo.
What is the name of the land seen?	Hvad er Navnet paa Landet, vi see?	Kannong-attekarpa nuna tekkursarput?
What is the water's name?	Hvad er Vandets Navn?	Imang una kannong attekarpa?
Do you know the land?	Kjender Du Landet?	Nuna ilirsaraïuk?
Can we sail through this channel?	Kunne vi sejle gjennem dette Sund?	Ugona ikkerasakut akkutiksakarpa?
Is the water deep?	Er Vandet dybt?	Imak itisimava?
How deep?	Hvor dybt?	Kannong itirsiga?
How shallow?	Hvor grundt?	Kannong-ikkatiga?
Is there a river there?	Er der en Elv?	Ouane kogejtsiakarpa?
Point to the river.	Peeg efter Elven.	Kok tikoardlugo.
Which is the road?	Hvor er Vejen?	Sukut pissaugut?
Go before us.	Gaae foran.	Siulersortigut.
When is it high water?	Naar bliver Vandet höjt?	Kakugo ullissava?
When is it low water?	Naar lavt Vande?	Kakugo tinnissava?
Can we anchor?	Kan vi ankre?	Kisarsinnavogut?
Are you a pilot?	Er du Lods?	Ilisimarsovit?
I want a pilot.	Jegvilde have Lods.	Ilisimarsomik piomagalloarponga.
Are you going on shore?	Gaaer du i Land?	Ikaissavit (siksamut)?
May we land?	Maae vi lande?	Ikarkovisigut, v. aposinnavogut?
Will you come back?	Vil du komme tilbage.	Utissavit (tamannga)?
When will you?	Hvor vil du hen?	Sumut pissavit?
Come to us again.	Kom igjen til os.	Uterfigisigut.
Do you sleep on shore?	Vil du sove i Land?	Nuname sinissavit?
Do you come to-morrow?	Kommer du imorgen?	Akkago ikaissavit?
Come back to-morrow.	Kom igjen imorgen.	Akkago ama ikkardlutit.
Come in two days.	Kom i overmorgen.	Akkagoane ikarniarit.
Is there a good harbour?	Er der god Havn?	Ajungitsomik kisarfikarpa?
Is the harbour bad?	Er Havnen slet?	Kisarfik ajorpa?
Is the bottom rocky?	Er der Steen i Bunden?	Nakka ujarakarpa?
Is the bottom mud?	Er der Dynd?	Nakka mauvarnarpa?
Is the bottom sand?	Er der Sand?	Nakka syorakarpa?
Is the bottom clay?	Er der Leer?	Nakka marrakarpa?

ENGLISH.	DANISH.	ESQUIMAUX.
What mark is that?	Hvad Mærke er dette?	Sunauna nællunærkotak?
Is there a current?	Er der en Ström?	Sarfakarpa?
Which way does it go?	Hvad Vey gaaer den?	Sumut sarfarpa?
Is the current strong?	Er Strömmen stærk?	Sarfarkulukpa?
I shall go on shore.	Jeg vil gaae i Land.	Apôssaunga.
I shall not go on shore.	Jeg gaaer ej i Land.	Apôssengilanga.
I shall sleep on shore.	Jeg vil sove i Land.	Nuname sinissaunga.
My boat is on shore.	Min Baad er i Land.	Umiajtsiara siksamepok.
A man is on shore.	En Mand er i Land.	Siksame kivgakarponga.
Is the landing good?	Er Landeplasen god?	Apôneng ajornangila?
Is there reindeer there?	Er der Rensdyr?	Tuktokarpa?
Are foxes there?	Er der Ræve?	Teriauniakarpa?
Are hares there?	Er der Harer?	Ukadlekarpa?
Are bears there?	Er der Björne?	Nennokarpa?
I shall take a rope on shore.	Jeg vil före en Line i Land?	Siksame pittukomarpaka.
Make fast the rope.	Gjör Touget fast.	Pittuta sukaglugo.
Cut the rope.	Kap Touget!	Pittouta kippivdlugo!
Loose the rope.	Los!	Pittursardlugo!
Make fast.	Fast!	Pittuglugo!
RELATING TO WIND AND WEATHER.	OM VIND OG VEJR.	SILLAMIK ANNOREMIGLO.
What do you think of the weather?	Hvad tænker du om Vejret?	Silla kannong—èssesugaïuk?
Do you think the wind will continue?	Tænker du at Vinden vil blive ved?	Annore tajmàeginnaissanerpok?
Will the wind change?	Vil Vinden forandres?	(See, A)
Shall we have rain?	Vil det regne?	Siedlilissaua?
Shall we have snow?	Vil det snee?	Apissaua?
Shall it be calm?	Bliver det stille?	Kaïtsyssava?
Shall it blow?	Vil det blæse?	Annordlilissaua?
Will it be fair wind?	Faae vi god Vind?	Orkomiaissaugut?
Will the weather be good?	Bliver Vej ret godt?	Silla ajyssengila?
Has there been snow?	Har det sneet?	Aputekaralloarpise?
Has there been wind?	Har det blæst?	Annordleralloarpa?
Has there been rain?	Har det regnet?	Siedleralloarpa?
Has there been frost?	Har det frosset?	Issekaralloarpa?
Does it freeze?	Fryser det?	Issekarpa?
It freezes.	Det fryser.	Issekau.
It did freeze hard.	Det frös haardt.	Issekulukalloarkau.
Frostbitten.	Som har Frost.	Krerisimarsok.
Are you frostbitten?	Har du Frost?	Krerisimavit?
Is there ice there?	Er der Iis der?	Tersane sikkokarpa?
There is much ice.	Meget Iis.	Sikkokarkulukpok.
There is little ice.	Lidt Iis.	Ingmangoak.
There is plenty of water.	Vand nok.	Akkutiksakarpok* (p c).
No water.	Ingen Vand.	Akkutiksakangilak.

* Propr. There is way! akkutiksakarpa? is there way?

ENGLISH.	DANISH.	ESQUIMAUX.
No ice.	Ingen Iis.	Sikkongilak.
Icebergs.	Iisfjelde.	Illulirsæt.
Is the ice broken up?	Er isen brudt?	Sikkoærnpa sikkoærupok?
Is it frozen over?	Er der lagt til?	Sikkoïnangolerpa?
There is no ice.	Der er ingen Iis.	Sikkokangilak.
The ice is not broken.	Isen er ikke brudt.	Sikkoærusimangilak.
There is no water.	Der er ingen Vand.	Sikkoinavok, v. akkutiksakangilak
The weather was bad.	Vejret var ondt.	Silla ajoralloarpok
The weather was good.	Vejret var godt.	Silla ajungikalloarpok.
The weather was foggy.	Vejret var taaget.	Silla pyolirksovok.
The weather was clear.	Vejret var klart.	Silla ûlaralloarpok.
In thick weather.	I tykt Vejr.	Silla pyorsorsomet.
In bad weather.	I ondt Vejr.	Silla ajormet.
In good weather.	I godt Vejr.	Silla ajungimet.
I think a fog is coming on.	Det bliver vist taaget.	Pyolissakokau.
I think the weather will continue as we have it now.	Jeg tænker Vejret vil blive det samme.	Silla tajmâeginnaissakokau.
It is a fair wind.	Det er god Vind.	Arkomiarpogut.
It is a foul wind.	Det er Modvind.	Arksorpogut.
It is a calm.	Det er Stille.	Kaitsorpok.
A baffling wind.	Det er omlöbende.	Annorè nellinginak.
It is a hard gale.	Det blæser op.	Nektimalerpok.
This has been a mild season.	Det har været mildt.	Kickalloarpok.
This has been a bad season.	Det har været uroligt.	Annordleïnaralloarpok.
There has been much wind.	Det har blæst meget.	Annordleinaralloarpok.
There has been much cold.	Det har været meget koldt.	Issekulukalloarkau.
Is there ice there west?	Er der Iis Vest paa?	Sammane sikkokarpa?
Is there ice there north?	Er der Iis Nord paa?	Auane sikkokarpa?
Is there ice there south?	Er der Iis Syd paa?	Kanane sikkokarpa?
Is there ice there east?	Er der Iis Œst paa?	Pauane sikkokarpa?
The winter was very cold.	I Vinter var det koldt.	Okiok issekulukalloarkau.
The spring was a bad season.	I Foraar var det uroligt Vejr.	Upernigavta annordleralloarpok.
ARMS, &c.		
Knives.	Knive.	Saveet (one, savik).
Spears.	Spyde.	Kallugirsæt.
Bows.	Buer.	Pissiksit.
Arrows.	Pile.	Karksut.
Guns.	Kanoner.	Auleirksoit.
Muskets.	Flinte.	Aulejsit.
Cutlasses.	Sabler.	Pænnæt.
SUNDRIES.	ADSKILLIGT.	NELLINGINAK.
Books.	Böger.	Attuækkæt.
Compasses.	Compasser.	Nellunærkotit.

ENGLISH.	DANISH.	ESQUIMAUX.
Canvas.	Sejldug.	Tingerdlautiksak.
Casks.	Huer.	Neseet.
Shoes.	Skoe.	Atteraursæt.
Blankets.	Lagener.	Tungit.
Skin (outer jacket).	Yder Pelts.	Nejtsek.
Skin (inner jacket).	Under Pelts.	Tingmirsæt.
Trousers.	Buxer.	Kardleet.
Boots.	Stövler.	Kaungit (sing. kamik).
Shoes.		See before, or isigamæt.
Scissors.	Sax.	Krejutik.
Razor.	Ragekniv.	Ungiaut.
Needles.	Synaale.	Merkutit.
Thread.	Traad.	Yalursæt.
Corks.	Propper.	Simeet.
I wish to sell (it).	Jeg vil sælge.	Tunniomagalloarpara.
I wish to buy (it).	Jeg vil kjöbe.	Pissiniaromagalloarpara.
I wish to exchange (it).	Jeg vil bytte.	Taursiomagalloarpara.
I wont sell (it).	Jeg vil ikke sælge.	Tunniomangilara.
I wont buy (it).	Jeg vil ikke kjöbe.	Pissiniaromangilara.
I wont exchange (it).	Jeg vil ikke bytte.	Taursiniaromangilara.
VARIOUS.		
I want to borrow it.	Jeg vilde laane det.	Attartoromagalloarpara.
Will you lend?	Vil du laane.	Attorkoviuk?
I will lend it.	Jeg vil laane.	Attorkoara.
I will not lend it.	Jeg vil ikke laane.	Attorkongilara.
How many?	Hvormange?	Kapsit?
Where are you going?	Hvorhen vil du?	Sumut pissavit?
When do you come again?	Naar kommer du igjen?	Kakugo utissavit?
Are you going far away?	Skal du langt bort?	Ungesiksomun audlaissavit?
Are you going north?	Skal du nord paa?	Auonga pissavit?
Are you going south?	Shal du syd paa?	Kauonga pissavit?
Are you going east?	Skal du öster paa?	Pauonga pissavit?
Are you going west?	Skal du vester paa?	Sammunga pissavit?
Do you walk?	Skal du gaae?	Pissÿssavit?
Do you take a sledge?	Skal du kjöre?	Kremuksissavit?
Are you alone?	Er du allene?	Kissingorpit?
Who is with you?	Hvo er med dig?	Kina illegaïuk?
What do you ask for?	Hvad vil du?	Sumik?
What will you take for?	Hvad vil du have derfor?	Sumik?
What news have you?	Hvad Nÿt har du?	Sumik tussaralloarpit?
Very good news.	Godt Nÿt.	Tussækketin ajungilet.
Very bad news.	Onde Tidender.	Tussækketin ajorpæt.
It is war.	Der er Krig.	Sekkuaursokarpok.

ENGLISH.	DANISH.	ESQUIMAUX.
It is peace.	Der er Fred.	Sekkuaursokangilak.
There is a quarrel.	Der er Strid.	Sekkolirsarput.
They fight.	De slaaes.	Panikput.
They have fought.	De have slaaets.	Panikalloarput.
Will fight (they).	De ville slaaes.	Panissaput.
Are you armed?	Er du bevæbnet?	Sekkokarpit.
I have been attacked.	Jeg blev anfaldt.	Pångnekarponga.
I beat him.	Jeg slog ham.	Ajugavonga.
I was beaten.	Jeg blev slaaet.	Arktorsartipanga.
He is wounded.	Han er saaret.	Ikkilersimavok.
He is killed.	Han er dræbt.	Tokotipok.
Where are you come from?	Hvorfra er du?	Sumit aggerpit?
Where do you belong to?	Hvor hörer du hjemme?	Suna nunagaïuk?
Where are you going?	Hvorhen skal du?	Sumut pissavit?
When are you going?	Naar reyser du?	Kakugo audlaissavit?
Where are they going?	Hvor sklle de hen?	Sumut pissapæt?
Where do they belong to?	Hvor have de hjemme?	Suna nunagaæt?
When are they going?	Naar sklle de rejse.	Kakugo audlaissapæt?
How far?	Hvor langt?	Kaunok ungesiksigirsomut?
Which way?	Hvad Veÿ?	Suknt?
By water.	Til Vands.	Imakut.
By land.	Over Land.	Nunakut.
Stop where you are till I come back.	Bie hvor du er til jeg kommer igjen.	Tersanêgit utilerserdlunga.
Do not wait for me.	Bie ikke efter mig.	Utakkrissengilarma.
Wait for me here.	Bie her efter mig.	Tamane utakkrinianga.
Wait for me there.	Bie der efter mig.	Ikane utakkrinianga.
Are you ready to go?	Er du færdig at gaae?	Enerpit audlarkudlutit?
When will you be ready?	Naar bliver du færdig?	Kakugo enissavit?
Do you believe it?	Troer du det?	Operaïuk?
Do you advise?	Mener du?	Isumakarpit?
Why don't you answer?	Hvi svarer du eÿ?	Saag akkingilatit?
Have you any thing for me, or any one else?	Har du noget til mig eller nogen anden?	Uamnut kimudloneen adlanmut sumik pekkarpit?
Do you like it?	Kan du lide det?	Illuaraïuk?
Don't like it.	Kan du ikke lide det.	Illuaringiliuk.
What is the matter?	Hvad erder?	Sumik?
Where shall we meet?	Hvor skal vi mödes?	Sume nellautsomarpogut?
Will you attempt, or try?	Vil du pröve det?	Okataissaviuk?
Is that true?	Er det sandt?	Illomut!
Is that not true.	Er det ikke sandt?	Seglo?
A disturbance has broken out among the —.	Der er kommen Ufred imellem —.	Ikingutigeegungnærput.
Send a party of men.	Send nogle Folk.	Innuïn illejt kailit.
I will send men.	Jeg vil sende Folk.	Kivgat audlartissavaka.

ENGLISH.	DANISH.	ESQUIMAUX.
Do not meddle.	Bryd dig ikke herom.	Sÿssersok.
You ought to change your resolution.	Du skulde betænke dig.	Tajma pissengikalloarpotit.
I give my consent.	Jeg samtÿkker.	Tajmaikile or akkoerara.
I will not give consent.	Jeg vil ikke samtykke.	Ajornakau.
I will leave you.	Jeg forlader Dig.	Kremeissauagit.
I can wait no longer.	Jeg kan ikke bie.	Audlaromarponga.
I will detain you.	Jeg vil opholde dig.	Unnikkogalloarpagit.
It is unnecessary.	Det behöves ikke.	Pirsariakangilak.
It is not right.	Det er uret.	Illuangilak, v. ajorpok.
Will you dine?	Vil du spise?	Nerrissavit.
I have dined.	Jeg har spiist.	Nerriræerponga.
Bring your friend here.	Lad din Ven komme hid.	Illet tamaunga pile.
Bring here your family.	Lad din Familie komme hid.	Nulliet krittornetidlo kaïlit.
Do not forget.	Glem ikke.	Puïorkrennæk.
I do not know.	Jeg veed ikke.	Nælluvonga.
I must take time to consider of it.	Jeg vil betænke mig derpaa.	Assukiak, erkarsautigiomarpara.
A skin under jacket.	En Underpelts.	Tingmirsæt.
A skin upper jacket.	En Overpelts.	Nejtsek.
Skin trousers.	Skindbuxer.	Kardleet.
Boots.	Stövler.	Kaungit.
Shoes.	Skoe.	Atteraursæt.
Stockings.	Strömper.	Allersit.
Gloves.	Handsker.	Aketit.
A wooden or natural leg.	Et Been.	Neehu—nio (pronounced, neeo).
VESSELS, &c.		
Sleep on board.	Sove ambord.	Umiarsoarne siningnek.
Sleep on shore.	Sove iland.	Nuname siningnek.
You must not sleep on board.	Du maà ej sove ombord.	Umiarsoarne sinissengilatit.
I require immediate help.	Hjelp mig strax.	Ikiorsinga erngrenak.
Will you give me help?	Vil du hjelpe mig?	Ikiyssavinga?
I will help you.	Jeg vil hjelpe dig?	Ikiÿssauagit.
I will not help you.	Jeg vil ikke hjelpe dig.	Ikiyssengilagit.
Give me a rope.	Giv mig en Line.	Aklunaursak kaïrsuk.
I will give you a rope.	Jeg vil give dig en L.	Akklunaursamik tunnissauagit.
I cannot.	Jeg kan ej.	Ajornakau.
An anchor.	Et Anker.	Kisak.
A cable.	Et Kabeltoug.	Aklunaursarsoak.
Files.	File.	Aggiutit.
Hammer.	Hammer.	Kavtak.
Axe.	Öxe.	Ullimaut.
Chalk.	Kride.	Aglaut.
Nails.	Söm.	Kikitsæt.
Carpenters' tools.	Tommermands Redskab.	Sennetit.

ENGLISH.	DANISH.	ESQUIMAUX.
Lead.	Blÿ.	Akertlok.
Harpoon.	Harpun.	Tukak.
Shovel.	Skovl.	Nivaut.
Spade.	Spade.	Tuggaut.
Wooden shovel.	Træskovl.	Nivaut.
PROVISIONS.		
Beef (fresh).	Færsk Kjöd.	Nekkre.
Beef (salt).	Salt Kjöd.	Nekkre tarajornitsok.
Fish (fresh).	Færsk Fisk.	Nerpik.
Fish (salt).	Salt Fisk.	Nerpik tarajornitsok.
Bread.	Bröd.	Timiursak, v. tigek.
Pease.	Ærter.	Ærtæt.
Spirits.	Spiritus.	Sillærunartok.
Butter.	Smör.	Pôngnek.
Eggs.	Æg.	Manneet.
Milk.	Melk.	Imuk.
Oil.	Olie.	Olie.
Medicines.	Medicin.	Nekkursautit.
Whiskey.	Brœndeviin.	Sillakangitsok.
Rum.	Rum.	Sillakangitsok aukpadlartok.
Beer.	Öl.	Imiak.
Water.	Vand.	Imek.
Wine.	Viin.	Vine.
Cheese.	Ost.	Imuk.
Coffee.	Caffe.	Kaffe.
Sugar.	Sukker.	Sukko.
Tea.	Thee.	The.
Plums.	Svedsker.	Kiggutiglit.
Raisins.	Rosiner.	Serkordluktut.
Barley.	Grÿn.	Suaursæt.
Syrup.	Syrup.	Mamanga.
Vinegar (acetum).	Ædike.	Sernartok.
RELATING TO HEALTH.		
Are you well?	Er du rask?	Ajungilatit?
Is he well?	Er han rask?	Ajungila?
Are they well?	Ere de raske	Ajungilæt?
I am well.	Jeg er rask.	Ajungilanga.
We are well.	Vi ere raske.	Ajungilagut.
They are well.	De ere raske.	Ajungilæt.
I am not well.	Jeg er ikke rask.	Ajorponga.
I am very ill.	Jeg er meget daarlig.	Napparsimakulukponga.
They are ill (unwell).	De ere daarlige.	Napparsimaput.

ENGLISH.	DANISH.	ESQUIMAUX.
Is your wife well?	Er din Kone rask?	Nulliet ajungila?
Is your family well?	Er din Familie rask?	Krittornetin ajungilœt?
Is your husband well?	Er din Mand rask?	Uveen ajungila?
I have been sick.	Jeg har været syg.	Napparsimagalloarponga.
You have been sick.	Du har været sÿg.	Napparsimagalloarpotit.
Are many sick?	Ere mange syge?	Kapseet napparsimapœt?
How many are sick?	Hvor mange ere syge?	Kapsit napparsimapœt?
What is the sickness?	Hvad er den Sygdom?	Suna nappautigæt?
Have you a doctor?	Have I en Doctor?	Nekkursaîrsokarpise?
I will send you a doctor.	Jeg vil sende Jer en Doctor.	Nekkursaîrsok kakÿssauara.
Send for the doctor.	Send Bud til Doctoren.	Nekkursaîrsok kaïle.
Is he or she alive?	Er han eller hun levende?	Innuva?
Is he or she dead?	Er han eller hun död?	Tokosimava?
He or she is alive.	Han eller hun lever.	Innuvok.
He or she is dead.	Han eller hun er död.	Tokosivamok.
My son is well.	Min Sön er rask.	Ernera ajungilak.
My daughter is well.	Min Datter er rask.	Panniga ajungilak.
My son is not well.	Min Sön er ikke rask	Ernera napparsimavok.
My daughter is not well.	Min Datter er ikke rask.	Panniga napparsimavok.
Where are the sick?	Hvor ere de Syge?	Napparsimersut nau?
My doctor is sick.	Min Doctor er sÿg.	Nekkursaïrsiga napparsimavok.
My doctor is dead.	Min Doctor er död.	Nekkursaïrsiga tokovok.
RELATING TO VESSELS, &c.		
Is the ship large?	Er Skibet stort?	Umiarsoït angissimapæt?
How large?	Hvor stort?	Kannong aktigæt?
How small?	Hvor lille?	Kannok miktigæt.
How many men?	Hvor mange Mand?	Innuee kapsiopæt?
She is large.	Det er stort.	Angikaut.
She is not large.	Det er ikke stort.	Angingilæt.
Have you any letters?	Har du Breve?	Aglekkœnnik pekkarpit?
Send letters.	Send Breve.	Aglekkæt neksiudlugit.
I have letters.	Jeg har Breve.	Aglekkœnnik pekkarponga.
I have no letters.	Jeg har ingen Breve.	Aglekkœnnik pekkangilanga.
The vessel in sight is.	Hvader det Skib i Sigte.	Kikun okko umiarsoït.
A ship	Et Skib.	Umiarsoït.
A boat with men.	En Baad.	Umiajtsiait.
A packet (a launch).	En Barkasse.	Umiaitsiarsoit.
Are you on shore?	Er du paa Land?	Tullekpit?
Is your vessel leaky?	Er jert Skib læk?	Umiarsoæse asserorpæt?
Do you leak much?	Lækker I meget?	Asserorkulukput?
We leak much.	Vi lække meget.	Asserorkulukput.
Are you in distress?	Er Ti Nöd?	Nauværpise?
I want assistance.	Jeg onsker Hjelp.	Ikiorteksarsisukponga.

ENGLISH.	DANISH.	ESQUIMAUX.
I am on shore.	Jeger i Land.	Apoponga.
My ship is on shore.	Mil Skib er i Land.	Umiarsoaka nunaliput.
The leak increases.	Lækken bliver större.	Asserornerrogiartorput.
The leak is stopped.	Lækken er stoppet.	Asserorungnærput.
Come back.	Kom tilbage.	Uterit.
Go away.	Gaae væk.	Arvsærit, v. audlarit.
I want to come.	Jeg vil komme.	Aggissaunga.
I want to go.	Jeg vil gaae.	Audlaïssaunga.
I want you to stay.	Jeg vilde have dig til at blive.	Tersanékoagit.
BIRDS.	FUGLE.	TINGMIRSÆT.
Eagle (vultur albicilla).	Örn.	Nektoralik.
Falcon (falco islandicus).	Falk.	Kirsoviârsuk.
Snow owl (stryx nictea).	Hvid Ugle.	Opik.
Raven (corvus corax).	Ravn.	Tullugak.
White partridge (tetroa lacopus).	Rype.	Akeiksek.
Willow partridge (fringilla laponica).	Markspurven.	Narksamiutak.
Willow partridge (fringilla linaria).		Akpamiutak.
Willow partridge (motacilla œnanthe)	Steensqvetten.	Kussektâk.
Snow bunting (emberiza nivalis).	Iisfugl (Sneef).	Kopananarsuk.
Bernacle (anas bernicala).	Radgaas.	Nerdlek.
Gold eye (clougala anas).	Hviinand.	Kærtlutorpiârsuk.
Harlequin (anas histronica).	Strömand.	Tornaviarsuk.
Mallard (anas boschas).	Vildand.	Kongmuktajok, v. kærtlutok.
King duck (anas spectabilis).	Pukkelnæbbet Edderf. (femina).	Arnauiartak.
Eider duck (anas mollissima).	Edderfugl.	Mitek (plur. merkdelineatunt).
Goosander (mergus merganser).	Gunland.	Parârsuk.
Red-breasted Meganser (mergus serrator).	Fiskeand.	Paik, v. nyaliksak.
Great Auk (alca impennis).	Geÿrfugl.	Isarokitsok.
Razor bill (alca torda).	Klub alke.	Akparnak, v. akpartluk.
Black bill (alca pica).	Alke.	Akpa.
Little auk or rotch (alca alle).	Söekonge.	Akpalliârsuk.
Fulmar petrel (procellaria glacialis).	Mallemukken.	Kakordluk.
Shearwater (procellaria puffinus).	Enkekone; Skrabe.	Kakordlungnak.
North guilemot (colymbus glacialis).	Ömmer.	Tudlik.
Red-throated guilemot (colymbus septentionalis).	Loom.	Karksauk.
Great tern (sterna trirundo).	Tærne.	Imerkotejlak.
Xeme (larus Sabini, larus collaris).*		Kongæserutilik.
Black-backed gull (larus marinus).	Svartbaggen.	Naïardlurksoak.
Kittywake (larus tridactylus).	Krykkie.	Tatarak.

* Not known. I have seen it in Capt. Ross's First Voyage, and can baptize it *Kongæserutilik*, viz., "that with the neck-kerchief."

ENGLISH.	DANISH.	ESQUIMAUX.
Ivory gull (larus candidus).	Den hvide Mange.	Nûjanârsuk.
Glaucus gull (larus glaucus).	Blaamaagen.	Naianak.
Cormorant (pelicanus carbo).	Skarv.	Okaitsok.
Crested cormorant(pelicanus cristatus)	Topskarven.	Tingmik.
Gannet (pelicanus bassonus).	Havsule.	Kuksuk.
Snipe (scolopax gallinago).	Hossegjög.	Siggruktôk.
Jardreka (scolopax jardreka).	Domsneppen.	Sargvarsurksoak.
Sandpiper (tringa striata).	Strandsneppen.	Sargvârsuk.
Sandpiper (tringa interpres).	Tolken.	Telligvak.
Sandpiper (tringa lobata).	Nordvestfugl.	Nellonmirsortok.
Sandpiper (tringa alpina).	Landsneppe.	Tòjuk.
Plover (charadrius apricurius).	Brokfugl.	Kajordlék.
Ringed plover (char. stiaticula).	Pÿtfugl.	Tukavàjok.
Puffin (alca arctica).	Söepapagojen.	Killangâk.
Puffin (uria grylle).	Teist.	Serfak, v. kernektârsuk.
Pintail duck (anas hyemalis).	Angletaske.	Aglek.
Parasitic gull (cataracta parasitica).	Struntjager.	Meriarsaïrsok, v. isingak.
Horned owl (strix otus).	Hornugle.	Siutitôk.
Plain falcon (falco rusticolus).	Spællet falk.	Kirksoviarsuk millakulartok.
Eider duck (anas mellissima).	Ederfuglehan.	Amaulik.
King duck (anas spectabilis).	Osterboygds Edderf.	Kdeliningalik.
ANIMALS.	DYR.	NERSSUTIT.
Polar bear (ursus maritimus).	Björu.	Nennok.
Arctic fox (canis lagopus varietas nigra).	Ræv.	Kernektâk.
Wolf (canis lupus).		Amarok.
Hare (cetraria islandus).	Hare.	Ukalek.
Reindeer (cervus tarandus).	Rhensdyr.	Tukto.
Walrus (trichecus rosmaurus).	Hvalros.	Auvek.
Seals (phocæ).	Sælhunde.	Puïrsit.
Hooded seal (phoca cristata).	Klapmyds.	Nejtsersoak.
Common seal (phoca vitulina).	Spraglet Sælhund.	Kassigiak.
Harp seal (phoca Grœnlandica).	Svartisden.	Atak.
Great seal (phoca barbata).	Remmesæl.	Takamugak, v. urksuk.
Rough seal (phoca hispida).	Fjord sæl.	(Junior) millaktôk.
White seal (phoca leporina).	Söeharen.	Ukalerajek.
Small seal (ph. barb. pullus).	Un Uksakunge.	Terkigluk.
Fœtus of a seal, or its unborn youag.	Iblau ufødt Sæl	Iblau.
Sea unicorn (monodon monoceros).	Narhval.	Kernektak.
Dolphin (delphinis delphis).	Marsviin.	Nesa.
Wolverine (gulo luscus).		Kaeweek.
Whales, &c. (cete).	Hvalfisk.	Arfek.
(balena physalus).	Finnefisk.	Tunnolik.

ENGLISH.	DANISH.	ESQUIMAUX.
Whales, &c. (balena musculus).		Kreporkarnak.
(balena rostrata).	Sværdfisk.	Tikàgulik.
(balena mystietus).	Bardehvalen.	Arfavek, v. sokalik.
White whale (delphinus albicans)	Hvedfisk.	Krelelluak.
Fish (salmo rivalis).	Bæköred.	Aunârdlek, v. ekallugak.
Salmon (salmo scorpio).		Krebseriksok.
(salmo alpinus).		Ivisarok.
Codfish (gadus reglesinus).	Kuller.	Misarkoruak.
(gadus callarius).	Kabliau.	Sàraudlik.
(gadus morpua).	Skrijtersk.	Sarndlirksoak.
(gadus barbatus).	Torsk.	Ogak.
Hallibut (pleuronectes hippoglossus).	Helleflynder.	Nettarnak.
Eel (angulla vulgaris).	Aal.	Nimeriak.
Corriphine (coryphæna rupestris).	Borglax.	Iugmingoak.
Mytilus edulis.	Musling.	Uïdlok.
Antique labrus (labrus exoletus).	Blaastaal.	Kreblernak.
Sepia loligo.	Blæksprutten.	Amikôk.
Lobster (cancer norvegirus).	Hummer.	Naularnak.
A bee.	En Bie.	Egytsak.
Pike-headed whale (balæna boops).	Butskop.	Kreporkâk.
Gunnel blenny (blennius gunnellus).	Tangsprel.	Kurksaunak.
Ascaris vermicularis.	Barneorm.	Koartak.
Physeter macrocephalus.	Eachelot.	Kigutilik.
Aranea saccata.	Edderkop.	Ausick.
Rough seal (phoca hispida).	Fjordsæl.	Nejtsek.
Areolated blenny (blenn. lumpenus).	Tangspret.	Tejàrnak.
Musca stercoraria.		Anariak.
Tabanus Grœnlandicus.	Vandbie.	Miluïak.
Musca vivax. Volucella lapponica.		Milmarsuk.
Musca vomitoria.	Spyflue.	Nivingak.
Pool salmon (salmo stagnalis).	En Öreil.	Ekallukâk.
Mya byssifera.	Gaberskjæl.	Menningoak.
Mya truncata.	Sandskjæl	Usursak.
Avis.	Faar.	Saua.
Capra.	Dotta nu ring.	Sanaursak.
Lernæa.	Sililuluk.	Massinnio.
Beroe.	Uportaanligt.	Ippiarsursak.
Medusa.	Wolf.	Nuertlek.
Medusa capillata.		Nuertlersoak.
River bullhead (cottus gobio).	Grundling.	Ujarangmio.
White shark (squalus carcharias).	Hay.	Ekallurksoak.
Lepus timidus.	Hare.	Ukalek.

ENGLISH.	DANISH.	ESQUIMAUX.
ICE.	IIS.	
On salt water	Paa salt Vand	Sikko.
On fresh water	Paa serok Vand	Sermek.
Iceblink	Iisblink	Sermersoak.
Heavy ice	Storiis	Sikkorsoak.
New thin ice	Tyndiis	Sikkoak.
On the earth	Paa Jorden	Nillersoak.
Even ice	Jevn	Mannerarsoak.
Blue	Blaa	Annardlok.
Bay ice	Fjordiis	Kaksuk.
Lain in a kettle to melt		Imiugak.
Iceberg	Iisfjeld	Illuliak.
Small streaming		Kavalerngit.
Fast on the beach	Iisfjör	Kaïngok.
Moveable by the beach		Ivksinek.
Pieces at sea (drift)		Navlornerit.
Icicle	Iistap	Kussugak.
On the inside of a window		Illo.
Produced when water from beneath goes over the fast ice of a river		Særsernek.

CHRONOMETERS.

Ever since the year 1794, my attention has been much devoted to the practical use of chronometers, both while I belonged to the Honourable East India Company's service, and in the Royal Navy, where I had, when serving under the gallant Lord de Saumarez, the charge of the navigation of both the Channel and the Baltic fleet.

On taking command of the expedition fitted out for the discovery of a North-west Passage, my first care was to obtain good chronometers, and also as many of them as possible. My own chronometer was made by the late justly celebrated Earnshaw, and was certainly a very superior one; I therefore took it as the standard for comparison, with the whole thirteen. Several of these were the property of private persons, who either lent them to the expedition, or sent them on trial: of the latter description were those sent by Messrs. Parkinson and Frodsham, who sent two with a memorandum that their rate would increase to fourteen seconds and then remain steady: a circumstance which actually took place, and which went to prove that they had discovered some new principle, in their regulation or construction, and my report on them could not be but very favourable. Since this every expedition has been furnished by Parkinson and Frodsham with these valuable machines, and the reports on their performance have been uniformly favourable. On this voyage I purchased of them the pocket chronometer 1081, which was distinguished as being that made for Sir E. Parry, on his attempt to reach the North Pole, as well as for its uniform rate. These makers also kindly sent with me a box chronometer at their own risk, which could not but be a great acquisition. Both of these performed to admiration; the box chronometer, until we left Victoria harbour, where it was purposely allowed to run down that it might be more easily carried, and the pocket one during the whole time. On our arrival they were both returned to the makers, and being desirous to make public the principle on which these instruments

P

have been brought to such perfection, and reserving my own observations on it for the conclusion of this article, I shall give their answer to my request in their own words.

4, *Change Alley, May* 15, 1834.

SIR,

IN compliance with your desire to be furnished with a report of the condition of the two chronometers of our make, which you took with you in your late Expedition to the Arctic Regions, we have examined them with the most careful and minute attention, and find them in an excellent state: indeed, very far more perfect than could have been expected after such a length of time, and the severe trials which they must have undergone.

With regard to their peculiar construction, which you at the same time requested us to describe, as you were desirous of publishing it for the benefit of science and navigation generally, we have no hesitation in complying with your wishes; so far as is consistent with justice to ourselves, and we hope that our communication may prove useful.

The *peculiar principle* which we have discovered is of the highest importance in giving the final adjustment to chronometers, as by it we are enabled, *in all cases*, to give permanence to their rates, within the limits of exactness requisite in navigation.

We beg, in the first place, to disclaim all intention of insinuating that in the mechanical construction of our instruments there is any thing superior to, or materially different from, those made by other respectable makers; for we are well aware, that all chronometers lately made by intelligent artists, are on the same mechanical principle. But the fact is notorious, that of several instruments made with equal care, reference being had only to their mechanical construction, some are found to perform well, and others indifferently; while nothing can be discovered in the workmanship which will in any way account for the variation.

Chronometers in general, as at present constructed, are found progressively to accelerate on their rates, and in many instances this takes place to such an extent, that a new rate is required, rendering them ill suited for long voyages; on the contrary, others have a continual disposition to lose on their rates, and are therefore equally unsuited to the wants of the seaman.

But whether the rates of chronometers were accelerated or retarded in use, there existed no *recognised* or *known* remedy for the evil, UNTIL WE MADE THE DISCOVERY, which it is one object of this communication to record our claim to. Some artists have trusted to *time* for its correction; and a writer in a scientific journal* has recently

* Nautical Magazine.

even assigned the period when the cure might be expected to be completed: but *time* being no party to the bargain, generally left the instruments thus turned over to its benevolence to pursue their vagaries without interference.

The cause, which the writer alluded to has assigned for this acceleration, is the use of tempered balance-springs; now tempered balance-springs have been in use for more than half a century, and forty years ago they were made by ourselves. If time, therefore, could have cured the defects of the tempered balance-spring, as stated in the paper above alluded to, these old chronometers would now have been excellent instruments, which certainly they are not in general found to be.

The consequence has been, that the rates of most of the chronometers at this moment in existence, can only be considered constant for short intervals of time. Many years have clapsed since our attention was drawn to this peculiarity, from several mortifying circumstances which occurred in our own experience; and after satisfying ourselves that it was in vain to look for the cause of so perplexing a phenomenon in the *mechanical construction* of the instrument, we resolved to examine the *physical condition* of the materials of which the balance and its spring are made: and we discovered that the greater part, if not the whole of the discrepances, were owing to circumstances in this *physical condition.*

After many experiments and much investigation, we had the good fortune to discover the means of correcting this physical peculiarity, either completely, or so nearly, that we can now undertake (after ascertaining the tendency) so to alter the physical properties of the balance and its spring, as to make ANY chronometer, whose mechanical construction is otherwise satisfactory, perform with sufficient exactness for every purpose for which chronometers are generally required.

The acceleration of chronometers on their rates, hitherto unexplained in the history of chronometers, is produced by the constant action of winding and unwinding the balance-spring, which, in chronometers beating half seconds, takes place two hundred and forty times in each minute, and it is thereby deprived of a portion of its elasticity. It becomes consequently stiffer, stronger, and more stubborn; and as the motions of the balance (the measurer of time) are regulated by this spring, the vibrations become more rapid, and are performed in less time.

The cause of chronometers losing on their rates, is also generally to be traced to the physical imperfection of the balance-and-spring; which, contrary to what takes place in the tempered spring, becomes relaxed by constant action, combined with other causes; and consequently has less power over the vibrations of the balance. But independently of all accidental circumstances, the chronometer is continually changing its rate, with every alteration of tension in the balance-spring.

P 2

The scientific artist may, indeed, give to this spring the isochronal property, so far that under given and constant circumstances, unequal arcs of vibration in the balance, will be performed in equal time; but this adjustment will in no degree counteract the effect occasioned by change of tension to which we have been adverting.

We do not allude in the preceding remarks to defective compensation for change of temperature, but to that gradual deviation from the rate which many chronometers are found to exhibit, and to an extent that often interferes with their usefulness.

It is true that all chronometer makers do occasionally produce instruments, which, for a sufficient length of time, keep steady rates; but they do so only from accidental circumstances, of which the makers themselves are not always aware. They approximate to the correction which we have discovered the means of making *in all cases.*

In our researches on this subject, we have found that the defect in the correction for change of temperature, is amongst the least of the difficulties to be contended with; and the value of the principle of adjustment which we have discovered has been eminently proved by the accurate performance of our chronometers, which have been exposed to the severities of the arctic winters, in all the Polar voyages. In one of those voyages, *eleven* out of *fifteen* chronometers stopped from the cold; whilst FOUR made by us, (all of ours that were sent) maintained the same rates at Melville island that they were found to have in London after the return of the expedition.

The chronometrical parts of our chronometers consisting of the compensation balance and the detached escapement, are the same as invented before 1766, by the eminently distinguished artist, M. Le Roy, of Paris, with the important improvement of the detant on a spring instead of on pivots, as made by the late Mr. Earnshaw; together with some minor but useful alterations in the execution and arrangement suggested by our own experience.

We have said before, that chronometers made by the same artist do not always perform equally well, although the same workmen are employed, the same labour is bestowed, and the same attention paid to each. Several modern artists have endeavoured to remedy this defect by means of mechanical contrivances, some of which display considerable ingenuity and are apparently very plausible; but, however beautiful in theory, these contrivances have produced no practical advantage; no one has yet discovered the seat of the disease, or the cause of so remarkable an effect. We reassert that no *mechanical contrivance* can remedy the defect: it is only to be remedied by a knowledge of the principle which we have discovered.

Le Roy's original inventions of the balance for compensating for changes of temperature, and the escapement, were entitled, from their beautiful simplicity, to the reward so justly bestowed upon him; and with the improvement above alluded to, by our countryman Earnshaw, continue unrivalled: in fact they are generally adopted by all intelligent chronometer-makers.

We consider that the best balance is that composed of laminæ of brass and steel, when properly proportioned, and worked so that the particles are placed under no particular or partial constraint, which might prevent their free and natural action throughout the whole periphery of the balance. This we consider an important requisite; for to the want of affinity in the condition of the particles, we attribute some of the irregularities observed in the rates of chronometers, when subject to the rigorous test of daily comparison—more particularly after sudden changes of temperature. There are inherent defects in the shape of the balance, which prevent its affording theoretically the means of a perfect compensation; but it is doubtful whether other forms, which appear preferable in theory, would be found in practice to answer so well.

As evidence of our possessing means peculiar to ourselves, of bringing a chronometer to keep a steady rate, we may mention the fact, amongst numerous other instances, and we do it with much satisfaction, that of the *eight* chronometers entitled to the prizes for the most accurate performance during the last three annual public trials at the Royal Observatory, at Greenwich, *five* were constructed by us, and adjusted on the *principle peculiar to ourselves.*

We may add, that within the last fifteen years, during which period we have been adjusting our chronometers on THIS PRINCIPLE, we have had extensive experience of its efficacy, having made and sold more than twice as many marine chronometers as any other maker has done during thirty years;—the best proof that the public have appreciated our discovery.

Attempts have recently been made to introduce *glass* in the construction of the balance-spring; and the first performance of some of the instruments in which this alteration was introduced, was very satisfactory.

There is, however, reason to apprehend that this *material* will not be found to give to the instrument a *permanent* rate, as one of the very best of them has, in the course of a few months, deviated from its rate to the amount of seven seconds a day: while another chronometer, under the same circumstances, on the usual construction, with a steel balance-spring, and which at the last public trial (1833) was second in performance to one made by us, kept a remarkably steady rate.

We may also be allowed to state, that on this trial (1833), sixty chronometers were sent by various makers; and at the termination, the numbers were reduced to ten, *four* of which were made by us; and the extreme variation of each, in the twelve months, was considerably within the limits fixed in 1828 for the reward of Three Hundred Pounds. Three of them made less error than our chronometer, No. 1410, in 1828;

for which we then received the premium of Three Hundred Pounds. The extreme variation of these five chronometers was as follows:

In 1828,	No. 1410	in twelve months	″ ‴ 1.41	actual extreme variation.
1833	679	ditto	0.98	
	1600	ditto	1.31	
	460	ditto	1.24	
	1502	ditto	1.52	

In 1830, one of our chronometers was entitled to the second prize, and some others of our making were within the limits.

In the trial of 1831, the chronometers made by us obtained the *whole of the three prizes*, and another was fifth on the trial list. We may be excused for making particular reference to the trials of this year, from the remarkable circumstance, that in all the preceding years, from 1822, when the trials for prizes were first established, a period in which several hundreds of chronometers had been sent for trial, but four had performed within one second of extreme variation in the twelve months; whilst in this trial the WHOLE of our four chronometers went within less than a second of extreme variation; the following being the extreme variations as published by the Astronomer Royal:

No. 311	in twelve months	″ ‴ 0.70	actual extreme variation.
2	ditto	0.86	
665	ditto	0.89	
1	ditto	0.99	

In 1832 and 1833, chronometers made by us were entitled to prizes; and several others of our manufacture have been frequently within the limits prescribed by the Government, forming a large proportion of the best chronometers submitted to *public trial.*

It has been repeatedly suggested to us, that a PRINCIPLE so important as ours has proved to be, should be imparted to the public, as every thing tending to the improvement of chronometers is a matter of national concernment. We are willing to give up to the public the benefit of our knowledge and experience in these matters, on receiving, as others have done, an adequate compensation for the value which the discovery is of to us in our private business; but we hold ourselves justified in withholding an explanation of the principle, until it either ceases to be of importance to us, or we are adequately remunerated for disclosing it.

Government having directed that the public trials of chronometers at Greenwich, for prizes, shall cease after the present year, a few remarks on the origin of those trials, and on the favourable effect which they have had on the art of chronometer making, may not inappropriately close our observations.

Notwithstanding the encouragement which Government had long afforded to the art, by purchasing chronometers largely, and at liberal prices, for the use of the navy; and the very considerable rewards which had been given to three of the leading artists (3000*l.* each) for the superior performance of some instruments made by them, yet the general state of the art was much below what was generally believed, and might have been expected.

Aware of this fact, and desirous that the art which we exercised should participate in the general improvement, we, in 1818, addressed a letter to J. W. Croker, Esq., at that time Secretary to the Admiralty, respectfully suggesting that Government might further and most essentially aid the progress of the art, by giving *frequent and small rewards to ingenious workmen who made instruments that actually performed well, without reference to the principles on which they were constructed.*

The public trials at the Royal Observatory commenced in 1820, and the performance of the chronometers on the first trial proved the correctness of the opinion which we had formed as to the general state of the art of chronometer making. The prizes of 300*l.* and 200*l.* were that year adjudged to chronometers which Government would not at the present time purchase at any price.

Several of the chronometers which we sent on trial in the various scientific expeditions to the Polar Seas and towards the Equator, having performed satisfactorily, we sent some of our experimental chronometers to Greenwich on trial, a few years after the public trials were first established; and the opportunity thus afforded us of having the effect of our successive alterations tested by daily observation, enabled us to detect many minute sources of error, which we should otherwise most probably never have discovered.

The opportunity, too, of returning for trial chronometers which, having performed unsatisfactorily we had endeavoured to improve, gradually led us to the discovery of the principle which enables us now to control at pleasure, and to counteract, any general tendency in chronometers to deviate from their rates.

We are, Sir,

Yours, respectfully,

PARKINSON & FRODSHAM.

To Capt. Sir John Ross, R.N.,
&c. &c. &c.

Those who have perused the above statement from Messrs. Parkinson and Frodsham, and are at all interested in the improvement of navigation, cannot but be desirous that a fair trial should be given to this important discovery; and if it is found that chronometers which are the production of respectable artisans, and which from causes hitherto unknown deviate from their rates, so as to be comparatively useless, can be corrected by the application of their principle, so as to become sufficiently perfect for the purposes of navigation, by maintaining the uniform rate within the limits prescribed by Government, no one will deny, that this important discovery should be made public, and that such discovery is fully entitled to a liberal compensation; and I cannot conclude this article without recommending it to the serious attention of those whose duty it is to inquire into and reward merit.

Mr. Murray, a very respectable chronometer-maker of London, being desirous to establish the excellent going of his chronometers, sent No. 620 eight day, 634 two day, and 558 one day, all box chronometers, which could not be a great acquisition to us; and it is but justice to say that they were excellent instruments, for although they all gained at first, they obtained a constant rate, from which they did not deviate whilst in my possession. I regret much that it was not in my power to bring them home, as I have no doubt they would have been found perfect, with the exception of one which met with an accident.

In addition to No. 571, box chronometer, and of 1081 for the pocket, of Parkinson and Frodsham I purchased No. 418, pocket chronometer, of Barraud, which I knew to be good, having it formerly in my possession; but the main spring gave way soon after we sailed, which reduced my number to five. These were under the charge of Commander Ross, until July, 1831, after which they were all under my own care, and the only two that were brought home were those by Parkinson and Frodsham.

NEW THEORY OF THE AURORA, BY SIR JOHN ROSS

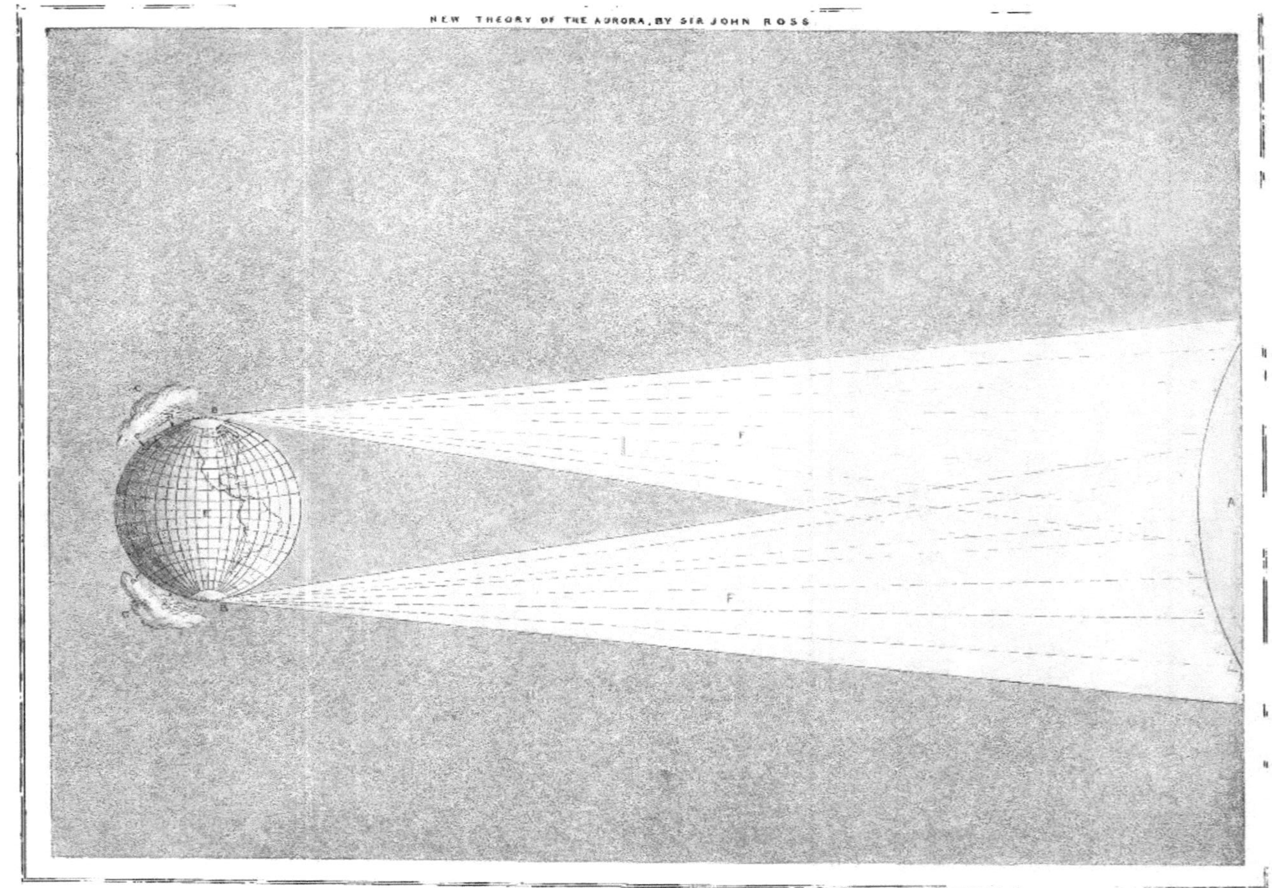

AURORA BOREALIS.

NEW THEORY.

Many theories have been proposed during the last century, to account for the nature and appearance of this beautiful phenomenon, but to each of these, and to all, objections have been made, that I think cannot be justly applied to the following, which has been founded on a long series of observations made carefully by myself on this interesting subject, and under circumstances peculiarly advantageous.

Before I proceeded on my voyage of 1818, my attention was directed to the phenomenon of the Aurora by the late Dr. Wollaston, who had collected, with great pains, much information on the subject, which he kindly transmitted to me, as well as his own observations, from which, however, he came to no other conclusion than a supposition that "the Aurora was beyond the atmosphere of the earth."

As the expedition which I commanded in 1818 did not winter in the Arctic Regions, my observations during that voyage were confined to the months of September and October, during which time the ships were moving in a southerly direction from the

Q

latitude of 74° to 58° north, when it was observed that from the latitude of 74° until 66°, the phenomenon was seen to the *southward,* particularly at midnight; but when the ship had passed to the southward of the latitude of 66°, it was seen to the *northward.* In several instances the Aurora was distinctly observed to be between the two ships, and also between the ships and the icebergs; proving unquestionably that it could not be at that time beyond the atmosphere of the earth. This indeed was the only fact which I completely established during that voyage, but which was a conclusion that led me to inquire how its proximity to the earth was to be accounted for. Both at my observatory in Scotland, and during my late and long-protracted residence in the Arctic Regions, my attention has been particularly directed to this interesting subject, and my conclusions are, that *the splendid phenomenon, called the Aurora, is entirely occasioned by the action of the sun's rays upon the vast body of icy and of snowy plains and mountains which surround the poles.*

The rays of the sun, *in the first instance,* are reflected, from uneven, plain, or variegated surfaces, of the coloured, icy, or snow-clad substances, which are presented to them at the point of incidence by the rotation of the earth, and passing over the poles reach and illuminate clouds which are only rendered visible to us by such illumination, these clouds having positive, negative, and reflecting qualities, possess the power of producing all the surprising effects which have been observed by distributing the rays they have received, and as they receive them, in every direction; and according to the state of the atmosphere, give additional variety to the original colours as reflected from the point of incidence; and further, if due regard is paid to the properties of light, its connexion both with magnetism and electricity may be satisfactorily explained.

In support of this theory—In the first place, we have the fact, that when the spectator's position on the earth is to the northward of the 69° of north latitude, the Aurora is generally observed to bear to the southward, very seldom to the northward of east or west, and never in that direction or in the north, unless the sun is in opposition, or a region of icy or snowy substance is between the spectator and the bearings of the sun; although the illuminated clouds which I have mentioned might there, as in a lower latitude, very possibly reflect the rays they have received in every horizontal, as well as vertical direction.

Secondly. The atmosphere between the sun and the spectator is always clear, whether he is to the southward or northward of the Aurora. When he is looking at the Aurora from a high latitude, towards it in the south, the sun is then at his back to the north; and if the sky becomes cloudy in that (the northern) direction it is fatal, the Aurora immediately disappears, because the rays are intercepted by an impenetrable cloud. In like manner, when the spectator observes the Aurora bearing to the eastward or westward, if a cloud or fog intervenes between his position and the sun, it immediately disappears.

Thirdly. When the spectator sees the Aurora to the *northward*, he is always to the *southward* of the icy regions, and at that time the sky in the direction of the sun is always clear; should a cloud intervene, either above or below the point of incidence, the phenomenon will disappear.

When the rays of the sun are reflected from a vast plain of icy substance to stationary and to us invisible clouds, it follows that the Aurora will remain a long time without changing, the rays being then reflected as from a circular or globular mirror, the angle of incidence and reflection remaining the same; but the moment that these rays arrive (by the earth's rotation) at water, or at some non-reflecting substance or surface, the Aurora suddenly disappears, as it does by an intervening cloud, which is a fact I have had confirmed by many observations.

With regard to the action of the Aurora on the magnetic needle, I need only say, that in common with every other kind of light, it has the property of affecting the needle or combining with magnetism. The effects of the Aurora on the needle were the same as the sudden approach of a naked candle, or when the light of a lamp was concentrated by a lens on the needle delicately suspended at a distance of eighty-four yards: an experiment which I repeatedly tried at Sheriff's harbour. With regard to electricity, it is notorious that there is less in the Arctic Regions than in any other place; and, during my first voyage, the electrometer was never moved by the electric fluid, although often tried.

The position of the Aurora Borealis in the heavens, depends much on the depression of the sun below the horizon of the spectator, on its bearings, and on the nature of the surface which first receives the sun's rays, at the point of incidence, which if uneven will produce the *capra saltans*, or merry dancers; if the surface is even it will produce the *irabs*, or beam, provided the illuminated cloud is tranquil, but if not it will produce the *sagitta*, or *faces* (pencil rays, or torch); and if the rays are conveyed from thence by a second reflection, which is very often the case, the *bothinia*, or cave, will appear with the pencil rays ascending; the *corona* and *pithiæ* depend also on the shape of the clouds as well as their positive and negative qualities.

The colours of the Aurora depend on several circumstances: First, on the colours of the objects which originally receive the sun's rays at the incidental point. Secondly, on the state and qualities of the atmosphere, through which the reflected rays pass before they reach the clouds which they are to illuminate, and thereby render visible to the spectator not only the clouds themselves, but the various colours which the rays have then assumed. Thirdly, by the nature and composition of the cloud itself; however, it is most probable that the colour depends oftener or more materially on the colour of the objects which first receive the sun's rays at the incidental point, from whence they proceed by the laws of reflection, according to the various oblique directions of that surface; since the observations of Captain Cook, and other antarctic navigators, represent that the Aurora Australis has always "a clear white light," and that no coloured ice has been observed in the antarctic regions; while, on the contrary, ice of every colour has been observed by myself and others to exist in great abundance in the Arctic Regions.

The reason that the Aurora is not always visible, is evidently because the sky near the pole is often cloudy and foggy, particularly in the spring and autumn, and when it is considered that the Aurora cannot be visible unless the atmosphere is clear on *both sides of the pole* in the direction of the sun, it will appear probable that it does not often happen; and in summer of course the Aurora cannot be seen in latitudes where the sun is then above the horizon below the pole, but I have often observed an appearance in the sky resembling the pencil rays of an aurora, with the exception that the illumination of the clouds was overpowered by the light of the day; and as the sun was then always in opposition to the northward, I can have no doubt but that this phenomenon was an aurora, caused by the rays of the sun reflected from the circumpolar mountains of ice to the clouds: and I may add, that this appearance has been noticed by several navigators of the Polar Regions.

The noise of the Aurora, described by some as resembling a silken flag exposed to a fresh breeze, and by others as that of a rushing noise like fireworks playing off, was never heard or observed, on any of the recent Arctic voyages, and it may be concluded that such a noise does not take place in these regions: if, however, it is insisted upon to be the fact in more southern latitudes, it may probably be occasioned by the combination of the Aurora with electric matter, which is not found in the north.

Since this paper was read at that excellent institution, the British Association for the advancement of Science, I have had the satisfaction of learning that several of its most distinguished members had made observations corroborative of my theory; among which I may mention those of W. L. Wharton, Esq., of Dryburn, Durham, who has kindly transmitted to me the copy of an article he wrote in the *Durham Advertiser*, November, 1830. In this case, the Aurora was seen at eleven, P. M., when it was considerably to the westward of north at twelve (midnight), the summit of the luminous arch was due north. He adds, "Those who may have remarked the radiations of the Aurora have probably been struck by their similarity to those beams of light which radiate from the sun when partially observed by a cloudy atmosphere. They may also have observed with us that the radiations for the most part appear to proceed from that spot under the horizon in which the sun would be seen, if not concealed by the body of the earth, and that the summits of the accompanying arches of light are always seen directly above the same spot. Is it not then possible that the phenomena of the Aurora may originate in the light of the sun refracted at an immense elevation above us, after glancing over the nebulous strata of a distant part of the earth's atmosphere?"—In like manner, the registers of the Aurora in all the recent voyages to the Polar Regions corroborate my theory, although different conclusions, or conjectures, were hazarded respecting its nature and origin, and to which I must refer my readers as they are too numerous for insertion.

I may conclude by adding, that my theory has been submitted to the celebrated Professor Schumacher and others, who made no objections to it.

JOHN ROSS.

EXPLANATION OF THE PLATE.

A—The sun as at the Equinox.

B B—The points of incidence.

D D—Positions of the spectators.

C C—Clouds rendered visible by the reflected rays.

E—The earth as at the Equinox.

F F—The rays of the sun.

This diagram represents the sun's rays acting on the icy or snow-covered part of the earth, and being reflected over the poles reach clouds which are rendered visible by illumination; and having themselves reflecting qualities, distribute them upwards, downwards, or in any other direction, and owing to the rotation of the earth, are changing or steadfast according to the nature of the surface at the incidental point which first receives the rays.

NATURAL HISTORY.

*A

ACCOUNT

OF THE OBJECTS IN THE SEVERAL DEPARTMENTS OF

NATURAL HISTORY,

SEEN AND DISCOVERED DURING THE PRESENT EXPEDITION.

BY CAPTAIN JAMES CLARK ROSS, R.N., F.R.S., F.R.A.S., F.L.S., &c.

HAVING placed the department of Natural History under the exclusive charge of my Nephew, Captain J. C. Ross, whose acquirements in this branch of knowledge have been long known to the public, from the results of the former voyages in which he was engaged, I am indebted to him for the following pages; which have been drawn up by himself, with the assistance of those friends whom he has noticed in his own Preface.

JOHN ROSS.

PREFACE.

The recent publication of the Fauna Boreali Americana, by Dr. Richardson, has rendered a detailed account of the Zoology of the Arctic Regions quite unnecessary. Nearly all the quadrupeds and birds that were met with in the course of our voyage in the Victory having fallen under the notice of that distinguished traveller and naturalist, they have there been described with accuracy, and illustrated by beautifully coloured engravings, so that nothing further is now left to be desired.

In the following brief notice the arrangement of Cuvier, in the Règne Animal, has been adopted, and in nearly all cases a reference is given to Dr. Richardson's descriptions in the Fauna Boreali Americana, and to the valuable Zoological notices appended to the several narratives of the Expeditions of Discovery to those Regions, under the command of Sir W. E. Parry and Sir John Franklin, where will be found all that is interesting both to the general reader and the naturalist.

I have much pleasure in expressing my obligations to Dr. Richardson for his observations on four species of Salmon brought home by me: his intimate acquaintance with the various species of that extensive and interesting genus inhabiting the lakes and rivers of the North American Continent, will give a high value to that portion of the notice of the Fishes.

The rest of our collection having been necessarily abandoned with the Victory, a short and very imperfect account has been drawn up from my rough notes taken at the time, which, from my being but little acquainted with that branch of Natural History, is of course very defective.

To my friend Mr. Curtis, my warmest acknowledgments are due for his valuable remarks on the few Insects which I was able to bring to England, and the very beautiful drawings and engravings which accompany them.

The liberal and kind assistance I have received from Mr. Richard Owen, in drawing up the catalogue of the Marine Invertebrate Animals, requires my best thanks; particularly for his careful and elegant dissection of the new genus which he has named "Rossia;" peculiarly valuable at a time when the internal organization of the inferior orders of animated nature has become so extensively used in their classification.

J. C. R.

ZOOLOGY.

BY COMMANDER (NOW CAPTAIN) JAMES CLARK ROSS, R.N., F.R.S., F.L.S., &c.

1.—URSUS MARITIMUS (*Polar Bear*).

URSUS MARITIMUS.—*Cuv: Règ. An.*—vol. i., p. 137.
Rich: Faun. Bor. Amer.—p. 30.
Fab: Faun. Grœnl.—p. 22.

Is found in greater numbers in the neighbourhood of Port Bowen, and Batty Bay, in Prince Regent's Inlet, than in any other part of the Polar Regions that I have visited in the course of the several expeditions of discovery. This circumstance, probably, arises from Lancaster Sound being but seldom covered by permanently fixed ice; and therefore affording them means of subsistence during the severity of an Arctic winter; and also from its being most remote from the usual winter residence of any of the Esquimaux, who alone dispute the sovereignty of the north with this monarch of its ferine inhabitants.

During our stay at Fury Beach many of these animals came about us, and several were killed. At that time we were fortunately in no want of provisions, but some of our party, tempted by the fine appearance of the meat, made a hearty meal off the first one that was shot. All that partook of it soon after complained of a violent headache, which, with some, continued two or three days, and was followed by the skin pealing off the face, hands, and arms; and in some, who had probably partaken more largely, off the whole body.

On a former occasion I witnessed a somewhat similar occurrence, when, on Sir Edward Parry's Polar journey, having lived for several days wholly on two bears that were shot, the skin pealed off the feet, legs, and arms of many of the party. It was then attributed rather to the *quantity* than the *quality* of the meat, and to our having been for some time previous on very short allowance of provision. The Esquimaux eat its flesh without experiencing any such inconvenience; but the liver is always given to the dogs, and that may possibly be the noxious part. The Esquimaux of Boothia Felix killed several during their stay in our neighbourhood in 1830—all males.

The males are considerably larger than the females, as will be seen by the following measurements, being the average of nine males and seven females taken by myself:

	Male.	Female.
Length from snout to the end of the tail	94 inches	78.7 inches
snout to shoulder .	33.5 . .	26.3
snout to occiput .	18.4 . .	15.6
Circumference before the eyes . .	20.4 . .	15.8
at broadest part of the head .	32.2 .	28
at largest part of the abdomen .	65.2 . .	57.6
Length of alimentary canal . .	61 feet .	52 feet
Weight	900 lbs. .	700 lbs.

The weight varies very much according to the season and condition of the animal.

The largest of the above measured 101.5 inches in length, and weighed 1028 lbs., although in poor condition.

2.—GULO LUSCUS (*Wolverene*).

GULO LUSCUS.—*Cuv: Règ. An.*—vol. i., p. 141.
Rich: Faun. Bor. Amer.—p. 41.
Sab. in Supp. to Appx. to Parry's 1st Voy.—p. clxxxiv.

Kā ŏ wēēk.—Esquimaux of Boothia Felix.
Kab le a rioo.—Esquimaux of Melville Peninsula.

Some traces of the existence of this animal in the highest northern latitudes were observed on two of the preceding Arctic expeditions; but none of the animals were seen on either of those occasions: although we now know that it remains throughout the winter as far north as the 70° of latitude, and is not, like some other animals of that rigorous climate, subject to any change of colour from the most intense cold.

A few days previous to the arrival of the Esquimaux near Felix Harbour, in January, 1830, the tracks of this animal were first seen; and soon after, the skins of two old and two young ones were brought to the ship by the natives, who had taken them in traps built of stones.

During each of the following winters their tracks were occasionally seen, and at Victoria Harbour they were very numerous. There, in the middle of the winter, two or three months before we abandoned the ship, we were one day surprised by a visit from one, which pressed hard by hunger, had climbed the snow wall that surrounded our vessel, and came boldly on deck, where our crew were walking for exercise. Undismayed at the presence of twelve or fourteen men, he seized upon a canister which had some meat in it, and was in so ravenous a state that whilst busily engaged at his feast he suffered me to pass a noose over his head, by which he was immediately secured and strangled. By discharging the contents of two secretory organs, it emitted a most insupportable stench. These secretory vessels are about the size of a walnut, and discharge a fluid of a yellowish-brown colour, and of the consistence of honey, by the rectum, when hard pressed by its enemies.

The descriptions of authors are sufficiently accurate; but the following dimensions may be useful:

Length from snout to the insertion of the tail .	28.4 inches
of the tail	9.8 (vertebræ)
of the hair of the tail .	6
	44.2 inches
Length from snout to shoulder . . .	11.2 inches
to occiput	6.5
Extreme breadth of head	4.1
Circumference at ensiform cartilage .	14.5
at neck	10.6
at broadest part of the head .	13

Vertebræ—Cervical 7
Dorsal 15 (10 true and 5 false ribs)
Lumbral 5
Sacral 3 (now in one)
Caudal 15

It was a female, and weighed 27½ lb.

*B

3.—MUSTELA ERMINEA (*Ermine*).

MUSTELA ERMINEA.—*Cuv: Règ. Anim.*—vol. i., p. 145.
Rich: Faun. Bor. Amer.—p. 46.

These beautiful and elegant little animals were by no means numerous; but their tracks were occasionally seen during the winter, following those of the Lemmings, upon which they chiefly subsist during that inclement part of the year. It is almost impossible to tame them, preferring rather to die than live in confinement. One that came on board of our ship and was taken, although treated with the greatest kindness, its restless and vicious nature so completely exhausted it, that it died at the end of a week or ten days. The Ermine assumes its winter dress early in September, and again changes to brown towards the end of May. It is the great enemy of the Lemming, and in its turn is preyed upon by the Fox.

It is 18 inches long, and weighs 5½ oz.

4.—CANIS LUPUS OCCIDENTALIS (*American Wolf*).

CANIS LUPUS.—*Cuv: Règ. Anim.*—vol. i., p. 150.
CANIS LUPUS OCCIDENTALIS.—*Rich: Faun. Bor. Amer.*—p. 60.

Considerable numbers of this animal were seen on the narrow Isthmus of Boothia, where they arrive early in the spring to intercept the Reindeer on their way to the north. None were killed by us during our late voyage, owing to their extreme wariness; but their tracks were occasionally seen during each of the winters. They are very troublesome to the Esquimaux, robbing their hoards, tearing the skin covering off their canoes, and killing their dogs. It is a remarkable circumstance, that a single wolf will go amongst any number of Esquimaux dogs, and carry off any one from amongst them without the others attempting to attack it. Such is their extreme dread of the Wolf, that they begin to tremble and howl whenever they are aware of its approach. The Wolf will seldom attack a man, except when starving; but if alone and *unarmed*, it will not care to get out of his way.

ARCTIC FOX.

5.—CANIS LAGOPUS (*Arctic Fox*).

CANIS LAGOPUS.—*Cuv: Règ. Anim.*—vol. i., p. 153.
Rich: Faun. Bor. Amer.—p. 83.
Sabine, in Franklin's 1st Journey—p. 658.
Rich: Appendix to Parry's 2d Voy.—p. 299.

Inhabits the highest northern latitudes throughout the winter, and is provided with the finest and thickest fur, to enable it to withstand the intense cold of those regions.

The young generally migrate to the southward late in the autumn, and collect in vast multitudes on the shores of Hudson Bay: they return early the following spring along the sea-coast to the northward, and seldom again leave the spot they select as a breeding place.

The summer fur of this beautiful animal is admirably described by Mr. Sabine, *loc. cit.*; and the winter dress by Dr. Richardson, *ut supra*, where an interesting detail of its habits is given.

In most of the individuals taken in February we observed that the long hairs on the back and loins are tipped with black, to the extent which they project beyond the rest of the fur: this is particularly the case in the females.

It brings forth from six to eight young early in June. In July, 1831, one of their burrows was discovered on the sandy margin of a lake; it had several passages, each opening into a common cell, beyond which was an inner cell, where the young, six in number, were taken. They were precisely of the same colour as the old ones at that season of the year. Hearne says, that "the young are all over of a sooty black;" this probably refers to the following variety of the Arctic Fox. In the outer cell, and in the several passages leading to it, we found great numbers of the two species of Lemming, several Ermine, and the bones of hares, fish, and ducks, in great quantities. Four of the young foxes were kept alive till the end of the following winter, and were a great amusement to our crew by their playfulness, as they soon became very tame. They never attained the pure white of the old Fox, a dusky lead colour remaining about the face and sides of the body.

There is a remarkable difference in the disposition of these animals, some being easily tamed, whilst others remain savage and untractable, notwithstanding the kindest treatment. The females are much more vicious than the males. A Dog Fox that lived several months became so tame in a short time, that he regularly attended our dinner-table like a dog, and was always allowed to go at large about the cabin.

*B 2

A pair kept for the purpose of watching the changes of their fur, threw off their winter dress during the first week in June; the female a few days earlier than the male. Towards the end of September the brown fur of summer gradually became of an ash colour, and by the middle of October was perfectly white: from that period it continued rapidly to increase in thickness until the end of November, when the last of the two died, having lived in confinement nearly ten months.

The flesh of the young Fox is white, and well flavoured. Dr. Richardson says, "Captain Franklin's party agreed with Hearne in comparing the flavour of a young Arctic Fox to that of the American Hare." Captain Lyon considered it to "resemble the flesh of the kid;" whilst those of our party, who were the first to taste them, named them "lambs," from their resemblance in flavour to very young lamb. The flesh of the old Fox is by no means so palatable; and the water it is boiled in becomes so acrid as to excoriate the mouth and tongue. During our late expedition, they constituted one of the principal luxuries of our table, and were always reserved for holidays and great occasions. We ate them boiled—or more frequently after being parboiled, *roasted* in a pitch kettle.

They were taken by us in considerable numbers, and formed a valuable addition to our provisions when meat was very scarce.

The females are somewhat smaller than the males, and generally in poorer condition. The average weight of twenty males being 7 lb. 4 oz.; of twenty females, 5 lb. 11 oz.

	Males.	Females.
Length from snout to insertion of tail .	22.4 inches .	21.8 inches
to end of vertebræ of tail	35 .	33.5

Length of fur in each 2.7 inches beyond the vertebræ of the tail.

Length of the head measured with callipers	5.5 inches
Mean length of the alimentary canal . .	86.7
of the intestinum cæcum .	4.5

6.—CANIS LAGOPUS (*Var. β. Fuliginosus*).

Canis Lagopus Fuliginosus.—*Rich: Faun. Bor. Amer.*—p. 89.

This variety of the Arctic Fox is much more rare than the preceding, only three individuals having been captured out of fifty of the pure white kind. Indeed in a country which presents an unvaried white surface, they must have extreme difficulty in surprising their prey, and be much more exposed to the persecutions of its enemies.

It is somewhat larger in its measurements than the white variety.

		Male.
Length from snout to insertion of the tail	.	23.7 inches
to end of vertebræ of the tail	. .	36.2
of the head measured with callipers		5.7

7.—ARVICOLA HUDSONIA (*Hudson's Bay Lemming*).

LEMMUS HUDSONIUS.—*Cuv: Règ. Anim.*—vol. i., p. 207.
ARVICOLA HUDSONIA.—*Rich: Faun. Bor. Amer.*—p. 132.
Rich: App. to Parry's 2d Voy.—p. 308.

The smallest of the quadrupeds of the Polar Regions, and has been found in the highest latitude that has yet been attained: even on the ice of the Polar Ocean, to the northward of the 82° of latitude, the skeleton of one was found.*

It has never been met with far in the interior of the country, preferring to congregate during the summer months along the sea-shores, where amongst large loose stones they rear their young, and find shelter from their numerous enemies. In the winter season, each individual makes a nest of dried grass, on the surface of the earth, beneath the snow, and has many passages in different directions from its nest, along which it passes in search of food. It seldom appears during the winter, but its tracks are occasionally to be met with even in the coldest weather; but from the whiteness of its fur, and the rapidity with which it burrows beneath the surface of the snow, it is seldom taken at that season of the year.

It feeds chiefly on the roots of *Polygonum Viviparum*, on grasses, vetches, and during the summer on almost every kind of plant the country produces; but is nevertheless fond of animal food, even to devouring its own species; and the salmon hoards of the Esquimaux frequently furnish provision to numbers of these animals during the winter.

* See Appendix to Parry's Polar Journey, p. 190.

It brings forth from four to eight young at various periods of the year: thus one taken by us in March had four young *in utero*, nearly matured; and a nest with six young ones, blind, naked, and helpless, was found on 12th July; they abandoned their nest on the 22d.

It is easily tamed, and fond of being caressed; one that had been but a few days confined, escaped during the night, and was found next morning on the ice alongside the ship: on putting down its cage, which it recognised in the servant's hand, it immediately went into it. It lived for several months in the cabin; but finding that, unlike what occurred to our tame hares under similar circumstances, it retained its summer fur, I was induced to try the effect of exposing it for a short time to the winter temperature.

It was accordingly placed on deck in a cage, on the 1st of February; and next morning, after having been exposed to a temperature of 30° below zero, the fur on the cheeks and a patch on each shoulder had become perfectly white. On the following day the patches on each shoulder had extended considerably, and the posterior part of the body and flanks had turned to a dirty white: during the next four days the change continued but slowly, and at the end of a week it was entirely white, with the exception of a dark band across the shoulders, prolonged posteriorly down to the middle of the back, forming a kind of saddle, where the colour of the fur had not changed in the smallest degree. The thermometer continued between 30° and 40° below zero until the 18th, without producing any further change, when the poor little sufferer perished from the severity of the cold.

On examining the skin, it appeared that all the white parts of the fur were longer than the unchanged portions; and that the ends of the fur only were white, so far as they exceeded in length the dark-coloured fur; and by removing these white tips with a pair of scissars, it again appeared in its dark summer dress, but slightly changed in colour, and precisely the same length as before the experiment.

8.—ARVICOLA TRIMUCRONATA (*Back's Lemming*).

ARVICOLA TRIMUCRONATA.—*Rich: App. to Parry's 2d Voy.*—p. 309.

Although seen by us on the coast of Boothia Felix in considerable numbers, it is not so generally to be met with in the Arctic Regions as the preceding species.

The individual specimen from which Dr. Richardson's very accurate description was drawn, was taken by Captain Back (in honour of whom it has been named) on Point Lake, in latitude 65° N. It was a female of smaller dimensions than those we have generally met with; for Dr. Richardson states it to be a little *inferior* in size to the Hudson's Bay Lemming: whereas a comparison of the average measurements and weight of above twenty of each species is in favour of the latter.

No specimens of this species were obtained during the winter; but it is more than probable that, like the preceding species, it is white during that season.

The first fur of the young, as in the Hudson's Bay Lemming, is rather more obscure than that of the parents; and even in this early state the two species are easily distinguishable by their colour, the trimucronate thumb not being at first so very apparent.

9.—ARCTOMYS PARRYI (*Parry's Marmot*).

ARCTOMYS PARRYI.—*Sab: in App. to Franklin's 1st Journey.*
Rich: in App. to Parry's 2d Voy.
Rich: in Faun. Bor. Amer.—p. 158.

None of these animals were seen during our late voyage in the Victory; nor do I believe they have ever been found far north of the Arctic Circle. I notice it here merely to mention that some of the dresses of the Esquimaux who had lately left Repulse Bay were made of its skins. These people told us that it was very numerous in those parts.

10.—LEPUS GLACIALIS (*Polar Hare*).

LEPUS GLACIALIS.—*Rich: Faun. Bor. Amer.*—p. 221.
LEPUS TIMIDUS.—*Fab: Faun. Grœnl.*—p. 25.

There is scarcely a spot in the Arctic Regions, the most desolate and steril that can be conceived, where this animal is not to be found, and that too throughout the winter:

nor does it seek to shelter itself from the inclemency of the weather by burrowing in the snow, but is found generally sitting solitary under the lee of a large stone, where the snow-drift as it passes along seems in some measure to afford a protection from the bitterness of the blast that impels it, by collecting around and half burying the animal beneath it.

It is accordingly provided with a remarkably fine, thick, woolly fur, admirably calculated to withstand the most intense cold.

In summer it is found chiefly at the foot and sides of gentle acclivities, where amongst the large loose stones it finds some secure retreat to bring forth its young. A female killed by one of our party at Sheriff Harbour, on the 7th of June, had four young *in utero*, perfectly mature, 5½ inches long, and of a dark gray colour. In one shot by us at Igloolik, on the 2d of June, six young were found, not quite so far advanced; and Fabricius, who states that he has himself seen eight young *in utero*, says it brings forth many young towards the end of June. One taken by us on the 28th of June a few days after its birth, soon became sufficiently tame to eat from our hands, and was allowed to run loose about the cabin. During the summer, we fed it on such plants as the country produced, and stored up a quantity of grass and astragali for its winter consumption; but it preferred to share with us whatever our table could afford, and would enjoy pease soup, plum pudding, bread, barley soup, sugar, rice, and even cheese, with us. It could not endure to be caressed, but was exceedingly fond of company, and would sit for hours listening to a conversation, which was no sooner ended than he would retire to his cabin: he was a continual source of amusement by his sagacity and playfulness, until in the middle of winter, when playing some of his pranks, he struck his head against one of the beams, and was ever after subject to fits. He lived and thrived nevertheless throughout the winter, and died in the following summer after fifteen months' confinement.

Although constantly in a temperature never much below the freezing point, its fur assumed its white colour as early as those that were running wild, and exposed to the climate; and although it cast its winter coat early in May, it was replaced by a pure white fur; from which, it is probable that the old males are not subject to the same change as the females in summer. Fabricius says, that "the Greenland Hare is white both in summer and winter." Amongst the inhabitants of Greenland, one Esquimaux woman was found who spun some of the beautiful white wool of the Hare into a thread, and knitted several pairs of gloves; one pair of which, notwithstanding the native filthiness of the Esquimaux, came into my possession beautifully white. It very much resembles the Angola wool, but is still more soft.

11.—CERVUS TARANDUS (*Reindeer*).

CERVUS TARANDUS.—*Cuv: Règ. Anim.*—vol. i., p. 261.
Rich: Faun. Bor. Amer.—p. 238.
Rich: App. Parry's 2d Voy.—p. 326.

Although this animal was seen in great numbers on the Isthmus of Boothia, only one individual was killed in the course of our late voyage. It was a fine buck, of larger size than ordinary, and weighed 250 lb.; the average of those killed at Spitzbergen and Melville Island did not exceed half that weight.

The does arrived about the middle of April, the bucks nearly a month later; and herds of several hundreds were seen about the Isthmus towards the end of May. Numbers of the fawns, which at that period are in a very weak state, are killed by the natives, who hunt them with their dogs; and the does themselves often fall victims to their attachment to their offspring.

The natives of Boothia depend chiefly on the skins of these animals for their beds and clothing; their bows and spears are principally made from their horns, which being softened by steeping in water are easily cut into shape, even with their rude knives; and the sinews of the Reindeer make the best thread. The paunch, termed by them *ner-rook-kah*, is esteemed a great delicacy; and its contents is the only vegetable food which the natives ever taste.

It feeds on the usneæ, alectoriæ, cetrariæ, and other lichens in the early part of spring; but as the summer advances, the young and tender grass fattens it so quickly, that in August they have been killed with several inches thick of fat on their haunches. In this state the meat is equal to the finest English venison; but is most tasteless and insipid when in poor condition.

Dr. Richardson *loc. cit.* has given a most detailed and interesting account of the several uses to which every part of this animal is put, and the various ways by which it is captured or killed in different parts of the American continent.

The natives of Boothia seldom hunt it in the spring, and then the bow and arrow is their only mode of killing it; but in the autumn, as the animal returns from the north in fine condition, they are destroyed in great numbers by parties of the natives driving them into the water, whilst others in canoes kill them with spears at their leisure.

Although they migrate, towards the middle of September, to milder climes, yet stragglers are occasionally seen in the winter.

*c

Length from snout to insertion of tail .	70	inches
length of tail . .	5.2	
hair of the tail .	2	
Extreme length . .	77.2	

Height at fore shoulder . . .	51	inches
hind quarter	53	
Girth behind the fore legs	55	

12.—OVIBOS MUSCHATUS (*Musk Ox*).

Ovibos Muschatus.—*Rich: Faun. Bor. Amer.*—p. 271.
Bos Muschatus.—*Cuv: Règ. Anim.*—p. 281.
Sabine, in App. to Franklin's 1st Journey—vol. i., p. 668.
Rich: in App. to Parry's 2d Voy.—p. 331.
Musk Ox.—*Hearne's Journey*—p. 137. *Pennant, Arctic Zool.*—vol. i., p. 9.

Oo ming mak.—Esquimaux.

The circumstance of this animal and the Reindeer having been found in Melville Island, led to the belief that a chain of islands, at no great distance from each other, connected Melville Island with the shores of the continent. The recent discovery of the Isthmus of Boothia, and the fact that the continent of America extends to the 74th degree of north latitude, affords an easy solution of the route by which this animal visits the North Georgian Islands. They are said by the natives to be very numerous between the Isthmus of Boothia and Repulse Bay; but are not found to the westward, the whole country being of low limestone formation, whilst the rugged granite hills are the favourite resort of the Musk Ox.

On one of my surveying excursions from the ship, in April, 1830, we were fortunate in meeting with two of these animals, which we killed; they were both males, in very fine condition. We found the meat most excellent food, and quite free from any musky flavour, although the skin smelt strongly of it. The account of the manner in which the natives hunt this animal will be found in the narrative.

The Esquimaux informed us, that at Aw-wuk-too-teak the Musk Ox is frequently seen in considerable numbers. It is not so highly valued by them as the Reindeer; its hide being too thick and hard for clothing, is used only for beds.

The dung of the Musk Ox, as well as of the Reindeer, when fresh, is considered a delicacy by the natives.

There is an excellent drawing of the Musk Ox in Captain Parry's Narrative of his First Voyage, p. 257, by Lieut. Beechy. The description by Dr. Richardson is most accurate; and a very fine specimen brought from Melville Island is preserved in the British Museum.

13.—PHOCA FŒTIDA (*Rough Seal*).

PHOCA FŒTIDA.—*Cuv: Règ. Anim.*—vol. i., p. 168.
Fab: Faun. Grœnl.—p. 13.
Rich: App. to Parry's 2d Voy.—p. 332.
ROUGH SEAL.—*Penn: Quad.*—vol. ii., p. 278; and *Arctic Zool.*—vol. i., p. 160.

Inhabits the seas both on the east and west sides of the Isthmus of Boothia, and constitutes the principal means of subsistence to the inhabitants during eight or nine months of every year.

In July, August, and September, the Reindeer and Salmon afford to the Esquimaux an agreeable and salutary change. The skins of the Reindeer supply them with beds and clothes; but it is the Rough Seal on which they wholly depend for their winter's food; when all other animals have retired to a more temperate climate, the Seal is sought by the Esquimaux, whose dogs are trained to hunt over the extensive floes of level ice, and to scent out the concealed breathing-holes of the Rough Seal. So soon as one is discovered, a snow wall is built round it, to protect the huntsman from the bitterness of the passing breeze; where, with his spear uplifted, he will sit for hours until his victim rises to breathe, and falls an easy sacrifice to his unerring aim. In this manner, a party of thirty hunters killed 150 of these animals during the first two months they remained in our neighbourhood; the fishery for ten or twelve miles round was then completely exhausted; so they broke up into several smaller parties, and dispersed in various directions. In the month of May, the Rough Seal, with its young, lie basking in the sun, close to holes in the ice, and are at that time very difficult to approach; but the natives imitate both their cry and action so exactly as to deceive the animals until they get sufficiently near to strike them with their spear. Fabricius says, it is the most heedless of all the Seals, as well on the ice as in the water: from our experience, we would certainly give them a very different character, for none of our sportsmen were ever able to get sufficiently near to shoot them. The natives of Boothia say they are not in their prime until the third year; and we never heard them complain of the offensive smell, which their more fastidious brethren in Greenland are said to dislike so extremely. The blood of the Rough Seal answers all the purposes of glue.

The Rough Seal resembles our common Seal, *P. Vitulina*, the principal differences being in the more diminutive size of the *P. Fœtida*, its being clothed with a more woolly coat, and some slight differences in its colour; all of which may indeed be fairly attributed to difference of food and climate.

The average length from the snout to the extremity of the tail, of twenty measured by me, was 55 inches, the hind flippers extending 9 inches beyond the end of the tail; and the average weight of the same number was 199 lb.: the circumference immediately behind the fore-flippers being 49.7 inches. The females are larger than the males.

The average length of the young, when between five and six months old, was 38 inches; the weight 49 lb.; circumference as above, 28.6 inches; length of the alimentary canal, 49 feet 8 inches; and of the cæcum, 3½ inches.

It feeds chiefly on the *Mysis fluxuosus* and other small *Cancri*.

14.—PHOCA GRŒNLANDICA (*Harp Seal*).

PHOCA GRŒNLANDICA.—*Cuv: Règ. Anim.*—vol. i., p. 168.
Egede, Grænl.—p. 62, fig. A.
HARP SEAL.—*Penn: Arct. Zool.*—vol. i., p. 163.

Kai ro lik.—Esquimaux of Boothia.

Unlike the preceding species, it is seldom met with on the fixed ice of the bays and inlets, but prefers the loose floating floes which constitute what is termed by the whale fishers "the middle ice" of Baffin's Bay and Davis Straits. It is, however, occasionally met with near the coast of Greenland.

We have never seen it in any part of Prince Regent's Inlet; but from the natives of Boothia we obtained several skins of this Seal, which they describe as being sometimes very numerous on the west side of the Isthmus, but is much more scarce than the preceding species. They have never seen any of this species on the east side of the Isthmus of Boothia.

15.—PHOCA BARBATA (*Great Seal*).

Phoca Barbata.—*Cuv: Règ. Anim.*—vol. i., p. 168.
Fab: Faun. Grœnl.—p. 15.

Oo ge ook.—Esquimaux.

Is the largest of the Seals inhabiting the Polar Seas. It is but seldom sought after by the natives of Boothia, as it approaches the shores only in the summer season, when the salmon fishery wholly engrosses their attention. In winter it seeks those parts of the Arctic Ocean which are seldom, if ever, frozen over for any length of time.

No specimens were obtained.

16.—TRICHECHUS ROSMARUS (*Walrus*).

Trichechus Rosmarus.—*Cuv: Règ. Anim.*—vol. i., p. 171.
Fab: Faun. Grœnl.—p. 11.

I we ak.—Esquimaux.

Inhabits the west coast of Baffin's Bay, and is occasionally seen in the northern part of Prince Regent's Inlet, but the natives of Boothia have never seen a Walrus; and although we found amongst them several articles made from the tusks of that animal, they were all brought from Repulse Bay, where it abounds.

No specimens were obtained.

17.—DELPHINAPTERUS BELUGA (*White Whale*).

DELPHINAPTERUS BELUGA.—*Cuv: Règ. Anim.*—vol. i., p. 290.
DELPHINUS ALBICANS.—*Fab: Faun. Grænl.*—p. 50.
Scoresby's Arctic Regions—vol. ii., pl. xiv.

Seen abundantly in Prince Regent's Inlet, but none were taken by us.

18.—MONODON MONOCEROS (*Narwhal*).

MONODON MONOCEROS.—*Cuv: Règ. Anim.*—vol. i., p. 292.
Fab: Faun. Grænl.—p. 29.
Scoresby's Arctic Regions—vol. ii., pl. xv.

The Narwhal, or Sea Unicorn, though occasionally seen in great numbers in the upper part of Baffin's Bay and Prince Regent's Inlet, are but seldom killed, from the great difficulty of surprising them when sleeping on the surface of the water, and the very short time they remain up when they rise to breathe.

The oil produced from its blubber is considered superior to that of the Whale; and the horn is valuable. Two or three years ago, several hundreds of these animals were found dead along the west coast of Baffin's Bay by the vessels employed in the whale-fishery; and I was informed by Captain Humphreys, of the Isabella, that of a great many examined by him, the males only have the horn-shaped spiral tooth.

Fabricius says, that both male and female have this horn; and that sometimes, but very seldom, the male has two of equal size. A specimen of this may be seen in the valuable museum of the Royal College of Surgeons; and an account of a female Narwhal, which had a horn similar to the male, is given in the 13th volume of the Transactions of the Linnæan Society, p. 620; but both these cases are of rare occurrence.

The largest horn I have seen measured 8½ feet. In all the males the rudiments of a second horn or tooth is present; and in the female are two such rudimental teeth, each about 8 inches in length.

A female killed in June had one young *in utero*, nearly matured, of a bluish-brown colour, nearly 5 feet long.

Several skeletons of this animal were seen by us as we travelled along the eastern coast of the Peninsula of Boothia, but only one horn was found amongst them; it measured 7 feet in length, 9½ inches in circumference at its insertion, and weighed 14lb. 6oz.

19.—BALÆNA MYSTICETUS (*Black Whale*).

BALÆNA MYSTICETUS.—*Cuv: Règ. Anim.*—vol. i., p. 296.
Fab: Faun. Grœnl.—p. 32.
Scoresby's Arctic Regions—vol. ii., pl. xii.

The capture of the Whale, which gives employment to several thousands of our seamen, and has annually produced, on an average of the last twenty years, between eleven and twelve thousand tons of oil, and from five to six hundred tons of whalebone; has of late years greatly declined, owing to the increasing difficulties attending the fishery. Wearied by the incessant persecutions of man, the Whale has lately abandoned all the accessible parts of the Spitzbergen Sea, where it was by no means unusual to see sixty or seventy sail of British vessels engaged in its capture.

On the east side of Baffin's Bay, as far as the 72° of latitude, abundance of Whales of a large size were to be found, some few years ago; but, like the fishery in the Spitzbergen Sea, this also was deserted. The Whales retired to the westward of the then considered impenetrable barrier of ice that occupies the middle of Baffin's Bay.

In 1818 that barrier was passed by the first Expedition of Discovery, sent by the government to those regions; where the haunts of the Whale and the nursery for its young were laid open to the fishermen, whose daring enterprise and perseverance in following the track of the discoverers, were amply rewarded for the first few years by most abundant success; since the produce that in any one year has been brought to England from those newly-discovered portions of the Arctic Seas, is more than sufficient to cover the whole expenses of all the Expeditions of Discovery that have been sent, during the last twenty years, to those regions: and yet people, not aware of this circumstance, are perpetually asking what benefit can result to this country from such undertakings!

The Whale, however, still continues to retire from the persecutions of man; and the numbers of its young which are annually destroyed without remorse by the avaricious but imprudent fishermen, must soon exhaust the fishery; and search must then be made far to the westward of Baffin's Bay, and to the eastward of Spitzbergen, for their places of retreat.

We found them in considerable numbers as low as the latitude of 71° N, along the western shore of Prince Regent's Inlet; and the whole line of coast is crowded with the remains of Esquimaux winter huts, which had been chiefly constructed of the crown bones of the young Whale.

The natives of the Isthmus of Boothia say, that it is but rarely seen either on the east or west side of the Isthmus; and they, not being sufficiently well prepared, or in sufficient numbers, never venture to attack it. Only two were seen by us during the three years we were frozen up in that neighbourhood.

A most interesting account of the Whale fishery is given by Captain Scoresby, *loc. cit.*, where its importance to Great Britain, as a nursery for seamen, employment of capital, and as a source of national wealth, is made sufficiently manifest.

BIRDS.

1.—FALCO ISLANDICUS (*Jerfalcon*).

FALCO ISLANDICUS.—*Rich: Faun. Bor. Amer.*—vol. ii., p. 27. *Lath: Ind. Orn.*—vol. i., p. 32.
Cuv: Règ. Anim.—vol. i., p. 323.
Sab: Greenl. Birds, in Trans. Lin. Soc.—vol. xii., p. 528. *Temm.*—vol. i., p. 17.
WHITE JERFALCON.—*Lath: Syn.*—vol. i., p. 83; and *Supp.*—p. 21.

Several were seen about Victoria Harbour, pursuing the packs of young Grouse, in August and September, 1832; and a pair built their nest a short distance to the south of Felix Harbour. No specimens, however, were obtained by us.

2.—STRIX NYCTEA (*Snowy Owl*).

STRIX NYCTEA.—*Rich: Faun. Bor. Amer.*—vol. ii., p. 88. *Lath: Ind. Orn.*—vol. i., p. 57.
Cuv: Règ. Anim.—vol. i., p. 345. *Temm.*—vol. i., p. 82.
Fab: Faun. Grœnl.—p. 60; and in *Appendices to Parry's 1st, 2d, and 3d Voyages.*
SNOWY OWL AND WHITE OWL.—*Arct. Zool.*—vol. ii., p. 233. *Lath: Syn.*—vol. i., p. 132.

Was occasionally seen throughout the winter about Victoria Harbour, where several pairs had bred in the preceding autumn, but none were obtained by us.

*D

3.—ALAUDA CORNUTA (*Shore Lark*).

ALAUDA CORNUTA.—*Rich: Faun. Bor. Amer.*—vol. ii., p. 245.
ALAUDA ALPESTRIS.—*Forst: Phil. Trans.*—lxii., p. 398. *Lat: Ind. Orn.*—vol. ii., p. 498.
Cuv: Règ. Anim.—vol. p. 400. *Temm.*—vol. i., p. 279.
Rich: App. to Parry's 2d Voyage—p. 343.
SHORE LARK.—*Penn: Arct. Zool.*—vol. ii., p. 392.

One shot by us, near Felix Harbour, agreed well with the descriptions of authors. Two others were all that were seen by us; it is therefore but rarely met with above the 70° of latitude.

4.—SYLVIA ŒNANTHE (*Wheatear*).

SYLVIA ŒNANTHE.—*Temm.*—vol. i., p. 135. *Lath: Ind. Orn.*—vol. ii., p. 529.
Sabine, in Trans. Linn. Soc.—vol. xii., p. 531.
MOTACILLA ŒNANTHE.—*Cuv: Règ. Anim.*—vol. i., p. 382.
Fab: Faun. Grænl.—p. 122.
WHEATEAR.—*Lath: Syn.*—vol. iv., p. 465. *Arct. Zool.*—vol. ii., p. 420.

One of these little birds was observed flying round the ship in Felix Harbour on the 2d of May, 1830, and was found dead alongside, the next morning: having arrived before the ground was sufficiently uncovered to enable it to procure its food, it had perished from want. It is the only instance of this bird having been met with in Arctic America, in the course of our several Expeditions to those regions.

I do not find it mentioned by Dr. Richardson, in the "Fauna Boreali Americana." Fabricius found it in Greenland; and several were seen by us, on our first voyage, off Cape Farewell, in October, 1818.

5.—EMBERIZA NIVALIS (*Snow Bunting*).

EMBERIZA NIVALIS.—*Rich: Faun. Bor. Amer.*—vol. ii., p. 246. *Lath: Ind. Orn.*—vol. i., p. 397.
Cuv: Rég. Anim.—vol. i., p. 405. *Temm.*—p. 319. *Gmel.*—vol. i., p. 866.
Fab: Faun. Grœnl.—p. 117. *Sabine, in Trans. Linn. Soc.*—vol. xii., p. 532.
Rich: in App. to Parry's 2d Voyage.—p. 343.
SNOW BUNTING.—*Brit. Zool.*—vol. i., p. 444. *Arct. Zool.*—vol. ii., p. 355.
Lath: Syn.—vol. iii., p. 161.

Abounds in all parts of the Arctic Regions, between the middle or end of April and the end of September.

6.—PLECTROPHANES LAPPONICA (*Lapland Finch*).

PLECTROPHANES LAPPONICA.—*Ross, in App. to Parry's 3d Voyage*—p. 97.
Selby, in Trans. Lin. Soc.—vol. xv., p. 156, pl. 1 (young).
Rich: Faun. Bor. Amer.—p. 248, pl. 48 (excellent).
PLECTROPHANES CALCARATA.—*Meyer: Tasch.*—vol. iii., p. 176.
EMBERIZA CALCARATA.—*Temm.*—vol. i., p. 322. *Rich: in App. to Parry's 2d Voyage*—p. 345.
LAPLAND FINCH.—*Arct. Zool.*—vol. ii., p. 377. *Lath: Syn.*—vol. iii., p. 263.

Is by no means numerous in the higher northern latitudes. A nest with five eggs was brought on board early in July, 1830.

7.—CORVUS CORAX (*Raven*).

CORVUS CORAX.—*Rich: Faun. Bor. Amer.*—vol. ii., p. 290. *Lath: Ind. Orn.*—vol. i., p. 150.
Cuv: Rég. Anim.—vol. i., p. 420.—*Temm.* p. 107. *Gmel.*—vol. i., p. 364.
Fab: Faun. Grœnl.—p. 62. *Rich: App. to Parry's 2d Voyage*—p. 343.
Ross, App. to Parry's 3d Voyage—p. 97.
RAVEN—*Lath: Syn.*—vol. i., p. 367. *Arct. Zool.*—vol. ii., p. 245.

This is one of the few birds that are capable of braving the severity of an Arctic

*D 2

winter and of enduring the scorching rays of a tropical sun, without any change being produced in its plumage by the extremes of climate. Cuvier and other authors mention, that in the north it is frequently found more or less white: we never saw any thing corroborative of such an observation. It preserves its plumage and peculiar characteristics, unchanged, in every part of the globe.

8.—TETRAO LAGOPUS MUTUS (*Ptarmigan*).

TETRAO LAGOPUS MUTUS.—*Rich: Faun. Bor. Amer.*—vol. ii., p. 350.
TETRAO LAGOPUS.—*Cuv: Règ. Anim.*—vol. i., p. 482. *Lath: Ind. Orn.*—vol. ii. p. 639.
Fab: Faun. Grœnl.—p. 114. *Sab: Supp. to Parry's 1st Voyage*—p. cxcvii.
Rich: App. to Parry's 2d Voyage—p. 350.
Ross, App. to Parry's 3d Voy.—p. 99; and *App. to Parry's Polar Voy.*—p. 193.
PTARMIGAN.—*Brit. Zool.*—vol. i., p. 359, pl. 57. *Lath: Syn.*—vol. iv., p. 744. *Arct. Zool.*—p. 315.

Is not so numerous in the higher northern latitudes as the two following species. A pair was shot on the east side of the Peninsula of Boothia, in latitude 71° nearly; and three or four more were obtained at Felix Harbour.

9.—TETRAO LAGOPUS SALICETI (*Willow Grouse*).

TETRAO LAGOPUS SALICETI.—*Rich: Faun. Bor. Amer.*—vol. ii., p. 351.
TETRAO SALICETI.—*Cuv: Règ. Anim.*—vol. i., p. 483. *Temm.*—vol. ii., p. 471.
Sabine, App. to Franklin's 1st Journey—p. 681.
Rich: App. to Parry's 2d Voyage—p. 347.
TETRAO ALBUS.—*Lath: Ind. Orn.*—vol. ii., p. 639. *Gmel.*—vol. i., p. 750.
Ross, App. to Parry's 3d Voyage—p. 101.
WHITE GROUSE.—*Lath: Syn.*—vol. iv., p. 743. *Arct. Zool.*—vol. ii., p. 308.
WILLOW PARTRIDGE.—*Hearne's Travels*—p. 338.

Inhabits both shores of the inlet to the west of Boothia; but is not to be found on the east side of the Peninsula, seeming to prefer the low limestone formation to that of the high rugged granite, which appears more peculiarly adapted to the habits of the Rock Grouse and the Ptarmigan.

10.—TETRAO LAGOPUS RUPESTRIS (*Rock Grouse*).

TETRAO LAGOPUS RUPESTRIS.—*Rich: Faun. Bor. Amer.*—vol. ii., p. 354, pl. 64, fem.
TETRAO RUPESTRIS.—*Sab: Supp. to Parry's 1st Voyage*—p. cxcv.
Rich: App. to Parry's 2d Voyage—p. 348.
Ross, App. to Parry's 3d Voyage—p. 99.
Lath: Ind. Orn.—vol. ii., p. 640. *Gmel.*—vol. i., p. 751.
ROCK GROUSE.—*Arct. Zool.*—vol. ii., No. 184. *Lath: Syn. Supp.*—p. 217.

Is much more numerous in the higher northern latitudes than either of the two preceding species. It frequents the eastern side of the Peninsula of Boothia; but was not found to the westward.

11.—COLUMBA MIGRATORIA (*Passenger Pigeon*).

COLUMBA MIGRATORIA.—*Rich: Faun. Bor. Amer.*—vol. ii., p. 363.
Sab: App. to Franklin's Journey—p. 679.
Cuv: Règ. Anim.—vol. i., p. 488.
Forster, in Phil. Trans. Roy. Soc.—vol. lxii., p. 398.
PASSENGER PIGEON.—*Arct. Zool.*—vol. ii., p. 322.

A young male bird flew on board the Victory during a storm, whilst crossing Baffin's Bay in latitude 73½° N, on the 31st of July, 1829. It has never before been seen beyond the sixty-second degree of latitude; and the circumstance of our having met with it so far to the northward, is a singular and interesting fact.

It is well known, from the dreadful devastation it commits in the rice-fields of America; and the accounts which authors give of the inconceivable multitudes that occasionally assemble together, are quite incredible. See Wilson's "American Ornithology," vol. ii., p. 299.

12.—CHARADRIUS SEMIPALMATUS (*American Ring Plover*).

CHARADRIUS SEMIPALMATUS.—*Rich: Faun. Bor. Amer.*—vol. ii., p. 367.
CHARADRIUS HIATICULA.—*Temm.*—p. 539. *Cuv: Règ. Anim.*—vol. i., p. 501.
Sabine, in Franklin's Journey—p. 684.
Sab: Supp. to Parry's 1st Voyage—p. cc.
Rich: App. to Parry's 2d Voyage—p. 351.
Sab: in Trans. Linn. Soc.—vol. xii., No. 10.

Very numerous during the summer months in Boothia, inhabiting the marshy grounds, and feeding chiefly on the larvæ of the *Tipula Arctica* (of Curtis).

---

13. CHARADRIUS PLUVIALIS (*Golden Plover*).

CHARADRIUS PLUVIALIS.—*Rich: Faun. Bor. Amer.*—vol. ii., p. 369.
Cuv: Règ. Anim.—vol. i., p. 501. *Lath: Ind. Orn.*—vol. ii., p. 740.
Gmel.—vol. i., p. 688. *Fab: Faun. Grœnl.*—No. 79.
Temm.—vol. ii., p. 535. *Sabine, Franklin's Journey*—p. 683.
Sabine, Supp. to Parry's 1st Voyage—p. cxcix.
Ross, App. to Parry's 3d Voyage—p. 683.
GOLDEN PLOVER.—*Arct. Zool.*—vol. ii., p. 483.

Abundant during the breeding season in most parts of the Arctic Regions. We found them plentifully in the neighbourhood of Felix Harbour, feeding in the marshes, in company with the preceding species.

14.—VANELLUS MELANOGASTER (*Grey Lapwing*).

VANELLUS MELANOGASTER.—*Rich: Faun. Bor. Amer.*—vol ii., p. 370.
Cuv: Règ. Anim.—vol. i., p. 502.
Sabine, Franklin's Journey—p. 684.
Rich: App. to Parry's 2d Voyage—p. 352.
SWISS SANDPIPER.—*Arct. Zool.*—vol. ii., p. 478.

Is somewhat larger than the Golden Plover, with which it has been frequently confounded. It is also more rarely met with; but was found by us breeding near the margins of the marshes immediately to the south-west of Fury Point, in considerable numbers.

Some specimens were also obtained near Felix Harbour.

15.—STREPSILAS INTERPRES (*Turnstone*).

STREPSILAS INTERPRES.—*Rich: Faun. Bor. Amer.*—vol. ii., p. 371.
Cuv: Règ. Anim.—vol. i., p. 529.
STREPSILAS COLLARIS.—*Temm.*—vol. ii., p. 553. *Sabine, Franklin's Journey*—p. 684.
Sab: Supp. to Parry's 1st Voyage—p. cc.
Rich: App. to Parry's 2d Voyage—p. 352.
TURNSTONE.—*Edwards*—pl. 141.

Is still more rare than the preceding, and only one specimen was obtained, early in July, at Felix Harbour; it was a female in full breeding plumage. Some others were seen by us, as we travelled along the coast between Victoria Harbour and Fury Point, about the middle and towards the end of June.

16.—GRUS CANADENSIS (*Brown Crane*).

GRUS CANADENSIS.—*Rich: Faun. Bor. Amer.*—vol. ii., p. 373. *Cuv: Règ. Anim.*—vol. i., p. 510.
BROWN CRANE.—*Penn: Arct. Zool.*—vol. ii., p. 443.

Several individuals of a species of Crane were seen by us in the neighbourhood of Fury Beach; they were probably of the abovenamed species, but as no specimen was obtained, it cannot be identified with certainty.

17.—TRINGA MARITIMA (*Purple Sandpiper*).

TRINGA MARITIMA.—*Rich: Faun. Bor. Amer.*—vol. ii., p. 382. *Cuv: Règ. Anim.*—vol. i., p. 525.
Sab: Trans. Linn. Soc.—vol. xii., p. 532. *Temm.*—vol. ii., p 619.
Sab: Supp. to Parry's 1st Voy.—p. cci. *Rich: App. to Parry's 2d Voy.*—p. 354.
STRIATED SANDPIPER.—*Arct. Zool.*—vol. ii., p. 472. *Lath: Syn.*—vol. v., p. 176.

But few individuals of this species were seen near our watering stations; we found them, however, in considerable numbers near Fury Point; and at Melville Island, on a former voyage, they were very numerous.

18.—TRINGA ALPINA (*American Dunlin*).

TRINGA ALPINA.—*Rich: Faun. Bor. Amer.*—vol. ii., p. 383.
Sabine, Trans. Linn. Soc.—vol. xii., p. 533.
TRINGA VARIABILIS.—*Sabine, Franklin's Journey*—p. 686. *Temm.*—vol. ii., p. 612.
Sab: Supp. to Parry's 1st Voyage—p. cc.
Rich: App. to Parry's 2d Voyage—p. 353.
DUNLIN.—*Penn: Arct. Zool.*—vol. ii., p 476.

Is very abundant during the breeding season near Felix Harbour, building its nest in the marshes and by the sides of the lakes.

19.—PHALAROPUS FULICARIUS (*Flat-billed Phalarope*).

PHALAROPUS FULICARIUS.—*Rich: Faun. Bor. Amer.*—vol. ii., p. 407.
PHALAROPUS PLATYRHYNCHUS.—*Cuv: Règ. Anim.*—vol. i., p. 528. *Temm.*—vol. ii., p. 712.
Sabine, Trans. Linn. Soc.—vol. xii., p. 536.
Sab: Supp. to Parry's 1st Voyage—p. cci.
Rich: App. to Parry's 2d Voyage—p. 355.
Ross, App. to Parry's 3d Voyage—p. 102.

Temminck's and Sabine's descriptions are excellent. Dr. Richardson's is taken from an individual killed in the Columbia River, and is of unusually small dimensions: of above twenty measured by me, the smallest exceeded 8 inches in length, and the average of that number was rather more than 8⅓ inches; he states the extreme length of his specimen to be only 7 inches. The females are larger than the males. Twelve of them together weighed 21 ounces, or 1¾ ounces each.

20.—STERNA ARCTICA (*Arctic Tern*).

STERNA ARCTICA.—*Rich: Faun. Bor. Amer.*—vol. ii., p. 414. *Temm.*—vol. ii., p. 742.
Sabine, Franklin's Journey—p. 694. *Sab: Supp. to Parry's 1st Voy.*—p. ccii.
Rich: App. to Parry's 2d Voyage—p. 356.
Ross, App. to Parry's 3d Voyage—p. 103; and *App. to Parry's Polar Voyage*—p. 194.

Very scarce, both to the east and west of the Peninsula of Boothia, only five or six having been seen by us during the three years we were in that neighbourhood.

It has lately been found abundantly on the west coast of Ireland, in the winter season.

21.—LARUS GLAUCUS (*Glaucous Gull*).

LARUS GLAUCUS.—*Rich: Faun. Bor. Amer.*—vol. ii., p. 417.
Cuv: Règ. Anim.—vol. i., p. 556. *Temm.*—vol. ii., p. 757.
Sab: Trans. Linn. Soc.—vol. xii., p. 543.
Sab: App. to Parry's 1st Voyage—p. cciii.
Ross, App. to Parry's 3d Voyage—p. 103.
GLAUCOUS GULL.—*Arct. Zool.*—vol. ii., p. 532. *Lath: Syn.*—vol. vi., p. 374.

Numbers of this magnificent species of Gull built their nests on the upper part of the face of a high precipice, two or three miles to the south of Felix Harbour; and the whole line of precipitous rock that forms the western shore of Prince Regent's Inlet, is annually resorted to by them in the breeding season. Although feeding chiefly on fish, the young bird is scarcely inferior either in delicacy of flavour or colour to the tenderest chicken: the old ones, however, are not quite so palateable, and smell most offensively after being kept a day or two.

22.—LARUS ARGENTATUS (*Black-winged Silvery Gull*).

LARUS ARGENTATUS.—*Gmel.*—vol. i., p. 600. *Temm.*—vol. ii., p. 764.
Rich: App. to Parry's 2d Voyage—p. 358.
Ross, App. to Parry's 3d Voyage—p. 104.
SILVERY GULL—*Arct. Zool.*—vol. ii., p. 533. *Lath: Syn.*—vol. vi., p. 375.
HERRING GULL.—*Arct. Zool.*—vol. ii., p. 527.

The individuals of this species obtained during our late voyage, agreed sufficiently with the descriptions above referred to, except perhaps that the markings on the primary quill feathers are not quite so dark as in European specimens.

Dr. Richardson has referred the examples of this bird, brought to England on our former voyages from Melville Island and Melville Peninsula, to the Larus Argentatoides of the Prince of Musignano. (*Faun: Bor. Amer.*—p. 417.)

23.—LARUS LEUCOPTERUS (*White-winged Silvery Gull*).

LARUS LEUCOPTERUS.—*Rich: Faun. Bor. Amer.*—vol. ii., p. 418.
LARUS ARGENTATUS.—*Sab: Trans. Linn. Soc.*—vol. xii., p. 546.
LARUS ARCTICUS.—*M'Gillivray, Wer. Trans.*—vol. v., p. 268.

This bird abounds in Greenland and Iceland, and was first described many years ago by Dr. Edmonstone, of Shetland, in the Wernerian Transactions, under the name of the "Less Iceland Gull," from its general resemblance, except in size, to the *L. Glaucus*, which he had before described under the name of Iceland Gull. Captain Sabine, in his "Memoir on the Birds of Greenland," *loc. cit.*, was disposed to have considered this a new and undescribed species; but in deference to Mr. Temminck, who conceived that the absence of the dark markings on the wings might be occasioned by the severity of the climate in which it was found, he classed it with the preceding species. Its distinctive characters are now, however, sufficiently well known: the specimens obtained by us during our late voyage, agreed most exactly with Captain Sabine's description above referred to.

It was found breeding on the face of the same precipice with the Glaucous, but at a much less height, and in greater numbers.

It is not unfrequently met with at the Shetland Islands in the winter season, and may therefore be added to our catalogue of British Birds.

24.—LARUS EBURNEUS (*Ivory Gull*).

LARUS EBURNEUS.—*Rich: Faun. Bor. Amer.*—vol. ii., p. 419.
Phipps's Voyage, App.—p. 187. *Gmel.*—vol. i., p. 596.
Lath: Ind. Orn.—vol. ii. p. 816. *Temm.*—vol. ii., p. 769.
Sab: in Trans. Linn. Soc.—vol. xii., p. 548.
Supp. to Parry's 1st Voyage—p. cciv.
LARUS CANDIDUS.—*Fab: Faun. Grænl.*—p. 103, No. 67.
IVORY GULL.—*Penn: Arct. Zool.*—vol. ii., p. 529.

Although extremely numerous in Baffin's Bay, and frequently met with during our former voyages in the vicinity of Port Bowen, one of its breeding-places, yet few were seen by us after passing to the southward of that part of Prince Regent's Inlet: and only one specimen was obtained.

This beautiful species of Gull has lately visited the western shores of Ireland.

25.—LARUS TRIDACTYLUS (*Kittiwake*).

LARUS TRIDACTYLUS.—*Rich: Faun. Bor. Amer.*—vol. ii., p. 423. *Temm.*—vol. ii., p. 774.
Fab: Faun. Grænl.—p. 98. *Lath: Ind. Orn.*—vol. ii., p. 817.
Sab: Supp. to Parry's 1st Voyage—p. ccv.
Rich: App. to Parry's 2d Voyage—p. 359.
Ross, in App. to Parry's 3d Voy.—p. 105; and *Polar Journey*—p. 195.
KITTIWAKE.—*Penn: Arct. Zool.*—vol. ii., p. 529. *Brit. Zool.*—vol. ii., p. 186.
Lath: Syn.—vol. vi., p. 393.

*E 2

Inhabits all parts of the Arctic Regions, and has been met with in the highest latitudes yet attained by man. It is extremely numerous during the summer season along the west coast of Prince Regent's Inlet; where, in several places that are peculiarly well fitted for breeding stations, they congregate in inconceivable numbers.

We killed enough to supply our party with several excellent meals, and found them delicious food, perfectly free from any unpleasant flavour.

26.—LARUS ROSSII (*Cuneate-tailed Gull*).

LARUS ROSSII.—*Rich: Faun. Bor. Amer.*—vol. ii., p. 427.
Rich: App. to Parry's 2d Voyage—p. 359.
Ross, App. to Parry's Polar Voyage—p. 195.
Wilson's Illust. Zool.—vol. i., pl. 8.
LARUS ROSEUS.—*Jardine and Selby, Orn. Illust.*—p. 1, pl. 14.

Was discovered near Igloolik in June, 1823, where only two specimens were obtained, although many others were seen: it has since been found abundantly on the east side of Spitzbergen, and several pairs were observed by Sir Edward Parry's party beyond the 82° of latitude.* It is noticed here as occasionally visiting Boothia, on the authority of Mr. Abernethy, who reported to me that he had seen one fly over the ship in Felix Harbour. He had accompanied Sir Edward Parry on his Polar Journey, during which it was frequently seen; and, although unsuccessfully, eagerly pursued as an object of more than ordinary interest, from the circumstance of only two specimens of it having reached England: he is therefore not very likely to have been mistaken.

Dr. Richardson has accurately described its plumage; but the measures having been taken from the dried skin, differ triflingly from those taken by me of the recent specimens, *ut infra:*

Extreme length from the tip of the beak to the end of the tail .	13.6 inches
to the angle of the mouth .	1.3
Length of the tarsus	1.2
middle toe and nail	1.2

Extent of wing, 30 inches. Weight, 6 ounces.

* See Parry's Narrative of his Polar Journey, p. 81.

27.—LARUS SABINI (*Fork-tailed Gull*).

LARUS SABINI.—*Rich: Faun. Bor. Amer.*—vol. ii., p. 428.
Sabine (*Mr.*), *Trans. Linn. Soc.*—vol. xii., p. 520, pl. 29 (very good).
Sabine (*Capt.*), *Trans. Linn. Soc.*—vol. xii., p. 551; and *Supp. to Parry's 1st Voyage*—p. ccv.
Rich: App. to Parry's 2d Voyage—p. 360.
Ross, App. to Parry's Polar Voyage—p. 195.
XEMA COLLARIS.—*Leach, in Ross's Voyage*, oct. edit.—vol. ii., p. 164.

Was discovered by Captain Sabine on the three islands of Baffin, during Captain Ross's first voyage to these regions in 1818, and described by Mr. Sabine with minute accuracy in the Transactions of the Linnæan Society, *loc. cit.*

Since that period it has been found in many parts of the Arctic Regions; at Spitzbergen, Igloolik, and Behring's Straits; and by our party as we travelled along the coast, a little to the southward of Cape Garry. I have no doubt that the low land where it was met with, is one of its breeding-places.

I have lately heard that it has also been found on the west coast of Ireland, so that it has a much more extensive range than was at first supposed; and it is the more extraordinary that it remained so long unknown to naturalists.

Only one specimen was obtained by us at Felix Harbour; it was shot by Dr. M'Diarmid, and was the only one seen during our three years' residence in that quarter. The Esquimaux informed me that it breeds in great numbers on the low land west of Neityelle.

Dr. Leach founds its generic distinction on the forcature of the tail: for a similar reason the *L. Rossii* should also form the type of a new genus, no other known Gull having a cuneiform tail.

28.—LESTRIS POMARINUS (*Pomarine Jager*).

LESTRIS POMARINUS.—*Rich: Faun. Bor. Amer.*—vol. ii., p. 427. *Temm.* vol. ii., p. 793.
Sab: Supp. to Parry's 1st Voyage—p. ccvi. *Rich: App. to Parry's 2d Voyage*—p. 361.
Ross, App. to Parry's 2d Voyage—p. 105; and *Parry's Polar Voyage*—p. 196.

Is a larger bird and much more scarce than the common Arctic Jager. It varies very much in colour, according to age, some being entirely of a uniform blackish-brown, and others more or less marked with lighter colours.

A nest with two eggs was found near Fury Point, by the margin of a small lake.

29.—LESTRIS PARASITICUS (*Arctic Jager*).

LESTRIS PARASITICUS.—*Rich: Faun. Bor. Amer.*—vol. ii., p. 430. *Temm.*—vol. ii., p. 796. *Sab: Trans. Linn. Soc.*—vol. xii., p. 551. *Supp. to Parry's 1st Voyage*—p. ccvi. *Rich: App. to Parry's 2d Voyage*—p. 361. *Ross, App. to Parry's 3d Voyage*—p. 105; and *App. to Parry's Polar Voyage*—p. 196.
CATHARACTA PARASITICA.—*Fab: Faun. Grœnl.*—p. 103.

The form and relative length of the central tail feathers of this bird vary so much according to age and other circumstances, as to have induced the belief of the existence of several distinct, but very nearly allied, species, and the differences observed in the plumage of the immature birds, materially tended to strengthen this idea. Temminck and Sabine were the first to point out the mistakes that preceding authors had made, and by giving accurate descriptions of the bird in every state of plumage from the egg to maturity, have prevented a recurrence of similar errors.

30.—PROCELLARIA GLACIALIS (*Fulmer Petrel*).

PROCELLARIA GLACIALIS.—*Temm.*—vol. ii., p. 802. *Lath: Ind. Orn.*—vol. ii., p. 823. *Fab: Faun. Grœnl.*—p. 86. *Gmel.* vol. i., p. 562. *Sab: Supp. to Parry's 1st Voyage*—p. ccvi. *Ross, App. to Parry's 3d Voyage*—p. 106; and *App. to Parry's Polar Voyage*—p. 196.
FULMER PETREL.—*Lath: Syn.*—vol. iv., p. 403. *Penn: Arct. Zool.*—vol. ii., p. 534. *Brit. Zool.*—vol. ii., p. 203.

Abounds in most parts of the North Atlantic Ocean, but is peculiarly numerous in Hudson's Bay, Davis's Strait, and Baffin's Bay. It is also occasionally met with to the westward of Lancaster Sound, and in Regent's Inlet, following the whale ships, and availing themselves of the success of the fishermen, by feeding off the carcase of the whale after it has been deprived of its blubber and turned adrift. It is often of essential service to those employed in the capture of the whale, by guiding them to those places where the fish are most numerous, and by giving notice of the first appearance of those animals at the surface of the water, by crowding to the spot from all quarters.

31.—SOMATERIA SPECTABILIS (*King Duck*).

SOMATERIA SPECTABILIS.—*Rich: Faun. Bor. Amer.*—vol. ii., p. 447.
ANAS SPECTABILIS.—*Temm.*—vol. ii., p. 851. *Gmel.*—vol. i., p. 507. *Lath: Ind. Orn.*—vol. ii., p. 845. *Fab: Faun. Grœnl.*—p. 63. *Sab: in Trans. Linn. Soc.*—vol. xii., p. 553. *Sab: Supp. to Parry's 1st Voyage*—p. ccvii. *Rich: App. to Parry's 2d Voyage*—p. 371. *Ross, App. to Parry's 3d Voyage*—p. 106.
KING DUCK.—*Penn. Brit. Zool.*—vol. ii., p. 246. *Arct. Zool.*—vol. ii., p. 554. *Lath: Syn.*—vol. vi., p. 473.

Vast numbers of this beautiful duck resort annually to the shores and islands of the Artic Regions in the breeding season, and have on many occasions afforded a valuable and salutary supply of fresh provision to the crews of the vessels employed on those seas. On our late voyage, comparatively few were obtained, although seen in very great numbers. They do not retire far to the south during the winter, but assemble in large flocks; the males by themselves, and the females with their young brood, are often met with in the Atlantic Ocean, far distant from any land, where the numerous crustaceous and other marine animals afford them abundance of food.

32.—SOMATERIA MOLLISSIMA (*Eider Duck*).

SOMATERIA MOLLISSIMA.—*Rich: Faun. Bor. Amer.*—vol. ii., p. 44.
ANAS MOLLISSIMA.—*Temm.*—vol. ii., p. 848. *Gmel.*—vol. i., p. 514. *Lath: Ind. Orn.*—vol. ii. p. 845. *Fab: Faun. Grœnl.*—p. 68. *Sab: Supp. to Parry's 1st Voyage*—p. ccviii. *Rich: App. to Parry's 2d Voyage*—p. 370. *Ross, App. to Parry's 3d Voyage*—p. 106; and *Polar Voyage*—p. 197.
EIDER DUCK.—*Penn: Brit. Zool.*—vol. ii., p. 243. *Arct. Zool.*—vol. ii., p. 553. *Lath: Syn.*—vol. vi., p. 470.

Is so similar in its habits to the preceding species, that the same remarks equally apply to both. This is, however, more generally known as a European bird, and is famous for the beautifully elastic down from which it receives its name. That of the *S. Spectabilis* is equally excellent, and is collected in great quantities by the inhabitants of the Danish colonies in Greenland, and forms a valuable source of revenue to Denmark. Vast quantities of this down is also collected on the coast of Norway, and in some parts of Sweden.

33.—HERALDA GLACIALIS (*Long-tailed Duck*).

HERALDA GLACIALIS.—*Rich: Faun. Bor. Amer.*—vol. ii., p. 460.
ANAS GLACIALIS.—*Temm.*—vol. ii., p. 860. *Gmel.*—vol. i., p. 529. *Lath: Ind. Orn.*—vol. ii., p. 864. *Sab: Trans. Linn. Soc.*—vol. xii., p. 555. *App. to Parry's 1st Voyage*—p. ccviii. *Rich: App. to Parry's 2d Voyage*—p. 373.
ANAS HIEMALIS.—*Fab: Faun. Grœnl.*—p. 71.
LONG-TAILED DUCK.—*Penn: Brit. Zool.*—vol. ii., p. 268. *Arct. Zool.*—vol. ii., p. 566. *Lath: Syn.*—vol. vi., p. 468.

The most noisy and most numerous of the ducks that visit the shores of Boothia. Being a quicker diver, and of more rapid and irregular flight, fewer of this species than of the other were shot. Its down is equally valuable with that of the two preceding species, but is of a darker colour. Its flesh is most excellent food.

The peculiar structure of the trachea of this and the two preceding birds, are described and figured by Captain Sabine, *loc. cit.*

34.—ANSER BERNICLA (*Brent Goose*).

ANSER BERNICLA.—*Rich: Faun. Bor. Amer.*—vol. ii., p. 469.
ANAS BERNICLA.—*Temm.*—vol. ii., p. 825. *Gmel.*—vol. i., p. 513. *Lath: Ind. Orn.*—vol. ii., p. 844. *Fab: Faun. Grœnl.*—p. 41. *Sab: in Franklin's Journey*—p. 698. *Sab: Supp. to Parry's 1st Voyage*—p. 207. *Rich: in App. to Parry's 2d Voyage*—p. 367. *Ross, Parry's Polar Voyage*—p. 196.
BRENT GOOSE.—*Penn: Brit. Zool.*—vol. ii., p. 151. *Arct. Zool.*—vol. ii., p. 551. *Lath: Syn.*—vol. vi. p. 467.

This well-known winter inhabitant of the lochs and friths of the Scottish coast, is found during the summer months in the highest northern latitude that has yet been reached, but in no great numbers. It did not remain in the neighbourhood of Felix Harbour to breed, but several large flocks were seen on their way to the northward, of which only a few were shot. We found them in greater numbers near Fury Point, and along the low line of coast to the southward, which, abounding with extensive fresh-water lakes, is probably one of their breeding stations.

35.—ANSER HUTCHINSII (*The Less Canada Goose*).

ANSER HUTCHINSII.—*Rich: Faun. Bor. Amer.*—vol. ii., p. 470.
ANAS BERNICLA, β.—*Rich: App. to Parry's 2d Voyage*—p. 368.

These birds arrived in flocks about the middle of June, in the neighbourhood of Felix Harbour, and soon after dispersed in pairs to their breeding places. At Igloolik, the only place where we had before met with them, their nests were found in the marshes near the sea; but on this occasion several pairs constructed their nests on a ledge of rock near the foot of a high precipice; immediately above them the dovekies, looms, several species of gulls, and near its summit the jerfalcon and raven built their nests.

From three to four eggs were found in each nest, of a pure white, and of an oval form, measuring 3.1 inches by 2.1, and weighing from 1800 to 2000 grains.

The female bird is smaller than the male; to the measurements given by Dr. Richardson, which are very accurate, we may add that its extent of wing is fifty-two inches, and that it averages about four pounds and a half in weight.

Its flesh is of a most exquisite flavour.

---

*f

36.—COLYMBUS GLACIALIS (*Great Northern Diver*).

COLYMBUS GLACIALIS.—*Rich: Faun. Bor. Amer.*—vol. ii., p. 474.
Temm.—vol. ii., p. 910. *Fab: Faun. Græn.*—p. 97.
Sab: Franklin's Journey—p. 703.
NORTHERN DIVER.—*Penn: Brit. Zool.*—vol. ii., pp. 165, 167, pl. 30. *Arct. Zool.*—vol. ii, p. 518.

Only three specimens of this magnificent bird were obtained, and in each of these a most striking difference was observed in the colour of the bill, from the usual descriptions of authors. In our specimens the bill being of a very light horn colour, whilst in the European bird it is described as being black. There are other differences in the relative measurements of our bird, which will be more manifest by comparing the dimensions given by Dr. Richardson, *loc. cit.*, with the mean of the measurements of our three specimens.

Extreme length .	36 inches.	Mean of our specimens	31.4 inches
Tail . . .	4	. . . .	2.7
Bill above .	3.1	.	3.65
to rictus .	4.6	. . . . .	5.42
Tarsus . .	4.4		4.2
Extent of wing	48	. .	58
Weight . .		10 pounds.	

Thus it appears that our bird, though four inches and a half shorter, has a bill eight-tenths of an inch longer, and ten inches greater extent of wing than that described by Dr. Richardson. I should have been disposed to agree with Wilson in supposing that there are two species, and have assigned to the Boothian Divers a new specific name; but on communicating with my friend Joseph Sabine, Esq., whose ornithological experience is only exceeded by the ready assistance he affords to whoever may wish to avail themselves of his high authority, I am now induced to concur with him in the belief that the lighter colour of the bill may be occasioned by age, more especially as no difference of any importance could be detected in the colours of the plumage.

37.—COLYMBUS ARCTICUS (*Black-throated Diver*).

COLYMBUS ARCTICUS.—*Rich: Faun. Bor. Amer.*—vol. ii., p. 475.
Temm.—vol. ii., p. 913. *Rich: App. to Parry's 2d Voyage*—p. 376.
BLACK-THROATED DIVER.—*Penn: Arct. Zool.*—vol. ii., p. 520.

This beautiful species of Diver was but rarely met with by us, and only two specimens were obtained.

It is found abundantly in Greenland, which seems to be its chief breeding place. The natives make an inner dress of the richly-coloured velvet-like plumage of the throat of this and the following species, which being worn next to the skin, is the warmest and most luxurious dress that can be made.

38.—COLYMBUS SEPTENTRIONALIS (*Red-throated Diver*).

COLYMBUS SEPTENTRIONALIS.—*Rich: Faun. Bor. Amer.*—vol. ii., p. 475. *Temm.*—vol. ii., p. 916.
Gmel.—vol. i., p. 586. *Lath: Ind. Orn.*—vol. ii., p. 801.
Fab: Faun. Grœnl.—p. 94. *Sab: Trans. Linn. Soc.*—vol. xii.,
p. 542. *Supp. to Parry's 1st Voyage*—p. ccix. *Rich.*
App. to Parry's 2d Voyage—p. 337. *Ross, App. to Parry's*
3d Voyage—p. 106; and *Parry's Polar Voyage*—p. 197.
RED-THROATED DIVER.—*Penn: Brit. Zool.*—vol. ii., p. 169. *Arct. Zool.*—vol. ii., p. 520.
Lath: Syn.—vol. vi., p. 344.

Much more abundant in Boothia than either of the two preceding species, and has been found in every part of the Arctic Regions visited by the late expeditions.

*P 2

39.—URIA BRUNNICHII (*Brunnichs Guillemot*).

URIA BRUNNICHII.—*Rich: Faun. Bor. Amer.*—vol. ii., p. 477. *Temm.*—vol. ii., p. 924. *Sab: Trans. Linn. Soc.*—vol. xii., p. 538. *Supp. to Parry's 1st Voy.*—p. ccix. *Rich: App. to Parry's 2d Voy.*—p. 377. *Ross, App. to Parry's 3d Voy.*—p. 106; and *Parry's Polar Voyage*—p. 197.

Captain Sabine, in his valuable memoir on the birds of Greenland, was the first to point out the mistaken notions of preceding authors with respect to this bird, and to rescue it from the confusion into which wrong synonyms and imperfect descriptions had involved it; and in distinguishing it by the name of Brunnich, paid a well-merited tribute to the indefatigable research and accuracy in observation of that learned naturalist.

It abounds in Baffin's Bay, and is found in most parts of the Arctic Seas. I have also met with it at Unst, the northernmost of the Shetland Islands, and in several parts of Scotland; but it has ever been confounded by authors, with the Uria Troille, which it so nearly resembles.

Captain Sabine and Brunnich * have clearly marked the distinctive specific characters of this species.

40.—URIA GRYLLE (*Black Guillemot*).

URIA GRYLLE.—*Rich: Faun. Bor. Amer.*—vol. ii., p. 478. *Temm.*—vol. ii., p. 925. *Fab: Faun. Grænl.*—p. 92. *Sab: Trans. Linn. Soc.*—vol. xii., p. 540. *Sab: Supp. to Parry's 1st Voy.*—p. ccix. *Rich: App. to Parry's 2d Voy.*—p. 377. *Ross, App. to Parry's 3d Voyage*—p. 107; and *Polar Voyage*—p. 197.

BLACK GUILLEMOT.—*Penn: Brit. Zool.*—vol. ii., p. 163. *Arct. Zool.*—vol. ii., p. 516.

This well-known beautiful little bird is found during the summer months in all parts of the Arctic Seas, and is the only water-fowl that remains in very high northern latitudes throughout the winter.

* Brunnichii Ornithologia Borealis (Uria Troille), No. 109.

Dr. Richardson has already described its plumage, during that season of the year, with minute accuracy, from some specimens that were shot by me near Igloolik, in March, 1823. One individual only was obtained by us during the winter, although several others were seen off Fury Point, in February, 1833.

It was subsequently met with in great numbers as we travelled along the high precipitous land between Fury Point and Batty Bay, where they collected in vast quantities during the breeding season, affording to our party many delicious meals, and proving a valuable addition to our then scanty stock of provision. Several thousands were shot by our sportsmen, and by means of this providential supply of fresh food, several of the men, that had been long afflicted with that most dreadful malady, the sea scurvy, were restored to health.

It is not equal in flavour to the preceding species, but is much more numerous and more extensively dispersed along the coasts of the Arctic Seas.

41.—URIA ALLE (*Little Guillemot*).

URIA ALLE.—*Rich: Faun. Bor. Amer.*—vol. ii., p. 479. *Temm.*—vol. ii., p. 928. *Sab: Supp. to Parry's 1st Voyage*—p. ccx. *Ross, App. to Parry's 3d Voyage*—p. 107; and *Parry's Polar Voyage*—p. 197.

ALCA ALLE.—*Sab: Trans. Linn. Soc.*—vol. xii., p. 554. *Fab: Faun. Grænl.*—p. 84.

LITTLE AUK.—*Penn: Arct. Zool.*—vol. ii., p. 512. *Lath: Syn.*—vol. v., p. 327.

Collect during the breeding season in vast numbers along the north and east coast of Baffin's Bay, but are seldom to be met with far to the westward of Lancaster Sound. A few were seen by us near Leopold Island, and two or three specimens were obtained.

FISH.

I.—CYCLOPTERUS MINUTUS.

CYCLOPTERUS MINUTUS.—*Pallas, Spicil. Zool.*—vol. vii., p. 12, pl. 3, figs. 7—9.
Fab : Faun. Grœnl.—p. 135.

Pallas's description of this extraordinary and beautiful little fish is most perfect. It is the *Cycloptère Menu* of Lacepède,* the *Bouclier Menu* of Bonnaterre,† and probably the small species of this genus, alluded to by Mr. Couch, in his paper on the "Natural History of Fishes found in Cornwall," published in the fourteenth volume of the Transactions of the Linnæan Society, p. 87.

It is found in many parts of the Atlantic Ocean; Fabricius observed it in the southern parts of Greenland, and great numbers were taken by us from amongst the extensive floating patches of seaweed that are met with off that coast; but it has never been seen at any great distance to the northward of the Arctic circle.

It rarely much exceeds an inch in length, and is therefore not used by the natives of Greenland as food, but constitutes the chief means of subsistence to the several species of gulls which are seen hovering over those banks of seaweed in astonishing numbers.

* Histoire Naturelle des Poissons—tome ii., p. 60.

† Planches de l'Encyclopédie Méthodique.

2.—LIPARIS COMMUNIS.

LIPARIS COMMUNIS.—*Sab: in App. to Parry's 1st Voyage*—p. ccxii.
CYCLOPTERUS LIPARIS.—*Lacepède, Hist. Nat. Poissons*—vol. ii., p. 69.
Fab: Faun. Grœnl.—p. 135, var. 1.
Bloch.—pl. 123, fig. 3. *Ross, App. to Parry's Polar Voy.*—p. 199
CYCLOPTERUS GELATINOSUS?—*Pallas, Spicil. Zool.*—vol. vii., p. 21, pl. 3, fig. 1.

Was found in company with the preceding, but less numerous; it extends its range to the highest northern latitudes, having been found at Spitzbergen, Melville Island, Kamschatka, and in almost every part of the Arctic Seas that has been visited by the late Expeditions of Discovery.

Several specimens were obtained by us near Felix Harbour, all of which belong to the first variety of this species, noticed by Otho Fabricius, *loc. cit.*, and may eventually prove to be a distinct species, although the descriptions of authors and figures quoted may equally apply to both varieties, except in the size, and in the absence of the two cirrhi in the upper lip, which are wanting in the individual under consideration.

The average length of our variety, from the tip of the snout to the insertion of the tail, is somewhat more than three inches, whilst that of the larger variety, mentioned by Fabricius, is often a foot, and by other authors said to attain sixteen to eighteen inches.

The sucking apparatus consists of thirteen tubercles, arranged in a circular form, about one-third of an inch in diameter, and placed exactly between the snout and the vent.

3.—OPHIDIUM PARRII.

OPHIDIUM PARRII.—*Ross, App. to Parry's 3d Voyage*—p. 109.
Ross, App. to Parry's Polar Voyage—p. 199.

This species, which was discovered several years ago in Prince Regent's Inlet, during Sir Edward Parry's third voyage to the Arctic Seas, belongs to

Cuvier,* subgenus *Les Fierasfers,* and for the same reason to the second subgenus of Lacepède,† distinguished by the absence of "*barbillons aux mâchoires.*"

A single individual of this very rare species, not exceeding four inches in length, was ejected from the stomach of a glaucous gull, shot by us near Felix Harbour. It agreed sufficiently well with the description above quoted.

4.—OPHIDIUM VIRIDE.

OPHIDIUM VIRIDE.—*Fab: Faun. Grœnl.*—p. 141.
Ross, App. to Parry's 3d Voyage—p. 110.
OPHIDIUM UNERNAK.—*Lacepède, Hist. Nat. des Poissons*—vol. ii., p. 282.

Like the preceding species, was but rarely met with by us; a few individuals were obtained from among the patches of seaweed off the west coast of Greenland, in July, 1829, agreeing very exactly with the excellent description of Otho Fabricius, *loc. cit.*

5.—GADUS MORHUA (*Common Codfish*).

GADUS MORHUA.—*Cuv: Rég. Anim.*—vol. ii., p. 330. *Tete de la Morue*—pl. 10.
Lacepède, Hist. Nat. des Poissons—vol. ii., p. 369, pl. 10, fig. 1

O-wuk.—Esquimaux of Boothia.

Becalmed off the west coast of Greenland, in latitude 65½° N, a number of very fine codfish were caught by our crew. The bank on which they were found, consists of coarse sand, broken shells, and small stones, with from eighteen to thirty fathoms water over it.

* Règne Animal—vol. ii., p. 359.

† Histoire Naturelle des Poissons—vol. ii., p. 278.

There are several other banks of considerable extent along that coast, where the cod-fish assemble in the autumn in astonishing numbers; and although so near to some of the Danish colonies, but little advantage is derived from those fisheries, which if properly managed would doubtless prove of very great benefit to the inhabitants of that part of the country, as an article of food, and of considerable value to Denmark in a commercial point of view.

We observed much difference in the number of the rays of the dorsal fins, from those given by Lacepède. In all those examined by me, without a single exception, the second back fin contained a greater number of rays than either the first or third; although there was considerable variation in those of some individuals.

The following dimensions are taken from an average of fifteen different fishes, varying in length from twenty-nine to forty-six inches, and in weight from eight to thirty-five pounds:

Length from the tip of the snout to the end of the tail . .	36.7 inches
of the head to the posterior part of the gill covers .	9.1
of the tail (from its insertion)	5.2
Depth of the tail	7.4

Average weight, 16 lb. 2 oz.

B 7. P 18. V 6. A 19, 20. D 14, 20, 17. C 38 to 40.

This fish had never before been found during any of the preceding Arctic expeditions, although frequently sought for; but on our late voyage we purchased a number of a smaller size, much resembling in colour the rock codling of our coast, from a party of Esquimaux, who were fishing for them through holes in the ice, that covered the inlet on the west side of the peninsula of Boothia, near Cape Isabella, in June, 1831. Those obtained from the natives varied from fourteen to twenty-five inches in length, but we were told by them that those taken in the autumn at a short distance to the westward often exceeded three feet.

The alimentary canal of the largest examined by me rather exceeded twice the length of the body, and was furnished with two hundred and fifty simple cylindrical cœca.

6.—GADUS CALLARIAS.

GADUS CALLARIAS.—*Lacepède, Hist. Nat. des Poissons*—vol. ii., p. 409.
Cuv: Règ. Anim.—vol. ii., p. 332.
Fab: Faun. Grœnl.—p. 144.

Il-lit-oke.—Esquimaux of Boothia.

This species of codfish is found abundantly in the Baltic, the White Sea, and along the whole of the continental coast line of the north of Europe. Fabricius describes it as being very numerous in many parts of Greenland; and our having found it on the north coast of the American continent, along the shores of the inlet to the west of the peninsula of Boothia, is an interesting feature in its history. At the same time, the fact that the only four species of fish which were found by us in that inlet, being also common to Davis's Strait and Baffin's Bay, may be considered an additional proof (if any be still wanting) of a water communication between these two seas. It is also worthy of remark, that only two of these four species inhabit the sea on the east side of the isthmus of Boothia.

From the middle of May until near the end of June the seal-fishery is very unproductive, and attended with great labour and difficulty; the salmon do not arrive until the rivers begin to pour their waters into the sea; and during the interval, the Esquimaux assemble along the shores of that inlet, and procure a sure and abundant supply of this fish. At that period of the year it is in very poor condition, and nothing but absolute necessity could induce the natives to seek a kind of food which they dislike so much. Our party had been on very short allowance of provisions previous to meeting the Esquimaux who were engaged in its capture, and this providential supply of provisions was of essential benefit to us, and we all thought it excellent food.

It is not improbable that the three specimens of a species of *Merlangus?* mentioned by Captain Sabine,* as having been found frozen in the ice that covered Winter Harbour, in Melville Island, belongs to this species, although from the mutilated state of the specimens, he was unable to determine their identity. The number of fin rays given by him agree very nearly with the average of a number examined by me. It seldom much

* Supp. to Parry's 1st Voyage—p. ccxii.

exceeds fourteen inches in length, but some specimens were obtained nearly a foot and a half long, from which the following dimensions are given :

Length from the tip of the snout to the end of the tail .	17.3 inches
of the head to the posterior part of the gill covers .	4.5
of the tail (centre rays)	1.2
from the tip of the snout to the vent . . .	8.6

Fin Rays: B 7. P 19. V 6. A 22, 22. D 12, 19, 23. C 40 to 44.

Alimentary canal, fourteen inches. Cæcal appendages forty-two, varying from an inch and a half to half an inch in length. Cirrhus on the lower jaw 0.7 of an inch long.

7.—MERLANGUS POLARIS.

MERLANGUS POLARIS.—*Sab: Supp. to Parry's 1st Voyage*—p. ccxi.
Ross, App. to Parry's Polar Voyage—p. 199.

This little fish inhabits the northern seas as far as we have hitherto been able to penetrate towards the pole; having been found in lat. $82\frac{3}{4}$° N, swimming near the surface of the sea, amongst the broken fragments of ice, and affording to the gulls and other seafowl their chief source of subsistence.

During our late voyage we found them wherever we went; great numbers were taken by us from between the cracks in the ice, which covered the harbour of Batty Bay, in July, 1833, and contributed greatly to support the strength of our party, when on a very small allowance of provisions.

At that period of the year it is much infested with the *Lernæa gadina*, which attaches itself to the gills of the fish.

It does not quit the Arctic Seas during the winter, several having been taken in a net at Felix Harbour during that season.

It seldom exceeds ten inches in length.

8.—BLENNIUS POLARIS.

BLENNIUS POLARIS.—*Sab: Supp. to Parry's 1st Voyage*—p. ccxii.
Ross. App. to Parry's Polar Voyage—p. 200.

B. *imberbis, pinnis anali, caudali, dorsalique, unitis.* (Sabine.)

Like the *Merlangus Polaris,* it well deserves the specific name bestowed on it by Captain Sabine, from its having been found in the highest northern latitudes. It is, however, by no means numerous, and only one specimen was obtained during our late voyage; it was taken from the stomach of a *Gadus Callarias,* that was caught in the inlet on the west side of the peninsula of Boothia, and agreed, so far as its mutilated state would admit of comparison, with Captain Sabine's description, *loc. cit.*

9.—COTTUS QUADRICORNIS.

COTTUS QUADRICORNIS.—*Lacepède, Hist. Nat. des Poissons*—vol. iii., p. 241.
Sab: Supp. to Parry's 1st Voyage—p. ccxiii.
Ross, App. to Parry's 3d Voyage—p. 111.
Bloch, Ich.—vol. iii., p. 146, pl. 108.
COTTUS SCORPOIDES.—*Fab: Faun. Grœnl.*—p. 157.

Kan-ny-yoke.—Esquimaux of Boothia.

Is abundant along the west coast of Greenland, but is more rarely met with in the higher northern latitudes. Two or three individuals were taken in a net in Felix Harbour, and several were captured by the natives on the west side of the peninsula of Boothia, differing in no respect from the excellent description and plate in the Ichthology of Bloch.

Fabricius observes of the *Cottus Scorpius,* that although in daily use, it is the favourite food of the Greenlanders, and is considered wholesome for the sick; and of the *Cottus Scorpoides,* that it is less savoury; the natives of Boothia, however, prize it very highly, preferring it to the codfish or salmon.

It is also worthy of remark, that the Esquimaux of Boothia apply the same name to this fish that the Greenlanders do to the *C. Scorpius* of Fabricius.

10.—COTTUS POLARIS.

COTTUS POLARIS.—*Sab: Supp. to Parry's 1st Voyage*—p. ccxiii.

C. *imberbis, capite spinis duabus, operculis spinis quatuor, armatis.* (Sabine.)

This species of Cottus was found abundantly in pools of water, left by the falling of the tide, near the mouths of rivers, or streams of fresh water, on the east side of the isthmus of Boothia, and particularly so along the low shores of Sheriff Harbour. Those examined by me agreed very nearly with Captain Sabine's description, excepting, only, some slight difference in the number of the fin rays, which from the average of a great many noted by me, but varying considerably with each other, I found to be as follows:

P 15. V 5. A 15. D 8, 13. C 12 to 14.

It seldom exceeds two inches in length, and from its numbers, affords a supply of food to the gulls, ducks, and other waterfowl that resort to those regions to breed.

11.—PLEURONECTES HIPPOGLOSSUS.

PLEURONECTES HIPPOGLOSSUS.—*Lacepède, Hist. Nat. des Poissons*—vol. iv., p. 601.
Cuv: Rég. Anim.—vol. ii., p. 340.
Fab: Faun. Grænl.—p. 161.
PLEURONECTE FLÉTAN.—*Bloch, Ich.*—pl. 47.
HALIBUT.—*Penn. Brit. Zool.*—vol. iii., p. 184.

The common Halibut of our shores is found abundantly near the west coast of Greenland, but it seldom attains to a very great size. The largest seen by O. Fabricius did not much exceed four feet in length: those taken by us varied in this from thirty-eight to forty-four inches; and in weight from twenty-two to forty-one pounds. According to Lacepède, it has been captured near the coasts of Iceland and Norway, of a most enormous magnitude, rivalling in size some of the smaller species of the whale kind; and Pennant, who had himself seen one that weighed three hundred pounds, says, that much larger ones are frequently taken near Iceland. The following dimensions are the average of ten, that we took off the west coast of Greenland, in July, 1829, from the same bank as the *Gadus Morhua* of this notice.

Length from the tip of the snout to the end of the tail	43.1 inches
of the head to the posterior part of the gill covers	10.7
of the tail (centre ray)	6.0
of the rays of the anal and dorsal fins . .	4.3
Breadth of the tail . . .	13.3
of the body	21.1

Average weight, 34¾ lb.

Number of fin rays: B 7. P $\frac{1}{1}\frac{1}{6}$. V 6. D 99. A 77. C 17.

SALMONES,

BY JOHN RICHARDSON, M.D., F.R.S., &c.

The following notices of four specimens of *trout*, brought from Boothia Felix by Captain James Clark Ross, are drawn up in very general terms, that they may not occupy more space than that assigned to the other objects of Natural History, described in the Appendix; but figures, with the characters of the species in minute detail, will be given in the third volume of the "Fauna Boreali Americana," now preparing for publication.

The first species is, as far as we know, peculiar to the inlet in which it was found. It would have been highly interesting to have detected the same species of salmon in Coronation Gulf and Regent's Inlet, but the *Salmo Hearnii* and *Mackenzii*, and several species of *Coregonus*, found in the former, were not seen in the latter; neither have the *S. salar*, or common salmon, which frequents the rivers from Labrador to the forty-second parallel of latitude, nor an undescribed species, resembling the *Gorbuscha* of Kamtschatka, which abounds in New Caledonia, been hitherto detected in the American Polar Seas; nor does the *S. namaycush* (Pennant), a gigantic trout, which exists abundantly in all the great American lakes, appear to have been observed in the waters of Boothia Felix. The last species, however, that is mentioned in the following notices, is common in all parts of the fur countries; and it is probable that *S. alipes* and *nitidus* have also an extensive range, though want of more southern specimens have prevented us from ascertaining the fact.

SALMO ROSSII (*Ross's Arctic Salmon*).

ICON.—*Faun. Bor. Amer.*—pl. 80, and the head pl. 85, fig. 2.

This salmon, named *Eekalook* by the Esquimaux, was found in vast numbers* in the sea near the mouths of rivers, and furnished an agreeable article of diet to the members of the Expedition. It is quite distinct from any species that we have had an opportunity of seeing in other parts of America, and it does not agree with the character of any of those described in the History of Kamtschatka, as quoted in "Arctic Zoology," except perhaps with the *Salmo malma* (Steller) or *Golet* of the Russians, which corresponds with it in its comparatively slender cylindrical form, small scales, scarlet spots on the sides, and the colours of some other parts. But the *Golet*, instead of being found only in the sea, ascends rivers to their very sources, and does not congregate in shoals like the *Salmo Rossii.* None of the Scandinavian salmons described by Nilsson have any resemblance to *S. Rossii.*

The most remarkable peculiarities of this species, are the truncated form of the upper jaw; the length of the lower one, which considerably exceeds the distance between the tip of the snout and nape of the neck; and the smallness and form of its scales. These are imbedded in a mucous skin, which entirely covers them, except their small truncated tips, that project and feel very rough to the touch in the dried specimen. The scales are rather remote, being nowhere tiled. The teeth in the jaws are remarkably obtuse. In addition to the row on each side of the tongue, which exists in all the other *Truttæ*, there are two or more rows of smaller teeth, crowded across the tip of that organ. Two drawings by Captain Ross, with the inspection of the dried skin, enable us to describe the colours as follows: Back, top of the head, dorsal and caudal fins intermediate between oil-green and hair-brown; sides pearl-grey and silvery, with a blush of lilac, marked near the lateral line with scattered round dots of carmine. The belly varies from tile-red to arterial blood-red; the sides of the head are nacry. When the fish is out of season, the colour of the lower parts fades to a

* Some idea may be formed of the amazing numbers in which the *Salmo Rossii* visit the rivers of Boothia Felix, by mentioning that from a single haul of a small-sized seine net, we landed 3378 salmon, varying in weight from two to fourteen pounds, and averaging something more than four; the whole rather exceeded six tons weight. A great many more were enclosed in the net, but escaped through some holes that were for some time unobserved, and others by leaping over it.—J. C. Ross.

dusky-orange. The flesh is reddish, of different tints in different individuals, being best flavoured when the colour is most intense.

The length of the specimen which was brought home is thirty-four inches, of which the head forms one-fifth.

The following are the numbers of the rays of the fins:

Br. 12, 13. D 13—0. P 14. V 10. A 11. C 21$\frac{6}{6}$.

SALMO ALIPES (*Long-finned Char*)

ICON.—*Faun. Bor. Amer.*—pl. 81, and the head pl. 86, fig. 1.

This species, which with several other kinds, is included by the Esquimaux under the general appellation of *Eekalook-peedook*, was found in a small lake, whose waters were discharged into the sea by a rivulet about half a mile long. The smallness of its scales, and the vomerine teeth being confined to the anterior knob, characterize it as belonging to the subdivision *Salvelini* or Chars of Nilsson. Its form is slender, its jaws are of nearly equal length, and it differs from all its congeners, that we have seen, in the great comparative length of its fins. The scales are small and crowded, but not tiled; they are covered with a thin epidermis, and do not exhibit the projecting naked tips, which give so peculiar a character to the skin of *Salmo Rossii*. Even in the dried specimen they are perfectly smooth to the touch. No description of the colours of this species was furnished to us, but as far as can be judged from the tints remaining in the prepared skin, the upper parts were hair-brown, the sides paler, with yellowish spots, and the belly white or yellow; the under fins more or less deeply orange.

The length of the specimen is twenty-four inches, of which the head measures one-fifth.

Fins: Br. 11, 12. P 15. D 13—0. V 9. A 10 or 11. C 19$\frac{6}{6}$.

SALMO NITIDUS (*The Angmalook*).

ICON.—*Faun. Bor. Amer.*—pl. 82, fig. 1, and head pl. 86, fig. 2.

This fish, which is also to be ranked among the Chars, was found in the same lake with the preceding one, to which it bears much resemblance in the form of the parts of

*h

the head, and in the size and general character of the scales; it differs from it, however, in having a thicker body, a ventricose belly, and short fins. Its upper jaw, too, is comparatively shorter, the distance from the tip of the snout to the extremity of the labials, when applied to the top of the head, falling about an inch short of the nape instead of reaching to it as in the preceding species. Its colours are described as follows by Captain J. C. Ross: "The body above the lateral line is of a deep green, softening towards the belly, which, posteriorly to the pectorals, is of a beautiful yellowish-red. There are several rows of ocellate red spots, confined chiefly to the space between the lateral line and the yellowish-red of the belly, and varying in size, the largest being as big as a pea. The dorsal fins are of the colour of the back. The pectorals, ventrals, and anals, are dusky-red, their first rays white."

The length of the specimen is twenty inches, of which the head forms more than one-fifth.

Fins: Br. 11, 12. P 17. D 14—0. V 10. A 12. C 21$\frac{4}{6}$.

SALMO HOODII (*The Masamacush*).

ICON.—*Faun. Bor. Amer.*—pl. 82, fig. 2, pl. 83, fig. 2, and head pl. 87, fig. 1.

This Char is well known throughout the fur countries, being found in every river and lake. Its Cree name is *Masàw-mæcoos.* It resembles the two preceding Chars in its scales, but differs from them in the shortness of its jaws, and from the rest of the genus in the peculiar smallness of its head, which forms only one-sixth of the total length. Plate 82, fig. 2, above quoted, is copied from a drawing made from a recent specimen taken at Cumberland House, on the Saskatchewan, lat. 54°, by the lamented officer whose name it bears; while plate 83, fig. 2, is from the dried skin brought home by Captain J. C. Ross. An individual killed at Fort Enterprise, in March, 1821, exhibited the following colours: Back and sides intermediate between olive-green and clove-brown, bestudded with moderately large roundish spots of yellowish-grey, the colour becoming more dilute as it descends on the sides; the belly and under jaw are white, and there are a few bluish-grey dots in the latter: there are also some small and regular dots on the caudal and dorsal fins; irides honey-yellow, scales having merely a moderate degree of lustre; there is a row of teeth across the tip of the tongue, and a few scattered ones on its centre, as well as the usual row on each side.

The length of the specimen from Boothia Felix is twenty-one inches.

Fins: Br. 10, 11. P 15. D 12—0. V 10. A 11. C 19$\frac{8}{8}$.

INSECTS.

DESCRIPTIONS, &c.

OF THE

INSECTS BROUGHT HOME BY COMMANDER JAMES CLARK ROSS, R.N., F.R.S., &c.

BY JOHN CURTIS, ESQ., F.L.S., &c.

However delighted the naturalist may be with the productions of his native soil, he cannot fail to take a deep interest in objects that are transported from distant regions, possessing, as they do, the charms of novelty, and frequently presenting to him new types of form, or at least species, that he has never before had the opportunity of investigating.

The little collection of Insects lately brought from the Arctic Regions by Commander Ross, is consequently highly interesting, and the observations interspersed through the following pages, from his notes, contain data and information that are very important to the entomologist.

I may here briefly observe, that all the forms in the collection of Insects are strictly European, and the greatest variety, as well as number, was found amongst the Lepidoptera, but this might arise from the insects of that order being larger and more conspicuous, and consequently more likely to attract the attention, than smaller and sometimes almost inanimate objects. I think it very probable, however, that the Coleoptera are less abundant in the Polar Regions than the Hymenoptera, Lepidoptera, and Diptera.

*n 2

ORDER COLEOPTERA.

Fam.—DYTISCIDÆ.

Gen. 95.*—COLYMBETES. (*Clairv.*)

1. *Mœstus*, narrow, ovate, somewhat piceous, legs castaneous, female very finely shagreened.

Length three lines, breadth one line and a half.

Antennæ yellowish-brown, ochreous at the base, trophi ochreous, palpi black at the apex; head with two ferruginous spots at the base, and an impressed line and puncture on each side the base of the clypeus; thorax with an impressed punctured line all round, deepest at the anterior margin, and a large puncture on each side; elytra very long, slightly convex, piceous and shining, with a violaceous tint in the male, dull greenish and finely shagreened in the female; the lateral margins obscure ochre, a few punctures are scattered over them, forming two or three indistinct lines; legs castaneous, underside of thighs and posterior tibiæ piceous.

This is the only beetle contained in the collection, and was found in the lakes not uncommonly; I believe specimens are also in the cabinets of the Zoological Society, that were brought home by the late Captain Lyon.

Two large beetles were captured on the 23d of June, 1831, and another on the 14th of July; they were found under stones, but were obliged to be abandoned with other valuable portions of the collections in Natural History.

ORDER DERMAPTERA.

Gen. 442.—FORFICULA. (*Linn.*)

An earwig was taken on the 23d of June, 1831, "they were scarce," Commander Ross adds, "but several were found under stones."

* The numbers of the genera refer to Curtis's Guide to an Arrangement of British Insects.

Pl. 3

ORDER HYMENOPTERA.

Fam.—ICHNEUMONIDÆ.

Gen. 484.—ICHNEUMON. (*Linn.*)

2. *Lariæ.* Antennæ curled; rufous, tips of antennæ, head, underside of the trunk, with the coxæ, and a spot and a broad stripe on the abdomen black.

Plate A, fig. 1.

Length five lines, breadth ten lines.

Clothed with very short brownish pubescence, pale castaneous, minutely punctured; antennæ and head black, the former filiform, the basal joint rufous, third and four following joints paler red; trunk black, the upper surface of the mesothorax and scutellum rufous and shining, metathorax dull and darker above, with a black furcate stripe down the back; abdomen ovate, very thickly punctured, a black dot at the base of the second segment, the third with a broad black stripe down the middle, concave on each side, the remainder black with a rufous spot on each side at the base of the fourth segment, petiole rather short, narrowed at the base; wings tinged with yellowish fuscous, nervures and stigma ferruginous ochre, areolet quinquangular; legs rather stout, coxæ and trochanters black, the former with a red spot on the upper side in the hinder pair.

This Ichneumon infested the larvæ of the *Laria Rossii*, from which it was bred early in July, another was taken on the 8th of the same month, but they were not very numerous.

Gen. 516.—EPHIALTES. (*Grav.*)

A fragment only of a female was preserved, but from the existence of the specimen it might be inferred that fir trees or stumps were in the neighbourhood. The metathorax, abdomen, sheaths of the oviduct, and posterior coxæ and trochanters are black, the remainder of the legs red, the tarsi dusky at the apex; oviduct ochreous; inferior wings transparent, nervures piceous. It is similar in form to *E. Carbonarius* (Christ.), but considerably smaller I believe.

Gen. 529.—CAMPOPLEX? (*Grav.*)

3. *Arcticus*. Black, legs fulvous.

Length four lines, breadth seven lines and a half.

Black and pubescent; antennæ as long as the insect, subsetaceous and not very slender; head and thorax thickly but minutely punctured, the former short, the latter subglobose, abdomen shining, clavate, and slightly compressed at the apex, peduncle rather short; wings transparent, areolet very small, subtrigonate, with the base angulated, and the nervures uniting at the apex before they reach the marginal cell; nervures and stigma piceous, the latter narrow; legs fulvous, coxæ, trochanters, and tips of tarsi black; the spurs to the four posterior tibiæ rather long and slender.

Gen. 554.—MICROGASTER. (*Lat.*)

4. *Unicolor*. Black, wings nearly colourless.

Length one line one-third, breadth three lines.

Black, thickly and minutely punctured, base of the tibiæ dirty ochre, spurs at the apex brighter; wings transparent but stained with black, nervures and stigma ochreous brown, areolet imperfect.*

A male was bred from a cluster of cocoons, enveloped in a silky ball, resembling those containing the eggs of some spiders.

Fam.—FORMICIDÆ.

Gen. 661.—MYRMICA. (*Lat.*)

5. *Rubra*. (Linn.)

"In great numbers under stones."

Fam.—APIDÆ.

Gen. 723.—BOMBUS. (*Lat.*)

6. *Kirbiellus*. Black, anterior and posterior margins of the thorax and base and apex of abdomen clothed with yellowish hairs.

* Vide Curtis's British Entomology—vol. vii., folio and plate 321.

Male	$7\frac{1}{2}$ lines long,	16 lines broad
Female	10 . . .	20
Neuter	7 . . .	13

Male. Black, antennæ as long as the thorax, compressed at the apex; face and crown of head clothed with long yellow and black hairs; thorax yellow with hairs, having a transverse black band between the wings, basal half of abdomen yellow, the remainder orange, with a narrow black band across the middle; wings slightly yellow at the costa, the posterior margin slightly stained with brown, nervures piceous; basal joint of tarsi clothed inside with bright ferruginous hairs; spurs, base of claws, and apex of tarsi ochreous.

Female, pl. A, fig. 2.

Black, a broad margin in front of the thorax, hinder margin of scutellum, and the abdomen, excepting the third segment and the apex, clothed with long yellow-ochreous hairs; wings yellowish, excepting the posterior margin, the nervures piceous; inside of the tarsi with the pile bright ferruginous; tips of spurs, apical joint of tarsi, and base of claws subcastaneous.

Neuter. Similar to the female but much smaller, the hairs beyond the black band on the abdomen are generally orange, and the whole of the tarsi, excepting the basal joint, is subcastaneous.

I have named this bee, which seemed to be the most abundant species, after my esteemed friend the Reverend William Kirby.

7. *Polaris.* Black, clothed with yellow hairs above, with a black band across the thorax, and an indistinct one across the abdomen.

Male	6 lines long,	15 lines broad
Female	10 .	20

Male. Black, clothed with yellow hairs; head black, with a patch of yellow hairs on the face, and another on the back part of the head, a blackish band across the centre of the thorax, and an indistinct narrow one on the third and fourth segments of the abdomen, the apex orange; inside of tarsi clothed with yellowish pile.

Female. Black, a broad band across the anterior portion of the thorax, the scutellum, and abdomen clothed with long yellow hairs, whitish towards the apex of the abdomen, with a few black hairs on the sides of the third segment, a band of the same colour on the fourth, and a very slight one on the fifth segment; the tarsi clothed with black pile internally, the outside of the basal joints brownish, the edges ferruginous.

A pair only of this species was preserved, in size and many respects it resembles *B. Kirbiellus*, but the indistinct and somewhat double band of black hairs across the abdomen will distinguish it, and the yellow pile inside of the tarsi in the male and the black in the female, are sufficient characters I think to justify its being separated from the former species.

8. *Arcticus*. (Kirby in the Supplement to the Appendix of Captain Parry's 1st Voyage, p. ccxvi.)

An imperfect male was the only specimen brought home of the species.

As Commander Ross's observations embrace the above three species, I shall be under the necessity of imbodying them; but that is of little importance, as their habits must be very similar.

"The largest bee seems to be the earliest insect on the wing; it is generally seen early in June, but the smaller specimens do not appear until the middle or end of July." It may be observed that the females are the largest, and the next in size the males; these make their appearance first, and the neuters, or working class, come later, when more flowers probably are out, and their labours are less interrupted by unsettled weather.

"The first female was seen on the 7th of June, 1830, they were very abundant on the 2d of July, and on the 14th a neuter was taken; on the following day they were very numerous, and the females less abundant, but a few were observed as late as the 18th of August, soon after which time they seem in a very weak state."

"In 1831 the first bee was seen on the 19th of June, on the 26th two females, and on the 8th of July several were captured; on the 14th many females, on the succeeding day some neuters, and on the 27th of August, 1832, a large bee was seen."

ORDER TRICHOPTERA.

Fam.—PHRYGANIDÆ.

Gen. 760.—TINODES? (*Leach.*)

9. *Hirtipes*. Slate colour, wings pale fuscous.

Length two lines and a half, breadth nine lines.

Pale slate colour, sparingly clothed with long whitish hairs; head small; eyes prominent, as well as two ocelli; wings pale ochreous fuscous, pubescent and glossy, superior elongated and narrow, gradually narrowed to the base; cilia short; inferior wings iridiscent; tibiæ and tarsi dull ochreous, with numerous short black bristles inside, and especially beneath the latter; the four posterior tibiæ furnished with ochreous spurs at the apex.

This insect has the habit of a Tinodes, but the neuration of the wings does not quite agree with any in my possession, and it has but one pair of spurs to the posterior tibiæ; if, therefore, the antennæ were not wanting, I should be disposed to give it a generic name.

ORDER LEPIDOPTERA.

Fam.—PAPILIONIDÆ.

Gen. 767.—COLIAS. (*Fab.*)

10. ***Boothii.*** Yellow, posterior margins blackish, cilia rosy; a black spot on the superior wings, the disc orange, and a spot of the same colour on the inferior.

Expansion of wings two inches.

Pl. A, fig. 3 ♂, 4 ♀, 5 underside of ♀.

Male. Antennæ crimson, the club beneath ochreous, above brown: thorax and abdomen black, clothed with long whitish hairs, rosy on the collar and head: wings sulphur colour, freckled with black at the base, and at the posterior margins forming a dentated fimbria, which vanishes before reaching the anal angle; costa and cilia rosy, the nervures sometimes rather dark in the superior wings, with a large space of orange not approaching the costa or posterior margin; at the apex of the discoidal cell is a black sublunulate spot; inferior wings with a large orange spot on the disc, and sometimes a small one above it; *underside* thickly freckled with black, especially the inferior wings, but less so at the posterior margins; the entire edges of the wings are rosy; superior with a whitish dot on the black spot, which is variously formed; inferior with a large and small whitish spot on the disc, surrounded with reddish-chestnut colour, forming two tails towards the posterior margin, a spot of the same colour at the base, and frequently a lunate brown spot on the upper edge; legs rosy.

Female. Similar to the male, but the black freckled fimbria to the wings is broader

*i

and ornamented with seven large yellow spots in the superior, and six in the inferior, which are, excepting these spots, entirely freckled with black, and have a greenish tinge ; the *underside* is darker and brighter than in the male, the inferior wings and the freckled parts of the superior are green, parallel to the posterior margin is a line of subtrigonate spots, very distinct and black in the superior, and reddish-brown in the inferior wings.

A small specimen of the male, I observe, has indistinct yellow spots on the fimbria of the superior wings, and the castaneous comet-shaped spots on the underside of the inferior are very small, and in one female the black spot in the upper, and the orange spots in the inferior wings are very large, and in another female the upperside very much resembles the male.

At the request of Commander Ross, I have named this handsome insect after Felix Booth, Esq., the munificent patron of the Expedition.

11. *Chione.* *Male,* yellow, superior wings orange on the disc, with an orange spot near the centre of all the wings. *Female?* with the nervures and a spot near the disc black, with a broad black fimbria spotted yellow.

Expansion one inch eight lines to one inch ten lines.

Pl. A, fig. 6, ♂.

Male similar to *C. Boothii,* but the spot at the apex of the discoidal cell is orange, and the posterior margins of the wings are very slightly freckled with black ; the underside in some examples resembles the female rather than the male of the same species.

Female, greenish sulphur, superior wings slightly orange on the disc, with the nervures and a lunulate spot black, a broad black fimbria bearing six or seven small sulphureous spots ; inferior with a similar fimbria, but less perfect, and an orange spot on the disc ; *underside* pale greenish sulphur, similar to *C. Boothii,* but having only one comet-shaped spot on the under wings.

Knowing how variable some species of the genus Colias are,* I have great doubts if this be any more than a variety of *C. Boothii.* There are other specimens, which I believe are varieties of the female occasioned by age and other circumstances, being much paler, with the black of the nervures very much suffused, so much so in one specimen, as to render nearly the whole of the superior wings of the same colour as the fimbria.

" These butterflies generally appear about the middle of July, as well as the two

* I need only instance *P. Electra* Linn. (*C. Edusa* Fab.), which is of a deep orange colour, yet the female is sometimes met with of a pale yellow, and during my visit to the south of France, I took one of these females paired with a male of the usual orange colour

following species, they are chiefly found upon the *Oxytropis Campestris* and *O. Arctica*, two papilionaceous plants; they were captured from the 14th of July to the 13th of August, 1830, and on the 19th were in a very wasted state; on the 14th of July, of the following year, one Colias only was taken."

Gen. 770.—HIPPARCHIA. (*Fab.*)

12. *Rossii.* Brownish-black, antennæ ochreous, superior wings with two rufous spots, with a black centre; having a white pupil also on the underside.

Expansion of wings two inches.

Pl. A, fig. 7, underside of male.

Male blackish; palpi rather long and very hairy; antennæ slender and ochreous, the club elongated; wings rounded, blackish-brown, with a slight bloom of violet, superior with two red spots towards the apex, with a black pupil, the superior one the smaller, cilia dull ochre, indistinctly spotted with brown; *underside* with the disc of the superior wings chestnut colour, and two red spots towards the apex, each having a white pupil and black ocellus; inferior freckled and variegated with ochre, forming several spots towards the base, and an indistinct band beyond the centre, on the external edge of which are four ochreous dots; inside of four posterior legs pale ochreous.

Female blackish, with an ochreous shade, the rufous spots towards the apex paler, with the black pupil more or less distinct, and one or two smaller rufous spots between them and the posterior angle; the antennæ are dotted with black on the upper side, and the club is dark above and very much compressed; *underside* with the superior wings more rust-coloured, and the two spots ochreous; the spots and fascia on the inferior wings more distinct, the margins of the latter, especially the hinder one, dentated.

This very distinct Papilio, I have the pleasure of dedicating to my friend Commander James Clark Ross, F. R. S., &c., whose zeal for natural history is equalled only by that enterprise and energy which have characterized all his undertakings, and carried him so successfully through his various voyages to the Arctic Regions.

Five specimens only were brought home, "they were scarce, and frequented the precipitous faces of dark-coloured rocks and loose stones. I never found," says Commander Ross, "any of them on flowers of any kind. A few specimens were obtained on the 18th and 25th of July, 1830, and one on the 14th of the same month the year following."

*i 2

13. *Subhyalina.* Wings semitransparent, fuscous, costa freckled with black and white, two small black spots towards the apex with white pupils, most distinct on the underside.

Expansion one inch eleven lines.

Male black, antennæ ochreous, the club elongated; wings semitransparent, pale fuscous, nervures ochreous, costa black, freckled with white; two indistinct white dots towards the apex with blackish ocelli, cilia whitish, spotted with black; *underside* of superior wings similar to the upper, but the ocellated spots are distinct, and the surface, excepting the disc, is mottled with ochre and pale black, brightest at the apex; inferior wings spotted and mottled with black and dirty white, forming a waved and curved pale line beyond the middle, with three or four whitish dots beyond it.

A single male was preserved, and probably was taken with the last species, of which, at first sight, I thought it had been only an old and faded specimen, but on examination it proved to be in good condition.

Gen. 775.—MELITÆA. (*Fab.*)

14. *Tarquinius.* Wings tawny, spotted with black, inferior wings beneath with several pearly spots edged with black, an irregular pearly line beyond the middle, and seven spots of the same on the margin.

Expansion from one inch six lines to one inch ten lines.

Black, antennæ with a large spoon-shaped club, the tip and underside tawny; palpi somewhat ochreous beneath, freckled with scarlet outside; wings tawny orange, black at the base, superior with three long black spots on the discoidal cell, and a waved line across the middle formed of black crescents, beyond is a row of six black spots, and close to the posterior margin a line of ʌ's, alternating with the same number of spots, which variegate the white cilia; inferior similarly marked; *underside,* superior wings paler, sometimes ochreous at the tip, variegated with ferruginous, the spots from the upper side apparent, but smaller and fainter; inferior wings reddish-brown, a little variegated with ochre, with three pearly spots at the base, a v shaped one, and two larger elongate-trigonate spots, margined with black beyond them, across the middle is a row of black ʌ's, with an irregular line of pearly crescents, with six small black spots beyond it, and seven pearly spots on the margin, edged internally with black ʌ's, the superior margin is also pearly, the cilia pale ochreous spotted with black; legs dull ochreous, thighs scarlet on the upperside.

As this insect does not agree with the *P. Tullia* of O. Fabricius, and I have reason to believe that several species have been detected in the Polar Regions, I have carefully described it and given it a name.

M. Tarquinius was an abundant species, and like the Coliades was found feeding on the flowers of *Oxytropis Campestris* and *O. Arctica*; specimens were captured on the 10th of June, and between the 2d and 14th of July, 1830, they were most abundant; in 1831 the first butterfly seen was one of this species; this was the 10th of July, and on the 14th two more were taken. Commander Ross was so fortunate as to discover the caterpillar apparently of this species, from its structure resembling those larvæ that are known of the European Melitææ. "I do not know the caterpillar of any of the butterflies, unless it be that of the Melitæa, of which I made the following description. It measured exactly an inch in length, by 0.22 of an inch, it was composed of thirteen segments besides the hindermost one; the first and last segments with two, the second and twelfth segments with four, and all the other segments of the body with six prickles or horns, and disposed in rows and equidistant on each side of the back. Colour dark brown, with a line of white spots along each side. Some caterpillars I have seen entirely of a blackish-brown, or rather brownish-black; one that was found under a stone in the middle of March, and of course perfectly hard frozen, showed symptoms of life in half an hour after being brought into the cabin, and in less than an hour it was walking about the table. It is thus described in my note book, and differs so much from the others, that it probably belongs to another species. Length 0.75 of an inch; three rows of prickles on each side of the back; twelve ribs or segments and a white dorsal line along the back; colour above brownish-black, beneath clove-brown." It possibly may be the same caterpillar in an earlier stage, as the different skins vary considerably.

Gen. 779.—POLYOMMATUS. (*Lat.*)

15. *Franklinii.* Silvery grey, with a black ocellated dot on the centre of each wing, beneath brown, with numerous white spots, those on the upper wing with large black pupils, in the under wings with only small ones or none.

Expansion from eleven to thirteen lines.

Pl. A, figs. 8 and 9.

Black with bluish hairs, palpi bluish white, margins of eyes silvery white; antennæ dotted with white, club orange, excepting the back; wings greyish powdered with silvery green, especially at the base, the spots on the underside slightly visible, a black spot on the disc on each wing with a whitish margin; the edges of the wings fuscous, the posterior with a line of indistinct whitish ocelli along the margin; cilia white; *underside*, superior wings with a white spot towards the base, and another on the disc with a long black pupil, beyond them is a curved line of six black spots ocellated with white, and near the posterior margin the same number of indistinct kidney-shaped blackish spots margined with white; inferior wings fuscous freckled with gold, but blue at the base, five whitish spots towards the base, the three outer ones with black pupils, four similar ones in a line beyond the middle, touching a row of eight whitish lunules bearing blackish spots, two towards the centre being the largest, and sometimes crescent-shaped; legs bluish-white.

I have named this pretty species after Sir John Franklin, whose overland expeditions in the Northern Regions have so greatly contributed to our knowledge of the geography and natural history of that part of the world.

"Only two individuals of this species were taken; they were feeding on *Astragalus Alpinus* near the end of July."

Fam.—BOMBYCIDÆ, or ARCTIIDÆ.

Gen. 814.—LARIA. (*Schr.*)

16. *Rossii.* Transparent grey, superior wings with two blackish waved lines forming a fascia across the middle, with a spot between them, and a similar sinuated line beyond them; inferior wings cream colour, ochreous inside with a blackish fimbria.

Expansion of male one inch eight lines, female one inch ten lines.

Pl. A, fig. 10.

Male yellowish-grey, a spot on each shoulder, and the abdomen darker; superior wings semitransparent, the costa blackish interrupted with grey, a waved blackish line before and another beyond the middle, with a crescent-shaped spot at the extremity of the discoidal cell, and a very sinuated and dentated line near to the posterior margin; cilia blackish, spotted with ochre; inferior wings cream colour, the abdominal margin ochreous, as well as the cilia, with a blackish fimbria.

Female apparently paler, but very much injured.

I have named this very distinct moth after Captain Ross, who first penetrated these inhospitable regions, and to whom we are indebted for many additions to our zoological collections.

It is a very abundant insect, especially in the caterpillar state, for about a hundred were collected on the 16th of June, 1832, near Fury Beach; the first that was seen in the previous year was on the 19th of June, and several more on the 23d. The caterpillar is large and hairy, of a beautiful shining velvety black, the hairs being somewhat ochreous, there are two tufts of black hair on the back, followed by two of orange. A great number of them are destroyed by several kinds of flies and ichneumons, one of which is represented at fig. 1; but those that arrive at maturity spin a close web, about the size of the silkworm's, and covered outside with its hairs, the pupa is piceous and shining, and the back thickly clothed with long brownish-ochre hairs its whole length; the moth appears about the beginning of August. The following interesting experiments I have transcribed from Commander Ross's MSS. "About thirty of the caterpillars were put into a box in the middle of September, and after being exposed to the severe winter temperature of the next three months, they were brought into a warm cabin, where in less than two hours, every one of them returned to life, and continued for a whole day walking about; they were again exposed to the air at a temperature of about 40° below zero, and became immediately hard frozen; in this state they remained a week, and on being brought again into the cabin, only twenty-three came to life: these were at the end of four hours put out once more into the air, and again hard frozen; after another week they were brought in, when only eleven were restored to life; a fourth time they were exposed to the winter temperature, and only two returned to life on being again brought into the cabin; these two survived the winter, and in May an imperfect *Laria* was produced from one, and six flies from the other; both of them formed cocoons, but that which produced the flies was not so perfect as the other." The caterpillar "feeds mostly on the *Saxifraga tricuspidata* and *S. oppositifolia*.

Gen. 820.—EYPREPIA. (*Ochs.*)

17. *Hyperboreus.* Castaneous brown, superior wings with a spot on the costa, and an interrupted stripe towards the hinder margin cream colour; inferior wings with an orange band across the middle, bearing a brown spot; the margin orange also.

Expansion one inch eleven lines.

Male castaneous brown, antennæ black, the rays short; the superior wings with a cream coloured spot at the middle of the costa, and a waved stripe of the same colour near the posterior margin, nearly divided in the middle; inferior wings ochreous freckled with scarlet, castaneous brown at the base, an elongated spot at the middle, and a sinuated fascia beyond it of the same colour; margin of the abdomen, upper side of the thighs, and underside of wings vermilion, variegated with the ochre and brown of the upper surface.

On the 8th of August, this splendid moth was brought on board by one of the men, it was the only one seen, and too much injured for drawing. In a former voyage a similar insect was brought home by Captain Lyon, this may therefore be only a remarkable variety.

Fam.—NOCTUIDÆ.

Gen. 849.—HADENA.* (*Schr.*)

18. *Richardsoni.* Brown and pale grey, the upper wings with an ear-shaped and two other spots on the disc, and two denticulated strigæ beyond them; inferior, dirty white, the base and a fimbria fuscous.

Expansion one inch five lines.

Pl. A, fig. 11.

Male pale grey, palpi and antennæ black, the latter ciliated beneath;† head and thorax variegated with black; abdomen fuscous; superior wings brown, the costa spotted with grey and black, two grey waved strigæ near the base edged with black, with a small black oval attached to the second, above it is a small black ring united to a larger ear-shaped spot, beyond them is a curved denticulated grey striga edged inside with black, and a darker one near to the posterior margin; cilia whitish, spotted with black; inferior wings ochreous white, a lunulate spot on the disc, the base and fimbria pale black; legs spotted with black; wings beneath yellowish-white, with a fuscous lunulate spot on the disc of each, and a fimbria of the same colour.

I have named this very distinct moth after Dr. Richardson, the friend and companion of Sir John Franklin.

Two males only were brought home, they were captured on the 25th of July, 1830, and it was by no means a numerous species. It considerably resembles the *Noctua Lappo* of Godart, but is at once distinguished by the white on the under wings, and it is worthy of remark, that the only specimen I have seen of that moth was captured in Forfarshire, Scotland, and presented to me by Charles Lyell, Esq.

* For the character of this genus, see Curtis's Brit. Ent.—fol. 308.

† The tips are represented as in the specimen; they appear to be broken off.

FAM.—PHALÆNIDÆ.

GEN.—PSYCHOPHORA. (*Kirby.*)

Antennæ rather short and setaceous, bipectinated in the male, simple in the female; the rays very short at the base, and vanishing towards the apex; each joint producing two, which are clavate and pubescent (fig. 7 *a*); *maxillæ* long and spiral; *palpi* porrected horizontally, short and very hairy, projecting a little beyond the head; *head* and *eyes* rather small; *thorax* subglobose and hairy; *abdomen* short subcylindric, tufted at the apex in the male with a pair of horney incurved spoon-shaped forceps; *wings*, superior subtrigonate, the apex a little angulated in the female; *legs*, posterior a little the longest; tibiæ, anterior short, with an internal spine, the others longer, with a pair of spurs at the apex, the posterior with a pair also below the middle; claws simple and distinct.

19. *Sabini.* (Kirby.) Cinereous, superior wings with an obscure dark patch at the base, and a slightly angulated fascia across the middle narrowed at the interior margin, the edges sinuated, with a dot on the disc; inferior wings paler, with two obscure transverse lines; underside whitish-cinereous, with a fuscous spot on the costa; the cilia spotted fuscous.

Expansion from one inch to one inch and two lines.

Plate A, fig. 12, male; fig. 7, the head in profile.

Mr. Kirby's description being incomplete, from his want of perfect specimens, I have endeavoured to supply the deficiency by giving the generic characters. When I published the genus Psodos (*Treit.**), I thought, from the observations of Mr. Kirby, that *P. trepidaria* might be allied to his genus Psycophora, if not synonymous, but I am now satisfied that it is considerably removed from it. It bears considerable resemblance to the genus Thera (*Ste*), but is most probably allied to Zerynthia.†

GEN. 915.—OPORABIA. (*Ste?*)

20. *Punctipes.* Cinereous, superior wings with an oblique fascia, and several pale waved strigæ; legs spotted with white.

* Curtis's Brit. Ent.—vol. ix., pl. 424. † Ib.—vol. vii., pl. 296.

*K

Expansion one inch and two lines.

Antennæ blackish, setaceous, pubescent beneath; maxillæ long and spiral; palpi short, not very thickly clothed with scales; superior wings cinereous, with a darker patch at the base, a faint oblique fascia across the middle; narrowed towards the interior margin, the edges crenated, with two very waved pale lines between it and the base, and three beyond it, and a dot on the disc; cilia spotted; legs fuscous, tips of all the joints of the tarsi, of the tibiæ, and a spot on the centre of the latter, white; the middle tibiæ are spurred at the apex.

An imperfect specimen, wanting the body and under wings, was brought home.

Fam.—TORTRICIDÆ.

*Gen. 960.—ORTHOTÆNIA. (*Ste.*)

21. *Bentleyana.* (Don.) Ochreous brown, superior wings variegated with numerous whitish silvery spots, forming irregular lines, with a distinct round one at the centre, the costa spotted brown and white, each of the white dots bearing a brown one; inferior wings pale fuscous.

Expansion from ten to twelve lines.

Bentleyana. *Don: Brit. Ins.*—vol. x., pl. 357, fig. 1.

Pinetana. *Hub: Tort.*—pl. 10, fig. 57?

I believe several specimens were taken the 2d of July, 1830, and the 14th of the same month the following year. This is an interesting discovery, as it shows the distribution and times of appearance of a small moth. In ascending Schichallien in company with my friend Mr. Dale, on the 11th of July, 1825, we met with this insect in great abundance on the north side, near and at the top, upon the turf amongst the rocks; we found it in a subsequent year amongst heath, at an elevation of about 1000 feet, on mountains in the neighbourhood of Ambleside in the middle of June, and afterwards at Trafford, near Manchester.

22. *Septentrionana.* Dark brown, superior wings with a darker oblique fascia, the costa spotted with white; inferior wings fuscous white.

Expansion seven lines.

Blackish-brown, superior wings somewhat variegated with grey, with an indistinct oblique band across the middle, narrowest at the costa, which is marked with six or

* Curtis's Brit. Ent.—vol. viii., fol. 364.

seven silvery white rays, several of them divided by a darker line; cilia ochreous white, spotted at the base with brown; inferior wings, legs, and underside, pale fuscous white.

The box contained two specimens of this small Tortrix, which resembles a little the *T. hybridana* of Hübner, pl. 38, fig. 238.

Gen. 964.—ARGYROTOSA? (*Ste.*)

23. *Parryana.* Grey, superior wings with an angulated brown band near the base, an incomplete one across the middle, and the apex of the same colour.

Expansion eight lines.

Pl. A, fig. 13.

Brown, head and sides of thorax inclining to ferruginous, apex of abdomen ochreous; superior wings pale grey, with a lilac tinge, and delicately tessellated with brown, an angulated brown band near the base, indistinct at the costa, and another at the middle, vanishing at the interior margin, very narrow at the costa, and angulated and dilated outside at the disc, a round spot of the same colour at the tip, and three smaller ones approaching it on the costa; inferior wings a little paler, the margin and cilia ochreous-fuscous.

The antennæ were broken off of the only specimen preserved of this very distinct Tortrix, which I have named after Sir William Edward Parry.

ORDER XIII.—HEMIPTERA.

Fam.—ACANTHIDÆ.

Gen. 1094.—ACANTHIA. (*Lat.*)

24. *Stellata.* Blackish sericeous, elytra with a pale spot at the centre, and several at the apex; legs ochreous.

Length three lines.

Black, clothed with very short shining hairs; thorax transverse; the edges beneath subochreous, as well as the centre of the antepectus; scutellum rather large; elytra with the costa reflexed at the base, a semitransparent spot at the base, another on the disc, and eight or nine arranged in a circle on the submembranous apex; margins of abdominal segments beneath ochreous, and forming a row of dots down each side; legs dirty ochre somewhat freckled with piceous.

The head is wanting to the only specimen I have seen; it most resembles *A. Zosteræ* of Fabricius, but is very distinct from my examples of that insect; as some of its larvæ or pupæ were found, it is probably not uncommon in the Polar Regions.

Gen. 1094 *a.*—PEDETICUS? (*Lap.*)

25. *Variegatus.* Black, sides of thorax and numerous spots on the elytra whitish ochre; legs spotted with white and ochre.

Length two lines and one-third.

Black, clothed with shining pubescence and black hairs; eyes large, very globose and prominent, subferruginous striped with black, the clypeus, excepting a stripe down the middle, apex of the labrum, internal margin of the eyes, and a triangular spot on each side beneath, ochreous; thorax trapezate, gibbose on the back, with a fovea at the centre, the base very concave, the sides pale ochreous; elytra with a pale ochreous patch near the base, another beyond the middle, and a semiorbicular one at the apex, divided into several spots by the black nervures, each bearing a blackish dot; legs hairy; antepectus, coxæ, trochanters, and base of thighs, excepting the anterior, whitish ochre, the thighs striped beneath with black; the tips, two broad bands on the tibiæ, excepting the posterior, and the apical portion of the basal joint of the tarsi, ochreous.

ORDER XV.—DIPTERA.

Fam.—CULICIDÆ.

Gen. 1137.—CULEX. (*Linn.*)

26. *Caspius.* (Pall.) Black, head and thorax griseous, abdomen with seven white bands.

From two to three lines long, from four to six broad.

C. Pipiens. *Fab: Faun. Grœnl.*—p. 209, n. 171.

Several females, but not one male, were brought home; this may be accounted for, either from the males appearing earlier or later, or from their not being sanguinary; I have frequently for a week together found the females of *Culex annulatus* congregated in summer-houses in gardens, without being able to discover a single male.*

Commander Ross remarks, "Of this genus only one species was observed. It first appeared about the 10th of July, on the 15th it became very numerous, and on the 22d so extremely troublesome, as to prevent the necessary duties of the ship. They were in perfect clouds over the marshes, and their larvæ constitute the principal food of the trout that inhabit the lakes. It was only in the beautiful summer of 1830 that we found them so very numerous. On the 13th of August of that year they came out again after the rain, but were no longer very troublesome, being apparently nipped by the frost at night; indeed soon after this time the ground was again covered with snow, and all entomological observations were terminated."

Fam.—TIPULIDÆ.

†Gen. 1140.—CHIRONOMUS. (*Meig.*)

27. *Polaris.* (Kirb.) Black hairy, wings lacteous, iridescent, the costa fuscous, with the nervures darker, halteres dirty ochre.

Length three lines and three-fourths, breadth six lines.

Ch. Polaris. *Kirby in Supp. to App. of Capt. Parry's 1st Voyage*—p. ccxviii.

Pl. A, fig. 14, female; fig. 2, head of same in profile.

No males of this species were brought home, and only three females, none of which retained their first pair of legs, which are therefore merely sketched in the plate to show their situation.

28. *Borealis.* Black, thorax grey, abdomen with seven whitish rings; costa fuscous; legs lurid.

Length three lines, breadth six lines.

Black, basal joint of antennæ ochreous; thorax hoary; abdomen clothed with long subdepressed yellowish hairs, the margins of the segments shining whitish or silvery; wings lacteous, opalescent, the costa fuscous, the nervures darker; halteres yellowish; legs dull castaneous ochre, tips of the thighs and tarsi fuscous.

Only one specimen has come under my observation, and that had lost its antennæ and some of its legs.

* Curtis's Brit. Ent.—vol. xii., fol. 537. † Ib.—vol. ii., fol. 90.

Gen. 1160.—TIPULA. (*Linn.*)

Division A with the fourth cell of the wings peduncled.

29. *Arctica.* Cinereous, wings clouded with brown; legs subferruginous, tarsi fuscous. Length ten lines and a half or eleven lines, breadth one inch and seven to eight lines. Pl. A, fig. 15, female; fig. 4, underside of apex of abdomen of the same.

Silky slate colour; thorax with a brown line down the centre, a stripe of the same colour on each side, furcate at the base; abdomen more cinereous, the incisures slightly ochreous, the apex horny, with a large oval piceous and shining shield above, terminated by two moveable, lanceolate, serrated, and ferruginous lobes, curved at the apex, the penultimate joint furnished with two long slender spines beneath (fig. 4); wings clouded with brown, forming a spot on the stigma and another behind it, and leaving several large transparent and irregularly-formed spots along the disc, the costa and base are ochreous, the nervures dark brown; halteres dull and pale ochreous, fuscous at the tip; legs dull ferruginous, tips of thighs, tibiæ, and tarsi, black.

Specimens only of the female were preserved, and none of them had antennæ, or the anterior feet. "They appeared," says Commander Ross, "about the same time as the Culex, and were equally numerous. Their larvæ are the principal food of the plover and other birds that seek their prey in the marshes, as was proved on the 27th of June, when great numbers of the larvæ of the Tipula? were taken from the stomach of a gull that had been feeding in the marshes."

This fine species of Tipula is remarkable for the singular termination to the apex of the abdomen, being, I imagine, an extraordinary development of the sexual organs. I have never seen any other species like it in this respect, excepting one lately described under the name of *T. montana*,* which has the same horny shield and broad serrated forceps, and it is worthy to be observed that this species is attached to elevated districts in the north, having only been found on Skiddaw and mountains of Scotland in July, by Mr. Dale and myself.

Fam.—SYRPHIDÆ.

†Gen. 1245.—HELOPHILUS. (*Meig.*)

39. *Bilineatus.* Black, pubescent, two pale lines on the thorax, six lunulate spots on the abdomen, the first two yellow, as well as the base of the tibiæ.

* Curtis's Brit. Ent.—vol. xi., fol. 493, no. 9 *a*. † Ib.—vol. ix., fol. 429.

Length four lines and a half to six lines, breadth nine to ten lines and a half.

Black, clothed with short yellowish pubescence; face yellow or white with very short hairs, excepting a black shining space down the middle; antennæ brown except at the base, the seta ochreous; thorax with two narrow yellow lines down the fore part of the back; scutellum dull ochreous; abdomen with a rather large bright ochreous trigonate-lunate spot on each side at the base, and colouring the sides of the first segment beneath, the two following with a transverse yellow lunate spot on each side, the first pair sometimes being bright ochreous outside; base of wings and costa tinged with dull yellow, stigmatic spot fuscous, nervures black, alulæ and halteres ochreous; base of the tibiæ, and sometimes the apex of the thighs, ochreous.

The box contains three specimens.

Fam.—MUSCIDÆ.

Gen. 1276.—TACHINA. (*Ill.*)

31. *Hirta.* Black, very bristly, face silvery, hairs on back of head grey, scutellum subochreous.

Length six lines, breadth ten lines.

Black, pubescent, and covered with long bristles, especially the abdomen; head trigonate, silvery-white, excepting the crown, the hairs behind the eyes grey; eyes naked; antennæ with the third joint long and elliptical, seta stout at the base; thorax with four indistinct whitish lines before; scutellum tawny except at the base; wings similar to fig. 23, tab. 41, of Meigen, yellowish-brown at the base; squamulæ ochreous.

A single specimen was preserved, which I believe was bred from the Laria.

Gen. 1287.—ANTHOMYIA. (*Meig.?*)

32. *Dubia.* Cinereous, eyes margined with white, thorax with three fuscous stripes Two lines long, three lines and a half broad.

Grey-ash colour, sparingly pilose; antennæ with the basal joint minute, the second subtrigonate, third scarcely larger and oblong; eyes reddish-brown, face dull shining white, crown of head ash colour; thorax with three fuscous stripes down the back, and an indistinct one on each side; wings rather broad, iridescent, the nervures and legs black.

I have little doubt of this small fly being an Anthomyia, but as neither of the specimens had any setæ to the antennæ, I cannot determine the genus with certainty.

*Gen. 1293.—SCATOPHAGA. (*Meig.*)

33. *Apicalis.* Cinereous, very pubescent, face, apex of abdomen, and legs, castaneous.

Male, four lines two-thirds long, eleven broad; *female*, four lines long, nine broad.

Male. Cinereous, thickly clothed with fine long brown hairs, especially the abdomen and legs; antennæ blackish, two basal joints rufous, seta slightly pubescent only; lip horny and black; head with a furcate space before the crown, the face and palpi reddish-orange; thorax with a double ash-coloured line down the middle, and an obscure one on each side; abdomen elongate-ovate, with the margin of the third segment, and the following joints, entirely ferruginous; wings tinged with yellow, the costa and base of a much deeper and brighter colour, the nervures ochreous, excepting the two transverse ones, which are fuscous, and suffused, as well as the longitudinal ones connecting them; halteres and legs pale castaneous.

Female much less hairy, especially the abdomen and legs, the former being ovate, the second segment sometimes having the margin ferruginous, and a greater portion of the third, as well as the apex, of the same colour.

A male and two females of this handsome species were preserved.

34. *Fucorum.* (Fall.) "Obscure cinereous; thorax with four black lines; palpi, antennæ, and legs, black."—*Meig.*

Male, length three lines, breadth six lines; *female* rather smaller.

Meig: Syst. Besch.—vol. v., p. 253, n. 14; tab. 45, f. 29.

This insect is common in Sweden amongst seaweeds, from which circumstance Fallen has named it *Fucorum.* Commander Ross brought home a pair of flies that agree so well with the above description of Meigen, that I consider them identical.

* Curtis's Brit. Ent.—vol. ix., fol. 405.

MARINE INVERTEBRATE ANIMALS.

The following account of the Marine Invertebrate Animals, inhabiting those parts of the Arctic Ocean visited in the course of our late expedition, is very incomplete owing to nearly the whole collection having been necessarily abandoned with the Victory. Some few, however, of those that were considered to be most interesting, as forming the types of new genera, were brought by us to England, and specimens of each have been deposited in the valuable museum of the Royal College of Surgeons.

The arrangement and generic characters adopted in this notice, is that of Latreille in the last edition of Cuvier's "Règne Animal."

J. C. R.

CRUSTACEA—DECAPODA.

I.—CRANGON BOREAS.

CRANGON BOREAS.—*Lat. Cuv. Règ. Anim.*—vol. iv., p. 94.
Lam: Hist. Nat. des Anim. sans Vert.—vol. v., p. 201.
Sab: Supp. to Parry's 1st Voyage—p. ccxxxv.
Ross, App. to Parry's 3d Voyage—p. 120; and *Polar Voy.*—p. 205.
CANCER BOREAS.—*Phipps's Voyage, Appendix*—p. 194, plate 11, fig. 1.
Zool. Dan.—vol. iv., p. 14, plate 32, fig. 1.

Several specimens of this very fine species of Crangon were obtained, by means of

* L

a dredge, near Felix Harbour. It was also taken at a short distance from the west coast of Greenland, but seems to have entirely escaped the notice of Fabricius. We have in former voyages found it abundantly in various other parts of the Arctic Seas, but nowhere so numerously as near the Low Island (of Phipps), Spitzbergen, where it was first discovered. It has recently been brought from the shores of Kamtschatka and California, by Captain Beechey, as have also several hitherto undescribed species of Crustacea, but of which no account, it is much to be regretted, has yet been published.

2.—SABINEA SEPTEMCARINATA.

Char. Gen.—*Antennæ superiores* setis duabus in eâdem ferè lineâ horizontali insertis: interiore longiore. *Inferiores corpore breviores*, setaceæ, squamâ ad apicem externè unidentatâ pedunculo adnexâ: articulo primo ad squamæ medium non producto.

Palpi pediformes articulis quatuor exsertis; duobus ultimus longitudine æqualibus.

Pedes decem; par anticum majus compressum subdidactylum par secundum *brevissimum tenue inunguiculatum,* par tertium tenue præcedente longiore subcrassiore ungue simplici instructum; paria 4 et 5 præcedente crassiora unguibus compressis instructa.

Char. Sp.—*Sabinea* thorace septemcarinato; carinis serratis.

CRANGON SEPTEMCARINATUS.—*Sab: Supp. to Parry's 1st Voyage*—p. ccxxxvi., pl. 2, fig. 11—13.
Ross, App. to Parry's Polar Voyage—p. 205.

Owing to the peculiar formation of the second pair of legs, in this singular animal, it has become necessary to establish a new genus, of which it is the only known species; and I have much pleasure in dedicating it to my friend, Captain Edward Sabine, of the Royal Artillery, by whom it was discovered in the west coast of Davis's Straits, during Sir Edward Parry's first voyage to those regions. His very accurate description is as follows: "Length four inches; colour varied, red and white above, white beneath; thorax seven carinate, the three lateral carinæ on each side serrate, the middle one with strong spines; rostrum short, curving down between the eyes, grooved in the centre; the five upper carinæ carried on in very faint rudiments along the back; the terminal setæ of the superior antennæ inserted nearly in the same horizontal line, the interior one being the longest; the first joint of the inferior antennæ scarcely produced beyond the middle of the squama; a strong spine in the abdomen directed forward between the chelate legs; the last joint of the pediform palpi subacuminate,

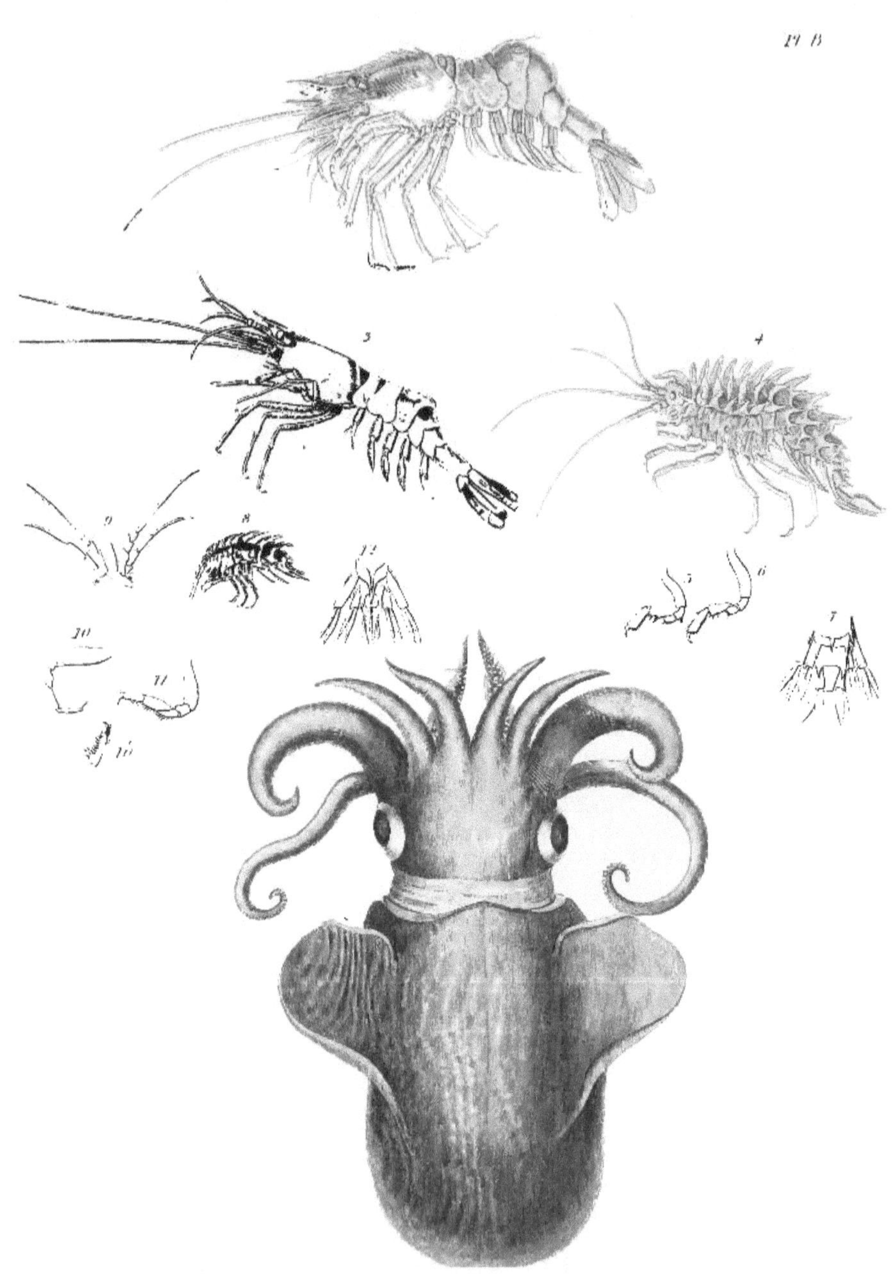

rather longer than the preceding; second pair of legs slender, very short, bristled, and unarmed, in which last essential point it differs from the *Pontophilus spinosus* of Dr. Leach, *Mal. Pod. Brit.*, t. 37, to which in other respects this species bears a near resemblance."

It is more rarely met with in the Arctic Seas than the Crangon Boreas, but a few specimens were obtained near Felix Harbour. It was also found in a previous voyage near the island of Igloolik in considerable numbers.

3.—HIPPOLITE ACULEATA.

ALPHEUS ACULEATUS.—*Sab: Supp. to Parry's 1st Voyage*—p. ccxxxvii., pl. 2, figs. 9 & 10.
Ross, App. to Parry's 3d Voyage—p. 120; and *Polar Voyage*—p. 206.
CANCER ACULEATUS.—*Fab: Faun. Grœnl.*—p. 239.

A. (H.) thoracis carinâ dentibus quatuor, margine antico trispinoso, segmentis utrinque aculeatis, palpis pediformibus apice spinulosis. (*Sabine.*)

The Alpheus Aculeatus and A. Polaris of Sabine, belong to the genus Hippolite of Leach (*Mal. Pod. Brit.*), on account of the second pair of claws being shorter than the first. This arrangement, which appears to be now universally agreed to by naturalists, is adopted by Latreille in the "Règne Animal," and is therefore followed in this notice. It is an abundant species in the Arctic Seas.

4.—HIPPOLITE SOWERBEI.

Plate B, fig. 2.

HIPPOLITE SOWERBEI.—*Leach, Mala. Pod. Brit.*—t. 39.
GAMMARUS SPINOSUS.—*Sowerby, Brit. Mis.*—vol. ii., pl. 21.

H. rostro alto obtuso supra multi-serrato, apice emarginato serrulato; subtus uni-serrato. (*Leach.*)

This species was first described by Mr. George Sowerby, in the "British Miscellany," *loc. cit.* It was taken near the Scottish coast; and Dr. Leach received an imperfect specimen from the Firth of Forth, but it appears to be of very rare occurrence in those parts. During one of our former voyages, we found it near the island of Igloolik in considerable numbers, associated with the preceding and following species. Some specimens were obtained by us, through a hole in the ice, at Felix Harbour, in the very depth of winter.

The general form of the rostrum agrees with that figured by Dr. Leach, but many have it simply emarginate at the apex, and not serrulate.

It differs from the two following species in the dentations of the carina of the thorax, extending along its whole length; and in the upper part of the third segment of the body being produced posteriorly in a strong spine.

5.—HIPPOLITE BOREALIS. (*n. s.*)

Plate B, fig. 3.

Hipp. thoracis dimidio posteriore lævi, anteriore sub-carinato, margine anteriore utrinque bi-spinoso.

The principal differences, as compared with the A. (H.) Polaris of Sabine, consist in the absence of, or very slightly marked, dentations on the thoracic carina; in having only two spines, instead of three, on either side of the anterior margin of the thorax (that at the junction of the lateral margin being wanting in H. Polaris); in the superior antennæ being proportionally longer; and in being of a paler yellow colour, without the red spots and markings of the H. Polaris. As in the specimens of H. Polaris obtained by me, the middle lamella of the tail has from eight to ten minute spines along each side, and is terminated by several strong setæ, the margins of the rest of the plates of the tail are beautifully ciliated, excepting on the exterior edge of the lateral plates, which are toothed at their posterior angle.

Dr. Leach takes his specific characters from the rostral dentations, but these, as Captain Sabine justly remarks, in his description of *Alpheus* (*Hippolite*) *Polaris*, agree in no two specimens of that species, as to number, nor the rostrum as to shape.

H. Borealis was found associated with the preceding species, and was dredged up from a depth of eighty fathoms off Elizabeth Harbour. It was also found in considerable numbers near the island of Igloolik on a preceding voyage.

6.—HIPPOLITE POLARIS.

ALPHEUS POLARIS.—*Sab: Supp. to Parry's 1st Voyage*—p. ccxxxviii., pl. 2, figs. 5—8.
Ross, App. to Parry's Polar Voyage—p. 206.

A. thoracis dimidio posteriore lævi, anteriore carinato serrato; chelis et unguibus apice nigris. (*Sabine.*)

The excellent description and plate referred to above, render any further remark unnecessary, except that the rostral dentations are usually more numerous, both above and beneath.

It is an abundant species in the Arctic Seas.

7.—MYSIS FLEXUOSUS.

MYSIS FLEXUOSUS.—*Lam: Hist. Nat. Anim. sans Vert.*—vol. v., p. 200.
CANCER FLEXUOSUS.—*Mull: Zool. Dan.*—vol. ii., p. 34, pl. 66.
CANCER MULTIPES.—*Montague, in Trans. Linn. Soc.*—vol. ix., tab. 5, fig. 3.
CANCER OCULATUS.—*Fab: Faun. Grœnl.*—p. 245, pl. 1, figs. A and B.
PRAUNUS FLEXUOSUS.—*Leach, in Edin. Encycl.*—vol. vii., p. 401.

Though but sparingly found in the seas of Europe, it inhabits some parts of the Arctic Ocean in amazing numbers, and constitutes the principal food of the prodigious shoals of salmon, that resort thither in the months of July and August, and upon which the inhabitants of Boothia depend, in a great measure, for their winter store of provisions. It is also the chief food of the whale, by which such a prodigious quantity of fat is produced in the body of that immense animal.

During the summer they assemble in vast myriads at the mouths of rivers, but in the winter are more generally distributed along the whole line of coast, and, together with the Argonauta Arctica, are to be seen in every crack that opens with the tide, even at the coldest period of the year.

It is called by the natives Il-le-ak-kak.

AMPHIPODA.

8.—THEMISTO GAUDICHAUDII.

TH. corpore elongato, luteo; capite globoso; antennis inferioribus longioribus; pedibus inæqualibus, quinto pari longissimo; caudæ appendicibus planis, ciliatis. (*Guer.*)

This singular animal was first described by M. F. E. Guérin, in a paper entitled "Mémoire sur le Nouveau Genre Thémisto," &c., communicated to the Society of Natural History at Paris, August 29, 1828, and published soon after in the fourth volume of the memoirs of that society.

The specific name is in honour of Dr. Gaudichaud, one of the naturalists of the corvette *La Coquille*, during a voyage round the world, under the command of Captain Duperrey, by whom it was collected, together with a number of other curious specimens of marine invertebrate animals.

M. Guérin's minute and accurate description is exceedingly well illustrated by a lithographic delineation of the various parts that compose this singular and interesting genus. The individual selected for description was smaller than those met with by us during our late voyage to the Arctic Regions, our specimens being as large as M. Guérin's second or magnified figure; in every other particular they agree with his description, of which the following is an extract:

"Corps oblong, composé de douze segmens;* tête occupée entièrement par deux yeux à réseau, arrondie, non prolongée inférieurement en rostre. Quatre antennes, les supérieures plus courtes que la tête, courbées au bout; les inférieures beaucoup plus longues. Quatorze pieds; les quatre premiers courts, dirigés en avant, couchés sur la bouche, et représentant les deux dernières paires de pieds-machoires des crustacés supérieurs; les quatre suivans beaucoup plus grands, terminés par un crochet dirigé

* Not including the head.

vers la queue; la cinquième paire trés-longue dirigée vers la bouche, ayant l'avant-dernier article grêle, fort long, garni d'épines en dedans et terminé par un crochet; les quatre derniers, de moitié plus courts, dirigés et conformés de même, mais sans dents à l'avant-dernier article. Queue terminée par six appendices natatoires longs, aplatis, bifides à l'extremité; trois paires de filets également natatoires sous les trois premiers segmens de la queue."

It is most nearly allied to Hyperia of Latreille and Phrosina of Risso,* but differs from the former in the great length of the fifth pair of legs, and in the inferior antennæ being longer than the superior; and from Phrosina, in the greater length of the antennæ, and in the head not being prolonged inferiorly *en rostre*.

It is a singular circumstance in the history of this animal, that it has hitherto been found only in the vicinity of the Falkland Islands, and near the west coast of the peninsula of Boothia.

9.—GAMMARUS NUGAX.

GAMMARUS NUGAX.—*Sab: Supp. to Parry's 1st Voyage*—p. ccxxix.
TALITRUS NUGAX.—*Ross, App. to Parry's 3d Voyage*—p. 119; and *Polar Voyage*—p. 205.
CANCER NUGAX.—*App. to Phipps's Voyage*—p. 192, pl. 12, fig. 3.

By reason of the small superadded setæ on the upper antennæ of the Cancer Nugax (*Phipps*), I have referred it to the genus *Gammarus*, although it does not participate in all the characters assigned to that genus by Latreille. The lower antennæ being longer than the upper, it belongs to Lamarck's genus *Talitrus*. This last character, together with the second pair of feet, being elongate, and terminated by a flattened setose articulation, without a claw, render the establishment of a new genus necessary for its proper arrangement.

It is a very numerous inhabitant of the Arctic Seas.

* Cuvier Règne Animal—vol.iv., p. 117.

10.—GAMMARUS AMPULLA.

GAMMARUS AMPULLA.—*Sab: Supp. to Parry's 1st Voyage*—p. ccxxix.
Ross, App. to Parry's Polar Voyage—p. 204.
CANCER AMPULLA.—*Phipps's Voyage, Appendix*—p. 192, pl. 12, fig. 2.

In this species the superior antennæ, which have also the superadded seta, are one-half shorter than the inferior; the second pair of feet are unguiculate, not setose, but the work is very minute. The fifth and sixth pairs have femoral laminæ, but less than those of the seventh pair.

It is by no means abundant in the Arctic Seas, excepting near the Low Island (of Phipps), Spitzbergen, where it was first discovered. Some few specimens were obtained near Felix Harbour.

11.—GAMMARUS BOREUS.

GAMMARUS BOREUS.—*Sab: Supp. to Parry's 1st Voyage*—p. ccxxix.
Ross, App. to Parry's 3d Voyage—p. 119; and *Polar Voyage*—p. 204.
SQUILLA PULEX.—*Degeer, Ins.*—vol. vii., p. 525, pl. 33, figs. 1 and 2.

G. caudæ dorso spinoso, oculis lunatis, pedibus quatuor anticis chelatis, pari septimo præcedentibus longiore. (*Sabine.*)

Is found abundantly along the shores of the north-east part of the American continent, and its contiguous islands, but especially so near the estuaries of rivers, seeming to prefer the brackish to the salt water of the ocean.

12.—GAMMARUS LORICATUS.

GAMMARUS LORICATUS.—*Sab: Supp. to Parry's 1st Voyage*—p. ccxxxi., pl. 1, fig. 7.
Ross, App. to Parry's 3d Voyage—p. 118; and *Polar Voyage*—p. 204.

G. rostro corniformi deflexo, dorso carinato, segmentis postice et acute productis. (*Sabine.*)

The specimens obtained in Prince Regent's Inlet agreed generally with Captain Sabine's description, but some few, taken at the same time, approached more nearly to Fabricius's* description of *Oniscus serratus;* the three posterior pairs of legs being much shorter than those of *G. loricatus,* but longer in proportion than those of *O. serratus,* when compared with the third and fourth pairs. In some specimens the rostrum was so very minute, as hardly to be distinguishable, whilst in others it was very large.

It is an abundant species.

13.—GAMMARUS SABINI.

GAMMARUS SABINI.—*Leach, Ross's Voyage*—oct. ed., vol. ii., p. 178.
Sab: Supp. to Parry's 1st Voyage—p. ccxxxii., pl. 1, figs. 8—11.
Ross, App. to Parry's 3d Voyage—p. 118; and *Polar Voyage*—p. 204.

G. segmentibus dorsalibus postice falcato productis, capite inter antennas acumine minuto.

This species was found abundantly in Prince Regent's Inlet, and near Felix Harbour.

* Fauna Grœnlandica—p. 262.

*m

14.—AMPHITHOE EDVARDSI.

TALITRUS EDVARDSI.—*Sab: Supp. to Parry's 1st Voyage*—p. ccxxxiii., pl. 2, figs. 1—4.
Ross, App. to Parry's 3d Voyage—p. 119; and *Polar Voyage*—p. 205.

T. (A.) rostro corniformi, antennis subæqualibus, corpore ovato depresso, caudâ compressâ tricarinatâ spinosâ.

The *Talitrus Edvardsi* of Sabine, belongs to the genus *Amphithoe* of Leach, which is adopted by Latreille. The excellent description and plate above referred to, render any further remark unnecessary.

It is an abundant species in the Arctic Seas, more especially near the island of Igloolik, where it was taken on a former voyage in very great numbers.

Nov. Gen.—ACANTHONOTUS. (*Owen, MS.*)

Char. Gen.—Antennæ subæquales, 4-articulatæ, articulo ultimo e plurimis segmentis efformato, articulo tertio superiarum brevissimo. Pedes 4-antici, monodactyli, filiformes, articulo ultimo primi paris serrato. Rostrum productum acutum, incurvatum. Oculi parvi.

15.—ACANTHONOTUS CRISTATUS.

Char. Sp.—A. segmentis 4-anticis in cristâ continuâ supernis elevatis; reliquis in spinis retrorsum inclinatis productis.

Acanthonotus cristatus, which forms the type of a new genus, closely allied to *Talitrus* of Latreille, was first discovered near the island of Igloolik, during Sir Edward Parry's second voyage; but as no account of the Marine Invertebrate Animals brought home on that occasion was published, it has hitherto escaped unnoticed. In the course of our late voyage a few specimens, both of this and the following new genus, were obtained at Felix Harbour.

To the generic and specific characters given above we may add, that all the segments of the body are produced inferiorly into long spines, that of the fourth being the broadest and longest; of the dorsal spines, the fifth and sixth are the longer.

The *femora* of the three last pairs of legs are produced posteriorly into long spines, and the penultimate segment has two spines.

The first and second joints of the superior antennæ are terminated above by a spine; the third joint is the shortest.

The toe of the first foot is serrate, having about eight teeth, and the claw is clothed with fine hairs on the exterior surface, as represented, highly magnified, in fig. 10', plate B.

Plate B, fig. 8, represents a side view of *Acanthonotus cristatus* of the natural size.

Fig. 9, a magnified view of the upper part of the head and antennæ.

Figs. 10 and 11. Magnified view of the two first pairs of legs: and fig. 10' shows the peculiar formation of the toe and claw of the first pair.

Fig. 12. Magnified view of the three posterior segments, and middle plate of the tail; together with the lateral and terminal styliform processes.

Nov. Gen.—ACANTHOSOMA. (*Owen, MS.*)

Char. Gen.—Antennæ inequales, superiores dimidio breviores, articulo ultimo e plurimis segmentis efformato, articulis tertiis et secundis superiorum æqualibus. Pedes 4-antici, monodactyli, filiformes, articulo ultimo primi paris unguiculato. Rostrum productum acutum undulatum. Oculi parvi.

16.—ACANTHOSOMA HYSTRIX.

Char. Spec.—A. segmentis 9-anticis spinis septem armatis.

This very distinct genus is more common at Felix Harbour than the preceding; it was taken at Igloolik on a former voyage in considerable numbers.

On each of the first nine segments of the body there are seven spines, forming in the aggregate seven longitudinal rows, protecting the back and sides of the body; in addition to these there are two spines above the eyes, one on each side of the rostrum;

this part is white, curved over the head, and directed forward; the eyes are small and white. The tenth segment of the body has only five spines; the fourth and fifth caudal segments having three, and the others only two spines.

The *femora* of the three posterior pairs of legs are each armed with two strong spines posteriorly, of which those on the last are the largest and strongest. The two posterior caudal segments are each furnished with a double styliform process, of which the anterior is the longer. The middle plate of the tail is truncate, with two styliform processes, similar to those of the preceding genus.

Plate B, fig. 4, represents a large-sized specimen of the *Acanthosoma Hystrix.*

Figs. 5 and 6, a magnified view of the two anterior pairs of legs.

Fig. 7, the three posterior segments and middle plate of the tail, together with the lateral and terminal styliform processes.

MOLLUSCA—CEPHALOPODA.

Nov. Gen.—ROSSIA. (*Owen.*)

A single specimen of a small species of Cephalopoda was taken near the beach at Elwin Bay, Prince Regent's Inlet, on the 29th of August, 1832. It was preserved in spirits, and brought to England; and I am indebted to the friendship of Mr. Owen, Assistant Conservator of the Museum of the Royal College of Surgeons, for the following account of this remarkable animal, accompanied with illustrations of his dissections, which have been engraved by Mr. I. Curtis, F.L.S., &c.

J. C. R.

"The small Cephalopod which you have brought from the Arctic Regions to this country, proves to be the type of a new genus. It differs from *Loligo* and *Sepioteuthis* in the form, proportions, and position of its lateral fins, and in the extent of its horny dorsal style, or *gladius*;* in these respects, it bears a closer affinity to *Sepiola* (Leach); it differs, however, from *Sepiola* generically in having the anterior margin of the mantle free in the whole of its circumference; its natural position is therefore interme-

* This is the term by which Aristotle designates the horny plate of the Loligines:—" Τῇ μὲν οὖν σηπίᾳ, καὶ τῇ τευθίδι καὶ τῷ τεύθῳ ἐντός ἐστι τὰ στερεὰ ἐν τῷ πρανεῖ του σώματος, ἃ καλουσι τὸ μεν σήπιον, τὸ δὲ ξίφος. Sub dorso firma pars sepiæ loligini ac lolio continetur; illius *sepium*, horum *gladium* vocant.—*Hist. Animal.*, lib. iv., c. 1. 12mo. Ed. Schneider.

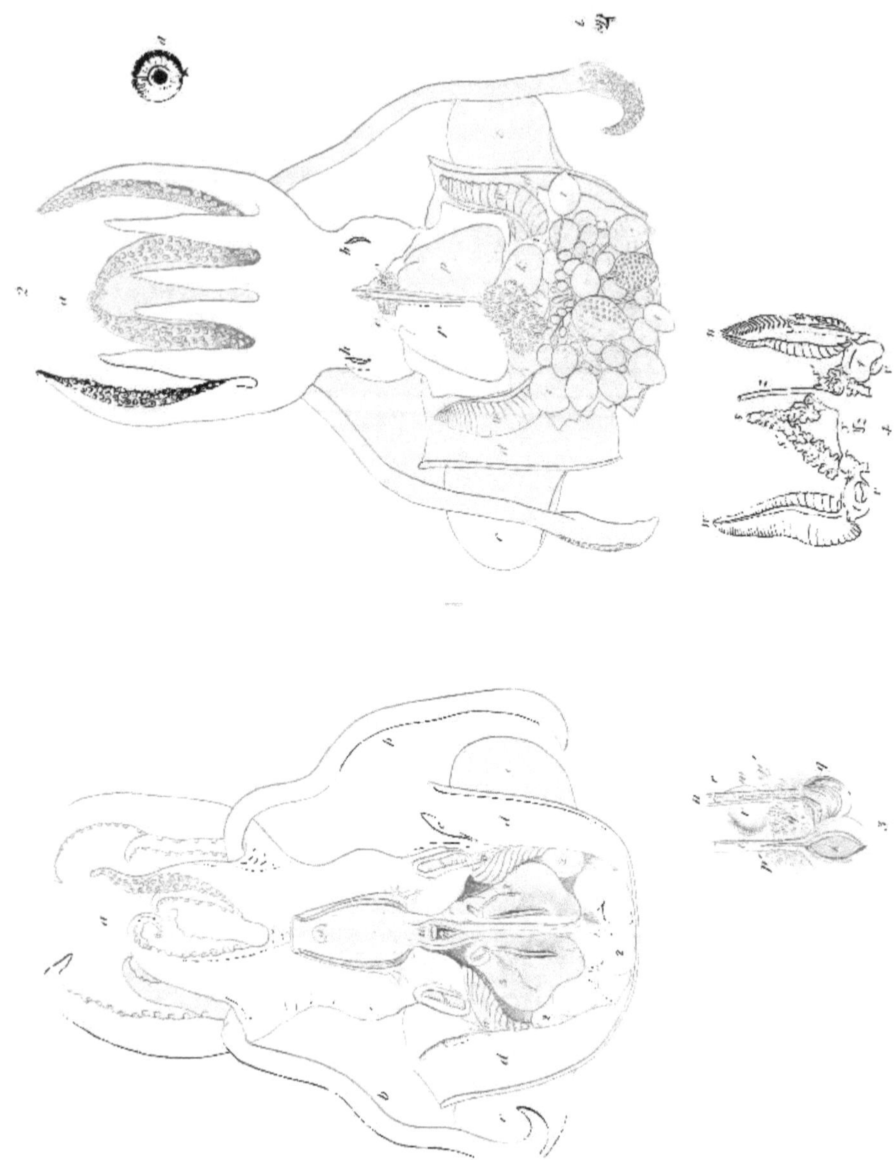

diate to *Sepiola* and *Sepioteuthis*, which it connects together as well by its intermediate size, as by the peculiarities of its structure.

I propose to call the genus *Rossia*, in honour of the Commander of an Expedition, at once so honourable to the enterprising character of the British seaman, and so interesting in its scientific results.

Class—CEPHALOPODA. (*Cuvier.*)

Order—DIBRANCHIATA.

Tribe—DECACERA.

Family—LOLIGINIDÆ.

Genus—ROSSIA.

CHAR. GEN.—*Corpus* ventricosum; duabus pinnis latis rotundatis, subdorsalibus, antrorsum positis; margine antico pallii libero.

Brachia subbrevia, triedra; acetabulis pedunculatis, pedunculis brevissimis; ad basin brachiorum in duabus seriebus alternantibus, ad apicem in plurimis seriebus aggregatis. Ordo longitudinis parium brachiorum, 1, 2, 4, 3.

Tentacula longitudine corpus æquantia, ad apicem acetabulis pedunculatis minimis obsita.

Gladius, corneus, longitudine lin. ix. æquans; inferius parum dilatatus.

CHAR. SP.—*Rossia palpebrosa.*

From the obvious uncertainty of deducing a stable specific character from the only known representative of its genus, I have limited myself to proposing a *nomen triviale*, taken from the remarkable development of the skin surrounding the eyeball, by means of which this animal evidently possesses the power of defending the eye, as the pulmonated Vertebrata do by means of their more regularly-formed eyelids. The utility of this provision, in seas abounding with fragments of ice, is obvious. Fig. 1, pl. B, from a sketch by Captain Ross, shows the appearance of the eyes while the animal was alive; fig. 2, pl. C, *h.* shows the closing of the eyelid after death.

The admeasurements of the specimen were as follow, but it must be borne in mind that it had shrunk in all its dimensions in consequence of having been macerated in spirit.

	Inches.	Lines.
Length from the end of the visceral sac to the end of the longest tentacle	5	0
Ditto from the end of the visceral sac to the anterior margin of the mantle	1	9

	Inches.	Lines.
Length from the end of the visceral sac to the interspace of the first or middle pair of dorsal brachia	3	2
Ditto of the tentacle	4	2
Breadth of the body (exclusive of the fins) . . .	1	8
Ditto of the head, across the eyes . .	1	3

The specimen presented a dull dusky brown colour, over the whole of the dorsal and lateral aspects, and over the exterior of the arms. The pigment producing this hue was disposed in minute close-set points. Captain Ross's drawing of the recent animal exhibits a greenish metallic lustre, reflected from these surfaces, slight remains of which are still perceptible in the specimen. The ventral surface is of a light ash colour.

The form of the abdomen or visceral segment of the body is more ventricose than in *Sepiola*. The anterior margin of the mantle projects slightly forwards at the middle of its dorsal aspect, as in *Sepioteuthis*, and is reflected downwards for about half an inch before being continued upon the back part of the head. There is a transverse groove on either side of the mantle, about a line behind its anterior margin: this part is colourless anterior to the grooves, as in *Sepiola*.

The fins are short, semicircular, dorsal in their position, but nearer the sides of the body, and placed more forwards than in *Sepiola vulgaris*; the interspace between their origins is to the breadth of the body as 3 to 4, while in *Sepiola vulgaris* it is as 3 to 5. They project laterally from the body, with a slight inclination forwards. They measure in length one inch, in breadth ten lines.

The *brachia* are proportionately shorter and thicker than in *Sepiola*, more resembling those of *Sepia*, but not having the same relative dimensions as in that genus, e. g. the third, and not the fourth pair, is the longest (counting from the dorsal aspect), but the fourth pair is proportionately longer than in *Sepiola*. They measure,

The first pair, one inch.
The second pair, one inch three lines.
The third pair, one inch nine lines.
The fourth pair, one inch five lines.

They present the usual three-sided pyramidal form, with the internal facet beset with the suckers or acetabula. These are of a globular figure, supported by very short sub-lateral peduncles. Commencing from the base of the arms, the suckers are arranged in a double alternate series; this disposition prevails along the whole of the first pair, along three-fourths of the second pair, and along about half of the third and fourth pairs of arms, beyond which the suckers are aggregated into irregular transverse rows of from three to five, diminishing in size to the apex of the arm. In this respect there is an intermediate structure between *Sepiola*, in which the suckers are in a double alternate series along the whole arm; and *Sepia*, in which they are aggregated from the commencement. The horny cup in each acetabulum has its margins entire: and its diameter is equal to one-third of the fleshy sphere in which it is implanted.

The tentacles or proboscides * are round, and slightly dilated at their extremities, which are beset for about nine lines by minute and close-set suckers; these diminish in size towards the extremity of the tentacle, and the largest of them do not exceed one-fiftieth of an inch in diameter. The horny cup of these acetabula is proportionately larger than in those of the brachia, and their pedicles are longer. (See *b*, pl. C.) A narrow membranous expansion is extended along the sides of the dilated extremities of the tentacle.

The tentacula emerge from within the membrane extended between the third and fourth pairs of brachia, but this interbrachial fold, though of greater breadth, does not connect the arms together for a greater extent than the membrane between the third and second, or that between the second and first pairs of legs; but there is no corresponding fold between the ventral pair of arms. In this respect *Rossia* resembles *Sepiola* and *Sepia*; in all of which, therefore, the interbrachial membranes have obviously other uses than to protect the tentacles, which can be retracted into a cavity below the base of the arms; they probably serve, but in a minor degree than in *Octopus*, as a retropulsive fin.

The eyes of the specimen were of large size, forming the usual convexity on each side of the head; they were, however, as has been before mentioned, almost completely hidden from view by the contraction of the lower eyelid principally, the opening of the fold corresponding to the transparent portion of the integument continued over the eyeball (for the animal cannot be said to possess a true cornea), was of a longitudinal figure, and dorsal in its position. In *Sepiola* there is a slight fold beneath the eye, corresponding to the largely developed eyelid in *Rossia*, but there is a greater proportionate breadth of the head at this part in *Sepiola*.

The siphon or funnel extends to within a line of the interbrachial membrane of the ventral pair of arms, resembling in this respect *Sepiola* rather than *Sepia*, or *Sepioteuthis*, where the funnel reaches only half-way between that part and the margin of

* This superadded pair of elongated arms were termed by Aristotle προβοσκίδαι, in contradistinction to the ordinary eight arms, which he calls πόδες.—*Hist. Animal.*, lib. iv., c. 1.

the mantle. It is depressed and tapers towards the extremity; within the tube, and two lines distant from the end, there is the small valve, which exists in all the Cephalopods that have locomotive organs adapted for propelling them forwards. On either side of the base of the funnel there is an oblong cartilaginous depression, surrounded by a raised margin, to which a corresponding projection on the inner side of the mantle is adapted. This structure for strengthening the attachment between the mantle and the head is met with in all the *Decacera*, and in *Ocythoë*, but does not exist in *Octopus*. The membranous expansions from the sides of the base of the funnel, corresponding to the '*callottes*' in *Octopus*, extend in *Rossia* around the anal aperture.

The rudimentary dorsal shell, or gladius, is not more than nine lines in length, and one line and a half in breadth at its lower and dilated half; there is a longitudinal mesial ridge on its external surface, and a corresponding groove with lateral ridges on the opposite side; it is of a firm texture, and brown colour anteriorly, but becomes thin, soft, white, and cartilaginous at its posterior extremity.

The digestive organs of *Rossia* resemble those of *Sepiola*, with the exception of the laminated pancreatic cæcum being of a simpler form, and the follicles appended to the biliary ducts being more developed; these are larger, indeed, than in any Cephalopod in which this structure has been found. The horny mandibles, and their surrounding fleshy lips, present no peculiarity worthy of remark. The outer lip, as in *Sepiola*, is more contracted than in *Sepia*. The œsophagus descends in the dorsal interspace of the hepatic lobes without dilating to form a crop. The muscular stomach is lined with a cuticle, but is not so strong as in *Octopus*. The laminated cæcum is a simple oval cavity, as in *Nautilus*, without spiral appendage. The biliary secretion enters it between two of the widest laminæ, which are continued onwards some way into the intestine. The gut ascends without any convolution on the opposite side of the liver, and terminates between the two muscles which connect the base of the funnel with the ventral side of the mantle, and which, from their disposition, serve as a sphincter to the intestine.

The lower pair of salivary glands are lobulated, and of the usual proportionate size. The liver is bilobed, each lobe notched at its upper end, and expanding towards the lower end. Besides the proper capsule, which has a smooth glistening surface, the liver is contained in a strong peritoneal cavity. The two biliary ducts emerge from the lower end and immediately branch out into a mass of larger and simpler follicles, which are arborescent, and extend their ramifications half an inch from the ducts, forming a mass, which conceals the upper halves of both the stomach and rudimentary pancreas. The ink-bag is situated between the liver and the muscles which surround the arms, close to which its duct enters the intestine. The ink is black, of the same tint as the china-ink.

The organs of circulation, in the form of the systemic ventricle and of the spongy *venæ cavæ*, resemble those of *Sepioteuthis* more than those of *Sepiola;* the branchial ventricles are proportionately larger than in any other Cephalopod. The *vena cava*, after its division, becomes dilated and cellular, but the cells are not produced outwardly into distinct pendulous follicles, the exterior of the vein presents simply a folded or convoluted appearance. The branchial ventricles are of a transversely oblong figure, four lines in length, and three in breadth: they have the small fleshy appendages, as in *Sepiola*, *Sepoteuthis*, and other true decapods. The fleshy stem of the branchia, through which the branchial artery passes is very broad. The branchial vein dilates into a sinus or auricle, before terminating in the systemic ventricle. This is of a cylindrical form, tapering at its lateral extremities where the blood enters, and bent upwards at the right side to give off the greater aorta; the lesser aorta comes off from the middle of the opposite side of the ventricle.

The larger aorta ascends with the œsophagus between the lobes of the liver, the smaller one descends to supply the ovary principally. The specimen was a female, and had been taken at the season of reproduction. The ovary occupied the lower half of the dorsal aspect of the abdomen; it was filled with numerous bodies, varying in size from one line to six in the transverse diameter, and with as various figures, some being spherical, others oval, some pyriform, and a few rendered angular by external pressure, but all having their superfices more or less reticulated, as in *Sepia*, &c., in consequence of the honeycombed glandular structure of their parietes. These bodies, which are appended by delicate peduncles, of various length, to one point of the membranous ovary, are commonly regarded as the ova,* but they are, in fact, the glandular calyces, which secrete the true ova; the analogous parts in the Nautilus I have termed *capsulæ oviferæ:* they correspond to the Graafian follicles or ovisacs of the Vertebrata. The ova in these ovisacs exhibited in *Rossia* various stages of development indicative of an internal impregnation: many of the reticulate ovisacs were collapsed, having discharged their ova; nine of the ova so discharged, were situated in the single oviduct. The ova which still remained within the capsules had the smooth transparent cortical membrane perfectly formed, and differed from the ova in the oviduct only in the tenuity of this membrane. The discharged ova measured five lines in the long and four in the short diameters. The oviduct was wide, thin, and membranous; it passed along the ventral aspect of the ovary and pericardium towards the left side: its termination was thickened, and beset with transverse glandular folds, as in *Nautilus*, and was situated immediately behind the two large superadded

* See Grant on the Anatomy of *Sepiola*, in Zool. Trans.—vol. i., p. 84, pl. 11, fig. 12.

*N

glands. These bodies have been described in Sepiola,* as the oviducts, but they are equally distinct from the true efferent tube in that genus as in *Rossia;* the true oviduct being single in *Sepiola*, as in *Sepia*, and forming by its termination the crescentic glandular organ, which lies between and behind the two large accessory glands above mentioned; of which the function is to secrete the adhesive substance which connects the ova, after they have passed out of the oviduct, and before they are discharged by the funnel. Filamentary processes of the secretion were hanging from the ducts of the glands in the specimen here described. They are composed of numerous transverse laminæ, the secretion of which passes into a central longitudinal fissure, where it is moulded into the filamentary form. In *Nautilus* these glands are united at the mesial plane, and the corresponding organ is single in the pectinibranchiate mollusks.

EXPLANATION OF THE FIGURES.

Plate B.

Fig. 1. *Rossia palpebrosa*, from the dorsal aspect.

Plate C.

Fig. 1. *Rossia palpebrosa*, with the mantle and funnel laid open on the ventral aspect, showing the infundibular valve, the ova in the oviduct, and other viscera *in situ*.

Fig. 2. The same laid open on the dorsal aspect, and the capsule of the liver removed, showing the ovisacs, and the relative position of the viscera on this side of the abdomen.

Fig. 3. The digestive canal laid open.

Fig. 4. The branchia, and organs of circulation.

The same letters indicate the same parts in each figure:—*a*, the eight brachia; *a'*, one of the brachial suckers magnified; *b*, the two tentacula; *b'*, a tentacular sucker magnified; *c*, the fins; *d*, the inside of the mantle; *e e*, the processes which enter *f f*, the cavities at the base of the funnel; *g*, the infundibular valve; *h*, the opening of the eyelids; *i*, the œsophagus; *k*, the muscular stomach; *l*, the pancreas; *m*, the intestine; *n*, the anus; *o*, lower salivary glands; *p p*, liver; *p' p'*, hepatic ducts; *q*, hepatic follicles; *r*, ink-bag; *s*, vena cava; *s' s'*, its glandular auricular portions going to *t t*, the branchial ventricles; *v v*, their fleshy appendages; *w w*, the branchiæ;

* See Grant on the Anatomy of *Sepiola*, in Zool. Trans.—vol. i., p. 84, pl. 11, fig. 10.

r r, systemic sinuses; *y*, systemic ventricle; *z*, aortæ; 1 1, ovisacs in the ovary appended to filamentary pedicles; 2 2, ova in the oviduct; 3 3, glands which secrete the *nidamentum*, or connecting substance of the ova.

R. O."

PTEROPODA.

2.—CLIO BOREALIS.

CLIO BOREALIS.—*Cuv: Rég. Anim.*—vol. iii., p. 27. *Lamarck*—vol. vi., p. 286.
CLIO LIMACINA.—*Phipps, Ellis Zooph.*—p. 15, figs. 9 and 10.
Leach, Ross's Voyage—oct. edit., vol. ii. p. 172.
Sab: Supp. to Parry's 1st Voyage—p. ccxxxix.
Ross, App. to Parry's 3d Voy.—p. 120; and *Parry's Polar Voy.*—p. 206.
CLIO RETUSA.—*Fab: Faun. Grœnl.*—p. 334.
CLIONE PAPILIONACEA.—*Pallas, Spicil. Zool.*—vol. x., p. 37, pl. 1, figs. 18 and 19.

Very numerous in most parts of the Arctic Ocean. Less abundant in Regent's Inlet and the Gulf of Boothia.

3.—LIMACINA ARCTICA.

LIMACINA ARCTICA.—*Cuv: Rég. Anim.*—vol. iii., p. 28.
Lamarck—vol. vi., p. 290.
Leach, Ross's Voyage—oct. edit., vol. ii., p. 172.
Sab: Supp. to Parry's 1st Voyage—p. ccxxxix.
Ross, App. to Parry's 3d Voyage—p. 120. *Parry's Polar Voyage*—p. 206.
ARGONAUTA ARCTICA.—*Fab: Faun. Grœnl.*—p. 386.

A very abundant species; peopling as it were the Polar Seas, and constituting the chief source of subsistence to the Greenland whale. It is indeed most truly wonderful that so small and apparently insignificant an animal can be made to fulfil the most important purposes; from the smallest species of crustacea to the enormous whale, all derive their food directly or indirectly from this little creature. It is in fact to the inhabitants of the Arctic Ocean, what the vegetable kingdom is to the inhabitants of the land—the foundation of animal existence.

ACEPHALA.

4.—BOLTENIA RENIFORMIS.

BOLTENIA RENIFORMIS.—*Mac Leay, Trans. Linn. Soc.*—vol. xiv., p. 536, pl. 18.
ASCIDIA GLOBIFERA.—*Sab: Supp. to Parry's 1st Voyage*—
ASCIDIA CLAVATA.—*Fab: Faun. Grænl.*—p. 303.

CHAR. SP.—B. obscura scabriuscula, corpore subreniformi, orificiis subprominentibus, pedunculo terminali. (*Mac Leay.*)

A single specimen of this extraordinary animal was dredged up from a depth of seventy fathoms, near Elizabeth Harbour. I can add nothing to Mr. Mac Leay's admirable description, except that the colour of the body is a very light brown, that of the pedicle darker.

5.—CYSTINGIA GRIFFITHSII.

CYSTINGIA GRIFFITHSII.—*Mac Leay, Trans. Linn. Soc.*—vol. xiv., p. 540, pl. 19.

C. ovata globosa cineracea glabra semipellucida, pedunculo vix longitudine corporis. (*Mac Leay.*)

This interesting species is of very rare occurrence, even in those seas where it was first discovered; a single specimen, taken in Fox's Channel, during Sir Edward Parry's third voyage to the Arctic Regions, fortunately for science came under the notice of Mr. Mac Leay, and, together with two other species of Ascidiæ from the same place, was the occasion of his learned memoir on the "Anatomy of the Natural Group of *Tunicata*," *loc. cit.*

Two specimens were obtained by us near Felix Harbour, but as these were abandoned with the rest of our collection, it is probable that the individual from which Mr. Mac Leay's description and drawings were taken, is the only specimen ever brought to England.

GEOLOGY.

BY CAPTAIN SIR JOHN ROSS, *C.B.*, *K.S.A.*, *K.C.S.*, &c.

GEOLOGICAL NOTICE RESPECTING THAT PART OF THE AMERICAN LAND VISITED DURING OUR VOYAGE.

I MAY commence with James's Island, of which Sir E. Parry examined the southern and eastern coasts; my observations which are peculiarly scanty for this part of our voyage, are limited to the northern shore, to which the name of North Devon has been given. I must at the same time say, that under my previous familiarity with the neighbouring and opposed shore of America, I formed the conclusions here drawn, more from a comparison of the physiognomy of the little known with that which had been far better studied, than from observations which our very brief intimacy with this coast afforded me no means of making.

My acquaintance with the shore in question begins at Cape York, and extends to Possession Bay. The whole of this line presented that succession of limestone, which from its similarity, in every particular, of picturesque forms, positions, and mineral characters, I had determined, when on the American shore, and with ample opportunities of examination, to be a "deposit" or "series," so resembling that which the geologists of England term mountain limestone, that it must be discriminated by this name, unless, as I do not yet know, the American philosophers have applied another term to their great calcareous formations.

Of the interior country on this shore, I must speak with more reserve; yet drawing such inferences as I here give, from the same source, namely, the exceeding similarity of character in the forms of the land on the two sides of the passage which includes Barrow's Strait and Prince Regent's Inlet. It will immediately be seen, that on the American shore, the limestone skirts the bases of chains of hills which consist chiefly, or, to our observation at least, most conspicuously of granite, including some portions of the primary stratified rocks, which might have been more extensive than I had the means of ascertaining. Now, the same exact character of outline and general aspect pervaded the interior of James's Island, as far as that was visible; where a range of mountains possessing the same conical irregular forms as those on the American shore, rose at the back of the assignable limestone hills. I could not but conclude that their geological nature was the same; while some specimens of gneiss, of green compact felspar, and of granite, picked up on the beaches where our boats landed, served to confirm this conclusion: and the more so, from their absolute identity with the analogous rocks which I had collected along the shore from Fury Beach to the isthmus of Boothia.

If I have thus referred to my first and far more detailed observations on the geological structure of the American shore, I may commence at Cape Northeast, being the north-eastern part of America, sufficiently noted in the chart appended to this work.

At this place, the forms of the land alone might, to a practised eye, have disclosed the nature of the fundamental rocks; since the hills present those outlines, so well known, by which this limestone is characterized; the stratification equally indicating the mineral constitutions of the rock, in those cliffs and ravines, where it is peculiarly exposed; as the examination of specimens at more leisure, with the long continued contact which I could command throughout a space of many miles, could leave no doubt of the truth of these conclusions, from the point in question, as far as Fury Beach.

I must now observe, that from Northeast Cape onwards to Adelaide Bay, I could obtain no sight of any interior hills, of the same conical and irregular character as I had become so well acquainted with on the more southern parts of this shore. Every visible hill was flat-topped, so as to convince me that it was a part of the same calcareous range. But at the bottom of Cresswell Bay, I first began to see a range of interior hills, of a very different character: and subsequent observation, accompanied by a long experience of the nature of the rocks, which I could examine at hand, having taught me that the hills of this character consisted of primary rocks, and far most extensively, of granite, it is at this point that I must first note my assurance of the existence of a range of granitic and its associated rocks, on this coast; forming the fundamental structure of this country, and covered, or rather skirted, as is usual, by a range of the secondary, and, for the most part, calcareous series.

As well as I could estimate, the distance of this primary interior range of mountains, from the sea-shore, judging at least by that of their summits, is about thirty miles. But from that, somewhat indeterminate point, of course, the ridge, if ridge it be, which appears so to the eye, inclines towards the sea line, and, in its progress thence, reaches the shore at Port Logan. The limestone which I have already mentioned, disappears in consequence, and I met with it no more on this eastern coast; recovering it only to the westward of the isthmus of Boothia, near Neitchillee.

I must now, therefore, note as much of its peculiarities as may enable geologists to form that judgment of its analogy to the rocks they have defined on which I have no right to decide, from my very imperfect acquaintance with this subject. I presume, of course, that they will call it "the mountain limestone," because this is the name which I have seen applied to rocks resembling it in character, and, as far as I understand those subjects, in position: but this however I must leave to the more competent.

From Northeast Cape to Adelaide Bay, it presents those forms which distinguish the limestone district of Yorkshire, but with far more decided shapes in some parts of this line, of which the analogies and resemblances may be seen in Derbyshire, though in the most remarkable places, these are very like to some scenery which I remember seeing in a French picturesque work, representing the scenery and antiquities of Pola, in Istria.

It would be to repeat what must be well known to every one interested in this subject, to say, that the fractures which the precipices of this rock present, are frequently such as to display the appearance of castles and towers, as the smaller ones are apt to exhibit the appearances of niches and statues, so as to confer on them a singular and striking variety of architectural effect, which, under peculiar circumstances, is even very deceptive. Of these apings of the works of art, we had an abundant and various display; that I could not make pictures of what I saw, from the extreme severity of the weather, and the difficult circumstances in which I was almost invariably placed, might possibly be regretted on the score of art, but can be of no moment for the present end, where the general fact and its bearings are so well understood by all whom geology can interest.

If this leading and striking character is not sufficient to satisfy geologists respecting the precise nature of this limestone, as it regards the systems of the earth which they have adopted, I suppose that this presumed character will be confirmed by its mineral nature, and by that of the organic remains which it contains. In different places, the former exhibits all those various characters, in texture and colour, which I have seen in collections of specimens of this particular limestone, as well as in several parts of Scotland, where this rock has been pointed out to me, though it would be superfluous for me to describe what is well known to every geologist. And if sometimes pure and somewhat marble-like in its texture, so it is argillaceous and dull, when it approaches to those shales into which it gradually passes, and with which it is interstratified.

It is in its shales also, as I understand is usual with all limestones, that the organic remains which it contains are chiefly found; though, as is not uncommon elsewhere, some of these occur only in that compact and almost pure calcareous rock, of which they form a part. If, even, I were better informed on this subject, so as to know the distinctions of rocks which are derivable from shells, I could not pretend to distinguish fragments, nor even the more perfect shells, by their present names in the modern systems; since I have had no means of keeping my knowledge up to the level of the improvements in this branch of science. Suffice it to say, that such organic remains, or shells, as I found, consisted of corals, of entrochi, of terebratulæ, and of others which I will not, or need not, pretend to name; as of all I may say, that they bore such a general resemblance to those of the "mountain limestone" of England and Scotland, which I have seen in collections, as will doubtless satisfy others respecting that in which I am not inclined to take any further concern than may be necessary for allowing others to form those conclusions, which it would be presumptuous in me to draw.

To terminate the history of this limestone, I need only remark in addition, that after ceasing at Port Logan, where the primary rocks reach the shore, it recurs at Neitchillee, to the southward of the isthmus of Boothia, and that it was thence traced for about two hundred miles to the westward, towards Cape Franklin, where our knowledge of this coast ends. On this long line, however, no mountains of this rock, such as I have described as occupying so great a range of country, occurred. In general, the shores were barely skirted by low strata of a calcareous stone, frequently schistose, intermixed with shales; as they were often so encumbered with fragments and blocks of the primary rocks, as well as of the limestone in question, that I could not often be sure that the fundamental strata were present. The geological conclusion that I was compelled to draw was, nevertheless, the same; namely, that the primary district of this portion of the American coast was skirted throughout its whole extent, with the exception of that line on which the sea met those rocks, by a series of secondary strata, of which this peculiar limestone was the leading and almost the exclusive member.

I ought now, according to the usual doctrines of geology, as I understand them, to have also found the red sandstone, which holds a place between this limestone and the primary srtata. I must, however, observe, that on the whole of the long line which I examined at various times, extending from Northeast Cape to the Western Sea, that rock was never found in its position: whether owing to its real absence, or to the difficulty of seeing shores so often, and for such long periods, covered with ice and snow, or to my own negligence of this subject, where there was so much of more importance to engage my attention, I cannot now presume to say. Several fragments of a sandstone were however picked up on the shores, at various and distant places; as, for example, near Batty Bay, at Fury Beach, at Victoria Harbour and at other places which I need not name, proving the existence of sandstone strata in the vicinity, or at least somewhere on this coast.

But according to more practised judgments than my own, these specimens are inadequate to prove whether the rock whence they have been derived belongs to the lowest red sandstone, or to that which is termed red marl. That they are red, brown, and mottled, sometimes soft, and at others very hard, is all that I can say respecting them; and this diversity of character is, as I am informed, well known to occur in both the sandstones in question.

But there is one fact whence I am told I may conclude, that in some parts of this shore, at least, the collected specimens must have been derived from the red marl, whatever may be the case with respect to the southern part of the same line. This is the occurrence of gypsum in the vicinity of Northeast Cape: a mineral which geologists have hitherto referred to this series. But I must leave that matter to their judgments, as I have nothing more to suggest on the subject of these rocks, since I am not possessed of any other evidence than that which I have stated. It is only needful to add, that as I saw no strata superior to the limestone, and obtained no specimens likely to have been derived from any series higher than the red marl, as the several friends whom I have consulted admit; so I may, I presume, conclude that the secondary strata of this shore are limited to the rocks which I have described: a fact which, if I have read sufficiently on this subject, is exactly conformable to what occurs very widely in the northern portion of the North American continent.

Having already said of the primary land of this coast, that it forms ridges of hills more interior than those of limestone wherever these occur, I must now observe that it reaches the shore at Port Logan, and occupies the remainder of that coast to the southward, together with the valley of lakes that crosses the isthmus, as far as Lake Wittersted, where it is once more skirted by the flat limestone already described. Of the geography of this class of rocks, I can, of course, give no further description, since the climate and the snow united, prevented all research into the interior, and all minute examination, for the most part, of what was accessible.

To say that what I saw and could not touch, consisted of granite, is more than, as I am told, I ought to affirm, since geologists seem agreed that it is difficult to judge of

*o

primary mountains by their physiognomy alone. Even when more near the eye, I will not say how often I may not have mistaken gneiss for granite; yet this latter rock seemed to me to predominate through all the ridges, as it was also that which I found far most frequently whenever I could obtain actual contact with the rocks.

That it presented the usual variety of external character, I need scarcely say, and that it included a great variety of mineral aspect or composition is what I can now but remember, without being able to describe. Only three varieties appear among the very few specimens which I brought home; namely, one of red felspar, white quartz, and hornblende, one of the same felspar and quartz, with white mica, and a third of pale felspar and quartz, with a dark variety of this mineral. In one place I noted that a large mass of this rock was thickly studded with garnets; but having brought home no specimens, I cannot now describe it more particularly.

Having found no specimens of gneiss in this small rescued collection, and having but little recollection of the places where I saw this rock, I can give no account of it. Commander Ross appears to have met with it more extensively than I did, but as this branch of natural history was not under his charge, I cannot derive from his recollection, any facts sufficiently positive to state, either respecting its geography or its mineral characters. I shall only note, that in Felix Harbour, I found hornblende schist, belonging to this series, as I am informed, together with that compact green felspar, which is known to be one of its inmates. That I saw common slate, or argillaceous schistus, in Victoria Harbour, and in one or two other places, is all that I can now recollect respecting that rock; while one of the engraved plates represents a part of a stratum associated with another of gneiss, traversed, as it appears, by a granite vein, and the whole intersected by one of quartz.

The last rock which I have to notice is trap. A considerable mass of this occurs at Saumarez River, and it is also represented in one of the plates; the only other place where I noticed it was near Elizabeth Harbour, where numerous veins traverse the granitic hills which skirt this shore.

Of mere minerals, I found agate pebbles in one place, with veins of white, pink, and yellow quartz, near Elizabeth Harbour, and copper ore near Agnew River and Lord Lindsay River.

The hills are often covered with granite boulders, offering the usual difficulty so often discussed: but I saw no other alluvia than those which are easily referred to the flowing of water during the summer thaws, and to the action of the waves on the shores.

REPORT ON INSTRUMENTS.

My transit instrument was made by Mr. T. Jones, of Charing Cross, for my observatory at North-west Castle, Wigtonshire, where I had it in use four years. Its telescope was thirty-six inches in length, with an object-glass two inches and five-eighths aperture, and was an excellent instrument: it was the whole time under the charge of Commander Ross.

My theodolite was nine inches in diameter, with double telescope, and was made also by Jones, for the late Captain Bartholomew.

The diurnal variation instrument was made by Mr. Dollond, whose instructions I received respecting its use, and was the same which had been made for Sir John Franklin. I had also two altitude instruments made by Jones, which were supplied to me from the Colonial Office, and which I used to determine the height of the Eastern over the Western Sea. I had three dipping-needles, one made by Jones, which was with Sir Edward Parry; one by Pope, and one of my own construction. We had five sextants; an instrument sent by Mr. Warre, which was the invention of Lieut. Drummond, R.A., being a compass with apparatus for finding the latitude and longitude attached to it, and was a very ingenious invention; but, as the compass had ceased to traverse where we wintered, it could not be tried. My telescope for occultations was sixty-six inches focal length, with an aperture of three inches and five-eighths; the object-glass by Tully. I had also Barlow's apparatus, and Gilbert's azimuth compass, and six others; two marine and one mountain barometer. Rowland's and Tyrrel's perspective instruments, the former was found of great value as

*o 2

the greatest tyro in drawing could not fail to delineate the land correctly with it. The deep sea clamms, Dr. Marcet's water-bottle, Massey's patent log, and other instruments of minor importance, were, with the exception of Jones's dipping-needle, two sextants, and two spyglasses, left at Victoria harbour, where they were buried on the north side of the bay; but I have no doubt but they would be discovered and destroyed by the natives.

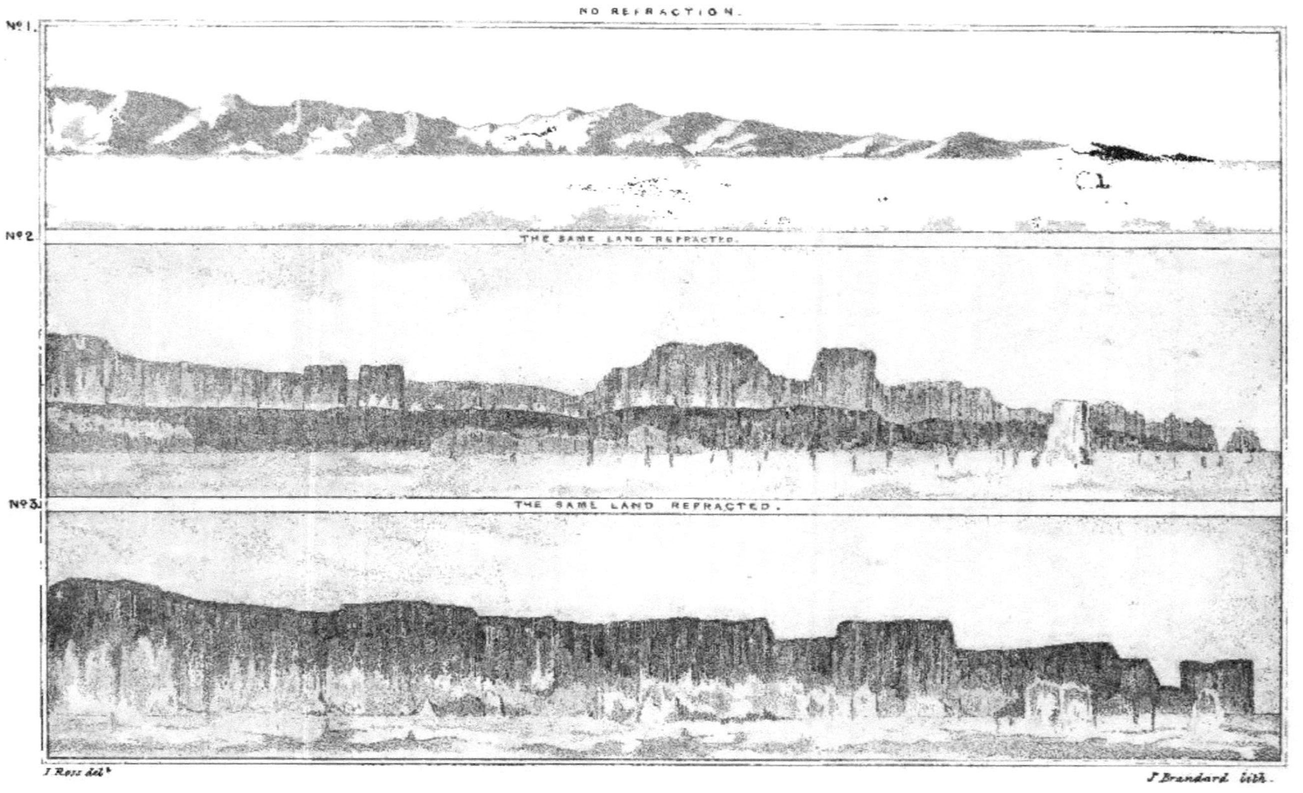
NO REFRACTION.
No 1.
No 2.
THE SAME LAND REFRACTED.
No 3.
THE SAME LAND REFRACTED.
J Ross delt
J Brandard lith.

TERRESTRIAL REFRACTION.

Those who pass a year northward of the Arctic Circle, during the spring and autumn, are amazed at the extraordinary appearance of the objects around them, which are often changed in shape so totally different from what they really are, that it is quite impossible to take correct sketches, or make any thing like a true estimate of the distance of the land, which, in the course of a few minutes, is often so much changed as not to have any thing like the natural or true outline. Captain Scoresby gives some extraordinary instances of both land and ships seen at an immense distance, and on our first voyage it is recorded, that Cape Clarence was seen from the deck at the distance of one hundred and twenty miles, the ship being at that time two degrees of latitude south of the cape; and, indeed, it was only in the spring after our arrival at Felix harbour, that we discovered the land to the east-south-east of us, with many intervening islands. But the most remarkable circumstance which occurred during our observations was the uneven current of refraction raising an intermediate body (an iceberg or island) above the more distant land, which at the time of no refraction was considerably higher. This fact at once shows the fallacy of setting up a mark or board at a distance of a few miles to observe a star setting behind it; and which could be no proof of the inaccuracy of the table of refractions in the Nautical Almanac, which, indeed, I found by all my observations to be wonderfully correct. I cannot omit to mention an extraordinary instance of unusual refraction, which took place on the 22d of September, 1832, when we were at North End Cape, lat. 73° 53′ north, long. 90° west. The weather was very clear, and, in an east-north-east bearing, no land could be seen.

I was watching the rising of the sun, with my eyes fixed to the spot, when I saw the sun emerge; in an instant his lower limb was his full diameter above the horizon, without his figure being changed; in this position he remained about half a minute, then fell, his lower limb being dipped about one-eighth of the diameter; he then assumed various amorphous forms, continued varying for five minutes, and at length assumed the proper form.

The plate is given to show the land in three different states:

First, as with no refraction, distant fourteen miles.

The second is the same land, with an iceberg four miles distant raised above the land.

The third, the same refracted in a different way on the same day.

These outlines are taken by Ronald's invaluable instruments which I had fixed on a point of land sixteen feet above the level of the sea, and by which the figure could be traced with the greatest precision, and with which I made above three hundred observations, tending to confirm what I have stated. These observations were taken during the first week in May, 1831.

ANALYSIS OF FLUIDS, &c.

I AM indebted for the following article to my friend Mr. Thomas Rymer Jones, who, in conjunction with Mr. Hemmings, submitted the articles I gave them to a careful examination, and made the following report, which requires no comment, as the acquirements of these gentlemen are known to qualify them highly for such an investigation.

1.—SEA-WATER FROM PADLIAK OR SPENCE BAY.

This water was taken from the sea by me on the 4th of June, 1830, and carefully preserved in a bottle with a ground glass stopper, and was never out of my possession, having been carried by me the whole length of our fatiguing journey to Fury beach; in order to establish the specific gravity and component parts of the water in the sea of King William, or that to the westward of the isthmus of Boothia.

The specific gravity of this water was 1.011 at a temperature of sixty-four degrees of Fahrenheit, and a wine pint contains 116,97 grains, of which matter—viz.:

	GRAINS.
Magnesia .	5.81
Chloride of sodium	92.5
Sulphate of lime	7.67
Sulphuric acid .	4.39—besides that contained in the sulphate of lime.
Muriatic acid	5.65—besides that contained in the muriate of soda.

The salts therefore contained in the water are most probably—

	GRAINS.
Muriate of magnesia .	8.7
Sulphate of magnesia .	8.26
Chloride of sodium (dry salt) .	9.25
Sulphate of lime .	7.47
	116.93

2.—BRINE FROM FURY BEACH.

Having found this fluid in a beef-cask at Fury beach on our return to winter there, and still in a fluid state while the temperature was below zero, I made use of it as an artificial horizon: and as it was subsequently exposed to a temperature of forty degrees below zero (at which point the finest mercury freezes) without being frozen, I thought it worth while to preserve some for analysis, and the following is Mr. Jones's report:

The specific gravity of this brine was 1.171 at a temperature of sixty-four degrees of Fahrenheit. Two fluid drachms contained thirty-one grains and a quarter of solid matter, of which twenty-eight grains were pure chloride of sodium, the remainder contained traces of sulphates of magnesia and lime, and a small quantity of animal matter; a portion placed in a thin glass tube was submitted in succession to the action of some of the most powerful freezing mixtures without undergoing congelation.

3.—WATER FROM THE RIVER SAUMAREZ.

This river, which is in the latitude of seventy degrees north, was found flowing and unfrozen by us early in May, 1830, and, according to the account of the natives, never freezes. As the cause of this phenomenon was unexplained, and might be attributed to the nature of the water, I took some carefully out of the river and found its temperature then at thirty-three degrees of Fahrenheit; since which it was, like that of the western sea, never out of my possession, but kept in a bottle with a ground glass stopper, and carried by me from the time the Victory was abandoned until our return, when it was handed to Mr. Jones, and the following is his report:

Specific gravity of the water from this river is 1.004 at sixty-four degrees of Fahrenheit. This was found to contain a minute portion of the chloride of sodium, and traces of the sulphate of lime.

From this it must appear that the nature or component parts of the water could not be the reason that it did not freeze, and it must therefore be attributed to springs in the bottom of the Great Lake, out of which it flows, and which we estimated to be about three hundred feet above the level of the sea. This chain of lakes was about fifteen miles long, and in some places, three miles wide.

4.—WINE FROM FURY BEACH.

This wine had been lying four years in cask on the beach before we arrived, when we took it on board, and bottled it, after which it was four years in my possession.

Sherry—specific gravity 0.991 at temperature 64 degrees of Fahrenheit.
Port wine—ditto ditto 0.981 ditto ditto.

5.—RUM FROM FURY BEACH.

This is under the same circumstances as the last.

Specific gravity 0.910.

These articles had undergone no change, except, probably, a diminution of strength sufficiently indicated by the specific gravity. The same may be also said of a bottle of brandy cherries which were brought home, *without being opened*, the fruit not having been in the least decomposed. In addition to this, I may mention a bottle of the cordial called " Parfaite Amour," which, although exposed to the severest test, had lost neither colour nor flavour.

6.—LEMON JUICE.

This had been exposed in casks for eight years in Fury beach, and we were of opinion that it had lost much of its antiscorbutic qualities, from its want of the expected effect on those who were afflicted with scurvy; and our opinions seem to have been well founded, according to the following report:

The lemon juice has undergone a partial decomposition, but still contains a considerable

*p

proportion of citric acid; the decomposition being principally in the *vegetable* matter, seems to imply that citric acid alone is not a check to that dreadful malady the scurvy.

7.—THE MUSTARD

Had, as might be expected, lost the greater part of its pungency.

STATE OF PROVISIONS.

The provisions of which the following account is given, had been lying exposed to the climate for eight years, in the latitude of seventy-three degrees and forty-seven minutes north, and longitude of ninety-one degrees and forty-seven minutes west, and very little above high-water mark.

The preserved meats, with few exceptions, were the manufacture of Messrs. Gamble and Co., and being enclosed in tin cases, could not be discovered by animals who depend on the sense of smelling: these were cylinders of various sizes, the ends of each becoming concave or convex, according to the degrees of contraction or expansion caused by the climate, secured them against bursting from its effects, and the contents were found to be in nearly the original state: these consisted of beef, roasted and boiled, veal, mutton, spiced meat of various kinds, turnips, parsnips, and carrots, all of which were found to be in excellent preservation. The soups, which were preserved in quantities, from a quart to a gallon, were excellent, and we left a considerable quantity behind, but no meat of any kind.

The flour, which was preserved in iron-bound casks, and had been likewise exposed for eight years to the climate, was found to be in good condition; for although in many cases the hoops had slackened, so as to admit the moisture into the cask, it penetrated but a short way, while the whole of the interior was perfectly sound. The bread, of which there were many casks, was in a good or bad state, according to the soundness of the cask which contained it, and we employed ourselves in separating the bad from the good, and put all into repaired casks. A part of this, and also of the flour, is sufficient, with the addition of the remaining soup, to sustain the life of twelve men for a year. Owing to the pickles being also in cask, they had suffered much, the vinegar having leaked out of most of them: fifty of these, and twenty-five of lemon juice, are also left, at a little distance south of the house, and covered with coals, as the most effectual way of preserving both.

PHILOSOPHICAL OBSERVATIONS.

ON COLD.

Having already devoted much in Chapter XIII. of the Narrative on this subject, as it regards the human body, it only remains to publish my experiments on its effect on other substances. I shall begin with those on ice, which were repeated yearly: the thickness of the ice was measured regularly, both on a lake and in the sea, every month, and was found to increase until the end of May, when it had arrived at its maximum thickness, which in the sea was ten feet, and the lake eleven; the proportion being so much more on fresh than on salt water. In the months of February and March, when the temperature of the air was at fifty degrees below zero, the temperature of the ice gradually diminished between the surface and the water, which was, immediately below the ice, at the temperature of twenty-seven degrees; showing that to freeze sea-water below the ice (where no air was to be found) required a temperature five degrees lower than the freezing point of Fahrenheit. This was done by excavating a large shaft in the ice, and, as it deepened, a horizontal hole was bored large enough to admit the thermometer at every foot in depth, until we arrived at the water, in which a thermometer was immediately immersed, and the result obtained, the further detail of which need not be presented.

ITS EFFECTS ON SNOW.

The same experiments were made on snow, with proportional results: twelve feet depth of snow being equal in the resistance of cold to seven feet of ice. It was from these experiments that I determined on covering our miserable canvas habitation at Fury beach with ice, which was accomplished by watering the snow walls as they were constructed, and also the roof; the former being made from seven to nine feet thick, and the latter from four to six. This we found effectual against cold until the mercury had

*P 2

frozen; after which, the frost penetrated more or less according to the force of the wind. The general effects of the cold on the snow as it fell, was to pulverize it, so that when a strong breeze came it rose and filled the air like dust, to a considerable height. On the other hand, the valleys, and every place into which the wind had forced the snow, became so hard as to bear being formed into blocks, like Ashlar work, of large dimensions, and rolled into the sledges without damage, and thus we were enabled to build the walls of our huts with considerable rapidity, our first care on halting being to find a place where the snow was hard.

ITS EFFECTS ON MERCURY.

The effect of cold on mercury depended materially on its purity, and I observed that the longer or the oftener it was used, it froze the sooner. It was at first imagined that the lead of the trough which is generally used in artificial horizons, amalgamated with the mercury, but I always used a wooden trough, and a glass bottle to keep it in; notwithstanding which the scum, which was always greatest in cold weather, was equally large, and every year the mercury which had been used, froze at a higher temperature, until it reached to thirty-one degrees, being eight degrees higher than the usual point; while mercury, which had not been exposed, retained its purity. We went through the usual experiments of freezing it in a pistol-bullet mould, and firing the ball through an inch board; as also the finest almond oil, which froze at fifteen degrees, and became very hard at thirty degrees, so as to penetrate, when formed into a bullet, through an inch plank at the distance of five yards.

The effect of cold on various metals was found to be the same as has been often published; but perhaps the loss of magnetic power, in no less than twelve needles of compass cards, which were found on Fury beach, may be most properly attributed to cold, as they were found with the needle pointing north, south, east, and west, and all alike deprived of their magnetic property. The effects of cold on the icebergs was the most striking; as soon after the thermometer had sunk below zero, icebergs were heard renting and tumbling to pieces with tremendous noise; and in the spring, these immense masses were seen, like as many mountains after the devastation of an earthquake. It has been supposed that the cold also had the effect of giving the green and blue colour to the ice; but, although these colours were deeper and more general after than before winter, still I do not think the fact to be sufficiently proved, that the cold is the only cause.

SURGEON'S REPORT.

REPORT

OF

DR. GEORGE M'DIARMID, SURGEON OF THE VICTORY,

ON THE SICK OF THE CREW.

THE following interesting Report of the Sick on board the Victory, was intended for the Narrative; but Dr. M'Diarmid, to whom I am now indebted for it, was unexpectedly appointed to a vessel which was ordered suddenly to India, and sailed before he could prepare it for publication; and he has only returned in time for its insertion in the Appendix. The Report may appear short, as that of so great a length of time, but it is Dr. M'Diarmid's intention to give to the public a fuller account than the prescribed limits of this Appendix could admit of. It has always given me great pleasure to do justice to his uniform zeal and attention, both as regards his profession and other duties; and it has also afforded me much gratification that his conduct has been duly appreciated by the Lords of the Admiralty, who, having dispensed with the usual term of servitude in the Royal Navy, promoted him to the rank, successively, of Assistant-Surgeon and full Surgeon in his Majesty's naval service soon after his return.

JOHN ROSS.

SURGEON'S REPORT.

July 13, 1829.—Our armourer was on this day attacked with pulmonary inflammation; he had, as we subsequently learned, previously suffered from the same malady, and had not been long discharged from one of the London hospitals, when he proffered his services in this expedition. It had been Sir John Ross's intention, soon after the commencement of the voyage, to send him home in one of the whale ships, I having already reported my patient as unfit for further service, but no opportunity presented itself for his return. The poor fellow's case terminated in confirmed consumption, and, although his death was probably in some degree accelerated by the severity of the climate, I think that most likely his disease would have terminated fatally had he remained in England; and I question whether, had he been at home, he could have received more attention, or met with more kindness, even from his relatives, than he experienced at the hands of his shipmates. One wish of his only remained ungratified—he dreaded having his remains deposited in a foreign land, and often expressed vain regrets, that he could not return home to expire on his native soil.

July 27, 1829.—On this day, John Wood, seaman, aged twenty-two, a healthy and robust young man, fractured both the bones of his left leg in jumping into the launch. The cure was completed within two months by ordinary means, nature effecting the union, and the doctor getting the credit of it.

This man was, nine months after his recovery from this accident, severely afflicted with sea-scurvy, and likewise, subsequently in 1833; and as it has been observed, especially by the medical officers attached to Anson's expedition in his Voyage round the World, that fractures become disunited under the ravages of this malady, I think it proper to observe, that in this instance nothing of the kind occurred, although scorbutic symptoms made their appearance so soon after the fractured bones had become consolidated. The symptoms of his first attack, in 1830, were soon controlled; in 1833, however, the disease assumed a more malignant and violent character, and rapidly attained its worst and most deplorable form: the gums were absorbed almost to the edge of the sockets of the teeth, and had become black and putrid, livid patches appeared on the limbs, the legs became œdematous, and the powers of life were prostrated even to repeated faintings. This melancholy state was rendered still more distressing from the bad quality of the lime juice which we had obtained from the stores of the Fury, and which having become decomposed by time, was almost inefficient; yet, in spite of the severity of the disease, and its protracted continuance during a period of four months, I never discovered any indications of disunion in the broken limb. It may, however, be observed, that Lord Anson's men were destitute of all kinds of fresh provisions, and, therefore, not only could not cure, but were unable even to mitigate the progress of the horrible malady which raged among them.

July 24, 1831.—Anthony Buck, aged twenty-four. As this man's case, blindness after epilepsy, is referred to in the Report of the Committee of the House of Commons, it may be, perhaps, interesting to give a short outline of it. In May of this year, he had suffered from snow blindness, which had probably left a disposition to cerebral disease. On the day above mentioned, when on a fishing party seventeen miles from the ship, he had his first attack of epilepsy, from which he recovered with impaired vision of the left eye. On the eleventh of October, he had a second attack still more violent, causing nearly total blindness of both eyes. The fits recurred at irregular intervals for two months, and eventually disappeared, leaving him, however, nearly blind. It cannot be of much interest to trace the various remedies used in this case; but it may be reasonably hoped that the sight may be eventually though gradually recovered; since it is most probable that the blindness depends only on a loss of nervous energy in the retina, from the violence of the fits, a degree of impaired vision being a common consequence of such cases.*

* Since writing the above, I have been told that Buck has partially recovered his sight. Such cases are sometimes fairly referred to organic lesion, but are more usually functional diseases simply.

The second fatal case under my care was one of dropsy (ascites). James Dickson had been on a fishing party two months before the manifestation of dropsical symptoms. He had fallen into the water, and had slept through the night in his wet clothes. His general health from this period was gradually disturbed, and I attribute his malady to the suppressed perspiration consequent upon exposure to damp and cold. On the 20th of October, 1831, he complained of pain and tightness of the abdomen, which, on examination, was found to be swollen and tense. Aperients and diuretics were ordered, as also mercurials to promote the action of the absorbent system, due attention being paid to the function of the skin. I combated the accumulation of fluid with varying success, until the latter end of December, when the tension became extreme, and he was tapped. The operation, as usual, gave him only temporary relief; and, gradually sinking, he died on the 10th of January, 1832.

It is worth while to notice, that at various times during the course of this complaint, symptoms of scurvy made their appearance. So again in Buck's case (epilepsy) the same disease occasionally manifested itself; again in Henry Eyre's case (the cook), who was affected with rheumatism; and in short, in nearly all the cases, the same scorbutic symptoms were mixed up with the proper characteristics of each disease. Even consumption, absolute as it is in our climate, was modified by the same controlling diathesis. The experienced statistical investigator will, in the history of all atmospheric constitutions, observe the same phenomenon in all parts of the world. The cholera epidemic, which stalked like a malignant giant over a great part of the globe, spreading death and desolation in its course, asserted the same controlling influence over disease in general, as has been remarked by most writers on that disease. So again in districts where ague prevails, most diseases receive some additional intermittent character which in other regions do not properly belong to them.

From the experience of former voyagers, and from a consideration of the common causes of scurvy in a northern region, we had sufficiently been taught, that no precaution, however strict, no policy, however comprehensive, could ensure a crew from the occasional ravages of this debilitating malady. The absurdity of attributing it to the single cause of salt provisions, would have been inferior to the pathological views even of the earliest investigators of disease; for the ancients tell us, that not any one cause produces disease, but that is assumed in common parlance as the cause which seems chiefly to have contributed to the effect. Every depressing agent contributes to establish the scorbutic condition. No wonder, then, that at one period a vexatious confinement with no probable limits, and the most harassing disappointments, hope almost chased away by despair, provisions at times scanty, and a deficiency of all comfortable clothing, should have rendered the constitutions of a great part of our little crew obnoxious to this northern enemy. There were times when the spirits of the crew, like our thermometers, were below zero; and such a condition, conjointly with the causes above mentioned, not only introduced some severe cases, but likewise in a degree baffled our efforts at a cure. The means of prevention were rigidly enforced, and the importance of exercise, by walking, and occasionally dancing, was never lost sight of. Humidity was carefully watched as a known enemy; and to the various ingenious contrivances of former expeditions, an original and successful invention for condensing vapour was superadded. Regular nutritious diet, and plenty of it, should be the rule in serving out the provisions for a northern expedition: we may be disposed to express disgust at witnessing an Esquimaux meal, and indeed nothing can well be more revolting to an European of even ordinary refinement; but let us recollect that the common dietetic rule in the days of Augustan polity was "semper quamplurimum assumere dummodo hunc concoquat," and we must leave the savage on a par with the Roman courtier, since they have equally the same limit to the work of refection—the utter impossibility of eating more. Let it be distinctly understood, that I am not advocating gluttony, but merely recording what I believe to be a fact, that very liberal feeding is indispensable to a due generation and preservation of heat in such a climate, and therefore indispensable to the prevention of scurvy.

Seventeen of our crew, in all, were more or less sufferers from this complaint: one only fell a victim to it. So long as we had a store of good lime-juice, good clothing, generous diet, and a favourable condition of cheerfulness, it was not difficult to arrest or control the slighter cases which appeared; but when, in the winter of 1832, and spring of 1833, after deserting the ship, the men had to contend with depression of mind, and a scanty diet (a diet which would have suited a Pythagorean better than a sailor, for we had scarcely any animal food, while our clothing had become almost unserviceable), the development of severe scurvy at once served to heighten our misery, and to show how poor a defence a vegetable regimen (chiefly farinaceous) is, when the causes above named are conjointly exerting their depressing influence.

*Q 2

Here again I may note, that those who were slightly affected at the time they left the ship, were so far benefited by the daily exercise of walking from Victoria harbour to Fury beach, a distance of between two and three hundred miles, that on their arrival at the latter place every man had undergone a spontaneous cure. But it was during our stay at the Fury's stores that the worst form of the disease appeared.

Mr. Chimham Thomas was one of those who had been scorbutic on leaving the ship, and also at various times for two years before. Like several others, he had experienced a spontaneous cure during the journey to the stores, and from July, 1832, to November of the same year, had remained free from the disease; but, under the causes above referred to, his symptoms claimed my notice. On the 12th of November, he was so seriously ill, that with a paucity of all means of controlling the disease, I from the first had apprehensions of the result. There was, indeed, lime-juice found among the Fury's provisions, but seven years had sufficed to render it inert. Neither had I much to expect from exercise; for although it were easy from the commencement to place a sentinel over such a patient on board a man-of-war, admonition was all that in our situation could be had recourse to. We had indeed plenty of good flour, carrots, parsnips, vegetable soup, peas, &c.; but it was impossible to get the men to persist in such food, neither, under the complication of such depressing causes, can it be relied on with any certainty as an antidote. After struggling with the usual appalling symptoms for three months, debilitated by recurrent hæmorrhage from the nose, and his life prolonged by friction, and such excitants as our limited means allowed, a miserable death closed an existence still more miserable. Another case, previously recited (John Wood), promised to be equally severe; but, as it did not occur until March of 1833, he had all the benefit of the warm season, and of a change of diet, which our shooting parties afforded us in the summer months, so that by July he was out of danger.

The other fifteen cases were of various extent, and all did well: and I may here notice, that in all, a disposition to constipation rather than to diarrhœa characterized the disease. It might be supposed that, as scurvy is as familiar to the natives as the snow by which they are surrounded, some new remedy, either external or internal, might have been learned from them. With the direct causes of the complaint they were as conversant as the most learned of us: they say it follows a want of provisions, and they know well that good living and active exercise are indispensable to the cure. Their sole internal medicine is train oil. This is, in fact, their panacea; and, if it fail, the conjurer is their only refuge.

All northern expeditions have furnished cases of frostbite, or, as we call the milder affections in our own temperate region, chilblains, for they differ only in degree. With due care, these accidents ought not to occur, but to be at all times on our guard is almost impossible. Security is mortals' chiefest enemy, and a long immunity from suffering renders us negligent of danger. In all, we had about a dozen cases. That of George Taylor, one of the mates, demands distinct observation. This poor fellow had gone out with a travelling party, and was at the time about forty miles from the ship. In the morning, he had put on a wet stocking; when on his journey, he felt his foot cold and benumbed, but imprudently persisted in walking without noticing it. In the evening, when ordered by Captain James Ross to put on the usual night-stockings, he discovered that the whole of his foot was frostbitten up to above the ankle. I did not see the case till his return, three days afterwards; Captain James Ross had judiciously ordered the limb to be rubbed with snow, and to be immersed in ice-cold water. On examination I found the foot much swollen, painful, and in a state of incipient gangrene: anodyne poultices were applied, but it soon became necessary to amputate, a measure which the man urged me to delay till Sir John Ross's return, and which I at length performed with a favourable result. The other cases were of minor importance, and all did well.

If the preservation of a uniform temperature by external means be of the highest importance, it must be admitted that the due and vigorous generation of caloric by a proper selection of food is not less so. The natural food of this climate seems well adapted to the purpose. Every one knows that solar caloric, caloric by combustion, and that generated by animal life, are the three chief sources by which our temperature is sustained. Now, it seems but reasonable that in a region where our supply from the two first is so exceedingly limited, the more active evolution from the last source should compensate for the deficiency. It is not so difficult, though certainly far from easy, to explain the laws of heat when exerted on inanimate matter, so as to produce the known vacillations of atmospheric temperature. But to explain these laws as influencing, and influenced by, the laws of vitality—in other words, to show how the affinities of matter are antagonized by the power of vitality (or that we may not lead our readers to suppose there is any want of harmony in the code of laws by which Divine Providence at once governs the animate and inanimate, we will not say antagonized, but nicely balanced), this indeed has long puzzled, and will still puzzle, philosophers the most acute. There are, however, some facts upon which we can reason with interest and advantage to future navigators; and we have a theory fairly grounded on those facts, which has now withstood the test of nearly half a century, and which has been indeed modified by the careful process of induction from experiments,* but which has never been altogether refuted. To this I deem it my indispensable duty to direct the attention of any of my medical brethren, who may hereafter chance to visit these regions; for what is notoriously said of air in all parts of the world, may here also be said of heat, "we must have it or we die."

To the physiologist, and the general philosopher, my remarks, perhaps, appear commonplace, and certainly not original, but let him bear in mind that they are recorded only as a means of directing my successors to the importance of this subject, and to the necessity of adapting the *victûs ratio* accordingly. To proceed then, there are three modes by which heat is probably generated within the body—by the chemical decomposition which takes place in respiration, by the influence of the brain and nervous system, in some degree perhaps analogous to its development by galvanic influence, and by the process of digestion and nutrition.

If it be acknowledged that combustion goes on more rapidly in cold weather, and that this is wisely pre-ordained, the same remark applies to respiration, in which the imaginative poet and the cold philosopher alike recognise the resemblance. The heat generated will partly depend on the rapidity of the union of the impurities of the blood and the consequent liberation of caloric.

But it will partly depend on the quantity of carbon and hydrogen contained, and taken in with the food. On this ground alone, I expect the patience of my readers; for it will follow, if this be admitted, that such provisions should be selected for these expeditions as may have been found to contain these elements in the largest possible

* *Vide* Crawford's Experiments, Spalding on the Diving Bell, and the more recent experiments of Brodie, Phillip, and Le Gallois.

excess, loosely combined, and in the most favourable state for elimination. We all know that articles of an opposite chemical constitution lower the temperature, such as nitre, acids, mineral and vegetable, and hence the failure of lime juice as an anti-scorbutic, unless aided by nutritious food. On reference to the food destined by nature for the support of the Esquimaux, we find it almost exclusively hydro-carbonaceous, oil, blubber, fish, and flesh, the two latter of which cannot be too fat for them. Here we see a strong analogy between their process of nutrition and that of combustion; nearly the same materials, the same play of affinities, the same results, the same change of latent into sensible caloric. That persons of a weakly digestion have no great conservative power with regard to temperature, is a matter beyond doubt; and the converse seems equally manifest. It is here we have to regard the felicity of an Esquimaux-constitution, for whatsoever improvement our appetites underwent among them, their inherent digestive powers exceeded ours out of all reasonable proportion.

If I am rightly understood, my readers must see that I contend that the gross diet of northern tribes is not a matter of chance, but in harmony with the slow but constant changes which are continually going on around them; and intended to enable them to resist cold, and to vigorously generate heat. Thus, as we witnessed, the mother was enabled safely to expose her naked infant, but a few days born, to an atmosphere of seventy-five degrees below our freezing point for several minutes; the heat being rapidly generated by the one, and as tenaciously retained by the other, for the child during this time was feeding at the breast. The influence of the nervous system in evolving heat is now generally admitted; its elimination in the process of digestion and nutrition, although not less certain, is still more difficult of explanation.

On a review of the journal of all the cases which came under my care, I can scarcely find room, in the limited space allowed me here, to do more than merely state that pneumonia, colds, simple fevers, and some cases of gastric disease, constituted the chief part of them. Duly considering the various difficulties and privations suffered by the crew, our mortality of three individuals will not be deemed either numerous or extraordinary.

CAPTAIN BACK.

Before this sheet was put to the press, this intrepid and persevering officer arrived in London. It will be recollected, that in the spring of 1833, he volunteered his services in the most praiseworthy and disinterested manner to search for me and my companions, who had then been absent nearly four years. Immediately after our providential return, despatches were sent to him, which he received in May, 1834; and at the same time, directions to continue his survey of Great Slave river, the very existence of which was doubtful, principally with the view of uniting the coast between Cape Turnagain and Commander Ross's furthest beacon. The result of this enterprise has proved that the line of coast to the southward of the Isthmus of Boothia had not been completely examined, and that the information received by Commander Ross from the Esquimaux, making into a bay the land between the isthmus and Matty island, was incorreet; and thus opening a new field for conjecture; but, although it is very probable that the land to the westward of that inlet is an island, I am not of opinion that the western sea joins with Prince Regent's inlet. No one will deny that Captain Back, whose zeal, intelligence, and perseverance, has done so much, will be the fittest person to finish the work he has begun; and I have learnt with peculiar pleasure, that his Majesty, our august sovereign, having dispensed with the term of servitude established by the regulations of the navy to qualify him for the next step, has promoted him to the rank of Captain, as a reward (the most honourable) for his eminent services, and which will render it unnecessary for him to serve on board a ship, before he takes the command of another land expedition, which I hope he will soon undertake by order of government.

I cannot conclude without offering my grateful thanks, to the corporations of London, Hull, the Trinity of Hull, Liverpool, Bristol, and Wicklow, who have each conferred their freedom upon me, as also to the sovereigns of Russia, Prussia, Sweden, Denmark, France, Belgium, and above four thousand individuals, who have presented me with splendid and flattering testimonials of the sense they have entertained of my humble endeavours in the cause of science, but more especially for the kind interest which has been so universally felt for me and my companions.

BIOGRAPHY

OF

THE VICTORY'S CREW.

BIOGRAPHY

OF

THE VICTORY'S CREW.

This short Biographical Sketch of the Men, composing the Crew of the Victory, may not be found uninteresting to my Readers.

MR. THOMAS BLANKY, First Mate.

Mr. Blanky was born at Whitby, in the year 1800; is five feet seven inches high, stout made, has a fair complexion, with light hair: went to sea at eleven years of age, and served an apprenticeship of six years in a collier, between Shields and London, on board two vessels, called the Liberty and the Property, after which he was one year in the coasting trade, and two years in the Greenland fishery, on board the Volunteer, of Whitby, where he filled the situation of line manager. He was twelve months in the Swan, revenue cutter, from which he went second mate of the Latona, for one voyage in the timber trade: after making a voyage as second mate of the Lord Wellington to Dantzic, he went two voyages first mate of a collier. In the year 1824 he volunteered to serve on board his Majesty's discovery ship, the Griper, Captain Lyon, and was on board her on that disastrous voyage to Cumberland strait. On her return he entered on board the Navigator, as second mate, and made a voyage to Alexandria; and then as first mate of the Sprightly, to Riga, and two voyages in the coal trade. In 1827 Sir E. Parry's attempt to reach the North Pole was undertaken, and he volunteered on board the Hecla as a leading man; but this attempt being also unsuccessful, he returned to the merchant service, making a voyage to Quebec, and another to St.

*R 2

Petersburg, as first mate of the Almira; after which he joined an uncle as mate, who was master and owner of a schooner, but was wrecked soon after on Flamborough Head. When he joined the Victory as first mate, he had been eighteen years at sea, and had become an excellent seaman, of which he gave several remarkable proofs. I may mention that on the morning of the 12th of August, when his presence of mind and decision saved the ship from being thrown into the breakers of a heavy pack of ice. His education having been neglected in his youth, he attended very diligently to instructions given him on the voyage, and became an excellent navigator. Having been before a shipmate of Commander Ross, he naturally attached himself to him, and from whom he received much instruction. Although he was the spokesman on most of the occasions of discontent, particularly on the march from Victoria harbour to Fury beach, I do not blame him so much as those at whose instigation he committed the act of insubordination, and I had no hesitation in giving him my strongest recommendation to A. Chapman, Esq., M.P., who appointed him mate of one of his ships, which led to his obtaining the command of a merchant ship, and which all along seemed to be the sole object of his ambition.

MR. THOMAS ABERNETHY, Second Mate.

Mr. Abernethy was born at Peterhead, in Scotland, in the year 1802, and was nearly six feet high, straight, and well made; had a florid complexion, dark eyes and hair, an aquiline nose, and was decidedly the best-looking man in the ship. He went to sea at the early age of ten, and served an apprenticeship of four years in the Friends, of Peterhead, in which he went one voyage to the West Indies, and two to Greenland: afterwards he went three voyages to Davis's straits, in the Hannibal; and after which he entered and continued in the coasting, Oporto, and American trade. In 1824 he joined the Fury, Captain Hoppner, and was wrecked in Prince Regent's inlet, sharing the hardships of that unfortunate voyage. After making a voyage in a merchant ship, he volunteered his services in the Polar Expedition of 1827, and was one of the most meritorious of Captain Sir Edward Parry's crew: for this, after serving the necessary time on board a ship of the line, he was promoted to the Blossom sloop of war, as gunner, and married the daughter of Mr. Fiddis, the carpenter who was with me and Sir E. Parry on all the previous voyages to the Arctic Regions. When he volunteered with me in the Victory, he had been seventeen years at sea, and was in my opinion the most steady and active, as well as the most powerful man in the ship: he was one of those who volunteered to proceed to the westward, on the first journey with Commander Ross. I had no hesitation in recommending him strongly to the Admiralty, and he was accordingly promoted to his Majesty's ship Seringapatam, as a reward for his meritorious services.

MR. GEORGE TAYLOR, Third Mate.

Mr. Taylor was born at Lancaster in the year 1800; is five feet four inches and a half high; has blue eyes, brown hair, and a good complexion. He served his apprenticeship of five years to the trade of a ship carpenter, at Ulverston, in Lancashire, in the building-yard of James Hart, Esq. A short period after his time was served, he entered as carpenter of a merchant vessel, and served three years as second mate and carpenter of the Six Sisters, of Liverpool, employed in the timber trade, and subsequently in another ship belonging to Hull, before he joined the Victory steam-vessel, where I found him doing duty as master when I purchased her at Liverpool. He volunteered in the first instance to carry the vessel to London, where he was employed while the vessel was fitting out, and behaved himself so well that I made him third mate. In 1830, while on a journey with Commander Ross, he got his right foot frostbitten; and being in the first instance neglected, ended in the amputation of his foot, two inches above the toes, since which he was unable to do any active duty, but was nevertheless very useful. He could walk very little during the remaining three years, and he had often to be carried on the sledge on our march from Victoria harbour to Fury beach. In 1832, on leaving Batty, on the 1st of October, we attempted to carry him on the substitute for a sledge, which we made from the staves of casks; but being quite unable, we were obliged to leave him twice, and I myself returned with the empty sledge to bring him, for which he was always grateful. He was one of the most trusty I had of the crew, and was the person who detected William Light, the steward, purloining my allowance of provisions. When he returned home I provided for him a situation in the Dock-yard, but he preferred going to Liverpool, where his wife and family were, and had been supported by Sir Felix Booth in his absence.

MR. CHIMHAM THOMAS, Carpenter.

Mr. Thomas was born at Devonport in 1792; was five feet three inches high, blue eyes, and sallow complexion. His father was a caulker in his Majesty's Dock-yard at

Plymouth, and he served his apprenticeship of seven years to a shipwright with Mr. Tucker, the master builder. He was employed in His Majesty's Dock-yard until the year 1814, when he volunteered to serve on the Lakes in America, assisted in the building of the St. Lawrence of one hundred guns, and Psyche frigate, and several small vessels—shared in several actions, and returned to England in 1824, after ten years' arduous service. On his homeward passage he suffered shipwreck in the Mary, of Liverpool, on the coast of Ayrshire, losing all his hard-earned property. Having entered on board his Majesty's ship Boadicea, Commodore Sir James Brisbane, as carpenter's mate, he sailed to the East Indies, where he served two years, during which time he was chiefly at Rangoon, Arrawadda, &c., on board the flotilla opposed to the Burmese; was in several storming parties, and was the next man to Captain Dawson when he was killed attacking a large stockade. In 1826 he was appointed carpenter of the Slaney, by Admiral Gage, and from thence to the Eurydice, in which ship he returned to England. He volunteered on board the Victory in 1829, only the day before she left Woolwich, and was promptly granted leave of absence by the Lords of the Admiralty, to enable him to join. Mr. Thomas was a most excellent workman, and could produce very high testimonials of his character and conduct: but his constitution was worn out by his servitude in the East Indies and America, and could not withstand the severe trials which it was now exposed to, and he sunk under the combined effects of cold and fatigue at the age of thirty-nine years, leaving a widow (to whom he had been only a year married), and a daughter, to deplore his loss.

ALEXANDER BRUNTON, Chief Engineer.

Alexander Brunton was born at Temple, in Midlothian, is five feet four inches high, blue eyes and brown hair, sallow complexion, having much the appearance of a half-worn tradesman. He served his apprenticeship to Mr. Stevenson, the Engineer, at Edinburgh, with whom he continued some time afterwards as a workman; he set up in business for himself at Leith, as a scale-beam and edge-tool maker, but failed, and entered into several steam-vessels as engineer. Having served five years, he came to London; and after working at printing-machine making, for some time, he got into Messrs. Maudslay's manufactory, where he was five years; from thence he went to Messrs. Braithwaite's, and joined the Victory in 1829; having been one of those employed in constructing the engine. I considered him a great acquisition, especially as he had a strong recommendation from his masters; he had hard work certainly until the 21st of August, as he had almost daily to repair one part or another of the engine; but it was then given up, and his place was a complete sinecure for some time: he is an excellent but a very slow workman. At Fury beach, he was employed making tin utensils for the officers and men, and it was calculated that each tin-pot he made (taking his high wages into consideration) cost about 1*l.*! He had no less than 617*l.* 15*s.* to receive when he returned, yet he was not contented, and was one of those who sent a petition to the Admiralty to recover the value of clothes which had been furnished to him to keep him from perishing with cold. When we abandoned the ship, he was one of the most useless. Since his arrival, he has married a widow and set up a "Gin Palace," called the "Crown and Cushion," in the Borough!

ALLAN MACINNES, Second Engineer.

Alexander Macinnes was born in the year 1808, at the isle of Mull, in Argyllshire; he is five feet seven inches high, stout made, of a swarthy complexion, and marked with the smallpox. He was the son of a farmer, but served his apprenticeship, first to a baker, then to an engineer at Gloucester. He had been five years in steam-vessels before he volunteered to the Victory. His situation would also have been a sinecure, after the steam-engine was given up, but he was wanted in his calling as a baker, and was found very useful while at Fury beach, where he made excellent bread. On our return home, he went to see his friends in the North, he returned in spring last, and applied to me for a recommendation to Messrs. Maudslay and Field, which I readily gave him: but in a few days after he signed the same petition with Brunton to recover the value of clothes, &c., which had been in like manner furnished to him, although he had received 169*l.* 18*s.* 8*d.* of wages, not more than half of which he was entitled to by law, which was an act of ingratitude I did not expect, and of which he has since repented.

JAMES MARSLIN, Armourer.

James Marslin was born in 1793, at Bristol: he was five feet seven inches high, sallow complexion, and slight made; recommended to me by Mr. Blanky, the mate, who had formerly been his shipmate. Until after the ship had sailed, he managed to keep from us that he was labouring under any complaint; but we had no sooner left the land, than it was discovered that he was in a consumption, and he confessed that he had been discharged from an hospital for that complaint only a few months before:

he did scarcely any duty, and I had determined on sending him home by the first whaler I could meet with, but unfortunately for him as well as ourselves, we never met with any, and he continued gradually to sink under his complaint, until the 20th of January, when he died, at Felix harbour, and was buried on M'Diarmid's island. His wages (being claimed by two different parties) were paid into the hands of the Accountant-general of his Majesty's Navy. He seemed to be an inoffensive man, and departed this life quite prepared for the great change.

ROBERT SHREEVE, Carpenter's Mate.

Robert Shreeve was born in 1806, at Teddington, in Norfolk, is five feet eight inches and a half high, blue eyes, and complexion sallow; is the son of a farmer, and was never before at sea. After being at school in Bury St. Edmond's, he served seven years' apprenticeship to a joiner and house carpenter; he afterwards came to London, and was employed at various places for several years before he came to Mr. Braithwaite's, at New Road; and from whence he volunteered to serve in the Victory. He was a useful person, but had very indifferent health, and was not well calculated for such a service. Having had quite enough of the sea, he declined entering in his Majesty's service, and having received 166*l.* 9*s.* of wages, he set up for himself as carpenter and undertaker.

JOSEPH CURTIS, Harpooner.

Joseph Curtis was born in the year 1805, at Rotherhithe, is five feet four inches and seven-eighths high, blue eyes, dark complexion, and brown hair; his father was a tailor, and he went to sea at the early age of ten years, having served his time in the coal trade on board the Flora and Nancy of London. He entered the Davis straits' fishery in the Eliza whaler, and was also a voyage to Greenland in the Everett; but the most remarkable event of his life, is, his having been on board the Dundee whaler of London, when she was frozen up in Davis's strait, and passed the whole of the winter in the ice, during which, the ship's company had three times abandoned the ship, expecting that she would be crushed to pieces by the ice; their sufferings also from hunger and cold were great, but they returned in safety after the insurance had been paid to the owner. Since that event, he had been both in the coasting and timber trade, and came from a steam-vessel to the Victory. He was not a powerful man, and therefore not well calculated for such a service as ours, but he was an excellent seaman, and his conduct being uniformly good, I gave him a strong recommendation, and he was sent, by Admiralty order, to the Excellent, to prepare for being made a gunner in the royal navy.

JOHN PARK, Seaman.

John Park was born in 1803, at Bridport, in Dorsetshire, is five feet seven inches high, of a sallow complexion, with light blue eyes. His father, who belonged to the Dock-yard at Portsmouth, had him bound seven years apprentice to a hair-dresser, a trade he did not like, and when his time was out he went to sea in 1821, on board his Majesty's ship Euryalus, in which he served three years, when he was paid off, and immediately joined the Glasgow; on board of which he also served three years in the Mediterranean. Being asked by me, "What was the most remarkable event in his life?" he answered, that he "had shaved the Duke of Devonshire in a gale on board the Glasgow." I then asked, "Were you not on board her at the battle of Navarino?" he replied, "Oh, yes, but that was nothing." His father having lost his life in the American lakes, where he had volunteered to serve, his mother married Mr. More, gunner of the Tenodos, who was formerly in the Hecla, and who recommended him to me. He was a very active, willing young man, and useful in his calling as a barber, but too delicate in constitution for this service. Being a good seaman, and having always conducted himself well, I gave him a strong recommendation, and he was, with Curtis, sent by Admiralty order to the Excellent, to prepare for a gunner's warrant in the royal navy.

RICHARD WALL, Harpooner.

Richard Wall was born at North Shields, in the year 1803; is five feet five inches and a half high, has small features, blue eyes, and a sallow complexion, with dark hair. He served his apprenticeship of seven years to the sea in the Mary and Joseph, in the Madeira, Gibraltar, and coal trade, and after his time was served he went a voyage to Archangel; he was afterwards both in the East India and West India merchant service. His father was a sailor, and having been twenty-three years in the navy, retired as a pensioner. He is an excellent seaman, though not powerful; was one of the best men we had; and in consequence of his good conduct he obtained a good situation in his Majesty's Dock-yard at Deptford.

*s

ANTHONY BUCK, Seaman.

Anthony Buck was born in 1807, at Whitby; is five feet seven inches and three-eighths high, slenderly made, strong features, with dark eyes, complexion, and hair. He had been at sea eleven years before he joined the Victory in 1829: he was seven voyages in the whale fishery, but latterly in the Manchester to the Mediterranean. This man, when he entered, appeared to be in perfect health; but in 1831, while at the river Lindsay, he was seized with epilepsy, and it turned out that he had been at the hospital of Malta for the same complaint. His entering with us was therefore an act of folly to himself and cruelty to us, which was as unaccountable as inexcusable; he was of course a burden to us ever since he was seized with the first fit, and was very near being numbered among the dead. His father was a sailor in the merchant service, but we did not know of any other relations. He became latterly nearly blind, and he was one of those we had to carry on a sledge after leaving Fury beach. Besides his wages, he received a share of a small subscription; but under the circumstances the Admiralty did not entertain his petition for additional remuneration, and he returned to his parish.

JOHN WOOD, Seaman.

John Wood was born in 1809, at East Wemyss, in Fifeshire: he is five feet seven inches high, stout made, his complexion and hair fair, with blue eyes, and flat broad face. He served four years to the sea in the American trade, sailing from Kirkaldy; he was afterwards several voyages in the West India and Quebec trade, and joined the Victory in 1829. In July the same year he broke his leg, by jumping from the ship to the launch to secure her while towing, and we were therefore deprived of his services during the remainder of the outward voyage; and he was never a useful man. He was attacked with scurvy every winter, and was nearly perishing from the effects of that malignant disease at Fury beach, from whence we had to carry him on a sledge to Batty bay. His constitution was not calculated for such an expedition, or indeed for the sea service; and he retired, after receiving his wages, for which he had done so little, to his friends in the North.

DAVID WOOD, Seaman.

David Wood was born in 1805, in Midlothian; is only five feet two inches and a half high, has a fair and freckled complexion, with light blue eyes. His father was a sailor, who had served long in the navy, and lost his life in his Majesty's service. He served four years apprenticeship out of Kirkaldy, in the Davis straits' trade, on board the Dryad whaler, and went afterwards in the Baltic trade, having been twelve years at sea before he joined the John, where he was in the situation of *Schemer*, the person who has charge of the hold. He did not join the mutineers of that ship, but volunteered for the Victory after it took place, in a very handsome manner. His constitution was delicate, but he was nevertheless a very useful person. He was one of the two who were on the topgallant-yard when the foremast-head gave way, but got down just in time; the other was John Park, who was also saved. David Wood returned to recruit his health in his native climate, and has not since been heard of.

GEORGE BAXTER, Ordinary Seaman.

George Baxter was born in 1806, at Kinghorn, in Scotland, where his father kept a public garden; he is five feet six inches and a half high, fair complexion, blue eyes. and light hair. He had never been at sea, and entered on board the John as what is called a *green hand:* he did not join the mutineers of the John, and entered after the mutiny, for which I gave him the rating of an ordinary seaman. His constitution was rather delicate, but latterly he held out well; and on our arrival, after receiving his pay, he returned to his friends, since which he has not made to me any application for employment, which I should consider him entitled to, in consequence of his good conduct.

JAMES DIXON, Ordinary Seaman.

James Dixon was born in 1807, at Tanery, parish of Clanduff, in the county Down: he was five feet eight inches high, and the stoutest man in the ship; he had a florid complexion, with blue eyes and rather dark hair. His father was a sixty-acre farmer. and brought his son up to labour. When about eighteen he went to England as a packman, and the whole substance of the family was laid out in Irish linen, which he was to

*s 2

sell; but he did not succeed, and returned after having lost or spent all, and was at last reduced to sweeping the chimneys of steam-vessels. He entered on board the John as a *green hand*, and did not join the mutineers, but entered in the Victory after the mutiny. He was one of those whose heart failed him, and after having a severe cold, he fell into a state of despondency, from which he never recovered; having given himself up in despair he wished to die—and from the circumstances under which we were then reduced it was perhaps better that he did not remain long enough to inculcate that feeling among the rest of the crew—he died on the 14th of January, 1832: his wages have been paid into the hands of the Accountant-general, but have not yet been claimed.

BARNARD LAUGHY, Ordinary Seaman.

Barnard Laughy was born at Belfast in the year 1810; he is five feet five inches and a half high, of a sallow complexion, and a little marked with the smallpox; he has blue eyes, brown hair, and has a strong Irish accent. His father was an Irish labourer, who came to Scotland and settled on the estate of Colonel M'Douall, of Logan. He had never been at sea, except in fishing-vessels, but was recommended by Mr. Gibson, factor to Colonel M'Douall as a hard-working lad, who would do to feed the fire of the steam-boiler · his constitution was, however, not calculated for such a voyage, and he was one of those who generally gave out soonest. His conduct was, nevertheless, good; and I procured him a situation in the Coast-guard, which was very acceptable to him, as he managed to lose the whole of his money before he got the length of his father's house.

HENRY EYRE, Ship's Cook.

This man, who was fifty years of age, was an old sailor; having been formerly cook of the Griper, with Captain Hoppner, he made some money, and set up a public-house, which he called "The North Pole." His story was that he was robbed of the money he had laid by to pay his bills, and therefore failed: but he was so addicted to drinking that he could not keep sober, and the receipt of his wages was fatal to him, as he died from intoxication a few days after. He was carried to the grave by his shipmates, who subscribed for a monument to his memory.

WILLIAM LIGHT, Steward.

This man was born in 1800, at Medbury, in Devon; he was five feet seven inches high, and by his account had been fourteen years at sea. Having been in two of the former voyages to the Arctic seas, it was considered that he would be an acquisition, and he was entered as steward, in which capacity he had served before: but he turned out to be the very worst subject we had. He was always shamming, or complaining of some pain or other which incapacitated him for any thing but washing; and was therefore excused *harder* duties, and allowed to *wash* linen and *mend* stockings. He was often in the sick list, especially in spring, and was decidedly the most useless person in the ship, as well as the most discontented. This man has been circulating the most scandalous falsehoods, as to my treatment of the crew; and has been furnishing materials for a narrative of the expedition, with which the public have been attempted to be deluded, in the form of numbers, published weekly, and as he possessed no journal or record of the voyage, the greatest part of his pretended narrative is fabulous, and I suspect that the publisher is a considerable loser by the shilling trash. He attended, for some time, at the Panorama in Leicester Square, and amused his hearers with wonderful adventures, in which he always figured as the chief actor, although he was, of all the men on the expedition, the least fond of fatigue or hard work; and instead of his lie in carrying me thirty miles, it was he himself that was carried. In consequence of his unfounded calumnies against me he was dismissed by the proprietor: but as, were I to give his *previous* history, and a true and full account of his conduct during the voyage, I might be supposed to harbour vindictive feelings towards him, I desist in doing so.

It was indeed with great pain I was compelled, conscientiously, to except him from my recommendation of the crew to Government for future employment; but I hope that the good qualities of which he so loudly boasts, will be better appreciated by those with whom he may be hereafter connected.

The interest which this expedition created, will be best expressed by my stating that I could have manned my ship with officers of my own rank, while several offered also to bear a part of the expense, if I would take them on any terms; it was also productive of many curious applications, of which the following is an amusing specimen:

(Copy.)

Gosport, March 31, 1829.

HON. SIR,

Singular it will appear, but true; three nights following, a person appeared to me in a dream, and said, "Go with Captain Ross, he will be crowned with *success*." And not having the smallest thought of such things before, and reading of dreams having led to great discoveries, I put some confidence in this, and make bold to offer my services, should a man of my description be wanted. I am thirty-eight years old, good constitution, and understand all the undermentioned branches, and have no objection to make myself useful in all to meet satisfaction from my commander: cooking in all its branches; baking; butchering; preserving all kinds of poultry in cases, retaining their proper flavour, dead for any time; portable soups; broths; brawn; preserved meat of every kind; game; stuffing birds, and setting them up in their skins; preserving, &c. &c. If any of these professions would be of any utility in the voyage, I should be happy to join the expedition. I have been three voyages to the East Indies with one captain now in London, four years and a half in the flag-ship Victory—left four days ago at my own request—can produce discharge and certificates to any gentleman's satisfaction, being all the time as cook to the gentlemen on board; and should you not have ordered your portable soups, it would be a great saving to let me make them: in fact, we can always renew the stock, when we can obtain fresh meat on the voyage. Honoured Sir, you will confer an honour on me by answering these few lines.

Your most humble and obedient servant will be truly thankful,

M. L., Castle Inn, Gosport.

This application would, of course, have been treated as coming from some one who chose to amuse himself, but having met with an officer of the Victory who actually knew the man, and gave him an excellent character, and being really in search of a cook, I wrote to him that he might join the expedition under my direction, as cook, if he could produce certificates of his discharge, and if the references to his character were found to justify the account he gave of himself, but that he must lose no time. In answer, I received a note to inform me that I might depend on his joining the ship on Friday; instead of him, however, a letter came from his wife, of which the following is a copy, and which closed the transaction.

April 9, 1829.

Sir,

I have just found out that my husband has made an engagement with you to join your expedition, through a dream, *without consulting me*; I must beg to tell you, sir, that he shall not go—I will not let him have his clothes. He must be mad ever to think of leaving a comfortable home, to be frozen in with ice, or torn to pieces with bears; therefore, I am determined he shall not leave Gosport, so I hope you will not expect him.

Yours, Sir, &c., and so forth,

MARY L.

The interest which the expedition excited, was indeed intense; but it was nothing compared to the feeling which was every where roused by our arrival. Subscriptions were proposed, and it was believed that 20,000*l*. might easily have been raised, but Ministers took up the cause so liberally as to induce me to depend solely on them, by, in the first instance, paying the men their *double* wages until the ship was lost, and *full* wages up to the day of their arrival—which was far more than they were entitled to by law under any circumstances—and with this they had every reason to be contented, for in fact they were entitled to nothing after the mutiny of the John; they all agreed by acclamation to *run all risks* for the promise of double pay if they succeeded, or *nothing if not*. My nephew Commander Ross, was put on full pay for a year, and then to receive his promotion. Mr. Thom was appointed to the Canopus, and the Surgeon made full Surgeon in the navy. And, although the remuneration which I received was small, compared to what I might have had by a subscription, it was sufficient to cover my losses, and to enable me to recover some of my property which had been sacrificed in my absence; however, I had an opportunity of refuting calumnies which had been industriously circulated against me for many years, and, above all, I had the honour of receiving valuable testimonials of high approbation from almost every sovereign in Europe, as well as from our most excellent King.

The subscriptions which were begun in various parts of the kingdom, were discountenanced by me; but, although I did not receive or pocket one farthing of what may have been subscribed, I have reason to believe that the generous public have been imposed upon by those who pretended they were receiving subscriptions for the survivors of the expedition.

APPENDIX.

METEOROLOGY.

METEOROLOGY.

METEOROLOGY being considered of much importance by the scientific world, great attention was paid to this interesting department, which was undertaken by Mr. Thom, whose duty led him to be more constantly on board the ship: the excellent form of a register invented and given to me by Captain Beaufort was adopted, and the men were severally instructed to read off the degrees shown by Fahrenheit's thermometer, which was placed on the ice, in a canvas tent, at a convenient distance from the ship. Its altitude was registered every hour, and at the same time the direction and force of the wind, and the state of the weather, in a manner which will be manifest in the following table, to which directions are prefixed. The first column in the table is the day of the month; the second column is the direction of the wind; the third column is the force of the wind, denoted by figures in the following manner:

0. Calm.
1. Light air, or just sufficient to give steerage way.

2. Light breeze	or that in which a man-of-war with all sail set, and clean full, would go in smooth water.	1 to 2 knots.
3. Gentle breeze		3 to 4 knots.
4. Moderate breeze		5 to 6 knots.
5. Fresh breeze	or that which a well-conditioned man of war could carry in chase full and by.	Royals.
6. Strong breeze		Single-reefed topsails, and topgallant sails.
7. Moderate gale		Double-reefed topsails.
8. Fresh gale		Triple-reefed topsails.
9. Strong gale		Close-reefed topsails, and courses.

10. A whole gale, or that which scarcely could bear the close-reefed main topsail and foresail.
11. A storm, or that which would reduce her to storm staysails.
12. A hurricane, or that which no canvas could withstand.

a 2

Fourth column denotes the state of the weather by the following letters of the alphabet:

b—Blue sky; whether clear or hazy weather.
c—Clouds; detached, passing clouds.
d—Drizzling rain—drift snow in winter.
f—Foggy. f.—Thick fog.
g—Gloomy; dark weather.
h—Hail.
l—Lightning.
m—Misty, hazy atmosphere.
o—Overcast, or whole sky covered with clouds.
p—Passing, temporary showers.
q—Squally.
r—Rain. r.—Continued rain.
s—Snow.
t—Thunder.
u—Ugly, threatening appearances.
v—Visible; clear atmosphere.
w—Wet dew.

By the combination of these letters all the ordinary phenomena of the weather may be expressed with facility. Examples: 1st, b c m signifies, "Blue sky, with passing clouds, and hazy atmosphere." 2d, g v, "Gloomy; dark weather, but distant objects visible." 3d, qq p d l tt, "Very hard squalls, with passing showers of drizzle, and accompanied with lightning, and with very heavy thunder."

N.B.—In the following tables the first column expresses the day of the month; the second the direction of the wind expressed fractionally, thus $\frac{4}{NNW}$: that is, 4 hours at NNW; the numerator expressing the number of hours, and the denominator the direction: in like manner the force of the wind, state of the weather, and temperature, are expressed; the numerator being always hours beginning after midnight.

METEOROLOGICAL OBSERVATIONS OF THE VICTORY DISCOVERY SHIP, TAKEN ON THE ICE, AND REGISTERED HOURLY.

Days of Month.	Direction of Wind.	Force of Wind.	State of Weather.	OCTOBER, 1829. Temperature in Shade.	+	−	Mean.
1	NW. S. SSE. WbN.	[illegible]	[illegible]	[illegible]	20°	17°	+19°.54
2	Northly. NW.	[illegible]	[illegible]	[illegible]	22	18	18.98
3	NW. N. NNW. NW. N.	[illegible]	[illegible]	[illegible]	21	19	17.54
4	NW. NNW. N.	[illegible]	[illegible]	[illegible]	20	14	18.21
5	NNW. N. SW. S. NNW.	[illegible]	[illegible]	[illegible]	17	15	15.88
6	NNW. NW. South.	[illegible]	[illegible]	[illegible]	20	12	17.75
7	SSW. South. SE. varble.	[illegible]	[illegible]	[illegible]	16	12	14.125
8	SE. EbN. & varble.	[illegible]	[illegible]	[illegible]	24	19	21.17
9	EbN. SbE. N. NNW.	[illegible]	[illegible]	[illegible]	22	12	17.06
10	NbW.	[illegible]	[illegible]	[illegible]	14	9	11.48
11	NWbW. NNW. NW.	[illegible]	[illegible]	[illegible]	15	10	13.33
12	NW.	[illegible]	[illegible]	[illegible]	18	11	14.93
13	West. WNW. WbS.	[illegible]	[illegible]	[illegible]	20	10	12.00
14	NW. WNW. NW.	[illegible]	[illegible]	[illegible]	22	17	18.41
15	NW.	[illegible]	[illegible]	[illegible]	18	7	14.52
16	NWly.	[illegible]	[illegible]	[illegible]	14	6	9.42
17	NW.	[illegible]	[illegible]	[illegible]	14	8	10.13
18	NW. SW. NW. WbS.	[illegible]	[illegible]	[illegible]	7	0	4.35
19	Calm. South. Calm.	[illegible]	[illegible]	[illegible]	10	½	4.25
20	Calm. NNW.	[illegible]	[illegible]	[illegible]	7	0	2.25
21	NNW. NW. NbW.	[illegible]	[illegible]	[illegible]	5	2	1.08
22	WNW. SbE. West.	[illegible]	[illegible]	[illegible]	−2	+6	−1.81
23	WbN. NW. WSW.	[illegible]	[illegible]	[illegible]	6	6	1.69
24	SW. WSW. SWbS.	[illegible]	[illegible]	[illegible]	+16½	2	+1.01
25	SSW. NW. North.	[illegible]	[illegible]	[illegible]	18	−7	6.18
26	NNW. NNE. NEbN.	[illegible]	[illegible]	[illegible]	−2	6	−3.54
27	NWbN. WNW.	[illegible]	[illegible]	[illegible]	1	11	4.875
28	W, WNW. SWbS. N. NNE.	[illegible]	[illegible]	[illegible]	7	13½	11.07
29	NNE. NWbN. NW. NNW.	[illegible]	[illegible]	[illegible]	+4	5	+0.46
30	C. W. S. ESE. NW. SW.	[illegible]	[illegible]	[illegible]	3	12	−2.68
31	WNW. SW. WNW. W. SW.	[illegible]	[illegible]	[illegible]	−8	16½	14.17

VARIATION.
N. 150, NbW. 99, NNW. 111, NWbN. 120, NW. 682, NWbW. 20, WNW. 73, WbN. 31. — North Westerly 454
W. 68, WbS. 46, WSW. 46, SWbW. 0, SW. 112, SWbS. 54, SSW. 27, SbW. 0. — South Westerly 116
S. 41, SbE. 30, SSE. 0, SEbE. 0, SE. 18, SEbS. 0, ESE. 20, EbS. 0. — South Easterly 63
E. 0, EbN. 117, ENE. 0, NEbE. 0, NE. 0, NEbN. 12, NNE. 77, NbE. 0. — North Easterly 60

Total. 699 hours. 45 do. calm. 744 — 31 days.

	+	−	Mean
Highest, lowest, and mean temperature	+24	16½	7.94+
Total force of the Wind			1976

METEOROLOGICAL OBSERVATIONS OF THE VICTORY DISCOVERY SHIP, TAKEN ON THE ICE, AND REGISTERED HOURLY.

	Days of Month.	Direction of Wind.	Force of Wind.	State of Weather.	NOVEMBER, 1829. Temperature in Shade.	+	—	Mean.
⊕	1	5 North. 11 NW. 4 NNE. 4 North.	[illegible]	[illegible]	[illegible]	$\bar{2}$°	$\bar{8}$°	$\bar{5}$°
	2	1 C. 8 WSW. 6 SW. 9 WNW.	[illegible]	[illegible]	[illegible]	4½	21	10.02
☽	3	16 WNW. 8 Calm.	[illegible]	[illegible]	[illegible]	5	14	10.19
	4	4 ENE. 8 NEbE. 8 NEbN. 1 NNE.	[illegible]	[illegible]	[illegible]	0	7	3.28
	5	6 NNE. 6 N. 0 NNW. 4 NNE.	[illegible]	[illegible]	[illegible]	4	13	7.75
	6	12 NNE. 12 NbE.	[illegible]	[illegible]	[illegible]	3	5	3.77
	7	8 NbE. 9 North. 8 NNW.	[illegible]	[illegible]	[illegible]	+5	−2	+2.29
⊕	8	4 NEbN. 14 NNE. 6 SSW.	[illegible]	[illegible]	[illegible]	6	10	0.54
	9	1 SSW. 4 C. 5 S. 4 C. 8 SW.	[illegible]	[illegible]	[illegible]	−9	15	−11.90
	10	4 C. 4 Vble. Wy. 4 C. 8 S. 4 C.	[illegible]	[illegible]	[illegible]	15	23	18.58
	11	8 C. 1 NE. 8 NNW. 7 NNE.	[illegible]	[illegible]	[illegible]	8	23	18.25
	12	12 N. 4 NW. 5 NE. 3 NEbE.	[illegible]	[illegible]	[illegible]	+26	6	+7.77
	13	4 NNE. 4 C. 4 ENE. 2 SE. 5 C. 5 ESE.	[illegible]	[illegible]	[illegible]	26	+5	15.60
	14	12 NE. 4 NEbE. 8 NEbN.	[illegible]	[illegible]	[illegible]	10	4	5.92
⊕	15	6 Calm. 4 NE. 14 NbN.	[illegible]	[illegible]	[illegible]	6	1½	3.00
	16	24 NNE.	[illegible]	[illegible]	[illegible]	7½	−1	2.56
☾	17	17 NEbN. 7 NEbE.	[illegible]	[illegible]	[illegible]	8	4	3.17
	18	4 NNE. 20 NE.	[illegible]	[illegible]	[illegible]	7	3	1.10
	19	24 NEbN.	[illegible]	[illegible]	[illegible]	7	−0	+4.10
	20	16 NEbN. 8 NNE.	[illegible]	[illegible]	[illegible]	9	3	6.25
	21	4 NEbN. 8 North. 12 NNE.	[illegible]	[illegible]	[illegible]	9	−1	5.83
⊕	22	5 NNE. 19 Calm.	[illegible]	[illegible]	[illegible]	−2	9	−5.18
	23	16 NNE. 8 South.	[illegible]	[illegible]	[illegible]	5½	18	11.67
	24	3 C. 4 SSW. 3 C. 4 North.	[illegible]	[illegible]	[illegible]	8	18	13.67
	25	3 NEbN. 7 NE. 2 NNW. 12 NW.	[illegible]	[illegible]	[illegible]	7	13	7.19
●	26	2 NW. 4 NbW. 6 C. 6 NE. 3 SW. NW.	[illegible]	[illegible]	[illegible]	5	17	12.21
	27	1 North. 11 Calm. 12 South.	[illegible]	[illegible]	[illegible]	18	27	22.58
	28	4 SW. 8 NNE. 8 SW. 4 South.	[illegible]	[illegible]	[illegible]	22	26	24.25
⊕	29	7 Calm. 11 North. 6 Calm.	[illegible]	[illegible]	[illegible]	21	31½	23.06
	30	4 North. 8 NW. 11 NEbN. 1 S.	[illegible]	[illegible]	[illegible]	33	37	35.04

ABSTRACT.

63 N.302.	0 NbW.4.	24 NNW.90.	0 NWbN.0.	41 NW.142.	0 NWbW.0.	22 WNW.49.	0 WbN.0.
4 W.16.	0 WbS.0.	8 WSW.10.	0 SWbW.0.	32 SW.45.	0 SWbS.0.	13 SSW.13.	0 SbW.0.
38 S.34.	0 SbE.0.	0 SSE.0.	0 SEbS.0.	2 SE.4.	0 SEbE.0.	0 ESE.26.	0 EbS.0.
0 E.0.	0 EbN.0.	4 ENE.4.	22 NEbE.43.	54 NE.136.	147 NEbN.227.	134 NNE.309.	20 NbE.125.

North Westerly = 152
South Westerly = 57
South Easterly = 49
North Easterly = 341

Total. 599 hours. 121 do. calm. 720 = 30 days.

Highest, Lowest, and Mean Temperature + 26 − 37 − 3.58

Total force of the Wind 1649

METEOROLOGICAL OBSERVATIONS OF THE VICTORY DISCOVERY SHIP, TAKEN ON THE ICE, AND REGISTERED HOURLY.

Days of Month.	Direction of Wind.	Force of Wind.	State of Weather.	DECEMBER, 1829. Temperature in Shade.	+	−	Mean.
1	NbE. E. SW. North.	[illegible]	[illegible]	[illegible]	31°	35°	32.09
2	Calm. East.	[illegible]	[illegible]	[illegible]	26	34	30.90
3	Calm. East.	[illegible]	[illegible]	[illegible]	10	24	19.14
4	NNW. C. NW. C. SSE.	[illegible]	[illegible]	[illegible]	10	17	15.54
5	NE. NW. SSW.	[illegible]	[illegible]	[illegible]	8	19½	16.46
6	West. SSW. South.	[illegible]	[illegible]	[illegible]	14	18	16.17
7	SW. Calm.	[illegible]	[illegible]	[illegible]	12	23	17.13
8	Calm. NNE. NW.	[illegible]	[illegible]	[illegible]	16	24	18.77
9	ESE. W. Varble. S. Calm.	[illegible]	[illegible]	[illegible]	17	26	20.79
10	South. SW. West.	[illegible]	[illegible]	[illegible]	28	33	30.12
11	S. C. N. SSW.	[illegible]	[illegible]	[illegible]	16	27	20.01
12	SSW. C. NNE. NNW.	[illegible]	[illegible]	[illegible]	23	25½	23.69
13	NNW. NW.	[illegible]	[illegible]	[illegible]	20	26	22.58
14	WNW. NNW. NW. North.	[illegible]	[illegible]	[illegible]	16½	20	18.02
15	NW. North.	[illegible]	[illegible]	[illegible]	18	27	21.63
16	NNW. NW. West.	[illegible]	[illegible]	[illegible]	25½	31	28.65
17	West. WNW. S. varble. E. SSW. S. C.	[illegible]	[illegible]	[illegible]	31	36	34.13
18	Calm. E. NNE. N. NE.	[illegible]	[illegible]	[illegible]	19½	33	24.83
19	NE. NbE.	[illegible]	[illegible]	[illegible]	17	22	20.08
20	NNW. N. NWbN. N. NE. NW.	[illegible]	[illegible]	[illegible]	21	22	20.71
21	SW. NNE. Calm.	[illegible]	[illegible]	[illegible]	16	20	17.02
22	C. Varble. Sly. S. Calm.	[illegible]	[illegible]	[illegible]	21	27	25.73
23	S. SSE. SW. SSW. Calm.	[illegible]	[illegible]	[illegible]	16	20	18.21
24	C. W. C. N. NbE.	[illegible]	[illegible]	[illegible]	16	21½	18.71
25	N. NNE. N. C. S. NNE.	[illegible]	[illegible]	[illegible]	16	22	18.96
26	Calm. Varble.	[illegible]	[illegible]	[illegible]	22	29½	21.90
27	Varble. Sly. C. SSW. SW. W. SW. SSW. S.	[illegible]	[illegible]	[illegible]	29	32	30.13
28	SSW. Calm. N. WNW.	[illegible]	[illegible]	[illegible]	25	31	30.51
29	C. W. C. W. C.	[illegible]	[illegible]	[illegible]	30	37	31.13
30	C. NW. NW. North.	[illegible]	[illegible]	[illegible]	27	37	29.15
31	North. NW.	[illegible]	[illegible]	[illegible]	15	25	19.25

ABSTRACT. [illegible]

North Westerly —229
South Westerly —131
South Easterly — 95
North Easterly —121

Total. 579 hours. 165 do. calm. 744 ÷ 31 days.

Highest, Lowest, and Mean Temperature – 8 – 37 – 23.08

Total force of the Wind 1614

METEOROLOGICAL OBSERVATIONS OF THE VICTORY DISCOVERY SHIP, TAKEN ON THE ICE, AND REGISTERED HOURLY.

	Days of Month.	Direction of Wind.	Force of Wind.	State of Weather.	JANUARY, 1830. Temperature in Shade.	Max.	Min.	Mean.
	1	NNW. N. SW. SbW. S. SSW. W.	[illegible]	b. g. b.	[illegible]	13½°	23°	19°.56
	2	SSE. SW. SSW.	[illegible]	b. g. o. cg. b.	[illegible]	17	20	18.40
⊕	3	SbW. SSW. SbW.	[illegible]	g. o. g. o. os.	[illegible]	11	19	14.95
	4	SSW. Vble. Wy. SbW.	[illegible]	cs. g. o. os. o.	[illegible]	7	13	9.38
	5	Calm. Vble. Wy. Calm. NNE.	[illegible]	o. os. o. b. g.	[illegible]	5	11½	7.64
	6	Vble. Sy. NNW. Calm. NNW.	[illegible]	b. g. b. c.	[illegible]	8	16	13.25
	7	NbW. S. E. Calm.	[illegible]	c. g. b. c.	[illegible]	8	13	9.17
⊕	8	NbW. Calm. SW.	[illegible]	b. g. gr. b.	[illegible]	9½	27	20.29
	9	SW. Vble. Sy. SW. S.	[illegible]	b. g. b.	[illegible]	27	38	32.18
⊕	10	SSE. Calm. SSW. NW.	[illegible]	b.	[illegible]	34	39½	37.27
	11	Calm. SW. NNW. SW.	[illegible]	b.	[illegible]	30½	37	34.00
	12	SW. SSW. W. NW.	[illegible]	b. o. b. g.	[illegible]	32	37	34.07
	13	NW. NNW.	[illegible]	o. g. b. o. b.	[illegible]	27	35	32.25
	14	NNW. N. NbW.	[illegible]	o. b. g. o. g. b.	[illegible]	36	42	38.56
	15	NNW.	[illegible]	g. m. g. o. g. b.	[illegible]	39	41	40.4
	16	NNW.	[illegible]	g. b.	[illegible]	37	44	39.88
⊕	17	Calm. N. NNE. N.	[illegible]	b. os.	[illegible]	31	45	39.40
	18	NbW.	[illegible]	s. d.	[illegible]	9	32	17.96
	19	North.	[illegible]	s. d. b. g. b.	[illegible]	9	25	17.92
	20	North. NW. SW.	[illegible]	b. g. b.	[illegible]	26	40	33.79
	21	N. SW. W. NW. Calm.	[illegible]	b.	[illegible]	38	42	40.06
	22	Calm. Vble. Wy. E. Calm.	[illegible]	b.	[illegible]	34	40	38.11
	23	Calm. NW. SW. Vble. Sy. Calm.	[illegible]	b.	[illegible]	35	40	38.13
⊕	24	SW. Calm. South. NNE.	[illegible]	b. gs. g. o. cs. o.	[illegible]	21	35	29.8
	25	NNE. SW. SE. NNE.	[illegible]	os. o. b.	[illegible]	21½	29	25.81
	26	NNE. SSW.	[illegible]	b. g. b.	[illegible]	28	36	31.96
	27	SSW. North.	[illegible]	b.	[illegible]	26½	33½	28.58
	28	North.	[illegible]	b. gs. g. b.	[illegible]	15	29	20.77
	29	SW. NbW. S. SW.	[illegible]	b. gb. b.	[illegible]	17	28	21.31
	30	SSW. Calm. S. Calm.	[illegible]	b.	[illegible]	27½	34	30.42
+	31	Calm. N. E. ENE.	[illegible]	b. g. b. o. os.	[illegible]	27	34½	29.77

ABSTRACT.

N. 396.	NbW. 275.	NNW. 197.	NWbN. 0.	NW. 62.	NWbW. 0.	WNW. 0.	WbN. 0.	North Westerly — 325	Total. 657 hours. 87 do. calm. 744 — 31 days.
W. 57.	WbS. 0.	WSW. 0.	SWbW. 0.	SW. 251.	SWbS. 0.	SSW. 129.	SbW. 67.	South Westerly — 230	
S. 79.	SbE. 0.	SSE. 29.	SEbS. 0.	SE. 5.	SEbE. 0.	ESE. 0.	EbS. 0.	South Easterly — 62	
E. 5.	EbN. 0.	ENE. 10.	NEbE. 0.	NE. 0.	NEbN. 0.	NNE. 71.	NbE. 0.	North Easterly — 40	

Highest, Lowest, and Mean Temperature — 5 — 45 33.13

Total force of the Wind 1656

METEOROLOGICAL OBSERVATIONS OF THE VICTORY DISCOVERY SHIP, TAKEN ON THE ICE, AND REGISTERED HOURLY.

Days of Month.	Direction of Wind.	Force of Wind.	State of Weather.	FEBRUARY, 1830. Temperature in Shade.	+	−	Mean.
1	ENE. Calm. KNE. Vble.	[illegible]	[illegible]	[illegible]	25°	27°	25°.88
2	Calm. South. Variable Wly. S. Calm.	[illegible]	[illegible]	[illegible]	25	38	32.5
3	Calm. Southly. Calm.	[illegible]	[illegible]	[illegible]	38	43	39.88
4	Calm. Variable Ely. C. Ebs. Calm.	[illegible]	[illegible]	[illegible]	38	44	42.19
5	Calm. NE. Calm. N. Calm.	[illegible]	[illegible]	[illegible]	40	44	42.71
6	Calm. Vble E. Vble Wly. NE. Calm.	[illegible]	[illegible]	[illegible]	31½	43½	40.83
7	Calm. SE. SW. SSW. South.	[illegible]	[illegible]	[illegible]	39½	47	42.85
8	SW. NNE. S. SW. S.	[illegible]	[illegible]	[illegible]	32	44½	40.48
9	South. SW. South.	[illegible]	[illegible]	[illegible]	43	47	45.1
10	SSW. S. NE. SW. South.	[illegible]	[illegible]	[illegible]	45	47	46.42
11	Calm. NNE. SW. NE. Calm.	[illegible]	[illegible]	[illegible]	41	47	46.44
12	C. SW. WSW. Vble Wly. C. N. ENE.	[illegible]	[illegible]	[illegible]	40	47	44.58
13	North. NE. South.	[illegible]	[illegible]	[illegible]	39	45½	43.23
14	S. N. Calm. S. SW.	[illegible]	[illegible]	[illegible]	35	43½	40.84
15	SW. SSW.	[illegible]	[illegible]	[illegible]	39	45	43.23
16	Calm. NNE. North.	[illegible]	[illegible]	[illegible]	30	45	39.22
17	NEbN.	[illegible]	[illegible]	[illegible]	16½	27	20.08
18	NEbN.	[illegible]	[illegible]	[illegible]	9	18½	13.44
19	North.	[illegible]	[illegible]	[illegible]	7½	17½	12.60
20	North. NE. North.	[illegible]	[illegible]	[illegible]	5	12	8.98
21	North. NNE. Calm.	[illegible]	[illegible]	[illegible]	0	17	6.13
22	S. Calm. S. SE.	[illegible]	[illegible]	[illegible]	12	21½	17.77
23	Calm. South.	[illegible]	[illegible]	[illegible]	+1½	15	5.63
24	S. Calm. S. Calm.	[illegible]	[illegible]	[illegible]	−3	11½	5.25
25	North. NNE.	[illegible]	[illegible]	[illegible]	6½	17	14.31
26	NNE. North.	[illegible]	[illegible]	[illegible]	15	22½	19.42
27	NNE. Calm. NE. North.	[illegible]	[illegible]	[illegible]	18	32	25.42
28	C. NNW. NW. W. SSW.	[illegible]	[illegible]	[illegible]	22	38½	31.98

ABSTRACT.

N.247. NbW.0. NNW.5. NWbN.0. NW.9. NWbW.0. WNW.0. WbN.0. North Westerly 101
W.41. WbS.0. WSW.15. SWbW.0. SW.151. SWbS.0. SSW.98. SbW.0. South Westerly 119
S.129. SbE.0. SSE.0. SEbS.0. SE.6. SEbE.0. ESE.0. EbS.2. South Easterly 102
E.3. EbN.0. ENE.10. NEbE.0. NE.11. NEbN.145. NNE.155. NbE.0. North Easterly 169

Total. 491 hours. 12 do. wind variable. 169 do. calm. 672 28 days.

Highest, Lowest, and Mean Temperature + 1½ − 47 − 29.9

Total force of the Wind . . 1058

METEOROLOGICAL OBSERVATIONS OF THE VICTORY DISCOVERY SHIP, TAKEN ON THE ICE, AND REGISTERED HOURLY.

Days of Month.	Direction of Wind.	Force of Wind.	State of Weather.	MARCH, 1830. Temperature in Shade.	+	−	Mean.
1	[illegible]	[illegible]	[illegible]	[illegible]	−29°	−39°	−34°.17
2	[illegible]	[illegible]	[illegible]	[illegible]	25	40	34.15
3	[illegible]	[illegible]	[illegible]	[illegible]	26	41½	34.75
4	[illegible]	[illegible]	[illegible]	[illegible]	21	37	31.69
5	[illegible]	[illegible]	[illegible]	[illegible]	24	39	34.00
6	[illegible]	[illegible]	[illegible]	[illegible]	19½	40	28.56
7	[illegible]	[illegible]	[illegible]	[illegible]	14	29	22.27
8	[illegible]	[illegible]	[illegible]	[illegible]	17	29	21.19
9	[illegible]	[illegible]	[illegible]	[illegible]	13	29	24.10
10	[illegible]	[illegible]	[illegible]	[illegible]	13½	32	25.17
11	[illegible]	[illegible]	[illegible]	[illegible]	15	34	27.42
12	[illegible]	[illegible]	[illegible]	[illegible]	19	37	29.23
13	[illegible]	[illegible]	[illegible]	[illegible]	19	39	29.81
14	[illegible]	[illegible]	[illegible]	[illegible]	22	42	33.00
15	[illegible]	[illegible]	[illegible]	[illegible]	16	39	29.90
16	[illegible]	[illegible]	[illegible]	[illegible]	21	40	33.5
17	[illegible]	[illegible]	[illegible]	[illegible]	21	42	34.25
18	[illegible]	[illegible]	[illegible]	[illegible]	16½	41	32.08
19	[illegible]	[illegible]	[illegible]	[illegible]	19	39	28.77
20	[illegible]	[illegible]	[illegible]	[illegible]	13	38	24.29
21	[illegible]	[illegible]	[illegible]	[illegible]	14	29	22.81
22	[illegible]	[illegible]	[illegible]	[illegible]	5	29	18.06
23	[illegible]	[illegible]	[illegible]	[illegible]	+1	21	8.90
24	[illegible]	[illegible]	[illegible]	[illegible]	15	12	+1.79
25	[illegible]	[illegible]	[illegible]	[illegible]	5	17	−4.23
26	[illegible]	[illegible]	[illegible]	[illegible]	2	23	13.06
27	[illegible]	[illegible]	[illegible]	[illegible]	−4	25	13.92
28	[illegible]	[illegible]	[illegible]	[illegible]	+7	13	1.7
29	[illegible]	[illegible]	[illegible]	[illegible]	15	9	0.38
30	[illegible]	[illegible]	[illegible]	[illegible]	16½	1	+7.48
31	[illegible]	[illegible]	[illegible]	[illegible]	20	+4	9.69

ABSTRACT.

N.209.	NbW.8.	NNW.60.	NWbN.0.	NW.50.	NWbW.0.	WNW.11.	WbN.0.	North Westerly = 212
W.83.	WbS.9.	WSW.23.	SWbW.0.	SW.87.	SWbS.4.	SSW.17.	SbW.8.	South Westerly = 162
S.34.	SbE.0.	SSE.1.	SEbS.0.	SE.4.	SEbE.0.	ESE.0.	EbS.0.	South Easterly = 31
E.14.	EbN.0.	ENE.4.	NEbE.2.	NE.97.	NEbN.3.	NNE.99.	NbE.0.	North Easterly = 105

Total. 510 hours. 234 do. calm.

744 — 31 days.

Highest, Lowest, and Mean Temperature +20 −42 −20.93

Total force of the Wind . . . 862

METEOROLOGICAL OBSERVATIONS OF THE VICTORY DISCOVERY SHIP, TAKEN ON THE ICE, AND REGISTERED HOURLY.

Days of Month.	Direction of Wind	Force of Wind.	State of Weather.	APRIL, 1830. Temperature in Shade.	+	−	Mean.
1	3 S. 1 SE. 4 SSE. 4 SSW. 4 SW. 8 WSW. 1 NW.	[illegible]	[illegible]	[illegible]	+11°	+5°	+7°.52
2	NW. NE. S. SSE. Calm.	[illegible]	[illegible]	[illegible]	22	−13½	6.02
3	South. Calm. SSW.	[illegible]	[illegible]	[illegible]	16	18	−3.67
4	SSE. C. S. SSE. S. SE. SSE.	[illegible]	[illegible]	[illegible]	5	16	8.06
5	SSE.	[illegible]	[illegible]	[illegible]	4½	7	0.31
6	SSE. SE. E. S. SSW. SW.	[illegible]	[illegible]	[illegible]	27	5	+12.29
7	SSE. Variable Ely. SE.	[illegible]	[illegible]	[illegible]	14	5	6.67
8	C. SSE. C. Variable Ely. SW. S.	[illegible]	[illegible]	[illegible]	17	5	9.13
9	S. SW. W. Variable Sly. WSW.	[illegible]	[illegible]	[illegible]	6	14	−4.04
10	SW. SbW. SW. West	[illegible]	[illegible]	[illegible]	8	17	7.04
11	West, C. SW. SW. SSE.	[illegible]	[illegible]	[illegible]	24	1	+ 9.04
12	SW. SSE. SW. SE.	[illegible]	[illegible]	[illegible]	19	+3	12.01
13	SE. SE. SSW. S. SSW. SW.	[illegible]	[illegible]	[illegible]	31	7	19.60
14	SW. WSW. North	[illegible]	[illegible]	[illegible]	14	2	7.00
15	S. SSE. C. SSE.	[illegible]	[illegible]	[illegible]	17	1	8.33
16	Calm. W. SW.	[illegible]	[illegible]	[illegible]	14	2	6.79
17	C. SSW. SE. SSE. C. S.	[illegible]	[illegible]	[illegible]	19½	0	6.69
18	C. W. SbE. SSE. S. SSE. C.	[illegible]	[illegible]	[illegible]	11	−7	2.84
19	WSW. Variable Stod. W. SE. SSW.	[illegible]	[illegible]	[illegible]	8	13	−2.75
20	SW. C. W. WSW. WSW.	[illegible]	[illegible]	[illegible]	0	17	8.96
21	W. S. SSW. W. SW.	[illegible]	[illegible]	[illegible]	−1	17	8.14
22	SSW. S. SSW.	[illegible]	[illegible]	[illegible]	9	17	12.79
23	C. SE. SSE. C. SE.	[illegible]	[illegible]	[illegible]	1	20	10.79
24	SE. SE. SW. SW. S. SSE. S.	[illegible]	[illegible]	[illegible]	0	21	10.13
25	S. SSE. S. SW. SSW.	[illegible]	[illegible]	[illegible]	−1	15	6.89
26	NbW. SSW. C. SW. SW.	[illegible]	[illegible]	[illegible]	0	15	4.18
27	SSW. SSW. SW. WSW.	[illegible]	[illegible]	[illegible]	6	8	2.23
28	SW. S. SSW. SbW. S.	[illegible]	[illegible]	[illegible]	1	13	5.10
29	SbW. SSW. SSE. SSW.	[illegible]	[illegible]	[illegible]	−2	15	7.02
30	S. SW. S. SSE. SE.	[illegible]	[illegible]	[illegible]	+8	9	−2.79

ABSTRACT.

[illegible]

North Westerly	216
South Westerly	300
South Easterly	63
North Easterly	191

Total. 670 hours. 50 do. calm. 720 = 30 days.

Highest, Lowest, and Mean Temperature + 31 − 21 + 1.365

Total force of the Wind 1780

METEOROLOGICAL OBSERVATIONS OF THE VICTORY DISCOVERY SHIP, TAKEN ON THE ICE, AND REGISTERED HOURLY.

Days of Month.	Direction of Wind.	Force of Wind.	State of Weather.	MAY, 1830. Temperature in Shade.	+	−	Mean.
1	NE. N. SSW. WNW. N. W. NbE. N.	[illegible]	b.g.c.g.b.g.o.b.g.o.	[illegible]	+18	0°	+8°.23
2	N. NNE.	[illegible]	o.c.b. g. c.	[illegible]	18	+7	13.06
3	NNW. NbW. N. NNE. NE. C.	[illegible]	c. o. g. b. e. g.	[illegible]	19	6	12.58
4	SbW. WSW. West. South.	[illegible]	g. b. g.	[illegible]	19	5	13.19
5	SW. W. SSW. W. SW. WSW. SW. WSW. W.	[illegible]	g. r. g.	[illegible]	12	2	8.29
6	W. C. WSW. W. SW. South.	[illegible]	b. g. c.	[illegible]	18	0	10.38
7	NE. SSE. SWbS. WSW. WNW.	[illegible]	g. o. os. o. g.	[illegible]	28	7	17.10
8	WNW. West.	[illegible]	q. b. q.	[illegible]	11	1	6.81
9	S. SSW. WNW. S. ESE. East.	[illegible]	b. c. b. os.	[illegible]	18	−1	8.54
10	FbN. SW. NNW.	[illegible]	os. b. c. b.	[illegible]	10	+2	6.23
11	NNW. WNW. W. N.	[illegible]	c. g. b. g. b.	[illegible]	14	0	6.44
12	C. W. NE. NNE. WNW. W. SW. C. W.	[illegible]	b. q.	[illegible]	11	−1	6.56
13	SW. S. W. ENW. NW. WbN. Vbly. S. W. WSW. W. NE. NNW. C. W.	[illegible]	b. c. b. c. b.	[illegible]	15	+1	9.56
14	W. NW. S. W. NW.	[illegible]	b.	[illegible]	15	4	10.29
15	SE. WSW. VbleSW. S. SE. S. SW. SSW.	[illegible]	b. g.	[illegible]	18	4	13.48
16	SbE. SE. E. ESE.	[illegible]	gs. os. b.	[illegible]	16	9	13.29
17	East.	[illegible]	b. g. os. b. o.	[illegible]	21	8	16.27
18	E. S. E. SNE.	[illegible]	q. os. o. q. os.	[illegible]	30	17	23.5
19	SNE.	[illegible]	os. g. o. os.	[illegible]	22	12	18.38
20	NNW. NW. N. NNE. N. SNE. N.	[illegible]	g. os. q. os. o. os. o.	[illegible]	20	12	15.90
21	NNE. N. NE. NNE. N.	[illegible]	o. c. b.	[illegible]	19	8	14.48
22	NNW. N. NNW. NNE. NW.	[illegible]	b.	[illegible]	18	8	14.71
23	NW. NNW. N. NNE. NbW.	[illegible]	b. g. b.	[illegible]	21	11	16.52
24	NbW. NNW. NNE.	[illegible]	b.	[illegible]	22	11	17.63
25	NNW. N. NNE. Calm.	[illegible]	b.	[illegible]	21	11½	17.81
26	C. S. SE. E. WNW. SW. W. SW. SE. NW. W. C.	[illegible]	b. f. q. b.	[illegible]	25	11	18.21
27	E. NE. SE. S. SW. W. NW. C. NNE. C.	[illegible]	b.	[illegible]	27	13	20.81
28	C. NE. SW. S. SW. W. NNW. SW.	[illegible]	b. f. o. b.	[illegible]	31	16	24.81
29	C. NE. W. NW. S. SSW. S. SW. C. N. C. NNE. E.	[illegible]	b.	[illegible]	34	23	29.99
30	C. SSW. C. SSW. E. S. NNE. NE. NbE.	[illegible]	b. f.	[illegible]	37	23	30.48
31	Variable Easterly.	[illegible]	f. f. f.	[illegible]	33	26	29.96

ABSTRACT.

N. 146.	NbW. 23.	NNW. 163.	NWbN. 0.	NW. 73.	NWbW. 0.	WNW. 125.	WbN. 10.	North Westerly — 223
W. 115.	WbS. 0.	WSW. 70.	SWbW. 0.	SW. 71.	SWbS. 9.	SSW. 31.	SbW. 10.	South Westerly — 142
S. 79.	SbE. 13.	SSE. 7.	SEbS. 0.	SE. 41.	SEbE. 1.	ESE. 10.	EbS. 0.	South Easterly — 109
E. 192.	EbN. 8.	ENE. 0.	NEbE. 0.	NE. 88.	NEbN. 0.	NNE. 258.	NbE. 4.	North Easterly — 235

Total. 700 hours. 44 do. calm. 744 — 31 days.

Highest, Lowest, and Mean Temperature +37 −1 +15.27

Total force of the Wind . . . 1512

METEOROLOGICAL OBSERVATIONS OF THE VICTORY DISCOVERY SHIP, TAKEN ON THE ICE, AND REGISTERED HOURLY.

	Days of Month	Direction of Wind.	Force of Wind.	State of Weather.	JUNE, 1830. Temperature in Shade.	+	−	Mean.
	1	N. C. S.	[illegible]	b. f. m. f. f.	[illegible]	+32°	+27°	+29°.48
	2	S. C. VSly. C. NNE.	[illegible]	b. m. b.	[illegible]	36	26	31.83
	3	NW. NNW. N. NNW. NNE. N.	[illegible]	b. bc. b. bc. b.	[illegible]	31	28	31.44
	4	NNW. NNE. North.	[illegible]	b. bc. b.	[illegible]	35	27½	31.85
	5	NNW. North.	[illegible]	b.	[illegible]	32	26	29.00
+	6	N. NNW. N. NNE.	[illegible]	b. c.	[illegible]	31	26	30.13
	7	NNE. S. W. NW. W. SSW.	[illegible]	g. q. og. n. bc. c. bc.	[illegible]	40	28	32.98
	8	SSW. SW. SSW. NE. SSW. Calm.	[illegible]	c. b. bc. b.	[illegible]	55	30	40.10
	9	C. NE. C. SSW. SW.	[illegible]	b.	[illegible]	46	31	38.08
	10	SSW. S. SW. SSW.	[illegible]	b.	[illegible]	49	30	38.04
	11	SW. W. SW. W. SW.	[illegible]	b. g. m. f. o. c. b. f. c.	[illegible]	42	30½	35.04
	12	WSW. SE. C. NW. SW. S. C. S.	[illegible]	f. m. o. o. cl. g. b.	[illegible]	49	32	38.66
+	13	SW. W. NW. N. NE. NNW. SSW. WNW.	[illegible]	c. os. o. b.	[illegible]	40	30	33.92
	14	WNW. W. Variable. Sly. E. NE.	[illegible]	c. os. b. c. os. g. b. qs.	[illegible]	46	28	36.08
	15	NE. NNE. N. NE. E. S. SW. W. NE. C. N.	[illegible]	os. o. g. os. g. os. os.	[illegible]	46	29	35.51
	16	NW. W. NW. N. C. SW. SE. / NE. N. NW. NNE. E. NE. NNE.	[illegible]	os. o. c. os. b. os. o. g. o. g.	[illegible]	50	31	37.92
	17	C. SW. C. NE.	[illegible]	c. o. g. r.	[illegible]	50	30½	38.38
	18	NE. ENE. N. C. NE.	[illegible]	b. g. c. b.	[illegible]	58	31	38.13
	19	NE. Calm. NNE.	[illegible]	g. m. r. f. g. c. qs. r. f. o. c.	[illegible]	48	31	35.77
+	20	N. C. E. C. SW.	[illegible]	c. g. b. o.	[illegible]	62	33	47.29
	21	NE. East. NNE.	[illegible]	b. ql. of. f. fr. f.	[illegible]	51	31	40.80
	22	NE. C. SW. C. S.	[illegible]	b. f. o. b. o. b. g. r.	[illegible]	46	35	39.90
	23	S. SW. NNE. SbW.	[illegible]	c. g. b.	[illegible]	46	33	39.63
	24	C. SbW. East. NE.	[illegible]	b. r. is. s. sr. r.	[illegible]	48	33	38.5
	25	NNE. S. SSE. SSW. W.	[illegible]	s. b. sc. b.	[illegible]	49	31	40.00
	26	W. ENE. W. C. W.	[illegible]	b. gs. b.	[illegible]	62	33	42.37
⊕	27	West.	[illegible]	b. bc. b. os. b. os. b.	[illegible]	49	33	40.54
	28	W. WSW. NNE.	[illegible]	b. os. or. b. os.	[illegible]	50	33	40.21
	29	Calm. NEbN. NNE.	[illegible]	b. c. f. b. f. b.	[illegible]	42	33	37.21
	30	NNE. NE. North.	[illegible]	c. fs. fr. fs. os. b. os. o. c.	[illegible]	47	32	37.25

ABSTRACT.

N. 131.	NbW. 0.	NNW. 125.	NWbN. 0.	NW. 25.	NWbW. 0.	WNW. 5.	WbN. 0.	North Westerly 133	Total. 649 hours. 71 do. calm. 720 — 30 days.
W. 77.	WbS. 0.	WSW. 8.	SWbW. 0.	SW. 129.	SWbS. 0.	SSW. 100.	SbW. 27.	South Westerly 210	
S. 14.	SbE. 0.	SSE. 2.	SEbS. 0.	SE. 2.	SEbE. 0.	ESE. 0.	EbS. 0.	South Easterly 42	
E. 14.	EbN. 0.	ENE. 0.	NEbE. 12.	NE. 175.	NEbN. 16.	NNE. 316.	NbE. 0.	North Easterly 261	

Highest, Lowest, and Mean Temperature +62 +26 +36.76

Total force of the Wind 1125

METEOROLOGICAL OBSERVATIONS OF THE VICTORY DISCOVERY SHIP, TAKEN ON THE ICE, AND REGISTERED HOURLY.

Days of Month.	Direction of Wind.	Force of Wind.	State of Weather.	JULY, 1830. Temperature in Shade.	+	−	Mean.
1	4/North. 11/NNW. 5/SWbW. 4/NW.	4/3. 2/4. 13/3. 3/2. 2/1.	2/b. 5/bq. 2/b. 3/bq. 5/b. 3/bc. 4/b.	+1/35°. 1/37°. 1/39°. 1/40°. 2/41°. 2/42°. 1/41°. 2/44°. 2/45°. 3/44°. 2/42°. 2/40°. 1/39°. 1/38°. 2/37°.	+45°	+35°	+40.96
2	4/NW. 2/SW. 14/Vble. Wy. 4/NNW.	2/2. 22/1.	24/b.	+3/36. 1/38. 1/42. 1/44. 1/46. 1/48. 2/46. 1/47. 2/49. 1/50. 1/51. 1/50. 1/49. 1/47. 1/45. 1/43. 1/38. 3/36.	51	36	43.5
3	8/North. 8/NNE. 8/North.	8/2. 6/1. 2/2. 5/3. 1/4. 2/5.	4/b. 2/fr. 4/b. 14/c.	+2/36. 2/32. 4/34. 2/35. 1/36. 5/37. 8/36.	37	32	35.46
4	24/North.	5/3. 1/4. 2/3. 1/4. 16/3. 2/2.	13/c. 3/b. 2/c. 6/b.	+1/37. 1/43. 1/40. 5/42. 1/43. 9/42. 1/41. 3/40. 1/38. 1/36.	43	36	40.88
5	5/North. 1/NNW. 18/North.	5/3. 1/2. 3/3. 11/2. 1/3. 4/2.	24/b.	+3/43. 1/45. 2/51. 1/48. 3/45. 1/46. 1/46½. 4/48. 1/47. 1/46. 1/47. 2/46.	51	43	46.40
6	5/NNW. 9/NNE. 6/SSW. 4/East.	9/1. 4/2. 10/1.	18/b. 2/g. 4/b.	+2/46. 2/42. 1/44. 2/46. 1/48. 2/49. 1/48. 2/53. 2/48. 2/47. 2/44. 2/40. 3/42.	53	40	45.42
7	9/NNE. 1/NE. 1/E. 1/NNE. 1/S. 1/Vble. 4/SSW. 7/C.	7/1. 4/2. 8/1. 7/0.	24/b.	+1/43. 1/44. 1/46. 2/48. 2/49. 1/50. 1/44. 1/42. 1/44. 1/45. 1/50. 4/53. 1/52. 1/51. 1/46. 1/40. 1/38. 1/34. 1/35. 1/32.	53	32	45.70
8	5/NNW. 1/C. 6/SE. 4/N. 1/NE. 1/SE. 6/NNE.	2/1. 2/2. 1/1. 1/0. 10/1. 1/2. 5/1. 2/2.	21/b. 3/g.	+1/46. 2/47. 2/45. 1/48. 1/50. 1/52. 1/54. 1/55. 1/57. 1/59. 2/60. 1/55. 1/49. 1/51. 1/40. 1/39. 4/38. 1/37.	60	37	47.13
9	24/NE.	17/2. 7/1.	6/b. 6/or. 1/o. 3/or. 8/o.	+1/35. 1/37. 5/38. 1/37. 2/38. 1/37. 3/38. 2/36. 2/35. 3/37. 3/36.	38	35	36.70
10	5/C. 1/S. 2/W. 8/SSW. 4/C. 4/NNE.	5/0. 2/1. 9/2. 4/0. 1/1. 3/2.	11/b. 3/o. 1/q. 9/c.	+2/36. 2/37. 1/38. 1/39. 1/37. 1/36. 1/38. 2/39. 1/41. 1/43. 1/42. 2/39. 1/41. 2/42. 1/41. 1/40. 1/39. 1/38. 1/37.	44	36	39.13
11	4/NNW. 8/WSW. 12/NNE.	1/1. 1/3. 2/2. 1/3. 3/2. 16/1.	3/c. 1/b. 4/c. 6/b. 3/c. 7/o. 1/or.	+1/38. 2/37. 1/38. 1/40. 1/43. 2/42. 1/46. 1/48. 1/50. 2/52. 2/50. 1/48. 1/46. 1/42. 1/41. 1/40. 1/37. 1/36. 2/35.	52	35	43.13
12	4/SSW. 3/NW. 13/NNW. 4/NW.	4/4. 4/3. 2/3. 4/3. 1/2. 5/3. 1/2.	6/or. 1/o. 6/c. 2/o. 9/or.	+3/35. 3/36. 1/38. 1/40. 1/41. 1/43. 1/45. 1/46. 2/45. 1/44½. 1/44. 1/42. 1/41. 2/40. 1/39. 3/38.	46	35	40.02
13	1/NW. 1/C. 7/N. 7/NNE. 2/C. 4/NEbN.	2/1. 2/1. 1/0. 8/2. 4/1. 2/0. 4/1.	12/or. 6/o. 6/or.	+1/38. 3/39. 1/37. 3/36. 5/35. 1/36. 7/37. 4/38.	39	35	36.92
14	5/NNW. 9/NNE. 2/E. 4/C. 4/N.	2/1. 4/2. 8/1. 4/0. 2/1. 2/2. 2/1.	6/or. 2/o. 1/l. 2/f. 1/f. 5/b. 4/c.	+3/39. 1/42. 1/40. 1/38. 1/46. 1/42. 1/46. 1/48. 1/49. 1/51. 2/52. 1/53. 3/54. 1/50. 1/45. 1/42. 1/40. 1/38. 1/37.	54	37	45.08
15	8/NE. 5/Calm. 11/North.	8/1. 5/0. 9/1. 2/2.	24/b.	+3/37. 1/39. 1/42. 1/44. 1/46. 2/48. 1/49. 1/55. 1/60. 2/61. 1/59. 1/55. 3/54. 1/51. 1/50. 1/48. 1/46. 1/44. 1/42.	61	37	49.04
16	24/North.	5/1. 4/0. 3/3. 6/4. 2/3. 1/4. 2/3. 1/0.	23/b. 1/bq.	+1/42. 1/44. 4/46. 4/47. 4/48. 1/47. 3/46. 2/45. 1/42. 1/40. 1/39. 1/37.	48	37	45.13
17	5/NbW. 16/NNW. 3/NW.	3/7. 3/6. 1/5. 3/4. 11/3. 3/4.	2/g. 4/c. 2/b. 9/c. 2/or. 6/o. 3/g. 3/c.	+2/38. 1/39. 3/40. 1/41. 2/42. 1/44. 1/45. 1/46. 1/45. 1/44. 1/43. 1/42. 1/41. 2/40. 1/39. 4/46.	46	38	41.21
18	7/NW. 7/N. 4/Vble. 6/Calm.	2/4. 4/3. 2/2. 4/3. 2/4. 1/3. 1/2. 2/1. 6/0.	4/c. 20/b.	+5/46. 1/42. 2/44. 2/46. 1/47. 1/48½. 1/49. 2/50. 1/49½. 1/49. 1/48. 3/49. 1/48. 1/47. 1/46.	50	40	45.88
19	4/S. 3/NW. 11/Calm. 6/NNE.	7/3. 11/0. 1/1. 1/4. 4/1.	24/b.	+1/46. 2/47. 2/49. 2/50. 1/51. 1/52. 1/53. 2/55. 1/52. 1/58. 1/59. 1/60. 1/58. 1/57. 1/54. 2/50. 1/48. 1/45. 1/42.	60	42	51.96
20	4/NNW. 12/N. 1/Calm. 7/North.	3/2. 3/3. 1/2. 2/1. 2/2. 1/4. 3/2. 1/1. 1/0. 2/2. 4/3. 1/4.	24/b.	+2/40. 1/42. 1/44. 1/46. 1/47. 1/48. 2/49. 1/50. 1/52. 1/54. 1/50. 2/57. 1/53. 1/57. 1/51½. 2/50. 2/48. 1/44. 1/42.	57	40	48.44
21	12/NNW. 4/Calm. 6/NbW. 2/Calm.	1/4. 2/3. 2/1. 2/2. 2/1. 4/0. 2/1. 2/2. 2/1. 2/0.	4/bq. 20/b.	+1/41. 2/40. 1/41. 1/42. 1/44. 1/48. 2/52. 2/55. 1/55. 1/56. 1/57. 1/59. 1/60. 1/58. 2/55. 1/47. 2/45. 2/43. 1/42.	60	40	49.29
22	2/NW. 1/C. 9/W. 8/C. 1/E. 1/S. 1/SW. 1/Calm.	2/1. 1/0. 3/1. 3/2. 3/1. 8/0. 3/1. 1/0.	24/b.	+1/43. 1/45. 1/47. 1/48. 1/49. 1/50. 1/52. 1/54. 1/56. 1/57. 1/59. 1/60. 1/63. 1/66. 1/69. 1/70. 1/66. 1/65. 2/62. 1/58. 1/44. 1/46. 1/44.	70	43	55.21
23	1/C. 2/SE. 5/Calm. 2/SW. 4/SSW. 2/SEbE. 8/C.	1/0. 1/2. 1/1. 5/0. 8/1. 8/0.	24/b.	+1/44. 2/46. 1/47. 1/48. 2/50. 1/52. 1/54. 1/56. 1/57. 1/58. 1/60. 1/64. 1/66. 2/67. 1/66. 1/58. 1/56. 1/53. 1/50. 2/48.	67	44	54.63
24	5/C. 4/SbE. 2/C. 1/SE. 2/S. 6/C.	8/0. 5/1. 2/0. 3/1. 6/0.	24/b.	+1/47. 1/48. 1/49. 1/50. 1/51. 2/52. 2/53. 1/56. 1/60. 1/62. 1/61. 2/60. 1/61. 1/60. 1/59. 1/56. 1/52. 1/50. 1/48. 1/44. 1/42.	62	42	53.58
25	4/S. 6/SE. 5/SW. 2/S. 4/SE. 2/C.	6/1. 2/3. 2/2. 5/3. 1/2. 4/1. 2/0.	8/b. 4/c. 12/b.	+1/47. 2/46. 1/48. 1/50. 1/52. 1/56. 1/57. 1/49. 1/44½. 1/50. 1/52. 1/54. 1/56. 1/57. 2/58. 1/56. 1/54. 2/52. 1/51. 1/49. 1/44.	58	44	51.69
26	3/N. 3/C. 1/SE. 1/Calm. 16/NNE.	3/2. 3/0. 1/1. 1/0. 4/1. 1/2. 1/1. 4/2.	4/c. 3/q. 2/o. 15/or.	+2/44. 2/40. 1/42. 2/43. 1/44. 1/46. 2/47. 1/43. 1/42. 1/40. 1/39. 2/38. 2/37½. 1/37. 2/35. 2/34.	47	34	40.45
27	1/N. 1/C. 6/NNE. 1/N. 1/C. 2/NNE. 5/W. 4/SW. 8/W.	1/1. 1/0. 3/1. 1/0. 2/1. 1/2. [illegible]	8/cr. 1/c. 4/or. 1/c. 10/b.	+2/35. 2/38. 2/40. 2/42. 2/43. 1/44. 1/45. 1/46. 1/48. 2/49. 1/46. 1/44. 2/42. 1/41. 1/40. 2/39.	49	35	42.08
28	4/W. 2/SW. 2/SSE. 3/NW. 6/SW. 5/SE. 1/C. 1/N.	[illegible]	4/b. 6/c. 2/q. 4/b. 2/c. 6/b.	+1/36. 2/35. 2/36. 1/38. 1/40. 1/42. 1/41. 1/46. 1/48. 1/49. 1/50. 1/56. 2/60. 1/59. 1/58. 1/56. 1/58. 1/47. 1/48. 1/43. 2/44.	60	35	47.29
29	24/NNE.	20/1. 4/2.	2/c. 18/b. 4/c.	+2/36. 2/37. 2/39. 2/40. 2/41. 3/40. 1/44. 3/45. 3/44. 2/43. 2/42.	45	36	41.13
30	24/North.	21/1. 3/2.	4/q. 4/b. 8/c. 3/gr. 2/c. 3/gr.	+1/40. 2/38. 1/39. 1/40. 1/42. 1/43. 1/41. 4/42. 1/40. 2/39. 1/38. 3/37. 5/36.	43	36	39.00
31	2/NNE. 4/ENE. 18/North.	1/1. 3/2. 3/1. 1/2. 1/4. 13/4. 1/2.	10/q. 2/or. 2/c. 10/g.	+1/34. 1/35. 2/37. 1/38. 1/39. 1/40. 1/41. 2/42. 1/43. 1/44. 1/46. 1/45. 1/44. 1/42. 5/40.	46	34	41.13

ABSTRACT.

191/N. 180.	11/NbW. 41.	84/NNW. 225.	0/NWbN. 0.	36/NW. 23.	5/NWbW. 11.	0/WNW. 0.	0/WbN. 0.	North Westerly —327	Total. 637 hours. 5 do. wind vble. 102 do. calm. 744 = 31 days.
43/W. 97.	0/WbS. 0.	8/WSW. 13.	0/SWbW. 0.	21/SW. 42.	0/SWbS. 0.	21/SSW. 29.	0/SbW. 0.	South Westerly — 93	
15/S. 18.	5/SbE. 5.	2/SSE. 3.	0/SEbS. 0.	26/SE. 31.	2/SEbE. 2.	0/ESE. 0.	0/EbS. 0.	South Easterly — 50	
8/E. 6.	0/EbN. 0.	4/ENE. 0.	0/NEbE. 0.	34/NE. 52.	4/NEbN. 4.	117/NNE. 147.	0/NbE. 0.	North Easterly —167	

Highest, Lowest, and Mean Temperature +70 + 32 +44.57

Total force of the Wind 1303

METEOROLOGICAL OBSERVATIONS OF THE VICTORY DISCOVERY SHIP, TAKEN ON THE ICE, AND REGISTERED HOURLY.

Days of Month.	Direction of Wind.	Force of Wind.	State of Weather.	AUGUST, 1830. Temperature in Shade.	+	−	Mean.
1	North. Vble Sly. N. Vble Sly. North.	[illegible]	b.	[illegible]	+45°	+39°	+41°.50
2	NW. North.	[illegible]	[illegible]	[illegible]	42	33	38.96
3	North. W. S. Vble Sly. North.	[illegible]	b.	[illegible]	56	38	47.00
4	NbW. NW. N. NE. S. E. S. N.	[illegible]	b. c.	[illegible]	56	40	47.25
5	NNW. Vble. S. NW. N.	[illegible]	b. c. g. [illegible]	[illegible]	58	39	47.83
6	N. NW. Vble Sly. N. S. NNE.	[illegible]	c. cr. b. bv. b.	[illegible]	56	36	44.00
7	[illegible]	[illegible]	[illegible]	[illegible]	44	31	39.71
8	NNW. N. NNE. NbW. NNW.	[illegible]	[illegible]	[illegible]	48	36	39.67
9	WbN. SE. SW. S. N. SW. N.	[illegible]	[illegible]	[illegible]	42	36	39.38
10	NWbW. SW. NNW. Calm.	[illegible]	[illegible]	[illegible]	41	38	39.81
11	C. SWbW. W. Vble Sly. S. Vble Sly.	[illegible]	qr. g. c. cq.	[illegible]	43	35	39.67
12	[illegible] NE. SE. SW.	[illegible]	c. cf. c.	[illegible]	40	36	38.42
13	N. C. NE. S.	[illegible]	c. cr. c. b.	[illegible]	43	36	39.30
14	[illegible] Vble Wly. SE. S.	[illegible]	[illegible]	[illegible]	48	31	40.5
15	[illegible]	[illegible]	[illegible]	[illegible]	43	31	39.58
16	[illegible]	[illegible]	[illegible]	[illegible]	44	36	39.30
17	C. SW. SE. Vble Sly. SE. E. C.	[illegible]	[illegible]	[illegible]	41	34	37.46
18	[illegible]	[illegible]	[illegible]	[illegible]	46	34	39.17
19	NNW. NW. NNW. N. NW. NNW.	[illegible]	g. c. b.	[illegible]	48	36	41.19
20	NW. Vble Sly. NE. SNE.	[illegible]	[illegible]	[illegible]	46	35	41.00
21	SNE. N. NNW. NWbN. NW.	[illegible]	[illegible]	[illegible]	46	34	39.98
22	NW.	[illegible]	c. b.	[illegible]	53	38	45.00
23	NW.	[illegible]	[illegible]	[illegible]	48	36	42.65
24	NWbN. N. NNE. N. NEbN.	[illegible]	[illegible]	[illegible]	42	35	39.58
25	NbE. NE.	[illegible]	c.	[illegible]	38	36	36.88
26	NE. NNE. North.	[illegible]	[illegible]	[illegible]	41	36	37.83
27	North. NbW. NNW. N.	[illegible]	c.	[illegible]	43	36	39.73
28	NbW. NNW. NWbN. NbW.	[illegible]	[illegible]	[illegible]	44	36	39.71
29	NNW.	[illegible]	[illegible]	[illegible]	43	36	38.67
30	NNW. NW. WNW.	[illegible]	[illegible]	[illegible]	41	35	38.80
31	[illegible]	[illegible]	[illegible]	[illegible]	42½	33	37.40

ABSTRACT.

[illegible]	North Westerly - 140	Total. 699 hours. 16 do. wind variable. 29 do. calm.	Highest, Lowest, and Mean Temperature +58 +33 +40.87
[illegible]	South Westerly - 87		
[illegible]	South Easterly - 73		Total force of the Wind 1996
[illegible]	North Easterly - 99	744 — 31 days.	

METEOROLOGICAL OBSERVATIONS OF THE VICTORY DISCOVERY SHIP, TAKEN ON THE ICE, AND REGISTERED HOURLY.

	Days of Month.	Direction of Wind.	Force of Wind.	State of Weather.	SEPTEMBER, 1830. Temperature in Shade.	+	−	Mean.
	1	S. NW. W. WNW. W. WNW. NW. N. NbW.	[illegible]	[illegible]	[illegible]	+32	+29	+30.35
	2	S. NNW. NbW. NW. NWbN. N. NbW.	[illegible]	[illegible]	[illegible]	35	30	32.90
	3	NbW. NW. NWbN. NNW.	[illegible]	[illegible]	[illegible]	35	29¼	32.5
	4	NNW. NWbN. NW. NNW. WNW. S. SbW. NW. NNW. NbW.	[illegible]	[illegible]	[illegible]	38	28	30.92
⊕	5	WSW. SbW. S. E. ENE. NE.	[illegible]	[illegible]	[illegible]	33	29	31.60
	6	NNE. North. NbW.	[illegible]	[illegible]	[illegible]	31½	27	29.77
	7	North. NbW.	[illegible]	[illegible]	[illegible]	36	27	31.67
	8	North. NbW. NW. NNW.	[illegible]	[illegible]	[illegible]	34	29	30.85
	9	NbW. N. WbS. NW. N. NW.	[illegible]	[illegible]	[illegible]	34	29	31.42
	10	S. NNW. NW. W. Vble Wy. WNW. Vble Sy. S.	[illegible]	[illegible]	[illegible]	32	28	29.79
	11	Vble Wly. W. NW. Vble Sly. S. C.	[illegible]	[illegible]	[illegible]	32	18	26.01
⊕	12	Vble & C. C. S. SWbS. SbW. Vble Sly.	[illegible]	[illegible]	[illegible]	41	16	29.60
	13	SWbS. Calm. South.	[illegible]	[illegible]	[illegible]	43	29	38.04
	14	S. C. Vble Sly. S. SW. S.	[illegible]	[illegible]	[illegible]	41	29	34.46
	15	S. SbW. SSW. SW. SWbW. Vble. Wly. C. WSW.	[illegible]	[illegible]	[illegible]	43	30	36.42
	16	S.W. Vble. EbS. WbS. WSW. W. Vble. W. NW. WbN. WbS. W.	[illegible]	[illegible]	[illegible]	40	29	34.23
	17	WNW. NW. WNW. Vble Wly. WNW. W. WSW. VbleNWly. W. WbS. WSW. SW.	[illegible]	[illegible]	[illegible]	40	25	31.75
	18	SSW. S. SbW. S. SbE. SSE. SE. SbE. NNE. N. NbW.	[illegible]	[illegible]	[illegible]	36	24	30.23
⊕	19	N. NW. WNW. W. WNW. WbS. SW. W. SSW. Vble. WSW. WbS.	[illegible]	[illegible]	[illegible]	28	22	24.88
	20	SWbW. Wly. WSW. S. SW. WSW. S. SSE. SSW. S.	[illegible]	[illegible]	[illegible]	32	24	27.42
	21	S. SE. SSE. SE. E. ENE. NE. NNE. NbW. NNW. NW.	[illegible]	[illegible]	[illegible]	27	14	22.58
	22	Vble N to W. NbW. N. NNW.	[illegible]	[illegible]	[illegible]	27	14	23.67
	23	NNW. NbW. N. NNE. NE. NEbE.	[illegible]	[illegible]	[illegible]	26	22	23.42
	24	NEbE. NbW. NbE. ENE. EbN.	[illegible]	[illegible]	[illegible]	29	22	26.09
	25	EbN. NE. NEbN. NNE.	[illegible]	[illegible]	[illegible]	30	27¼	28.8
⊕	26	NNE. N. NNE. N. NbW. NNW.	[illegible]	[illegible]	[illegible]	30	12	24.27
	27	NNW. WbN. SW. WbN. WSW. W. SW.	[illegible]	[illegible]	[illegible]	17½	7	11.4
	28	W. NW. WSW. WbS. WSW. W. WbN. NW. NbW. N. NW. NbW. NW. NWbN.	[illegible]	[illegible]	[illegible]	17	7	13.04
	29	NWbN. WNW. NW. NbW. NW. NWbW. W. WbS. W. WSW.	[illegible]	[illegible]	[illegible]	16	5	12.98
	30	WSW. NW. WbN. W. WbS. N. NW. W. WSW. SW. Vble. N.	[illegible]	[illegible]	[illegible]	15	7	11.5

ABSTRACT.

97/N.494. 68/NbW.432. 69/NNW.391. 14/NWbN.63. 14/NW.159. 2/NWbW.5. 29/WNW.79. 17/WbN.39.
45/W.169. 17/WbS.38. 31/WSW.79. 7/SWbW.23. 19/SW.73. 9/SWbS.23. 14/SSW.45. 11/SbW.26.
37/S.186. 5/SbE.17. 8/SSE.22. 0/SEbS.0. 5/SE.11. 0/SEbE.0. 0/ESE.0. 1/EbS.2.
3/E.6. 18/EbN.77. 4/ENE.12. 6/NEbE.23. 26/NE.76. 4/NEbN.76. 29/NNE.113. 1/NbE.11.

North Westerly = 418
South Westerly — 157
South Easterly — 106
North Easterly — 93

Total. 696 hours. 7 do. wind variable. 17 do. calm. 720 = 30 days.

Highest, Lowest, and Mean Temperature +43 + 5 +27.42

Total force of the Wind 2633

METEOROLOGICAL OBSERVATIONS OF THE VICTORY DISCOVERY SHIP, TAKEN ON THE ICE, AND REGISTERED HOURLY.

Days of Month.	Direction of Wind.	Force of Wind.	State of Weather.	OCTOBER, 1830. Temperature in Shade.	+	−	Mean
1	NWbN. NW. WNW. NW. Vble. Wly. SW. WSW. W.	[illegible]	[illegible]	[illegible]	19½	10	15°.27
2	WbS. West. NW. West.	[illegible]	[illegible]	[illegible]	19	12	14.92
3	W. WbN. WNW. WbN. W. WbN.	[illegible]	[illegible]	[illegible]	19	14	16.46
4	W. NW. WbN. WSW. W. WbN. WbS. WSW. SWbW.	[illegible]	[illegible]	[illegible]	20	15	18.42
5	SW. SSW. S. Vble. Sly. S. SbW. N. N. NbE. NNE. N. NNW.	[illegible]	[illegible]	[illegible]	23½	13	18.90
6	NWbW. NNW. NW. WNW. WbN. WbS. C. W.	[illegible]	[illegible]	[illegible]	15	8	12.48
7	W. SW. W. S. SW. W. WSW. SW. WSW. W.	[illegible]	[illegible]	[illegible]	17	7	13.29
8	W. WNW. W. WNW. NW. N. NE.	[illegible]	[illegible]	[illegible]	12	5	9.23
9	NEbN. N. WNW. Calm.	[illegible]	[illegible]	[illegible]	14	2	10.00
10	WNW. C. SE. C. SWbS. Calm	[illegible]	[illegible]	[illegible]	10	0	4.04
11	SE. WNW. C. W. Ely. SSW. Calm.	[illegible]	[illegible]	[illegible]	12	3	6.00
12	SW. W. C. NW. NE. North	[illegible]	[illegible]	[illegible]	10	6	7.92
13	N. C. NW. SW. NW.	[illegible]	[illegible]	[illegible]	8	1	4.31
14	SW. C. SEly. E. Sly. SbE. South.	[illegible]	[illegible]	[illegible]	22	0	6.34
15	S. SSW. SW. WSW. SE. WSW. SW.	[illegible]	[illegible]	[illegible]	24	14	18.23
16	W. NE. WSW. SbE. E. SE. ENE. NNE. N. NNE.	[illegible]	[illegible]	[illegible]	18	18	18.00
17	NNE. NW. WNW. NW. W. WSW. W. WbS.	[illegible]	[illegible]	[illegible]	18	7	12.75
18	WSW. SW. SWbS. SW.	[illegible]	[illegible]	[illegible]	12	8	10.50
19	SW. S. SW.	[illegible]	[illegible]	[illegible]	13	3½	7.19
20	SW. SSW. S. C. W. Easterly.	[illegible]	[illegible]	[illegible]	12	4	9.42
21	Vble E. to SSW. SE. East.	[illegible]	[illegible]	[illegible]	13	6	9.43
22	NE. East.	[illegible]	[illegible]	[illegible]	18	12	15.19
23	NE. N. NbW. NW.	[illegible]	[illegible]	[illegible]	22	18	20.79
24	NNW. NW.	[illegible]	[illegible]	[illegible]	21	10½	16.09
25	NWbW. W. WbS. C. WSW. Wly. C. WNW.	[illegible]	[illegible]	[illegible]	9	−½	3.40
26	NNE. NW. NNW.	[illegible]	[illegible]	[illegible]	10	+6	7.90
27	NW. Calm. Westerly.	[illegible]	[illegible]	[illegible]	10	8	9.27
28	W. WSW. SW. West.	[illegible]	[illegible]	[illegible]	7	−12	−3.81
29	E. SE. E. NNE. Easly. EbS.	[illegible]	[illegible]	[illegible]	6	9	+0.08
30	E. S. SW. SSE. SW. South.	[illegible]	[illegible]	[illegible]	9	+2	4.52
31	SbE. SE. South.	[illegible]	[illegible]	[illegible]	24	8	19.38

ABSTRACT.

N. 33.	NbW. 12.	NNW. 116.	NWbN. 10.	NW. 205.	NWbW. 10.	WNW. 100.	WbN. 87.	North Westerly 233	Total. 694 hours.
W. 266.	WbS. 11.	WSW. 182.	SWbW. 3.	SW. 255.	SWbS. 27.	SSW. 29.	SbW. 5.	South Westerly 211	1 do. wind variable.
S. 165.	SbE. 33.	SSE. 10.	SEbS. 0.	SE. 95.	SEbE. 6.	ESE. 0.	EbS. 13.	South Easterly 110	49 do. calm.
E. 170.	EbN. 0.	ENE. 2.	NEbE. 0.	NE. 75.	NEbN. 13.	NNE. 121.	NbE. 5.	North Easterly 107	744 31 days.

Highest, Lowest, and Mean Temperature +24 − 12 +10.95

Total force of the Wind . . . 2135

C

METEOROLOGICAL OBSERVATIONS OF THE VICTORY DISCOVERY SHIP, TAKEN ON THE ICE, AND REGISTERED HOURLY.

Days of Month.	Direction of Wind.	Force of Wind.	State of Weather.	NOVEMBER, 1830. Temperature in Shade.	+	−	Mean.
1	[illegible]	[illegible]	[illegible]	[illegible]	+ 24°	+ 18°	+ 21°.38
2	[illegible]	[illegible]	[illegible]	[illegible]	18	−4	5.92
3	[illegible]	[illegible]	[illegible]	[illegible]	0	6	−3.00
4	[illegible]	[illegible]	[illegible]	[illegible]	+24	+2	+14.40
5	[illegible]	[illegible]	[illegible]	[illegible]	24	14	19.75
6	[illegible]	[illegible]	[illegible]	[illegible]	22	16	19.02
7	[illegible]	[illegible]	[illegible]	[illegible]	17	12	14.06
8	[illegible]	[illegible]	[illegible]	[illegible]	13	4	7.94
9	[illegible]	[illegible]	[illegible]	[illegible]	10	2	5.96
10	[illegible]	[illegible]	[illegible]	[illegible]	+1	−16	−8.75
11	[illegible]	[illegible]	[illegible]	[illegible]	−2	9	5.42
12	[illegible]	[illegible]	[illegible]	[illegible]	6	11	8.83
13	[illegible]	[illegible]	[illegible]	[illegible]	12	24	16.60
14	[illegible]	[illegible]	[illegible]	[illegible]	24	30	27.33
15	[illegible]	[illegible]	[illegible]	[illegible]	26	32	28.21
16	[illegible]	[illegible]	[illegible]	[illegible]	19	32	28.08
17	[illegible]	[illegible]	[illegible]	[illegible]	13	21	17.42
18	[illegible]	[illegible]	[illegible]	[illegible]	11	20	13.71
19	[illegible]	[illegible]	[illegible]	[illegible]	23	35	28.93
20	[illegible]	[illegible]	[illegible]	[illegible]	25	35	29.71
21	[illegible]	[illegible]	[illegible]	[illegible]	18	25	21.38
22	[illegible]	[illegible]	[illegible]	[illegible]	21	26	23.63
23	[illegible]	[illegible]	[illegible]	[illegible]	25	35½	30.25
24	[illegible]	[illegible]	[illegible]	[illegible]	34	37	35.83
25	[illegible]	[illegible]	[illegible]	[illegible]	37	41	39.00
26	[illegible]	[illegible]	[illegible]	[illegible]	17	40	27.49
27	[illegible]	[illegible]	[illegible]	[illegible]	17	23	20.31
28	[illegible]	[illegible]	[illegible]	[illegible]	11	16	13.21
29	[illegible]	[illegible]	[illegible]	[illegible]	9	15½	12.29
30	[illegible]	[illegible]	[illegible]	[illegible]	12	21	15.63

ABSTRACT. [illegible]

North Westerly — 275
South Westerly — 137
South Easterly — 142
North Easterly — 44

Total. 598 hours.
14 do. wind variable.
108 do. calm.
720 — 30 days.

Highest, Lowest, and Mean Temperature + 24 − 41 − 11.45

Total force of the Wind 1409

METEOROLOGICAL OBSERVATIONS OF THE VICTORY DISCOVERY SHIP, TAKEN ON THE ICE, AND REGISTERED HOURLY.

Days of Month.	Direction of Wind.	Force of Wind.	State of Weather.	DECEMBER, 1830. Temperature in Shade.	+	−	Mean.
1	S. SSE. W. SW. East.	[illegible]	b. os. o. c. o. os.	[illegible]	13°	23°	17°.96
2	SE. C. SE. S. SE. S. SbE.	[illegible]	os. o. os.	[illegible]	+2	13	5.98
3	SbE. S. WSW. West.	[illegible]	os. o. cb.	[illegible]	6	1	+3.48
4	SW. WSW. SW. S. WSW. SW.	[illegible]	cb. c. b. c. b.	[illegible]	−2	19	−10.92
5	SW. WSW. W. Ely. E. SE. SSE.	[illegible]	o. b. o. os. o. os	[illegible]	6½	19	11.62
6	S. SE. S. SSW. S. WSW.	[illegible]	o. os. o. c. b.	[illegible]	5	9	6.38
7	SW. C. S. SSE. SSW.	[illegible]	c. e. c. g. o. c.	[illegible]	7	12	9.35
8	S. SW. W. SW. S. SW. Calm.	[illegible]	o. os. b. g. b. g. b.	[illegible]	11	18	15.17
9	C. SW. W. NW. SSW. NW.	[illegible]	b. o. b. o. os.	[illegible]	11	19½	15.65
10	S. NW. W. C. NW. South.	[illegible]	g. b. g. b. c. b. g.	[illegible]	9	19	16.27
11	S. SW. WSW. S. C. W. Calm	[illegible]	b. c. o. g. b.	[illegible]	19	23	20.21
12	SSW. C. NW. S. Calm.	[illegible]	b. g. o. g. b	[illegible]	23	25½	23.96
13	NW. C. S. C. S. SSW. C.	[illegible]	b	[illegible]	26	32	29.13
14	C. S. C. SW. W. NW. C.	[illegible]	b.	[illegible]	30	33	32.29
15	S. NNW. N. NNW.	[illegible]	q. ov. os. od. o. o. bd	[illegible]	18	30	21.41
16	NNW.	[illegible]	b. o. b. bq.	[illegible]	20	37	31.42
17	NNW. N. NWbN.	[illegible]	bd. od. od. bqd. bd.	[illegible]	14	19	16.67
18	NNW. NW. WNW. NW. SE. E.	[illegible]	b. c. b.	[illegible]	16	25	19.48
19	SE. W. SW. W. Calm.	[illegible]	b.	[illegible]	25	27½	26.50
20	SSE. SW. C. South.	[illegible]	b. g. o. q. o. os. q	[illegible]	24	27	25.96
21	SE. NW. North	[illegible]	q. b. cb. b.	[illegible]	23	28	25.48
22	NNW. NW. North.	[illegible]	b. bd. qd. o. qd. od. bd.	[illegible]	21	28½	26.19
23	NNW. SE.	[illegible]	osq. + os. osd. qd. o. os.	[illegible]	11	21	16.06
24	SE. C. W. SW. SSW.	[illegible]	os. g. b. g. b. g. c. b.	[illegible]	12	19½	17.98
25	W. WNW. SSW. SW. S.	[illegible]	g. os. q. q. b.	[illegible]	15	21	17.17
26	SE. SSE. E. ESE. NEbS. SSE.	[illegible]	c. b. o. os. c. b.	[illegible]	22	27½	24.67
27	Sly. C. SE. ESE. SE. EbS.	[illegible]	b. c. q. o. os.	[illegible]	20	28	24.00
28	SE. ESE. NNE. N. E.	[illegible]	os. o. os.	[illegible]	8½	19	13.38
29	EbS. S. SSE. S. NW. W. WNW.	[illegible]	o. b. c. b. o. g. b.	[illegible]	11	30	23.00
30	S. C. Vble. SbW. S. C.	[illegible]	b.	[illegible]	32	41	36.79
31	C. SW. S. C. NW.	[illegible]	b.	[illegible]	42	47	13.94

ABSTRACT.

N. 265.	NbW. 0.	NNW. 392.	NWbN. 64.	NW. 57.	NWbW. 0.	WNW. 29.	WbN. 0.	North Westerly — 221	Total. 621 hours. 4 do. wind vble. 119 do. calm. 744 — 31 days.
W. 92.	WbS. 0.	WSW. 56.	SWbW. 0.	SW. 61.	SWbS. 0.	SSW. 60.	SbW. 4.	South Westerly — 158	
S. 229.	SbE. 10.	SSE. 35.	SEbS. 9.	SE. 150.	SEbE. 0.	ESE. 29.	EbS. 25.	South Easterly — 238	
E. 35.	EbN. 0.	ENE. 0.	NEbE. 0.	NE. 0.	NEbN. 0.	NNE. 12.	NbE. 0.	North Easterly — 22	

Highest, Lowest, and Mean Temperature +6 −47 −20.24

Total force of the Wind . . . 1811

METEOROLOGICAL OBSERVATIONS OF THE VICTORY DISCOVERY SHIP, TAKEN ON THE ICE, AND REGISTERED HOURLY.

Days of Month.	Direction of Wind.	Force of Wind.	State of Weather.	JANUARY, 1831. Temperature in Shade.	+	—	Mean.
1	Calm. Ely. SE. Westerly.	[illegible]	b. c. b.	NB. at 9 P. M. by Diff. Ther. 47. [illegible]	—45	—47	—46°.25
2	NW. Calm. NW. Calm.	[illegible]	b.	Do. at 4h. at 8h. at 12h. [illegible]	46	55	48.00
3	Calm. Vble Wly. Calm.	[illegible]	b.	A. M. D.T. 4h. 6h. Noon 2h. 8h. [illegible]	47½	51½	49.30
4	S. C. Sly. SE. Calm. SE.	[illegible]	b.	D.T. [illegible]	49	56½	53.30
5	SW. C. S. SW. Calm.	[illegible]	b.	D.T. [illegible]	49	59½	55.04
6	NW. C. NW. SbW. NbW. C. SE.	[illegible]	b. c. q. os. o. c. b.	D.T. Ther. [illegible]	36	49½	42.08
7	C. Ely. Vble +. SW. C. S. Calm.	[illegible]	b.	[illegible]	44	46	45.13
8	C. Sly. C. WNW. SbE. Calm.	[illegible]	b.	[illegible]	45	45	45.00
9	S. C. NW. N. NE. C. Se.	[illegible]	b.	DT. [illegible]	38	49	44.63
10	S. NW. SW. N. W. S.	[illegible]	b. b. g. b.	[illegible]	24	45	36.04
11	South. WNW. SW.	[illegible]	g. b. g. o. g. o.	[illegible]	19	29	24.08
12	SW. W. NW. W. N. NW.	[illegible]	os o. os. c. g. o.	[illegible]	14	18½	15.46
13	C. NW. N. W. NW. C. NW. SW. NE. C. WSW	[illegible]	o. b. q.	[illegible]	14½	24	20.42
14	SW. S. SSE. SW. SbE.	[illegible]	q. o. os. osq. o.	[illegible]	9	23	15.29
15	S. SE. SbE.	[illegible]	o. g. c. g. o. os.	[illegible]	4	9	7.37
16	Nly. NW. N. NNW.	[illegible]	os. o. os. o.	[illegible]	+2½	3½	1.15
17	NW. W. SW. S. SE. WbN. NW. NWbN.	[illegible]	q. o. os. osq. os. o. os.	[illegible]	—3½	19	9.31
18	NWbN. NNW. NW.	[illegible]	os. osd. osq. os. od. qd.	[illegible]	9½	17½	13.52
19	NNW. NW. NbW.	[illegible]	q. b. qd. q. b.	[illegible]	17	22	19.42
20	NW. NNW. North.	[illegible]	b. bd. b. q. o. q. o.	[illegible]	21	25	23.75
21	WNW. NW. N. NNW.	[illegible]	o. os. o.	[illegible]	12	20	15.08
22	NW. WNW. NW. N.	[illegible]	o. os. o. g. o. bc. os. o. q.	[illegible]	7	12	9.75
23	N. NNW. NW. NNE.	[illegible]	q. b. qq. osq. osd. q. d. qd. b.	[illegible]	8	15	11.58
24	N. NNW. NbW. NW. N.	[illegible]	b. q. o. g. b. q.	[illegible]	8	15½	12.52
25	N. W. SW. N. SbW. C.	[illegible]	q. o. q. c. b. q. b. g.	[illegible]	8	14	10.20
26	S. C. EbS. S. W. N. S.	[illegible]	c. b. c. b. c. g. o. c. b.	[illegible]	9	17	14.14
27	NWbW. NW. W. SW. W. SSE. SW.	[illegible]	b. o. c. o. c. b.	[illegible]	12	20½	17.00
28	S. N. S. C. N. NW.	[illegible]	b. c. b. c.	[illegible]	21	26	24.02
29	N. Sly. N. NW. W. NW. C. WbS.	[illegible]	o. q. c. b. c.	[illegible]	19	24	21.92
30	NNW. C. Wly. NNE. SE. C.	[illegible]	c. g. c.	[illegible]	19½	21½	20.23
31	W. NW. N. NNW.	[illegible]	b. o. od.	[illegible]	2½	22	11.90

ABSTRACT.

N. 275. NbW. 76. NNW. 284. NWbN. 80. NW. 380. NWbW. 4. WNW. 34. WbN. 17.
W. 82. WbS. 5. WSW. 5. SWbW. 0. SW. 163. SWbS. 0. SSW. 0. SbW. 14.
S. 105. SbE. 19. SSE. 19. SEbS. 0. SE. 26. SEbE. 0. ESE. 0. EbS. 0.
E. 6. EbN. 0. ENE. 0. NEbE. 0. NE. 4. NEbN. 0. NNE. 30. NbE. 0.

North Westerly — 329
South Westerly — 133
South Easterly — 131
North Easterly — 2?

Total. 615 hours. 2 do. wind variable. 127 do. calm. 744 — 31 days.

Highest, Lowest, and Mean Temperature +2½ —59½ —25.43

Total force of the Wind . . 1657

METEOROLOGICAL OBSERVATIONS OF THE VICTORY DISCOVERY SHIP, TAKEN ON THE ICE, AND REGISTERED HOURLY.

Days of Month.	Direction of Wind.	Force of Wind.	State of Weather.	FEBRUARY, 1831. Temperature in Shade.	+	−	Mean.
1	NNW. S. NNE. N. NNW.	[illegible]	[illegible]	[illegible]	6°	3°	2°.60
2	NW. N. ENE. NNW. NW.	[illegible]	[illegible]	[illegible]	9½	+4	6.94
3	N. SNW. NW. WNW. SW. S. SE. E. S. SbW.	[illegible]	[illegible]	[illegible]	6	−½	3.67
4	South. SSW.	[illegible]	[illegible]	[illegible]	−1	17	−8.73
5	SW. S. SW. SSW.	[illegible]	[illegible]	[illegible]	12	25½	18.10
6	SSW. SW. S. NW. WbN.	[illegible]	[illegible]	[illegible]	21	32	24.38
7	WNW. W. NW. N. C. E.	[illegible]	[illegible]	[illegible]	27	34	31.42
8	S. C. SE. Vble. C. W.	[illegible]	[illegible]	[illegible]	26	37	34.21
9	SW. S. SSW. SW. W. NW.	[illegible]	[illegible]	[illegible]	26	37	30.56
10	NW. SE. C. S. SW.	[illegible]	[illegible]	[illegible]	38	44	40.48
11	S. SSE. S. North.	[illegible]	[illegible]	[illegible]	35	42	39.13
12	NW. S. WSW. C. NW. SW. NW.	[illegible]	[illegible]	[illegible]	39	43½	41.38
13	W. WSW. NNW. NNW. NbS. NW. C. S. C. SW. C.	[illegible]	[illegible]	[illegible]	39½	44½	42.73
14	NW. W. NW. C. S. SSW.	[illegible]	[illegible]	[illegible]	39½	47	42.83
15	NNW. C. W. N. Sly. SW. C.	[illegible]	[illegible]	[illegible]	40	47	44.19
16	C. SE. ESE. S. SW. C.	[illegible]	[illegible]	[illegible]	44	48	46.63
17	C. NNW. SW. S. WbS. C. NW.	[illegible]	[illegible]	[illegible]	45½	48½	47.40
18	W. NW. C. NW. West.	[illegible]	[illegible]	[illegible]	44½	48	46.73
19	NW. S. NE. W. N. NW. SW.	[illegible]	[illegible]	[illegible]	42½	47	45.70
20	C. SE. C. SW.	[illegible]	[illegible]	[illegible]	47	49	47.98
21	SW. SW. S. W. SW. SSW. SW.	[illegible]	[illegible]	[illegible]	42½	48	45.35
22	SW. S. SW. S. Calm vble.	[illegible]	[illegible]	[illegible]	33	45	41.21
23	N. W. SW. SE.	[illegible]	[illegible]	[illegible]	18	44½	29.88
24	S. NW. N. NNW. NW. W. NW. WNW. S.	[illegible]	[illegible]	[illegible]	17	28½	21.15
25	SW. S. SE. S. W. NE. SW. W. SSW. NW.	[illegible]	[illegible]	[illegible]	29	41½	32.29
26	C. SE. S. WSW.	[illegible]	[illegible]	[illegible]	31	44½	10.71
27	Calm. S. Calm.	[illegible]	[illegible]	[illegible]	40	46½	13.65
28	SSW. WSW. W. SSbW. Vble. SW.	[illegible]	[illegible]	[illegible]	39½	47	43.58

ABSTRACT. [illegible]

North Westerly 194. South Westerly 212. South Easterly 154. North Easterly 11.

Total. 578 hours. 12 do. wind variable. 2 do. calm. 672 28 days.

Highest, Lowest, and Mean Temperature + 9½ − 49 − 32.46

Total force of the Wind 1333

METEOROLOGICAL OBSERVATIONS OF THE VICTORY DISCOVERY SHIP, TAKEN ON THE ICE, AND REGISTERED HOURLY.

	Days of Month.	Direction of Wind.	Force of Wind.	State of Weather.	MARCH, 1831. Temperature in Shade.	+	−	Mean.
	1	C.S.NW.N.W.NW.NNW.NW.S.C.	[illegible]	b.	[illegible]	33	43	38°.75
	2	NW.C.EbS.SE.SW.C.Vble+.NW.	[illegible]	cb. b.	[illegible]	34½	43½	40.75
	3	W. SW. S. SE. S. SbW. NW.	[illegible]	b.c.od.o.qd.q.c.od.b.q.c.	[illegible]	29	38½	34.73
	4	C. SW. S. Wly. NW. Calm.	[illegible]	b.	[illegible]	33	44	39.83
	5	SW. WNW. NW. NNW. NW. C. SW.	[illegible]	qs. os. q. b. bd. qd. q. b.	[illegible]	35	42	38.98
☾ ⊕	6	W.C.S.SE.SW.NW.SW.W.C.W.C.	[illegible]	b. g. b.	[illegible]	29½	43	36.67
	7	S. C. E. S. Wly. C. S. SE. Vble+.	[illegible]	b.	[illegible]	28	42	35.98
	8	E. N. NW. SW. S. Vble+. C. S. WSW. C.	[illegible]	b.	[illegible]	30½	44	39.85
	9	C. S. Vble+. SW. N. Sly. C. SW. SSW.	[illegible]	b. q. b.	[illegible]	29	44	37.54
	10	ESE. C. Sly. NW. C. SW. C.	[illegible]	b.	[illegible]	29	43	38.38
	11	C.SSE.C.NW.WSW.S.SW.WNW.	[illegible]	b.	[illegible]	22½	41	32.5
	12	C. Wly. Vble+. C. Wly. C.	[illegible]	b. q. b.	[illegible]	23	37½	32.00
⊕	13	C. NE. C. Varble Sly. W. C. Wly. C.	[illegible]	b.	[illegible]	21½	38	31.46
	14	S. SW. Ely. SW. C. S. N. NW. C.	[illegible]	b. g. b.	[illegible]	22	37	29.10
	15	S. Vbl. SSE. WNW. Sly. SW. WSW. SSW.	[illegible]	a. bc. b. q. qds. osd. bd.	[illegible]	20	38	29.65
	16	WNW. WSW. WbS. W. NNW. NW. NSW. NW. C. S.	[illegible]	os. bd. ods. b.	[illegible]	23	36	29.38
	17	Vble+. ESE. S. E. S. SSE. SW. Calm.	[illegible]	b. q. b. q. b.	[illegible]	28	40	34.73
	18	S. SW. W. WSW. NWbW. NW. WNW. W. C.	[illegible]	b. q. b.	[illegible]	30	41½	37.13
	19	C. SW. Vble+. C. W. NW. W. NW.	[illegible]	b. q. b. c. b.	[illegible]	30	46	40.06
☽ ⊕	20	SW. W. WNW. W. Calm.	[illegible]	b. q. b.	[illegible]	36	48	42.85
	21	C. S. SbW. WSW. Calm.	[illegible]	b.	[illegible]	37	51	44.27
	22	C. WNW. C. SbS. W. S. C.	[illegible]	b.	[illegible]	34½	49	41.67
	23	SE. C. S. C. S. Sly. C. W. S.	[illegible]	b.	[illegible]	33	47½	42.18
	24	SSW. Sly. S. NW. NNW. NW. N. NNE.	[illegible]	o. os. o. b. bc. c. b. g. b.	[illegible]	26	44½	38.63
	25	SW. SW. Vble+. WSW. SSW. SW. SSW.	[illegible]	b. q. c.	[illegible]	28½	45	36.81
	26	S.SW. W. Vble. SE. W. C. SW. S. Calm.	[illegible]	c. b. q. o. os. b. c.	[illegible]	21	37	28.33
⊙ ⊕	27	C. NW. NE. N. ENE. NE. EbN. NE. N.	[illegible]	b. bc. os. g. bc.	[illegible]	21½	37½	28.17
	28	NNW. NW. NWbN. S. W. SW. Sly. SW.	[illegible]	b. bd. b. c.	[illegible]	22	37½	32.29
	29	SW. S. SW. SSW. S. SSE. SW. WSW.	[illegible]	o. bd. b. bc.	[illegible]	20½	36	28.80
	30	SbW. W. E. SW. S. ENE. NE. N. NNW.	[illegible]	bc. c. os. o. os.	[illegible]	12½	30½	21.88
	31	NW. N. W. WSW. SW. S. E. Calm.	[illegible]	os. o. c. o. c. cs. os. o. q. b.	[illegible]	8½	22	15.79

ABSTRACT.

N. 17	SbW. 0.	NNW. 79.	NWbN. 13.	NW. 81.	NWbW. 0.	WNW. 71.	WbN. 0.	North Westerly — 158	Total. 539 hours. 32 do. wind variable. 173 do. calm. 744 — 31 days.
W. 83.	WbS. 27.	WSW. 56.	SWbW. 0.	SW. 169.	SWbS. 0.	SSW. 44.	SbW. 30.	South Westerly — 185	
S. 178	SbE. 0.	SSE. 20.	SEbS. 2.	SE. 24.	SEbE. 6.	ESE. 8.	EbS. 2.	South Easterly — 147	
E. 14.	EbN. 8.	ENE. 16.	NEbE. 0.	NE. 32.	NEbN. 0.	NNE. 7.	NbE. 0.	North Easterly — 41	

Highest, Lowest, and Mean Temperature −8½−51−34.74

Total force of the Wind 1067

METEOROLOGICAL OBSERVATIONS OF THE VICTORY DISCOVERY SHIP, TAKEN ON THE ICE, AND REGISTERED HOURLY.

Days of Month.	Direction of Wind	Force of Wind.	State of Weather.	APRIL, 1831. Temperature in Shade.	+	–	Mean.
1	Wbs. WSW. NNE. Sly W. Sly.	[illegible]	[illegible]	[illegible]	7°	25	15°.19
2	[illegible]	[illegible]	[illegible]	[illegible]	+3½	15	4.5
3	NW. N. NNE. NNW. NW.	[illegible]	[illegible]	[illegible]	1½	7½	3.90
4	NNW. N. NNE. N. NW. NNW	[illegible]	[illegible]	[illegible]	–2	12	6.77
5	NNW. N. Wly. NW. C. NW.	[illegible]	[illegible]	[illegible]	5	17	11 71
6	N. NW. NNW. Nly. N. NW.	[illegible]	[illegible]	[illegible]	6	20½	13.42
7	NNW. Calm. NNW.	[illegible]	[illegible]	[illegible]	6½	17	11.48
8	NW. NWbW. W. NW. W. C. NW. C.	[illegible]	[illegible]	[illegible]	2	21	12.08
9	NW. SWly. Sly. N. NNW. N.	[illegible]	[illegible]	[illegible]	4	21	16.08
10	NW. NNW. NW. NNW. NW.	[illegible]	[illegible]	[illegible]	11	23	16.96
11	NNW. Vble+. SSW. S. SW.	[illegible]	[illegible]	[illegible]	1	21	11.81
12	SW. S. SSE. WSW. N. SW. Nly. C.	[illegible]	[illegible]	[illegible]	5½	24½	16.35
13	NNE. NE. E. NE. NNE. N. NNE.	[illegible]	[illegible]	[illegible]	5½	19	10.60
14	NNE. North.	[illegible]	[illegible]	[illegible]	0½	11	5.91
15	NNW. NW. N. NNW.	[illegible]	[illegible]	[illegible]	+4	8	3.61
16	NWbN. N. NNW. C. NNW.	[illegible]	[illegible]	[illegible]	2	14½	5.77
17	NW. C. Vble+. Nly. C. NW. N. C. NW.	[illegible]	[illegible]	[illegible]	4	19	8.04
18	W. SW. S. SbE. S. W. SW. C.	[illegible]	[illegible]	[illegible]	–2	15	6.48
19	S. C. S. SW. S. SSE. SE.	[illegible]	[illegible]	[illegible]	+10	5½	+3.92
20	SE. ESE. E. ENE. NNW. Wly. NNE. N. C.	[illegible]	[illegible]	[illegible]	+17½	+10	11.83
21	C. SW. NW. S. SEbS. C. ESE. NNE. NW.	[illegible]	[illegible]	[illegible]	30	11	19.08
22	E. NNW. WNW. SSW. NNE. NNW. NNE. NNW. C.	[illegible]	[illegible]	[illegible]	21½	2	13.5
23	SE. NE. NbW. NNW. N.	[illegible]	[illegible]	[illegible]	13	–13	.40
24	NNW. NWbN. NNW. NWbN.	[illegible]	[illegible]	[illegible]	3	15	–7.04
25	NW. NWbN. NW. NWly. N. C. WNW.	[illegible]	[illegible]	[illegible]	6	13	3.77
26	WSW. C. WNW. S. NW. N. ENE.	[illegible]	[illegible]	[illegible]	9½	17	2.54
27	NEbN. NNE. N. NNW. NW. NNW.	[illegible]	[illegible]	[illegible]	9	+0	5.35
28	NNW. NW. W. WbN. W. WbN. WbN. NW.	[illegible]	[illegible]	[illegible]	5	–17	2.46
29	WNW. C. WNW. NW.	[illegible]	[illegible]	[illegible]	8	18½	4.81
30	S. NE. SW. C. W. WSW. S. SSW.	[illegible]	[illegible]	[illegible]	8	14½	4.04

ABSTRACT.

N. 334. NbW. 6. NNW. 191. NWbN. 111. NW. 325. NWbW. 2. WNW. 78. WbN. 63.
W. 102. WbS. 15. WSW. 11. SWbW. 0. SW. 69. SWbS. 0. SSW. 16. SbW. 0.
S. 58. SbE. 16. SSE. 47. SEbS. 4. SE. 17. SEbE. 0. ESE. 3. EbS. 0.
E. 4. EbN. 0. ENE. 17. NEbE. 0. NE. 8. NEbN. 16. NNE. 101. NbE. 0.

North Westerly	800
South Westerly	103
South Easterly	63
North Easterly	71

Total.
624 hours.
7 do. wind variable.
54 do. calm.
720 30 days.

Highest, Lowest, and Mean Temperature +30 –25 – 6.44

Total force of the Wind 1695

METEOROLOGICAL OBSERVATIONS OF THE VICTORY DISCOVERY SHIP, TAKEN ON THE ICE, AND REGISTERED HOURLY.

	Days of Month.	Direction of Wind.	Force of Wind.	State of Weather.	MAY, 1831. Temperature in Shade.	+	−	Mean
⊕	1	17 Calm. 1 West. 6 NE.	[illegible]	20 b. 1 bc. 2 bcs. 1 c.	[illegible]	12	16	−.48
	2	6 NNE. 10 N. 2 ENE. 6 SE.	[illegible]	oc. bc. bcd. bc. b. bc. o.	[illegible]	6	1	+2.17
	3	6 ESE. 2 NNE. 4 NE. 6 N. 2 NNE. 4 NNW.	[illegible]	o. g. b.	[illegible]	10	2	3.29
	4	1 NW. 6 C. 1 SE. 2 C. 4 S. 4 Vble+. 6 C.	[illegible]	24 b.	[illegible]	20	3	7.71
	5	4 S. 4 W. 1 NW. 1 SW. 2 Vble+. 4 Sly. 2 WbN. 6 C.	[illegible]	24 b.	[illegible]	21	4	8.23
	6	4 Vble+. 2 NE. 1 E. 1 SE. 1 C. 5 Vble+. 1 S. 2 NW. 4 C.	[illegible]	24 b.	[illegible]	20	4½	7.71
	7	2 NW. 1 N. 1 NNE. 4 WNW. 16 N.	[illegible]	24 b.	[illegible]	19½	1	6.81
⊕	8	4 SSW. 4 C. 4 S. 6 Wly. 2 SW. 4 NNW.	[illegible]	24 b.	[illegible]	21	1	10.10
	9	4 NWbN. 8 NW. 3 NNW. 5 N. 2 NbW. 2 C.	[illegible]	24 b.	[illegible]	21½	1	11.13
	10	4 N. 13 NW. 5 NEbE. 1 NNE.	[illegible]	24 b.	[illegible]	22½	+3	13.13
	11	12 NbW. 5 NWbW. 7 NWbN.	[illegible]	b. g. c. cd. bcq.	[illegible]	19	4	11.77
	12	24 NNW.	[illegible]	b. bd. b. bdq. bd.	[illegible]	19½	7	13.54
	13	22 NNW. 1 NWbN. 1 NW.	[illegible]	bd. b. bd. b. bd. b.	[illegible]	22½	9	16.06
	14	4 NNW. 16 NW. 2 WSW. 2 W.	[illegible]	c. b.	[illegible]	32	10	20.27
⊕	15	2 W. 6 C. 10 NNE. 6 Calm.	[illegible]	24 b.	[illegible]	32	10	20.06
	16	2 SE. 1 S. 5 SSE. 10 SW. 6 SWbW.	[illegible]	b. bc.	[illegible]	29½	8½	18.65
	17	4 SW. 2 C. 14 SSE. 2 C. 2 NNE.	[illegible]	bc. c. o. g.	[illegible]	28	12	20.81
	18	3 NNE. 5 N. 12 NNE. 4 N.	[illegible]	o. os. od. bd. b.	[illegible]	24	11	19.65
	19	5 N. 3 NW. 12 SE. 4 N.	[illegible]	b. q.	[illegible]	32½	10	21.67
	20	1 NNE. 1 N. 1 NW. 4 WNW. 4 W. 7 NW. 2 WNW. 3 C. 3 WSW.	[illegible]	o. g. bc. b.	[illegible]	24	8½	17.06
	21	7 SW. 7 SE. 6 S. 4 ESE.	[illegible]	b. bc. bcs. bc. o. os.	[illegible]	25	8	16.81
⊕	22	6 ESE. 4 E. 2 ENE. 4 NE. 5 N. 3 NE.	[illegible]	os. sd. oc. bcd. os. bc.	[illegible]	22	14	18.19
	23	8 NNW. 2 NE. 2 SE. 12 N.	[illegible]	b. q. od.	[illegible]	30½	12	24.12
	24	24 North.	[illegible]	od. qsd. bcd. bcosd. bcd. bc. b	[illegible]	33	20	26.38
	25	5 WNW. 4 W. 8 SW. 7 WSW.	[illegible]	b. bc. bqc. bc. bgc. gs. os.	[illegible]	34	17	27.23
	26	5 NNE. 9 NbW. 4 NW. 6 WSW.	[illegible]	os. o. bc. os. o.	[illegible]	34	20	25.44
	27	8 SW. 10 W. 2 SSE. 3 SE. 1 NE.	[illegible]	qc. qcd qc. o. od. bc. bcs. qs.	[illegible]	36	13	24.77
	28	2 NW. 2 NbE. 2 NE. 3 NNE. 3 NE. 4 ENE. 2 E. 2 N. 4 NE.	[illegible]	qs. bc. bcs. bc. os. bc. qc. bc.	[illegible]	34	20	25.60
⊕	29	4 E. 4 NE. 11 N. 1 NW. 4 NNW.	[illegible]	oc. bc. bcd. qcd.	[illegible]	25	13	19.38
	30	2 NNW. 2 NW. 9 WNW. 11 W.	[illegible]	bc. b. bc. q. qs. os.	[illegible]	34	11	20.09
	31	24 West.	[illegible]	os. cs. bc. qs.	[illegible]	28	16	20.5

ABSTRACT.

N. 119.	NbW. 49.	WNW. 300.	NWbN. 49.	NW. 163.	NWbW. 25.	WNW. 42.	WbN. 4.	North Westerly = 320
W. 165.	WbS. 0.	WSW. 30.	SWbW. 15.	SW. 68.	SWbS. 0.	SSW. 4.	SbW. 0.	South Westerly = 135
S. 31.	SbE. 0.	SSE. 32.	SEbS. 0.	SE. 32.	SEbE. 0.	ESE. 61.	EbS. 0.	South Easterly = 95
E. 30.	EbN. 0.	ENE. 23.	NEbE. 6.	NE. 123.	NEbN. 0.	NNE. 111.	NbE. 4.	North Easterly = 109

Total. 659 hours. 15 do. wind variable. 70 do. calm. 744 = 31 days.

Highest, Lowest, and Mean Temperature +36 −16 +16.02

Total force of the Wind 1876

METEOROLOGICAL OBSERVATIONS OF THE VICTORY DISCOVERY SHIP, TAKEN ON THE ICE, AND REGISTERED HOURLY.

	Days of Month	Direction of Wind.	Force of Wind.	State of Weather.	JUNE, 1831. Temperature in Shade.	+	−	Mean.
	1	7 W. 11 SW.	[illegible]	2 qcs. 2 bc. 16 osd. 2 bc. 2 q.	[illegible]	+24°	+15°	+19°.90
	2	2 SWbS. 7 SWbW. 8 SW. 3 SSW. 1 NW. 1 SSW. 1 NW.	[illegible]	4 q. 12 osd. 6 os. 2 osd.	[illegible]	30	18	24.10
	3	8 West. 10 WSW. 6 SW.	[illegible]	1 o. 1 oc. 20 bc. 2 os.	[illegible]	32	14	23.19
	4	3 W. 18 NW. 1 W. 2 WSW.	[illegible]	1 q. 4 bc. 3 b. 16 bc.	[illegible]	30½	14½	21.96
+	5	8 W. 10 WNW. 6 WSW.	[illegible]	6 b. 1 bcd. 17 b.	[illegible]	30	15	23.21
	6	5 WSW. 1 C. 3 S. 4 C. 3 SWbS. 2 SW. 3 WSW.	[illegible]	20 bc. 4 b.	[illegible]	33	14	24.10
	7	2 SbW. 1 N. 1 NW. 3 SSW. 1 SE. 4 SSE. 4 E. 4 ESE. 2 SE. 2 SEbS.	[illegible]	4 bc. 0 b. 4 bc. 4 os. 8 ods. 2 o.	[illegible]	32	15	25.34
	8	2 SbE. 2 S. 4 SE to E. 4 S. 12 Calm.	[illegible]	2 o. 1 os. 1 bcs. 7 bc. 6 o. 1 qs. 3 os. 1 bc.	[illegible]	37	29	32.58
	9	1 C. 5 WSW. 2 NSE. 4 N. 8 NNW. 4 NW.	[illegible]	4 bc. 7 qc. 6 bc. 2 q. 7 bc.	[illegible]	37	24½	30.52
	10	11 WNW. 3 NNW. 4 NWbN. 4 N.	[illegible]	4 bc. 6 b. 12 o. 4 q.	[illegible]	38	20½	26.21
	11	20 NW. 4 WbN.	[illegible]	22 o. 1 od. 2 os.	[illegible]	36½	26	32.71
+	12	2 NW. 22 West.	[illegible]	2 o. 2 os. 15 osd. 4 bcd. 2 bc.	[illegible]	32	20	25.77
	13	1 SSW. 22 SW. 1 WSW.	[illegible]	2 bc. 2 b. 1 b. 11 b. 8 bc.	[illegible]	35	18	27.08
	14	3 WSW. 13 West. 8 Calm.	[illegible]	3 bc. 1 o. 2 bc. 3 o. 4 os. 11 bc.	[illegible]	40½	22	31.71
	15	3 SW. 2 C. 4 SSW. 6 WSW. 6 SE. 2 SbE. 2 C.	[illegible]	4 b. 3 bc. 13 b. 4 q.	[illegible]	41	26	33.23
	16	4 SE. 1 N. 2 NbW. 4 NW. 4 SW. 2 +. 6 Calm.	[illegible]	3 qs. 3 q. 2 qs. 4 c. 12 b.	[illegible]	42	26	34.19
	17	3 SE. 1 S. 3 NE. 1 S. 3 C. 1 SW. 8 +. 3 N. 1 NW.	[illegible]	24 b.	[illegible]	41	24	34.94
	18	3 C. 6 NW. 3 C. 5 NW. 1 C. 2 NW. 1 C.	[illegible]	9 c. 4 b. 3 c. 4 b. 4 c.	[illegible]	41	28	35.08
+	19	8 NW. 16 North.	[illegible]	8 b. 4 c. 12 o.	[illegible]	49	32	39.58
	20	2 N. 2 W. 1 NW. 2 C. 1 NW. 1 N. 1 C. 12 SSW. 1 SE. 1 S.	[illegible]	24 b.	[illegible]	52	32	40.90
	21	13 SW. 5 S. 1 W. 5 NW.	[illegible]	3 c. 2 of. 6 o. 4 c. 4 b.	[illegible]	40	32	34.38
	22	2 SW. 2 N. 4 SWbN. 4 N. 4 NW. 8 NSW.	[illegible]	c. cs. c. cb. c. mb. c. cb.	[illegible]	40	31½	35.42
	23	4 NSW. 3 C. 3 NSW. 1 S. 5 SSE. 8 SW.	[illegible]	8 b. 1 bc. 11 b. 1 g. 3 of.	[illegible]	52	30½	38.60
	24	6 SW. 10 S. 2 SW. 2 S. 2 SW. 2 S.	[illegible]	4 of. 2 c. 2 of. 1 c. 15 b.	[illegible]	40	30	35.38
	25	1 S. 11 SW. 0 WSW. 2 W. 1 WSW.	[illegible]	c. g. o. bc. c. bc. c. bc	[illegible]	38	34	36.28
⊕	26	4 Wly. 4 C. 4 N. 6 S. 2 C. 4 SE.	[illegible]	2 o. 2 qr. 1 o. 13 bc. 2 b. 4 g.	[illegible]	39	31	36.38
	27	2 SW. 11 S. 5 SW. 6 W.	[illegible]	4 o. 4 co. 4 b. 1 c. 3 o. 0 cf.	[illegible]	39	33	35.75
	28	4 Wly. 3 NW. 1 C. 4 SW. 12 S.	[illegible]	cr. c. oc. g. o. bc. b. c.	[illegible]	42	32	37.27
	29	10 SW. 1 C. 1 S. 4 SSE. 8 S.	[illegible]	4 c. 4 f. 1 bc. 12 f. 2 bcf. 2 bc. 8 c.	[illegible]	40	31	35.52
	30	12 SW. 12 WNW.	[illegible]	4 bc. 1 cs. 1 c. 2 bc. 4 c. 4 bcs. 2 b. 6 bc.	[illegible]	38	33	35.54

ABSTRACT.

13 N.122.	NbW.1.	21 NNW.61.	NWbN.30.	149 NW.255.	0 NWbW.0.	52 WNW.160.	4 WbN.13.	North Westerly = 238
81 W.231.	0 WbS.0.	34 WSW.61.	7 SWbW.31.	119 SW.357.	4 SWbS.8.	25 SSW.52.	0 SbW.0.	South Westerly = 283
71 S.155.	4 SbE.8.	11 SSE.25.	2 SEbS.6.	10 SE.23.	0 SEbE.0.	4 ESE.18.	0 EbS.0.	South Easterly = 111
6 E.17.	0 EbN.0.	0 ENE.0.	0 NEbE.0.	7 NE.9.	0 NEbN.0.	2 NNE.7.	0 NbE.0.	North Easterly = 15

Total.
647 hours.
8 do. wind variable.
65 do. calm.
720 = 30 days.

Highest, Lowest, and Mean Temperature +52 +14 +31.56

Total force of the Wind 1715

d

METEOROLOGICAL OBSERVATIONS OF THE VICTORY DISCOVERY SHIP, TAKEN ON THE ICE, AND REGISTERED HOURLY.

Days of Month.	Direction of Wind.	Force of Wind.	State of Weather.	JULY, 1831. Temperature in Shade.	+	−	Mean.
1	WNW. SW. WSW. WNW. NW.	[illegible]	[illegible]	[illegible]	39°	33	35°.69
2	NW. NNW. NW. NWbW.	[illegible]	[illegible]	[illegible]	38	31	34.64
3	NW. WNW. W. S. W. SW.	[illegible]	[illegible]	[illegible]	40	34	37.42
4	W. S. SW. SSE. S. SSE. SE.	[illegible]	[illegible]	[illegible]	38	32	36.23
5	SE. East.	[illegible]	[illegible]	[illegible]	34	32	33.29
6	NE. ENE. NE. NNE. NE. NNE.	[illegible]	[illegible]	[illegible]	38	32	35.5
7	N. NW. N. NWbN. NNE. NNW. N. SW. NNE. SW.	[illegible]	[illegible]	[illegible]	41	34	38.77
8	SW. N. NNW. W. SW. S. SSE. SE. SW. WSW. SW.	[illegible]	[illegible]	[illegible]	43	37	40.50
9	SW. N. NW. WNW. NW. N. NE. C. W. N. NNE.	[illegible]	[illegible]	[illegible]	38	34	36.23
10	NNE. N. NNW. NbW. NNE.	[illegible]	[illegible]	[illegible]	38	32	35.85
11	NNE. NbE.	[illegible]	[illegible]	[illegible]	37	34	35.38
12	NNE. NNW. Vble SEly. SE. S. W. SW. NW. NNW. NNE.	[illegible]	[illegible]	[illegible]	40	34	36.92
13	WSW. NE. C. E. ESE. SE. S. Ely. SW. S. SSW.	[illegible]	[illegible]	[illegible]	40	33	36.10
14	SE. SW. S. ESE. E. ESE.	[illegible]	[illegible]	[illegible]	39	33	35.33
15	East. NE. NNE. NEbN.	[illegible]	[illegible]	[illegible]	39	33	35 25
16	North. NE. NNE.	[illegible]	[illegible]	[illegible]	44	34	40.15
17	NE. NNE	[illegible]	[illegible]	[illegible]	44	34	39.00
18	NE. N. NE. North.	[illegible]	[illegible]	[illegible]	44	32	39.52
19	North. SE.	[illegible]	[illegible]	[illegible]	48	37	42.75
20	S. Sly. N. SbE. S. NW. NE. E. S. E. S.	[illegible]	[illegible]	[illegible]	46	35	39.81
21	C. SbE. N. S. SbE. SE. SSE.	[illegible]	[illegible]	[illegible]	44	34	38.73
22	SSE. SW. SbE. N. S. SSE.	[illegible]	[illegible]	[illegible]	45	34	39 52
23	SSE. W. Calm. NE.	[illegible]	[illegible]	[illegible]	42	33	37.54
24	C. SSE. SE. EbN. E. C. North.	[illegible]	[illegible]	[illegible]	44	33	39 13
25	C. E. EbS. East.	[illegible]	[illegible]	[illegible]	41	33	38.00
26	SE. E. SE. E. C. ENE.	[illegible]	[illegible]	[illegible]	42	33	37.67
27	C. N. NE. S. C.	[illegible]	[illegible]	[illegible]	48	36	40.60
28	C. E. NW. N. C.	[illegible]	[illegible]	[illegible]	41	35	38.54
29	North. Vble NWbW. NNW.	[illegible]	[illegible]	[illegible]	41	36	38.92
30	Vble from NW. Calm.	[illegible]	[illegible]	[illegible]	50	36	41.92
31	NW. N to NW. Vble W to NE.	[illegible]	[illegible]	[illegible]	44	37	41.31

ABSTRACT.

N. 180.	NbW. 33.	NNW. 114.	NWbN. 17.	NW. 134.	NWbW. 20.	WNW. 109.	WbN. 0.	North Westerly = 205	Total. 678 hours.
W. 100.	WbS. 0.	WSW. 19.	SWbW. 0.	SW. 74.	SWbS. 0.	SSW. 1.	SbW. 0.	South Westerly = 61	22 do. wind variable.
S. 116.	SbE. 32.	SSE. 85.	SEbS. 0.	SE. 94.	SEbE. 0.	ESE. 20.	EbS. 11.	South Easterly = 155	45 do. calm.
E. 102.	EbN. 2.	ENE. 34.	NEbE. 0.	NE. 149.	NEbN. 19.	NNE. 192.	NbE. 121.	North Easterly = 255	744 = 31 days.

Highest, Lowest, and Mean Temperature + 50 + 32 + 37.94

Total force of the Wind 1775

METEOROLOGICAL OBSERVATIONS OF THE VICTORY DISCOVERY SHIP, TAKEN ON THE ICE, AND REGISTERED HOURLY.

Days of Month.	Direction of Wind.	Force of Wind.	State of Weather.	AUGUST, 1831. Temperature in Shade.	+	−	Mean.
1	SW. W. E. NEly to ESE. NE. Wly.	[illegible]	bc. b. bc.	[illegible]	49	36	41°.29
2	WNW. SW. W. WSW. S.	[illegible]	o. bc. b.	[illegible]	54	40	47.41
3	W. Wly. W. S. WSW. SW. S.	[illegible]	c. bc. b. bc.	[illegible]	52	40	44.91
4	S. SbW. WSW. W. WSW. SW. SWbW.	[illegible]	c. g. or. c.	[illegible]	46	36	41.00
5	WNW. W. WbS. WNW. W. SW. C.	[illegible]	b. c. bc. c.	[illegible]	40	36	38.17
6	C. N. NE. E. S. Ely. Calm.	[illegible]	c. b. bc. b.	[illegible]	41	31	37.08
7	WNW. NW. Nly. ESE. S. W.	[illegible]	c. b. c. cb. c. bc.	[illegible]	41	33	37.29
8	W. WbN. NW. WbN. NW. WNW. Wly. WNW. NW.	[illegible]	c.	[illegible]	44	32	37.62
9	WSW. W. C. S. Ely E. NE. ENE.	[illegible]	bc. b. bc. b. c. o.	[illegible]	50½	31	40.98
10	ENE. E. NEbE. ENE. NE.	[illegible]	bc. f. or. c. cr. b. of.	[illegible]	35	32	33.81
11	ENE. NE. NEbE. NNE. Nly. NE. N.	[illegible]	ofr. of.	[illegible]	37	33	35.15
12	N. NNW. NNE. NNW. N. NW.	[illegible]	c. q. b. bc. q. bc.	[illegible]	39	34	36.56
13	WNW. NE. N. Ely. SE. S. C. N.	[illegible]	c. b. c.	[illegible]	44½	34½	40.15
14	C. NE. C. ENE. C. N. +. N. NEbE. E. NE.	[illegible]	b. bc. f. bc. c.	[illegible]	41	34	36.88
15	E. ENE. E. ESE. E. ESE. E.	[illegible]	o. or. c. or. o. or. ofr.	[illegible]	36	34	35.33
16	Ely. E. ESE. +. South.	[illegible]	or. ors. os. ofr. of.	[illegible]	35	33	33.96
17	SSW. S. Ely. C. SE. Calm.	[illegible]	b. ofs. of. ofs. of. ofr. of. ofr. of.	[illegible]	38	33	35.06
18	C. NW. NNW. C. SSE. NE. NNW.	[illegible]	ofs. of. cfc. c. cf. bc. cf.	[illegible]	41	33	36.17
19	NNW. Wly. NWbN. NE. NNE. NE. +. NNW. C. NNW. WNW.	[illegible]	cf. cb. c. bc. b. bc. b. bc. c.	[illegible]	48	35	40.29
20	C. NWbW. NW. C. Nly. S. SW. WSW. WbN. WSW. SW. W.	[illegible]	bc. c. b. bc.	[illegible]	44	37	40.04
21	W. WNW. NE. Ely. ENE. NEbE. NE.	[illegible]	bc. c. of. ofr. ofr. cfr. cr. cfr.	[illegible]	38	32	35.13
22	N. NNE. N. NWbN. NW. NNW.	[illegible]	cfr. cr. bc. b. bc.	[illegible]	33	28½	31.91
23	NW. NWbN. C. N.	[illegible]	of. cfr. of. fs. br. b. bc. o.	[illegible]	38	29	34.08
24	NNW. NWbN. N. SE. SSE. S. C.	[illegible]	o. of. c. bc. b. bc. o.	[illegible]	37	29	33.01
25	SbE. C. SW. S. SE. Ely. C. S. C. SWbW. S. WSW. N.	[illegible]	c. of. f. bc. c.	[illegible]	42	30	34.83
26	N. NNW. NW. NEly. SE. S. SSE. S. SSE. S.	[illegible]	bc. cf. b. bc.	[illegible]	36	33½	34.79
27	SSE. S. SW. S. Sly. +. ENE. +. NE. Ely. SE. SSE. S. SbW.	[illegible]	[illegible]	[illegible]	40	32	36.29
28	S. WSW. W. WNW. W. WbN.	[illegible]	c. bc. os. bc. c.	[illegible]	36	29½	32.32
29	WbS. WNW. N. NW. WNW. W. WNW. N.	[illegible]	[illegible]	[illegible]	31	21	27.92
30	N. NNW. NNE. N. NbW. NNW.	[illegible]	bc. b. os. bc. b. bc. b. bc. b.	[illegible]	34	21	29.51
31	N. Sly. SE. SW. +.	[illegible]	b. bc. cf. bc. qbc.	[illegible]	34	26	29.79

SUMMARY.			
[illegible]	North Westerly — 267	Total. 687 hours. 14 do. wind variable. 43 do. calm. 741 — 31 days.	Highest, Lowest, and Mean Temperature +51+21+36.51
[illegible]	South Westerly — 134		
[illegible]	South Easterly — 130		Total force of the Wind . . 2001
[illegible]	North Easterly 182		

METEOROLOGICAL OBSERVATIONS OF THE VICTORY DISCOVERY SHIP, TAKEN ON THE ICE, AND REGISTERED HOURLY.

Days of Month.	Direction of Wind.	Force of Wind.	State of Weather.	SEPTEMBER, 1831. Temperature in Shade.	+	−	Mean.
1	SW. Sly. SbW. S. E. +Vble. C.	[illegible]	beq. bc. o. or.	+30°. 31°. 32°. 33°. 34°. 36°. 35°. 34°.	+36°	+30°	+33°.83
2	C.Vble.N.NbW.NW.NWbW.SWbN. C. NNW.	[illegible]	or. os. or. o. o. o. bc. of.	+34. 33. 34. 33. 34. 35. 35½. 35. 34. 33½. 33.	35½	33	33.98
3	N. NWbN. NNW. N. NbE.	[illegible]	bf.cf.o.bc.os.oqs.o.c.cq.cqf.	+33. 32. 31½. 32. 33. 33½. 34. 33½. 33. 32. 32½. 32. 31½. 31. 30.	34	30	32.42
4	NNW. N. NbW.	[illegible]	oqf. oq. cq. oq. cq. cq.	+30. 29. 28. 27. 26. 27. 28. 30. 29. 26. 27.	30	26	28.04
5	NNW. NWbN. NW.	[illegible]	oqs. cq. os. oqs. os. osq.	+27. 26. 27. 28. 28½. 29. 28. 27. 26.	29	26	27.44
6	NWbN. NNW. NW.	[illegible]	oqs. os. o. c. os. o. cs.	+25. 26. 27. 28. 28½. 29. 28. 27½. 27.	29	25	27.17
7	NNW. NW. NWbN. NbW. NNW. N.	[illegible]	o. c. os. o. os. o. c. o. c. qs. bq.	+27. 28. 28½. 29. 30. 29. 28. 27.	30	27	28.15
8	W. SSW. Sly. S. SE.	[illegible]	o. b. osq. cq. bcq. cq. b. bc.	+26. 25½. 26. 24. 21½. 25. 27. 28. 29. 28. 27. 28. 26½.	29	24	27.06
9	N. NNW. Sly. SE. S. SSW. +Vble. West.	[illegible]	b. bc. bq. b. cq. b.	+25½. 25. 24. 25. 26. 27. 28. 29. 30. 31½. 31. 30. 28. 27. 26½. 25½. 25½. 24.	31½	22½	26.44
10	W. SSW. Sly. S. SE.	[illegible]	bc. bcm. cf. c. of. o. of. os. o. cf.	+24. 23. 23½. 26. 23½. 24. 23. 24.	26	23	23.92
11	SSE. S. SSW. Ely. SSE. S. SE. C. NW.	[illegible]	of. os. c. o. os. o. c. of. cf.	+24. 25½. 28. 29. 31½. 33. 33. 32.	33	24	29.00
12	N. NWbN. NbW. N. NNW. C. NE.	[illegible]	o. cb. of. c. cs. c. o. c. cf. os. c. b.	+32. 31. 30. 29. 28. 26. 25. 27½. 25. 22. 22½. 23.	32	22	27.25
13	N. SW. E. NNW. Nly. N. NNW. NWbN.	[illegible]	b. c. o. ob. o. ob. os. o. bc. bq.	+22. 24. 25. 24. 23. 22. 20. 19. 18.	25	18	21.97
14	NNW.	[illegible]	bq. b. bq.	+18. 19. 20. 21. 22. 23. 22. 21. 20. 19. 18.	23	18	19.83
15	NNW.	[illegible]	b. o. cb. c.	+17½. 17. 16. 18. 19. 20. 22. 23. 24. 25. 26. 24. 23½. 23. 25½.	26	16	21.48
16	NNW. Westly.	[illegible]	o. c. o. cb. o. c. bc.	+25. 28. 27. 28. 29. 30. 32. 31½. 31. 32. 31. 30. 28. 27.	32	25	29.23
17	W. WSW. WNW. C. Vble. NE. C.	[illegible]	o. c. bc. c. o.	+26. 27. 26. 27. 28. 27½. 28. 27. 26.	28	26	26.73
18	NWbW. WNW. N. NbE. NNW. N. NNW. NWbN.	[illegible]	bc.cs.of.ofs.of.c.cs.o.os.o.oq.cbq.	+26. 27. 26. 24. 23. 22. 20. 19. 18. 17. 16. 16. 17½.	27	16	20.35
19	NWbN. NNW. NWbN. NW. +. SWbS.	[illegible]	b. bc. c. br. b. bc.	+18. 19. 18. 19. 20. 20½. 21. 22. 21. 20. 19. 18. 17. 19.	22	17	19.04
20	SSW. Sly. SEtoSW. SbW. S. SSW. SW.	[illegible]	c. bc. bf. bc. c. os. oqs.	+20. 21. 22. 21. 20. 21. 22. 23. 24. 25. 26. 27.	27	20	22.92
21	WSW. SW. SbW. Sly. NNW. NbW.	[illegible]	oqs. os.	+28. 29. 30. 31. 32. 32½. 32. 30. 29. 27. 26. 24. 22.	32½	22	29.52
22	NbW. N. NWbN. NW. C. NNW.	[illegible]	o. bc. c. b. bc. c. b.	+21. 20. 19. 18. 17. 18. 18. 17. 16. 17. 18.	21	16	17.25
23	NW. Wly. NW. WNW. Wly. NbW.	[illegible]	c. c. cb. c. bc. b. bc.	+17. 18. 17. 16. 14. 15. 15½. 16. 17. 18. 19. 18. 17. 16. 15. 14. 13. 12. 10. 9.	19	9	16.23
24	+. C. W. WSW. Vble. WSW. SW.	[illegible]	b. bc. o. of. o.	+8. 7. 8. 9. 12. 12. 13. 14. 14½. 14. 15. 16.	16	8	12.15
25	C. SW. WSW. SE. ESE. EbS. ESE.	[illegible]	bc. o. os.	+16. 19. 18. 19. 20. 21. 22. 23. 22. 20. 19. 18. 17.	23	16	19.00
26	NE. NNE. N. NbE. NNE. N. NE. EbS.	[illegible]	os. cs. bd. os. od. qd. bc. dq.	+14. 13. 12. 13½. 13. 14. 13. 12. 10. 9. 10. 12. 14. 16. 17.	17	9	11.61
27	EbS. NNE. NbE. NNW. N.	[illegible]	bc. b. bc. b. q. bc. b.	+17. 16. 15. 14. 11. 10. 9. 10. 11. 10½. 10. 9. 8. 7. 8. 7. 6½. 6.	17	6	10.31
28	N. NbE. NE. EbN. ENE.	[illegible]	bc. o. od. os.	+8. 7. 8. 8½. 9. 10. 11. 12. 14. 16. 18. 19. 20. 21. 22. 23. 24. 25.	25	7	13.44
29	E. EbN. ESE. EbN. East.	[illegible]	os. o. oh. o. os. o. c. bc. b.	+26. 28. 29. 28. 26. 25. 24. 23. 22. 23.	29	22	26.70
30	NE. NNE. North.	[illegible]	c. bc. b. bc. of. bc. b. of. bf.	+23. 22½. 22. 21. 22. 20. 18. 17. 16. 18. 17. 16½. 16.	23	16	19.67

ABSTRACT.

N.	NbW.	NNW.	NWbN.	NW.	NWbW.	WNW.	WbN.	North Westerly 554	Total. 661 hours. 25 do. wind variable. 34 do. calm. 720 = 30 days.
W.	WbS.	WSW.	SWbW.	SW.	SWbS.	SSW.	SbW.	South Westerly 101	
S.	SbE.	SSE.	SEbS.	SE.	SEbE.	ESE.	EbS.	South Easterly 101	
E.	EbN.	ENE.	NEbE.	NE.	NEbN.	NNE.	NbE.	North Easterly 105	

Highest, Lowest, and Mean Temperature + 36 + 6 +23.4

Total force of the Wind 2441

METEOROLOGICAL OBSERVATIONS OF THE VICTORY DISCOVERY SHIP, TAKEN ON THE ICE, AND REGISTERED HOURLY.

Days of Month.	Direction of Wind.	Force of Wind.	State of Weather.	OCTOBER, 1831. Temperature in Shade.	+	—	Mean.
1	N. NW. WNW. C. NW. N. C.	[illegible]	[illegible]	[illegible]	15°	7°	11°.25
2	C. S. C. SSW. S. C. +Vble.	[illegible]	[illegible]	[illegible]	29	13	22.21
3	SW.W.SSE.SSW.+Vble N.W.NNW.C.	[illegible]	[illegible]	[illegible]	26	13	19.54
4	C. SE. SbW. SW. S.	[illegible]	[illegible]	[illegible]	20	14	16.42
5	S. SSW. SW. S. Sly.	[illegible]	[illegible]	[illegible]	20	8	16.21
6	SSE. SE. C. SSE. SW. C. N.	[illegible]	[illegible]	[illegible]	24	8	18.10
7	N. NbW. NNW. N.	[illegible]	[illegible]	[illegible]	19	16½	18.08
8	North.	[illegible]	[illegible]	[illegible]	16	12½	15.60
9	N. NNW. N. NbW.	[illegible]	[illegible]	[illegible]	13	8	10.97
10	NbW. NNW. NbW.	[illegible]	[illegible]	[illegible]	8	4	5.33
11	NbW. NNW.	[illegible]	[illegible]	[illegible]	8	5	6.73
12	NNW. ENE. +Vble. NNW.	[illegible]	[illegible]	[illegible]	14	7	10.94
13	+. NNE. ESE. SSE. SE.	[illegible]	[illegible]	[illegible]	18	9	13.13
14	SE. SW. S. SSE. C. SSE.	[illegible]	[illegible]	[illegible]	22	13	18.48
15	SSE. C. S. SSW. Wly. +. Wly.	[illegible]	[illegible]	[illegible]	19	10	16.56
16	SSW. SW. S. SSW. WSW. C.	[illegible]	[illegible]	[illegible]	22	8	17.63
17	WSW. S. SEbS. SSE. SEbS.	[illegible]	[illegible]	[illegible]	24	22	22.90
18	SE. E.WSW. SSE. WSW. NNW. ESE.	[illegible]	[illegible]	[illegible]	26	24	25.09
19	C. SSE. S. SSW. W. SSW. +Vble.	[illegible]	[illegible]	[illegible]	25	21	23.33
20	W. NE. NbW. NNW. N.	[illegible]	[illegible]	[illegible]	22	−2	10.63
21	North. NbW.	[illegible]	[illegible]	[illegible]	−2	6	−3.85
22	NbW. C. Nly. C. ESE. E. C. NNW. E.	[illegible]	[illegible]	[illegible]	6	11	9.17
23	S. SSW. Sly. +Vble. S.+Vble. C. North.	[illegible]	[illegible]	[illegible]	+2	8	3.60
24	NbW. NW. NbW.	[illegible]	[illegible]	[illegible]	−9	23	17.40
25	NbW.	[illegible]	[illegible]	[illegible]	+3½	20	7.85
26	N. NNW. SE. ESE. E. NE. N.	[illegible]	[illegible]	[illegible]	16	0	+6.48
27	N. NNE. N. NE.	[illegible]	[illegible]	[illegible]	2½	5	−1.23
28	NNE. North.	[illegible]	[illegible]	[illegible]	8	0	+3.70
29	North.	[illegible]	[illegible]	[illegible]	0	2½	−1.27
30	NNW. Ely. S. Wly. SE. E. SW.	[illegible]	[illegible]	[illegible]	−2	11	5.21
31	S. SSE. SW. E. SE. S.	[illegible]	[illegible]	[illegible]	+17	11½	+1.15

ABSTRACT.

N. 56. NbW. 15. NNW. 306. NWbN. 0. NW. 15. NWbW. 0. WNW. 2. WbN. 0.
W. 11. WbS. 0. WSW. 20. SWbW. 0. SW. 70. SWbS. 0. SSW. 70. SbW. 12.
S. 126. SbE. 0. SSE. 51. SEbS. 21. SE. 46. SEbE. 0. ESE. 22. EbS. 0.
E. 58. EbN. 0. ENE. 1. NEbE. 0. NE. 30. NEbN. 0. NNE. 60. NbE. 0.

North Westerly — 331
South Westerly 115
South Easterly — 152
North Easterly — 63

Total.
664 hours.
24 do. wind variable.
56 do. calm.
744 = 31 days.

Highest, Lowest, and Mean Temperature +29 −23 +8.32

Total force of the Wind 2044

METEOROLOGICAL OBSERVATIONS OF THE VICTORY DISCOVERY SHIP, TAKEN ON THE ICE, AND REGISTERED HOURLY.

Days of Month.	Direction of Wind.	Force of Wind.	State of Weather.	NOVEMBER, 1831. Temperature in Shade.	+	—	Mean.
1	[illegible]	[illegible]	[illegible]	[illegible]	+20	+11½	+17°.13
2	[illegible]	[illegible]	[illegible]	[illegible]	14	0	6.10
3	[illegible]	[illegible]	[illegible]	[illegible]	13	4	7.83
4	[illegible]	[illegible]	[illegible]	[illegible]	13½	−2	8.06
5	[illegible]	[illegible]	[illegible]	[illegible]	3	2	0.83
6	[illegible]	[illegible]	[illegible]	[illegible]	−2	17	−11.69
7	[illegible]	[illegible]	[illegible]	[illegible]	3	19	13.46
8	[illegible]	[illegible]	[illegible]	[illegible]	+10	3	+ 6.33
9	[illegible]	[illegible]	[illegible]	[illegible]	16	+8	11.21
10	[illegible]	[illegible]	[illegible]	[illegible]	17	12	14.92
11	[illegible]	[illegible]	[illegible]	[illegible]	18	13	16.5
12	[illegible]	[illegible]	[illegible]	[illegible]	14½	−2	4.48
13	[illegible]	[illegible]	[illegible]	[illegible]	10½	+6	8.52
14	[illegible]	[illegible]	[illegible]	[illegible]	9	−5½	2.25
15	[illegible]	[illegible]	[illegible]	[illegible]	0	20	−12.29
16	[illegible]	[illegible]	[illegible]	[illegible]	0	18	12.25
17	[illegible]	[illegible]	[illegible]	[illegible]	+19	+3	+13.92
18	[illegible]	[illegible]	[illegible]	[illegible]	19	8	13.69
19	[illegible]	[illegible]	[illegible]	[illegible]	19	3	12.92
20	[illegible]	[illegible]	[illegible]	[illegible]	9	0	4.58
21	[illegible]	[illegible]	[illegible]	[illegible]	8	−7½	0.98
22	[illegible]	[illegible]	[illegible]	[illegible]	14	+5	9.02
23	[illegible]	[illegible]	[illegible]	[illegible]	6	−8	2.25
24	[illegible]	[illegible]	[illegible]	[illegible]	−9	18	−13.75
25	[illegible]	[illegible]	[illegible]	[illegible]	0	15	6.60
26	[illegible]	[illegible]	[illegible]	[illegible]	11	20	15.42
27	[illegible]	[illegible]	[illegible]	[illegible]	16	24	20.17
28	[illegible]	[illegible]	[illegible]	[illegible]	22	30	25.38
29	[illegible]	[illegible]	[illegible]	[illegible]	26	32½	29.29
30	[illegible]	[illegible]	[illegible]	[illegible]	33	42	38.16

ABSTRACT.

N.489.	NbW.409.	NNW.114.	NWbN.0.	NW.93.	NWbW.0.	WNW.5.	WbN.0.
W.52.	WbS.0.	WSW.0.	SWbW.0.	SW.13.	SWbS.0.	SSW.73.	SbW.5.
S.134.	SbE.42.	SSE.123.	SEbS.2.	SE.110.	SEbE.0.	ESE.4.	EbS.2.
E.39.	EbN.0.	ENE.6.	NEbE.0.	NE.4.	NEbN.0.	NNE.0.	NbE.0.

North Westerly — 235
South Westerly — 51
South Easterly — 249
North Easterly — 27

Total.
564 hours.
15 do. wind variable.
141 do. calm.
720 — 30 days.

Highest, Lowest, and Mean Temperature +20 −42 − 1.23

Total force of the Wind . . . 1449

METEOROLOGICAL OBSERVATIONS OF THE VICTORY DISCOVERY SHIP, TAKEN ON THE ICE, AND REGISTERED HOURLY.

Days of Month.	Direction of Wind.	Force of Wind.	State of Weather.	DECEMBER, 1831. Temperature in Shade.	+	−	Mean.
1	C. +. SE. C. Sly. NW. Calm.	[illegible]	b.	[illegible]	40°	42°	41.40
2	NW. S. C. SE. +. NW. Sly. North.	[illegible]	b. bd.	[illegible]	23	40	37.69
3	North. NNW. NbW.	[illegible]	bd. cd. bd.	[illegible]	13	22	17.13
4	NNW.	[illegible]	bd. od. cd. bd.	[illegible]	8	12	8.52
5	NNW.	[illegible]	[illegible]	[illegible]	6	8	7.10
6	N. NNW. +. NW. E.	[illegible]	bcd. b. bc. b.	[illegible]	8	26½	18.29
7	NNW. NNE. N. NW. SW. S. E. S. SSE. S. SE. SSE. Ely. C.	[illegible]	b. c. os. o. b.	[illegible]	13	21	17.90
8	N. NW. N. NNW.	[illegible]	[illegible]	[illegible]	12	16	13.81
9	NNW. NW. N. E. N.	[illegible]	[illegible]	[illegible]	10	16	11.60
10	North. NNW.	[illegible]	b. bc. os. b.	[illegible]	14	22½	18.01
11	North. NNW.	[illegible]	bd. b.	[illegible]	22	25	23.60
12	North. NNW. N. East.	[illegible]	b.	[illegible]	22½	26½	24.44
13	NEly. C. E. C. E. +. SE. N.	[illegible]	b. bc. b.	[illegible]	25	32	28.83
14	North. NNW. North.	[illegible]	b. bc.bcd.bc. b.	[illegible]	18	29	21.17
15	North. NNW.	[illegible]	b. bd. cd. bd. b.	[illegible]	6	18	10.19
16	NNW. N. NNW.	[illegible]	b. bc. cd. osg.	[illegible]	2	8	5.00
17	NW. NNW. NW. WSW. C. NW.	[illegible]	[illegible]	[illegible]	7	22	15.48
18	NSW. N. +. SE. Ely. C. SE. C.	[illegible]	b. o. b.	[illegible]	22	35½	28.40
19	C. N. NNW. C.	[illegible]	b. bc. bd. b.	[illegible]	28	36	30.31
20	C. SE. NW. SE. S. SE. E. NNW. NW.	[illegible]	b. bc. c. cd. bcd.	[illegible]	8	35	25.77
21	NW. WbS. Calm.	[illegible]	bcd. b.	[illegible]	8	24	12.65
22	C. NW. Wly. NW. E. W. C. NNW. NE. C.	[illegible]	b.	[illegible]	26	39	33.33
23	ESE. C. N to SE. +. NE. C.	[illegible]	b.	[illegible]	35½	39½	36.81
24	C. +. SE. C. E. Calm.	[illegible]	b. bc. c. bc. b.	[illegible]	20	34½	25.61
25	C. S. SE. SSE. NW. W.	[illegible]	bc. os. c. c. b.	[illegible]	14	29	20.46
26	SE. C. SE. +. SE. C.	[illegible]	b.	[illegible]	31	37	35.60
27	C. Sly. +. SSE. C. SE. C.	[illegible]	b.	[illegible]	36	39	37.54
28	NW. E. SW to E. W. C.	[illegible]	b.	[illegible]	36	37½	36.90
29	C. E. NW. E. C.	[illegible]	b. os. b. bc. b. o. b.	[illegible]	30	38	34.85
30	C. SSE. +. Calm.	[illegible]	b. os. o. c. b.	[illegible]	27	39	31.79
31	C. S. Sly. SW. S. SE.	[illegible]	b. c. os.	[illegible]	27	39	32.5

ABSTRACT.

N. 28	NbW. 129	NNW. 113	NWbN. 0	NW. 257	NWbW. 0	WNW. 0	WbN. 0	North Westerly 371	Total. 556 hours, 16 do. wind vble. 152 do. calm.
W. 13	WbS. 2	WSW. 1	SWbW. 0	SW. 20	SWbS. 0	SSW. 0	SbW. 0	South Westerly 23	
S. 15	SbE. 0	SSE. 14	SEbS. 0	SE. 61	SEbE. 0	ESE. 4	EbS. 0	South Easterly 100	
E. 51	EbN. 0	ENE. 0	NEbE. 0	NE. 7	NEbN. 0	NNE. 5	NbE. 0	North Easterly 62	744 — 31 days.

Highest, Lowest, and Mean Temperature −2 −42 −23.96

Total force of the Wind . . 2277

METEOROLOGICAL OBSERVATIONS OF THE VICTORY DISCOVERY SHIP, TAKEN ON THE ICE, AND REGISTERED HOURLY.

Days of Month.	Direction of Wind.	Force of Wind.	State of Weather.	JANUARY, 1832. Temperature in Shade.	+	−	Mean.
1	4/S. 2/W. 4/NW. 10/NbW. 6/Calm.	4/1. 1/2. 2/3. 4/4. 2/5. 1/2. 2/3. 2/2. 6/0.	1/c. 3/b. 2/bc. 2/bd. 5/cd. 11/b.	−1/26½°. 2/26°. 1/26½°. 3/27°. 1/26°. 1/28°. 2/29°. 2/29½°. 1/30°. 2/29°. 3/34°. 1/33½°. 1/36°. 3/37°.	26	37°	30°.31
2	2/Wly. 1/S. 5/C. 4/SSE. 12/SSW.	3/1. 5/0. 3/1. 2/2. 1/3. 5/4. 2/8. 3/7.	8/b. 9/bc. 3/os. 4/bcqd.	−5/38. 3/37½. 2/37. 1/36½. 1/36. 1/32. 1/31. 1/29. 4/27. 1/27½. 1/27. 1/26. 1/25. 1/26.	25	38	32.52
3	18/SSW. 4/Calm. 2/NNE.	2/5. 1/4. 1/2. 4/5. 1/4. 3/3. 2/3. 3/4. 1/3. 4/0. 2/1.	2/bcqd. 3/b. 3/os. 8/od. 2/bc. 6/b.	−1/26. 1/25½. 1/26. 1/26½. 1/25. 1/24. 1/23. 1/22. 6/24. 1/27. 1/30. 1/31. 1/32. 1/35. 2/36.	22	36	27.02
4	9/Calm. 3/S. 12/NNW.	9/0. 4/1. 2/2. 4/3. 1/4. 1/3. 2/4. 1/5.	9/b. 7/bc. 7/b. 1/bc.	−1/38. 7/39½. 1/36. 1/38. 1/39½. 2/40. 3/39. 4/39½. 2/39. 2/37.	36	40	38.95
5	8/NbW. 14/NNW. 2/Calm.	2/5. 1/6. 2/7. 1/6. 1/5. 2/4. 2/5. 6/6. 2/5. 1/4. 1/2. 1/1. 2/0.	6/bd. 18/b.	−1/37. 2/36. 1/37. 2/37½. 3/37. 5/38. 1/37. 1/38. 1/39. 2/40.	36	40	36.92
6	6/C. 1/SE. 1/C. 4/+. 2/WNW. 3/+. 3/SEbE. 4/C.	6/0. 1/1. 1/0. 12/1. 4/0.	8/b. 2/bc. 2/b. 1/ql. 3/g. 8/b.	−4/45. 1/37. 1/43. 6/44. 1/44½. 7/45. 4/45½.	44	47	44.90
7	1/C. 11/NbW. 12/NNW.	1/0. 2/1. 1/5. 2/3. 2/4. 3/5. 1/6. 2/5. 4/3. 1/3. 1/6. 4/3.	8/b. 2/bg. 2/g. 12/b.	−1/46. 2/43. 3/36½. 4/36. 1/35½. 3/35. 1/35½. 1/35. 2/34½. 2/34. 2/33½. 2/34.	33½	46	36.19
8	4/C. 3/S. 4/C. 6/S. 4/NNW. 3/C.	4/0. 3/1. 4/0. 2/1. 1/2. 1/3. 1/2. 1/1. 2/2. 2/1. 3/0.	24/b.	−2/34. 1/36. 1/38½. 1/40. 1/41½. 1/41. 1/42. 3/41. 1/42. 1/43. 1/41. 1/43½. 1/44. 1/43½. 3/44. 4/44.	34	44½	41.75
9	2/Ely. 2/C. 3/NE. 1/C. 4/N. 3/C. 1/NE. 8/C.	2/1. 2/0. 3/1. 1/0. 4/1. 3/0. 1/2. 8/0.	24/b.	−2/45. 5/45½. 1/46. 1/46½. 1/47. 1/46. 1/46½. 1/46. 1/46½. 1/47. 1/44. 1/42. 2/42½. 2/43.	42	47	44.92
10	12/Calm. 4/+. 8/Calm.	12/0. 1/1. 8/0.	20/b. 2/g. 2/bg.	−3/43. 1/42½. 1/45. 1/44½. 1/44. 2/43½. 2/44. 4/45. 1/44½. 2/43½. 1/42½. 1/40. 1/38. 1/37½.	37½	45	43.15
11	7/S. 1/C. 4/SE. 12/SSE.	1/1. 3/2. 3/1. 1/0. 3/2. 1/3. 1/4. 5/5. 2/6. 4/5.	6/b. 1/qs. 17/os.	−1/38. 2/37. 1/35½. 1/35. 1/34. 1/32. 1/31½. 1/26. 1/25. 1/24. 1/22. 3/20. 5/18. 1/16. 3/15.	15	38	24.5
12	12/S. 6/SE. 2/C. 4/NNW.	2/6. 1/5. 1/6. 2/5. 2/4. 3/3. 2/2. 2/1. 2/0. 3/2. 1/1.	6/osd. 13/os. 1/u. 3/os. 1/u.	−1/16. 1/15. 5/14. 1/13½. 4/13. 8/12. 2/13. 2/12.	12	16	13.02
13	4/NbW. 20/NNW.	1/2. 16/3. 2/4. 5/5.	24/os.	−4/12. 4/13. 1/12½. 1/13. 1/14. 1/16. 1/17. 3/18. 1/20. 2/22. 3/24. 2/25.	12	25	17.19
14	24/NNW.	1/4. 1/5. 1/6. 1/7. 5/8. 1/7. 1/8. 3/9. 1/10. 1/9. 8/10.	24/od.	−3/26. 1/25½. 6/26. 2/27. 3/26. 2/27. 5/27½. 1/28. 1/30.	25½	30	26.71
15	8/NNW. 4/NW. 4/+. 2/NNW. 4/C. 2/SE.	6/10. 2/9. 1/8. 1/2. 1/8. 1/6. 1/2. 3/3. 2/1. 4/0. 1/2. 1/1.	4/cd. 5/bd. 6/qd. 9/b.	−1/28. 1/28½. 1/25. 3/28. 1/29. 2/30. 1/27. 1/28. 2/30. 1/28. 3/26. 1/27. 1/28. 1/29. 1/30. 1/30½.	27	30½	28.38
16	4/S. 4/SSE. 4/Sly. 4/SSW. 4/SE. 4/Sly.	2/3. 2/4. 12/3. 8/1.	12/bc. 6/o. 1/bc. 1/o. 2/bc. 2/cg.	−1/30½. 1/30. 5/28. 1/29. 1/27. 1/26. 1/25. 2/22. 1/21. 1/20. 1/18. 1/19. 1/20. 2/22. 1/21. 2/19. 1/18.	18	30½	23.78
17	2/SSE. 6/SE. 4/+. 3/N. 1/NNW. 4/N. 4/NNW.	8/3. 2/2. 2/1. 3/3. 3/2. 1/4. 5/5.	7/c. 1/o. 4/uc. 7/os. 1/oc. 4/o.	−1/16. 1/15. 1/14. 1/13. 2/12. 2/10½. 1/11. 1/9. 2/8½. 3/8. 1/9. 2/8. 5/9. 1/8.	8	16	10.08
18	8/NNW. 3/+. 1/NNW. 2/C. 6/SE. 4/S.	4/5. 4/4. 3/3. 1/1. 2/0. 4/1. 1/2. 1/3. 1/1. 1/2. 1/3. 1/5.	2/g. 2/o. 15/c. 1/bc. 1/c.	−7/8. 2/10. 1/8. 4/10. 1/11. 2/10. 1/11. 2/12. 1/13½. 2/13. 2/12.	8	13½	10.06
19	5/NW. 1/C. 2/S. 4/SW. 8/SSW. 4/+.	1/3. 1/2. 3/1. 1/0. 3/3. 1/4. 4/5. 2/6. 3/4. 1/3. 1/5. 1/3. 1/5. 1/4.	4/cq. 1/bc. 1/o. 2/os. 2/o. 1/bc. 1/q. 2/os. 3/cd. 1/bcd. 1/b. 4/bc.	−1/14. 1/15. 1/16. 2/[illegible]. 1/17. 2/18. 1/21. 1/22. 3/20. 1/21. 1/22. 1/23. 3/25. 1/25½. 4/26.	14	26	21.15
20	4/SE. 1/N. 1/C. 1/SE. 1/E. 1/N. 15/NNW.	4/4. 1/3. 1/0. 1/2. 4/1. 1/2. 1/3. 1/4. 1/6. 2/7. 2/6. 1/7. 2/5. 1/5. 1/1.	3/cq. 2/os. 2/c. 1/o. 1/c. 11/cd. 4/c.	−2/27. 2/27½. 1/24. 2/23. 1/24. 1/21. 1/22. 1/18. 1/17. 1/15. 3/14. 4/16. 1/11. 1/15. 1/16. 1/16½.	10	27½	18.19
21	3/N. 1/C. 2/Sly. 2/NNW. 4/Sly. 4/EbS. 5/N. 3/NNW.	1/5. 1/2. 1/1. 1/0. 2/1. 2/2. 3/3. 1/3. 1/4. 2/2. 1/1. 3/3. 2/4. 1/7. 2/8.	8/b. 1/o. 11/os. 2/od. 2/obq.	−1/22. 1/23. 2/24. 6/26. 1/25½. 5/25. 3/26. 1/26½. 3/27. 1/28.	22	28	25.13
22	12/North. 12/NNW.	2/9. 9/10. 3/9. 1/10. 1/9. 1/8. 1/7. 2/6. 3/9. 1/8.	16/od. 8/bd.	−2/26. 1/27. 1/28. 2/29. 2/30. 2/33. 1/33½. 1/34½. 1/35. 3/36. 2/36½. 2/36. 1/34. 1/34½. 1/34. 1/33½.	27	36½	32.87
23	24/NNW.	10/9. 1/8. 5/7. 8/8.	1/bcd. 1/bd. 6/od. 12/cd. 4/bd.	−1/32. 1/31. 2/30. 2/28. 1/26. 1/28. 1/29. 2/30. 1/31. 2/31½. 2/32. 1/32½. 1/32. 3/31½. 1/32. 1/32½. 1/31½.	26	32½	30.63
24	24/North.	6/9. 2/6. 2/9. 1/10. 1/9. 2/8. 2/7. 3/8. 4/9. 3/10.	24/bd.	−1/32. 1/31½. 1/31. 4/30. 2/31. 3/30. 1/29. 2/28. 1/27. 3/24½. 1/24. 2/23. 3/21.	21	32	27.52
25	12/N. 4/NNW. 8/N.	6/9. 2/8. 2/7. 2/6. 2/7. 4/8. 6/7.	4/bd. 16/od. 4/bd.	−1/21. 1/20. 1/19. 2/18. 2/21. 1/19. 1/17. 1/18. 1/19. 3/16. 1/19. 8/20. 1/18½.	17	21	19.31
26	4/N. 4/NNW. 4/+. 4/W. 4/SW. 2/SSW. 2/SW.	2/7. 1/6. 2/5. 1/5. 1/3. 1/2. 4/1. 2/3. 3/4. 1/5. 2/6. 1/3. 1/4. 1/6. 1/5.	14/b. 6/c. 1/o. 3/cg.	−3/18. 2/20. 1/21. 1/22. 1/23. 1/24. 1/25. 1/27. 3/28. 1/26. 1/27. 1/28. 1/27. 1/26. 3/27. 3/26.	18	28	24.38
27	6/SSE. 4/SSW. 2/SW. 3/C. 1/S. 2/C. 1/W. 3/NNW.	4/5. 1/3. 1/7. 1/6. 1/7. 1/5. 1/4. 1/5. 1/4. 1/2. 1/1. 3/0. 1/1. 2/0. 1/2. 1/3. 2/4.	4/bc. 4/os. 1/o. 2/os. 2/o. 2/c. 4/bc. 5/b.	−1/25. 1/23. 2/22. 2/24. 1/23. 1/22. 2/20. 2/19. 1/18. 1/20. 2/23. 1/22. 2/19. 1/21. 1/23. 1/22. 1/24. 1/24½.	18	25	21.73
28	4/NNW. 6/NW. 4/SWbN. 10/NNW.	7/5. 3/4. 1/3. 1/4. 1/3. 1/4. 10/5.	24/b.	−1/25. 2/26. 2/24½. 1/23. 1/23½. 2/23. 2/24. 1/26. 1/25. 2/24. 1/25. 3/26. 1/24. 3/24½. 2/23.	23	26	24.44
29	24/North.	4/3. 3/2. 4/3. 1/4. 7/5. 4/6. 1/7.	4/b. 4/bc. 4/c. 8/b. 4/b.	−3/23. 1/24. 8/23. 1/22. 3/24. 1/25. 1/26. 1/26½. 1/27. 1/27½. 2/28. 1/30.	22	30	24.54
30	14/North. 2/SSE. 8/North.	7/6. 3/5. 6/6. 3/5. 4/6. 1/5.	6/b. 1/bc. 1/o. 6/od. 4/bcd. 8/b.	−6/30. 1/29. 1/26. 1/24. 1/22. 1/21. 1/20. 2/21. 2/20. 1/22. 1/21. 6/20.	20	30	23.71
31	3/North. 1/South. 20/NNW.	1/4. 1/3. 1/2. 2/1. 2/4. 1/3. 7/6. 2/5. 7/7.	10/b. 2/bd. 12/b.	−1/24. 1/27. 1/30. 1/31½. 1/32. 1/33. 1/33. 1/35½. 1/33½. 1/33. 1/32. 1/30. 2/29. 1/31½. 1/29. 3/28. 5/26.	24	35½	29.40

ABSTRACT.

130/N.796. 33/NbW.129. 215/NNW.1209. 4/NWbN.16. 17/NW.66. 0/NWbW.0. 2/WNW.2. 0/WbN.0.
9/W.23. 0/WbS.0. 0/WSW.0. 0/SWbW.0. 12/SW.52. 0/SWbS.0. 18/SSW.212. 0/SbW.0.
64/S.193. 0/SbE.0. 30/SSE.127. 0/SEbS.0. 36/SE.72. 0/SEbE.3. 0/ESE.0. 0/EbS.0.
5/E.9. 0/EbN.0. 0/ENE.0. 0/NEbE.0. 4/NE.5. 0/NEbN.0. 0/NNE.14. 0/NbE.0.

North Westerly = 404
South Westerly = 69
South Easterly = 131
North Easterly = 19

Total. 614 hours, 30 do. wind variable. 100 do. calm. 744 = 31 days.

Highest, Lowest, and Mean Temperature −8 −47 −27.52

Total force of the Wind 2937

METEOROLOGICAL OBSERVATIONS OF THE VICTORY DISCOVERY SHIP, TAKEN ON THE ICE, AND REGISTERED HOURLY.

	Days of Month.	Direction of Wind.	Force of Wind.	State of Weather.	FEBRUARY, 1832. Temperature in Shade.	+	−	Mean.
	1	NNW.	[illegible]	b. bd.	[illegible]	22	27°	24°.10
	2	NNW.	[illegible]	bd. c. bc.	[illegible]	12	23½	18.04
	3	C. N. +. 1SE. C. N. NNW. C. NNW.	[illegible]	bc. b. g. os.ps. o. bcs. bc. o.	[illegible]	13	20	16.29
	4	NNW. NbW. NNW.	[illegible]	b. bc. cs. os. o. c. bcd. c. b.	[illegible]	19	29½	22.98
+	5	NNW.	[illegible]	b. bd.	[illegible]	29½	35½	33.44
	6	NNW.	[illegible]	bd. od. bd. cd. bd.	[illegible]	27	36	29.95
	7	NNW.	[illegible]	bd.	[illegible]	24	30	27.06
	8	NNW. Calm.	[illegible]	bd. b.	[illegible]	22	35	26.00
	9	C. E. +. Ely. SE.	[illegible]	b. g. b.	[illegible]	35	38½	36.81
	10	S. SE. S to E. S. C.	[illegible]	b.	[illegible]	36½	40	38.60
	11	C. Ely. C. NNW. NW.	[illegible]	b. bc. o.	[illegible]	35½	39	37.21
+	12	NNW.	[illegible]	o. od. bc. b.	[illegible]	34½	37½	35.42
	13	NW. NNW. Calm.	[illegible]	bd. b.	[illegible]	32	39½	35.19
	14	C. S. E. SE. E. S. E. S.	[illegible]	b. bc.	[illegible]	37	41½	39.46
	15	S. SSE. SE. Calm.	[illegible]	c. bc. c. bc. b. bc. c.	[illegible]	34	39	37.71
	16	Sly. W. NNW. C. N. NW. NSW. W. NNW.	[illegible]	c. b. c. bc. c.	[illegible]	33	37	35.08
	17	NNW. Calm.	[illegible]	bc. b. bc. bcd. bc. b.	[illegible]	35	40½	37.73
	18	C. E. N. C. NNW. C. Sly NW. C. SE. E. NNW.	[illegible]	b. bc. b.	[illegible]	31	41	37.15
+	19	C. NNW. C. NNW.	[illegible]	b. g. cc. cfd. cd. bd. bg. b.	[illegible]	38	44½	41.02
	20	NNW.	[illegible]	b. bc. o. bcd. bgd. od. bd. bg. b.	[illegible]	38	44	41.06
	21	NNW. E. SE. W. NW. NNW.	[illegible]	bd. b.	[illegible]	34	40½	36.90
	22	NNW. C. E. NNW. Ely. NW. NE. +Vble.	[illegible]	b.	[illegible]	30	42½	37.34
	23	S. C. SE. C. +. NNW.	[illegible]	b. bc. c. b.	[illegible]	24	39	30.94
	24	NNW.	[illegible]	b. bd. b.	[illegible]	38½	41½	40.20
	25	NNW.	[illegible]	bd. bc. b.	[illegible]	33	40	36.02
+	26	NNW. C. Ely. SE.	[illegible]	bc. b. bc. b.	[illegible]	29	44	36.15
	27	E. SW. SSW. NNW. NbW.	[illegible]	b. c. cs. bc. b.	[illegible]	33	39½	36.66
	28	NNW. SE. NNW. S. SSE. E. C.	[illegible]	b. bc. o. bc.	[illegible]	31	39½	37.17
	29	SSE. SE. C. SSE. Ely. NbE. NNW.	[illegible]	bc. b. bc. c. os. bc. b. cs. bc. b.	[illegible]	31	38	35.19

ABSTRACT.

N. 25.	NbW. 16.	NNW. 235.	NWbN o.	NW. 77.	NWbW o.	WNW o.	WbN o.	North Westerly — 151	Total. 604 hours, 13 do. wind vble. 79 do. calm. 696 = 29 days.
W. 16.	WbS. o.	WSW. o.	SWbW o.	SW. 16.	SWbS. o.	SSW. 22.	SbW. o.	South Westerly — 19	
S. 90.	SbE. o.	SSE. 18.	SEbS o.	SE. 60.	SEbE. o.	ESE. 3.	EbS. o.	South Easterly — 92	
E. 14.	EbN. o.	ENE. o.	NEbE o.	NE. 5.	NEbN. o.	NNE. o.	NbE. 4.	North Easterly — 39	

Highest, Lowest, and Mean Temperature —12 —44½—33.69

Total force of the Wind . . . 2817

METEOROLOGICAL OBSERVATIONS OF THE VICTORY DISCOVERY SHIP, TAKEN ON THE ICE, AND REGISTERED HOURLY.

Days of Month.	Direction of Wind.	Force of Wind.	State of Weather.	MARCH, 1832. Temperature in Shade.	+	−	Mean.
1	8/NNW. 8/+. 4/North. 4/C.	2/3. 1/5. 3/4. 2/3. 1/2. 2/1. 1/2. 6/2. 4/0	6/b. 1/c. 4/cs. 13/b.	[illegible]	32°	43¼	38°.23
2	3/Wly. 2/NNW. 8/C. 4/Sly. 8/C.	3/1. 1/2. 8/0. 4/1. 8/0.	24/b.	[illegible]	34	45	40.13
3	3/C. 5/NNW. 4/C. 4/Sly. 3/SSE. 5/ESE.	3/0. 1/1. 4/0. 8/1. 3/2. 2/1. 3/2.	24/b.	[illegible]	32¾	41¼	38.40
4	1/NE. 3/C. 3/S to E. 3/C. 1/SE. 12/NNW.	1/1. 3/0. 4/1. 3/0. 1/1. 4/3. 4/4. 4/3.	12/b. 8/bc. 4/b.	[illegible]	38	45¾	41.08
5	11/NNW. 1/SE. 1/Nly. 5/C. 6/NW.	10/3. 2/1. 6/0. 2/2. 4/1.	24/b.	[illegible]	37	45¼	42.06
6	12/C. 4/SE. 1/SW. 3/E. 4/C.	12/0. 8/1. 4/0.	24/b.	[illegible]	37	48¼	43.60
7	1/C. 3/SE. 8/C. 4/NW. 4/C. 1/SW. 2/NNW. 1/C.	1/0. 3/1. 8/0. 2/1. 1/2. 1/1. 4/0. 1/2. 2/1. 1/0.	24/b.	[illegible]	33¼	44¼	40.81
8	1/NNW. 3/E. 3/SE. 3/S. 2/SSE. 2/S. 6/SSW. 1/C. 1/E. 1/NNW. 1/E.	1/2. 5/1. 11/2. 2/3. 2/1. 1/0. 1/1. 2/2.	8/b. 5/bc. 3/c. 8/b.	[illegible]	33	41	36.92
9	12/SSW. 3/S. 4/+. 1/W. 3/NE.	1/2. 1/3. 2/4. 5/5. 5/4. 3/3. 1/2. 3/1. 2/2. 1/3.	2/o. 1/bc. 1/ds. 5/ods. 1/od. 1/cd. 7/c. 6/b.	[illegible]	22	35¼	29.17
10	8/NNW. 1/N. 1/S. 2/SSE. 3/NW. 1/W. 1/WNW. 3/NNW. 4/C.	5/4. 1/3. 1/3. 1/2. 1/3. 1/2. 3/1. 2/2. 1/3. 4/1. 4/0.	24/b.	[illegible]	28	39	32.92
11	3/NNW. 1/C. 2/E. 1/SE. 1/W. 2/E. 5/C. 1/S. 4/NE. 4/C.	3/1. 1/2. 3/1. 1/2. 5/0. 5/1. 4/0.	7/b. 1/bc. 3/b. 1/bc. 3/b. 1/o. 4/cs. 4/b.	[illegible]	26	40¾	34.42
12	4/NW. 1/S. 2/C. 1/ESE. 4/C. 4/S to E. 4/C. 4/+.	5/1. 2/0. 1/1. 4/0. 4/1. 5/0. 4/1.	24/b.	[illegible]	26	40	34.69
13	2/C. 2/SSW. 2/C. 2/SE. 4/+. 12/NNW.	2/0. 2/1. 2/0. 6/1. 1/2. 4/3. 1/4. 4/6. 2/7.	12/b. 4/c. 2/g. 6/b.	[illegible]	26	40¼	33.98
14	24/NNW.	1/7. 1/8. 1/7. 5/8. 1/7. 3/8. 3/7. 2/6. 1/8.	21/bd. 3/b.	[illegible]	30¼	37	34.04
15	24/NNW.	3/8. 1/5. 2/7. 2/4. 2/5. 6/4. 1/5. 2/4. 5/5.	3/bd. 1/b. 2/bd. 2/b. 3/bd. 13/b.	[illegible]	31¼	36	34.02
16	19/NNW. 1/NW. 4/NNW.	1/3 2/2 1/1 1/3 2/4 1/3 4/4 3/2 3/3 1/2 1/1 2/2 1/3 1/4	21/b. 3/c.	[illegible]	25	35	31.25
17	5/NNW. 2/C. 1/SE. 4/Sly. 4/S. 2/W. 1/C. 1/S. 1/+. 3/Ely.	1/3. 2/4. 1/3. 1/2. 2/6. 1/2. 2/1. 1/2. 1/0. 5/1.	8/b. 2/q. 2/c. 2/bc. 3/c.	[illegible]	20	35¼	30.06
18	4/E. 4/C. 4/SSE. 3/C. 1/SSE. 4/Ely. 4/NNW.	4/1. 4/0. 4/1. 3/0. 5/1. 2/2. 4/3.	24/b.	[illegible]	18	34	28.46
19	4/NW. 20/NNW.	4/3. 1/3. 4/6. 3/5. 12/6.	5/b. 3/bd. 4/b. 8/bc. 3/b. 1/bc.	[illegible]	30	36	33.04
20	17/NNW. 2/C. 1/NW. 4/NNW.	1/7 1/8 1/7 1/8 1/7 5/6 4/5 2/4 1/2 2/0 1/1 3/3 1/4	5/bd. 19/b.	[illegible]	27	35	31.90
21	6/NNW. 2/SSE. 16/NNW.	1/4 1/2 2/1 2/3 1/1 1/2 2/3 2/6 2/3 2/6 4/7 4/8	6/b. 10/bc. 2/b. 4/bd.	[illegible]	21¼	33	28.33
22	24/NNW.	14/8. 6/7. 4/9.	24/b.	[illegible]	30	35¼	32.56
23	24/NNW.	4/9. 1/8. 1/7. 5/5. 1/6. 1/7. 13/6.	9/b. 2/bd. 13/b.	[illegible]	26	34	30.08
24	9/NNW. 3/Ely. 8/SE. 1/NW. 1/C. 2/NNW.	1/6 2/7 1/4 3/5 1/4 1/3 3/1 3/2 2/1 1/2 3/1 1/0 1/2 2/3	24/b.	[illegible]	19	38¼	28.67
25	4/NW. 20/NNW.	2/3. 1/2. 1/1. 4/2. 1/4. 3/5. 1/6. 3/7. 8/6.	9/b. 3/bd. 1/b. 3/bc. 8/b.	[illegible]	27¼	33	30.13
26	16/NNW. 5/NW. 1/Ely. 2/Calm.	6/8. 2/7. 3/6. 2/4. 5/3. 4/2. 2/8.	4/b. 6/bd. 14/b.	[illegible]	13	28	21.17
27	3/NNW. 1/C. 4/E. 12/C. 4/SE.	1/5. 1/4. 1/2. 1/0. 4/1. 12/0. 3/1. 1/2.	24/b.	[illegible]	12	32	23.08
28	3/NE. 1/NW. 2/C. 6/SSE. 3/SE. 3/SSW. 1/SE. 1/W. 2/SSE. 2/+.	4/2. 2/6. 3/1. 1/2. 2/3. 3/2. 1/4. 1/3. 4/2. 1/4. 2/0.	4/b. 4/q. 10/os. 2/o. 4/b.	[illegible]	4½	28	16.00
29	1/E. 1/SNE. 3/NNW. 1/N. 18/NNW.	1/1. 1/4. 2/5. 5/6. 15/7. 2/8.	2/b. 2/bc. 3/cd. 5/od. 12/osd.	[illegible]	14	22¼	18.71
30	16/NNW. 2/S to E. 6/Calm.	2/8 1/7 2/8 1/6 1/5 1/4 3/5 1/4 1/1 2/2 3/1 6/0.	4/osd. 7/od. 3/o. 2/g. 3/os. 1/bc. 4/os.	[illegible]	6	22¼	15.81
31	24/NNW.	1/1. 2/2. 1/4. 4/5. 3/4. 1/5. 2/6. 5/7. 5/8.	4/os. 12/od. 5/qd. 3/bd.	[illegible]	16	21	18.92

ABSTRACT.

7/N.13.	0/NbW.0.	371/NNW.1985.	0/NWbN.0.	14/NW.59.	0/NWbW.0.	1/WNW.1.	0/WbN.0.
0/W.13.	0/WbS.0.	0/WSW.0.	0/SWbW.0.	2/SW.3.	0/SWbS.0.	21/SSW.70.	0/SbW.0.
11/S.41.	0/SbE.0.	22/SSE.36.	0/SEbS.0.	32/SE.43.	0/SEbE.0.	6/ESE.9.	0/EbS.0.
37/E.42.	0/EbN.0.	0/ENE.0.	0/NEbE.0.	11/NE.13.	0/NEbN.0.	1/NNE.3.	0/NbE.0.

North Westerly — 413
South Westerly — 32
South Easterly — 91
North Easterly — 49

Total.
588 hours.
21 do. wind variable.
133 do. calm.
744 — 31 days.

Highest, Lowest, and Mean Temperature −4½ −48½ −31.37

Total force of the Wind 2289

METEOROLOGICAL TABLES.

The mountain barometer, from which the following observations were registered, was supplied by the Admiralty, and had been on the former voyage. It was constructed by Mr. Jones, of Charing Cross, and the scale graduated to hundreds, and was regularly observed by Mr. Thom.

VICTORY DISCOVERY SHIP, METEOROLOGICAL OBSERVATIONS.

REGISTER OF THE BAROMETER, CORRECTED FOR TEMPERATURE, CAPACITY, AND NEUTRAL POINT.

Days of Month.	NOVEMBER, 1829.			DECEMBER, 1829.			JANUARY, 1830.			FEBRUARY, 1830.			MARCH, 1830.			APRIL, 1830.		
	9 A. M.	5 P. M.	Midt.	9 A. M.	5 P. M.	Midt.	9 A. M	5 P. M.	Midt.	9 A. M.	5 P. M.	Midt.	9 A. M.	5 P. M.	Midt.	9 A. M.	5 P. M.	Midt.
1				29.950	29.922		30.057	30.000		29.795	29.765	29.785	30.185	30.025	29.891	29.959	29.780	29.700
2				29.900	29.850		29.840	29.835		29.805	29.939	30.000	29.842	29.862	29.860	29.743	29.810	29.024
3				29.815	29.880		29.780	29.735		30.042	30.060	30.098	29.900	30.035	30.040	29.854	29.994	30.111
4				29.960	29.975		29.620	29.660		30.100	30.115	30.100	30.040	30.042	30.450	30.260	30.400	30.476
5				29.930	29.780		29.710	29.740		30.070	30.000	29.990	30.045	29.995	29.943	30.460	30.115	29.900
6				29.675	29.682		29.840	29.760		30.000	29.980	29.985	29.980	29.912	29.900	29.330	29.210	29.485
7	29.415	29.420		29.426	29.406		29.580	29.480		29.920	29.875	29.803	29.995	30.022	30.000	29.500	29.561	29.575
8	29.450	29.750		29.668	29.733		29.595	29.700		29.745	29.645	29.700	30.022	30.022	29.995	29.564	29.715	29.777
9	29.655	29.700		29.748	29.752		30.025	30.045		29.715	29.793	29.810	29.989	30.003	29.990	29.533	29.584	29.740
10	29.875	29.825		29.743	29.710		30.155	30.045		29.827	29.835	29.800	30.010	29.930	29.829	30.148	30.322	30.435
11	29.716	29.525		29.635	29.738		29.700	29.600		29.805	29.810	29.810	29.745	29.682	29.680	30.495	30.523	30.500
12	29.801	29.002		29.948	29.996		29.245	29.240		30.085	30.225	30.248	29.662	29.645	29.648	30.480	30.360	30.182
13	29.800	29.375		30.000	29.985		29.460	29.540		30.165	30.000	29.811	29.716	29.815	29.840	29.940	29.899	29.915
14	29.685	29.755		29.639	29.700		29.755	29.865		29.822	29.925	30.000	29.935	29.912	29.919	30.040	30.143	39.190
15	29.795	29.900		29.896	29.994		29.940	29.995		30.320	30.503	30.634	29.918	29.948	29.930	30.240	30.235	30.240
16	29.935	29.742		29.780	29.723		30.065	30.135		30.705	30.765	30.750	29.937	30.002	30.000	30.321	30.283	30.200
17	29.683	29.819		29.880	29.960		30.095	30.025		30.682	30.633	30.612	30.002	30.002	29.980	30.082	30.045	30.052
18	29.896	29.800		29.845	29.881		29.155	28.920		30.535	30.470	30.425	30.005	30.025	30.051	30.045	30.045	30.040
19	29.735	29.742		29.924	30.095		29.100	29.240		30.422	30.428	30.427	30.123	30.187	30.200	30.045	30.015	30.040
20	29.825	29.864		30.210	30.215		29.398	29.500		30.444	30.471	30.484	30.248	30.261	30.261	30.040	29.965	30.050
21	29.550	29.519		30.284	29.865		29.705	29.710		30.565	30.540	30.521	30.187	30.161	30.175	30.020	29.990	29.980
22	29.345	29.372		29.693	29.540		29.460	29.395		30.520	30.480	30.400	30.183	30.181	30.117	30.020	30.120	30.182
23	29.365	29.360		29.405	29.440		29.300	29.395		30.320	30.185	30.131	30.035	29.918	29.867	30.075	30.040	30.985
24	29.430	29.430		29.500	29.575		29.408	29.465		29.955	29.875	29.812	29.791	29.788	29.790	29.880	29.800	29.815
25	29.240	29.266		29.780	29.895		29.640	29.720		29.750	29.800	29.820	29.890	29.967	29.980	29.915	29.936	29.938
26	29.520	29.685		30.073	30.090		29.805	29.828		29.842	29.862	29.900	30.005	30.085	30.000	29.936	29.945	29.932
27	29.820	29.900		30.215	30.240		29.680	29.785		29.972	30.078	30.080	30.119	30.109	30.105	29.280	30.000	29.920
28	29.945	29.905		30.375	30.380		29.735	29.710		30.262	30.318	30.315	30.103	30.147	30.225	29.955	29.955	29.940
29	30.162	30.160		30.422	30.430		29.630	29.645					30.235	30.305	30.362	30.100	30.140	30.130
30	30.182	30.105		30.370	30.260		29.800	29.980					30.300	30.290	30.270	30.030	30.000	30.100
31				30.100	30.090		30.075	29.950					30.290	30.223	30.100			
	29.702	29.663		29.896	29.896		29.689	29.696		30.114	30.12	30.116	30.014	30.018	30.013	29.976	29.997	30.018
	Mean Total, 29.682			Mean Total, 29.896			Mean Total, 29.692			Mean Total, 30.116			Mean Total, 30.015			Mean Total, 29.997		

VICTORY DISCOVERY SHIP, METEOROLOGICAL OBSERVATIONS.

REGISTER OF THE BAROMETER, CORRECTED FOR TEMPERATURE, CAPACITY, AND NEUTRAL POINT.

Days of Month	MAY, 1830.			JUNE, 1830.			JULY, 1830.			AUGUST, 1830.			SEPTEMBER, 1830.			OCTOBER, 1830.		
	9 A.M.	5 P.M.	Midt.	9 A.M.	5 P.M.	Midt.	9 A.M.	5 P.M.	Midt.	9 A.M.	5 P.M.	Midt.	9 A.M.	5 P.M.	Midt.	9 A.M.	5 P.M.	Midt.
1	30.280	30.032	29.777	30.542	30.485	30.545	29.621	29.606	29.638	30.040	30.030	30.018	29.942	29.560	29.540	30.123	30.182	30.065
2	29.810	29.800	29.772	30.463	30.250	30.150	29 722	29.796	29.798	30.030	30.000	29.981	29.602	29.745	29.875	30.018	29.962	29.861
3	29.830	29.900	29.960	30.000	29.950	30.012	29.775	29.800	29.825	29.960	29.915	29.899	29.911	29.995	29.981	29.815	29.815	29.832
4	30.020	30.057	30.046	30.012	30.020	30.050	29.987	30.024	29.906	29.895	29.880	29.809	30.133	30.085	30.000	29.787	29.718	29.700
5	30.080	30.100	30.116	30.050	30.080	30.145	30.138	30.242	30.000	29.805	29.725	29.711	29.520	29.422	29.200	29.662	29.421	29.532
6	30.200	30.200	30.186	30.151	30.204	30.263	30.313	30.390	30.362	29.690	29.650	29.591	29.400	29.468	29.505	29.778	29.800	29.881
7	30.132	30.100	30.210	30.301	30.322	30.435	30.390	30.365	30.346	29.560	29.495	29.471	29.650	29.722	29.781	29.882	29.880	29.556
8	30.240	30.380	30.320	30.450	30.395	30.411	30.305	30.125	30.019	29.465	29.420	29.428	29.900	30.015	29.982	29.963	29.998	29.911
9	30.420	30.295	30.291	30.448	30.385	30.314	29.765	29.475	29.521	29.405	29.365	29.361	29.985	30.022	30.024	30.182	30.244	30.215
10	30.175	30.258	30.321	30.268	30.283	30.111	29.590	29.752	29.842	29.295	29.295	29.300	29.980	29.955	29.784	30.218	30.218	30.128
11	30.342	30.345	30.311	30.183	30.118	30.111	29.750	29.675	29.579	29.360	29.520	29.600	30.090	30.025	30.000	30.193	30.193	30.128
12	30.312	30.263	30.229	30.213	30.184	30.111	29.385	29.329	29.355	29.800	29.900	29.911	30.078	30.053	29.991	30.098	30.098	30.065
13	30.205	30.195	30.160	30.066	30.071	30.061	29.605	29.721	29.621	29.998	30.020	30.000	30.035	30.103	30.100	30.065	30.140	30.181
14	30.225	30.205	30.160	30.218	30.298	30.321	29.785	29.805	29.726	30.020	30.040	30.030	30.122	30.105	30.045	30.200	29.958	29.641
15	30 178	30.125	30.060	30.371	30.283	30.271	29.748	29.770	29.726	30.045	30.040	30.030	29.100	29.915	29.900	29.782	29.975	29.950
16	30.005	29.880	29.935	30.270	30.109	30.121	29.715	29.732	29.726	30.040	30.035	29.960	29.935	29.918	29.873	29.982	29.783	29.593
17	30.020	30.025	30.060	30.221	30.335	30.240	29.790	29.800	29.801	29.990	30.025	30.039	29.908	29.868	29.830	29.733	29.878	29.900
18	30.140	30.192	30.291	30.374	30.412	30.356	29.915	29.915	29.901	30.085	30.060	29.988	29.705	29.585	29.680	30.013	30.102	30.057
19	30.333	30.380	30.380	30.365	30.219	30.160	29.915	29.915	29.903	29.991	29.958	29.833	29.900	29.964	29.960	29.995	29.897	29.867
20	30.380	30.395	30.435	30.261	30.322	30.247	29.920	29.990	29.940	29.900	29.860	29.872	30.035	30.084	30.039	29.766	29.744	29.697
21	30.435	30.440	30.480	30.200	30.085	30.019	30.000	29.980	29.951	29.962	30.085	30.039	29.842	29.795	29.720	29.710	29.700	29.666
22	30.500	30.560	30.621	29.958	29.855	29.825	29.964	29.964	29.983	30.060	30.076	30.015	29.730	29.975	30.015	29.617	29.580	29.555
23	30.660	30.640	30.581	29.850	29.998	30.000	29.990	30.000	29.983	30.125	30.192	29.709	30.093	30.025	29.900	29.538	29.522	29.531
24	30.518	30.435	30.411	29.875	29.825	29.738	29.994	29.800	29.891	30.098	30.095	29.601	29.660	29.394	29.300	29.612	29.680	29.688
25	30.400	30.395	30.305	29.795	29.787	29.747	29.870	29.775	29.728	30.198	30.205	29.729	29.400	29.420	29.486	29.790	29.801	29.801
26	30.384	30.282	30.261	29.700	29.732	29.728	29.660	29.450	29.366	29.895	29.880	29.785	29.598	29.728	29.785	29.801	29.872	29.915
27	30.322	30.300	30.261	29.800	29.790	29.728	29.270	29.600	29.885	29.882	29.982	29.788	29.803	29.828	29.720	30.002	30.067	30.107
28	30.268	30.180	30.100	29.757	29.821	29.791	29.920	30.100	30 042	29.952	29.900	29.819	29.693	29.800	29.800	30.173	30.198	30.145
29	30.119	30.200	30.240	29.790	29.820	29.779	30.090	30.075	30.081	29.850	29.845	29.819	29.900	29.903	29.980	30.077	29.915	29.825
30	30.396	30.414	30.474	29.760	29.780	29.711	29.995	29.868	29.866	29.845	29.838	29.819	30.004	30.027	30.140	29.861	29.837	29.825
31	30.538	30.500	30.445				29.900	30.020	30.017	29.800	29.680	29.575				29.618	29.513	29.515
	30.254	30.241	30.232	30.124	30.107	30.084	29.864	29.866	29.849	29.872	29.871	29.819	29.822	29.849	29.831	29.905	29.894	23.859
	Mean Total. 30.212			Mean Total. 30.105			Mean Total. 29.859			Mean Total. 29.854			Mean Total. 29.834			Mean Total. 29.886		

VICTORY DISCOVERY SHIP, METEOROLOGICAL OBSERVATIONS.

REGISTER OF THE BAROMETER, CORRECTED FOR TEMPERATURE, CAPACITY, AND NEUTRAL POINT.

Days of Month.	NOVEMBER, 1830.			DECEMBER, 1830.			JANUARY, 1831.			FEBRUARY, 1831.			MARCH, 1831.			APRIL, 1831.		
	9 A. M.	5 P. M.	Midt.	9 A. M.	5 P. M.	Midt.	9 A. M.	5 P. M.	Midt.	9 A. M.	5 P. M.	Midt.	9 A. M.	5 P. M.	Midt.	9 A. M.	5 P. M.	Midt.
1	29.621	29.738	29.855	30.544	30.513	30.487	30.195	30.300	30.320	29.860	29.845	29.800	29.741	29.745	29.777	30.214	30.158	30.100
2	30.099	30.220	30.189	30.339	30.237	30.172	30.343	30.364	30.320	29.840	29.830	29.600	29.760	29.843	29.821	30.214	30.360	30.420
3	30.160	30.035	29.914	30.138	30.111	30.140	30.280	30.258	30.206	29.498	29.835	30.031	29.821	29.798	29.800	30.440	30.440	30.400
4	29.477	29.461	29.372	30.215	30.416	30.360	30.305	30.533	30.640	30.320	30.448	30.444	29.883	29.903	29.820	30.340	30.330	30.310
5	29.189	29.297	29.323	30.334	30.301	30.271	30.714	30.690	30.601	30.560	30.600	30.535	29.882	30.078	30.141	30.300	30.[illegible]	30.266
6	29.190	29.178	29.237	30.255	30.262	30.271	30.500	30.440	30.481	30.458	30.280	30.271	30.119	30.130	30.125	30.181	30.079	29.930
7	29.419	29.546	29.580	30.374	30.478	30.481	30.335	30.300	30.300	30.270	30.280	30.290	30.128	30.066	30.000	29.740	29.603	29.555
8	29.589	29.589	29.560	30.565	30.632	30.631	30.300	30.305	30.300	30.290	30.290	30.280	29.921	29.893	29.866	29.493	29.500	29.516
9	29.683	29.803	29.885	30.646	30.698	30.664	30.310	30.300	30.250	30.200	30.160	30.200	29.878	29.991	30.000	29.630	29.760	29.800
10	30.115	30.211	29.901	30.660	30.632	30.590	30.161	30.135	30.100	30.244	30.240	30.185	30.048	30.089	30.055	29.795	29.810	29.620
11	29.611	29.593	29.748	30.538	30.457	30.356	29.953	29.990	29.914	30.080	30.000	29.970	30.040	30.040	30.041	29.642	29.720	29.750
12	29.897	30.010	30.044	30.284	30.232	30.147	29.995	30.077	30.135	30.045	30.070	30.043	30.086	30.102	30.060	29.880	29.960	29.980
13	30.278	30.500	30.581	30.068	30.018	29.938	30.311	30.360	30.380	29.960	29.884	29.786	30.055	30.055	30.060	29.922	29.884	29.830
14	30.660	30.662	30.625	29.938	29.930	29.938	30.247	30.020	29.900	29.680	29.638	29.560	30.076	30.109	30.161	29.838	29.838	29.840
15	30.605	30.600	30.600	29.945	30.012	30.000	29.729	29.618	29.600	29.470	29.481	29.475	30.229	30.131	30.100	29.860	29.900	29.966
16	30.494	30.390	30.285	29.989	29.921	29.812	29.580	29.622	29.710	29.538	29.610	29.670	29.960	30.000	30.035	30.040	30.120	30.140
17	30.083	29.879	29.955	29.788	29.740	29.706	29.636	29.582	29.522	29.760	29.860	29.942	29.962	29.978	29.918	30.272	30.[illegible]	30.370
18	29.718	29.720	29.756	29.708	29.843	29.940	29.694	29.718	29.765	30.025	30.146	30.226	29.846	29.854	29.820	30.352	30.136	30.049
19	29.882	29.949	29.979	30.042	30.038	29.999	29.842	29.898	29.900	30.260	30.218	30.125	29.794	29.782	29.740	29.898	29.860	29.675
20	30.023	30.060	30.045	30.054	30.100	30.151	30.000	30.100	30.101	30.140	30.144	30.160	29.708	29.716	29.701	29.620	29.700	29.725
21	30.122	30.144	30.153	30.335	30.481	30.485	30.155	30.206	30.251	30.032	29.920	29.700	29.664	29.592	29.520	29.744	29.877	29.900
22	30.165	30.168	30.162	30.322	30.027	29.819	30.391	30.500	30.500	29.713	29.660	29.590	29.458	29.458	29.510	29.900	30.040	30.120
23	30.200	30.208	30.233	29.705	29.780	29.680	30.418	30.330	30.306	29.413	29.240	29.040	29.633	29.744	29.777	30.145	30.222	30.176
24	30.286	30.345	30.361	29.680	29.629	29.461	30.350	30.390	30.396	29.038	29.360	29.570	29.820	29.880	29.844	30.163	30.180	30.176
25	30.380	30.340	30.289	29.322	29.300	29.418	30.320	30.200	30.685	29.780	29.875	30.157	29.880	29.880	29.840	30.097	30.061	30.125
26	30.243	30.238	30.276	29.599	29.682	29.707	29.894	29.863	29.880	29.990	30.075	30.300	29.880	29.778	29.735	30.018	29.963	29.874
27	30.238	30.238	30.208	29.753	29.798	29.793	30.000	30.062	30.046	30.323	30.379	30.380	29.758	29.818	29.818	29.624	29.572	29.620
28	30.205	30.200	30.155	29.770	29.758	29.714	30.050	30.050	29.950	30.248	30.059	29.900	29.879	29.902	29.880	29.720	29.840	29.820
29	30.179	30.241	30.306	29.878	29.960	29.960	29.855	29.800	29.753				29.873	29.925	29.931	29.840	29.948	30.055
30	30.415	30.518	30.540	29.900	29.920	29.912	29.740	29.900	30.041				29.940	29.957	29.930	30.188	30.240	30.260
31				29.980	30.020	30.090	30.138	30.093	29.976				29.989	30.071	30.123			
	30.007	30.036	30.037	30.086	30.094	30.068	30.121	30.129	30.136	29.965	29.979	29.972	29.894	29.914	29.901	29.967	29.984	29.979
	Mean Total. 30.027			Mean Total. 30.083			Mean Total. 30.129			Mean Total. 29.972			Mean Total. 29.903			Mean Total. 29.977		

REGISTER OF THE BAROMETER, CORRECTED FOR TEMPERATURE, CAPACITY, AND NEUTRAL POINT.

Days of Month.	MAY, 1831.			JUNE, 1831.			JULY, 1831.			AUGUST, 1831.			SEPTEMBER, 1831.			OCTOBER, 1831.		
	9 A. M.	5 P. M.	Midt.	9 A. M.	5 P. M.	Midt.	9 A. M.	5 P. M.	Midt.	9 A. M.	9 P. M.	Midt.	9 A. M.	5 P. M.	Midt.	9 A. M.	5 P. M.	Midt.
1	30.298	30.300	30.300	30.028	29.960	30.000	29.888	29.797	29.771	30.058	29.992	29.920	29.892	29.710	29.800	30.212	30.294	30.286
2	30.300	30.320	30.300	29.828	29.797	29.820	29.900	30.100	30.138	29.905	29.890	29.875	29.340	29.480	29.580	30.263	30.192	30.076
3	30.440	30.430	30.380	29.698	29.698	29.660	30.090	29.840	29.780	29.900	29.900	29.880	29.560	29.520	29.460	30.160	30.260	30.280
4	30.260	30.280	30.141	29.624	29.680	29.741	29.620	29.540	29.535	29.698	29.450	29.505	29.422	29.369	29.326	30.331	30.320	30.300
5	30.130	30.200	30.287	29.872	29.981	30.020	29.480	29.498	29.487	29.836	29.944	29.936	29.339	29.433	29.407	30.305	30.280	30.232
6	30.193	30.177	30.196	30.140	30.222	30.300	29.525	29.580	29.615	29.900	29.887	29.876	29.492	29.590	29.666	30.200	30.228	30.243
7	30.188	30.220	30.221	30.345	30.230	30.060	29.680	29.725	29.800	29.890	29.900	29.900	29.721	29.825	29.734	30.300	30.260	30.350
8	30.220	30.200	30.200	30.125	30.130	30.000	29.820	29.740	29.700	29.946	29.998	30.012	29.918	29.982	30.010	30.224	30.185	30.178
9	30.187	30.170	30.181	30.023	29.989	29.920	29.700	29.760	29.805	30.066	30.066	30.534	30.110	30.132	30.120	30.155	30.120	30.111
10	30.171	30.185	30.234	29.884	29.886	29.886	29.815	29.840	29.800	29.974	29.900	29.874	30.074	30.010	29.998	30.100	30.078	30.086
11	30.220	30.155	30.061	29.850	29.820	29.787	29.690	29.636	29.636	29.837	29.792	29.770	29.978	29.974	30.020	30.135	30.176	30.201
12	29.852	29.798	29.781	29.680	29.722	29.780	29.774	29.864	29.818	29.760	29.798	29.800	30.078	30.120	30.145	30.202	30.200	30.195
13	29.740	29.772	29.790	29.810	29.840	29.861	29.793	29.845	29.904	29.998	30.044	30.040	30.114	30.068	30.000	30.212	30.214	30.200
14	29.860	29.956	30.080	29.905	30.020	30.061	29.956	29.994	29.984	30.098	30.042	29.976	29.958	29.923	29.880	30.200	30.178	30.145
15	30.105	30.180	30.200	30.032	30.020	30.020	29.848	29.900	29.935	29.783	29.528	29.516	29.821	29.800	29.790	30.145	30.160	30.455
16	30.200	30.180	30.133	30.000	29.960	29.900	30.000	30.063	30.078	29.160	29.158	29.195	29.773	29.840	29.810	30.066	30.020	30.025
17	29.976	29.960	29.970	29.886	29.880	29.925	30.082	30.088	30.070	29.319	29.479	29.555	29.788	29.744	29.744	30.020	29.951	29.895
18	30.000	30.080	30.025	29.950	30.020	30.015	30.086	30.095	30.051	29.668	29.733	29.751	29.722	29.760	29.805	29.800	29.811	29.800
19	30.110	30.158	30.158	30.020	30.060	30.095	30.100	30.122	30.160	29.804	29.889	29.895	29.820	29.840	29.915	25.809	29.880	29.910
20	30.182	30.153	30.162	30.162	30.144	30.126	30 158	30.200	30.175	29.930	29.900	29.900	29.915	29.760	29.770	29.998	30.058	30.088
21	30.085	29.900	29.798	29.892	29.760	29.731	30.218	30.192	30.199	29.880	29.790	29.780	29.564	29.520	29.520	30.058	30.064	30.070
22	29.515	29.587	29.618	29.938	30.066	30.142	30.098	30.088	30.030	29.742	29.748	29.777	29.548	29.568	29.635	29.978	29.900	29.825
23	29.598	29.560	29.574	30.100	30.155	29.936	30.038	30.000	29.995	29.839	29.915	29.940	29.771	29.880	29.990	29.728	29.860	29.996
24	29.622	29.735	29.820	30.113	30.021	29.921	29.980	30.000	30.000	29.990	29.960	29.960	30.080	30.084	30.086	30.092	30.100	29.976
25	29.882	29.884	29.884	29.850	29.900	29.936	30.020	30.035	30.024	29.921	29.900	29.957	29.990	29.760	29.735	29.330	28.960	28.980
26	29.917	30.000	30.010	30.034	30.000	29.981	30.084	30.155	30.015	30.100	30.053	29.890	29.850	29.863	29.875	28.780	28.880	29.071
27	30.020	29.980	29.878	29.963	29.941	29.936	30.094	30.023	30.030	29.793	29.822	29.820	29.883	29.683	29.940	29.160	29.280	29.415
28	29.826	29.862	29.880	29.982	29.980	29.901	30.000	29.954	29.980	29.822	29.822	29.870	29.900	29.800	29.770	29.520	29.644	29.786
29	29.860	29.922	30.020	29.790	29.732	29.700	29.970	29.900	29.960	29.820	29.780	30.000	29.871	29.958	30.000	29.971	30.228	30.378
30	30.073	30.080	30.072	29.744	29.800	29.921	29.960	29.970	29.975	30.091	30.120	30.180	30.078	30.121	30.147	30.506	30.580	30.575
31	29.998	29.970	30.000				30.035	30.054	30.080	30.217	30.160	30.111				30.504	30.440	30.425
	30.034	30.044	30.044	29.942	29.947	29.936	29.919	29.922	29.92	29.863	29.85	29.871	29.812	29.81	29.822	30.008	30.026	30.05
	Mean Total. 30.04			Mean Total. 29.942			Mean Total. 29.92			Mean Total. 29.86			Mean Total. 29.815			Mean Total. 30.028		

REGISTER OF THE BAROMETER, CORRECTED FOR TEMPERATURE, CAPACITY, AND NEUTRAL POINT.

Days of Month.	NOVEMBER, 1831.			DECEMBER, 1831.			JANUARY, 1832.		
	9 A.M.	5 P.M.	Midt.	9 A.M.	5 P.M.	Midt.	9 A.M.	5 P.M.	Midt.
1	30.316	30.388	30.120	30.080	30.140	30.195	29.750	29.840	29.895
2	30.400	30.376	30.320	30.260	30.369	30.380	29.880	29.814	29.775
3	30.243	30.178	30.094	30.300	30.200	30.100	29.680	29.640	29.675
4	30.038	30.040	30.070	30.060	30.089	30.070	29.724	29.720	29.694
5	30.138	30.180	30.255	29.978	30.002	30.010	29.620	29.600	29.615
6	30.314	30.340	30.368	30.120	30.200	30.165	29.628	29.620	29.668
7	30.360	30.330	30.291	29.938	29.780	29.790	29.620	29.620	29.600
8	30.194	30.160	30.160	29.848	29.940	30.044	29.564	29.564	29.598
9	29.998	29.903	29.840	30.193	30.204	30.180	29.564	29.620	29.666
10	29.754	29.520	29.700	30.100	30.045	29.800	29.720	29.760	29.720
11	29.530	29.822	30.903	29.898	29.880	29.910	29.590	29.480	29.465
12	30.020	30.060	30.163	30.080	30.120	30.000	29.440	29.464	29.480
13	30.356	30.478	30.501	29.766	29.540	29.500	29.580	29.638	29.597
14	30.502	30.500	30.460	29.530	29.622	29.660	29.380	29.260	29.298
15	30.438	30.465	30.480	29.656	29.640	29.666	29.436	29.578	29.774
16	30.470	30.388	30.274	29.677	29.640	29.610	29.780	29.740	29.750
17	30.090	29.978	29.916	29.640	29.640	29.640	29.560	29.540	29.575
18	29.879	29.823	29.796	29.698	29.690	29.624	29.658	29.620	29.565
19	29.858	29.966	30.028	29.550	29.540	29.520	29.520	29.513	29.500
20	30.089	30.113	30.100	29.492	29.400	29.276	29.544	29.706	29.785
21	30.050	30.040	30.033	29.236	29.285	29.270	29.720	29.500	29.300
22	30.166	30.218	30.310	29.289	29.330	29.290	29.178	29.204	29.220
23	30.400	30.436	30.420	29.392	29.356	29.314	29.345	29.500	29.625
24	30.320	30.220	30.140	29.340	29.390	29.425	29.644	29.604	29.523
25	30.028	30.028	30.020	29.530	29.560	29.460	29.520	29.594	29.555
26	29.960	29.921	29.860	29.660	29.680	29.680	29.818	29.773	29.613
27	29.800	29.820	29.820	29.700	29.740	29.791	29.220	29.196	29.800
28	29.800	29.824	29.864	29.876	29.890	29.895	29.496	29.618	29.640
29	29.906	29.920	29.918	29.825	29.800	29.797	29.756	29.980	30.076
30	29.940	30.600	29.980	29.845	29.860	29.864	30.180	30.244	30.280
31				29.815	29.758	29.710	[illegible] 466	30.478	30.474
	30.112	30.114	30.15	29.783	29.785	29.763	29.628	29.646	29.671
	Mean Total. 30.125			Mean Total. 29.777			Mean Total. 29.648		

Days of Month.	FEBRUARY, 1832.			MARCH, 1832.			APRIL, 1832.		
	9 A.M.	5 P.M.	Midt.	9 A.M.	5 P.M.	Midt.	9 A.M.	5 P.M.	Midt.
1	30.340	30.240	30.140	29.715	29.781	29.800	29.740	29.760	29.754
2	30.060	29.960	29.894	29.822	29.830	29.835	29.742	29.660	29.675
3	29.745	29.660	29.660	29.857	29.897	29.800	29.780	29.960	29.990
4	29.700	29.700	29.710	29.996	30.088	30.100	30.080	30.080	30.174
5	29.838	29.930	29.921	30.238	30.310	30.320	30.120	30.135	30.140
6	29.900	29.840	29.840	30.418	30.440	30.412	30.100	30.090	30.073
7	29.870	29.940	29.910	30.340	30.260	30.296	29.880	29.720	29.800
8	30.054	30.200	30.156	30.026	29.892	29.800	30.120	30.260	30.200
9	30.260	30.100	30.360	29.580	29.525	29.540	29.945	29.680	29.614
10	29.869	29.744	29.840	29.760	29.958	30.008	29.576	29.676	29.800
11	29.813	29.938	29.320	30.100	30.180	30.188	29.968	30.042	30.060
12	30.033	30.040	30.090	30.240	30.200	30.198	30.048	30.060	30.060
13	30.200	30.240	30.221	30.100	30.020	29.804	30.038	30.060	30.080
14	30.080	29.936	29.880	29.940	29.793	29.760	30.106	30.114	30.111
15	29.778	29.710	29.750	29.760	29.840	29.880	30.138	30.140	30.102
16	29.740	29.700	29.680	29.936	29.942	29.910	30.110	30.100	30.032
17	29.620	29.670	29.665	29.956	29.960	29.480	29.934	29.990	30.100
18	29.638	29.624	29.680	30.048	30.140	30.160	30.020	29.940	29.900
19	29.640	29.700	29.781	30.178	30.180	30.100	29.840	29.760	29.720
20	29.998	30.240	30.280	30.180	30.200	30.200	29.680	29.720	29.720
21	30.380	30.380	30.240	30.180	30.138	30.140	29.680	29.870	29.902
22	29.940	29.600	29.520	30.080	30.066	30.050	30.010	30.100	30.120
23	29.280	29.300	29.370	29.896	29.798	29.780	30.140	30.120	30.120
24	29.475	29.540	29.500	29.760	29.820	29.823	30.158	30.300	30.300
25	29.600	29.688	29.740	29.820	29.700	29.800	30.340	30.344	30.380
26	29.740	29.840	29.835	29.660	29.820	29.920	30.370	30.320	30.270
27	29.660	29.740	29.800	30.040	30.134	30.200	30.240	30.192	30.140
28	29.876	29.800	29.770	30.180	30.168	30.136	29.988	29.942	29.980
29	29.656	29.620	29.666	30.032	30.000	29.960	29.910	29.976	29.920
30				29.000	29.840	29.800	30.062	30.100	30.080
31				29.700	29.690	29.700			
	29.858	29.863	29.835	29.953	29.987	29.964	29.995	30.007	30.01
	Mean Total. 29.852			Mean Total. 29.968			Mean Total. 30.004		

GENERAL ABSTRACT OF THE METEOROLOGICAL OBSERVATIONS OF THE VICTORY DISCOVERY SHIP, TAKEN ON THE ICE AND REGISTERED HOURLY. FELIX HARBOUR, LAT. 70° 0′ N, LONG. 91° 53′ W.

FROM OCTOBER, 1829, TO OCTOBER, 1830.

	Wind North-westerly		Wind South-westerly		Wind South-easterly		Wind North-easterly		Wind variable		Calm weather	Total No. of Hours	Total force of Wind	Mean daily force of Wind	State of Temperature in the Shade		
	Hours	Force	Hours	Force	Hours	Force	Hours	Force	Hours	Force	Hours				Max.	Min.	Mean
October	454	1278	116	323	69	129	60	246			45	744=31 days	1976	63.74	+24	−16½	+7.94
November	152	577	57	84	49	64	341	924			121	720=30	1649	51.9	+26	−37	−3.58
December	229	713	131	357	95	203	124	338			165	744=31	1611	52.07	−8	−37	−23.08
January	325	920	230	537	62	113	40	86			87	744=31	1656	53.42	−5	−45	−33.13
February	101	257	119	307	102	137	169	357	12		169	672=28	1058	37.8	+1½	−47	−29.9
March	212	341	162	261	31	42	105	218			234	744=31	862	27.8	+20	−42	−20.93
Result Total Winter 1829-30	1473	4086	815	1869	408	688	839	2169	12		821	4368=182	8812	47.79	+26	−47	−17.11
April	216	576	200	574	63	151	191	519			50	720=30	1820	60.67	+31	−21	+1.365
May	223	542	142	309	100	151	235	510			44	744=31	1512	48.78	+37	−1	+15.27
June	133	290	210	541	42	52	264	542			71	720=30	1425	47.5	+62	+26	+36.76
July	327	840	93	131	50	59	167	215	5	8	102	744=31	1303	42.03	+70	+32	+44.57
August	440	1377	87	196	73	109	99	289	16	25	29	744=31	1996	64.4	+58	+33	+40.87
September	340	1662	157	416	106	208	93	334	7	13	17	720=30	2633	87.76	+43	+5	+27.42
Result Total Summer 1830	1679	5287	889	2217	434	730	1049	2409	28	46	313	4392=183	10,689	58.52	+70	−21	+27.71

Remarks.—By referring to the Explanation at the beginning of the Meteorological Table, this Abstract will be readily understood. Beginning at the 1st of October, 1829, we have taken the six following for winter months, in which it will be manifest that the prevailing winds were north-westerly and next north-easterly, and that south-easterly winds were not only least prevalent but weakest, and that the total average of the wind was much greatest from the northward. The same remark is applicable to the summer months, and to these circumstances must be attributed the constant influx of ice and water to the Gulf of Boothia; added to which, the numerous and large rivers which discharge themselves into it, must consequently occasion and account for the strong current which Sir E. Parry found running to the eastward in Hecla and Fury strait.

GENERAL ABSTRACT OF THE METEOROLOGICAL OBSERVATIONS OF THE VICTORY DISCOVERY SHIP, TAKEN ON THE ICE AND REGISTERED HOURLY. SHERIFF'S HARBOUR, LAT. 70° 2′ N, LONG. 91° 52′ W.

FROM OCTOBER, 1830, TO OCTOBER, 1831.

	Wind North-westerly		Wind South-westerly		Wind South-easterly		Wind North-easterly		Wind variable		Calm weather	Total No. of Hours	Total force of Wind	Mean daily force of Wind	State of Temperature in the Shade		
	Hours	Force	Hours	Force	Hours	Force	Hours	Force	Hours	Force	Hours				Max.	Min.	Mean
October	233	605	244	818	110	317	107	389	1	6	49	744=31 days	2135	68.8	+24	—12	+10.95
November	275	828	137	180	142	279	44	108	14	14	108	720=30	1409	46.96	+24	—41	—11.45
December	211	981	150	253	238	526	22	47	4	4	119	744=31	1811	58.42	+6	—47	—20.24
January	329	1169	133	269	131	175	22	40	2	2	127	744=31	1655	53.45	+2½	—59½	—25.43
February	198	518	212	452	154	321	14	30	12	12	82	672=28	1333	47.62	+9½	—49	—32 46
March	158	285	193	430	147	234	41	77	32	41	173	744=31	1067	34.42	—8½	—51	—34.74
Result Total Winter 1830-1	1404	4386	1069	2402	922	1852	250	691	65	79	658	4368=182	9410	51.61	+24	—59½	—18.89
April	390	1462	105	220	93	155	71	187	7	9	54	720=30	2033	67.76	+30	—25	—6.44
May	320	1081	135	302	95	179	109	309	15	25	70	744=31	1896	61.16	+36	—16	+16.02
June	238	649	283	776	111	235	15	33	8	10	65	720=30	1703	56.77	+52	+14	+31.56
July	205	605	61	194	155	338	255	659	22	73	46	744=31	1869	60.26	+50	+32	+37.94
August	261	818	134	468	110	239	182	449	14	27	43	744=31	2001	64.55	+54	+24	+36.51
September	354	1592	101	225	101	181	105	411	25	32	34	720=30	2441	81.37	+36	+6	+23.4
Result Total Summer, 1831	1768	6207	819	2185	665	1327	737	2048	91	176	312	4392=183	11,943	65.31	+54	—25	+23.165

Remarks.—The wind during this winter prevailed from the north-westward, but the north-easterly winds were not so prevalent as during the former winter, the south-westerly winds being the next; this may account for the winter being so severe, as there can be no doubt that the wind came from a colder quarter, since in both this and the preceding summer we found the temperature colder as we approached the Magnetic Pole, which bore then nearly west from Sheriff's harbour. During the summer months the wind was decidedly most prevalent from the northward, particularly during the three latter months, which brought vast quantities of ice into the Gulf.

GENERAL ABSTRACT OF THE METEOROLOGICAL OBSERVATIONS OF THE VICTORY DISCOVERY SHIP, TAKEN ON THE ICE AND REGISTERED HOURLY. VICTORIA HARBOUR, LAT. 70° 9′ N, LONG. 91° 34′ W.

FROM OCTOBER, 1831, TO APRIL, 1832.

	Wind North-westerly		Wind South-westerly		Wind South-easterly		Wind North-easterly		Wind variable		Calm weather	Total No. of Hours	Total force of Wind	Mean daily force of Wind	State of Temperature in the Shade		
	Hours	Force	Hours	Force	Hours	Force	Hours	Force	Hours	Force	Hours				Max.	Min.	Mean
October	334	1394	115	219	152	246	63	152	24	33	56	744=31 days	2044	65.94	+29	—23	+8.32
November	235	830	54	152	248	447	27	49	15	19	141	720=30	1497	49.9	+20	—42	—1.23
December	371	2003	23	37	100	127	62	73	36	37	152	744=31	2277	73.45	—2	—42	—23.96
January	401	2218	69	287	131	345	13	28	30	59	100	744=31	2937	94 74	—8	—47	—27.52
February	454	2490	19	48	92	177	39	74	13	28	79	696=29	2817	97.38	—12	—44½	—33.69
March	413	2058	32	86	94	132	49	60	23	24	133	744=31	2360	76.13	—1½	—48½	—31.37
Result Total Winter 1831-2	2208	10993	312	829	817	1474	253	436	141	200	661	4392=183	13932	76.1	+29	—48½	—18.24

Remarks.—During this winter the force of the wind was much greater, particularly in the three last months. On this circumstance our hopes of relief were chiefly founded, as by the constant tempestuous weather the ice was kept in motion until late in the month of March, and being generally from the northward, the ice presented a vast space of huge amorphous hummocks.

DIURNAL VARIATION OF THE MAGNETIC NEEDLE.

The Diurnal Variation of the Magnetic Needle was a subject which attracted the attention of scientific men about the year 1759, when many experiments were made. Its motion westward was observed to commence about 8 A.M., and continue until 2 P.M., when it became stationary for some time, and afterwards moving gradually back until it attained its first position, its utmost extent of variation being 19′ 4″. It was also observed that at the time an Aurora Borealis was seen, its variation though irregular, was slowly eastward in the morning and westward in the evening, and in the night suddenly both ways in a very short time. These phenomena were attributed to the power of the sun in *heating* the eastern magnetic properties of the earth in the morning, and those of the western in the evening; this was demonstrated by placing a strong magnet on each side of a compass, so as to keep the needle in the magnetic meridian, and alternately screening the sun from each magnet, it was observed, that when the sun was shining on the eastern magnet only, that the needle moved to the westward. This hypothesis was also corroborated by the fact, that the diurnal variation was observed to be greater in the summer than in the winter at London, as will appear by the following table of the mean diurnal variation for each of the twelve months of the year 1759:

January	7′ 8″	July	13′ 14″
February	8′ 58″	August	12′ 19″
March	11′ 17″	September	11′ 43″
April	12′ 2″	October	10′ 36″
May	13′ 0″	November	8′ 9″
June	13′ 21″	December	6′ 58″

The maximum being in June, and the minimum being in December. Thus the regular diurnal variation was concluded to be occasioned by the heat of the sun, which, however, did not apply to the irregular variation; it was therefore supposed to be occasioned by some subterraneous heat which was at times unequally diffused. The above account will be sufficient to prove that the discovery of diurnal variation is not of a modern date, but we may pass over the experiments that were made subsequently, since none of them threw any light on the subject, until it attracted the attention of the late Captain Flinders, to whom also the discovery of the deviation of the magnetic needle is due.

On my voyage to the Arctic Regions in 1818, the phenomena of the magnet particularly attracted my attention, and although a paper has been published in the Transactions of the Royal Society, by Captain E. Sabine, the observations therein given are exclusively mine, that gentleman not having been even on board or present when they were made, but copied out of my note-book to which he had access. In both the editions of my narrative of that voyage, I have given, not only the observations themselves, and conclusions drawn from them, but rules for the correction for deviation, which are so simple, that any master of a merchant ship can as easily correct his course for the deviation peculiar to his ship as for the variation of the compass. Nor have these rules been superseded; for although Professor Barlow's ingenious plate has been described as "triumphant," it is by no means infallible, as it must be acknowledged that any alteration in the situation of the iron material on board the ship must affect its accuracy, and it cannot again be rectified without a good opportunity when the ship is at anchor; while it is at any rate a piece of expensive lumber, for which there is not the least necessity, if the easy rules I have given are put in practice.

During my late interesting voyage, I have not only had an opportunity of confirming all my former observations, but of adding many important facts, which our actual approach to the magnetic pole has put us in possession of. My first series of observations were made at Felix harbour, in lat. 69° 59', long. 92° west, where the variation was found to be 89° 45' west, and the dip 89° 55'. In order to carry on the observations on diurnal variation, which had been begun to the westward by Sir John Franklin, I was, by the liberality of Sir George Murray, then Colonial Secretary, furnished with several instruments which had been used by that scientific and persevering officer, among them the diurnal variation instrument constructed by Mr. Dolland, from whom I received the necessary instructions to use it. This instrument has already been described by Sir John Franklin, but its microscopes were since altered to make the arc more conveniently read off by them. Nevertheless, it was some time before I could use it to obtain any satisfactory result; my magnetic observatory was built entirely of snow, 200 yards distant from any metallic substance, and marks were put up for placing it in the true magnetic meridian. I soon found that this instrument, which had never before been put to such a test, required the greatest delicacy in its use. When the needle was nicely suspended by a single fibre of New Zealand flax, I found that it was materially disturbed by the approach of any metallic substance, by any sudden increase or decrease of light, and by alteration in the temperature; if I had a coat with brass buttons, or a watch in my pocket, I saw it move before I was within two yards of it; nor could I take five successive readings at each end of the needle, without observing that the increase of temperature caused by my looking through the microscopes had a considerable effect, and observing to a second was impossible, the needle having a constant tremulous motion. When too dark to observe without a light, I was obliged to take a paper lantern, and even then, when the lighted candle shining through the paper was held for the purpose of reading off the arc, it produced a horizontal motion in the needle, corresponding to the direction and strength of the light. We were now in a position so near the magnetic pole, that the natural or universal magnetic influence was at right angles with a magnetized needle, traversing on a point horizontally, and it was then at liberty to be acted upon by any other influence or power, without restraint, excepting from its friction on that point which was also materially lessened by the power of suspension already described; and by inspection of the Tables for April and May, 1830, it will be seen that it followed the sun, although protected from its rays by a snow hut covered with canvass, and had it been at the time immediately in the vicinity of the magnetic pole, there could be no doubt but it would have followed the sun completely round the compass. Again, it was, during the winter, when every thing magnetic is more sluggish, proved, that it was disturbed by and followed the light of a candle; that it was materially disturbed by a brilliant Aurora Borealis, particularly when that was of a deep red. I have therefore concluded, that light, of whatever kind, has the property of combining with the magnetic influence. Of electricity we had no opportunity of making experiments, there being less electric matter in the Arctic Regions than in any other place, as proved on my first voyage, when the electrometer was never affected by it. My second conclusion is, that metal of any kind will become in some degree magnetized, the microscopes became magnetic in June 1830, and after the brass instrument made by Mr. Dolland became affected, I suspended the needle through a glass barometer tube, and used a paper graduated card, which gave the observation to half a degree, and which, indeed, was as near as its tremulous motion would permit the eye to observe it on a silver arc. My third conclusion is, that it is affected by temperature.

So that my observations made during the first voyage were, in that respect, fully confirmed. The following table will clearly show the different periods on which the Diurnal Variation was greatest and least, as well as under what circumstances the differences took place.

VICTORY DISCOVERY SHIP, METEOROLOGICAL OBSERVATIONS.

REGISTER OF DIURNAL VARIATION FOR APRIL, 1850, BY DOLLOND'S DIURNAL VARIATION INSTRUMENT, TAKEN EVERY TWO HOURS, BEGINNING AT MIDNIGHT.

Days of the Month.	2	Velocity of Wind.	State of Weather.	Temperature.	4	Velocity of Wind.	State of Weather.	Temperature.	6	Velocity of Wind.	State of Weather.	Temperature.	8	Velocity of Wind.	State of Weather.	Temperature.	10	Velocity of Wind.	State of Weather.	Temperature.	Noon.	Velocity of Wind.	State of Weather.	Temperature.	For 24 Hours. Barometer at Midnight.	For 24 Hours. Direction of Wind.
1																									29.700	S.^{3} NNE.^{5} NW.^{16}
2																									29.824	
3	85.10.30	1	b	12°−	89.25.0	1	b	14°−	92.10.0	1	b	10°−	94.10.0	0	b	1°+	99.30.0	2	b	2°−	101.5.30	1	b	2°+	30.111	S.^{6} C.^{2} NNW.^{16}
4	84.31.0	1	b	11−	83.20.0	0	b	14	92.20.0	0	c	15	93.50.0	2	c	19−	96.55.0	1	c	9	99.45.0	1	g	4−	N. 645 30.176	NNE.^{10} NE.^{14}
5	87.25.0	5	g	7	90.0.0	1	g	6	92.10.0	3	g	6	93.45.0	3	os	2	96.15.0	4	os		97.40.0	4	gs	1+	29.900	NNE.^{24}
6	87.50.0	5	os	7+	92.2.0	5	os	7+	92.11.0	5	obs	9+	93.30.0	5	os	14+	95.35.0	6	os	14+	96.4.0	4	os	26	N. 296 29.485	NNE.^{11} ENE.^{6} SW.^{7}
7		1	c	5−	90.1.0	3	o	1−	92.12.0	5	c	2	94.0.0	5	c	9	96.01.0	5	c	9	97.3.0	4		8½	29.575	SSE.^{16} C.^{4} SE.^{4}
8	97.0.0	0	o	12+	90.0.0	2	os	12+	92.16.0	0	o	12	94.20.0	0	o	15	97.20.0	2	gs	16	96.21.0	2	gs	17	29.777	C.^{3} S.^{12} SW.^{6} C.^{3}
9	87.2.0	2	o	7−	96.30.0	1	o	5	92.15.30	2	os	2−		2	os		96.10.0	2	g	2	98.5.0	2	g	6	N. 4.9 29.790	S.^{4} W.^{2} WSW.^{12}
10	84.15.0	2	gos	16+	83.45.0	7	bs	16	92.40.1	4	b	15	95.0.0	6	b	14−	95.20.0	1	b	19	101.2.0	2	b	4−	30.131	SW.^{4} SSW.^{4} SW.^{12} W.^{4}
11	85.30.36	1	b	2	84.25.0	1	b		92.20.0	0	os	3+	94.40.0	0	os	6+	96.41.0	1	g	19	99.21.0	1	g	24½	30.510	WbS.^{5} C.^{3} SW.^{8} NNE.^{8}
12	87.25.15	3	gs	5	89.25.0	1	ogs	8	92.15.0	4	os	7−	94.25.0	1	os	10	95.50.0	2	os	12	98.25.0	3	o	13	30.182	SW.^{5} NNE.^{3} S.^{2} NNE.^{14}
13	86.31.0	6	o	16		5	os	18	92.15.0	5	o	18+	94.20.0	5	os	22	96.20.0	4	o	23	97.2.0	4	o	16	29.915	NE.^{11} SSW.^{7} SbSW.^{16}
14	96.21.0	1	b	6	85.45.0	3	g	6	92.5.30	3	gs	5	94.30.0	6	os	7	99.25.0	2	b	10	105.25.0	2	b	14	30.196	SW.^{10} WSW.^{10} N.^{4}
15	86.30.4	2	g	1	89.1.0	1	g	5	92.10.0	0	g	7	95.0.0	2	b	10	100.3.0	1	b	16	107.18.0	1	b	16	30.244	N.^{1} NNE.^{2} C.^{3} NNE.^{17}
16	87.1.0	0	c	2	89.33.0	3	c	5	92.21.0	5	b	4	94.32.0	2	b	4	98.45.0	2	b	10	99.12.0	2	b	14	30.290	C.^{9} W.^{13} SW.^{8}
17	84.2.30	0	b	2	87.21.0	0	b	2	92.11.0	1	b	1	95.17.36	1	b	7	101.3.15	2	b	9	108.21.0	1	b	11	30.052	C.^{6} SSW.^{6} NNE.^{6} E.^{2} N.^{2}
18	82.21.0	0	b	1−	86.3.0	1	b	8	92.14.0	1	b	1−	96.11.0	3	b	1	102.0.0	1	b	7	109.5.0	1	b	9	30.040	C.^{4} W.^{4} NE.^{1} NNE.^{8} E.^{6}
19	82.25.0	2	b	9	86.21.0	1	b	2−	92.10.0	2	b	2	96.22.0	5	b	2	101.50.0	5	b	2	108.21.0	6	b	5	30.040	WSW.^{8} W.^{8} NE.^{5} NNW.^{3}
20	85.41.0	2	g	12+	89.23.0	0	g	13	92.7.0	2	b	9	96.05.0	2	b	1−	99.0.0	3	g	2	99.25.0	4	g		30.050	NW.^{3} C.^{1} W.^{5} WSW.^{3} WNW.^{12}
21	84.42.0	2	b	16−	87.2.0	1	b	16	92.45.0	1	b	14	95.10.0	1	b	4	99.12.0	1	g	1−	101.7.0	2	g	1−	29.980	W.^{2} S.^{2} SSW.^{4} W.^{5} NW.^{11}
22	87.2.0	2	g	11	88.0.0	2	g	11	93.01.0	2	g	11	96.21.0	1	g	12	98.0.0	3	g	12	99.20.0	2	b	1	30.182	NNW.^{9} N.^{2} NNW.^{16}
23	84.12.0	0	b	19	87.0.0	0	b	20	92.20.0	3	g	16	94.17.0	1	g	11	99.21.0	1	b	6	101.9.0	1	b	1	29.985	C.^{3} NE.^{8} SSE.^{2} C.^{3} NW.^{16}
24	81.33.0	1	b	18	86.11.0	1	b	26	92.17.0	1	b	19	96.20.0	1	b	10	97.35.0	1	g	4	98.5.0	2	bs		29.815	NE.^{1½} SE.^{3} NW.^{3} N.^{6} NNE.^{6}
25		6	g	11		6	b	13	92.19.0	5	b	9	91.21.0	5	c	2		3	g	2		3	g	2	29.936	N.^{3} NNE.^{4} N.^{8} SW.^{2} NNW.^{5}
26	85.9.0	2	b	11	88.50.0	3	b	13		3	b	9		3	1		95.17.0	3	b	2	103.17.0	2	b		29.932	N.^{24}
27	83.25.0	0	b	6		1	bs	6	92.21.0	1	g	6	93.25.0	2	g	1½	95.15.0	1	g	1+	97.25.0	2	g	3½+	29.920	NNW.^{2} SSW.^{10} SW.^{7} WSW.^{5}
28	87.0.0	1	os	8	90.02.0	1	os	8	92.2.0	1	os	6		3	os	5		3	g	1−	98.7.0	3	g	1	29.910	SW.^{4} N.^{1}
29	88.0.0	3	g	11	89.10.0	3	g	11	92.15.0	2	g	9	94.11.0	2	g	4	99.15.0	2	b	3	104.16.0	2	b	2−	30.130	NNW.^{24}
30		0	g	8	93.15.0	1	o	5	92.25.0	0	os	3½	94.4.0	8	os	24½	97.05.0	7	os	7+	96.45.0	7	os	8+	30.100	S.^{2} NW.^{6} N.^{9} NNE.^{1} NE.^{2}

Days of the Month.	2	Velocity of Wind.	State of Weather.	Temperature.	4	Velocity of Wind.	State of Weather.	Temperature.	6	Velocity of Wind.	State of Weather.	Temperature.	8	Velocity of Wind.	State of Weather.	Temperature.	10	Velocity of Wind.	State of Weather.	Temperature.	Midnight.	Velocity of Wind.	State of Weather.	Temperature.
1																								
2																								
3	100.2.0	1	b	10°+	96.5.30	1	b	10°+	92.35.0	1	b	1°−	90.25.0	1	b	6°−	85.10.0	1	o	7°	83.21.0	1	b	11°−
4	98.30.0	1	g	1	94.20.0	2	g	5	92.20.0	2	b	5+	91.20.0	2	b	7	88.25.0	3	g	7½	86.11.0	3	g	8
5	97.0.0	5	os	1	91.0.0	7	os	2	92.5.0	8	os	3	91.15.0	8	os	4+	89.30.0	6	os	4+	87.30.0	5	os	4¼
6	95.30.30	4	os	26	94.30.0	1	os	2	92.1.0	4	os	15	91.30.0	6	os	6	89.0.0	5	os	2−	87.0.30	5	os	5−
7	96.24.0	4	o	9	91.55.0	2	o	10	92.10.0	1	o	10	91.0.0	1	o	18	88.30.0	2	o	12+	86.30.0	1	o	12
8	97.0.0	1	gs	17	91.0.0	2	gs	16	92.10.0	5	g	4	91.2.0	5	g	2−	89.0.0	5	g	4−	87.5.0	5	g	4
9	97.25.0	5	os		93.45.0	8	os	3−	92.20.0	8	os	4−	91.10.0	4	os	9	90.5.0	9	gs	13	87.35.0	10	gso	13
10	100.2.0	1	b	4	97.11.0	1	b	8+	93.0.0	2	b	1+	91.1.0	1	b	5	90.2.0	1	g	5	86.25.0	1	gs	1
11	100.20.0	1	b	18	98.25.0	1	b	22	92.20.0	1	b	14	90.25.0	2	b	8+	89.11.15	3	g	8+	87.16.0	3	gs	6+
12	99.1.30	1	o	18	94.15.0	4	o	19	92.5.0	4	o	16	91.5.0	3	o	14	90.25.0	3	os	13	87.10.0	5	os	11
13	97.2.30	3	o	11	94.20.0	3	os	21	92.25.0	3	os	17	91.15.0	4	os	12	89.22.0	3	gs	9	86.35.0	3	g	7
14	102.11.0	1	b	11	93.0.0	2	b	9	92.25.0	2	b	6	89.21.0	2	b	2	86.35.0	2	b	2	84.3.0	2	b	3
15	100.19.0	1	b	14	95.15.0	1	b	13	92.21.0	1	b	10	89.18.0	1	b	5	87.0.0	1	b	3	83.24.0	1	b	2−
16	100.0.0	3	b	10	98.30.0	3	b	10½	92.11.0	3	b	9	89.33.0	1	b	7	86.47.0	1	b	5	85.42.0	1	b	2+
17	101.6.0	1	b	14	99.6.0	1	b	10	92.15.0	1	b	7	86.51.0	0	b	4	85.25.0	1	b	2	81.30.0	2	b	2
18	102.7.0	1	b	11	100.0.0	1	b	16	92.25.0	1	b	9	86.40.0	1	b	4	84.23.0	0	b	6−	80.45.0	0	b	7−
19	102.1.0	6	b	2	99.49.30	1	b	1	92.05.0	2	b	8−	86.31.0	1	b	14−	84.41.0	4	b	16	82.29.0	3	b	16
20	98.5.0	6	os	3−	91.21.0	5	os	6−	92.10.0	7	os	5	90.2.0	7	os	7½	86.5.0	3	g	11	87.07.0	3	b	19
21	99.25.0	2	b	2	95.3.0	2	b	2	92.30.0	5	b	10	88.10.0	1	b	10	85.5.0	2	b	11	84.45.0	2	b	16
22	97.22.0	2	g	9	91.25.0	2	g	9	92.50.0	1	b	6	90.2.0	1	g	8	86.25.0	1	b	13	83.25.0	1	b	16½
23	100.11.0	1	b	3	96.33.0	0	b	1	92.22.0	0	b	6	88.3.0	1	b	12	84.21.0	1	b	13	83.45.0	1	b	15½
24	97.2.0	3	gs	2	94.2.0	2	gs	2		3	g	9	90.3.0	4	g	14	89.21.0	3	g	14		3	g	11
25	98.2.0	3	g	1+	93.3.0	4	gs		92.5.0	2	gs	1½	89.14.0	2	g	5	88.21.0	2	b	10	83.25.0	2	b	11
26	96.55.0	2	b		98.0.0	2	b		92.20.0	1	b		89.12.0	0	b	1½	80.0.0	1	b	4	85.0.0	1	g	5
27	96.15.0	3	g	6	95.22.0	2	g	11	92.25.0	2	g		90.21.0	5	g	1½	84.11.0	5	g	6	85.30.0	4	gs	7
28	97.31.0	3	g	1½	91.11.0	3	g	2	92.30.0	3	g	4	90.13.0	2	g	5	85.22.0	2	g	10	86.21.0	1	g	12
29	100.21.0	2	b	3	96.27.30	2	b	2	92.11.0	2	b	5	91.12.0	2	gs	7	83.17.0	2	g	9	87.07.0	2	b	9
30	94.15.0	7	os	7+	93.0.30	5	os	3+	91.23.0	8	os	6+		1	os	7		1	g	6		2	g	2

N.B.—Where blanks are left no observations were made. The directions of the winds are expressed as in the Meteorological Table, and the degrees of diurnal variation are read from north towards the west.

VICTORY DISCOVERY SHIP, METEOROLOGICAL OBSERVATIONS.

REGISTER OF THE VARIATION FOR MAY, 1830, BY DOLLAND'S DIURNAL VARIATION INSTRUMENT, TAKEN EVERY TWO HOURS, BEGINNING AT MIDNIGHT.

Days of the Month.	2				4				6				8				10				Noon.				For 24 Hours.	
		Velocity of Wind.	State of Weather.	Temperature.		Velocity of Wind.	State of Weather.	Temperature.		Velocity of Wind.	State of Weather.	Temperature.		Velocity of Wind.	State of Weather.	Temperature.		Velocity of Wind.	State of Weather.	Temperature.		Velocity of Wind.	State of Weather.	Temperature.	Barometer at Midnight.	Direction of Wind.
				+				+				+				+				+				+		
1	85.30.0	3	b	17	88.41.0	2	b	8	92.1.45	3	c	2	94.20.0	2	g	7½	94.4.0	1	g	13	98.42.0	2	b	18	29.777	4 6 5 2 2 NE. N. WNW. W. N.
♁ 2	87.55.0	8	o	8	89.30.0	6	c	10	92.10.0	5	b	11	95.30.0	1	b	12	99.22.0	3	b	14	102.7.0	2	b	16	29.772	4 20 N. NNE.
3	88.15.0	2	c	6	90.28.0	2	c	7	92.15.0	3	c	12	94.50.0	2	c	12	98.50.0	3	o	14	103.30.0	3	g	19	29.000	9 12 3 NWy. NEy. C.
4	89.20.0	1	g	10	90.25.0	1	g	16	92.00.0	2	g	13	95.0.0	1	g	18	100.15.0	2	b	29	111.25.0	3	b	18	30.046	3 4 3 4 SbW. WSW. W. S.
5	89.25.0	2	g	2	91.20.0	1	l	6	91.51.0	1	g	12	91.16.0	4	g	10	97.33.0	1	g	10	99.15.0	4	g	12	30.116	2 2 10 10 W. W. S. SW.
○ 6	95.21.0	0	b		88.11.0	1	b	1	92.25.0	2	g	8	95.0.0	3	g	12	97.12.0	2	g	16	99.0.0	2	g	18	30.186	7 5 3 14 E. WSW. SW. S.
7	88.42.0	2	g	8	89.12.0	1	g	10	92.30.0	1		15	97.0.0	2	o	21		3	os	24		3	os	28	30.210	8 8 0 NE. SSE. NW.
8	88.17.0	3	g	9	85.47.0	3	g	7	92.38.0	2	b	8	98.27.0	4	b	10	111.17.0	5	b	3	115.44.0	4	b	9	30.340	20 4 WNW. W.
⊕ 9	87.25.0	2	b		89.2.0	3	l	2½	92.32.0	3	b	7	88.32.0	2	b	8	110.0.0	3	b	9½	99.57.0	2	c	15	30.291	6 6 4 3 3 SSW. WNW. SE. SE. E.
10	89.24.0	4	os	4	89.31.0	3	b	3	91.5.0	4	b	1	89.55.0	3	b	7	102.29.0	4	b	9	107.22.0	4	b	10	30.321	2 5 19 EbN. NW. NNW.
11	86.13.0	2	c		89.45.0	1	g	2	91.20.0	1	b	5	98.12.0	3	b	6	102.2.0	2	b	8	110.10.0	2	b	11	30.311	15 5 3 1 NNW. WNW. W. N.
12	84.10.0	0	b		90.0.0	0	b	3	93.20½	0	b	5	98.12.0	1	b	7	101.17.0	1	b	9	113.2.0	1	b	9	30.229	7 4 8 2 2 C. NEy. WNW. E. W.
☾ 13	84.0.0	2	b	1½	89.24.0	4	b	9	92.11½	4	b	10	97.22.0	4	c	10½	103.01.0	2	b	14	112.22.0	2	b	14	30.160	2 4 NE. NW.
14	81.7.0	2	b	4	87.45.0	1	b	7	92.23.0	1	b	9	90.21.0	1	b	10	102.7.0	1	b	13	114.20.0	2	b	13	30.160	4 8 3 4 NW. S. W. NW.
15	84.22.0	1	b	6	86.41.0	1	b	14	90.0.0	2	b	14	95.51.0	1	b	16	105.25.0	1	b	16	111.11.0	2	b	17½	30.060	7 6 2 9 Wy. S. SE. SWy.
⊕ 16	88.22.0	2	gs	10	91.0.0	2	gs	16	92.26.0	3	os	15	94.10.0	3	os	18		3	b	16		3	b	16	29.935	6 8 7 3 SSE. SE. E. ESE.
17	85.57.0	3	b	8	90.2.0	2	g	9	92.2.0	4	os	11	91.00.0	6	os	15		7	os	17		6	os	20	30.060	24 East.
18		3	g	17		3	g	17		3	os	19		4	o	20		3	o	26½		2	o	29	30.201	14 2 5 3 E. S. E. NNE.
19	88.21.0	2	os	20	91.10.0	4	os	20	91.50.0	2	os	21	94.00.0	3	os	21	100.0.0	4	os	21	99.25.0	3	os	22	30.380	24 NNE.
○ 20	89.15.0	1	os	13	91.20.0	2	g	14	92.0.0	3	os	16	94.20.0	4	os	19	91.11.0	2	o	18	98.10.0	2	o	19	30.435	12 12 NWy. NE.
21	87.42.0	3	o	13	89.12.0	2	o	14	92.20.0	2	o	15	97.35.0	1	b	16	100.12.0	1	b	19	113.0.0	1	b	18	30.480	24 N to NE.
22	83.15.0	2	b	10	87.25.0	2	b	15	92.50.0	6	b	16	98.45.0	1	b	15	109.2.0	2	b	15½	116.3.0	2	b	16	30.621	6 6 4 4 3 NNW. N. NNW. NNE. N.
♁ 23	82.40.0	2	b	11		2	b	15		2	b	16		2	b	16		3	b	19		2	b	21	30.591	1 2 10 7 NW. NNW. N. NNE.
24	82.22.0	4	b	12	87.45.0	2	b	16	92.16.0	3	b	17	99.51.0	2	b	19	110.7.0	1	b	26	115.30.0	1	b	21	30.411	3 10 11 NbW. NNW. NNE.
25	81.27.0	3	b	14	86.36.0	2	b	17	92.17.0	3	b	18	99.25.0	2	b	19	110.15.0	2	b	20	116.25.0	2	b	20	30.305	5 13 6 NNW. NNE. C.
26	85.38.0	0	f	11	80.22.0	0	f	13	91.35.0	1	f	17	96.32.0	1	b	18	112.32.0	1	b	20	116.52.0	1	b	21	30.261	4 2 6 5 1 4 C. S. SE. W. SE. W.
☽ 27	83.49.0	0	b	14	87.07.0	0	b	14	92.10.0	1	b	17	98.36.0	1	b	10	109.23.0	1	b	22	111.8.0	1	b	24	30.261	4 6 4 6 C. NE. SE. W.
28	82.32.0	0	b	22	87.55.0	1	b	21	92.11.0	1	b	24½	96.50.0	1	b	22	106.5.0	1	b	24	112.50.0	2	b	28	30.240	2 8 3 6 4 1 C. NE. SW. NW.
29	83.22.0	0	b	25	85.03.0	1	b	27	92.14.0	1	b	28	99.27.0	1	b	30	116.22.0	1	b	32	115.20.0	1	b	34	30.100	24 Wy.
30	84.24.0	0	b	21	87.28.0	0	b	26	92.22.0	6	b	28	94.47.0	1	b	31	111.33.0	0	b	33½	116.27.0	1	b	36	30.474	6 8 10 C. SSW. Ey.
⊕ 31		2	f			1	f			1	f			1	fs			1	f			1	f		30.445	24 Ey.

Days of the Month.	2				4				6				8				10				Midnight.			
		Velocity of Wind.	State of Weather.	Temperature.		Velocity of Wind.	State of Weather.	Temperature.		Velocity of Wind.	State of Weather.	Temperature.		Velocity of Wind.	State of Weather.	Temperature.		Velocity of Wind.	State of Weather.	Temperature.		Velocity of Wind.	State of Weather.	Temperature.
				+				+				+				+				+				+
1	96.36.0	2	g	11	93.2.0	2	g	14	92.5.0	1	o	13	91.11.0	4	g	9	90.7.0	0	o	5	88.52.0	5	o	6
2	99.22.0	2	g	16	95.3.0	2	g	18	92.15.0	2	g	18	91.19.0	2	g	14	89.12.0	1	g	10	87.37.0	2	c	8
3	100.55.0	2	b	17	96.23.0	3	b	16	92.2.0	2	c	14	91.15.0	1	g	13	89.20.0	0	g	11	88.5.0	0	g	10
4	110.22.0	1	b	16	90.0.0	2	b	15	92.13.0	3	b	12	89.25.0	1	b	13½	88.34.0	3	g	9	88.10.0	2	g	5
5	97.11.0	4	g	12	94.12.0	3	g	11	92.20.0	4	g	10	91.21.0	4	g	8	89.18.0	4	g	4	87.25.0	3	g	2
6	97.05.0	2	g	18	91.31.0	2	g	17	92.21.0	2	g	15	90.41.0	2	g	11	87.50.0	2	b	9	87.48.0	1	c	6
7		1	os	27		4	os	21	92.18.0	2	os	16	90.0.0	2	os	15	89.7.0	2	o	12	86.16.0	2	g	12
8	106.3.0	3	b	7	99.7.0	1	b	6	92.5.0	3	b	7	90.22.0	4	b	7	89.11.0	7	g	2	88.21.0	5	g	1
9	100.22.0	1	b	16	90.12.0	1	b	14	92.7.0	2	b	10	90.19.0	2	os	9	92.45.0	1	os	7	88.18.0	1	os	6
10	97.25.0	3	c	12	97.2.0	3	b	11	92.9.0	2	b	9	88.13.0	2	b	8½	85.40.0	2	b	3	84.01.0	2	b	2
11	110.41.0	2	b	10	94.3.0	2	g	11	92.9.0	2	g	9	88.18.0	2	b	6	85.35.0	2	b	6	83.50.0	2	b	1
12	110.25.0	1	b	10	99.40.0	2	b	11	92.8.0	2	b	10	90.21.0	0	g	7	89.45.0	0	g	6	86.22.0	1	g	1
13	108.16.0	2	b	13	93.25.0	1	c	13	92.15.0	0	b	11½	88.5.0	1	b	9½	87.29.0	1	b	6	83.23.0	2	b	4½
14	107.11.0	3	b	14	90.15.0	3	b	15	92.4.0	3	b	15	87.30.0	2	b	11	84.41.0	1	b	8	80.25.0	1	b	4
15	103.5.0	1	b	19	99.5.0	1	b	16	92.1.0	1	b	14	87.25.0	1	b	11½	87.4.0	2	g	9	87.25.0	2	g	10
16	101.0.0	3	b	14	98.17.0	3	b	14	92.11.0	4	b	14	88.5.0	3	b	12½	85.12.0	2	b	10	82.21.0	2	b	9
17		4	b	21		3	b	24	92.22.0	4	b	21	87.45.0	2	b	20	87.30.0	1	o	18	87.02.0	3	o	17
18		1	g	30		1	g	29		1	g	26		1	g	26		2	g	22		2	os	20
19		3	g	21		3	g	20	92.35.0	3	g	18		3	g	16		4	o	12	89.01.0	2	os	12
20	96.15.0	2	os	20	94.5.0	2	os	20	92.45.0	3	os	18	91.12.0	2	o	11	90.0.0	3	o	14	86.31.0	1	o	13
21		2	b	16		2	b	15½	92.41.0	2	b	11½		1	b	12		2	b	10		2	b	9
22	110.45.0	2	b	19	97.2.0	2	b	17	92.47.0	2	b	16	87.25.0	2	b	14	83.17.0	2	b	13	89.21.0	2	b	11
23		3	b	20		2	b	19		3	g	18½		2	b	13		3	b	16		2	b	11½
24	109.30.0	2	b	22	98.43.0	2	b	22	92.0.0	2	b	20	86.37.0	2	b	17	82.45.0	4	b	13½	80.2.0	3	b	12
25	112.21.0	2	b	21	99.45.0	2	b	20	92.3.0	1	b	18	85.22.0	1	b	18	81.35.0	0	b	16	79.42.0	0	b	13
26	113.7.0	1	b	23	101.0.0	1	b	24	92.9.0	1	b	21½	84.51.0	1	b	20	81.41.0	1	b	16	80.17.0	0	b	14½
27	110.27.0	1	b	26½	101.1.0	1	b	26	91.17.0	1	b	25½	85.0.0	1	b	23	80.27.0	0	b	19	79.45.0	0	b	19
28	104.6.0	1	b	31	99.9.0	1	b	29½	92.5.0	2	b	28	88.25.0	2	f	27	88.5.0	3	o	27	80.10.0	1	b	25
29	110.0.0	1	b	34	101.0.0	1	b	33	92.4.0	0	b	32	84.0.0	0	b	32½	80.27.0	1	b	30	79.12.0	1	b	24
30	111.10.0	1	b	37	122.5.0	1	b	35	92.0.0	2	f	33		1	f	31		1	f	28		1	f	27
31		1	fs			1	f			2	f.			1	f.			1	f.			1	f.	

N.B.—Where blanks are left no observations were made. The directions of the winds are expressed as in the Meteorological Table, and the degrees are read from north towards the west.

DIP, &c. OF THE MAGNETIC NEEDLE.

I HAVE already mentioned that I was in possession of three dipping needles: one the construction of Mr. T. Jones, one by Mr. Pope, and the last by myself on the plan of Mr. Jennings. The two lastmentioned served to prove the accuracy of the first, which was used by me in the month of May, 1830, where I found the dip, by all three dipping needles, to be eighty-nine degrees and fifty-five minutes; and subsequently, at Padliak or Spence bay, where it was found to be eighty-nine degrees and fifty-six minutes, by six sets of observations taken on the two days which I remained there for the purpose: but the variation of the compass was found to be considerably less, being only sixty-eight degrees and thirty-five minutes west, making a difference of twenty degrees and twenty-five minutes, sufficient to indicate nearly where the Pole must be found. It is, however, but justice to say, that the position assigned to the Magnetic Pole by Commander Ross, was made entirely from his own observations, and if any discrepancies are found, I conceive that they must have proceeded from damage which the needle sustained while in my possession at Padliak; but which, if I may judge from the subsequent observations, was not so great as I at first apprehended.

I had also several observations on the magnetic force during the first year; but these I did not follow up, because it was evident that every winter, the magnetic force of the needle constructed for that purpose, had diminished probably from the severity of the climate: these needles are still in my possession.

The observations which I made on Sound, have so nearly the same result as those made on the preceding voyages, that they need not be detailed here; as also those on the Radiation of Solar Heat, the maximum of which was eighty-four degrees of Fahrenheit, in an ivory-mounted thermometer, suspended between two poles. While opposite to black-painted canvas it rose to ninety degrees.

g

LATITUDES AND LONGITUDES.

g 2

LATITUDES AND LONGITUDES.

FROM THE N.E. CAPE TO GULF OF BOOTHIA AND KING WILLIAM IV. SEA.

In the first Alphabetical Table the Latitudes and Longitudes of the new discoveries are given to the nearest minute. The names given by the natives are printed in *italics*, as are also those for which there was not room in the chart for their insertion.

This list will also explain the omissions and the discrepancies between the narrative and the chart, which arose from my unavoidable absence, whilst Commander Ross's narrative was printing; and by the chart having been printed and examined by His Majesty before I had received Commander Ross's narrative. Suffice it to remember, that the names on the chart are correct, and the latitudes and longitudes have been compared by Mr. C. Walker.

The second Alphabetical Table contains the Latitudes and Longitudes of Baffin's Bay, as verified by the observations of this voyage, some of which had been unwarrantably altered in some of the charts subsequently published; and the banks of the Isabella and Alexander, which had been expunged, have been resurveyed and restored to their places.

The third Table contains the Latitudes and Longitudes of the discoveries of Sir E. Parry, Sir John Franklin, and Captain Beechy, carefully abstracted from their charts by Mr. Charles Walker.

TABLE.—No. 1.

	N. Lat. ° ′	W. Long. ° ′
Abernethy, Cape	69.33	96.7
A'Court Bay .	71.34	94.40
Adam Island	69.16	96.10
Adelaide Bay . .	72.45	92.20
Adelaide, Cape, & Magnetic Pole of William IV. .	70.5	96.44
Adolphus Island	69.56	92.5
Adolphus Island .	69.52	96.59
Agnew River, (*Awatutiak River*)	70.42	92.32
Airey, Cape . .	71.23	94.8
Alexander, Cape	70.19	96.54
Allington, Cape	70.36	92.0
Arbuthnot Island	70.45	92.30
Artist's Bay . . .	69.37	94.34
Astronomical Society's Islands, (*Kayuktaguwik Island*) .	69.50	91.40
Athol Island	70.57	93.2
Auckland, Cape	69.21	94.10
Augherston, Cape .	71.27	94.27
Augusta Island	69.51	97.38
Augustus Island	69.47	96.52
Babbage Bay	71.28	94.36
Back's Bay	69.33	98.35
Batty Bay . . .	73.17	91.00
Beaufort's Islands, (*as changed by his Majesty's command*)	69.45	91.30
Bernard, Cape .	70.10	96.47
Best Harbour	70.13	91.20
Beverley Island	69.19	95.36
Biot Island .	69.40	91.0
Bjornsterna Bay	71.5	93.35
Black's Islands	69.50	91.48
Blair's Islands .	70.47	92.28
Blankey Island	69.34	95.17
Bowles Bay .	70.47	92.39
Bowles River, (Entrance of) .	69.26	93.30
Brown's Island .	72.1	95.21
Brunel Inlet . .	69.28	91.42
Cambridge, Cape .	69.34	94.46
Carl IV., Cape	69.43	95.45
Christian Monument	70.24	92.0
Christian, Cape	69.36	95.1
Clara, Cape	72.17	94 24
Copeland Islands .	70.7	91.45
Coults Lindsey Island	70.11	91.22
Culgruff, Cape	69.33	95.53
Cumberland, Cape	69.51	95.87
Curtis Lake .	69.26	93.18
Cuvier Island	69.10	91.1
Destrove, Cape	69.38	91.30
Dundas, Ann, Island	69.18	94.21
Dundas, Jane, Island	69.20	94.20
Dundas Mountains	69.26	93.5
Eclipse Harbour	70.30	92.5
Eden Bay	70.19	91.38
Edgworth, Cape	69.20	96.8

	N. Lat. ° ′	W. Long. ° ′
Elizabeth Harbour	70.38	92.8
Elliot Island	70.58	93.10
Elwyn Bay	73.29	90.45
Errol Island	69.48	96.39
Erskine Island	69.53	96.50
Esterhazy Bay	70.12	96.50
Esther, Cape	72.15	94.31
Fairbrother Island	69.39	93.1
Falkland Island	69.55	96.51
Faro Lina Bay, (*Caro Lina*)	69.4	94.32
Farrand, Cape	71.47	95.4
Faulkner, Cape	69.37	94.37
Fearnall Bay	72.16	94.30
Felix, Cape	69.55	97.55
Felix Harbour, (*Tingerahiu*)	70.0	91.53
Ferguson, Cutlar, Island	71.7	93.30
Fox Island	69.50	96.43
Francis II., Cape	70.14	96.51
Franklin, Jane, Cape	69.36	98.36
Franklin Point	69.30	99.5
Frederick Island	69.49	96.59
Frederick IV., Cape	69.38	95.6
Frederick William III., Cape	69.22	93.54
Garry, Cape	72.19	94.19
Goudy Island	70.12	91.18
George, Prince, River	69.34	96.37
Glasgow, Cape	69.42	97.19
Gloucester, Cape	69.48	95.52
Grimble Islands	71.54	95.20
Hardy Bay	69.30	91.41
Hardy, Cape	69.24	95.22
Harriet, Cape	69.6	94.30
Hansteen Lake	69.45	94.10
Hay, Dalrymple, Cape	71.10	93.45
Hazard Island	72.4	95.11
Hecla and Fury Islands	70.4	90.38
Hendon, North	70.1	91.58
Heytesbury, Cape	71.33	94.35
Hughes Hughes, Cape	69.30	95.18
Hull Bay	69.21	93.45
Jane River, (*Amitioke River*)	69.21	93.10
Jekyll Lake	69.45	93.25
Jones, Mary, Bay	70.22	91.55
Josephine Bay	69.36	94.40
Isabella, Cape	69.26	93.55
Kent, Duchess of, Bay	69.58	96.10
Keppel, Cape	69.52	92.15
Kjer, Cape, (*Tikipoke R.*)	69.43	90.45
Knight Island	70.51	92.46
Kall, Cape, (*Ornatioke R.*)	69.37	90.5
Lambert, Cape	69.36	95.27
Landon, Cape	69.5	95.27
Landseer, Cape, (*Padliak Cape*)	69.30	94.22
Lang River	72.11	94.52
Lawrence, Cape	69.36	94.30
Lax Harbour	70.22	91.30
Lax Island, (*Imaglooktook*)	70.23	91.30
Leiven Bay	70.16	96.51
Leopold Island	74.1	89.57
Lindsey, Lord, River, (*Titchik*)	70.9	92.23
Logan Port	71.17	94.41
Louis-Philippe, Cape	69.34	96.8
Manson, Cape	70.41	92.22
Margaret, Cape	70.9	91.28
Maria Gloria, Cape	69.40	95.17
Marjory Island	70.56	92.56
Maria Louisa, Cape	69.47	98.23
Martin's Islands	70.12	91.24
Mary, Cape	69.46	97.25
Matty Island	69.25	95.40
M'Culloch Island	69.26	94.0
M'Diarmid's Island	70.0	91.53
M'Dowall, Cape	71.23	94.6
Melbourne Island	69.15	95.45
Melville, Lady, Lake, (*Neitchillee Lake*)	69.26	93.0
Menchikoff Bay	71.38	94.46
Mildred Lake, (Entrance of)	69.4	94.30
Modina, Cape	69.35	96.30
Molke Bay	71.8	93.45
Moore, Carrick, Cape	71.12	93.50

	N. Lat. ° ′	W. Long. ° ′
Mundy Harbour . .	70.14	91.37
Munster Island, (*formerly Beaufort's Island*) . . .	69.58	96.56
Murray Bay	71.48	95.12
Nicholas I., Cape, (*Commander Ross's furthest N.W.*) .	70.25	96.56
Nordenskjold, Cape	71.14	94.52
Norfolk Bay . .	69.33	91.58
Norton, Cape .	69.14	96.0
Oakley Island .	70.54	92.49
Old Man of Hoy	71.1	93.18
Oliver Mount . .	72.8	94.51
Oscar Bay . .	69.44	95.30
Owen Lake	70.30	92.33
Palmerston, Cape	70.50	92.42
Palmerston, Point . .	69.24	93.41
Parry, Isabella Louisa, or Lady Parry Island . .	70.9	90.50
Parry Port, (Entrance of)	69.40	97.17
Pearson Island .	69.47	91.27
Peel Inlet .	69.13	96.7
Porter, Cape	69.11	94.30
Pouncet Island	70.33	91.55
Purcell Bay	71.41	94.52
Ramage Island .	69.42	91.10
Rodd Bay . .	73.54	90.10
Rodwell Bay	71.44	94.57
Ross, Andrew, Island	70.13	91.27
Rowley, Cape .	69.4	95.25
St. Catherine, Cape, (*Akwennok*)	70.23	91.35
St. Mary's Mount . .	71.15	94.10
Saumarez River, (*Koguloktok*)	70.4	92.25

	N. Lat. ° ′	W. Long. ° ′
Schumacher Island	69.55	91.37
Scoresby, Cape	71.43	94.46
Selkirk, Cape	69.56	96.9
Seppings, Cape .	73.46	90.12
Shee, Cape .	69.34	91.28
Sheridan, Cape	69.4	95.11
Sherriff Harbour	70.2	91.52
Slater Island	69.37	92.7
Somerset House	72.48	91.45
Sophia, Cape	69.36	96.47
South Island . .	69.50	91.26
Spence Bay, (Entrance of), (*Padliak Bay*) . .	69.25	93.45
Stanly E. River	70.15	92.15
Stillwell Bay .	71.24	94.20
Sullivan Bay, (Entrance of)	69.32	94.25
Susanna Island .	70.31	91.50
Sussex, Cape	69.43	95.30
Sydney, Sophia, Cape	69.48	97.30
Taylor, H., Cape .	69.40	91.28
Thompson's Islands	69.45	92.18
Tilson's Islands	69.45	92.30
Troughton Island	69.54	91.43
Union River, (Entrance of) .	72.35	95.00
Victoria Harbour .	70.9	91.34
Victory Point	69.38	98.36
Wall's Bay . .	69.49	98.14
Wellington Strait, (Entrance of)	69.34	96.0
Willersted Lake .	69.19	93.25
Wilson's Bay	71.50	95.25
Will. of Wirt., Cape	69.39	97.2
York, Cape .	73.50	86.30

TABLE.—No. II.

LATITUDES AND LONGITUDES OF PLACES IN BAFFIN'S BAY, DETERMINED 1818, 1833.

	N. Lat. ° ′	W. Long. ° ′
Adair, Cape	71.24	70.00
Agnes Monument Rock	70.37	67.30
Agnew, Cape	71.24	71.45
Alexander, Cape	77.43	75.30
——— Bank	69.9	65.00
Allison Bay	74.40	57.56
Antrobus, Cape	71.57	73.50
Arabella Rock	76.35	70.34
Ardrossan Bay	70.37	68.40
Aston, Cape	70.10	65.25
Athol, Cape	76.23	69.41
Baffin's Islands	74.41	57.25
Bank's Bay	74.46	76.08
Barnard's Mountains	75.55	81.00
Bathurst Bay	73.33	76.24
Beatrice, Cape	74.32	80.30
Bell's Isle	71.27	72.00
Beverley Cliffs	75.40	67.30
Bisson, Cape	69.10	65.20
Black Hook, Cape	71.27	55.31
Booth's Sound	76.49	70.50
Borthwick	65.54	61.10
Bowen, Cape	72.25	74.40
Brodie Bay	68.00	64.05
Broughton, Cape	67.47	63.30
Browne's Islands	75.29	60.09
Bruce Bay	70.28	67.32
Bushnan's Island	76.04	65.26
Bute Island	70.26	67.30
Byam Martin, Cape	73.33	77.10
Caledon, Cape	76.16	79.22
Campbell, Cape	64.06	65.12
Cargenholm, Cape	71.32	72.36
Carey's Islands	64.06	73.10
Catherine's Bay	73.30	81.50
Charlotte, Cape	74.32	79.30
Charles's Island	63.00	64.50
Chidley, Cape	68.37	53.33
Christian, Cape	70.35	67.37
Clarence, Cape	76.45	77.45
Clephane, Cape	65.45	61.00
Clyde River	70.21	67.30
Cobourg Bay	75.35	78.40
Cockburn, Cape	74.49	73.45
Coquin Sound	53.00	65.37
Coutt's, Cape	72.00	74.10
——— Inlet	71.58	74.12
Cranstoun, Cape	71.15	54.20
Crimson Cliffs, (*Beverley*)	76.00	68.30
Croker's Mountains	73.58	90.00
Cumberland Strait		
Cunningham, Cape	74.40	96.02
Dacre's, Cape	65.36	61.5
Dalrymple Rock	76.28	70.42
Darkhead, Cape	72.10	56.00
Desolation, Cape		
Devil's Thumb	74.16	57.56
Disco, N. End	70.12	59.12
——— S. End	69.11	56.30
Duck Islands	68.49	53.42

	N. Lat. ° ′	W. Long. ° ′
Dudley Digges, Cape	76.05	68.54
Duneira Bay	75.27	53.30
Durham, Cape	65.59	61.54
Dyer's, Cape	66.42	
Edward's Bay	76.38	78.30
Eglinton, Cape	70.49	78.30
Elizabeth's Bay	73.30	80.00
Enderby, Cape	63.45	65.30
Exeter Bay	66.30	61.00
Fanshawe, Cape	73.40	76.06
Four-Island Point	70.46	33.03
Frances, Cape	76.28	70.25
Fry, Cape	65.06	63.25
Gilbert Sound	67.42	33.20
Graham Moore, Cape	72.54	75.28
Gamble Bay	77.20	73.10
Hackluit Island		
Haig's Island	70.29	67.45
Hamilton's Bay	71.25	70.40
Hardwicke, Cape	76.30	78.58
Hathorn, Cape	71 30	72.20
Hay, Cape	73.35	80.35
Hope's Monument	72.26	80.45
Hewett, Cape	70.27	67.18
Hingston Bay	73.48	57.20
Hoare Bay	65.18	63.30
Home Bay	68.40	64.40
Hooper, Cape	68.06	64.36
Hoppner, Cape	76.56	70.48
Horse's Head	74.49	58.15
Horsburgh, Cape	74.35	73.45
Hurd, Cape	77.49	78.48
Hynd's Bay	66.33	61.0
Inglis Bay	65.47	61.50
Inmallick	76.00	66.46
Iron Mountains	76.10	65.24
Isabella, Cape	77.48	77.00

	N. Lat. ° ′	W. Long. ° ′
Isabella's Bank	{ 69.31 69.28	65.20 64.40
Jacob's Bay, (or N.E. Bay)	71.00	53.00
Jameson, Cape	71.45	73.30
Jones's Sound	76.20	78.10
Kater, Cape	69.39	65.40
Lady Ann Bay	75.54	80.00
Lancaster Sound	74.19	83.50
Lawson, Cape	71.45	55.36
Leifle Bay, (*or Love Bay, or Good Haven*)	69.10	54.40
Leopold, Cape	75.40	78.12
Lewis, Cape	75.31	59.0
Lindsay, Cape	76.06	79.24
Loch Ryan	65.06	65.55
Mackintosh, Cape	67.00	62.10
Martin Mountains	73.25	80.00
Mary Ann Island, or Cape	71.25	71.35
M'Culloch, Cape	72.13	74.24
M'Douall, Cape	71.24	70.58
M'Leay, Cape	70.15	66.35
Meikleham, Cape	65.18	63.00
Melville Bay, Lat. 76° 5′ to 75° 12′ Long. 60° to 64°.		
Melville, Cape	76.05	64.30
Melville's Monument	75.33	59.18
Merchant's Bay	67.38	64.20
Miller's Island	65.12	63.18
Morris, Cape	76.09	62.08
Mouat, Cape	77.29	78.00
Murdoch, Cape	76.08	61.28
Nias, Cape	63.38	65.58
North Ayr	70.00	72.10
North Bay Islands	68.19	53.47
North Galloway	71.00	73.00
Operniwick	73.25	57.26
Osborne, Cape	74.24	81.42

	N. Lat. ° ′	W. Long. ° ′
Paget, Cape	70.10	75.55
Parry, Cape	77.06	71.23
Petowack .	76.11	69.00
Possession Bay	73.33	77.28
Pond's Bay .	72.38	75.00
Prince Regent's Bay	76.10	64.50
	75.45	66.40
Prince William's Land .	72.30	78.00
Princess Charlotte's Monument	75.36	78.28
Queen Anne's Cape	66.24	53.20
Raleigh Mount	61.14	61.40
Red Head .	74.55	53.44
Reid's Bay	66.48	61.40
Robertson, Cape	77.24	71.36
Raper, Cape	69.54	65.20
Rosamond, Cape	74.10	83.17
Sabine Islands	75.29	60.09
Salmon Islands .	70.11	65.30
Savage Islands, or Wild Islands	67.44	53.40
Saumarez, Cape	77.30	73.52
Saunderson's Tower .	64.50	63.55
Sowallick (or Iron) Mountains	76.10	65.04
Scott's Bay . .	71.10	70.10
Shackleton, Cape	73.36	57.25
Sheffield Bay	65.30	62.40
Siddon, Cape .	75.17	59.00
Skene's Island	76.07	63.24
Smith's Sound	77.55	76.15
South East Bay	69.00	50.00
Stair, Cape .	77.43	70.55
St. Clair, Cape	64.15	65.05
Suffkowallick	76.00	57.00
Sugarloaf Island	74.02	57.30
Thom Islands .	75.40	60.00
Three Islands (of Baffin)	74.01	57.25
Unknown Island	71.00	53.45
Walker, Cape	75.46	59.54
Walsingham, Cape	66.00	61.10
Walter Bathurst, Cape	73.03	76.22
Warrender, Cape .	74.19	32.40
Waygatt Island, (N. E. Side) .	70.24	
Waygatt Strait, (N. Entrance)	70.26	
Whale Islands .	68.59	63.13
Whale Sound	77.15	71.20
White, Cape	76.35	70.36
Wilcox Point	74.10	57.45
Wollaston Island .	69.25	65.20
Wolstenholme Island	76.24	70.22
Wolstenholme Sound	76.29	70.00
Women's Islands	72.45	56.40
York, Cape	75.55	65.38

TABLE.—No. III.

SIR EDWARD PARRY'S FIRST VOYAGE.

	N. Lat. ° ′	W. Long. ° ′		N. Lat. ° ′	W. Long. ° ′
Cape Fisher	75.53	111.38	Lowther Island	74.35	97.40
Cape Mudge	75.55	110.8	Davy Island	74.32	98.55
Point Nias	75.38	110.36	Young Island	74.20	98.50
Point Ried	75.36	110.0	Cape Walker	74 7	97.42
Cape Beechy	75.5	113.3	Cape Bunny	74.8	95.15
Cape Edwards	75.8	112.30	Browne Island	74.45	96.36
Bushnan Cove	75.13	111.45	Somerville Island	74.40	96.25
Hooper Island	75.6	111.55	Griffith Island	74.35	95.40
Liddon's Gulf	75.5	112.30	Cornwallis Island	75.0	95.0
Cape Hoppner	74.58	112.50	Cape Bowden	75.3	92.20
Fife Harbour	74.50	110.38	Wellington Channel	75.0	93.0
Winter Harbour	74.48	110.50	Cape Martyr	74.38	95.10
Point Hearne	74.43	110.40	Barlow Inlet	74.45	93.50
Hecla and Griper Bay	74.45	110.30	Cape Hotham	74.40	93.50
Cape Dundas	74.28	114.0	Cape Gifford	74.9	93.50
Cape Hoy	74.23	113.10	Cape Rennell	74.8	93.20
Cape Providence	74.25	112.30	Garnier Bay	74.5	93.10
Sabine Island	75.45	109.30	Cunningham Inlet	74.6	94.0
Point Griffiths	75.5	106.5	Prince Leopold Island	74.0	90.0
Beverley Inlet	107.40	75.0	Cape Clarence	73.59	90.50
Point Palmer	108.8	74.55	Cape Seppings	73.50	90.20
Dealy Inlet	108.50	75.0	Point Innes	74.53	92.15
Bridport Inlet	109.0	75.0	Cape Spencer	74.47	92.8
Point Wakeham	74.48	110.15	Beechy Island	74.43	92.0
Cape Gilman	75.3	104.10	Cape Riley	74.41	91.47
Cape Cockburn	75.4	100.26	Caswall's Tower	74.45	91.12
Allison's Inlet	75.2	99.23	Cape Ricketts	74.38	91.10
Cape Capel	75.6	97.45	Rigby Bay	74.37	90.10
Bedford Bay	75.3	98.30	Cape Hurd	74.33	90.0
Baker Inlet	74.58	97.50	Cape Eardly Wilmot	74.40	91.20
Garrett Island	74.47	98.28	Gascoyne Inlet	74.40	91.22

	N. Lat. ° ′	W. Long. ° ′		N. Lat. ° ′	W. Long. ° ′
Cape Herschell	74.37	89.12	Cape Warrender	74.28	81.50
Maxwell Bay	74.35	89.0	Cape Osborn	74.40	80.26
Cape Fellfoot . .	74.33	88.25	Cape Beatrice .	74.45	80.20
Sir Benjamin Hobhouse Inlet .	74.27	87.10	Hope's Monument	74.43	80.30
Stratton Inlet .	74.27	87.0	Barrow's Strait	74.0	85.0
Burnet Inlet	74.25	86.40	Cape Crawford	73.50	84.10
Powell's Inlet	74.25	85.20	Admiralty Inlet	73.45	83.30
Brooking Inlet	74.25	85.5	Cape Franklin	73.42	83.15
Cape Bullen .	74.23	85.0	Cape Charles Yorke	73.53	82.50
Cape York	73.50	86.55	Wollaston Isles	73.50	80.50
Radstock Bay	74.40	91.0	Navy Board Inlet .	73.45	81.20
Eardly Bay .	73.48	87.15	Cape Castlereagh	73.50	80.45
Jackson's Inlet	73.17	89.0	Cape Hay	73.52	80.10
Port Bowden	73.13	89.5	Martin Mountains	73.43	79.20
App Harbour	72.27	89.52	Cape Liverpool	73.40	78.5
Fitzgerald Bay .	72.10	89.50	Cape Fanshawe .	73.35	77.33
Cape Kater .	71.50	90.10	Possession Bay and Mount .	73.30	77.23
Cape Horne	74.29	84.5	Cape Byam Martin	73.29	77.10
Cape Rosamond	74.33	84.0	Bathurst Bay .	73.26	77.10
Croker's Bay	74.40	83.20	Cape Walter Bathurst	73.23	76.50
Cape Pateshall	74.38	82.45			

SIR EDWARD PARRY'S SECOND VOYAGE.

	N. Lat.	W. Long.		N. Lat.	W. Long.
Autridge Bay	70.7	85.25	Bouverie Island	69.38	82.10
Whyte Inlet .	70.7	85.0	Mount Sabine	69.38	82.23
Gifford River .	70.0	82.0	Halse Creek	69.40	82.42
Cape Hallowell	69.58	85.26	Richards Bay	69.35	82.15
Cape Englefield	69.51	85.30	Cape Matthew Smith	69.25	82.2
Amherst Island .	69.48	83.55	Khemig	69.25	82.30
Arlagnarigo	69.15	85.15	Coxe Island	69.27	82.30
Siattoke .	68.18	87.30	Hooper Inlet . .	69.18	82.0
Aggrochiawik	68.5	86.15	Mogg Bay	69.14	82.5
Liddon Island	69.47	83.10	Neerlonacto .	69.30	81.40
Griffith's Creek	69.39	83.30	Igloolik Island	69.23	81.45
Crozier River	69.27	83.15	Arlagnuk .	69.12	81.25
Quilliam Creek	69.28	83.0	Pingitkalik .	69.2	81.15
Ormond Island	69.48	82.40	Murray Maxwell Inlet	69.50	80.40
Cape Ossory	69.44	82.31	Skeoch Bay	69.36	80.15
Cape Northeast	69.42	82.33	Cape Elwyn .	69.32	80.20

	N. Lat. ° ′	W. Long. ° ′		N. Lat. ° ′	W. Long. ° ′
Calthorpe Island	69.28	80.10	Agwisscowik .	68.31	81.45
Tangle Island	69.25	80.17	Ooglit .	68.23	81.32
Tern Island	69.33	80.52	Amitioke .	68.15	82.20
Cape Konig .	69.32	79.48	Cape Jermain	67.47	81.58
Ooglit Island	68.48	81.4			

FROM SIR JOHN FRANKLIN'S CHART.

Point Beechy	70.24	149.35	Point Calton	69.31	138.57
Point Back	70.24	149.20	Point Stokes	69.24	138.38
Guider Bay	70.21	149.8	Point Kay	69.19	138.10
Return Reef	70.25	148.45	Phillips Bay	69.15	138.15
Prudhoe Bay	70.22	148.35	Babbage River	69.12	138.10
Point Heald .	70.21	148.28	Point P. King	69.7	137.44
Yarborough Inlet	70.18	148.20	Point Sabine .	69.4	137.32
Point Chandos	70.20	148.8	Mount Conybeare	69.29	140.3
Point Anxiety	70.18	147.45	Mount Robinson .	69.22	140.40
Foggy Island .	70.15	147.36	Mountain Indian River	69.30	139.10
Lion and Reliance Reef	70.11	146.52	Mount Sedgwick .	68.58	138.55
Point Bullen	70.10	146.28	Barn Mountain	68.46	137.51
Point Thompson .	70.9	146.7	Cupola Mountain	68.44	137.55
Flaxman Island .	70.10	145.50	Mount Fitton	68.42	137.55
Point Brownlow	70.9	145.40	Mount Davies Gilbert	68.43	136.20
Sir T. Staines River	70.6	145.40	Pitt Island .	69.5	136.12
Canning River	70.4	145.30	Escape Reef	68.56	136.57
Boulder Island	70.3	144.58	Tent Island .	68.56	136.18
Camden Bay	70.4	144.40	Shoalwater Bay	68.54	136.25
Barter Island	70.5	143.50	Point Pillage	68.50	136.23
Point Manning	70.6	143.35	Pelly Isles	69.32	135.30
Point Sir H. Martin	70.4	143.0	Garry Isles .	69.27	135.36
Point Griffin	70.1	142.42	Kendall Isles	69.24	135.20
Point Humphreys	69.54	142.15	Whale Island	69.12	135.0
Beaufort Bay	69.46	141.50	Ellice Island	69.9	135.40
Mount Huskisson	69.35	142.5	Langley Island	69.0	135.10
Mount Greenough	69.30	143.20	Colville Island	68.50	135.50
Icy Reef . .	69.45	141.28	Halkett Island	68.30	135.0
Demarcation Point Winter Houses	69.40	141.0	Mount Gifford	68.12	135.24
Clarence River . .	69.36	140.45	Simpson Island	68.12	134.25
Backhouse River	69.35	140.28	Sacred Island	68.58	134.13
Sir P. Malcolm River	69.35	139.55	Smith Island	68.50	134.30
Herschell Island	69.35	139.0	Harrison Island	68.30	134.10

	N. Lat. ° ′	W. Long. ° ′		N. Lat. ° ′	W. Long. ° ′
M'Gillivray Island	68.10	134.0	Point Pierce .	69.48	122.30
Williams Island	68.37	134.10	Point Sir R. G. Keats .	69.49	122.0
Peel River .	67.40	134.30	Mount Colby .	69.36	121.55
Red River	67.25	133.30	Point Deas Thompson .	69.45	121.20
Fort Good Hope	67.27	130.51	Palgrave River .	69.41	121.10
Richards Island .	69.20	133.50	Roscoe River	69.40	121.1
Point Encounter	69.15	133.18	Mount Hooker .	69.36	121.33
Point Toker	69.38	132.20	Mount Rennell .	69.33	121.3
Refuge Cove	69.28	132.31	Point De Witt Clinton	69.33	120.27
Point Warren .	69.45	131.36	Buchanan River	69.23	120.0
Copland Hutchinson Bay	69.45	131.20	Point Tinney	69.20	119.40
Phillips Island	69.50	131.5	Croker Bay .	69.16	119.5
Atkinson Island .	69.54	130.43	Mount Sir H. Davy	69.0	118.47
M'Kinley Bay .	69.55	130.30	Sir G. Clerk's Island	69.25	118.35
Browell Cove	70.0	130.20	Point Clifton .	69.14	118.30
Cape Brown	70.11	129.50	Inman River	69.8	118.25
Russell Inlet	70.5	129.26	Point Wise .	69.3	118.0
Cape Dalhousie	70.16	129.20	Hoppner River	69.0	117.39
Campbell's Isles	69.30	129.0	Cape Young	68.56	116.55
Nicholson Island .	69.55	128.20	Harding River	68.50	117.3
Liverpool Bay .	70.10	128.20	Cape Hope	68.57	116.27
Point Sir P. Maitland	70.7	127.40	South's Bay	68.58	116.0
Harrowby Bay	70.10	127.20	Stapleton's Bay	68.55	116.20
Cape Bathurst .	70.35	127.30	Cape Bexley	69.0	115.50
Baillie's Islands	70.34	127.50	Point Cockburn .	68.52	115.0
Trail Point	70.20	126.30	Chantry Island	68.44	114.23
Point Fitton	70.12	126.15	M. Sutton Island	68.57	114.15
Cape Parry	70.5	123.33	Sir R. Liston Island	68.52	114.12
Booth Island	70.3	123.52	Lambert Island .	68.37	113.52
Moore Island	70.1	123.23	Bayfield Island	68.29	113.43
W. Horton River	69.56	126.0	Douglass Island .	68.26	113.46
Jardine River	69.42	125.40	Pasley's Cove	68.23	114.0
Burnett River	69.39	125.31	Mount Barrow .	68.20	113.54
Franklin Bay	69.40	125.0	Cape Krusenstern	68.22	113.44
Selwood Bay	69.50	124.0	Point Locker	68.12	113.56
Cracroft Bay	69.46	124.0	Saunders Islands	68.10	113.40
Wright Bay	69.41	124.0	Cape Hearne	68.11	114.51
Point Stivens	69.33	124.16	Basil Hall's Bay	68.15	115.0
Langton Bay	69.23	124.20	Cape Kendall	67.58	115.16
Burrow's Isles	69.48	123.30	Back's Inlet	67.57	115.50
Darnley Bay	69.40	123.10	Point Mackenzie .	67.51	115.30
Clapperton Island	69.41	123.16	Bloody Fall .	67.41	116.0
Cape Lyon . .	69.48	122.47	Copper Mine River	67.48	115.35

SIR JOHN FRANKLIN'S FIRST JOURNEY.

	N. Lat.	W. Long.		N. Lat.	W. Long.
	° ′	° ′		° ′	° ′
Sir G. Moore's Island, (largest) .	67.50	114.15	Tinney Cove	66.55	108.6
Lawford Islands, (centre) .	67.52	113.40	Ridcout Island	67.20	108.30
Port Epworth .	67.43	112.30	Fowler's Bay	67.22	108.20
Gray's Bay	67.47	111.55	Barry's Island	67.30	108.55
Wentzel's River	67.53	111.30	Point Everitt	67.42	108.42
Inman's Harbour	67.58	111.0	Fisher's Island	67.54	108.30
Cape Barrow	68.4	111.0	Buchan Bay	67.54	108.20
Galena Point .	67.54	110.40	Cape Croker	68.3	108.24
Detention Harbour	67.50	110.42	Warrender Bay	68.15	107.25
Moore Bay	67.45	110.20	Point Hay	68.15	107.40
Stockport Isles	67.47	110.10	Hurd's Islands	68.7	108.7
Marcet's Island	67.50	109.52	Point Beechy	68.6	108.16
Cheere's Islands	67.42	109.35	Walker's Bay	68.12	109.10
Hood's River	67.20	109.50	Porden's Isles	68.10	109.20
Baillie Bay .	67.20	109.20	Riley's Bay .	68.12	109.22
Point Wollaston .	67.33	109.24	Cape Flinders .	68.13	109.30
Back's River	66.30	107.52	Harry Cook's Island	68.10	109.48
Burnside River	66.37	108.16	Sir H. Davy Island	68.32	109.40
Young's Island	66.45	108.30	Point Turnagain	68.33	109.10
Elliot's Islands	66.54	108.45			

FROM CAPTAIN BEECHY'S CHART.

Point Barrow	71.12	156.10	Icy Cape	70.18	161.40
Elson Bay . .	71.22	156.6	Point Lay .	69.52	162.45
Franklin Extreme	71.20	156.4	Cape Beaufort	69.4	163.35
Cape Smyth	71.14	156.45	Vein of Coal	69.2	163.30
Refuge Inlet	71.6	157.0	Cape Sabine	68.54	164.34
Peard Bay .	70.52	158.20	Cape Lisburne	68.52	166.8
Seahorse Islands .	70.56	159.0	Cape Lewis	68.42	166.10
Point Franklin	70.58	158.45	Cape Dyer .	68.38	166.10
Wainwright Inlet .	70.36	159.45	Point Hope	68.20	166.40
Cape Collie .	70.38	159.55	Cape Thompson	68.7	165.52
Point Marsh	70.36	159.58	Cape Seppings	67.58	165.15
Blossom Shoals	70.23	161.45	Mulgrave Hills	67.36	163.40

	N. Lat. ° ′	W. Long. ° ′		N. Lat. ° ′	W. Long. ° ′
Cape Kruzenstern	67.9	163.37	Kruzenstern Island	65.47	168.52
Deviation Peak	67.5	161.0	Diomede Islands .	65.48	169 0
Hotham Inlet	66.50	162 0	Fairway Rock	65.39	168.43
Cape Blossom	66.44	162.25	Cape Prince of Wales	65.34	168.0
Cape Espenberg .	66.34	163.28	Cape York .	65.24	167.25
Kotzebue Sound	66.30	163.0	King's Island .	65.0	168.0
Bay of Good Hope	66.14	163.30	Conical Hill	65.40	167.30
Buckland River	66.10	161.0	King-a-ghee	65.36	167.50
Eschscholtz Bay .	66.20	161.30	Ei-dan-noo .	65.36	168.0
Choris Peninsula .	66.20	161.50	Point Jackson	65.22	166.45
Chamisso I. or E-ow-ick	66.14	161.45	Point Spencer	65.16	166.50
Spafarief Bay	66.6	161.50	Port Clarence	65.14	166.30
Cape Deceit	66.6	162.36	Grantly Harbour	65.16	166.20
Devil's Mount	66.20	164.25	Kow-e-rok	65.16	165.56
Cape Lowenstern .	66.16	165.35	Tokshook .	65.14	165.54
Schischmareff Inlet	66.20	165.30	Cape Douglas	65.0	166.40
Saritscheff Island	66.18	165.45	Cape Woolley	64.49	166.24
Ears .	66.0	166.0	Point Rodney	64.38	166.20
False Ears	65.48	163.10	Sledge Island	64.30	166.8
Ass's Ears . .	65.46	163.5	Behring's Strait .	66.6	169.40
Ratmanoff Island	65.50	169.0			

LIST

OF

SUBSCRIBERS

TO

CAPTAIN SIR JOHN ROSS's

Narrative

OF HIS

Residence in the Arctic Regions,

DURING THE YEARS [illegible] & 1833.

PUBLISHED WITH THE APPENDIX.

Royal Family of Great Britain.

His Most Excellent Majesty . THE KING		**Patron.**
Her Most Gracious Majesty . THE QUEEN		5 Copies.
Her Royal Highness . . . . The Duchess of Kent.		
Her Royal Highness . . . . The Princess Victoria.		
His Royal Highness . . . . The Duke of Cumberland.		
His Royal Highness . . . . The Duke of Sussex.		
His Royal Highness . . . . The Duke of Cambridge.		
His Royal Highness . . . . Prince George of Cambridge.		
His Royal Highness . . . . The late Duke of Gloucester.		

Foreign Princes.

His Imperial Majesty	Ferdinand I.	Emperor of Austria.	
His Imperial Majesty	Francis II.	late Emperor of Austria.	
His Imperial Majesty	Nicholas I.	Emperor of all the Russias,	4 Copies
Her Imperial Majesty	Alexandra	Empress of Russia.	
His Majesty	Louis Philippe . . .	King of the French.	
His Majesty	Frederick William III.	King of Prussia . . .	2 Copies.
His Majesty	Frederick VI. . . .	King of Denmark.	
His Majesty	Carl XIV. Johan . .	King of Sweden.	
His Majesty	Anthony	King of Saxony.	
His Majesty	William	King of Wirtemberg.	
His Majesty	Leopold I.	King of the Belgians.	
His Imperial Highness	Michael Pavlovitsch	Grand Duke of Russia.	
Her Imperial Highness . . .	Helena	Grand Duchess of Russia.	
His Royal and Serene Highness	Leopold II. . . .	Grand Duke of Tuscany.	
His Royal Highness	George V.	Grand Duke of Mecklenburg Strelitz.	
His Royal Highness	Frederick William	Prince Royal of Prussia.	
His Royal Highness	Joseph Francis Oscar	Crown Prince of Sweden.	
His Royal Highness	Christian Frederick	Crown Prince of Denmark.	
His Royal Highness	William Louis . . .	Prince of Prussia.	
His Royal Highness	Charles	Prince of Prussia.	
His Royal Highness	Adelbert	Prince of Prussia . . .	3 Copies.

ALPHABETICAL

LIST OF SUBSCRIBERS.

Aarons, E. L. Esq. St. James's-place, Aldgate
Abbey, John, Esq., Huddersfield
Abbott, Alex. S. Esq. Cambridge
Abbott, Jno. Esq. 10, Charlotte-st. Bedford-sq.
Abbott, Joseph, Esq. Solicitor, Middle Gloucester-street, Dublin
a'Beckett, Thos. T. Esq. 10, Staples Inn
Aberdein, Hy. Rt. Esq. Portreeve of Honiton
ABERGAVENNY, Rt. Hon. the Earl of
Aberystwith Book Society
Ablett, J. Esq. Llanbedr Hall, Denbighshire
Abraham, C. J. Esq. King's Coll. Cambridge
Abraham, Mrs. 10, Liverpool-street, New-road
Abraham, T. Esq. Taunton
Acherley, H. John, Esq. 3, Johnstone-st. Bath
Ackers, George, Esq. Moreton Hall, Cheshire
Ackroyd, Joseph, Esq. & Son, Halifax
Acland, Capt. J. P. Barnstaple
Acland, Sir Thos. D. Bart. Killerton. Devon
Acraman, Alfred, Esq. Gt. George-st. Bristol
Acraman, D. W. Esq. Low-crescent, Clifton
Acton, Mrs. Caroline, Southwold, Suffolk
Acton, Samuel, Esq. 32, Finsbury-square
Acton, William, Esq. Wolverton, Worcester
Adair, A. Esq. Heatherton-pk. near Wellington
Adair, J. Esq., Balkail, Glenluce
Adair, Rt. Shafto, Esq. Flexton Hall, Suffolk
Adam, Rear-Adml. Sir Chas. *M.P.* 14, Berkeley-square
Adam, J. G. Esq. 51, Cochran-street, Glasgow
Adam, Mr. Robert. 144, Queen-street Glasgow
Adams, Capt. Rd. Wamsfords, near Lymington
Adams, James, Esq. 4, Regent-ter. Edinburgh
Adams, John, Esq. King-street, Manchester
Adams, John, jun. Esq. Christ Church College, Oxford
Adams, Mr. S. jun. Ware
Adams, Rev. Wm. *D.D.* Halstead, Essex
Adams, W. Esq. 32, Trafalgar st. Walworth
Adamson, James, Esq. Ely-place
Adamson, Mr. Thomas, Seagate, Scotland
Adcock, S. Esq. Cambridge
Addington, Mr. L. 105, St. Martin's-lane
Addison, Mr. George, Bradford, Yorkshire
Addison, Joseph, Esq. King's-bench-walk
Addison, Ralph, Esq. Fleet-street
Adlam, Horatio, Esq. St. Christopher's
Adshead, Aaron, Esq. Stalybridge, Lancashire
Adshead, Josh. Esq. Mosley-st. Manchester
Adshead, Wm. Esq. Manchester
Agnew, Sir A. Bart. *M.P.* 14, Manchstr-bldgs
Agnew, Col. of Barnbarrow, 39, Devonshire-st.
Ainslie, Mrs. Colonel, Melville-st. Edinburgh
Ainslie, Mrs. Gilbert, Pembroke College Lodge, Cambridge
Ainslie, John, Esq. Waverton, near Liverpool
Aird, D. Esq. Clapton
AIRLIE, Right Hon. the Earl of
Aitchison, Captain, *R.N.*, Linkfield, Musselburgh, N. B.
Aitchison, George, Esq. Leith
Aitchison, Wm. Esq. Linkfield, Musselburgh
Albanellis, C. Esq. 21, York-st. Manchester
ALBEMARLE, Right Hon. the Earl of
Alcock, Thomas, Esq. Kingswood, Surrey
Aldam, W. Esq. Warmsworth, near Doncaster
Aldersey, Robt. Esq. Chester
Aldridge, G. Esq. Christchurch, Hants
Alduit, Robert Dawes, Esq. *R.N.*, H.M.S. Medea
Alexander, Boyd, Esq. 15, Hanover-terrace, Regent's-park
Alexander, Edward. Esq. 16, Sussex-place
Alexander, Edward, Esq. *F.S.A.* Halifax
Alexander, Henry, Esq. 6, Cork-street
Alexander, J. Esq. Upnor, Kent
Alexander, J. Esq. Newbury, Berks
Alexander, Mr. James, 42, Queen-st. Glasgow
Alexander, Lesley, Esq. 6, York-ter. Regnt's-pk
Alfry, Mr. Gloster-place, Brighton
Alington, Henry, Esq. Bayley Hall, Hertford
Alington, Rev. John, Little Barford, Beds. 4 Copies
Alington, Miss, Twywell, Northamptonshire. 4 Copies
Allan, T. Esq. 4, Hillside Crescent. Edinburgh
Allan, Wm. Esq. 30, Mosley-st. Manchester
Allason, Mr. W. Booksr. Nw Bond-st. 10 Copies
Allcock, J. J. Esq. Halesworth, Suffolk
Allcott, Mr. John, Bradford, Yorkshire
Allen, Mr. Daniel, 42, New Bond-street
Allen, Mr. George, Louth
Allen, Henry, Esq. the Lodge near the Hay, Brecknockshire
Allen, John, Esq. Cheltenham
Allen, John, Esq. Tovil, near Maidstone
Allen, Messrs. John and William, Falmouth
Allen, Miss, Talbot Inn, Market-st. Manchestr
Allen, Mr. Robert, 62, Buchanan-st. Glasgow
Allen, T. Esq. *R.N.* 1, Adam-place, Woolwich
Allen, Thos. Esq. Maidstone
Allen, William, Esq. 12, Lower Thames-street
Allen, Wm. Esq. Marsden-sq. Manchester
Allenby, Samuel, Esq. Maidenwell, near Louth
Allercot, Wm. Esq. St. Christopher's
Allin, T. M. Esq. Queen's College, Cambridge
Allingham, Mr. William, Bookseller, Reigate. 2 Copies
Allinson, Sam. Esq. 26, Lloyd-sq. Pentonville
Allport, Wm. Esq. Manchester
Allsopp, Samuel, Esq. Burton-on-Trent
Allman, Mr. Thos. Bookseller, 42, Holborn-hill
Alstone, T. Esq. 46, Claremont-pl. Glasgow
Alston, R. D. Esq. 126, Queen-st. Glasgow
Alt, Rev. Just Henry, *M.A.* Christ's Hospital
AMERICA, Library of the Congress of
Ames, George, Esq. Stoke Bishop, Bristol
Ames, Levi, Esq. 14, Hereford-street, London
Ammerschuler, C. Esq. Claremont, Surrey
Amory, William, Esq. 37, Devonshire-place
Amos, John, Esq. Fountain-st. Manchester
Amphlett, Richard, Esq. Monmouth
Amys, John Hewitt, Esq. Rickinghall, Suffolk
Anderdon, J. P. Esq. *F.R.S.* Farley Hill, Berks
Anderson, Adam, Esq. Huddersfield
Anderson, Alex. Esq. 24, Brompton-row
Anderson, Rev. Sir Charles, Bart. Lea, near Gainsborough
Anderson, Capt. D. A. Indian Navy, Trinity-street, Edinburgh
Anderson, Dr. 159, Vincent-street, Glasgow
Anderson, Francis, Esq. Westbury, Bristol
Anderson, Geo. Esq. Westgate-st. Newcastle-upon-Tyne
Anderson, Jno. Esq. Huddersfield
Anderson, John, Esq. 4 Gordon-st. Glasgow
Anderson, John, Esq. 2, Upper Bedford-place
Anderson, Mrs. Dennell Hill, Chepstow
Anderson, Philip, Esq. Corpus Christi College, Cambridge
Anderson, Robert, Esq. Alnwick. 17 Copies.
Anderson, Robt. Esq. 68, Glasford-st. Glasgow
Anderson, Rodney, Esq. Ludlow
Anderson, Thomas, Esq. Clapham-common
Anderson, Wm. Esq. Bedford Villa, Clifton
Anderson, Wm. Esq. Cobham, Surrey
Anderson, Wm. Esq. Cambridge
Andrew, E. Esq. 60, Church-st. Manchester
Andrew, John, Esq. Provost of Kilmarnock
Andrew, Wm. Esq. Mayor of Stockport
Andrews, Hy. Esq. Post Office, Manchester
Andrews, Jas. Esq. Bridewell, Liverpool
Andrews, Messrs. J. and Co. Booksellers, New Bond-street. 8 Copies
Andrews, Mrs. 7, Arlington-street. 2 Copies
Andrews, Mrs. Church-street, Manchester

i 2

Andrews, Mr. R. W. Dorchester
Angerstien, J. Esq. *M.P.* 23, St. James's-sq.
Annan, Mr. W. Booksllr, Croydon. 3 Copies
Ansell, Thomas, Esq. Harley-place, Bow
Antrobus, Sir Edmund, Bart. 146, Piccadilly
Antrobus, Gibbs W. Crawford, Esq. Eaton Hall, Macclesfield
Apothecaries, The Society of
Appleby, Mrs. Buston Vale, Northumberland
Applegarth, Mr. A. Crayford, Kent
Appleton, Mr. Hy. 26, Burton-st. Burton-cres.
Appleton, J. Esq. Fountain-street, Manchester
Appleyard, James, Esq. Warehouse-hill, Leeds
ARBUTHNOT, Right Hon. Lord Viscount
Arbuthnot, George, Esq. 25, Up. Wimpole-st.
Arch, Messrs. J. & A. 61, Cornhill. 15 Copies
Archbell, John, Esq. Huddersfield
Archdall, E. M. Esq. 69, Chancery-lane
Archdeacon, J. Esq. H.M.S. Excellent, Portsmouth Harbour
Archer, Thos. Esq. Cannon-st. Manchester
Archer, W. Esq. *R.N.* 22, Arundel-street
ARGYLE, His Grace the Duke of
Ariel, Myles, Esq. Ashley-place, near Bristol
Arkwright, Josh. Esq. Mark Hall, Harlow, Essex
Arlett, Henry, Esq. Pembroke College. For a Book Society
Arnfield, Mr. W. Northampton
Armistead, Messrs. J. & J. Water-lane, Leeds
Armitage, E. Esq. 4, Bank Bnildgs. Manchester
Armstrong, G. W. Esq. Redlion-st. Clerkenwell
Armstrong, R. Esq. 92, George-st. Manchester
Armytage, John, C. Esq. 1, Upper-st. Islington
Arnold, Mr. H. Bookseller, 45, Marchmont-st.
Arnold, Col. James R. Royal Engineers, Dover
Arnold, Mr. W. Seven Oaks, Kent
Arnold'sche, —. Buchhandlung, Dresden
Arrow, Mr. Henry, Seven Oaks, Kent
Arrowsmith, Jno. Esq. 33, East-st. Redlion-sq. 2 Copies
Artaria & Fortaine, Messrs. Booksellers, Mannheim, Germany. 2 Copies
Arthur, Capt. Jno. Brig Eleanor, Liverpool
Artillery, Royal, Woolwich, Library of
Artillery, Royal, Library of Non-commissioned Officers, at Woolwich
Arundell, W. A. H. Esq. Lifton Park, Devon
Ash, Richard, Esq. Cotham House, Bristol
ASHBURTON, Right Hon. Lord
Ashby-de-la-Zouch Permanent Library
Ashcroft, Wm. jun. Esq. 12, Butcher-row, Ratcliff
Ashe, Lieutenant-General, 162, Albany-street, Regent's-park
Asher, Mr. A. Bookseller, 90, Bartholomew-close. 2 Copies
Ashford Book Society
ASHLEY, Lord Viscount, *M.P.*
Ashley, Mr. James, Booksr. 22, Jermyn-street
Ashley, Mrs. Epsom, Surrey
Ashlin, John Meyson, Esq.
Ashton, Capt. Ship Cabotia, Liverpool
Ashton, Geo. Esq. Cannon-street, Manchester
Ashton, James, Esq. Bank-street, Manchester
Ashton, John, Esq. 15, New Cannon-street, Manchester
Ashton, John, Esq. St. Ives, Huntingdon
Ashton, Samuel, Esq. Pole Bank, Manchester
Ashton, Mr. Thomas, Torrington
Ashton, Wm. Esq. St. Ives, Hunts
Askew, John, Esq. Harbour Master, Seel-street, Liverpool
Askew, R. C. Esq. Arcade, Newcastle-upon-Tyne
Aspinal, James, Esq. Duke-street, Liverpool
Aspland, Mr. Wm. Bookseller, Waltham-cross. 3 Copies
Astbury, John, Esq. Mosley-st. Manchester
Aston, Charles G. Esq. Bridge-st. Manchester
Aston, Henry, Esq. 2, New Broad-street
Athenæum Journal
Atherley, Rev. A. Heavitree, near Exeter
Atlee, Falconer, Esq. Wandsworth
Atkins, J. Petty, Esq. Walbrook
Atkins, John, Esq. Alderman of London
Atkins, Capt. Robert, Nimrod, Liverpool
Atkinson, Christ. Esq. Ewart, Northumberland
Atkinson, Capt. Geo. Gt. Homer-st. Liverpool
Atkinson, George, Esq. Inner Temple-lane
Atkinson, J. R. Esq. Elmwood House, Leeds
Atkinson, T. W. Esq. St. John's College, Cambridge, and Yorkshire Gateside, near Sedbergh
Atkinson, John, Esq. 2, Exeter-street, Strand
Atkinson, Mr. John, Bookseller, Bradford, Yorkshire. 27 Copies
Atkinson, Rev. J. B. West Cowes
Atkinson, T. Esq. Bedford-st. North Shields
Atkinson, T. Esq. *R.N.* Rodwell, Weymouth
Atkinson, T. Esq. Charlton, near Salisbury
Atkinson, Wm. Esq. Pall-mall, Manchester
Attwood, Edward, Esq. Villiers-street, Bishop Wearmouth, Sunderland
Attwood, Rev. P. Wandsworth, Surrey
Aubertin, Miss, Banstead, Surrey
Aubrey, C. W. Esq. 22, Dorset-pl. Dorset-sq.
AUCKLAND, Right Hon. Lord, *K.C.B.*
Audibert, Mrs. 2, Gloucester-terrace
Audubon, John J. Esq. *F.R. & L.S.* 73, Margaret-street, Cavendish-square
Austen, H. Esq. Belle Vue, Seven Oaks, Kent
Austen, T. Esq. Kippington Park, Seven Oaks, Kent
Austin, Morgan, Esq. Redlion-st, Clerkenwell
Austria, the Private Library of H.M. the Emperor of
Author, Wm. Esq. York-street, Manchester
Avison, Thomas, Esq. Cook st. Liverpool
AVONMORE, Rt. Hon. Lord Viscount
Ayerst, R. G. Esq. Batts House, near Taunton
Ayre, Hy. Esq. 51, High-street, Manchester
Ayres, Captain

B.

Babbage, C. Esq. *K.H. F.R.S.* Dorset-street
Bacchus, Wm. Esq. 8, Tokenhouse-yard
Back, C. Esq. 1, Verulam-buildings, Gray's Inn
Back, Edward, Esq. St. Peter's, Norwich
Backhouse, Rev. J. B. Rector of Deal
Backhouse, Rev. R. D. Walmer, Kent
Bacon, Mr. John, Russell-street, Bermondsey
Bacon, Mr. Joshua B. Sidmouth-st. Regent-sq.
Bacon, N. C. Esq. North Walsham, Norfolk
Badnell, Rich. Esq. Farm Hill, Isle of Man
Bagehot, T. W. Esq. Langport
Bagge, E. Esq. Lynn, Norfolk
Bagge, Wm. Esq. Stradsett Hall, Norfolk
Bagle, Mr. J. 1, Abercrombie-street, Glasgow
BAGOT, Right Hon. Lord
Bagshaw, John, Esq. Brown-st. Manchester
Bagster, Mr. S. Bookseller, Paternoster-row
Bague, Lieut. Geo. *R.N.* 110, Sloane-street
Bahia, Book Society of
Bahia British Library
Bailey, C. H. Esq. Cannon-st. Manchester
Bailey, Henry W. Esq. Thetford, Norfolk
Bailey, W. B. Esq. Cannon-st. Manchester
Baillee, Charles, Esq. Advocate, 1, Moray-pl. Edinburgh
Baillie, Mrs. A. 33, Cavendish-square
Baillie, Mrs. Joanna, 33, Cavendish-square
Baillie, W. H. Esq. 33, Cavendish-square
Baily and Co. Messrs. Booksellers, Cornhill. 2 Copies
Baily, Francis, Esq. *F.R.S. F.L.S.* 37, Tavistock-place
Baily, Mrs. R. E. 41, Albion-st. Hyde-park
Bain, Mr. J. Bookslr, 1, Haymarket. 5 Copies
Bainbridge, John, Esq. 35, Southampton-row, Russell-square
Bainbridge, Thos. Esq. Croydon Lodge
Baird, Chas. Esq. St. Petersburgh
Baker, A. J. C. Esq. Cresswell, Northumberland
Baker, Sir Edwd. Bart. Ranstow, near Blandford
Baker, Rev. Francis, Wylye Rectory, near Salisbury
Baker, Geo. Esq. Bewdley, Worcestershire
Baker, H. Shenstone, Esq. Exeter Col. Oxford
Baker, J. & T. Esqrs. Gibraltar-pl. Chatham
Baker, Mr. John, Christchurch, Hants
Baker, R. Esq. West Hay, Wrington, Somerset
Baker, Samuel, Esq. Rochester
Baker, Rear-Admiral Sir Thos. *K.C.B. K.W.* Walmer, Dover
Baker, Lieut. W. H. *R.N.* Fort Moncrief, Hythe
Baker, Mr. W. Academy, Holloway
BALCARRES, Right Hon. the Earl of
BALCARRES, Right Hon. the Countess of
Bald, Hugh, Esq. Brecon
Baldock, Mr. D. Frinsbury, Kent
Baldock, Rev. R. Kingsnorth, Kent
Baldwin & Co. Messrs. Booksllrs. 11 Copies
Baldwin, Col. J. Dover
Baldwin, J. Esq. Park-square, Leeds
Baldwin, Mrs. Preston, Lancashire
Baldwin, Wriothesley, Esq. Maidstone
BALGRAY, Right Hon. Lord, Edinburgh
Ball, Mr. G. Bookseller, Chelsea
Ball, John, Esq. 9, Great St. Helen's
Balls, Henry, Esq. Cambridge
Bally, W. Esq. Sion-hill, Bath
Balmanno, Dr. 37, St. Vincent-st. Glasgow
Balston, W. Esq. Maidstone
Bancks, Hayward, & Fletcher, Messrs. Booksellers, Manchester. 8 Copies
Bandinel, Rev. Dr. Bulkeley, Bodleian Library, Oxford
BANDON, Right Hon. the Earl of
Banger, Thomas, Esq. Piddletown, Dorset
Bankes, Rev. E. Rectory, Corfe Castle, Wareham
Banks, D. Esq. Sheerness, Kent
Banks, George, Esq. Leeds
Banks, John, Esq. Halling, near Rochester
Baumgartner, Mr. Bookseller, Leipzig
Bannerman, A. Esq. Market-street, Manchester
Bannerman Mr. W. 25, Cochran-st. Glasgow
Baratty, Miss, Petersham
Barber, G. E. Esq. 13, York-road, Cheetham, Manchester
Barber, Joseph, Esq. Clapham-road
Barber, William, Esq. 2, Regent-square
Barclay, C. Esq. *M.P. F.S.A.* 43, Grosvnor-pl.
Barclay, D. Esq. 12, Austin-friars
Barclay, John, Esq. Stock Exchange
Barclay, Mr. James, 95, Farringdon-street
Bardsley, Dr. Jas. L. Piccadilly, Manchester

Barge, G. Esq. 19, Church-street, Manchester
BARHAM, Right Hon. Lord
Barham, Rev. C. H. Barming, near Maidstone
Baring, Rev. Frederick, Itchen Stoke
Baring, Sir Thomas, Bart. Stratton Park
Baring, W. B. Esq. *M.P.* 12, Gt. Stanhope-st.
Barker, F. D. Esq. Cambridge
Barker, J. Esq. Aldborough, Suffolk
Barker, James Thos. Esq. St. Saviour's Dock, Southwark
Barker, John, Esq. Print-street, Manchester
Barker, Thomas H. Esq. Albion-street, Leeds
Barker, William, Esq. 50, Mark-lane
Barklimore, Arch. Esq. 10, Charlotte-street, Bloomsbury
Barkway, Rev. F. Bungay, Suffolk
Barkworth, John, Esq. Anlaby, Hull
Barlow, J. H. Esq. 11, Angel-court
Barlow, J. Pratt, Esq. Godliman-street, Doctors Commons
Barlow, Jas. T. Esq. Gt. Suffolk-st. Borough
Barlow, Mrs. Holybourne, near Alton, Hants
Barlow, Rear-Admiral Sir Robert, *K.C.B.* Canterbury. 2 Copies
Barnard, Major-Gen. Sir A. *K.C.B. K.G.H.*
Barnard, Benjamin, Esq. Cornhill
Barnard, G. H. Esq. 17, Great St. Helen's
Barneby, J. Esq. *M.P.* Brockhampton, Herefordshire
Barneby, William, Esq. Worcester
Barned, J. Esq. 23, Rodney-street, Liverpool
Barnes, Dr. F. Master of Peter House College, Cambridge
Barnes, F. H. Esq. Counter-slip, Bristol
Barnes, Mr. G. King's Arms Library, Canterbury
Barnes, John, Esq. Stock Exchange
Barnes, R. Esq. Rustolme-road, Manchester
Barnes, Thos. Esq. George Inn, Cambridge
Barnes, W. M. Esq. *B.A.* Trinity College, Cambridge
Barnett, Benj. Esq. Spring Garden Cottage, Stepney
Barnett, F. Esq. Seven Oaks, Kent
Barnett, Mr. G. Eccleshall. 3 Copies
Barnett, John, Esq. 20, Charterhouse-square
Barnett, Mrs. R. Ramsgate, Kent
Barnett, R. C. Esq. 25, Chester-ter. Regnt's-pk
Barnett, R. Esq. Highgate Rise, Kentish-town
Barnett, Robt. Esq. Highgate Hill
Barnewall, Colonel, Oriental Club. 2 Copies
Barnstaple Book Club
Baron, George, Esq. Drewton Cave, Yorkshire
Baron, John, Esq. Russell-street, Bermondsey
Baroth, Chas. Esq. York-street, Manchester
Barr, John, Esq. St. Christopher's
Barr, William W. Esq. Leeds
Barraclough, Mr. Geo. Bookseller, Cambridge
Barras, Mrs. Latcham, Middlesex
Barratt. Thomas, Esq. Leicester
Barratt, Messrs. John & Sons, Cannon-street, Manchester
Barratty, Miss, Petersham
Barrett, Major C. R. Cheriton, Hants
Barrett, Mr. J. Bookseller, Brackley. 5 Copies
Barron, Mr. George William, 83, Oxford-street
Barrow, Simon, Esq. Lansdown-grove, Bath
Barrow, Capt. Thos. Wm. *H. E. I. C. S.* Enfield Chase
Barrowclough, Rich. Esq. Devonshire-place, Everton, Liverpool
Barry, John Smith, Esq. Foaty, County Cork
Bartells, Thomas, Esq. Distillery, Lambeth
Barter, Rev. R. S. College, Winchester

Bartholomew, John, Esq. 18, Brunswick-st. Glasgow
Bartholomew, R. Esq. 18, Brunswick-st. Glasgw
Bartholomew, W. Esq. Redlion-st. Clerkenwell
Bartlett, Thos. C. Esq. Wareham
Bartlett, Josiah, Esq. Lower Clapton, Middlx
Barton, Bernard, Esq. Woodbridge, Suffolk
Barton, Rev. J. East Church, Sheerness
Barton, R. W. Esq. Springwood, Manchester
Barton, Samuel, Esq. Manchester
Barton, T. Esq. St. John's Coll. Cambridge
Barton, W. H. Esq. Royal Mint
Bassett, Geo. Esq. High Hill, Kentish Town
Bassett, N. F. Esq. Mayor of Truro
Bastard, T. C. Esq. Charlton Musgrove, near Wincanton, Somerset
Batavia Book Club
Batcheler, Thos. Horatio, Esq. Gt. Yarmouth
Batcheller, W. King's Arms Library, Dover
Bate, Edw. Esq. *R.N.* Croom's-hill, Greenwich
Bate, Mrs. Frances, Bishopsteignton, Devon
Bate, Robert B. Esq. 20, Poultry
Bateman, C. Esq. Bertholly House, nr. Caerleon
Bateman, T. Esq. Spring-gardens, Manchester
Bates, Captain John, *R.N.* West Cowes
Bates, Mr. J. Long-lane, Bermondsey
Bateson, J. Esq. Park-square, Leeds. 2 Copies
Bateson, T. Esq. High Fields, Worthy, nr. Leeds
Bateson, T. jun. Esq. Aspining, near Leeds
BATH, Most Noble the Marquis of
Bath Literary Institution, Walks, Bath
Bath, the Corporation of
Bathurst, Sir F. Bart. Clarendon Park, Wilts
Batley, J. Esq. Armitage Bridge, Huddersfield
Batson, Hy. Esq. Rochett's House, Brentwood
Batson, T. R. Esq. Higham-place, Newcastle, Northumberland
Batten, Edward, Esq. Bank Coffee-house
Batten, John, Esq. Penzance
Battersby, Captain, Royal Engineers, Hull
Battey, Mr. James, Mars Steamer, Liverpool
Battley, Richard, Esq. 114, Fore-street
Batty, Mr. H. Bookseller, Ware. 2 Copies
Battye, R. C. Esq. Leeds
Battye, W. W. Esq. Mould-green, Huddersfield
Baugh, Mr. W. Bookseller, Ellesmere
Baxter, Wm. Esq. Dundee
Baxter, Mr. W. Bookseller, Lewes
Baylay, Rev. W. F. Canterbury
Bayldon, J. Esq. Jesus College, Cambridge
Bayley, Mr. Richard, jun. Newmarket
Bayley, Thos. K. Esq. Abbott's Leigh, Bristol
Baylis, Philip, Esq. Stoke Ash, Suffolk
Baynck, S. Esq. Willgate, Dundee
Bazely, Lieut. John, *R.N.* Dover
Beach, Col. Wm. Hicks, Oakley Hall, Basingstoke
Beadle, Joseph, Esq. Hull
Beadon, Edward, Esq. Taunton
Beadon, John, Esq. Gotten, near Taunton
Beadon, Lt. *R.N.* Grove Cottage, near Taunton
Beale, Mr. Thomas, Manchester
Beale, Mr. Thomas S. Cork
Bean, P. Esq. 5, Southampton-court, Queen-sq.
Beart, Lt. C. J. *R.N.* South Town, Yarmouth
Beasley, William, Esq. Dublin
Beatty, Sir W. Bart. *M.D.* Physician to Greenwich Hospital
BEAUCLERK, Adml. Lord Amelius, *K.C.B. K.G.H.*
Beauchamp, Geo. Esq. Ford-place, Thetford
Beauchamp, R. F. Esq. Watford House, near Taunton

Beaufort, Miss, Dublin
Beaufoy, Henry, Esq. South Lambeth
Beaumaris Book Society
Beaumont, Abraham, Esq. 300, Holborn
Beaumont, F. W. Esq. Dunmow, Essex
Beaumont, J. Esq. Dalton, near Huddersfield
Beaumont, Joseph, Esq. jun. Huddersfield
Beaumont, R. H. Esq. 21, Grosvenor-square
Beaumont, R. H. Esq. Gravesend
Beaver, H. Esq. Cheetham-hill, Manchester
Beaver, J. A. Esq. Oxford-road, Manchester
Beazley, Mr. W. Birmingham Steamer, Liverpool
Bebb, J. Esq. 20, Great Marlborough-street
Beck, S. Adams, Esq. Ironmonger's Hall
Beckwith, A. A. H. Esq. Norwich
Beckham, Horatio, Esq. Ipswich
Beckett, Christopher, Esq. Leeds
Beckett, Rev. George, Rector of Epworth
Beckett, Wm. Esq. Kirkstall Grange, Yorkshire
Beckton, J. Esq. Lower Mosley-st. Manchester
Beddome, J. R. Esq. Romsey, Hants
BEDFORD, His Grace the Duke of
Bedford, Rev. R. G. Devonshire Villa, Clifton
Bedford, Mrs. Stonehouse, Devon
Bedfordshire, East, Book Society
Bedingfeld, J. Esq. Ditchingham Hall, Norfolk
Bedwell, Bernard, Esq. 9, Canonbury
Bedwell, Philip, Esq. St. John's-st. Clrknwell
Bee, Messrs. W. & A. Tadcaster. 6 Copies
Beecham, W. P. Esq. Hawkhurst, Kent
Beecher, R. H. Esq. Cork
Beck, S. Adams, Esq. Ironmongers' Hall
Beeke, Rev. Henry, Dean of Bristol
Beer, Mr. William, Canterbury
Behrends, T. G. Esq. 12, Broad-street-bldgs.
Behrens, Jacob, Esq. 18, Somers-street, Leeds
Behrens, S. L. Esq. Mosley-st. Manchester
Beilby, Knot & Co. Messrs. Bkslrs. Birmingham.
Belcher, Wm. Esq. Highgate 3 Copies
BELFAST, Right Hon. the Earl of, *M.P.*
Bell, Ben. Esq. 29, St. Andrew's-sq. Edinburgh
Bell, Dr. David Wake, Topsham
Bell, Fred. B. Esq. Wallington, near Downham Market, Norfolk
Bell, Captain Geo. *R.N.* Belmont, Falmouth
Bell, Mr. Matthew, Bookseller, Richmond
Bell, Rannie & Co. Messrs. Leith
Bell, R. Esq. Collector of Customs, Southampton
Bell, Thomas, Esq. *F.R.S. F.L.S. F.G.S.* 17, New Broad-street
Bell, William, Esq. 19, Charterhouse-square
Bell, W. Esq. Rochester
Bellemois, Hippolite, Esq. Rouen
Bellman, E. Esq. Queen's College, Cambridge
Bence, H. B. Esq. Thorington Hall, Suffolk
Benckausen, Mr. De, Russian Consul-general
Bengal Mhow Military Library
Bengough, Geo. Esq. Cotham Lodge, Clifton
Benham, Mr. William Archibald, 65, Strand
Bennett, Mr. Charles, Redruth
Bennett, Edw. Esq. Princes-street, Manchester
Bennett, J. Henry, Esq. 6, Cavendish-crescent, Bath
Bennett, Jas. Esq. Almondbury, Yorkshire
Bennett, Wm. Esq. Free Press Office, Glasgow
Bensen, Rev. A. The Carse, Salisbury
Benson, Rev. Christopher, Worcester
Bentham, Mr. Bookseller, Manchester
Bentley, John, Esq. 130, Cheapside
Bentley, John, Esq. 4, Pump-court, Temple
Bently, Wm. sen. Esq. 81, Brunswick-street, Glasgow

Benyon, Thomas, Esq. Glednow
Berbice Reading Association
Berbidge, Edward, Esq. Stamford-hill
Berbidge, William, Esq. 74, Aldersgate-street
Berens, H. Esq. Sidcup, Kent
BERESFORD, Right Hon. General, Lord Viscount, *K.C.B. K.G.H. K.T.S. K.F.M.* and *K.F.*
Beresford, T. B. Esq. Christ Church, Oxford
Berger, Samuel, Esq. Upper Homerton
Berger, Samuel, Esq. Five Houses, Clapton
Berkeley, Charles A. Esq. Provost Marshal, St. Christopher's
Berkeley, John, Esq. Basseterre, St. Christopher's
Berkeley, Rev. J. Cotheridge, Worcester
Berkeley, R. jun. Esq. Spetchley, Worcestershire
Berlin, the Royal Mining Library of
Bernard, J. C. Esq. Cork
Bernard, James, Esq. Marble-st. Manchester
Bernard, Lady, 1, Bryanston-pl. Bryanston-sq.
Bernard, Dr. W. R. Cheltenham
Berners, Rev. Henry Denny, Archdeacon of Suffolk, Woolverstone Park, Ipswich
Berry, Lady, Ipswich
Berryman, Wm. jun. Esq. Wells, Somersetsh.
Berwick-upon-Tweed Subscription Library
BESSBOROUGH, Right Hon. the Earl of
Best, H. Esq. Thetford, Norfolk
Best, Lieut-Col. Jas. Rome House, Chatham
Best, W. B. Esq. Blackebrooke, Kidderminster
Bethell, R. Esq. *M.P.* 7, Richmond-terrace
Bettison, Mr. W. G. Library, Margate
Betts, J. T. Esq. Smithfield-bars
Betts, Mr. James, Winchester
Bevan, Charles J. Esq. 16, Devonshire-place
Bevan, John, Esq. Parade House, Redruth
Bevan, Dr. Robert, Monmouth
Beverly, C. J. Esq. Bethnal-green
Beverley, William, Esq. Commercial-st. Leeds
Bevis, Capt. *R.N.* West Cowes
Bewes, Thos. Esq. *M.P.* Beaumount House, Plymouth
BEXLEY, Right Hon. Lord
Bickerton, Lady A. H. 15, Circus, Bath
Bickley, Benjamin, Esq. Clifton
Biddulph, John, Esq. Charing-cross
Biddulph, Mrs. Myddleton, Chirk Castle
Biddulph, Rev. T. T. St. James's-sq. Bristol
Bidgood, Mr. A. M. 6, Vigo-street
Bidwell, L. S. Esq. Thetford, Norfolk
Bidwell, Mrs. Bury St. Edmund's
Biggs, Rich. H. Esq. 19, Small-street, Bristol
Bindloss, Wm. Esq. Cheapside, Manchester
Bingham, Colonel, Rochester
Bingham, John, Esq. Rose-hill, near Derby
Bingley, Robert, Esq. *F.R.S.* Royal Mint
Binliall, Edwin, Esq. Leeds
Binks, Mr. Doncaster
Binney, Lieut. John, Commander of H.M. Brig Pigeon, Falmouth
Binns, Godfrey, Esq. Deighton, Huddersfield
Binns, Thomas, Esq. 20, Essex-street, Strand
Binny, William, Esq. 23, India-st. Edinburgh
Binyon, Mr. Alfred, Mayfield Print Works, do
Binyon, B. Esq. 101, Market-st. Manchester
Binyon, Edwd. Esq. St. Ann's-sq. Manchester
Binyon, Thos. Esq. St. Ann's-sq. Manchester
Birch, Mr. H. Rochester
Birch, Jonathan, Esq. 45, Upper Gower-street
Birch, Samuel, Esq. Alderman of London
Birch, Mr. Wm. 10, High-st. Kensington
Birch, Wm. Esq. Back Mosley-st. Manchester
Bird, Edward, Esq. Glastonbury
Bird, Edward A. Esq. 29, Corn-street, Bristol
Bird, Lieut. Edward, *R.N.* 22, Arundel-street
Birdsall, Mr. J. Bookr. Northampton. 9 Copies
Birkbeck, Dr. George, Finsbury-square
Birkbeck, John, Esq. Anley House, near Settle
Birkett, E. L. Esq. Caius College, Cambridge
Birley, J. Esq. Back George-st. Manchester
Birt, Rev. Dr. John, Faversham
Birtwhistle, Mr. William, Bookseller, Halifax. 3 Copies
Bish, Thos. Esq. *M.P.* 2, St. James's-square
Bishop, George, Esq. South Villa, Regent's-park
Bishop, J. Esq. 18, York-place, Regent's-park
Bishop, Thos. Esq. Tenterden, Kent
Bishop, Lieut. Wm. *R.N.* Harleston, Norfolk
Bishop, Wm. Chatterley, Esq. *B.A.* St. John's College, Cambridge, and 9, Fitzwilliam-sq. east, Dublin
Bishopp, Dr. G. M. 10, Upper Gloucester-st. Dorset-square
Bisschop, F. Esq. Rue Kid Dorp, Antwerp
Bissett, Capt. *R.N.* Lymington
Bisshopp, Dr. Thornley Grange, Northampton
Bisshopp, Miss, Richmond, Surrey
BJORNSTJERNA, His Excellency the Count
Black, J. Esq. 109, Hope-street, Glasgow
Black, Mr. James, jun. 28, York-st. Glasgow
Black and Armstrong, Messrs. Booksellers, Tavistock-street. 50 Copies
Blackburn Ladies' Reading Society
Blackheath Reading Society
Blackmore, E. Esq. Princess-st. Manchester
Blackmore, E. Esq. 5, Mitre-court-chambers, Temple
Blackmore, Rev. R. Donhead St. Mary, Wilts
Blain, Saml. Esq. Brunswick-street, Liverpool
Blair, Alex. Esq. 13, Northumberland-street, Edinburgh
Blair, —. Esq. 45, Gloucester-place
Blair, Col. Thos. Dunskey, Port Patrick
Blair, Harrison, Esq. Cross-street, Manchester
Blair, Jas. Esq. Penninghame, Wigtonshire
Blair, Mrs. Lambert, Penninghame, Wigtonsh.
Blair, Mrs. Penninghame, Wigtonshire
Blake, E. P. Esq. Redgrove, Suffolk
Blake, George, Esq. Kitchen-street, Liverpool
Blake, Dr. Malachi, Taunton
Blake, Thos. Esq. West Cowes
Blakeney, J. H. Esq. 1, Fitzwilliam's-place, Dublin
Blakiston, Arthur, Esq. 38, Bedford-row
Blamey, Joel, Esq. Pool, near Redruth
Bland, Henry, Esq. York
Bland, W. Esq. Hartlip Place, Kent
Blandford, S. Esq. 20, Dover-street, Piccadilly
Blayds, Thomas, Esq. Leeds
Blayney, Thos. Esq. Evesham, Worcestershire
Bleeck, Alfred, Esq. Redcliff-parade, Bristol
Blegborough, R. Esq. Downing Coll. Camb.
Blencowe, Mrs. Rayne, Essex
Blencowe, R. W. Esq. Dawlish
Blick, Rev. F. Tamworth
Bligh, Capt. *R.N.* Milbrook, Southampton
Bligh, Mrs. Admiral, Crescent, Southampton
Bligh, R. Esq. 5, Upper Berkeley-place, Bristol
Blight, S. Esq. Falmouth
Blinkhorn, John, Esq. 5, Peel-st. Manchester
Bliston, Robt. Esq. Small Wood Manor Uttoxeter
Blois, Sir Chas. Bart. Cockfield Hall, Yoxford
Blundell, Capt. G. S. (Bengal Native Infantry), Taunton
Blundell, Dr. Thomas, Wisbeach
Blundell, William, Esq. Taunton
Blunt, Jos. Esq. 2, Upper Gower-street
Blunt, Jos. Esq. Liverpool-street, & 16, New Burlington-street
Blutram, Mr. J. At Messrs. Dixon & Sons, Friday-street, Manchester
Boase, Matthew John, Esq. Redruth
Bode, Frederick, Esq. 5, Chatham-place
Boger, J. Hext, Esq. Stonehouse, Devon
Bogle, Jas. jun. Esq. 196, Athol-place, Glasgow
Boghurst, J. Esq. Rochester
Bogue, J. Esq. 4, John-street, Bedford-row
Bohun, Richard, Esq. Beccles, Suffolk
Bolam, William, Esq. Newcastle
Bold, J. O. Esq. Edge-hill, Liverpool
Boldero, Rev. G. Ixworth, Suffolk
Boldero, J. Esq. Bury St. Edmund's
Boles, General, Exmouth, Devon
Bolitho, R. Foster, Esq. The Cliff, Penzance
Bolitho, Thomas, Esq. Penzance
Bolland, James, Esq. Leeds
Bolland, Right Hon. Mr. Baron, 4, Royal-terrace, Adelphi
Bolster, Mr. J. Bookseller, Cork. 10 Copies
BOLTON, Right Hon. Lord
Bolton, J. Esq. Walton's-bldgs. Manchester
Bolton, J. Esq. 13, Milburg-terrace, Dorset-sq.
Bolton, John, Esq. 92, Duke-street, Liverpool
Bolton, Thos. Esq. Brunswick-st. Liverpool
Bompass, Dr. George, Fishponds, Bristol
Bonar, A. Esq. Castle-crescent, Edinburgh
Bond, John, Esq. Grange, near Wareham
Bond, Mr. John, King-street, Yarmouth
Bond, Robert, Esq. Woodbine Cottage, West-end, Hampstead
Bond, Walter, M. Esq. Moy, Ireland
Bond, Wm. Henry, Esq. *R.N.* Falmouth
Bone, Mr. Joseph, Canterbury
Bonner, Rev. George, Cheltenham
Bonnett, Rev. C. S. Rectory, Avington
Bonnor, Rev. R. Maurice, Oswestry
Boobbyer, David, Esq. Stanhope-street, Strand
Booker, John, Esq. St. Petersburgh
Booker, J. W. Esq. Velendra, W. Cardiff
Boone, Messrs. T. and W. Booksellers, New Bond-street. 10 Copies
Booth, Sir Felix, Bart. 43, Portland-place. 10 Copies
Booth, Thos. Esq. Park Ironworks, nr Sheffield
Booth, Charles, Esq. Roydon Lodge, Essex
Booth, Geo. Esq. Brunswick-st. Liverpool
Booth, H. W. Esq. Christ College, Cambridge, and Roydon Lodge, Essex
Booth, John G. Esq. Crouch Hall, Hornsey. 2 Copies
Booth, Mr. J. Bookseller, Duke-street, Portland-place. 8 Copies
Booth, Miss, 43, Portland-place. 2 Copies
Booth & Pettit, Mess. 10, Lancaster-pl. Strand
Booth, William, Esq. dec. Roydon Lodge, Essex. 2 Copies
Borlase, Henry, Esq. Helston
Borlase, J. Esq. Mayor of Helston, Cornwall
Borlase, J. J. G. Esq. Truro
Borlase, John, Esq. Helston
Borough, Chas. Esq. St. Peter's-street, Derby
Borradaile, W. Esq. 5, Barge-yd. Bucklersbury
Bosanquet, Right Hon. Mr. Justice, 12 Montagu-place, Russell-square
Boss, Captain, John G. *R.N. M.P.*
Bossange and Co. Messrs. Booksellers, Great Marlborough-street

Botfield, Wm. Esq. Decker-hill, Shiffnal
Bottomley, James, Esq. Huddersfield
Bottomley, Mr. John, Bradford, Yorkshire
Bott, A. Esq. Berkeley-street west, Edgware-rd.
Boucher, Chas. Esq. Wisbeach, Norfolk
Bourchier, Charles, Esq. 66, Wimpole-street
Bourchier, Rev. Richard, Brightwalton, Berks
Bourdillon, G. Esq. Holybourn, Alton, Hants
Bourne, Mr. E. C. 19, Lamb's Conduit-street
Bourne, R. Esq. Hilderstone Hall, Staffordshire
Bourne, Timothy, Esq. 1, Exchange-al. Liverpool
Bouverie, E. Esq. Delapré Abbey
Bovill, Edw. Esq. Fairfields, Tiverton
Boville, J. W. Esq. Southampton
Bow, W. M. Esq. Broughton
Bowden, Captain, Falmouth
Bowden, J. S. Esq. 66, Aldermanbury
Bowen, Rev. P. Sheffield
Bower, Dr. Broxholm, near Doncaster
Bowerbank, J. S. Esq. 19, Critchill-place, New North-road
Bowle, Rev. J. Buona Vista, near Lymington
Bowles, Captain, *R.N.* 8, Hill-street
Bowles, Charles, Esq. Shaftesbury
Bowley, J. H. Esq. Cheltenham
Bowling, John, Esq. Scots Fusilier Guards, Guards' Hospital, Grosvenor-place
Bowyer, Miss A. 307, Holborn
Box, John, Esq. 68, Charlotte-st. Portland-pl.
Boxer, Capt. Edward, *R.N.* Dover
Boyd, Geo. W. Esq. Brunswick-st. Liverpool
Boyd, Mr. Isaac, 25, Church-st. Spitalfields
Boyd, Walter, Esq. Plaistow, Essex
Boyer, Herbert, Esq. Trafford-moss, Trafford-place, Manchester
Boyle, Right Hon. David, Lord Justice Clerk, 28, Charlotte-square, Edinburgh
Boyman, Captain, 1, Grosvenor-pl. Camberwell
Boys, Jacob. Esq. 60, Grand Parade, Brighton
Brace, Mr. Joseph, Willow-walk, Bermondsey
Brackenbury, Jas. Esq. Brown-st. Manchester
Brackenridge, G. W. Esq. University College, Oxford
Bradbury, Jas Esq. 20, Marsden-sq. Manchestr
Bradby, Rev. Thos. St. Mary's, Southampton
Bradfield, J. B. S. Esq. Stoke Ferry, Norfolk
Bradford, Rev. Wm. Mussage, Beaconsfield
Bradley, Mr. Tho. Gun Tavern, Lambeth-road
Bradley, Thomas S. Esq. Huddersfield
Braham, John, Esq. The Grange, Brompton
Braidley, Benj. Esq. Peel-street, Manchester
Braithwaite, Isaac, Esq. 64, Old Broad-st.
Braithwaite, J. Esq. 1, Bath-place, Fitzroy-sq. 3 Copies
Bramley, Richard, Esq. School Close, Leeds
Bramley, William, Esq. 2, Bedford-row
Brancker, Jas. Esq. Matthew street, Liverpool
Brancker, Sir Thomas, Rodney st. Liverpool
Brand, Mr. Robert, 1, Ingram-street, Glasgow
Brand, Mrs. Durham
Brandling, Chas. John, Esq. Middleton Lodge
Brandling, Rev. R. H. Gosforth House, Newcastle
Brandon, David, Esq. 27 Euston-square
Brandt, Robt. Esq. Norfolk-st. Manchester
Brasen, George, Esq. 7, Gray's-inn-square
Branson, Rev. R. J. *M.A.* Rectory, Armthorp
Brass, Wm. Esq. Cumberland-road, Bristol
Brawn, Mr. Wm. 9, Moore-place, Glasgow
Brawne, Rev. Dr. T. 98, Montrose-st. Glasgow
Bray, Joel, Esq. 63, St. Martin's-lane
BREADALBANE, Most Noble the Marquis of
Breffit, G. Esq. 4, Egremont-place, New-road

Brentford, Old, Book Society
Brenton, Rear Admiral Sir Jahleel, *K.C.B.* Lieutenant-Governor of Greenwich Hospital
Brett, J. Davy, Esq. Caius College, Cambridge
Brettle, George, Esq. 119, Wood-street
Brewer, John, Esq. 10, Saville-row, Walworth
Brewer, Mr. S. K. Bookseller, Brighton
Briandon, D. Esq. 27, Euston-sq. New-road
Briant, Miss Harriet, Bungay, Suffolk
Brice, Samuel, Esq. Frenchay
Briddon, Hy. Esq. Deansgate, Manchester
Bridge, C. Esq. Weymouth, Dorset
Bridge, S. F. Esq. Wellington
Bridge, Wm. Esq. Dorchester
Bridgeman, Hon. C. O. *R.N.* Knockin Hall
Bridgen, Mrs. Queen's-parade, Bristol
Bridges, B. C. Esq. Oriel College, Oxford
Bridges, Rev. Dr. T. E. President of Corpus Christi College, Oxford
Bridgett, Mr. Jos. Bridge-street, Derby
Brien, R. Esq., *R.N.* Spencer-st. Clerkenwell
Briggs, Rawdon, Esq. Wakefield
Briggs, Rawdon, jun. Esq. Halifax
Bright, R. Esq. Ham-grn. St. George's, nr. Bristol
Brighton Brunswick Book Club
——— Book Society
——— Ladies' Book Club
——— Literary & Scientific Institution
Brine, Capt. *R.N.* Boldre-hill, Lymington
Brinton, Miss, Speenhamland, Berks
Brisbane, Lieut.-Gen. Sir Thomas Macdougall, *K.C.B. G.C.H.* Makerstoun, Kelso
BRISTOL, The Most Noble the Marquis of
Bristol, The Corporation of 6 Copies
——— Library Society, King-street
Britton, Capt. John, Stratton place, Falmouth
Britton, Dr. S. G. Newport, Barnstaple
Broadbent, Samuel, Esq. Bradford, Yorkshire
Broadbent, T. Esq. 2 Marsden sq. Manchester
Broadhurst, Dan. Esq. Manchester
Broadley, Mrs. M. 9, Dorset-pl. Clapham-rd.
Broadmead, N. Esq. Langport
Broadrick, Wm. Esq. University Coll. Oxford
Broadwood, Rev. John, Finden, near Worthing
Brock, Rev. W. Rectory, Bishop's Waltham
Brocklehurst, J. Esq. *M.P.* Hardsfield House, Macclesfield
Brocklehurst, T. Esq. The Fence, Macclesfield
Brockman, R. T. Esq. Sandgate
Brockman, Rev. J. D. Cheriton, Kent
Brockman, Rev. W. Beachborough Hall, Kent
Broderip, W. J. Esq. 2, Raymond-buildings
Brodie, Sir B. C. Bart. *F.R.S.* 14, Saville-row
Brodie & Co. Messrs. Booksellers, Salisbury. 8 Copies
Brodie, J. C. Esq. Coulmony House, by Forres
Brodie, William Bird, Esq. *M.P.* Salisbury
Brodrick, J. B. Esq. Queen's Coll. Cambridge
Broke, Sir Philip, Bart. *K.C.B.* Broke Hall, near Ipswich
Bromley, B. Esq. Christ Church Coll. Oxford
Bromley, Sir Robert H. Bart.
Bromley, C. Esq. Southampton
Brook, G. H. Esq. Huddersfield
Brook, Richard, Esq. Poultry
Brook, Thomas, Esq. King's-arms-yard
Brook, Messrs. W. & R. Booksellers, Lincoln
Brook, William, Esq. Huddersfield
Brooke, E. Esq. Hanson's-court, Manchester
Brooke, Edward Basil, Major 67th Regt. St. Christopher's
Brooke, J. Esq. Armitage Bridge, Huddersfield
Brooke, J. Esq. Shepley Hall

Brooke, John, Esq. Stockport
Brooke, Lieut.-Genl. Wm. 12, Alfred-st. Bath
Brooke, P. jun. Esq. North-street, Leeds
Brooke, Z. Esq. 9, Arundel-st. Strand
Brookes, Robert, Esq. 3, Mount-st. Lambeth
Brooks, E. Esq. 26, Spital-square
Brooks, T. H. Esq. 25, Chancery-lane
Brooks, John, Esq. High-street, Manchester
Brooks, Robert, Esq. 90, Old Broad-street
Brooksbank, Thomas, Esq. 14, Gray's inn-sq.
Brotherton, Joseph, Esq. *M.P.* Manchester
Brough, Mr. A. Kidderminster
Brougham, Mrs. Booksr. Burslem. 4 Copies
Broughton, Rev. B. S. Foxley Park
Brown, Anthony, Esq. Alderman of London
Brown & Co. Messrs. Booksellers, Bristol
Brown, Mrs. Eliza, 43, Portland-pl. 2 Copies
Brown, Fountain, Esq. Park-place, Leeds
Brown, George, Esq. 1, Mall, Clifton, Bristol
Brown, Geo. Esq. 5, Stanhope-pl. Hyde-park
Brown, George, Esq. 101, Upper Thames-street
Brown, H. Williams, Esq. Leeds
Brown, J. Esq. 34, Fountain-st. Manchester
Brown, J. Esq. King James's Stairs, Shadwell
Brown, Jas. Esq. Dundee
Brown, James, Esq. Dundee
Brown, James, Esq. Leeds
Brown, John, Esq. 26 Chester-terrace, Regent's-park. 2 Copies
Brown, Mr. J. E. Booksr. Windsor. 5 Copies
Brown, Mr. J. Booksr. Penrith. 3 Copies
Brown, Mr. J. G. Bookseller, Leicester. 11 Copies
Brown, Rev. J. *M.A.* Trinity Coll. Cambridge
Brown, Robert, Esq. *F.R.S. F.L.S.*, &c. British Museum
Brown, Stephen, Esq. Colchester
Brown, Stephen, Esq. Jesus Coll. Cambridge
Brown, Thos. Esq. Master Attendant, Dockyard, Woolwich
Brown, Mr. Thomas, 36 Wood-st. Cheapside
Brown, W. W., Esq. Union Bank, Leeds
Brown, Wm. Esq. All Saints-place, Manchester
Browne, Alex. Esq. East Shore, Dundee
Browne, Alexander, Esq. Port Glasgow
Browne, Charles, Esq. Stock Exchange
Browne, Mr. C. Bear Inn, Great Yarmouth
Browne, F. H. Esq. St. John's College, Cambridge
Browne, Hon. Lieut.-Col. 5, Marlborough-buildings, Bath
Browne, Lieut.-Gen. G. Weymouth, Dorset
Browne, Matthew, Esq. Port Glasgow
Browne, Rev Thomas, *M.A.* Christ's Hospital
Browne, William, Esq. Shepton Mallet
Browne, W. J. Utten, Esq. Norwich
Browning, Mr. Edwin, 36, Little Windmill-street, Golden-square
Browning, Henry, Esq. 4, Gloucester-place
Browning, James, Esq. 113, St. John's-street
Browning, Thos. Esq. 5, South-sq. Gray's Inn. 3 Copies
Browning, W. H. Esq. St. John's-street
Browning, W. S. Esq. 8, Cumberland terrace, Regent's-park
Brownless, A. Esq. Goodhurst, Kent
BROWNLOW, Right Hon. the Earl of
Bruce, Mrs. Castle Eve Villa, near Poole
Bruce, Capt. Geo. Union Dockyard, Limehouse
Bruce, J. B. Esq. Magistrate, Duffryn, Aberdare, Glamorganshire
Bruce, Rev. J. Westbere, near Canterbury
Bruce, Sir Stuart, Bart. &c. Dublin Castle

Bruce, Thomas, Esq. Framlingham, Suffolk
Bruce, Thomas, Esq. High-street, Manchester
Brundrett, Jonathan, Esq. 10, King's-bench-walk, Temple
Brunel, M. J. Esq. 53, Parliament-street
Brunel, M. J. jun. Esq. 53, Parliament-street
Brunton, Wm. Esq. 12, Park-sq. Regent's-park
Bruton Book Society
Brutton, Chas. Esq. Northenhay Place, Exeter
BUCCLEUGH, His Grace the Duke of
Buchan, H. Esq. Southampton
Buchanan, John, Esq. 95, Candleriggs, Port Glasgow
Buchanan, R. Esq. 109, Fife-place, Glasgow
Buchanan, Robertson, Esq. 1, Walbrook-bdgs.
Buchanan, The Hon. A. H. Hales Hall, Salop
Buchanon, Mr. H. 241, Brandon-pl. Glasgow
Buck, Jno. Esq. 18, South-street, Finsbury
Buck, Lewis Wm. Esq. Hartland Abbey, Devon
Buck, S. Esq. Hartest, Suffolk
Buck, W. Esq. Bury St. Edmund's
BUCKINGHAM, Her Grace the Duchess of
Buckle, J. Esq. Wyelands, near Chepstow
Buckle, Joshua, Esq. York
Buckle, Miss, Britton Ferry, near Neath, Glamorganshire
Bucknell, George, Esq. Bermondsey
Buckton, G. Esq. Doctor's Commons
Buckton, John, Esq. Canterbury
Budd, John, Esq. Willesley, Barnstaple
Buenos Ayres, Library of
Bulgin, Mr. Bristol
Bulkeley, Sir Richard B. Williams, Bart. *M.P.* Baron-hill, Beaumaris
Buller, Sir John Yarde, Bart. 10, New-street, Spring-gardens
Bullin, Rear-Admiral, 13, Raby-place, Bath
Bullmore, W. H. Esq. Truro
Bullock, Geo. Esq. *B.A.* St. John's College, Cambridge
Bullock, H. Esq. Christ's College, Cambridge
Bullock, St. Geo. Esq. Clare Hall, Cambridge
Bulman, Harrison, Esq. Ellison-place, Newcastle-upon-Tyne
Bulmer, George, Esq. Crown-street, Leeds
BULOW, His Excellency the Baron, Prussian Embassy
Bumpus, Mr. Bookseller, 6, Holborn-bars. 7 Copies
Bund, T. H. Esq. Wick House, Worcester
Bunny, Edw. B. Esq. Speenhamland, Berks
Bunny, Jer. Esq. Northcote-street, Newbury
Bunting, J. P. Esq. King-street, Manchester
Bunyard, Mr. Thomas, Maidstone
Bunyon, R. J. Esq. New Bridge-st. Blackfriars
Burbidge, Mr. J. J. 130, Fleet-street
Burbidge, Thomas, Esq. Leicester
Burcham, C. Esq. Lynn Regis, Norfolk
Burcham, Rev. T. B. Trinity Coll. Cambridge
Burd, John, Esq. Gt. Chatham-st. Broughton
Burdikin, E. Esq. Market-street, Manchester
Burge, Mr. George, Herne Bay, Kent
Burgess and Hunt, Messrs. Ramsgate
Burgess, John Hy. Esq. Mayor of Glastonbury
Burgess, R. Esq. St. John's Coll. Cambridge
Burke, C. G. Esq. Christ's College, Cambridge
Burke, W. W. E. Esq. 3, Furnivals Inn
BURLINGTON, Right Hon. the Earl of
Burman, H. T. Esq. Caius College, Cambridge
Burn, J. G. Esq. Weukworth
Burnell, Miss, 29, Queen-street, Brompton
Burnett, J. F. Esq. Crayford, Kent
Burnett, J. H. Esq. 21, Charlotte-sq. Edinburg
Burney, H. Esq. Exeter College, Oxford
Burnie, John, Esq. 124, Bishopsgate-street
Burningham, Miss, Froyle, Alton, Hants
Burningham, T. Esq. Froyle, Alton, Hants
Burr, J. H. S. Esq. Christ Church, Oxford
Burrard, Capt. Sir Chas. Bart. *R.N.* Lyndhurst
Burrard, Rev. G. per Mr. Galpine, Lymington
Burrell, James F. Esq. Belvoir House, Fareham
Burrell, John, Esq. Durham
Burrill, Mr. H. Booksr. Chatham. 5 Copies
Burrough, Sir James, 16, Bedford-square
Burroughs, G. F. Esq. Shepton Mallet
Burrows, Dr. Samuel, Bath House, Bideford
Burslem Book Society
Burt, Thos. C. Esq. Somerfield-court, Sellinge, Kent
Burt James, Esq. Bond-street, Manchester
Burt, William, Esq. St. Giles's, Norwich
Burton, J. & J. Messrs. Leeds
Burton, Jas. Esq. Bridgewater-pl. Manchester
Bury St. Edmund's Public Library
Bury, Thos. Esq. Adelphi, Salford
Bush, J. Esq. 36, St. James's-pl. Kingsdown
Bush, Henry, Esq. Litfield House, Clifton
Bushby, Capt. Thos. *R.N.* Greenhithe, Kent
Bushby, W. P. Esq. 9, Exchange-al. Liverpool
Bushe, Right Hon. Charles Kendal, Lord Chief Justice of the King's Bench, Dublin
Bushe, T. Esq. 5. Fitzwilliam's-square, Dublin
Bushell, Wm. Esq. Portland-square, Bristol
Buston, Roger, Esq. Buston
Butcher, Lieut. *R.N.* Commander of the Redbreast Cutter
Butcher, William, Esq. Norwich
BUTE, Most Noble the Marquis of
Butler, D. Esq. Dunford House, near Wilton
Butler, G. S. Esq. Hill-place, Alton, Hants
Butler, R. Esq. 2, Kent-terrace, Regent's-park
Butler, T. D. Esq. 47, Castle-street, Liverpool
Butler, Thomas, Esq. 42, Trinity-sq. Tower-hill
Butler, Mr. W. T. Bookseller, Beaconsfield. 4 Copies
Butt, Rev. J. W. Bromley, Kent
Buttemur, Robert, Esq.
Butterfield, Mr. John, Bradford, Yorkshire
Butterworth, J. A. Esq. Cannon-st. Manchester
Buxton, J. M. Esq. Oxford-st. Manchester
By, Lieut-Col. Shernfold Park, Frant, Sussex
Byerley, Nicholas, Esq. 105, Holborn-hill
Byng, Mr. John, jun. Osmaston-road, Derby
Byrne, Mr. Thomas, Beaumaris. 3 Copies
Byrom, Miss, Eleanor, Quay-st. Manchester
Bywater, Dawson, & Co. Messrs. Pool-lane, Liverpool
Byzantium Book Club, Constantinople

C.

Cable, Samuel, Esq. St. Christopher's
Cadbury, William, Esq. Wellington
Caddell, David, Esq. Salisbury-square
Cadell, Mr. Thomas, Bookseller, Strand
Cadman, John, Esq. Leeds
Cagan, Hugh, Esq. Brunswick-st. Glasgow
Cain, James, Esq. Douglas, Isle of Man
Calcott, Captain B. Caynham Court, Salop
CALCUTTA, Right Hon. the Lord Bishop of
Calcutta Book Club
CALEDON, Right Hon. the Earl of. 2 Copies
Calkin & Budd, Messrs. Bkslrs. 118, Pall-mall. 4 Copies
Call, Mr. G. New Cross, Wolverhampton
Callan, Captain Thos. Ship Bland. Liverpool
Callender, Thos. P. Esq. Peel-st. Manchester
Callender, W. R. Esq. High-street, Manchester
Callicut, W. B. Esq. 4. York-place, Brompton
Callum, Mr. Charles, 48, Queen-st. Glasgow
Calman, Mr. John, Dundee
CALTHORPE, Right Hon. Lord
Calver, William, Esq. Ipswich
Calvert, Edmond, Esq.
Calvert, Mr. Edward, Rotten-row, Derby
Calvert, Dr. J. W. Blandford-pl. Regent's-pk
Calvert, Thomas, Esq. Kirstall-road, Leeds
Calvésche, —. Buchhandlung, Prague
Cambourne (Cornwall) Literary and Scientific Institution
Cambridge Book Society, Bull Inn, Cambridge
——— Caius College Library
——— Catherine Hall Library
——— Clare Hall Book Club
——— Corpus Christi College Library
——— Emanuel College Library
——— Jesus College Book Society
——— King's College Library
——— Magdalen College Library
——— Pembroke Hall Book Club
——— Queen's College Library
——— St. John's College Book Society
Cameron, Lieutenant-General, 11, Circus, Bath
Cameron, Patrick, Esq. Seagate, Scotland
Campbell, A. Esq. Blythewood, Glasgow
Campbell, Sir Arch. Bart. of Succoth, 1, Park-place, Edinburgh
Campbell, F. W. Esq. Birkfield Lodge, Ipswich
Campbell, J. Esq. 43, Buchanan-st. Glasgow
Campbell, J. C. Esq. Guernsey
Campbell, John, Esq. Budleigh, Devon
Campbell, Major H. C. Northend House, Portsmouth
Campbell, R. Esq. 127, Brunswick-st. Glasgow
Campbell, Rich. Esq. 11, Northumberland-street, Edinburgh
Campbell, W. Esq. 34, Candleriggs, Glasgow
CAMPERDOWN, Right Hon. the Earl of
Campion, Mr. Thomas, Cork
Camplin, Alderman Thomas, Bristol
Cancellor, Ellis, Esq. 15, Prince's-st. Lambeth
Cannan, D. Esq. Sambrook-ct. Basinghall-st.
Cannells, Mr. F. Liverpool
Canning, Right Hon. Sir Stratford, *M.P. G.C.B.* 29, Grosvenor-square
Cannon, Alexander, Esq. *R.N.* West Cowes
CANTERBURY, His Grace the Archbishop of
Canton Book Club
Cantwell, Robert, Esq. 25, Wimpole-street
Canwell, Mr. F. Liverpool
Capel, Captain, *R.N.* Swanage
Capel, John, Esq. 32, Russell-square
Capes, —, Esq. North-terrace, Camberwell
Capes, William, Esq. King-street, Manchester
Capper, Joseph, Esq. 4, Union-street, Bristol
Capper, Robert, Esq. Cheltenham
Carbis, Mr. John, Redruth
Carden, Thomas, Esq. Worcester
Cardwell, —. Esq. Cockpit-hill, Manchester
Carew, Admiral Sir B. Hallowell, *G.C.B.* dec. 2 Copies
Carew, Capt. Thos. *R.N.* Beckford House, Southampton
Carfrae, Colonel, Oriental Club
Carfrae, J. Esq. 19, Holloway-place, Holloway
Cargill, Thomas, Esq. Newcastle-upon-Tyne
Carkeet, William, Esq. Falmouth
CARLISLE, Right Hon. the Earl of

Carlisle, Sir Anthony, *F.R.S.* Langham-place
Carlisle, Thomas, Esq. Nelson Villa, Clifton
Carmac, Major, East India House
Carne, Edw. C. Esq. Kimberley-pl. Falmouth
Carne, John, Esq. Cottage, Falmouth
Carne, John, Esq. Lariggan, Penzance
Carne, William, Esq. Falmouth
Carnegie, James, Esq. Cork
Carpenter & Son, Messrs. Booksrs. Old Bond-st.
Carpenter, John, Esq. Mount Tavy, Tavistock
Carpenter, Mr. John, 11, King-street, Whitehall
Carpenter, Rev. J. Phillips, Grenofen, Tavistock
Carpenter, Rev. Lant, LL.D. Great George-st. Bristol
Carr, John, Esq. 30, Bedford-row
Carr, John, Esq. Walker, Northumberland
Carr, Mr. Wm. 15, Aston-place, Islington
Carrington, H. Esq. Caius College, Cambridge
Carter, Mr. C. 1, Chapel-road, Worthing
Carter, Dr. H. W. Canterbury
Carter, J. B. Esq. *M.P.* 21, Duke-st. Westmr.
Carter, T. W. Esq. Maidstone
Carter, Major, Great Malvern, Worcestershire
Carter, Miss, Library, Worthing
Carter, Capt. T. W. *R.N.* Ryde, Isle of Wight
Carter, Rev. W. D. Wye, Kent
Carthew, Edmund, Esq. Liskeard, Cornwall
Cartwell, Rev. J. *B.A.* Christ Coll. Cambridge
Cartwright, Mr. Francis, 62, Lr. Grosvenor-st.
Cartwright, Henry, Esq. Torquay, Devon
Cartwright, Major, Brackley, Northamptonshire
Cartwright, R. Esq. 35, Bloomsbury-square
Cartwright, Wm. Esq. Teignmouth, Devon
Carus, Rev. W. *M.A.* Trinity Coll. Cambridge
Carwick, Thomas, Esq. Hendon, Middlesex
Cary, Clarence Horatio, Esq. Bangor
Casacubertas, A. Esq. Plymouth Grove, Manchester
Casbolt, Henry, Esq. Diamond Estate, St. Christopher's
Case, J. Deane Esq. Abercrombie-sq. Lvrpool
Case, R. Edward, Esq. Clifton, Gloucestershire
Case, Rev. T. Bishops Caundle, Sherbourne
Cash, James, Esq. Piccadilly, Manchester
Caslon, Henry, Esq. Chiswell-street
Casson, William, Esq. Brown-st. Manchester
Castle, M. H. Esq. 1, Rodney-place, Clifton
Cathcart, John, Esq. Genoch, Glenluce
Cator, Captain B. *R.N.* Bexley, Kent
Cattermoul, Everet, Esq. Norwich
Cattley, S. W. Esq. 14, Queenhithe
Caulfield, Lieut.-Col. Oriental Club
Caulfield, William, Esq. Dublin
Cawood, John, Esq. Leeds
Cazalet, P. C. Esq. Kemp Town, Brighton
Cazenove, James, Esq. 6, Great Winchester-st.
Chadwell, Mr. Thomas, Bksllr. Peterborough. 2 Copies
Chadwick, W. Esq. Ackey, near Doncaster
Chaffey, Mr. H. T. Chard, Somersetshire
Chamley, Mr. Newcastle. Mr. Rankins
Challenger, Richard, Esq. St. Christopher's
Chalon, A. E. Esq. 42, Great Marlborough-st.
Challoner, Robert, Esq. Dublin
Chamberlayne, T. Esq. Cranbury Park, Hants
Chamberlin, Henry, jun. Esq. Norwich
Chamberlin, Robert, Esq. Norwich
Chambers, Sir Samuel, *R.N.* Bredgar, Kent
Champante, J. J. Esq. Belmont House, Taunton
Champernowne, H. Esq. Christ Church Coll. Oxford
Chandler, J. Esq. 7, Charles-st. Manchester-square

Chandler, L. Esq. 133, St. John's street
Chanter, T. B. Esq. Bideford
Chaplin, E. J. Esq. Magdalen Coll. Oxford
Chaplin, Frederick, Esq. Harlow, Essex
Chapman, David, Esq. 30, Miller-st. Glasgow
Chapman, F. Esq. Caius College, Cambridge
Chapman, J. Esq. 16, Grosvenor-st. Chorlton, Manchester
Chapman, Mr. John, 49, Albemarle-street
Chapman, Thos. Esq. Marshal of the King's Bench
Chapman, Wm. Francis, Esq. Hampstead
Chappel, W. T. Esq. Lemon-street, Truro
Chappell, Mr. J. 56, Skinner-street, Snow-hill
Charge, John, Esq. Chesterfield
Charlton, Edwin, Esq. 42, New Bridge-street
Charlton, J. Esq. 42, New Bridge-st. Blackfrs.
Charlton, W. Esq. Rochester
Charnley, Mr. Newcastle
Charnock, John, Esq. Woodhouse-lane, Leeds
Charter, T. M. Esq. Lynchfield House, near Taunton
Chatfield, Rev. R. *LL.D.* Vicar of Chatteris
Chatham and Rochester Philosophical, &c. Institution
Chatham Library
Chaytor, W. R. C. Esq. *M.P.* Witton Castle, Witton le Wear, Durham
Cheam School Library
Chenery, C. Esq. Warner's-yard, Mincing-lane
Cheney, E. H. Esq. Christ Church Coll. Oxford
Chennell, Mr. Thomas, Crown Inn, Guildford
Chepstow Reading Society
Chester Reading Society
CHEWTON, Right Hon. Lord Viscount
CHICHESTER, Right Reverend the Lord Bishop of
Chalcott, T. Esq. Pembroke House, Clifton
Child, George, Esq. Stony-street, Borough
Child, Mr. R. Store-street, Bedford-square
Child, Stephen, Esq. Stony-street, Borough. 2 Copies
Child, Stephen, jun. Esq. Stony-st. Borough
Children, John George, Esq. *F.R.S.* British Museum, Secretary of the Royal Society
Childs, John, Esq. Bungay, Suffolk
Chinchen & White, Messrs. Swanage
Chippendall, J. Esq. Mosley-rd. Manchester
Chisholm, Rev. Charles, Eastwell, Kent
Chisholm, Dr. R. Canterbury
Chitty, Joseph, jun. Esq. 6, Pump-ct. Temple
CHOLMONDELEY, Most Noble the Marquis of
Chorley, Henry, Esq. Calls, Leeds
Chorley, Miss E. Park-lane, Leeds
Christian, John, Esq. First Deemster, Milnetown, Isle of Man
Christophers, J. Esq. 12, New Broad-street
Church, Mr. S. 10, Gray's-place, Brompton
CHURCHILL, Captain Lord John Spencer, *R.N.* Kensington Palace
CHURCHILL, Hon. Lady Henrietta, Chesterfield
Churchill, James, Esq. Poole, Dorset
Churchill, Mr. John, Bookseller, 16, Princes-street, Leicester-square
Churchyard, Thomas, Esq. Melton, Suffolk
Clair, Capt. D. L. H. *R.N.* Staverton Court, Gloucester
Clapham, Messrs. J. & J. Leeds
Clapham, Thomas, Esq. Woodhouse, Leeds
Clare, J. Esq. 19, St. John's-sq. Clerkenwell
Clark, Andrew, Esq. Bear Garden, Southwark

Clark, Cyrus, Esq. Street, near Glastonbury
Clark, Ebr. Esq. 127, St. James's-st. Brighton
Clark, Mr. G. Bookseller, Dorchester
Clark, J. Esq. 3, Keppel-st. Russell-square
Clark, J. Esq. Trowbridge, Wilts
Clark, Jos. jun. Esq. Pollard-st. Manchester
Clark, J. P. Esq. 5, Sackville-st, Piccadilly
Clark, Rev. J. Grove House, Folkestone
Clark, Matthew, Esq. 9, Hanover-terrace, Regent's-park
Clark, Mr. Bookseller, Finch-lane
Clark, Mr. William, 80, St. John's-street-road
Clark, W. Esq. 74, St. John's-street
Clarke, A. Esq. 57, Brooke-street, Grosvenor-square
Clarke, Alexander, Esq. Academy, Newport, Isle of Wight
Clarke, Chas. M. Esq. 40, Norfolk-st. Strand
Clarke, Charles, Esq. Lincoln's-inn-fields, and Grove-road, St. John's-wood
Clarke, Sir Charles M. Bart. *M.D. F.R.S.* 10, Saville-row
Clarke, Mr. Edward, 144, Queen-st. Glasgow
Clarke, General, 48, Charlotte-st. Fitzroy-sq.
Clarke, George, Esq. Mosley-st. Manchester
Clarke, John, Esq. Fort Pitt, Chatham
Clarke, Mr. John, Bookslr. Horsham. 6 Copies
Clarke, Lieut. Pickering, *R.N.* Perrymead, Widcomb, Bath
Clarke, Rev. W. B. *A.M. F.G.S.* Stanley Green, Longfleet, Dorset
Clarke, Saml. Esq. Church-street, Manchester
Clarke, Thomas, Esq. *F.A.S.* Highgate Hill, Kentish Town
Clarke, W. R. Esq. Wymondham, Norfolk
Clarkson, W. G. Esq. 7, Bell yard, Doctors'-commons
Clavin, Miss Jane, S. York
Claxson, Rev. Dr. Gloucester
Claxton, Lieut. C. P. *R.N.* 10, St. Vincent-parade, Bristol
Claxton, Robt. Esq. H. M. Solicitor-general, St. Christopher's
Clay, John, Esq. Huddersfield
Clay, Miss, Tenant-street, Derby
Clay, Richard, Esq. Rose Villa, Huddersfield
Clay, Samuel, Esq. St. John's-street, West Smithfield
Clay, Mr. William, 50, West Smithfield
Claydon, Charles, Esq. Cambridge
Claye, Mr. Thomas, Bookseller, Stockport
Claye, Richard, Esq. King-street, Manchester
Clayette, Louis, Esq. Queen-st. Manchester
Claypon, Joseph, Esq. Hampstead Heath
Clayson, Capt. John, *R.N.* Deal
Clayton, Michael, Esq. Lincoln's Inn
Clayton, Mr. John, Bradford, Yorkshire
Clayton, Wm. Esq. Langcliff Place, near Settle, Yorkshire
Cleasby, Stephen, jun. Esq. 3 Cornwall-terrace, Regent's-park
Clegg, Benjamin, Esq. Cromford Court, near Manchester
Clegg, J. Esq. 5, Back Marsden-st. Manchester
Clegg, J. jun. Esq. Hodgson-sq. Manchester
Clegg, W. Esq. Cromford Court, near Manchester
Cleghorn, R. B. Esq. St. Kitt's, West Indies
Cleland, Col. St. Germain's-place, Blackheath
Cleland, J. Esq. 130, Upper Mill-st. Glasgow
Clements, Mr. R. Rochester
Clent, Mrs. Sarah, 37, Back, Bristol
CLEVELAND, His Grace the Duke of

Cliff, Thomas, Esq. Downend
Cliffe, Rev. L. A. Bishops Hull, near Taunton
Clifford, Capt. Sir Augustus, *C.B.* 86, Eaton-sq.
Clifford, Hon. C. Truham Hall, Lincolnshire
Clifford, James, Esq. Shardlow, Derby
Clinton, John, Esq. St. Christopher's. 2 Copies
Clive, Theophilus, Esq. Ryde, Isle of Wight
CLIVE, Right Hon. Lord Viscount, *M.P.*
CLONCURRY, Right Hon. Lord
Close, Wm. Esq. Rotherham, Yorkshire
Clowes, Rev. J. Broughton, Manchester
Coape, James, Esq. Christ's Coll. Cambridge
Coates, Henry, Esq. Colchester
Coates, Richard, Esq. Brown-st. Manchester
Coates, T. Esq. 42, Spring-gdns. Manchester
Coates, Mr. Booksr. 139, Cheapside. 3 Copies
Coates, Miss Walker, Drumsceeh, Edinburgh
Cobb, J. Esq. Hawkhurst, Kent
Cobbett, Mr. William, 106, St. Martin's-lane
Cobbold, Charles, Esq. Rose-hill, Ipswich
Cobden, R. Esq. Mosley-street, Manchester
Cochet, Vice-Admiral James, Bideford, Devon
Cock, Simon, Esq. 1, New Bank-buildings
Cockburn, Vice-Admiral Sir Geo. *G.C.B.* 4, Whitehall
Cockburn, Miss, Stratton-terrace, Falmouth
Cockburn, Lieut.-Gen. Sir Wm. Bart. *D.C.L.* 4, Lansdown-crescent, Bath
Cocker, Jonathan, Esq. Salford, Lancashire
Cockerell, Hon. Lady, Seizincot, Worcestersh.
Cockerell, James, Esq. Blackman-st. Borough
Cockerill, R. M. Esq. *R.N.* Oswestry
Cocking, Thomas, Esq. 19, Great Portland-st.
Codd, George, Esq. Town Clerk, Hull
Coe, Captain Thomas, *R.N.* Cambridge
Coffin, Richard Pine, Esq. Portledge, Devon
Cohen, B. Esq. 1, Wyndham-pl. Bryanston-sq.
Cohen, J. C. Esq. Stock Exchange
Cohen, Solomon, Esq. Pope's-head-alley
COIGNÉ, Le Duc de
Colby, Capt. David, *R.N.* Tichfield
Colchester Castle Society
Cole, G. C. Esq. Sevenoaks, Kent
Cole, Martin, Esq. Ipswich
Cole, Thos. Esq. 46, Fountain-st, Manchester
Coles, James, Esq. Old Change
Coles, Rev. T. H. Honington, Lincolnshire
Collett, B. Esq. Mathon Lodge, Worcestershire
Collier, John, Esq. *M.P.* Plymouth
Collier, Wm. Esq. Greengate, Manchester
Colling, John, Esq. Stock Exchange
Collingwood, H. J. W. Esq. Lilburn Tower, Northumberland
Collins, B. Esq. *R.N.* Christchurch, Hants
Collins, Charles, Esq. Stamford-hill
Collins, Mr. James, 115, Regent-street
Collins, Mr. Jones, Richmond, Surrey
Collins, Mrs. Charlton, Kent
Collins, P.H. Esq. Hatch, Beauchamp, Somst.
Collins, Robert, Esq. Redcliff-parade, Bristol
Collins, Mr. William, V. *R.N.* Harwich
Collinson, Mr. R. Booksr. Mansfield. 4 Copies
Colls, Charles, Esq. Huddersfield
Collyns, William, Esq. Kenton, Devon
Colman, G. Esq. 10, Holland-place, Brixton
Colmer, R. Esq. Abbot's Lodge, Sibton, Suffolk
Colpoys, Rev. J. Rectory, Droxford, Hants
Colquitt, S. M. Esq. *R.N.* Neptune Hotel, Liverpool
Colridge, Wm. Esq. 40, Dunlop-st. Glasgow
Colson, Rev. W. Piddlehinton, nr. Dorchester
Colston, E. F. Esq. Weymouth, Dorset

COLVILLE, Right Hon. Vice-Admiral Lord
Colville, Chas. Esq. Christ Church Coll. Oxford
Colyer, J. Esq. St. John's Cottage, Sevenoaks
Combe, Geo. Esq. 23, Charlotte-sq. Edinburgh
Comings, Richard, Esq. Cambridge
COMPTON, Right Hon. the Earl
Compton, H. Esq. Eddington, Berks
Comyn, Richard, Esq. 1, Queen-street-place
Comyns, Rev. J. Woodhouse, Bishopsteignton, Devon
Conlan, John, Esq. Dublin
Conn, Henry, Esq. Truro
Connell, James, Esq. Irving Academy
Connop, Rev. J. Bradfield Hall, Berks
Connor, Daniel, Esq. Bally Bricken, Cork
Conroy, Sir John, *K.C.H.* Kensington Palace
Considine, H. Esq. Trinity Coll. Cambridge
Consterdine, J. Esq. NewCannon-st. Manchestr
Conway, F. W. Esq. Dublin
Cook, James, Esq. New Mosley-st. Manchester
Cook, James, Esq. North-terrace, Camberwell
Cook, Rev. James, Newton Hall
Cook, John, Esq. Goodman's-yard, Minories
Cook, Mrs. Greenock, N.B.
Cook, Robt. K. Esq. Corpus Coll. Cambridge
Cook, Wm. Esq. 22, St. Paul's Churchyard
Cooke, Charles, Esq. 45, Doughty-street
Cooke, Isaac, Esq. Clifton, Bristol
Cooke, P. Davies, Esq. Awston, nr. Doncaster
Cooke, Samuel G. Esq. Colchester
Cooke, Sir W. B. Bt. Wheatley, nr. Doncaster
Cookes, Mrs. Woodhampton House, Worcestershire
Cookson, Capt. J. Royal Artillery, St. Christopher's
Cookson, J. Esq. York-crescent, Clifton
Cookson, Rev. Edward, Park-square, Leeds
Cooper, Sir Astley, Bart. *F.R.A.S.* Conduit-st.
Cooper, Col. F. G. Barton Grange, nr. Taunton
Cooper, Frdk. Esq. 7, Richmond-ter. Brighton
Cooper, Rev. G. F. Yetminster, Dorset
Cooper, E. J. Esq. *M.P.* Martree, Collooney, Ireland
Cooper, Rev. Mark, Barnsbury Park, Islington
Cooper, Richard, Esq. Monument-yard
Cooper, Rev. Sir W. H. 57, Portland-place
Cooper, Mr. Thomas, Stockport
Cooper, T. W. Esq. Old-street & Tottenham
Cooper, Thos. Esq. Bedford Hotel, Brighton
Cooper, William, Esq. Norwich
Coote, R. E. P. Esq. 19, York-crescent, Clifton
Coote, R. H. Esq. 1, Stone-bdgs. Lincoln's Inn
Coote, William, Esq. St. Ives, Huntingdon
Cope, Richard, Esq. Exchange-st. Manchester
Cope, W. Wadham, Esq. Old Bailey
Copeland, Thomas, Esq. *M.P.* Alderman of London. 57 Copies
Copenhagen, the Athenæum of
——— Classinian Library of
Copenhagen, Union of Students of
Copland, John, Esq. Surrey-street, Strand
Copling, John, Esq. *H.E.I.C.S.* Upper Tulse Hill, Surrey. 2 Copies
Coppin, Mr. Wm. Queen Adelaide Steamer, Liverpool
Coppinger, Wm. Esq. Cork
Corbett, Mr. William, 25, Bath-street, Glasgow
Corbould, Henry, Esq. 5, Crescent-place, Burton-crescent
Corfe, John D. Esq. 16, College-street, Bristol
Cornish, F. S. Esq. South Molton, Devon
Cornish, James, Esq. Falmouth
Cornish, William, Esq. Marazion, Cornwall

Cornwall Library, Truro
Corrall, P. Esq. Maidstone
Cortazzi, John, Esq. 22, Brunswick-square
Cosens, Captain E. S. Woolwich-road
Coste, T. Esq. Lower Mosley-st. Manchester
Costendiech, John, Esq. Lloyd's Coffee-house
Cutesworth, R. Esq. St. Helen's-place
Cottingham, George, Esq. Kersley House, near Bolton, Lancashire
Cotton, Benjamin, Esq. Cambridge
Cotton, C. R. Esq. Lewisham-road
Cotton, Mr. Edward, Rochester
Coulman, R.J. Esq. Wadworth Hall, Yorkshire
Coulman, Thos. Esq. Whitgift Hall, Yorkshire
Coulthurst, J. N. Esq. Gargrave House, Skipton
Court, Mr. Wm. Tolton Mill, Worcestershire
Courtauld, Samuel, Esq. Bocking, Essex
Courteney, Chas. Leslie, Esq. Christ Church College, Oxford
Coutts, Richard J. Esq. Mayor of Falmouth
Cousen, Mr. William, Bradford, Yorkshire
Cove, John, Esq. Bishopsteignton, Devon
Cove, Richard, Esq. Milford, near Salisbury
COVENTRY, Right Hon. the Earl of
Coventry, Charles, Esq. 71, Dean-street, Soho square
Coward, Noah, Esq. Treleigh, Redruth
Coward, W. Esq. Haberdashers-place, Hoxton
Cowie, Benj. G. Esq. Hill House, Esher, Surry
Cowing, Mr. J. James, Library, Barnet. 7 Copies
Cowling, John, Esq. Garden-court, Temple
Cowper, Henry, Esq. Tewin Water, Herts
Cowper, Dr. William, Glasgow College
Cowper, W. Esq. 193, Athol-place, Glasgow
Cox, Edw. S. Esq. Brailsford, near Derby
Cox, Henry, Esq. Park Fields, near Derby
Cox, J. Esq. Leazes-terrace, Newcastle-on-Tyne
Cox, John, Esq. Wrington, Somerset
Cox, Mrs. 3, Grove, Clapham Common
Cox, Thomas, Esq. Friar-gate, Derby
Coyney, W. Hill, Esq. Weston Coyney, near Newcastle-under-Lyne
Cozens, John, Esq. Sprowston Lodge, Norfolk
Craden, Mr. James, Bromley, Kent
Cragg, W. Esq. Threekingham, Lincolnshire
Craggs, Mr. Bookseller, Hull. 7 Copies
Cramer, Rev. Dr. Principal of New Inn Hall, Oxford
Cramer, J. T. Esq. Rathmore, Cork
Crane, John C. Esq. Bewdley
Crane, Mr. James, Cerne Abbas, Dorset
Crary, Mr. Liverpool
Crastie, Shafto, Esq. Crastie Hall
Craufurd, G. W. Esq. King's Coll. Cambridge
CRAVEN, Right Hon. the Earl of
Crawford, Colonel, Goodrich, near Ross
Crawford, W. H. Esq. Dublin
Crawley, Adml. 7, Green Park-buildings, Bath
Crawshaw, Thomas B. Esq. Huddersfield
Crawshay, R. Esq. George-yard, Up. Thames-st.
Crawshay, Wm. jun. Esq. George-yard, Upper Thames-street
Cresswell, John, B. Esq. New-court, Topsham
Crosswell, Mr. J. 121, Crawford-street
Crewdson, T. Esq. Longsight, Manchester
Crewe, Sir G. Bart. *M.P.* Calke Abbey, near Melbourne
Crewe, Rev. Henry, Breadsall, Derby
Crickitt, J. G. Esq. Doctors'-commons
Cringle, Capt. W. Smack Luna of Carron, Liverpool
Crine, William, Esq. Mosley-st. Manchester

Cristie, C. N. Esq. of Durie, 20, York-place, Edinburgh
Critchell, Wm. Esq. Ringwood, Hants
Critchley, T. Esq. 35, Mosley-st. Manchester
Crocker, Edward, Esq. King's-arms-yard
Crocker, P. Esq. Stourton, Wilts
Croft, James Robins, Esq. Liverpool
Croft, Venerable Archdeacon, Saltwood, Kent
Crofts, Mr. W. Bookseller, 19, Chancery-lane
Crofton, G. Esq. 61, St. Bartholomew's-close
Cronstadt, the Naval Library of
Crompton, Benjamin, Esq. Bury, Lancashire
Crompton, James, Esq. Kearsley, Lancashire
Crompton, John W. Esq. Leeds
Crook, James, Esq. Skinner-street, Snow-hill
Crook, John Chas. Esq. 32, Mecklenburg-sq.
Crookes, J. F. Esq. St. Bartholomew's Hospital
Croose, A. Esq. Fine Court, Bloomfield, Somst.
Crop, Jas. Esq. Gringley, near Gainsborough
Cropper, Edward, Esq. Liverpool
Cross, F. Esq. Great Duryard, near Exeter
Cross, Henry, Esq. Gainsborough
Cross, James, Esq. 8, Staple's Inn
Cross, John Brent, Esq. 4, Somerset-st. Bristol
Cross, Mr. J. Bookseller, Leeds. 4 Copies
Cross, Dr. Robert, Wisbeach
Cross, W. S. Esq. *B.A.* St. John's College, Cambridge
Crossfield, Abm. Esq. 91, Whitechapel-road
Crossfield, J. Esq. Abraham's-ct. Edinburgh
Crossland, James, Esq. Fenny, Huddersfield
Crossley, T. Esq. Cromford court, Manchester
Crossley, William, 2, York-street, Manchester
Crowder, R. B. Esq. 11, Pall-mall East
Crowley, Henry, Esq. Alton, Hants
Crowley, Mr. John, Wolverhampton
Crowther, Caleb, Esq. *M.D.* Wakefield
Crowther, Robert, Esq. Quay-st. Manchester
Croxon, Richard, Esq. Oswestry
Cruikshank, William, Esq. Furnival's Inn
Crum, Mr. John, 51, Cochran-street, Glasgow
Cryke, Capt. R. *R.N.* Albemarle Cottage, Stoke, Devon
Cudworth, John, Esq. Briggate, Leeds
Cuff, J. Esq. Freemasons' Tavern, Gt. Queen st.
Culme, Mrs. Wellington Court, Wellington
Culledge, Charles, Esq. March, Cambridge
Cumber, C. Esq. 13, Dickenson-st. Manchester
Cuming, J. Esq. Grey's Wood, Haslemere
Cummin, William, Esq. Kilmarnock
Cumming, Miss, Hill House, Taplow, near Maidenhead
Cundall, B. Esq. Norwich
Cunliffe, Col. Sir R. Bart. Acton, Denbighshire
Cunliffe, Thos. Esq. Church-st. Manchester
Cunningham, Capt. *R.N.* Battramsley Lodge, Lymington
Cunningham, J. Esq. 24, Upper Harley-street
Cunningham, J. Esq. Rodney-place, Clifton
Cunningham, R. Esq. Old Swan-wharf, Tower-st.
Cunningham, Mr. Thomas, Bookseller, Ashton-under-Lyne. 18 Copies
Cunow, Rev. G. A. Dukinfield
Curling, Daniel, Esq. Canonbury, Islington
Curling, Joseph, Esq. Herne Hill
Curling, Wm. Esq. Denmark-hill
Curling, Rev. William, 41, Trinity-square
Curling, Wm. Esq. Grove, Blackheath
Curran, Miss, Eshton Hall, near Skipton, Yorkshire
Currie & Bowman, Messrs. Bksllrs. Newcastle-upon-Tyne. 19 Copies
Currey, G. Esq. St. John's College, Cambridge
Currey, Robt. Esq. 106, Fleet-street
Curry, Mr. W. jun. & Co. Booksellers, 9, Upper Sackville-street, Dublin. 2 Copies
Curteis, Rev. Thomas, Seven Oaks, Kent
Curtis, Mr. Richard, Basingstoke
Curtis, A. T. Esq. St. John's Coll. Cambridge
Curtis, Richard, Esq. Acre-lane, Brixton
Curtis, Captain Timothy, *R.N.* Exmouth
Curtis, T. A. Esq. 8, Tokenhouse-yard
Curtis, William, Esq. Alton, Hants
Curtois, Rev. R. G. Chaplain to the Forces, Chatham
Cust, Richard, Esq. Carlisle
Cutbush, Mr. R. J. Maidstone
Cutler, Henry, Esq. Sidmouth, Devon
Cuttell, Josiah, Esq. Holmefirth, Huddersfield
Cutten, Charles, Esq. Clapham Rise
Cutto, A. W. Esq. 38, Canterbury-sq. Southwrk

D.

Dakins, Rev. Dr. Dean's-yard, Westminster
Dale, John, Esq. North Shields
Dalgleish, Andrew, Esq. Ingram-st. Glasgow
Dalgleish, Mr. G. 85, St. Vincent-st. Glasgow
DALHOUSIE, Right Hon. the Earl of
Dallas, Lieut.-Gen. Sir T. *G.C.B.* 36, Brock-street, Bath
Dallaway, J. Esq. *R.N.* Buckland, near Dover
Dalrymple, Lady Frances, 23, Up. Wimpole-st 2 Copies
Dalrymple, Lieut.-Col. Sir Adolphus, J. Bart. 129, Park-street
Dalston, John, jun. Esq. The Grange, nr. York
Dalton, Francis B. Esq. Huddersfield
Dalton, Jas. E. Esq. *B.A.* Queen's College, Cambridge
Dalton, Mr. W. H. Booksr. 28, Cockspur-st.
Dalway, Lieut. N. *R.N.* Sutherland Fort, Hythe
Daly, Mr. Denis, Lime-street, Liverpool
Damer, Hon. H. D. Milton Abbey, Blandford
Dancie, George Robert, Esq. 2, Mountjoy-street east, Dublin
Dando, Josh. Esq. Horfield Lodge
Daniel, Mr. Geo. Abergavenny
Daniel, Henry, Esq. 16, York-place, Clifton
Daniel, Thos. sen. Esq. Alderman of Bristol
Daniell, Edward, Esq. Colchester
Daniell, J. S. Esq. Blandford, Dorset
Danks, Mr. S. Bookseller, Bewdley. 7 Copies
Dansey, John, Esq. Blandford, Dorset
Dansey, Rev. Wm. Donhead St. Andrew's, Wilts
Danson, Edw. B. Esq. 2, New Broad-street
Danson, Miss, Preston, Lancashire
Darby, J. Esq. 10, Gt. George-st. Westminster
D'Arcy, Lt.-Col. Milford House, Lymington
Darell, E. Esq. Cale Hill, Charing, Kent
Darell, John, Esq. Jersey
Darlot, J. Esq. 39, East Cliff, Brighton
Darley, A. H. Esq. Christ Coll. Cambridge
Darling, Mr. Jas. Booksr. 22, Little Queen-st.
DARNLEY, late Right Hon. Earl of
Darter, Wm. Silver, Esq. Reading
DARTMOUTH, Right Hon. the Earl of
Darwell, Thos. Esq. Ridgefield, Manchester
Dashmen, Mr. Feltham, Middlesex
Dashwood, H. Esq. Corpus Christi College, Oxford
Dashwood, M. Esq. Downing Coll. Cambridge
Daubeny, E. Esq. Magdalen College, Oxford
Daubez, L. C. Esq. Truro
Davenport, C. Esq. Tunstall, Staffordshire
Davenport, Mr. D. A., Robert Napier steamer, Liverpool
Davey, Francis, Esq. Topsham, Devon
Davey, William, Esq. Redruth
Davids, J. Esq. West Cowes
Davidson, Mr. Rt. Brig Catherine, Liverpool
Davidson, Robt. Esq. 28, York-pl. Edinburgh
Davidson, Wm. Esq. 1, South Frederick-st. Glasgow
Davies, Rev. D. Studland, Dorset
Davies, Rev. G. Rochester
Davies, Henry, Esq. Monmouth
Davies, Mr. Jas. North and South American Coffee-house, Threadneedle-street
Davies, Mr. Js. Booksr. Holywell. 2 Copies
Davies, Miss, Oswestry
Davies, Mr. James, Bookseller, Holywell
Davies, Capt. Richard L. *R.N.* Penzance
Davies, Mr. R. Post-office, Merthyr Tydvil
Davies, R. Esq. 126, Holborn-hill
Davies, S. Esq. Wye, near Ashford, Kent
Davies, Wm. Esq. Merthyr Tydvil
Davis, Mr. A. J. Bull's-head-ct. Newgate-st.
Davis, Benj. Esq. 33, Cannon-st. Manchester
Davis, Dr. David, Park-st. Bristol
Davis, Mr. D. Allen-st. Goswell-street
Davis, Geo. jun. Esq. Mill-lane, Tooley-street
Davis, Gideon, Esq. Hamond Hill, Chatham
Davis, Horatio Nelson, Esq. Fenchurch-st.
Davis, Major H. J. 1, Devonshire-bldgs. Bath
Davis, Jas. Esq. Bridford, Dorset
Davis, W. Esq. Gravesend
Davy, Rev. C. W. Parkstone, Dorset
Davy, Rev. Dr. Martin, *F.R.* & *L.S.* Master of Caius College, Cambridge
Davy, John, Esq. St. Christopher's
Davys, Mr. John, Ashby-de-la-Zouch
Davys, Mr. Thomas, Ashby-de-la-Zouch
Dawes, H. Esq. 5, Cambridge-ter. Regent's-pk
Dawkins, Henry, Esq. Sandgate, Kent
Dawson, Dr. Jas. Mount-pleasant, Liverpool
Dawson, John, Esq. 9, Billiter-square
Dawson, J. Esq. Walton's-bldgs. Manchester
Dawson, John, Esq. Newcastle-upon-Tyne
Dawson, Mr. John, 25, Albemarle-street
Dawson, W. A. Esq. Abercrombie-terrace, Liverpool
Day, D. J. Esq. Rochester
Day, Mr. Frederick, Hemel Hempstead
Day, Hon. Judge, Dublin
Day, J. Esq. 3, Water-lane, Tower-street
Day, John, Esq. Beccles, Suffolk
Day, T. Esq. 9, Three-crown-sq. Southwark
Day, T. H. Esq. Baley Hill, Rochester
Day, Wm. Stuart, Esq. West Cowes
Day, W. W. Esq. Rochester
Day, William, Esq.
Daynes, Mr. John, Norwich
Deacon, Charles, E. Esq. Southampton
Deacon, H. Esq. Portsmouth
Deacon, J. Esq. Mabledon, Tunbridge Wells
Deacon, Saml. Esq. 3, Walbrook
Deake, Chas. Esq. Lamb-pl. New Cut, Bristol
Deakin, Miss Jane, Wem.
Deakin, Thomas, Esq. Adbaston House, near Eccleshall
Deakins, Wm. Esq. Stafford-row, Buckingham-gate
Dealy, Jas. Esq. Stock Exchange
Dean, G. Esq. Goswell-road
Dean, Thos. Esq. King-street, Manchester
Deane, Rev. H. Gillingham, near Shaftesbury

De Burgh, Hubert, Esq. West Drayton
Deck, Isaiah, Esq. Cambridge
Deedes, Wm. Esq. Sandling, Kent
Deedes, Rev. C. Hinxhill, Kent
DE GREY, Right Hon. the Earl
De Henry, Spencer, Esq. 8, Upper Grosvenor-street, and West Cowes
Deighton & Moxon, Messrs. Booksellers, York. 2 Copies
Deighton, Messrs. J. & J. W. Booksellers, Cambridge
Deighton, Mr. H. Bookr. Worcester. 44 Copies
De Jersey & Co. Messrs. Lower Mosley-street, Manchester
De Jersey, Dr. Romford, Essex
Delafosse, Rev. Danl. *A.M.* Richmond-green
De-la-Motte, Col. Peter, Fern Acres, Gerrard's-cross
De Lannoy, Richard, Esq. George-st. Manchstr.
Delavaud, G. Esq. 18, Marlboro'-bldgs. Bath
De Leon, D. M. Esq. Throgmorton-street
De Lisle, Consul-General of Rio de la Plata, Antwerp
Delmar, W. B. Esq. St. John's Coll. Cambridge
Delves, William, Esq. St. Christopher's
Dempster, R. Esq. 6, Marlboro'-pl. Brighton
Dempster, Mr. James, 6, South Hanover-st.
DENBIGH, Right Hon. the Earl of
Dench, L. Esq. Ely, Cambridge
Dendy, S. Esq. 16, Montagu-st. Russell-sq.
Denman, Thos. Esq. 23, Harley-street
Denmark, Dr. Alexander, Torquay, Devon
Denniston, Wm. Esq. Kelvin-grove, Glasgow
Dent, William, Esq. Worcester
Derby Permanent Library
Derby Philosophical Society
Derham, Robt. Esq. Leeds
Dering, Sir E. Bart. Surrenden-Dering, Kent
Desanges, F. Esq. Weaver-st. Spitalfields
DE SAUMAREZ, Right Hon. Admiral Lord, *G.C.B.*
Des Granges, Peter, Esq. 33, Cockspur-street
De Teissier, Mrs. Epsom, Surrey
Devas, Wm. Esq. Lawrence-lane
Devizes Literary Institution
Devon and Exeter Institution, Exeter
DEVONSHIRE, His Grace the Duke of
D'Ew, Dyer, Esq. Acre-lane
Dewe, Rev. S. Rochester
Dewer, Messrs. E. & R. 16, Old-street
Dewson, Mr. Francis, Packet Ship, C. Brandon, Liverpool
Dibsdall, Silas, Esq. Brunswick-sq. Bristol
Dickins, Thos. Esq. Vale Lodge, Leatherhead
Dickenson, Mr. George, Buckland, near Dover
Dickinson, Harvey, Esq. East India House
Dickinson, John, Esq. Lower-st. Islington
Dickinson, Miss, Farley Hill, Berks
Dickinson, Wm. Esq. East India House
Dickinson, J. Esq. Bartley Lodge, Southampton
Dickinson, Jonathan, Esq. Water-lane, Leeds
Dickinson, W. J. Esq. 5, Brunswick-pl. Leeds
Dickson, R. Esq. 3, Charlotte-row, Mansion House
Dighton, Major-Gen. J. Newland, Glostershire
Dillon, Col. 6, Chester-ter. Regent's-park
Dinsdale, J. Esq. Brunswick-pl. Regent's-pk.
Dinsdale, W. J. Esq. Brunswick-place, Regent's-park
Dinning, Henry, Esq. Newlands
Disbrowe, Sir Edward C., *K.C.H.* Envoy Extraordinary and Minister Plenipotentiary to Sweden

Dithelm, John, Esq. Pool-st. Manchester
Dix, Mr. John, Wellington
Dix, Robt. Esq. Ely, Cambridge
Dixon, Benjamin, Esq. Wakefield
Dixon, D. G. Esq. Maidenhead
Dixon, Dixon, Esq. Benton, Northumberland
Dixon, Geo. R. Esq. 15, King's-arms-yard
Dixon, John, Esq. Carlisle
Dixon, Peter, Esq. Carlisle
Dixon, Rev. W. H. Sutton-on-the-Forest, near York
Dixon, W. S. Esq. Manchester Basin, Liverpool
Dixon, Wm. Esq. 25, Chancery-lane
Dobbin, Captain, Milford
Dobbs and Co. Messrs. 134, Fleet-street
Dobie, Wm. Hy. Esq. 4, Queen Ann-street, Liverpool
Dobinson, Wm. Esq. Carlisle
Dobree, Augustus, Esq. Guernsey
Dobree, Rev. J. G. *M.A.* Holton, Suffolk
Dobson, A. H. Esq. 52, Fore-st. Cripplegate
Dobson, Benj. Esq. Park-place, Leeds
Dobson, John, Esq. New Bridge-street, Newcastle-upon-Tyne
Dobson, John, Esq. Secretary to Lloyd's
Dobson, Lieut.-Col. Mortimer, Berks
Dobson, Rev. John, Cornsbro' Vicarage, Doncaster
Dobson, Vice-Admiral Man, North Kilworth
Dodd, Mr. Postmaster, Woburn
Dodington, W. M. Esq. Horsington, Somerset
Dods, Dr. R. G. Rochester
Dodsleys, John, Esq. Skegby, Notts
Dodsworth, George, Esq. Gate Fulford, near York
Dodsworth, Rev. William, 3, Clarence-terrace, Regent's-park
Donaldson, Mr. J. 17, Exchange-sq. Glasgow
Donaldson, Mr. J. 105, St. Vincent-st. Glasgow
Doncaster Subscription Library
Donkin, Bryan, Esq. 6, Paragon, New Kent-rd.
Donkin, Henry, Esq. Durham
Dorehill, W. A. Esq. Chalk, near Gravesend
Dorling & Son, Messrs. Booksellers, Epsom. 17 Copies
Dorrington, W. Esq. St. Ann's-sq. Manchester
Dosseter, Mr. Thomas, 13, Poultry
Doughty, Ed. Esq. Upton House, near Poole
Douglas, Adml. J. E. 34, Charles-st. Berkley-sq.
Douglas, Henry Alex. Esq. Broad-street
Douglas, Jas. Esq. Great Yarmouth, Norfolk
Douglas, Jas. Esq. 7, Norfolk-st. Manchester
Douglas, Rev. P. H. Epsom, Surrey
Douglass, J. A. Esq. 1, Verulam-buildings, Gray's-inn
Douglass, J. H. Esq. Back-square, Manchester
Douglas, Mr. R. of Tain
Dove, Mrs. Lower Hill House, Ipswich
Dover, Jas. Esq. Boscombe Lodge, Hants
Dover, J. Esq. Three Cranes-whf. Southwk.-brdg.
Dover Philosophical Institution
Dowell, John, Esq. Wine-street, Bristol
Downes, John Fox, Esq. Ashford House, Salop
Downey, Lieut. John, *R.N.* Commander of H. M. Packet Briseis, Falmouth
Downs Messrs. Wm. & Co. Castletown, Isle of Man
DOWNSHIRE, Most Noble the Marquis of
Dowson, C. Esq. Limehouse Bridge Dock
Doyle, Captain John, Ship Ontario
Doyle, Genl. Sir John, Bart. *K.C.B.* 4, Somerset-street
Doyle, Rev. Thomas, London-road, Southwark

Drake, John, Esq. Back Hall, Bristol
Drake, Sir Thomas Trayton Fuller Eliott, Bart. Nutwell Court, near Exeter
Drax, J. M. S. E. Esq. Charboro' Park, near Blandford, Dorset. 2 Copies
Dreury, Jno. jun. Esq. Ashbourne-road, Derby
Drew, Benjamin, Esq. Bermondsey
Drew, Henry, Esq. 6, Nelson-square
Drew, J. W. Esq. Southampton
Drew, Simcoe, Esq. the Grange, Devon
Drew, Thomas, Esq. St. Christopher's
Dring & Fage, Messrs. 20, Tooley-street
Drinkald, John, Esq. Trinity-square, Tower
Driver, Mr. R. Southampton
Driver, Richard, Esq. Leeds
Driver, S. W. Esq. Farncombe, Godalming
Drummond, H. Home, Esq. of Blair Drummond, 128, Prince's-street, Edinburgh
Drury, Mr. J. Bookseller, Gainsboro'. 5 Copies
Dryden, —, Esq. Leith
Drysdale, Mr. A. Vulcan Steamer, Liverpool
Drysdale, Wm. C. Esq. 102, Leadenhall-st.
Dubbins, Mr. Edw. Regent Cottage, Brighton
DUBLIN, Right Hon. the Lord Mayor of (Arthur Perrin, Esq.)
Dublin, Royal Society of
Duboulay, Thos. Esq. Charlton, near Donhead, Wilts
Duckworth, Ellice, Esq. 42, Spring-gardens, Manchester
Dudman, Capt. Jos. *H.C.S.* Charlton, Kent
Duff, J. Gordon, Esq. 13, Harley-street
Duff, A. Esq. Advocate, 25, Charlotte-square, Edinburgh
Duff, T. A. Esq. 25, Melville-st. Edinburgh
Duge, C. J. Esq. 43, Princes-st. Rotherhithe
Duke, Dr. Patrick, 13, Great George-street
Dumaresq, Wm. Esq. Pelham-place, Alton
Dumbleton, Thos. Esq. 13, Upper Wimpole-st.
Dumernil fils, P. Esq. 66, Rue de la Vicomté Rouen
Dumfries Subscription Library
Dunbar, John, Esq. Limehouse
DUNCAN, Right Hon. the Lord Viscount
Duncan, Captain, *R.N.* Park-terrace, Blackheath
Duncan, George, Esq. Dundee
Duncan, Henry, Esq. 9, Cornwall-terrace
Duncan, Mr. James, Bookseller, Paternoster-row. 2 Copies
Duncan, Mr. Matthew, 50, Gordon-st. Glasgow
Duncan, Peter, Esq. Peter-st. Dundee
Dunckner & Humblot, Messrs. Booksellers, Berlin. 6 Copies
Duncombe, Lady Louisa, 23, Cavendish-sq.
Duncombe, Thomas Slingsby, Esq. *M.P.* 13, Arlington-street, Piccadilly
Duncombe, Hon. Wm. *M.P.* 23, Cavendish-square
Dundas, Hon. Robert, Somerset House
Dundas, Rear-Adm. Sir Thos. *K.C.B.* Albion-place, Reading
Dunlop, C. Esq. *M.P.* Talcross, Port Glasgow
Dunlop, Henry, Esq. Craigton, Glasgow
Dunlop, J. Esq. *M.P.* Dumfries
Dunlop, James, Esq. Port Glasgow
Dunn, Mr. G. Eldon-sq. Newcastle-upon-Tyne
Dunn, Mr. T. 6, Saville-place, Newcastle-upon-Tyne
Dunnett, Wm. Esq. King-street, Manchester
Dunston, John, Esq. Kaisfield, Devon
Durance, Mr. Wm. 1, Norfolk-place
Durand, P. Esq. Taunton

D'Urban, Capt. W. J. 25th Regt. Newport, near Exeter
D'Urban, Capt. W. D. *R.N.* Warminster
DURHAM, Right Hon. the Earl of
DURHAM, Right Rev. the Lord Bishop of
Durham Rev. the Dean and Chapter of
——— Subscription Library
Durrant, George, Esq. Norwich
Dyke, Rev. H. Hinton Rectory, near Brackley
Dyke, P. H. Esq. Lullingstone
Dykes, James, Esq. Port Glasgow
Dysart, Wm. Esq. Mile End Hall, near Stockport
Dyson, Rev. Francis, Tidworth, Wilts
Dyson, Colonel T. F. Manchester-square
Dyson, Thos. Esq. Diss, Norfolk
Dyson, Thos. Esq. Downham-market, Norfolk

E.

Eade, Mr. Matthew H. Redruth
Eadson, Saml. Esq. 16, Newmarket-buildings, Manchester
Eagle, Thomas, Esq. Rodercross-street
Eagle, William, Esq. Block House, Gravesend
Earnshaw, John, Esq. Hull
EAST INDIES, Honourable COMPANY of Merchants Trading to. 40 Copies
Easton, Mr. John, Brunswick Dock-master, Liverpool
Eastwood, Joshua, Esq. Meltham
Eastwood, Samuel, jun. Esq. Huddersfield
Ebsworth, G. T. Esq. Clare Hall, Cambridge
Eccles, Mr. W. Bookseller, Woodstock
Echam, Thomas, Esq. Cork
Eckstein & Son, Messrs. 13, High Holborn
Ecroyd, Mr. Benjamin, Bradford, Yorkshire
Eddowes, Mr. John, Bookseller, Shrewsbury. 4 Copies
Ede, Mr. R. B. Bookseller, Dorking. 4 Copies
Eden, J. Esq. Mount Pleasant, Liverpool
Eden, Rev. John, 8, Gloucester-place, Clifton
Eden, Ralph, Esq. Clerk to the Privy Seal, 26, Abingdon-street
Eden, Hon. & Rev. W. Beaksbourne, Kent
Edgell, H. Esq. 13, South-square, Gray's Inn.
EDINBURGH, Rt. Hon. the Lord Provost of
EDINBURGH, Rt. Hon. the Lord President of the Court of Session
————, Solicitors Library of
Edleston, Mr. Thomas, Cambridge
Edmeades, W. Esq. Norsted, Kent
Edmed, James, Esq. Gravesend
Edmeed, Jedediah Kerie, Esq. St. Christopher's
Edmonds, Charles, Esq. Change-alley
Edmonds, Christ. Esq. Bridge-st. Southwark
Edmonds, Mr. A. Booksllr. Shifnal. 3 Copies
Edmonds, Mr. W. Sittingbourne, Kent
Edmonstone, C. Esq. Trinity Coll. Cambridge
Edwards, Capt. Richd. *R.N.* Ringwood, Hants.
Edwards, Mr. E. Oswestry
Edwards, G. Esq. Halifax
Edwards, H. Esq. 53, Tavistock-square
Edwards, J. Esq. 36, Portman-pl. Edgeware-rd.
Edwards, J. B. Esq. Southwold, Suffolk
Edwards, James, Esq. Oswestry
Edwards, Mrs. M. Rhuabon
Edwards, Sam. C. Esq. Long Ashton, Bristol
Edwards, T. G. Esq. 8, York-ter. Regent's-pk.
Edwards, Mr. Thos. H.M. Steam Packet Office
Edwards, T. L. Esq. Trinity Coll. Cambridge
Edwards, Mr. Wm. Bookseller, Ave Maria-la. 2 Copies
Egan, Rev. J. Cork
Egan, T. S. Esq. Caius College, Cambridge
Egerton, F. T. Esq. Roche Court, Wilts
Egerton, Mr. Thos. Bookseller, Charing-cross
Egginton, John, Esq. Hull
Ekins, Vice-Adm. Sir C. *K.C.B.* Bishopsteignton, Devon
Elderton, Edward, M. Esq. 40, Queen-square
Eldrid, Edward, Esq. Fore-street, City
Elkins, Alfred, Esq. Foley-pl. Portland-place
Elkins, John, Esq. 59, Newman-street
Elkins, Mr. W. H. Bookseller, 85, Lombard-st. 2 Copies
Ellerman, Charles F. Esq. Consul-General for Hanover, Antwerp
Ellice, Capt. A. *R.N.* H.M.S. Ocean, Sheerness
Ellice, Rt. Hon. Edw. *M.P.* 3, Cleveland-sq
Ellin, Thomas, Esq. Sheffield
Ellinthorpe, J. S. Esq. 65, Brook-st. Chorlton-on-Medlock, Manchester
Elliot, Hon. Captain George, *R.N.*
Elliot, Hon. Henry, Trinity Coll. Cambridge
Elliot, Lieut.-Col. Barley House, Plymouth
Elliott, Rev. John, Minister, Peebles
Elliott, Mr. Ashford
Elliott, Mr. William, Speenhamland, Berks
Ellis, Charles, Esq. 25, Soho-square
Ellis, Mr. Henry, Exeter
Ellis, J. Esq. Barming, near Maidstone
Ellis, J. Esq. Wateringbury, Kent
Ellis, Mrs. 52, Connaught-terrace
Ellis, R. Esq. 4, Fitzwilliam's-square, Dublin
Ellis, Samuel, Esq. Stock Exchange
Ellis, Mr. William, 34, Old Steyne, Brighton
Ellis, Wynn, Esq. *M.P.* 30, Cadogan-place
Ellison, J. Esq. 2, Four Yards, Manchester
Ellison, Michael, Esq. Sheffield
Ellswood, A. Esq. Bungay, Suffolk
Elmslie, Mrs. Epsom, Surrey
Elrington, Major J. H. Tower of London
Elson, John, Esq. Bodmin
Elton, Chas. A. Esq. 6, Prince's-bdgs. Clifton
Elton, Capt. H. *R.N.* Lower-crescent, Clifton
Elton, John, Esq. Redland, Bristol
Elton, M. E. Esq. Widworthy Court, Devon
Elwes, Dudley, C. C. Esq. Stoke Bishop, Glos.
Elwes, J. H. Esq. Christ Church, Oxford
Elwin, W. Esq. Caius College, Cambridge
Emery, Miss Sarah, Glastonbury
Emery, Mr. St. Neots
Emly, Henry, Esq. 2, Middle-Temple-lane
Enderby, Mrs. Charles, Blackheath. 2 Copies
England, Rev. Dr. Stafford, Dorset
Ensor, Edmund, Esq. 125, Oxford-street
ERROLL, Right Hon. the D. Countess of
ERSKINE, Rt. Hon. Lady Augusta. 2 Copies
Erskine, Mrs. Bromley, Kent
Erskine, Right Hon. Thos. 1, Cumberland-pl.
Essell, George, Esq. Rochester
Essington, Wm. Esq. Malvern, Worcestershire
Estcourt, Rev. E. W. Newnton Rectory, near Tetbury
Estcourt, T. H. S. B. Esq. New Park, Devizes
ESTERHAZY, His Highness the Prince
Estridge, George, Esq. St. Christopher's
Etty, Walter, Esq. 31, Lombard-street
Euston, Mr. William, Rochester
Evans, Capt. Geo. *R.N.* 2, Wilton-crescent
Evans, Charles, Esq. Brown-street, Manchester
Evans, David, Esq. Bank, Merthyr Tydvil
Evans, Edw. jun. Esq. Basseterre, St. Christphr's
Evans, H. P. Esq. Novadd
Evans, Hugh Robert, Esq. Ely, Cambridge
Evans, J. Esq. 13, Tooke's-court, Chancery-la.
Evans, Mr. John, Mortimer-st. Cavendish-sq.
Evans, Mr. Josiah, Aberystwith. 2 Copies
Evans, Rev. John, *A.M.* Whitchurch, Salop
Evans, John M. Esq. St. Christopher's
Evans, Mr. M. Bookslr. Newport, Monmouth
Evans, Samuel, Esq. Mary's-gate, Derby
Evans, Thomas, Esq. Glastonbury
Evans, Thos. Esq. 60, Cannon-st. Manchester
Evans, William, Esq. 41, Grosvenor-place
Evans, Wm. Esq. *M.P.* Allestree, near Derby
Eveleigh, Samuel, Esq. 1, Plymouth-grove, Manchester
Everard, James, Esq. Lowestoft, Suffolk
Everard, Rev. Edw. *D.D.* the Wick, Brighton
Everest, J. B. Esq. Bodmin
Everett, B. Esq. Warminster, Wilts
Everington, William, Esq. 10, Ludgate-hill
Everitt, William, Esq. Catton, Norfolk
Every, Sir H. Bart. Egginton Hall, near Derby
Every, J. Esq. Old Park, near Dover
Ewart, John, Esq. Exchange-alley, Liverpool
Ewing, Sir K. Wm. Blythewood-sq. Glasgow
Ewing, Mr. R. John-Wood Steamer, Liverpool
EXETER, Most Noble the D. Marchioness of
———— Ladies' Book Club
———— Public Select Library
Eyles, Mr. George, Speenhamland, Berks
Eyres, W. Esq. Leeds
Eyson, P. B. Esq. 5, Ardwick-green, Manchester

F.

Faber, Chas. W. Esq. 89, Chancery-lane
Fagg, Thomas, Esq. 14, Wilmington-square
Fagg, R. Esq. Wilmington-square
Fairbain, P. Esq. Park-square, Leeds
Fairbairn, John, Esq. Newcastle-upon-Tyne
Fairbarn, Wm. Esq. Manchester
Fairbrother, P. Esq. 17, Gracechurch-street
Fairclough, Wm. Esq. Tabley-st. Liverpool
Fairrie, John, Esq. Church-lane, Whitechapel
Faith, G. Esq. 36, Mincing-lane
Faithful, Hy. Esq. Ship-street, Brighton
Faithfull, E. C. Esq. 5, King's-rd. Bedford-rw.
Falconer, A. Esq. Falconer Hall, Edinburgh
Falconer, Arch. Esq. Provost of Port Glasgow
Fallows, John, Esq. Stone, Staffordshire
FALMOUTH, Right Hon. the Earl of
Falmouth Public Library
Fancourt, Major, *M.P.* 1, Old Palace-yard
Fane, Capt. J. H. *R.N.* Green Park-buildings, Bath
Faraday, Mr. Robt. 114, Wardour-street, Soho
Farebrother, Chas. Esq. Alderman of London
Farmer, Thos. W. Esq. 79, Borough
Farnaby, Rev. Sir C. Bart. Wickham Court, Kent
FARNBOROUGH, Right Hon. Lord
Farquhar, James, Esq. Woburn-place
Farr, Fred. Wm. Esq. Beccles, Suffolk
Farr, W. Esq. Carno, Montgomeryshire
Farrand, F. Esq. Almonbury, Huddersfield
Farrand, Robt. Esq. 3, Park-street. 2 Copies
Farrer, Jas. Wm. Esq. 7, John-st. Berkeley-sq.
Farrer, Wm. Esq. Saham, Norfolk
Farrer, Wm. L. Esq. 66, Lincoln's-inn-fields
Farrow, Samuel, Esq. Diss, Norfolk
Fauke, W. Esq. Great Winchester-street, Torrington-square
Faulkner, Mr. B. Anglesea Hotel, Gosport

Fauntleroy, R. Esq. 2, Paragon, New Kent-rd.
Fauntleroy, Mr. Robt. Bookslr. Leadenhall-st.
Favell, Edward, Esq. Cambridge
Fawcett, R. M. Esq. Cambridge
Fayle, Rev. R. Wareham, Dorset
Fearnall, Wm. Esq. Union Dock, Limehouse. 3 Copies
Fearne, Joseph, Esq. Angel-court
Fearns, Miss, Acorn Bank, Westmorland
Featherstone, W. Esq. 17, Vere-street
Fector, J. M. Esq. *M.P.* Kersney Abbey, near Dover
Fedden, Olgar, Esq. Merrywood Hall, Bristol
Feilden, Rev. —, Langley, near Derby
Fell, M. E. Esq. Mitcham, Surrey
Fell, Rev. H. F. Cloudesley Parsonage, Islington
Fell, Jacob, Esq. Huddersfield
Fell, M. E. Esq. Mitcham, Surrey
Fellowes, Capt. Thos. *R.N.* Bradford Leigh, Wilts
Fellowes, Hon. Newton, *M.P.* Bryanston-sq.
Fenn, Joseph, Esq. Newgate-street
Fenn, Mr. Rob. Bookr. Charing Cross. 4 Copies
Fennell, Rev. Samuel, *B.D.* Queen's College, Cambridge
Fenton, Captain Thomas Charles, Chepstow
Fenton, Jas. C. Esq. Huddersfield
Fenwick, John, Esq. North Shields
Ferguson, Col. 48, Wilton-crescent
Ferguson, Captain James, Ship Henry Hoyle, Liverpool
Ferguson, J. Esq. Carlisle
Ferguson, John, Esq. 10, Cooper-st. Manchstr
Ferguson, Gen. Sir R. C. *M.P. G.C.B.* 5, Bolton-row
Ferguson, Joseph, Esq. Abbey-street, Carlisle
Fergusson, David, Esq. 15, Hutchinson-street, Glasgow
Fergusson, Right Hon. R. Cutlar, *M.P.* 17, Great Cumberland-street
Fernie, Joseph, Esq. Leadenhall-street
Ferrand, W. Esq. Harden Grange, near Bingley
FERRARD, Right Hon. Lord Viscount
Ferrier, J. Esq. Port Glasgow
Ferrier, R. E. Esq. 18, Park-ter. Regency-pk.
Ferris, John, Esq. Pydar-street, Truro
Ferris, Rich. Esq. 10, Richmond Hill, Clifton
Festing, Capt. H. Parkstone, near Poole, Dorset
FEVERSHAM, Right Hon. Lord
Few, Chas. Esq. Henrietta-st. Covent-garden
Few, Robert, Esq. Doughty-street
Ficklin, T. T. Esq. Cambridge
Field, John, Esq. Throgmorton-street
Fielden, J. Esq. *M.P.* 5, Peel-st. Manchester
Fielding, Messrs. George & G. H. Hull
Fielding, Rev. Hy. George-street, Manchester
Fielding, James, Esq. 6, New Cannon-street, Manchester
Fiftieth Regiment of Foot, Library of
Figgins, Vincent, Esq. West-st. Smithfield
Filmer, Sir E. Bart. East Sutton Park, Kent
Finch, Chas. jun. Esq. Cambridge
Finch, Mr. W. Rochester
Finch, W. Esq. Corpus Christi Coll. Cambridge
Findlay, R. S. Esq. Virginia-bldgs. Glasgow
Finlay, Alex. S. Esq. 8, St. Helen's-place
Finlay & Co. Messrs. 2 Copies
Finlay, Kirkman, Esq. Queen-street, Glasgow
Finnie, Archibald, Esq. Kilmarnock
Finnis, T. Q. Esq. 79, Great Tower-street
Firmin, Mr. P. V. 153, Strand

Firth, James F. Esq. Guildhall
Fisher, D. Esq. O.S.C. 15, Forth-st. Edinb.
Fisher, Edw. Esq. Longroyd Bridge, Huddersfield
Fisher, Francis, Esq. Jesus Coll. Cambridge
Fisher, Capt. J. *R.N.* Harbour-master's-office, St. Catherine's
Fisher, J. T. Esq. Otto Wells, Huddersfield
Fisher, Jas. Esq. Great Yarmouth
Fisher, John, Esq. Park Villa, Charlotte-street, Bristol
Fisher, Rev. G. J. Winfrith Rectory, Dorset
Fisher, Mr. T. M. 22, Tib-lane, Manchester
FITZCLARENCE, Lord Frederick
Fitzgerald, Rear Admiral, 26, Park-st. Bath
Fitz Gibbon, Hon. Col. R. H. *M.P.* 44, Belgrave-square
FITZMAURICE, Lord Henry P. Trinity College, Cambridge
FITZWILLIAM, Right Hon. the Earl of. 2 Copies
Fitzwilliam, Hon. George Wentworth, Trinity College, Cambridge
Fitzwilliam, Hon. W. T. S. Wentworth, Trinity College, Cambridge
Flack, C. J. Esq. Cavendish-bridge, Derby
Flack, Edward, Esq. Full-street, Derby
Fleck, Hugh, Esq. Basseterre, St. Christopher's
Fleischmann, Mr. C. A. Bookseller, Munich
Fleeming, Vice-Admiral, Hon. C. E. Sheerness
Fleming, Jas. P. Esq. 62, Miller-st. Glasgow
Fleming, Thos. Esq. Broughton View, Manchester
Flesham, P. F. Esq. Kent-street, Manchester
Fletcher, A. Esq. 6, Blythewood-sq. Glasgow
Fletcher, Mr. A. Redbridge, near Southampton
Fletcher and Co. Messrs. Paternoster-row
Fletcher, Chas. Esq. Gloucester
Fletcher, Captain, E. C. 1st Life Guards, 18, Sussex-place, Regent's-park
Fletcher, J. Esq. 6, New Broad-st. Manchester
Fletcher, Jas. Esq. 6, New Brown-street
Fletcher, John, Esq. Shiffnal
Fletcher, John Henry, Esq. Surveyor-General, Post Office, York
Fletcher, Jos. Esq. Union Dock, Limehouse. 3 Copies
Fletcher, Robt. Esq. Ashley Lodge, Montpelier, Bristol
Flew, John, Esq. Clear Mount, Weymouth
Flood, C. Esq. Bramble Hill, Honiton, Devon
Flood, John, Esq. Grace-street, Leeds
Flood, J. D. Esq. 42, Tothill-st. Westminster
Flooks, J. H. Esq. The Mount, near Wilton, Wilts
Flower, Henry, Esq. 4, King's-arms-yard
Flower, Rev. Mr. York
FOLEY, Right Hon. Lord
Fooks, T. B. Esq. Dartford, Kent
Footner, Wm. Esq. Romsey, Hants
Forbes, Sir Chas. Bart. 9, Fitzroy-square
Forbes, David, Esq. Douglas, Isle of Man
Forbes, G. Esq. 2, Mansion-house-place
Forbes, George, Esq. West Coates, Edinburgh
Forbes, J. H. Esq. Golder's Hill, Hampstead
Forbes, Sir J. Stuart, Bart. of Pitsligo, Greenhill, Edinburgh
Ford, Mr. W. Wolverhampton
Ford, Rich. Esq. Heavitree House, near Exeter
Forder, Robt. Esq. 4, Bugle-st. Southampton
Forester, Dr. Rich. F. Abbott's Hill, Derby
Formby, Rev. J. Frinsbury, Kent
Forrest, Sir Digory, Exmouth, Devon

Forrest, Mr. James, 23, Old Burlington-street
Forrester, G. Esq. Vauxhall Foundry, Liverpool
Forshall, Rev. J. *F.R.S.* British Museum
Forster, G. Esq. Alderman, Forth, Newcastle-upon-Tyne
Forster, James, Esq. 64, Old Broad-street
Forster, Rev. J. Crescent, Leicester
Fort, Lawrence, Esq. High-st. Manchester
Fortescue, Hon. Geo. Weare Gifford, Devon
Fortescue, T. Esq. Exeter College, Oxford
Fortescue, Wm. Esq. Smithfield-bars
Fortescue, W. Esq. Christ Church Coll. Oxford
Foth, Henry, Esq. Bridgewater-buildings
Foster, Aug. Esq. Warmwell House, Dorset
Foster, Rev. A. Kingston, near Taunton
Foster, Lieut. G. Commander H. M. Packet Lapwing, Falmouth
Foster, John, Esq. Town Hall, Liverpool
Foster, Mr. James, 10, Culver-street, Bristol
Foster, Mr. John, Kirby Lonsdale. 7 Copies
Foster, Rich. Esq. 3, Bedford-square
Foster, Richard, jun. Esq. Cambridge
Foster, Thos. Esq. Town Hall, Liverpool
Foster, Capt. W. Schooner Tampico, Liverpool
Foster, William, Esq. Lanwithan, Cornwall
Foulkes, Edw. Esq. Star-yard, Manchester
Fowler, Jas. Esq. 3, Lincoln's-inn-fields
Fox, Alfred, Esq. Falmouth
Fox, B. Esq. Chestnut Lodge, near Horsham
Fox, Dr. Brislington, near Bristol
Fox, Dr. Edw. Long, Brislington, Somerset
Fox, E. Berkley, Esq. 33, Montague-place, Bedford-square
Fox, George C. Esq. Falmouth
Fox, Mr. Hy. 57, Falkner-street, Manchester
Fox, J. Elliott, Esq. 40, Finsbury-crescent
Fox, Rev. Dr. John, Provost of Queen's College, Oxford
Fox, Lieut.-Col. *M.P.* Addison-rd. Kensington
Fox, Mr. Richard Gott, Bradford, Yorkshire
Fox, Robert Weare, Esq. Falmouth
Fox, Rev. Thos. H. L. Hinton St. Mary, Dorset
Fraland, Mr. James, 56, Wilson-st. Glasgow
Francis, Charles L. Esq. Wandsworth-road
Francis, Henry, Esq. Monument-yard
Francis, Robert, Esq. Canterbury
Francis, Samuel, Esq. Norwich
Frankland, Sir Robt. Bart. Thirkleby Park, Yorkshire
Franks, John, Esq. 16, Warwick-ct. Holborn
Fraser, Rev. Wm. St. Christopher's
Fraser, J. F. Esq. 15, Eaton-pl. Belgrave-sq.
Fraser, Gen. Sir John, *K.C.H.* CampdenHill
Fraser, Mr. Thos. 63, New Bond-street
Fraser, W. R. Esq. Trinity Coll. Cambridge
Frazer, Alex. Esq. Plymouth
Frederick, Lieut.-Col. 52, Berkeley-square
Freeling, Sir Francis, Bart. *F.R.S.* Post Office
Freeman, R. L. Esq. *R.N.* Dublin Castle
Freeman, John, Esq. Leamington-priors
Freeman, John, Esq. Gaines, near Worcester
Freeman, Spencer, Esq. Stowmarket, Suffolk
Frend, Richard, Esq. Mayor of Canterbury
Frend, Wm. Esq. 31, Upper Bedford-place, Russell-square
French, C. Esq. Hawkhurst, Kent
French, J. M. Esq. *F.R.A.S.*
Friend, John, Esq. Birchington, Kent
Fripp, W. Esq. Alderman, Cote House, Bristol
Frolich & Besch, Messrs. 11, Hanover-street, Hanover-square
Froost & Sons, Messrs. Nemarwket-lane, Manchester

Frost, John, Esq. 11, Wood-street, Cheapside
Frost, Messrs. Jos. & Isaac, 62, St. John's-square, Clerkenwell
Fry, Edmund and Son, Messrs. 4, Bishopsgate-st. within
Fry, Joseph James, Esq. Gloucester
Fry, Mr. Bookseller, Tunbridge
Frye, Rev. Dr. Crescent House, Brompton
Fryer, Chas. Esq. Cattistoke, Dorset
Fryer, F. W. Esq. Wimbourne, Dorset
Fryer, John, Esq. Chatteris, Cambridge
Fryer, Mr. Thomas, Northwich
Fryer, Thos. Chatteris, Cambridge
Fulcher, Rich. Esq. Bungay, Suffolk
Fuller, T. Esq. Stony Knolls, near Manchester
Fuller, Captain W. S. *R.N.* Brighton
Fuller, Mr. John, Dunmow, Essex
Fullerton, John, jun. Esq. Wellesbourne, Warwickshire
FULLORTON, Right Hon. Lord John, Edinburgh
Fullwood, B. Esq. 24, Somerset-place, Hoxton New Town
Funge, Mr. John, York-pl. City-road
Furley, R. Esq. Ashford, Kent
Furley, Robt. Esq. 17, Vere-street
Fyfe, Captain, *R.N.* 7, Albany-st. Edinburgh

G.

Gaddum, F. E. Esq. Pool-street, Manchester
Gadsby, John, Esq. Water-la. Manchester
GAGE, Right Hon. the Lord Viscount
Gage, Hon. W. Westbury House, Alton
Gaitskell, Lt.-Col. 29, Regency-sq. Brighton
Galbraith, H. A. Esq. Surgeon, Royal Asylum, Glasgow
Gale, E. Mornt, Esq. Upham, Bishop's Waltham
Gale, John Parrah, Esq. Bouverie-st. Fleet-st.
Galley, Thomas, Esq. Back-square, Mancheser
Galloway, Alexander, Esq. West-street, West Smithfield
Galpine, Mr. Lymington, Hants
Galton, J. H. Esq. Hadzor House, Worcestrsh.
Gandell, Edward, Esq. 10, Lombard-street
Gandell, George, Esq. 10, Lombard-street
Ganthony, R. P. Esq. Kennington Common
Garden, Mr. R. 302, St. Vincent-st. Glasgow
Gardiner, C. W. Esq. Coombe Lodge, Oxon
Gardiner, Rev. Dr. 10, Paragon-buildings, Bath
Gardiner, L. Esq. High-street, Manchester
Gardiner, R. Esq. Pall-mall, Manchester
Gardner, Rev. Dr. Lawrence, Sansaw, near Shrewsbury
Gardner, Mr. Henry, Sandwich
Gardner, Mr. Hereford
Gardner, Robert, Esq. Pall-mall, Manchester
Gare, Mr. Samuel, Chard, Somersetshire
Garey, E. B. Esq. 6, Upper Islington-terrace, Pentonville
Garland, Captain J. G. *R.N.* Leeson House, Isle of Purbeck, Dorset
Garland, Major John, *K.H.* Quatre-Bras Cottage, Muckleford, Dorset
Garland, N. Esq. Epsom, Surrey
Garlick, Joseph Prince, Esq. Leeds
Garmeson, Mr. J. Bookseller, 9, Temple-st. Whitefriars
Garnett, Mr. W. Bradford, Yorkshire
Garnett, Robt. Esq. St. James's-sq. Manchester
Garnier, Rev. Thos. Close, Winchester
Garniss, Mr. John, Queen's Dock, Liverpool

Garrard, Thomas, Esq. Chamberlain of Bristol
Garratt, John, Esq. Bishop's-court, near Exeter
Garratt, Mrs. 23, Royal-crescent, Bath
Garrett, P. Esq. Douglas, Isle of Man
Garry, Nicholas, Esq. 14, Stratton-st. Piccadilly
Garwood, Thomas, Esq. Wells, Norfolk
Garwood, William, Esq. York
Gaselee, Right Hon. Mr. Justice, Montagu-pl.
Gaskin, Rev. T. *M.A.* Jesus Coll. Cambridge
Gates, R. Esq. Bramley, Surrey
Gatliff, William, Esq. Leeds
Gatton, J. Howard, Esq. Hadgor House, Worcester. High Sheriff
Gavaron, Theodore, Esq. 27, Tavistock-square
Gay, J. Esq. 2, Queen-street, Southwark-bridge
Gaywood & Longworth, Messrs. 13, Grafton-street, Fitzroy-square
Gee, Joseph, Esq. Cottingham, near Hull
Gee, Robert, Esq. Hollywood, near Stockport
Gell, Philip, Esq. Hopton Hall, near Wirksworth, Derbyshire
Geltenes, J. Esq. Pembroke Coll. Cambridge
Geneste, Rev. Max. West Cowes
George, Alfred, Esq. Kingston Villa, Clifton
George, Mrs. Ann, Chepstow. 6 Copies
George, Chas. Esq. Abbott's Leigh, Bristol
George, John, jun. Esq. 192, Regent-street
George, Spark, Esq. Kirkstall, Leeds
Gerber, Wm. Esq. At Messrs. Rhomer, Brothers, & Co. Back George-street, Manchester
Gerold, Mr. C. Bookseller, Vienna
Gerrard, J. H. Esq. *D.C.L.* Principal of Bristol College
GEYMULLOR, Baron Henry V.
Gibb, Mr. H. W. Crown-street, Liverpool
Gibbes, Charles, Esq. 60, South Audley-street
Gibbins, B. Esq. Neath, Glamorganshire
Gibbins, Mr. John, Settle, Yorkshire. 5 Copies
Gibbons, J. Esq. 19, Goree Piazzas, Liverpool
Gibbons, Sir J. Bart. Stanwell-pl. Middlesex
Gibbs, Edward, Esq. 32, Fenchurch-street
Gibbs, G. H. Esq. 11, Bedford-square
Gibbs, James, Esq. Bath Cottage, Clifton
Gibson, Sir A. C. Maitland, Bart. Charlotte-square, Edinburgh
Gibson, Mr. Charles, Royal Oak, Ashford
Gibson, Edw. Esq. Mayor of Hull
Gibson, Mr. Francis, Saffron Walden
Gibson, J. Esq. Leazes-ter. Newcastle-on-Tyne
Gibson, John, Esq. Laboratory, Stratford
Gibson, N. Esq. 13, Saville-row, Newcastle-upon-Tyne
Gibson, R. Esq. Beckenham, Kent
Gibson, Thomas, Esq. Theberton House
Gibson, Mr. W. G. Saffron Walden
Gibson, Wood, Esq. Poolfold, Manchester
Giddy, Captain Charles, *R.N.* Penzance
Gidoin, Rev. J. L. Lympstone, Devon
Gilbert, A. Esq. Caius College, Cambridge
Gilbert, H. Esq. Pickshipton, near Devizes
Gilbert, Col. W. R. Cheltenham
Giles, John C. Esq. *R.N.* Woodside Cottage, Lymington
Giles, Captain Joseph, Wells
Giles, R. B. Esq. 52, York-crescent, Clifton
Gilfillan, Jas. Esq. 2, Rodney-st. Liverpool
Gilkison, David, Esq. Port Glasgow
Gill, Captain J. B. Brig Thetis, Liverpool
Gill, T. Esq. 1, Great Ormond-st. Bloomsbury
GILLIES, Right Hon. Lord, Edinburgh
Gillespie, Alex. jun. Esq. 13, America-square
Gillespie, R. Esq. 30, York-place, Baker-street
Gillett, John, Esq. Street, near Glastonbury

Gillett, W. E. Esq. Fairwater House, near Taunton
Gilliert, W. Esq. Commerce-court, Lord-street, Liverpool
Gillott, Mr. George, 36, Strand
Gipps, T. M. Esq. St. John's Coll. Cambridge
Girardot, J. C. Esq. Little Bookham, Surrey
Girdleston, S. Esq. Wisbeach, Norfolk
Girling, Captain T. A. Grove, Holt, Norfolk
Giron, Mr. J. F. Bookseller, Hemel Hempstead. 11 Copies
Gladdish, W. Esq. Cliff Cottage, Gravesend
Gladstone, R. Esq. Abercromby-sq. Liverpool
Gladstone, T. S. Esq. Chatham-st. Abercromby-square, Liverpool
Glaister, Wm. Esq. *M.A.* University College, Oxford
Glasgow Port Library
——— Public Library
Glennie, Rev. J. D. *A.M.* Sandgate, Kent
Glover, Rev. William S. Cumberland Villa
Glover, W. H. Esq. University Coll. Oxford
Goadsby, John, Esq. Water-lane, Manchester
Goadsby, Francis, jun. Esq. Salford
Goddard & Brown, Messrs. Booksellers, Hull. 9 Copies
Goddard, Mr. R. Rose and Crown, Wisbeach
Godden, Henry, Esq. Maidstone
Goding, James, Esq. 2, Belgrave-square
Goding, Thomas, Esq. Knightsbridge
Godson, Edward, Esq. 72, Aldersgate-street
Godwin, Richard, B. Esq. Mary's-gate, Derby
Godwin, Mr. Shadrach, Hemel Hempstead
Goffe, William, Esq. Falmouth
Golightly, Rev. C. P. Godalming
Gomersall, near Leeds, Book Society
Gompertz, Ben. Esq. *F.R.S.* Alliance Office
Goodenough, Dr. E. Dean of Wells
Goodhall, Rev. Dr. Provost of Eton
Goodhall, H. H. Esq. 55, Crutched-friars
Goodier, William, Esq. North Central Bank, Manchester
Gooding, John, Esq. Southwold, Suffolk
Goodman, George, Esq. Leeds
Goodman, John, Esq. Leeds
Goodman, John, Esq. Roundhay, near Leeds
Goodman, T. R. Esq. Trinity Coll. Cambridge.
Goodrich, R. Esq. 35, Amwell-st. Pentonville
Goodridge, J. Esq. Sturminster, Newton, Dorset
Goodsir, David, Esq. 71, Queen-st. Glasgow
Goodwin, Edm. Esq. Mosley-st. Manchester
Goodwin, William, Esq. Royal Mews
Goodyear, Mr. Thomas, 6, Aldersgate-street
Goold, Mr. John, Wimborne, Dorset
Goolden, John, Esq. Maesbury, Oswestry
Gordon, A. D. Esq. Rainbow-hill, Worcester
Gordon, Lt.-Col. Arthur, Port Hill, Bideford
Gordon, C. Esq. Wiscombe Park, near Honiton
Gordon, C. Esq. 40, Gower-st. Bedford-square
Gordon, H. M. Esq. 4, Lincoln's-inn-fields
Gordon, Dr. T. 5, Duchess-st. Gt. Wimpole-st.
Gore, Henry Jas. Esq. Merton College, Oxford
Gore, Thomas, Esq. Piccadilly, Manchester
Gore, Rev. William Charles, Barrow, Somerset
Gore, William Ormsby, Esq. *M.P.* Porkington Hall, Oswestry
Gosling, Robert, Esq. Dover-street, Piccadilly
Goss, James, Esq. Dawlish
Goss, Jno. Wm. Esq. Bull-wharf, Queenhithe
Gosse, Henry, Esq. Epsom, Surrey
Gosselin, M. H. Esq. Christ's Coll. Cambridge
Gossier, L'Abbé F. Rouen, Faubourg Beauvoisine, Rue du Nord, No. 1

Gott, Benjamin, Esq. Armley House, Leeds
Gott, John, Esq. Leeds
Gotelee, Mr. John, Bookseller, Hounslow
Goulburn, Edward, Esq. *M.P.* 21, Park-st Grosvenor-square
Gould, Rev. G. Fleet House, Weymouth, Dorset
Gould, John, Esq. Leigh-place, Ardwick, near Manchester
Gould, Mr. J. 20, Broad-st. Golden-square
Gouldsborough, John, Esq. 92, Market-street, Manchester
Gowan, P. Esq. 46, Lime-street
Gowan, Wm. Esq. St. Christopher's. 2 Copies
Gower, A. A. Esq. 14, Great Carter-lane, Doctors-commons
Gower, A. Lewis, Esq. 31, Finsbury-square
Gower, Edwin, Esq. 28, Coleman-street
Gower, R. F. Esq. 31, Finsbury-square
Grace, Capt. R. W. Castle House, Hampstead
Graeff, Edward John, Esq. Trafalgar-square
Graeff, John George, Esq. 4, Furnival's-inn
Grafton, J. S. Esq. Dover-street, Manchester
Graham, F. J. Esq. Carlisle
Graham, F. J. Esq. Postmr. Carlisle. 9 Copies
Graham, George, Esq. Dublin
Graham, Lady, 46, Grosvenor-place
Graham, Lieut.-Colonel, Mosknow, Carlisle
Graham, Sir Sandford, Bart. 1, Portland-place
Graham, Thomas, Esq. Turnham-green. 2 Copies
Graham, Rev. William, Arthurst, Longtown
Graham, W. Esq. jun. 70, Miller-st. Glasgow
GRANBY, Most Noble the Marquis of
Grange, Mr. Stephen, 126, Oxford-street
Granger, Edmund, Esq. Exeter
Grant, Alexander, Esq. 12, Arlington-street
Grant, Rev. Andrew, 68, Great King-street, Manchester
Grant, D. Esq. Cannon-street, Manchester
Grant, D. Esq. 37, York-place, Edinburgh
Grant, F. A. Esq. 1, Ulster-ter. Regent's-park
Grant, Rev. F. B. Dartford, Kent
Grant, George, Esq. 15, Rodney-st. Liverpool
Grant, Dr. George, Richmond-hill
Grant, M. Esq. 9, George-street, Edinburgh
Grant, Miss, Clifton Hill
Grant, Robert, Esq. 49, Melville-st. Edinburgh
Grant, Sir Thomas, 20, Leicester-square
Grant & Son, Messrs. Booksellers, 82, Prince's-street, Edinburgh
Grant, T. Esq. Collector of H. M. Customs, Bideford
Grant, W. Esq. Spring Side, nr. Bury, Lancashire
Grapel, Mr. W. Booksr. Liverpool. 8 Copies
Grave, John, Esq. Isle of Man. 14 Copies
Grave, Jos. Esq. Fountain-street, Manchester
Graves, John, Esq. 51, Call-lane, Leeds
Gray, Benj. Esq. Pollard-street, Manchester
Gray, John, Esq. Sherborne, Dorset
Gray, John, Esq. Wheatfield, near Bolton
Gray, Jonathan, Esq. York
Gray, Lieut.-Colonel, Lieut.-Governor of Pendennis Castle, Falmouth
Gray, Mrs. B. 95, Great Portland-street
Gray, Mr. Robert, 15, Gordon-street, Glasgow
Gray, Mrs. King-street, Manchester
Gray, Robert Alexander, Esq. Peckham Rye
Gray, W. Esq. 10, Brandon-place, Glasgow
Gray, Wm. jun. Esq. York
Gray, W. Esq. St. Christopher's
Greathead, A. H. Esq. Christ's Coll. Cambridge
Greaves, Capt. John, Barque Golden Fleece, Liverpool
Greaves, John, Esq. Crescent, Salford
Greaves, Mrs. S. King's Newton
Greaves, R. D. Esq. Leeds
Green, C. Esq. Wakefield
Green, Mr. F. High-street, Stoke Newington
Green, Mr. F. O. Market-street, Manchester
Green, H. C. jun. Esq. 94, Hatton-garden
Green, James, Esq. 22, Barbican
Green, Mr. James, Green's Hotel, Serle-street, Lincoln's-inn-fields
Green, Joseph H. Esq. 46, Lincoln's-inn-fields
Green, Mr. Bookseller, Knutsford
Green, Mr. T. St. Patrick Steam-packet Office, Clarence Dock, Liverpool
Green, Thomas, Esq. Huddersfield
Green, W. Esq. *F.C.* Worcester Coll. Oxford
Greene, Benjamin A. St. Ives, Huntingdon
Greene, Captain, B. *R.N.* Wickham, Hants
Greenhill, Mr. R. Ashford, Kent
Greenhow, Mr. Thomas, jun. Kendal
Greenland and Co. Messrs. Booksellers, 38, Poultry. 3 Copies
Greenshields, J. Esq. 15, Percy-street, Liverpool
Greenshields, John B. Esq. 125, Princes-street, Edinburgh
Greenslade, Mr. J. Booksr. Guernsey. 6 Copies
Greenup, Richard, Esq. *M.B.* Salisbury
Greenway, J. Commander *R.N.* St. Thomas's, Exeter
Greenwell, Colonel Sir Leonard, Commandant of the Garrison of Chatham
Greenwell, Rich. Esq. Fawcet-street, Bishop Wearmouth
Greenwell, Smith, Esq. 54, Great Surrey-street
Greenwich Reading Society
Greenwood, Rev. Dr. John, Christ's Hospital
Greenwood, R. Esq. Brookwood, Winchester
Greg, Robt. Hyde, Esq. Norcliffe, Cheshire
Greig, Admiral, Imperial Russian Navy, St. Petersburg
Gregor, Mrs. Ockley, Surrey
Gregory, G. Esq. Willesborough, Kent
Gregory, J. Esq. Clement's-inn
Greig, James, jun. Esq. *W.S.* 23, Forth-street, Edinburgh
Greig, Thomas, Esq. 10, Duke-st. Manchester
Greig, Woronzow, Esq. 2, Mitre-court, Temple
Grenade, Captain Gullen, *R.N.* Carlskrona
Gresham, John, Esq. Hull
Greville, Charles, Esq. Bristol
GREY, Right Hon. the Earl
Grey, Hon. W. B. 43, Charles-st. Berkeley-sq.
Grey, Sir George, *M.P.* 14, Eaton-place
Griffin, Mr. John, Hemel Hempstead
Griffin, Lieut. *R.N.* Stratton-place, Falmouth
Griffin, Mr. Robert, White Lion, Ely
Griffin, N. Esq. Portsea
Griffith, R. Esq. Fitzwilliam's-place, Dublin
Griffith, Rev. T. Llanfechan, Montgomeryshire
Griffiths, Lieut. S. *R.N.* Commander of H. M. Packet Swallow, Falmouth
Grimble, William, Esq. Cow-cross. 2 Copies
Grimsdell, Samuel, Esq. Sun-st. Bishopsgate
Grindlay, R. M. Esq. 8, St. Martin's-pl. Charing Cross. 2 Copies
Grisdale, Rev. L. Bolton, near Manchester
GROEBEN, Count de
Groombridge, Mr. R. Bookseller, 6, Panyer-alley. 2 Copies
Groos, Mr. C. T. Bookseller, Carlsruhe
GROSVENOR, Lord Robert, *M.P.*
Grote, Francis, Esq. Trinity Coll. Cambridge
Grote, George, Esq. *M.P.* Threadneedle-street
Grounds, David, Esq. 49, Threadneedle-street
Grout, George, Esq. Norwich
Grout, Joseph, Esq. Stamford Hill
Grove, Thos. Esq. Ferne House, Ferne, Wilts
Grove, Lieut. William, *R.N.* Holnest Lodge, Sherborne, Dorset
Grove, Rev. W. F. Teffont, near Mere, Wilts
Grundy, Thomas, Esq. Bury, Lancashire
Grussill, J. Esq. Pendennis Castle, Falmouth
Grylls, Glynn, Esq. Helston, Cornwall
Grylls, Rev. Richard Gerveys, sen. Alderman, Helston, Cornwall
Guest, W. Esq. Albion-buildings, Manchester
GUILDFORD, Right Hon. & Rev. the Earl of
Guise, Gen. Sir J. W. Bart. *K.C.B.* Rendcourt Park, Gloucester
Gullengrenade, Capt. Swedish Navy, Carlskrona
Gunnersall, Thomas Bedford, Esq. 10, Lombard-street
Gumprect, Mr. J. Buchanan-street, Glasgow
Gunn, Rev. D. Christchurch, Hants
Gunn, Rev. John, Chard, Somersetshire
Gunnell, Richard P. Esq. 7, Woburn-square
Gunnery, Mr. Jos. Edge-hill, Liverpool
Gunther, Mr. H. 7, Pratt-place, Camden Town
Guppy, Mrs. Sarah, Farway House, Clifton
Gurne, Mr. A. J. Mediterranean Packet Office
Gurney, D. Esq. North Runcton, Lynn, Norfolk
Gurney, Hudson, Esq. *F.R.S. V.P.S.A.* St. James's-square
Gustard, G. E. Esq. 1, Lancaster-pl. Strand
Gutteres, M. Esq. Sidmouth
Gutterson, Thomas, Esq. Chase Side, Enfield
Guy, Mr. Chelmsford
Gwillim, Lady, Staplefield Common, Sussex
Gwilt, John, Esq. Icklingham, Suffolk
Gwilt, Jos. Esq. Abingdon-street, Westminster
Gwyer, Joseph, Esq. Redcliff-parade, Bristol
Gwyer, W. O. Esq. Temple-street, Bristol
Gwynne, Lawrence, Esq. *LL.D.* Teignmouth

H.

Haberfield, Jno. Esq. Redcliff Parade, Bristol
HADDINGTON, Right Hon. the Earl of
HADDO, Right Hon. Lord
Haddon, Mr. Bookseller, Colchester
Hadfield, John, Esq. St. Ann's-st. Manchester
Hadlow, Mr. F. Faversham, Kent
Hadow, J. E. Esq. 5, Rood-lane
Hadwen, John, jun. Esq. near Huddersfield
Haggerstone, Sir Thos. Bart. Ellingham
Hague, John, Esq. Cranbrook, Kent
Haig, David, Esq. Lochrin, near Edinburgh
Haig, Geo. A. Esq. Bonnington, Leith
Haigh, John, Esq. Huddersfield
Haigh, Robt. Esq. Lochrin Distillery, Edinb.
Haines, G. C. Esq. Godalming
Haines, R. Esq. Godalming
Hains, Parton, Esq. Bishopsteignton, Devon
Hairby, Dr. J. Sablecote Cottage, Parkstone
Halden, R. G. Esq. Seagate
Hale, Wm. Esq. Colchester
Hales, Rev. Robert, Hillington, Norfolk
Halesworth Book Club
Halford, Sir Hy. Bart. *M.D. F.R.S. Pres.C.P.* Curzon-street
Halifax Subscription Library
——— New Subscription Library
Hall, Mr. Andrew, Peel-street Book Society, Manchester

Hailing, Mr. R. Bookseller, Upper York-street 2 Copies
Hall, B. P. Esq. Kensington-square
Hall, Mrs. Elizabeth, Gainsborough
Hall, Francis, Esq Hessle
Hall, George, Esq. Ely, Cambridge
Hall, Geo. Esq. Back Cannon-st. Manchester
Hall, Henry, Esq. Ashton-under-Lyne
Hall, J. O. Esq. 44, Queen-sq. Bloomsbury
Hall, Messrs. J. V. and Son, Booksellers, Maidstone. 8 Copies
Hall, James, Esq. Stalybridge, Yorkshire
Hall, Mr. James, St. James's, Barton, Bristol
Hall, Jno. jun. Esq. Bloomsbury Reading-rooms, Manchester
Hall, John, Esq. High-street, Winchester
Hall, John, Esq. St. Mary Axe
Hall, John, Esq. 1, Sussex-street, Manchester
Hall, Mr. John, Bookseller, Cambridge
Hall, Sir J. *K.C.H.* St. Catherine's Dockhouse
Hall & Marsh, Messrs. Booksellers, Speenhamland. 14 Copies
Hall, Robert, Esq. Leeds
Hall, Samuel G. Esq. 130, London Wall
Hall, Thos. Esq. Romsey, Hants
Hall, Dr. William, Leatherhead, Surrey
Hallett, F. Esq. 12, North-st. road, Brighton
Halliburton, Mr. J. Bksller, Coldstream, N.B.
Halliday, Rev. E. T. Yard House, Taunton
Holliday, Rev. Walter, St. Glenthorne, near Minehead, Somerset
Halsey, Thos. P. Esq. Christ Church, Oxford
Halsted, Admiral Sir L. W. *K.C.B.* Phœnix Lodge, Alton
Hamer, D. Esq. Glanyrafon
Hamilton, Major Gen. A. Kerr, Innerwick Lodge, Edinburgh
Hamilton, H. A. Esq. The Retreat, Topsham
Hamilton, Capt. H.M. Packet Service, Dover
Hamilton & Co. Messrs. Booksellers, London. 12 Copies
Hamilton, Jas, Esq. Woodland-ter. Falmouth
Hamilton, Rev. J. Canterbury
Hamilton, Hon. Robert, 2, Abercrombie-place, Edinburgh
Hamilton, Mr. Robt. Ship Dryope, Liverpool
Hamilton, Rev. R. W. East-parade, Leeds
Hamilton, Capt. W. A. B. *R.N.* DublinCastle
Hamilton, W. C. Esq. of Claighlan
Hamley, Joseph Esq. Bodmin
Hammersley, Chas. Esq. 25, Park-crescent
Hammett, James, Esq. 18, Lansdown-crescent, Bath
Hammond, Anthony, Esq. Stock Exchange
Hammond, George, Esq. Leeds
Hammond, William, Esq. 3, Russell-square
Hampton, J. Lewis, Esq. Hartlys, Beaumaris
Hanbury, Robt. Esq. Brick-lane, Spitalfields
Hancock, Jas. Esq. 54, Garside-st. Manchester
Hancock, Lieut. John, *R.N.* Swanage, Hants
Hanham, Rev. Sir J. Bart. Dean's-court, Wimborne
Hannaford, J. Esq. Christchurch, Hants
Hanley, W. L. Esq. 16, Ely-place
Hanmer, Latham, Esq. Everton Brow, Liverpool
Hanna, Captain John, Brig Rapier, Liverpool
Hannay, Dr. Port Patrick, North Britain
Hannay, Dr. J. H. 65, St. Vincent-st. Glasgow
Hannay, William, Esq. Nottingham
Hansard, James, Esq. 7, Southampton-street, Bloomsbury. 2 Copies
Hansard, Luke, Esq. 10, Bedford-square
Hansell, Thomas I. Esq. Hull
Hanson, Chas. jun. Esq. York
Hanson, John, Esq. Watling-st. Manchester
Hanson, Rev. W. H. *M.A.* Caius College, Cambridge
Hanwell, Vice-Adml. Joseph. Wareham
Harbottle, Thos. Esq. Fountain-st. Manchester
Harcourt, John, Esq. Artillery-st. Bermondsey
Hardacre, G. Esq. 12, Billiter-square
Harding, John, Esq. Waltham-cross
Harding, S. T. Esq. Cheetham Hill, Manchester
Harding, Rev. T. Bexley, Kent
Harding, W. Esq. Merchant's-sq. Manchester
Hardman, Thos. Esq. Broughton
Hardwick, P. Esq. *F.R.S. F.S.A.* 60, Russell-square
HARDWICKE, Right Hon. the Earl of. 2 Copies
Hardy, Dr. J. Doncaster
Hardy, J. Esq. Charminster, Dorset
Hardy, Jno. Esq. *M.P.* 7, Portland-place
Hardy, Thos. D. Esq. Record Office, Tower
Hardy, Rear-Adml. Sir T. M. Bart. *G.C.B.*
Hare, Chas. Esq. 19, Berkeley-square, Bristol
Hare, George, Esq. Huddersfield
Hare, Henry, Esq. Huddersfield
Hare, John, jun. Esq. Bristol
Hare, Hon. L. H. Lymington, Hants
Harford, J. Scandret, Esq. *F.R.S. D.C.L.* Blaise Castle, Bristol
Hargood, Adm. Sir William, *G.C.B., K.G.H.* Harley-street
Hargrave, William, Esq. Woodhouse-la. Leeds
Hargreave, John, jun. Esq. Bolton, Lancashire
Hargreave, James & Sons, Messrs. Mill Garth, Leeds
Hargreaves, Mr. James, Farnhill Hall, Skipton
Hargreaves, John, Esq. Marsden's-square, Manchester
Hargreaves, Mr. William, Bradford, Yorkshire
Hargreaves, W. Esq. Woodhouse-lane, Leeds
Harington, Capt. *R.N.* Kelston House, Ryde, Isle of Wight
Harland, Sir Robt. Bart. Orwell Park, Ipswich
Harlock, Jno. Esq. Ely, Cambridge
Harlock, Wm. Esq. Ely, Cambridge
Harman, Edw. Esq. Adam's-ct. Old Broad-st.
Harman, Henry, Esq. Tonbridge
Harman, Henry, Esq Adam's-ct. Old Broad-st.
Harman, Jerh. Esq. Adam's-ct. Old Broad-st
Harman, John, Esq.
Harman, T. Esq. Wombwell Hall, Northfleet
Harmer, James, Esq. Alderman of London
Harper, Edward, Esq. York
Harper, Moses, Esq. Barbourne Lodge, Worcester
Harper, W. jun. Esq. Trinity Coll. Cambridge
Harper, Wm. Esq.
Harpin, John, Esq. Burnlee, Huddersfield
Harries, Rev. Canon, Letterston, Pembrokeshire
Harrington, Thos. Esq. Old Steyne, Brighton
Harris, Chas. Pestell, Esq. Cambridge
Harris, Hy. Hemington, Esq. Cambridge
Harris, John, Esq. Surgeon, *F.L.S.* Exeter
Harris, Joseph, Esq. Chapel Villa, Toxteth Park, Liverpool
Harris, Quarles, jun. Esq. 9, Billiter-street
Harris, R. H. Esq. Botesdale, Suffolk
Harris, Samuel, Esq. Leicester
Harris, T. Esq. Sevenoaks, Kent
Harris, Wm. Esq. Corfe Mullen, Wimborne, Dorset
Harris, William, Esq. Worthing
Harrison, Abraham, Esq. Green Gate, Salford
Harrison, David, Esq. Stalybridge
Harrison, H. A. Esq. 33, Burton-street, Burton-crescent
Harrison, J. Esq. Newall's-bldgs. Manchester
Harrison, J. B. Esq. Southampton
Harrison, John, Esq. MelstonHall, nr. Ashbourn
Harrison, John, Esq. Dock-street, Leeds
Harrison, Rev. Matt. Church Oakley, Hants
Harrison, R. Esq. 2, Avenue-rd. Regent's-park
Harrison, Rob. Esq. 21, Keppel-st. Russell-sq.
Harrison, Robert, Esq. Silver-st. Hull
Harrison, T. C. Esq. 34, York-ter. Regent's-pk.
Harrison, Thos. jun. Esq. Wapping, Liverpool
Harrison, Wm. Esq. 45, Lincoln's-inn-fields
Harrod, James, Esq. Aylsham, Norfolk
Harrop, John, Esq. Stockport
Harrop, Mr. W. Thornton, near Bradford
Hart, J. Esq. Folkestone, Kent
Hart, John Geo. Esq. Stowmarket, Suffolk
Hart, Miss, Lee, Kent
Hart, Wm. Esq. King-street, Manchester
Harter, J. C. Esq. Chapel Walk, Manchester
Hartopp, Lady, Redland House, Clifton, Somrst.
Hartwright, W. Esq. 36, Pall-mall, Manchester
Harvey, Capt. E. Ship Howard, Liverpool
Harvey, G. R. Esq. Brabant-court, Philpot-la.
Harvey, Henry, Esq. Stock Exchange
Harvey, J. H. Esq. Newcastle-under-Lyne
Harvey, Lt.-Col. J. 10, Picardy-pl. Edinburgh
Harvey, John, Esq. Trinity Coll. Cambridge
Harvey, Thos. Esq. Northwold, Norfolk
Harvey, Thomas, Esq. Falmouth
Harvey, W. Esq. 40, Oldfield-rd. Manchester
Harwood, Rev. J. Deane, near Overton, Hants
Haslett, Mr. Jas. Chain Pier, Brighton
Hassall, Jos. Esq. 3, Pritchard-st. Bristol
Haster, Alex. Esq. 60, Ingram-street, Glasgow
Hastie, H. H. Esq. Pembroke Coll. Cambridge
HASTINGS, Most Noble the Marquis of
Hatchard, Messrs. J. and Son, 187, Piccadilly 7 Copies
Hatchett, C. Esq. Belle Vue House, Chelsea
Hatfield, George, Esq. Manchester
HATHERTON, Right Hon. Lord
Hathorn, George, Esq. 40, Brunswick-square
Hathorn, Hugh, Esq. Castlewig, N.B.
Haugh, Mrs. Doncaster
Hawker, Mrs. Pounsford House, near Taunton
Hawker, Lt.-Col. Peter, 2, Dorset-pl. Dorset-sq.
Hawkey, Joseph H. Esq. Penryn, Cornwall
Hawkin, Wm. Esq. Rockingham-st. Sheffield
Hawkings, James, Esq. Albion-pl. Blackfriars
Hawkins, Rev. Robt. Lamberhurst, Kent
Hawkins, W. Esq. Fouke's-buildings, Tower-st.
Hawksworth, Mrs. A. Bookseller, Tamworth. 3 Copies
Haworth, W. Esq. 11, Fountain-st. Manchester
Hawthorne, Matthew, I. Esq. 39, Keppel-st. Russell-square
Havergal, Rev. W. H. *A.M.* Astley, Worcester
Hay, Duncan, Esq. Rochester
Hay, Rev. E. Broughton-in-Craven, Yorkshire
Hay, Capt. Jas. George-st. Edinburgh
Hay, Sir Jas. D. Bt. Dunragit, Glenluce, N.B.
Hay, Sir John, Bart. *M.P.*
Hay, Hon. Sam. Eastwell House, Devizes
Hay, William, Esq. Park-square, Leeds
Hays, Mr. R. Bookseller, 234, Oxford-street
Hayde, Mr. B. R. 4, Burwood-pl. Edgware-rd.
Hayes, Christ. jun. Esq. 49, Upper Pitt-street
Haynes, Wm. Esq. St. Augustine-pl. Bristol
Haythorne, Mr. Alderman John, Hill House, Mangotsfield

Hayward, Edw. Esq. Temple, Suffolk
Hayward, J. Esq. Dartford, Kent
Hayward, Wm. Wk. Esq. Cambridge
Hazard, John, Esq. Old Brentford, 2 Copies
Hazell, John, Esq. St. Christopher's
Hazell, Mr. R. Maidstone, Kent
Head, Benjamin, Esq. Woodbridge, Suffolk
Head, Mr. Jeremiah, Stoke Cottage, Ipswich
Headland, Henry, Esq. 17, New Boswell-court
Headly, Wm. Esq. Cambridge
Healy, Mr. Wm. 130, Fleet-street
Heap, Edw. Barlow, Esq. Ashton-under-Lyne
Heap, Rev. Henry, *B.D.* Vicar of Bradford
Heap, John, Esq. 22, Bond-st. Manchester
Heard, Mr. Alderman John, Nottingham
Heath, Matthew, Esq. 12, Furnival's-inn
Heath, Matthew, jun. Esq. Stourport
Heathcoat, John, Esq. *M.P.* Tiverton, Devon
Heathcote, G. Esq. Trinity Coll. Cambridge
Heathcote, Sir Wm. Bart. Hursley Park
Heather, J. F. Esq. St. Peter's Coll. Cambridge
Heathes, Mr. T. Chieftain Steamer, Liverpool
Heathorn, John, Esq. Maidstone
Heaton, John, Esq. South-parade, Leeds
Heaton, Mr. J. Bookseller, Leeds. 19 Copies
Heaton, Mr. W. Newcastle
Heaviside, J. W. L. Esq. *M.A.* Sidney Coll. Cambridge
Heaward, Robt. Esq. Cleckheaton, Yorkshire
Heawood, Rev. E. Sevenoaks, Kent
Heawood, Joseph, Esq. Brinkway, Manchester
Heaword, J. Esq. Brinksway, near Stockport
Hebbert, Chas. Esq. Pall-mall East
Hebert, Robt. Esq. 13, Compton-ter. Islington
Heelis, Stephen, Esq. Princes-st. Manchester
Heisch, Fred. Esq. 16, America-sq. London
Helbert, H. J. Esq. 60, Gloster-pl. Portman-sq
Hellyer, Mr. P. Thos. Marine Library, Ryde
Hemingway, Mr. J. Low Moor, Yorkshire
Henderson, E. Esq. Coate's-cres. Edinburgh
Henderson, George, Esq. 23, Leman-street, Goodman's-fields
Henderson, Mr. S. G. Bookseller, Falmouth, Jamaica
Henderson, T. Esq. 19, Coate's-cres. Edinburgh
Hendrie, W. Esq. 7, Crescent-pl. Burton-cres.
Henley Reading Society
Henniker, Sir A. B. Bart. Thornham, Suffolk
Henry, Davy, Esq. 92, Stephen's-green, Dublin
Henry, Agard, Esq. Liverpool Water Works, Barnet-street
Henry, Lieut. John, *R.N.* Government Emigration Office, Bristol
Henry, Mrs. 11, Great Ormond-st. Bloomsbury
Hensley, Charles, Esq. Stock Exchange
Hensley, J. J. Esq. 35, Tavistock-square
Hensley, Thos. jun. Esq. Stock Exchange
Henslow, S. W. Esq. Clement's-inn
Henville, Rev. C. B. Vicar of Portsmouth
Herbert, H. A. Esq. Trinity Coll. Cambridge
Herbert, Mr. Hy. Bookslr. Wimborne, Dorset
Herbert, Mr. James, Sheerness
Herbert, Wm. Esq. Tottenham
Heritage, Capt. W. *R.N.* Cranbrook, Kent
Heron, Jos. Esq. Essex-street, Manchester
Herries, Rt. Hon. J. C. *M.P.*
Herries, Wm. Young, Esq. Edinburgh
HERVEY, Rt. Hon. Lord Alfred
HERVEY, Rt. Hon. Lord Charles
Heseltine, S. R. Esq. Stock Exchange
Heseltine, Wm. Esq. Turret House, South Lambeth
Hessing, W. A. G. Esq. 135, Regent-street

Heubner, Mr. J. G. Bookseller, Vienna
Heughan, Robt. Esq. North Shields
Hewett, Rt. Hon. Sir George, Bart. Freemantle Park, Southampton
Hewit —, Esq. Abingdon-street, Westminster
Hewitt, Capt. *R.N.* Lee Grove, Blackheath
Hewitt, Mr. J. Old Hummums, Covent-grdn.
Hewitt, Mr. Jos. Packlington-walk, Leicester
Hewitt, Thomas, Esq. Dublin
Hewlett, J. Esq. Fareham
Hewsworth, Hy. H. Esq. New Inn Hall, Oxford
Hext, Wm. Esq. Commander, *R.N.* Bodmin
Hey, Richard, Esq. York
Hey, Rev. Samuel, Ockbrook, Derby
Hey, William, Esq. Leeds
Hey, Wm. Esq. St. John's Coll. Cambridge
Heysham, T. C. Esq. Carlisle
Heywood, Robert, Esq. Bolton, Lancashire
Heywood, Dr. W. C. Blandford, Dorset
Heyworth, Ormerod, Esq. Water-st. Liverpool
Hibbert, Samuel, Esq. 78, Harley-street
Hibblethwaite, J. H. Esq. Woodhouse-lane, Leeds
Hichens, John, Esq. Redruth
Hickes, Aug. Esq. *R.N.* Berkeley, Gloucestersh.
Hick, Benj. Esq. Rose Hill, Bolton
Hicks, Benjamin, Esq. Bolton, Lancashire
Hicks, Francis, Esq. 25, St. John's Wood-rd.
Hicks, Mr. George, Wilson-street, Glasgow
Hicks, Mr. W. R. Bodmin
Hickson, R. Esq. Christ Church, Oxford
Higginbotham, Mosley W. Esq. Stockport
Higginbottom, Joseph, Esq. Ashton-under-Lyne
Higgins, J. G. Esq. Worcester Coll. Oxford
Higgins, W. Esq. Mount Pleasant-square, Manchester
Higginson, E. B. Esq. Saltmarshe, Herefordshire
Higgs, Mr. Samuel, Penzance
Higham, Geo. Esq. Huddersfield
Higham, Mr. L. J. Bookslr. 53, Chiswell-st.
Highbury Book Society
Highmore, N. Esq. Sherborne, Dorset
Hignett, Mrs. Ruth, Lambert-st. Liverpool
Hiley, Chs. Esq. Plainfield, nr. Poole, Dorset
HILL, Right Hon. Gen. Lord, *G.C.B. G.C.H.*
Hill, Edward, Esq. Water-street, Manchester
Hill, Henry, Esq. St. James's-place
Hill, Jas. Esq. Wisbeach, Norfolk
Hill, Capt. Jno. Smack Greyhound, Liverpool
Hill, Mr. John, Hill's Hotel, Charing-cross
Hill, Sir Rowland, Bart. *M.P.* Hawkstone
Hill, Capt. Thos. *R.N.* Greenhithe, Kent
Hill, Capt. Thomas, Ship Home, of Glasgow, Liverpool
Hill, Mr. Wm. Ship Corinthian, Liverpool
Hill, William, Esq. Guildford-street, Leeds
Hillary, Sir Wm. Bart. Fort Ann, Isle of Man
Hillhouse, George, Esq. Alderman of Bristol
Hillier, T. S. Esq. Woodhouse, Wolverhampton
Hills, E. Esq. Angel-terrace, Islington
Hills, Mr. Osborne, Bow, Middlesex
Hills, R. R. Esq. Norwich
Hills, Walter, Esq. Chatham
Hillyar, Sir James, 17, Montagu-square
Hillyer, Mr. P. Thos. Royal Marine Library, Ryde
Hilton, Thos. Esq. Bank-st. Manchester
Hinde, John, Esq. Sittingbourne, Kent
Hindle, Rev. Joseph, Gravesend
Hindley, Charles, Esq. *M.P.* Dukinfield
Hindley, Robt. Esq. Salford, Lancashire
Hindmarsh, Luke, Esq. Treasurer of Alnwick Library

Hird, Capt. *R.N.* Park-row, Greenwich
Hislop, Lt.-Gen. Sir T. Bart. *G.C.B.* Charlton
Hitchcock, G. Esq. 8, Watling-street
Hitchcock, H. W. Esq. Stock Exchange
Hitchcock, Mr. John, 13, Cork-street, Burlington-gardens
Hitchcock, Samuel, Esq. Brown-st. Manchester
Hoare, Chas. Esq. Luscombe, Dawlish
Hoare, Henry Arthur, Esq. Fleet-street
Hoare, Peter Richard, Esq. 37, Fleet-street
Hobbs, Wm. Esq. Church-st. Manchester
Hoblyn, Thos. Esq. *F.R.S.* Treasury
Hobson, C. Esq. 1, Gordon-pl. Tavistock-sq.
Hobson, J. Esq. Trinity College, Cambridge
Hobson, J. Esq. Royal Exchange-sq. Glasgow
Hobson, Jos. T. 11, Church-street, Liverpool
Hobson, Dr. Richard, Leeds
Hobson, R. Esq. St. James's-sq. Manchester
Hocking, Richard, Esq. Penzance
Hockings, Capt. Robert, *R.N.* Lymington
Hodge, Joseph, Esq. Truro
Hodge, R. M. Esq. Bosvigo Cottage, Truro
Hodges, Benj. G. Esq. Distillery, Church-street, Lambeth
Hodges, C. O. Esq. Lower Harley-pl. Clifton
Hodges, Thos. Law, Esq. *M.P.* Hempsted Park, Kent
Hodgkinson, Jno. Esq. 213, Upper Thames-st.
Hodgson, Mr. J. Bookseller, Belfast. 5 Copies
Hodgson, Mr. H. Bkslr. Wimpole-st. 6 Copies
Hodgson, Rich. Esq. 10, Salisbury-st. Strand
Hodgson, Samuel, Esq. Print-st. Manchester
Hodgson, Mr. Thos. Prince's Dock Master, Liverpool
Hodgson, T. Esq. Trinity College, Cambridge
Hodgson, W. N. Esq. Carlisle
Hodnett, W. Esq. St. Christopher's
Hoffman, Mr. Robert, 426, Strand
Hogarth, Rev. J. H. *D.C.L.* 52, Brompton-row
Holam, Mr. Henry, Ship Great Britain
Holchief, H. Esq. Geo. Washington, Liverpool
Holden, Mr. Preston, Lancashire
Holden, Mr. John, Ogle, Bolton
Holditch, Rev. H. *M.A.* Caius Coll. Cambridge
Holdridge, Capt. John, Ship General Williams, Liverpool
Hole, Richard, Esq. Daisy Bank, Manchester
Holehouse, S. Esq. *F.R.A.S.* 3, Charlton-cres. Islington
Holl, John, M. Esq. Kenwith Lodge, Devon
HOLLAND, Right Hon. Lord Vassall
Holland, C. D. Esq. Caius Coll. Cambridge
Holland, E. R. Esq. Marsden-sq. Manchester
Holliday, Rev. E. Chaplain of Plymouth Yard
Hollier, Mr. Hy. Bookseller, 62, Judd-st.
Hollingsdale, Mr. R. Stroud, Kent
Hollingworth, John, Esq. Bexley, Kent
Hollingworth, John, Esq. Maidstone
Holman, John, Esq. Folkestone
Holman, Joseph, Esq. Folkestone
Holman, Thomas, Esq. Folkestone
Holmes, Henry, Esq. Everton, Liverpool
Holmes, John, Esq. High Bailiff of Southwark
Holmes, Wm. Esq. 3, Lyon's-inn, Strand
Holmes, W. Esq. West Grove, Halifax
Holroyd, J. jun. Esq. Ripponden, Huddersfield
Holroyd, Rev. John, Leeds
Holroyd, Joseph, Esq. Grove House, Leeds
Holroyd, R. Esq. Bridgewater-pl. Manchester
Holroyde, E. Esq. Lower Millgate, Manchester
Holt, John, Esq. Back Mosley-st. Manchester
Holy, George, Esq. Sheffield
Holyland, T. Esq. 32, Cannon-st. Manchester

HOME, Right Hon. the Countess of
Homersham, Mr. George, Canterbury
Honridge, Sam. G. Esq. 1, Middle Temple-la.
HOOD, Right Hon. Lord Viscount
Hood, Jacomb, Esq. Bardon Park, Leicestershr.
Hookey, Francis, P. Esq.
Hookham, Mr. T. Bookseller, 15, Old Bond-st.
Hounden, J. D. Esq. Messrs. Hoare's, Fleet-st.
Hooper, Jas. Esq. 168, Upper Thames-street
Hooper, John, Esq. Poole, Dorset
Hope, Dr. Charles, Moray-place, Edinburgh
Hope, H.T. Esq. *M.P.* Duchess-st. Portlnd-pl.
Hope, R. W. Esq. Maze Hill
Hopes, William, Esq. Bank, Macclesfield
Hopcraft, Mr. P. Croughton-Hds. near Brackley
Hopkinson, James, Esq. Halifax
Hopps, J. Esq. 13, Brunswick-place, Leeds
Hordern, A. Esq. Oxley House, Wolverhampton
Hordern, H. Esq. Dunstall, Wolverhampton
Horn, H. G. Esq. 7, Heathcote-street, Mecklenburgh-square
Horn, Mr. Jonathan, Barnard Castle
Horne, — Esq. St. Ann's-square, Manchester
Horne, Edw. Esq. Mersey Hotel, Liverpool
Horne, Geo. L. H. Esq. 2, Lincoln's-inn-fields
Hornidge, Sam. G. Esq. 1, Middle Temple-la.
Horsfall, Chas. Esq. Everton, Liverpool
Horsfall, John, Esq. Hanover-square, Leeds
Horsman, W. Esq. 2, Anslie-pl. Edinburgh
Hose, Mr. J. C. True Sun Office, Strand
Hosking, Wm. Esq. *F.S.A.* Berner's-street
Hoskins, James, Esq. Gosport
Hoskyns, Sir Hungerford, Bart. Weymouth
Hough, Mr. C. Bookseller, Monmouth. 9 Copies
Houghton, George, Esq. London-rd. Leicester
Houghton, J. R. Esq. 2, Earl-st. Blackfriars
Houldsworth, Hy. Esq. Newton-st. Manchestr
Hovel, C. Esq. Canterbury
Hovell, Thos. Esq. 5 Houses, Upper Homerton
Howard, C. Esq. Albion-bldgs. Manchester
Howard, D. Esq. Portsea
Howard, F. Esq. Portsmouth
Howard, Mr. Hen. Falcon Inn, Waltham-cross
Howard, John William, Esq. 5, Mincing-lane
Howard, John, Esq. Leeds
Howard, Mr. T. St. Martin's-ct. Leicester-sq.
Howard, T. Esq. Granchester, near Cambridge
Howard, Thos. Esq. Herne Hill
Howard, Wm. Esq. Portwood, Stockport, near Manchester
Howarth, Mr. T. Booksllr. Knutsford. 3 Copies
HOWE, Right Hon. the Earl
Howe, Joseph, Esq. Coventry
Howe, J. A. Esq. St. Christopher's
Howe, Randal, Esq.
Howell, J. Esq. 10, Charles-st. St. James's
Howell, John, Esq. Queenhithe
Howell, Mrs. Sophia, Neath. 4 Copies
Howes, H. Esq. Caius College, Cambridge
Howman, Mrs. Beccles, Suffolk
Howman, Rev. A. E. Shiplake, Henley-on-Thms.
Howse, G. Esq Upper North-pl. Gray's-inn-rd.
Hoyle, Jas. Esq. 21, Fountain-st. Manchester
Hubbard, James, Esq. Leeds
Hubbersty, J. L. Esq. Queen's Coll. Cambridge
Hudson, Mr. Hy. Wheeler-street, Cambridge
Hudson & Nicholson, Messrs. Booksellers, Kendall. 4 Copies
Hudson, Joseph, Esq. 132, Oxford-street
Hudson, T. Esq. Camilla Lacy, near Dorking
Hudson, W. B. Esq. 27, Haymarket
Hudson's Bay Company, Fenchurch-street. 6 Copies
Hughes, Horatio, Esq. Aberystwith
Hughes, Mrs. Acton House
Hughes, Mr. Robert, Bookseller, Richmond, Surrey. 3 Copies
Hughes, Robt. jun. Esq. 46, Fountain-street, Manchester
Hughes, Thos. Esq. Musselburgh
Hughes, W. H. Esq. *M.P.* Ryde, Isle of Wight
Hughes, Wm. Esq. 35, Queen-square
Hugo, Samuel, Esq. Truro
Hulbert, Robt. S. Esq. Basingstoke
Hulkes, J. Esq. Hermitage, near Rochester
Hull, Col. William, Wimbledon. 6 Copies
Hull, Miss Hannah, Uxbridge
Hull, The Corporation of Mayor and Burgesses of. 2 Copies
—— Corporation of the Trinity House of
—— Lyceum Library
—— Mechanics' Institute
—— Subscription Library
Hullé, Jacob, Esq. 98, Lawrence Poultney-la.
Hulme, Wm. Esq. 25, Market-st. Manchester
Hulton, A. E. Esq. Trinity Coll. Cambridge
Hulton, F. Esq. Runcton, near Lynn, Norfolk
Hulton, Mrs. Preston, Barnfield, Southampton
Humble, Francis, Esq. Durham. 15 Copies
Humble, Mr. Michael, Woodside, Liverpool
HUMBOLDT, Baron Alex. Prussian Embassy
Hume, Rev. C. J. Meonstoke Rectory, Hants. 2 Copies
Hume, Gilbert Langdon, Esq. Corpus Christi College, Cambridge
Hume, Dr. John Robert, 9, Curzon-street
Hume, J. Esq. Seagate
Hume, J. D. Esq. 15, Russell-square
Hume, John, Esq. Dublin
Humphrey, R. P. Esq. Thorpe Mandeville, near Banbury
Humphrey, Captain, Hull
Humphreys, J. Esq. Market-st. Manchester
Humphreys, R. Esq. Ivy House, Clappedrum. 3 Copies
Humphris, Wm. Esq. 51, Leather-la. Holborn
Hungerford, R. B. Esq. Cork
Hunt, George, Esq. Southampton
Hunt, John, Esq. Ducie-place, Manchester
Hunt, Joseph, Esq. Newcastle-under-Lyne
Hunt, T. H. Esq. Mamhead Parsonage, Devon
Hunt, Rev. Thos. Felton, Oswestry
Hunt, Wm. Esq. jun. 23, Blenheim-ter. Leeds
Hunt, Wm. Andrews, Esq. East India House
Hunter, A. Esq. 5, North David-street, Edinburgh
Hunter, Adam, Esq. Leeds
Hunter, David, Esq. Blackness, Dundee
Hunter, Mr. David, Dundee
Hunter, Jameson, Esq. 110, Fenchurch-street
Hunter, Dr. R. North Hanover-st. Glasgow
Hunter, Mr. Rowland, Bookseller, St. Paul's Churchyard
Hunter, Samuel, Esq. Herald Office, Glasgow
Hunter, Thos. Esq. Wearmouth Walk, Bishop Wearmouth
Hunter, William, Esq. 14, Exchange-st.-East, Liverpool
Huntingford, G. W. Esq. New Coll. Oxford
Huntington, Miss, Hull
Hurle, J. Esq. King's Parade Cottage, Clifton
Hurst, John, Esq. Clapham-road
Hurst, J. C. Esq. Dartford, Kent
Hurst, Robert Henry, Esq. *M.P.* Horsham
Hurt, C. jun. Esq. Wirksworth, Derbyshire
Husenbeth, Chas. Fredk. Esq. St. James's-sq.
Huskisson, Capt. *R.N.* Governor of Greenwich Asylum
Hustler, Wm. Esq. Verulam-bldgs. Gray's-inn
Hutchings, Charles, Esq. Sherborne, Dorset
Hutchins, E. J. Esq. Dowlais, Merthyr Tydvil
Hutchins, Rev. Wm. Winnifred House, Bath
Hutchins, Wm. Esq. Battersea
Hutchinson, Captain E. *R.N.* 7, Grove-road, Lisson-grove
Hutchinson, Dr. Francis, Westgate-street, Newcastle-upon-Tyne
Hutchinson, Richard, Esq. Leeds
Huth, Frederick, Esq.
Hutt, William, Esq. *M.P.* 54, Conduit-street
Hutton, John, Esq. Marske, Yorkshire
Hutton, William, Esq. Gate Burton, near Gainsborough
Hutton, W. M. Esq. 5, Larkhall-lane, Clapham
Hyde, C. J. Esq. 3, Southampton-pl. New-rd.
Hyde, Geo. Esq. 3, Melbury-terrace, Dorset-sq.
Hyde, George, Esq. Norwich
Hyde, Mr. W. H. Bookseller, Newcastle, Staffordshire. 4 Copies
Hyder, W. Esq. Canterbury
Hyndman, J. B. Esq. Trinity Coll. Cambridge. 2 Copies

I.

Ibbetson, Mrs. 37, Wilton-crescent
Ichuster, Leo, Esq. 50, Spring-gardens, Manchester
Iceulden, John, Esq. Doctors'-commons
Ilbert, Wm. Roope, Esq. Horswell House, near Kingsbridge, Devon
Iley, Mr. M. Bookseller, Somerset-st. Portman-square. 2 Copies
Ilderton, Robert, Esq. Lemington Hall
Ilderton, Sanderson, Esq. Lemington Hall
Ing, Mrs. Martha, Mount Pleasant
Ingham, Robert, Esq. *M.P.* Westoe
Ingle, John, Esq. Stonehouse, Devon
Ingle, Thomas, Esq. Lynn Regis, Norfolk
Ingleby, C. Esq. Austwick, nr. Settle, Yorkshire
Inglis, Henry, Esq. Edinburgh
Ingpen, E. Esq. 27, Burton-st. Burton-crescent
Ingram, E. Esq. Town Malling, Kent
Ingram, G. Esq. Cranbrook, Kent
Ingram, Rev. Dr. James, President of Trinity College, Oxford
Ingram, Mr. John, 29, City-road
Innes, Captain, Mill-hill, Middlesex
Ipswich Literary Institution
IRELAND, Right Hon. the Lord Chief Justice of
Ireland, W. Esq. Aldermanbury
Irving, John, jun. Esq. New Broad-street
Irving, W. R. Esq. Trinity College, Cambridge
Isaacs, Elias, Esq. 51, St. Mary Axe
Isaacson, Harvest, Esq. Monmouth
Isaacson, Mr. J. 23, Bury-st. St. Mary Axe
Isaacson, Rev. J. *M.A.* St. John's College, Cambridge
Isherwood, John, Esq. Irwell-place, Broughton, near Manchester
Islington Literary and Scientific Society
Ismay, Mr. Wigton
Ivatt, Mr. Thomas, jun. George Inn, Cottenham, near Cambridge
Ives, Mrs. Catton, Norfolk

J.

Jack, Rev. Archibald, Tynemouth
Jackson, Captain, *R.N.* Milford
Jackson, Charles, Esq. Doncaster

l 2

Jackson, Mrs. Eliz. 4, Regent's-pl. Regent-sq.
Jackson, Mr. G. Booksllr. Hastings. 2 Copies
Jackson, J. S. Esq. District Bank, Manchester
Jackson, J. P. Esq. 1, Aubmrn-st. Manchester
Jackson, Messrs. J. & J. Booksellers, Louth. 5 Copies
Jackson, Rich. Esq. Parliament-st. Hull
Jackson, Robt. Esq. Burmantofis Grove, Leeds
Jackson, Wm. Esq. 8, Church-lane. Liverpool
Jackson, William G. Esq. Wisbeach, Norfolk
Jackson & Co. Messrs. Booksellers, St. Paul's Church-yard 6 Copies
Jacob, Ebenezer, Esq. *M.P.* 14, Manchester-buildings
Jameeson, Mr. R. 196, St. Vincent-st. Glasgow
James, Rev. Edward, Vicarage, Alton
James, Mr. F. Duke's Head, Rochester
James, Henry, Esq. Trinity Coll. Cambridge.
James, Hoskin, Esq. Town Clerk of Truro
James, Captain Joseph, *R.N.* Exeter
James, James, Esq. Stroud, Kent
James, Mr. Jameson, Leith
James, Lieut. R. B. *R.N.* Commander of H.M. Packet Spey, Falmouth
James, Robert, Esq. Glastonbury
James, W. B. Esq. 3, Gloucester-place, New-rd.
James, W. B. Esq. Brunswick-square, Bristol
James, Wm. Tice, Esq. Glastonbury
James, W. T. Esq. *R.N.* John's Coffee-house
James, William, Esq. Maidstone
Jameson, John, Esq. Edinburgh
Jameson, James, Esq. Leith
Jamieson, R. Esq. 32, Argyle-street, Glasgow
Janes, John, Esq. Stock Exchange
Janson, U. H. Esq. Pennsylvania Park, Exeter
Jardine, Sir Henry, Knt. 123, Prince's-street, Edinburgh
Jarrold & Son, Messrs. Booksellers, Norwich. 2 Copies
Jarvis, L. W. Esq. Lynn Regis, Norfolk
Jaulerry, Gerard, Esq. 16, King's-arms-yard
Java Sourabaya Book Club
Jebb, R. Esq. Chirk, Denbighshire
Jefferson, W. B. Esq. Ballabolt, Isle of Man
JEFFERY, Right Hon. Lord, Edinburgh
Jeffery & Son, Messrs. Booksellers, 4, Pall-mall
Jeffrey, Mr. W. R. Ashford, Kent
Jemmett, William, Esq. Ashford, Kent
Jenkins, Alfred, Esq. Trewergie, Redruth
Jenkins, C. E. Esq. 13, Great Prescot-street
Jenkins, George, Esq. Thames Ditton
Jenkins, James, Esq. Chepstow
Jenkins, Rev. William, Vicar of Sidmouth
Jenkins, Henry, Esq. Sidmouth, Devon
Jennard, William, Esq. Kemp Town, Brighton
Jenner, H. Esq. 1, Chesterfield-street
Jennett, Mr. T. Bookseller, Stockton-on-Tees
Jenney, W. Esq. Newton Hall, King's Newton, Derby
Jennings, G. Esq. Dover
Jennings, George, sen. Esq. Buckland
Jennings, J. Esq. Evershot, Dorset
Jephson, C. D. O. Esq. *M.P.* Mallow Castle, Mallow
Jerningham, Hon. E. S. Esq. 9, South Audley-st.
Jerningham, Hon. H. V. S. *M.P.* 11, Grosvenor-street
Jervis, Edward, Esq. Christ Church, Oxford
Jesse, Jos. Abbott, Esq. Princess-st. Manchester
Jessop, E. Esq. Storekeeper, Royal Dock-yard, Devonport
Jessopp, Francis, Esq. Wardwick, Derby
Jevons, Thos. Esq. Tabley-street, Liverpool
Jew, Mr. Thos. Booksllr. Gloucester. 3 Copies
Jewsbury, T. Esq. Market-street, Manchester
Jobling, John, Esq. 4, Eldon-pl. Newcastle-on-Tyne
Johnes, J. Esq. Dolecothy, Carmarthenshire
Johns, Edward, Esq. Penryn, Cornwall
Johnson, Mr. Edward, Croydon
Johnson, George, Esq. Addenbrook's Hospital, Cambridge
Johnson, Henry, Esq. 30, Crutched-friars
Johnson, J. Esq. Liverpool
Johnson, Mr. J. Bkslr. Sidney-st. Cambridge
Johnson, Dr. Jas. Physician Extraordinary to the King, 3, Suffolk-pl. Pall-mall
Johnson, James, Esq. High-street, Manchester
Johnson, Mr. James, Tudor-street
Johnson, Mr. James, Skylark Revenue Cruiser, Milford station
Johnson, Prior, Esq. Aldborough, Suffolk
Johnson, R. Esq. Bute Iron Works, Merthyr Tydvil
Johnson, S. Esq. Downing College, Cambridge
Johnson, Thos. Esq. St. Ann's-sq. Manchester
Johnson, Thomas, Esq. Alderman of London
Johnston, Dr. N. J. Suffolk-place
Johnston, James, Esq. of Straiton
Johnston, R. Esq. 10, Upper Thames-street
Joliffe, C. Esq. Alderney Cottage, near Poole, Dorset
Jolliffe, W. E. Esq. Southampton
Jones, A. Esq. Kirk Ella, Hull
Jones, Arthur, Esq. 13, Judd-place, East
Jones, C. Chadwicke, Esq. Mitre-ct. Temple
Jones, C. K. Esq. Downing Coll. Cambridge
Jones, D. E. Esq. 46, Salisbury-sq. Fleet-street
Jones, Eden Thos. Esq. Thornton Villa, Clifton
Jones, Edw. Esq. 3, Dale-street, Manchester
Jones, Mr. Edward, Pendre, Holywell
Jones, Mr. Edward, 157, Strand
Jones, Francis, Esq. 5, Ludgate-hill
Jones, H. Esq. York-st. Cheetham, Manchester
Jones, Mr. Hugh, Beaumaris
Jones, Rev. H. Wynne, Llansantfraid
Jones, Rev. H. A. *M.A.* Magdalen College, Cambridge
Jones, Col. Sir J. T. Bart. Royal Engineers Brighton
Jones, J. Esq. Friar-gate, Derby
Jones, J. Esq. New Cross, Wolverhampton
Jones, James, Esq. Bradford-st. Birmingham
Jones, Mr. Jasper, Bookseller, Shrewsbury
Jones, John, Esq. Stock Exchange
Jones, John, Esq. 44, Portland-place
Jones, John, Esq. Oswestry
Jones, John, Esq. Brecon
Jones, Mr. John, Portsea
Jones, Rev. M. W. Ospringe, Kent
Jones, W. Esq. Great Russell-st. Bloomsbury
Jones, Rich. Esq. 17, Juvenal-street, Liverpool
Jones, Capt. Theobald, *R.N.*
Jones, Captain Thomas, Liverpool
Jones, Lieut. Thomas, *R.N.* 2, Duchess-street
Jones, Mr. T. Saville place, Leicester-square
Jones, Thos. Esq. *F.R.A.S.* Charing-cross
Jones, Thomas Carr, Esq. 15, Cooper's-row
Jones, W. Esq. Hayle-place, near Maidstone
Jones, Mr. Walter, 15, High-street, Islington
Jones, Warren Willar, Esq. *B.A.* Caius Coll. Cambridge
Jones, Mr. William, Rhayader, South Wales. 2 Copies
Jones, William, Esq. Market-st. Manchester
Jones, William, Esq. Cardiff
Jones, William, Esq. Oldham
Jones, William, Esq. Crosby-square
Jortin, J. Esq. Charlotte-street, Bedford-square
Joule, Benjamin, Esq. Salford
Jowett, J. Esq. Mayor of Ashton-under-Lyne
Jowett, Miss, Bradford, Yorkshire
Joy, H. H. Esq. 11, Gt. Queen-st. Westminster
Joy, John, Esq. Cheam, Surrey
Joy, William, Esq. Northwold, Norfolk
Joyce, Mr. F. Southampton
Joyce, Miss Helen, Hampstead
Judd, William, Esq. Curzon Lodge, Old Brompton
Judge, James Bourne, Esq. Ramsgate

K.

Kalm, Mr. Von, Gentleman of the Chase, Court of Brunswick
KAROLYÉ, Count George, Vienna
KAROLYÉ, Count Stephen, Vienna
Kaslake, J. W. Esq. Magdalen Coll. Cambridge
Kay, Alexander, Esq. Provost of Dundee
Kay, Charles, Esq. Woodhouse-lane, Leeds
Kay, Robt. B. Esq. Friars Hill, Sussex
Kay, Samuel, Esq. Ashton
Kearney, J. Cuthbert, Esq. Garrett's Town
Kearney, Major, Queen's Bays, Norwich
Keasberry, Edward H. Esq. Fifehead, Dorset
Keay, James, Esq. 130, Prince's-st. Edinburgh
Keeling, Wm. Esq. *M.A.* St. John's College, Cambridge
Keeling, G. Esq. 6, New Cannon-st. Manchester
Keen, W. Esq. Canterbury
Keene, Charles, Esq. 102, New Bond-street
Keene, S. B. Esq. 7, Great Coram-street
Keene, Thomas, Esq. 6, Garlick-hill
Kekewich, Samuel Trehawke, Esq. Peamore, near Exeter
Kelland, P. Esq. Queen's College, Cambridge
Kelly, Thomas, Esq. Alderman of London
Kelly, Wm. Esq. Monte Cassino, Isle of Man
Kelsey, F. J. Esq. Harnham Cliff, Salisbury
Kemball, Lieut. W. H. *R.N.* 33, Queen-sq. Bristol
Kemp, Captain, Fort Pitt, Chatham
Kempson, Mr. Robert, Bookseller, 51, Lower Sackville-street, Dublin
Kendal, Friends' Book Society
Kendra, Wm. Esq. 33, Mill-street, Leeds
Kendrick, Mrs. Clovelly, Devon
Kendrick, Wm. Esq. 63, Stockwell, Glasgow
KENMURE, Right Hon. Lord Viscount
Kennaway, Mark, Esq. Exeter
Kennedy, Hon. J. 24, Bryanston-square
Kennedy, Mr. Robert, 59, Stockwell, Glasgow
Kennedy, Thomas, Esq. Havannah-st. Glasgow
Kennedy, W. Esq. 9, Duke-st. Manchester
Kennett, Mr. R. J. Bookseller, York-street
Kenrick, Miss, Peterborough
Kensington Book Society
Kensington, Edw. Esq. 17, St. Dunstan's-hill
Kent, B. Goolden, Esq. Levant Lodge, near Upton-upon-Severn
Kent, George, Esq. Falcon-street, London
Kent, John K. Esq. 33, Craven-street, Strand
Kent, William, Esq. Bathwick-hill, Bath
Kenworthy, J. Esq. Byrom-st. Manchester
Kenyon, Hon. Thomas, Pradoe
Keppel, Hon. Capt. Henry, *R.N.* 1, James-st. Adelphi
Keppel, Hon. T. R. *R.N.* 1, James-st. Adelphi
Keppel, Lieut. Jas. *R.N.* 1, James-st. Adelphi
Ker, John Bellenden, Esq. Southampton
Ker, John, Esq. 127, Brunswick-st. Glasgow

Ker, Thos. C. Esq. 11, Furnival's-inn
Ker, W. jun. Esq. 5, Covent-garden, Liverpool
Kerfoot, Tho. H. Esq. 9, Bread-st. Cheapside
Kernot, Price, & Co. Messrs. Commercial-road, Limehouse. 2 Copies
Kerr, Arch. Esq. 18, Glassford-street, Glasgow
Kerr, John, Esq. 2, Royal-cres. Edinburgh
KERR, Hon. Lord Mark
Kerr, Mr. W. Bookseller, Duke-st. Manchester-sq. 2 Copies
Kerr, Niven, Esq. 4, Great Winchester-street
Kerr, P. Esq. Marsden-square, Manchester
Kerrick, Richard Edward, Esq. Cambridge
Kerry, Mr. Richard, 20, Cork-street
Kerschner, J. Esq. 16, Wilmington-square
Kershaw, E. N. Esq. Catton Hall, Lichfield
Kershaw, James, Esq. High-street, Manchester
Kershaw, Rev. John, Maidstone
Kershaw, Mrs. Park-place, Leeds
Kettlewell, W. Esq. Clapham, Surrey
Key, Jonathan H. Esq. Hampstead
Key, Sir John, Bart. Bedford-square
Key, Lady, Bedford-square
Key, Mrs. S. Stone, Stafford. 3 Copies
Kibble, Mr. J. 30, South Hanover-st. Glasgow
Kibblewhite, James, Esq. Gray's-inn-place
KILDARE, Right Rev. the Lord Bishop of
Kilmarnock, Tradesmen's Library of
KILMOREY, Right Hon. the Earl of
Kinchant, R. H. Esq. Park Hall, Oswestry
Kinder, Mr. Wm. 25, Joan-st. Bedford-row
King, Capt. Andrew, *R.N.* Superintendent of Packets, Falmouth
King, Benj. Esq. Stowmarket, Suffolk
King, Mr. E. Bookseller, Wycombe
King, George, Esq. Redbridge, Southampton
King, Capt. Hon. J.W. *R.N.* Cranbrook, Kent
King, Captain J. *H.M.P.V.* Messenger
King, James, Esq. 4, Tavistock-place
King, Commander John, *R.N.* Portskewitt, near Chepstow
King, John, Esq. Corhampton House, near Droxford, Hants
King, John, Esq. 27, King-street, Portsea
King, Rev. Joshua, *D. D.* President of Queen's College, Cambridge
King, Knowles, Esq. Maidstone
King, Matthew, Esq. Port Glasgow
King, Mr. Bookseller, Leamington
King, R. M. Esq. Pyrland Hall, near Taunton
King, Samuel, Esq. Acorn-terrace, Limehouse
King, Mr. Thomas, Bookseller, Southampton
King, Thomas, Esq. Alvesdiston, Wilts
King, Messrs. W. & T. New-ct. Broad-street
King, Rev. Walker, Archdeacon of Rochester
KINGSBOROUGH, Rt. Hon. Lord Viscount
Kingsbury, M. B. Esq. Bungay, Suffolk
Kingsford, Alfred, Esq. Buckland, near Dover
Kingsford, Edward, Esq. Canterbury
Kingston, Thomas, Esq. 13, Crescent, Clifton
Kinnmard, A. Esq. St. Andrew's-st. Dundee
Kinsey, Rev. W. M. Cheltenham
Kinsman, Capt. R. J. Green Bank, Falmouth
Kinsman, Major, *R.M.* Stonehouse, Devon
Kipling, Mr. Robert, Barnard Castle. 4 Copies
Kirby, William, Esq. York
Kirk, Henry, Esq. Parrs House, Heaton Norris, Stockport
Kirk, Thomas, Esq. 10, Symonds-inn
Kirkley, Edward, Esq.
Kirkness, Capt. W. Stratton-place, Falmouth
Kirkman, J. Esq. 21, Mosley-st. Manchester
Kirkpatrick, G. Esq. Keston
Kirwan, E. Esq. King's College, Cambridge

Klage, Mr. C. Bookseller, Berlin. 5 Copies
Knatchbull, Rev. Dr. Wyndham, Smeeth, Kent
Knatchbull, Right Hon. Sir Edward, Bart. *M.P.* Merstham, Kent
Kneeshaw, Captain, *R.N.* Rochester
Knight, Charles, Esq. 22, Ludgate-street
Knight, Edward, jun. Esq. Chawton House, Alton, Hants
Knight, George Andrew, Esq. Truro
Knight, Mr. H. Poole, Dorset
Knight, I. Esq. 1, Greenwood-st. Manchester
Knight, J. Esq. New Walk, Leicester
Knight, Mr. James Young, Kirkgate, Leeds. 2 Copies
Knight, James, Esq. Southampton
Knight, James, Esq. Pall-mall, Manchester
Knight, Capt. James, jun. 9, Gloucester-sq. Southampton
Knight, John, Esq. Farnham, Hants
Knight, Mr. John, Crawley, Sussex. 4 Copies
Knight, Stephen, Esq. Portreath, near Redruth
Knight, T. Esq. Alton, Hants
Knight, Rev. W. Steventon Rectory, Hants
Knight, William, Esq. 1, Canonbury-place
Knill, J. Esq. 20, Addington-pl. Camberwell
Knowles, John, Esq. Crawley
Knowles, Josh. Esq. Church-street, Manchester
Knowles, W. Esq. Clifton, Gloucestershire
Knowles & Brown, Messrs. Rotherham, Yorksh.
Knox, George, Esq. Barnard Castle
Knox, Hon. Thos. St. John's Coll. Cambridge, and Barham House, Elstree
Knox, Mr. Robert, 13, Exchange-pl. Glasgow
Kray & Ruttray, Messrs. Dock-street, Dundee
Kruse, Mr. Peter, Chelsea
Krusenstern, Vice-Admiral, St. Petersburg
Krusenstierna, Capt. *R.N.* Carlskrona, Sweden
Kuller, Mr. James, Seagate, Dundee
Kusteman, Mjr. W. B. Brews House, Milverton
Kynaston, John, Esq. Poole, Dorset
Kyrke, James, Esq. Glascoed, near Wrexham

L.

Labouchere, Henry, Esq. *M.P.*
Labrey, Thos. Esq. Market-street, Manchester
Lace, F. J. Esq. Ingthorpe Grange, Yorkshire
Lachlan, J. Esq. Great Alie-street
Lacy, H. C. Esq. Kinyon Hall, Manchester
Lade, James, Esq. Port Glasgow, N.B.
Ladell, William, Esq. Braconsdale, Norfolk
Laen, Mr. T. *R.N.* Blackauton, near Dartmouth
Lafargue, Peter Augustus, Esq. Husband's Bosworth, Leicestershire
Laforest, William, Esq. 8, Bedford-row
Lagerstrale, Admiral, P. G. Carlskrona
Lahee, Chas. Esq. 32, Cheyne-walk, Chelsea
Laid, Thomas, Esq. Port Glasgow, N.B.
Laing, Mrs. C. 30, Gt. Coram-st. Brunswick-sq.
Laing & Forbes, Messrs. Booksellers, Glasgow. 5 Copies
Lake, Rev. A. West Walton, near Wisbeach
Lake, R. Esq. 29, Keppel-street, Russell-sq.
Lake, Mr. Wm. Bookseller, Uxbridge. 3 Copies
La Marche, J. B. Esq. High-st. Hull
Lambe, H. Y. Esq. Truro
Lambert, A. B. Esq. 26, Grosvenor-street
Lambert, C. Esq. Blendon Hall, Bexley, Kent
Lambert, J. Esq. Hawkhurst, Kent
Lamond, R. Esq. 60, Ingram-street, Glasgow
Lampeel, C. W. Esq. Clare Hall, Cambridge
Lancashire, Mr. T. G. Bookseller, Huddersfield. 64 Copies

Lander, D.O. Esq. Custom House, Poole, Dorset
Lane, Rev. Charlton, *A.M.* Eltham-place Kennington
Lane, Fred. Esq. Lynn, Norfolk
Lane, J. Esq. 30, Canonbury-square, Islington
Lane, John, Esq. Goldsmiths' Hall
Lane, Joseph, Esq. Cheadle, near Stockport
Lane, Michael, Esq. Braintree
Lane, William, Esq. Stockport
Lang, A. G. Esq. 62, Buchanan-st. Glasgow
Lang, David, Esq. 37, Virginia-street, Glasgow
Lang, Owen, Esq. Woolwich Dock-yard
Langdale, C. Esq. 9, Newton-ter. Kennington
Langdale, Hon. C. *M.P.* 20, Sackville-street
Langley, H. Esq. Dover
Langston, J. H. Esq. *M.P.* 143, Piccadilly
Langton, Capt. E. Gore, St. George's, Bristol
Langton, Col. Gore, *M.P.* Grosvenor-square
Langton, John Bicknell, Esq. Herne-hill
Langton, Zachary, Esq. 6, Bedford-row
Lankester, Thomas, Esq. Bewdley
Lapworth, Mr. R. Bookseller, Stratford-on-Avon. 8 Copies
Large, Mr. W. H. 12, Castle-square, Brighton
Larkins, Capt. Thomas, Quendon, Essex
Lascelles, Hon. Henry, 14, Hanover-square
Latham, W. Esq. 8, St. Ann's-street, Liverpool
La Touche, David Charles, Esq. Dublin
Latter, Edwd. A. Esq. 51, Ship-st. Brighton
Latter, R. B. Esq. Bromley, Kent
Launceston Public Subscription Library
Laurie, Sir Peter, Knt. Alderman of London
Laurie, Mr. R. H. Bookseller, 53, Fleet-street. 3 Copies
Lavender, Mr. Barton House, Ropley, Hants
Laver, Mr. C. 28, Speldhurst-st. Burton-cres.
Lavine, W. G. Esq. 16, Princess-st. Manchester
Law, G. Esq. 10, New-square, Lincoln's-inn
Law, James, Esq. Seagate, N.B.
Lawday, Thos. Esq. Avenue-de-Caen, Rouen
Lawdown, John, Esq. Albany-place, Glasgow
Lawford, Edward, Esq. Drapers' Hall
Lawford, Admiral John, Arundel-street, Strand
Lawford, John, Esq. Drapers' Hall
Lawrence, Isaac, Esq. Watling-street
Lawrie, John, Esq. 1, Robert-st. Adelphi
Lawrie, Patrick, Esq. West End, Hampstead
Laws, James E. Esq. Yarmouth, Norfolk
Lawson, Arch. Esq. 86, Miller-st. Glasgow
Lawson, De C. H. Esq. 6, Woodland-pl. Bath
Lawson, William, Esq. 39, St. Mary-at-hill
Lax, Charles, Esq. Wells, Somersetshire
Lax, Joseph, Esq. Bristol. 4 Copies
Layton Ladies' Book Society
Lea, Mr. J. E. Bkslr. Gloucester. 2 Copies
Leach, George, Esq. Stoke
Leach, Henry, Esq. Collector of H. M. Customs, Milford. 2 Copies
Leadbetter, Mr. J. 77, Queen-street, Glasgow
Leadbitter, John, Esq. York
Leaf, Edwin, Esq. East Dulwich. 2 Copies
Leaf, Mrs. East Dulwich
Leaf, William, Esq. Old 'Change
Leahy, Daniel, Esq. Shanancl, Cork
Leake, John, Esq. Stock Exchange
Lean, John Stuckey, Esq. South-hill, Shepton Mallet
Leather, J. W. Esq. Leeds
Le Blanc, T. Esq. 65, Paper-bldgs. Temple
Lecesne, L. C. Esq. 11, Fenchurch-buildings
Ledgard, G. Esq. Poole, Dorset
Lee, Chas. Esq. 20, Golden-square
Lee, Charles, Esq. Leeds
Lee, Daniel, Esq. 21, Cannon-st. Manchester

Lee, F. Valentine, Esq. Calthorpe-street, Mecklenburgh-square
Lee, G. Esq. 71. Lombard-street
Lee, Henry, jun. Esq. Chiswell-street
Lee, J. L. Esq. Bradford, Yorkshire
Lee, Dr. John, 31, Bedford-place, Russell-sq.
Lee, Mr. John, Booksr. Cheltenham. 2 Copies
Lee, Mr. John, Bradford, Yorkshire
Lee, L. L. Esq. 17. Old Broad-street
Lee, Lieut.-Col. Elford Breton, Topsham, Devon
Lee, Robert, Esq. Welton, Hull
Lee, Wm. Esq. Prospect House, Montpellier
Lee, William, Esq. St. Sidwell's, Exeter
Leechman, Jas. Esq. Melville-place, Glasgow
Leeds Literary Institution
——— New Subscription Library
——— Philosophical and Literary Society
Leefe, J. E. Esq. Trinity College, Cambridge
Lees, Adam, Esq. Ardwick, Manchester
Lees, J. Esq. Stamford-crescent, Ashton-under-Lyne
Leescombe, E. R. Esq. Christ Church, Oxford
Leese, Jos. jun. Esq. Ardwick, Manchester
Leeson, Robert, Esq. Dawlish, Devon
Le-Feuvre, W. Esq. Mayor of Southampton
Lefevre, Chas. S. Esq. *M.P.* 35, Eaton-place
Le Geyt, Mr. George Wm. Jersey. 4 Copies
Legg, S. Esq. 2, Great Knight Ryder-street
Legg, Thomas, sen. Esq. 230, Bermondsey
Legg, Thos. Esq. Abbey House, Bermondsey
Leggatt, H. Esq. Oakfield House, Worth, Sussex
Legge, Hon. Admiral, Sir A. K. *K.C.B* Blackheath
Legge, Hon. Captain, Blackheath
Legge, George, Esq. Ely, Cambridge
Legge, Rev. Geo. 7, Kington-buildings, Bristol
Legge, Hon. H. Dartmouth Grove, Blackheath
Legge, Hon. and Rev. Henry, Blackheath
Le Hunte, G. Esq. Trinity College, Cambridge
Leigh, C. Esq. Christ College, Cambridge
Leigh, Robert, Esq. Taunton
Leigh, W. Esq. 37, Market-st. Manchester
LEINSTER, His Grace the Duke of
Leir, Rev. Paul, Charlton Musgrove, Somerset
Leister, John, Esq. 32, Booth-st. Manchester
Leitch, Capt. John, Ship Montreal, Liverpool
Lemare, E. N. Esq. Broughton View, Manchester
Le Merchant, Rev. J. Newport, Isle of Wight
Lemon, Sir Charles, Bart. *M.P. F.R.S.* 46, Charles-street, Berkeley-square
Lemon, Mr. Palmer House Academy, Holloway
Leo, H. Esq. 4. Bond-street, Manchester
Leonard, Isaac, Esq. Portland-square, Bristol
Leonard, Isaac, Esq. 1, Brunswick-sq. Bristol
Leonard, Robert, Esq. Brislington, Bristol
Le-Pipre, P. Esq. Crown Office, Temple
Leslie, Mr. John, Bookseller, 52, Great Queen-street, Lincoln's-inn-fields
Lester, Major, W. H. *H.E.I.C.* Army, Taunton
Lestourgeon, Charles, Esq. Cambridge
Letham, Mr. Patrick, 49, Virginia-st. Glasgow
Lethbridge, J. H. Esq. Sandhill Park, Taunton
Lethbridge, Sir Thomas Buckler, Bart. Sandhill Park, near Taunton
Lett, John, Esq. Brixton Rise
Lett, Mrs. Mary, Mosley-street, Manchester
Letton, Mr. George, White Lion Inn, Wisbeach
Letts, Messrs. Booksellers, Royal Exchange. 13 Copies
Levesque, P. Esq. 29, Guildford-street
Levien, Edward, Esq. Stock Exchange
Levien, John, Esq. Stock Exchange
Levy, Mr. Charles, Rochester
Lewin, R. H. Esq. March, Cambridge
Lewin, Thomas, Esq. Bexley, Kent
Lewis, D. Esq. 28, Artillery-pl. West Finsbury
Lewis, D. B. Esq. Rochester
Lewis, Frances R. Esq. 227, Gt. Ancoats-st. Manchester
Lewis, Mr. J. 58, Gt. Russell-st. Bloomsbury
Lewis, James, Esq. 27, Great Russell-street
Lewis, Mr. Robert
Lewis, Capt. T. Locke, *R.E.* Exeter
Lewis, Mr. Thomas, J. Milford-haven
Lewis, Rev. Thos. 15, Compton-ter. Islington
Lewis, Thos. Esq. Foxdown, near Wellington
Lewis, Thomas, Esq. 70, Baker-street
Lewis, Thomas, Esq. 23, Park-street, Bristol
Ley, Rev. Carrington, Bere Regis, Dorset
Ley, James S. Esq. Durant House, Devon
Leyland, Rd. B. Esq. Walton Hall, Liverpool
Library of 50th Regt. of Foot
LICHFIELD, Rt. Hon. the Earl of
Lichfield Permanent Library
Liddle, Wm. Esq. 69, High John-st. Glasgow
Liebert, B. Esq. Halfmoon-street, Manchester
Liebieich, Edward E. Esq. Leeds
LIEVEN, His Highness the Prince of
LIEVEN, Prince Paul
Lignum, Dr. Bridge-street, Manchester
Lillie, James, Esq. Manchester
Lilly, F. Esq. Corn-exchange, Manchester
Lilly, R. F. Esq. Brunswick-square, Bristol
LINCOLN, The Earl of, *M.P.*
Lincoln Monthly Book Society
Lincoln's Inn Book Society
Lindo, Nathaniel, Esq. Throgmorton-street
Lindon, Wm. Esq. Cheetham-hill, Manchester
LINDSAY, Right Hon. Lord
Lindsay, Hon. H. H. 22. Berkeley-square
Lindsay, Hon. Hugh, 22, Berkeley-square
Lindsay, Thos. S. Esq. Dublin
Lindsell, Mr. H. Bookseller, 87, Wimpole-st. 2 Copies
Lisle, Rev. W. B. M. St. Fagan's, Glamorgansh.
LISTOWEL, Right Hon. the Earl of
Little, Mrs. Cripplegate House, Worcester
Little, Capt. T. Smack Swan, Liverpool
Littledale, Thomas, Esq. Liverpool
Littlehales, Rear-Adm. 6, Campden-pl. Bath
Livermore, James, Esq. 21, Tower-street
Liverpool, Clarendon Book Society of
Liverpool, English and French Book Society of
——— Friends' Book Society
——— Library
——— Union Book Society
Livesey, A. Esq. Church-street, Manchester
Living, Mr. William, Clapham-road-place
Livingstone, William, Esq. Huddersfield
Lizaur, J. A. D. Esq. 33, Chester-terrace
Llewellin, R. Esq. Holme Wood, Westbury
Llewellyn, Miss Mary, Cowbridge. 3 Copies
Lloyd, Dr. B. Provost of Trinity Coll. Dublin
Lloyd, D. Esq. Banker, Halesworth, Suffolk
Lloyd, E. J. Esq. Old Field House, Altringham, Manchester
Lloyd, Eyre, Esq. Beaumaris
Lloyd, Mr. E. Bkslr. 57, Harley-st. 4 Copies
Lloyd, Henry, Esq. Lombard-street
Lloyd, John, Esq. Cannon-street, Manchester
Lloyd, Richard Middleton, Esq. Wrexham
Lloyd, Sampson, Esq. Mosley-st. Manchester
Lloyd, Theo. Esq. Netherton House, Bewdley
Lloyd, Thomas P. Esq. 5, Old Broad-street
Lloyd, W. Esq. Aston Hall, Oswestry
Lloyd, William, Esq. Ludlow
Lloyd's, The Committee of
Lobb, Jos. Esq. Southampton
Lobb, William, Esq. 140, Aldersgate-street
Löbbeche, Mr. Frederick, Banker, Brunswick
Locke, J. B. Esq. 12, Church-st. Manchester
Locke, John, Esq. 2, Harcourt-buildings
Locke, T. B. Esq. Hessle-mount, Hull
Lockett, Mr. J. Apple-market, Manchester
Lockett, William J. Esq. Wardwick, Derby
Lockwood, Rev. C. B. Bury St. Edmund's
Lockwood, Mrs. Betchworth, Surrey
Lockwood, Miss, Betchworth, Surrey
Loder, Mr. R. Bookseller, Brighton. 6 Copies
Lodge, J. Esq. Magdalen College, Cambridge
Lodge, Mrs. Carlisle
Loft, Thomas C. Esq. Hull
LOFTUS, Lord Adam, Baliol College, Oxford
Loftus, Chas. Esq. Little Dunham, Norfolk
Log, T. Esq. Caius College, Cambridge
Lomas, Thos. Esq. Market-street, Manchester
Lomas, Thomas, Esq. Cannon-st. Manchester
Lomax, Mr. F. G. Bookslr. Lichfield. 6 Copies
Lomax, John, Esq. Bury, Lancashire
Lomax, Major-Gen. 9, Park-street, Bristol
Lomer, W. Esq. jun. 5, High-st. Southampton
LONDON, Right Hon. The Lord Mayor (H. Winchester, Esq.)
——— The Sheriffs of, and of Middlesex, (Mr. Alderman Harmer, and Mr. Alderman Wilson)
——— The Recorder of (Hon. C. Ewan Law)
——— The Chamberlain of (Sir James Shaw, Bart.)
——— The Town Clerk of (H. Woodthorpe, Esq. *LL.D. F.S.A.*)
——— The Common Sergeant (J. Mirehouse, Esq.)
——— The Remembrancer of (Edward Tyrrell, Esq.)
——— The City Solicitor (W. L. Newman, Esq.)
——— Royal College of Surgeons of
——— Assurance Company
——— Institution
——— King's College of
Long, Peter B. Esq. Ipswich
Long, Miss Tylney, Holmwood, Surrey
Long, Walter, Esq. Preshaw House, Alresford
Longdon, Robert, Esq. 32, Friar-gate, Derby
Longlands, Henry, Esq. Charlton, Kent
Longman & Co. Messrs. Paternoster-row. 112 Copies
Longe, Rev. Robert, Coddenham, Suffolk
Loraine, W. Esq. Eldon-st. Newcastle-on-Tyne
Lord, Mr. John, Church-row, Hampstead
Losack, Mr. R. West Malling, Kent
Loswenborg, P. C. S. 1st Lieutenant Swedish Royal Navy, Carlskrona
Lothian, T. Esq. 8, Chester-ter. Regent's-park
LOVAINE, Right Hon. Lord
Love, W. A. Esq. Downing Coll. Cambridge
Loveday, Major-Gen. 13, Grosvenor-pl. Bath
Lovejoy, Mr. G. Bookseller, Reading. 5 Copies
Lovejoy's Subscription Library, Reading
Lovelace, Mr. John, Bookseller, 10, Munster-street, Regent's-park. 3 Copies
Lovett, T. Esq. Fernhill Hall, Oswestry
Low, —. Esq. Lyndhurst, Hants
Low, Archibald, Esq. Portsea
Low, Mr. S. Bookseller, Lamb's Conduit-st. 3 Copies
Lowe, Rev. Thos. Hill, Precentor of Exeter
Lowndes, J. H. Esq. 46, Pall-mall, Manchester
Loyd, Edward, Esq. Bank, Manchester

Lucas, Charles. Esq. 21, Fenchurch-street
Lucas, Matthew Prime, Esq. Alderman of London
Lucas, R. C. Esq. University College, Oxford
Lucas, Robert, Esq. 53, Lincoln's-inn-fields
Luck, Richard, Esq. Rutland-street, Leicester
Lukyn, R. Esq. Faversham, Kent
Lumb, Henry, Esq. Wakefield
Lunnon, Mr. William
Lupton, Thomas, Esq. Leeds
Luscombe, S. Esq. Exeter
Lushington, E. S. Esq. Trinity Coll. Cambridge
Luxmoore, C. J. Esq. Rose-mount, Alphington
Lyall, George, Esq. *M.P.* 17, Park-crescent
Lyde, Lionel, Esq. 291, Regent-street
Lyle, W. G. Esq. 10, Gt. James-st. Bedford-rw
Lynch, John, jun. Esq. Tralee, Ireland
Lynch, Nicholas J. Esq. St. Christopher's
LYNDOCH, Right Hon. Genl. Lord, *G.C.B.*
Lyne, L. S. Esq. 4, Old Broad-street
Lyne, Thomas, Esq. Sevenoaks, Kent
Lynn, Rev. James, Gad's-hill House, near Rochester
Lynn, Watt, Esq. Sheffield
Lynn, Wm. Esq. Waterloo Hotel, Liverpool
Lyon, Rev. R. Sherborne, Dorset
Lys, M. Esq. Ridgway, near Lymington
LYTTELTON, Right Hon. Lord
LYTTELTON, Right Hon. the Dowager Lady, Great Malvern, Worcestershire. 2 Copies

M.

Maaivil, Jas. Esq. Crown and Anchor, Finsbury-pavement
Mac Allister, Alex. Esq. 50, Brunswick-street, Glasgow
Macallister, Mr. J. Queen's Court, Glasgow
Mac Bride, Mr. Hugh, Master of Clarence Dock, Liverpool
MACCLESFIELD, Right Hon. the Earl of
Macclesfield, Library of
Mac Culloch, James, Esq. Guernsey
Macdonald J. Esq. Secretary to the Highlands' Society
Macdonalds, —, Esq. 33, Abchurch-lane
Mac Dougal, Monteith and Co. Messrs. Mexico, South America
Mace, J. Ellis, Esq. Tenterden, Kent
Macfarlane, Rev. Dr. Principal of Glasgow College
Macfarlane, Major J. Frant, Sussex
Mac Gibbon, Walter, Esq. 26, Glassford-street, Glasgow
Macgowan, Dr. Edward, Exeter
Macgregor, Walter, P. Esq. Vauxhall Foundery, Liverpool
Mac Haffie, Wm. Esq. Tibb-street, Manchester
Mac Haffies, Mr. Jas. 21, St. Andrew's-sq. Glasgow
Mac Haffies, Mr. Robt. 42, West George-st. Glasgow
Machin, J. M. Esq. York Club, Waterloo-pl.
Machkeclmie, A. Esq. Hythe, Kent
Mac Indoe, A. Esq. 125, Virginia-st. Glasgow
Mac Intosh, C. Esq. Cross Basket, Glasgow
Mac Intyre, D. Esq. 40, Dunlop-st. Glasgow
Mackay, Captain, 6th Dragoons
Mackay, T. H. Esq. St. John's Coll. Cambridge
Mac Kay, Thos. G. Esq. 10, Walker-street Edinburgh
MACKENZIE, Right Hon. Lord, Edinburgh
Mackenzie, J. J. R. Esq. Trin. Col. Cambridge
Mackenzie James A. Stewart, Esq. *M.P.* 8, St. James's-place
Maclachlan, Walter, Esq. Port Glasgow, N. B.
Maclagan, Thos. Esq. Craftness, Aberfeldy, Perthshire
Maclea, Charles G. Esq. Water-lane, Leeds
Maclean, Dr. Allan, Colchester
Maclean, J. Esq. Broad-street Chambers
Mac Lean, James, Esq. Port Glasgow, N. B.
Mac Lellan, A. W. D. Esq. 70, Miller-st. Glasgow
Mac Leod, Colonel D. Oriental Club
Macnical, A. A. Esq. Lieut. Adjt. 1st Royal Regt.
Madras, Book Society of the Madras European Regiment
Magnus, Martin L. Esq. Steel-yard, Upper Thames-street
Magor, John P. Esq. Penventon, Redruth
Magrath, Sir George, *M.D. F.R.S.* Plymouth
Maher, Capt. M. C. *W.S.R.Y.C.* Taunton
Mahony, Rev. D. Cork
MAIDSTONE, Rt. Hon. Lord Viscount
Maidstone Literary Institution
Main, Mr. H. Manchester Steamer, Liverpool
Maine, Rev. John Thos. Rector of Husband's Bosworth, Leicestershire
Mainland, Mr. Wm. Brig Annie, Liverpool
Mainwaring, Lieut. B. *R.N.* Barton Cliff, Christchurch, Hants
Mainwaring, Sir H. Bart. Peover Hall, Cheshire
Mainwaring, Rev. Jas. Bramberof Park, Cheshire
Mair, John, Esq. 17, Vere-street
Maitland, Adam, Esq. of Dundrennan, Kirkcudbright
Maitland, Sir A. C. Gibson, Bart. Charlotte-sq. Edinburgh
Maitland, E. F. Esq. 11, Bryanstone-square. 2 Copies
Maitland, Rear-Admiral, Sir F. L. *K.C.B.* Portsmouth Dock-yard
Maitland, Rev. Garbes, Monigaff, Newton Stewart
Maitland, J. Esq. of Dundrennan, Kircudbright
Major, Jas. Esq. Mayor of Folkstone, Kent
Major, Wm. Esq. 260, Whitechapel-road
Majoribanks, E. Esq. 34, Wimpole-street
Makin, J. Esq. Broughton Mills, Manchester
Makins, Charles, Esq. Woodhouse-la. Leeds
Makinson, J. Esq. Market-street, Manchester
Malbon, Jas. Esq. 3, Newcastle-st. Strand
Malcolm, Jesse, Esq. 22, High-street, Hull
Male, W. H. Esq. Comptroller of His Majesty's Customs, St. Christopher's
Malin, R. Esq. 60, Deansgate, Manchester
Malkahen, Mr. Wm. Bookseller, Merthyr Tydvil. 18 Copies
Mallard, Peter, Esq. Stock Exchange
Mallard, Wm. Esq. Clarence-pl. Kingdown, Bristol
Mallcott, John, Esq. 12, Newgate-street
M'Alpine, James, Esq. Leith, N.B.
Mammatt, John, Esq. Ashby-de-la-Zouch
Manbey, Wm. Esq. Stratford
Manchester, Bloomsbury Reading-rooms
——— Exchange-street Library
——— Newell's-bldgs, Reading Society
——— Peel-street, Book Society
——— Portico Library, Mosley-street
——— Subscription Library
Mandell, Rev. H. D. Queen's Coll. Cambridge
Manico, P. Esq. 11, Southampton-st. Covent-garden
Manley, J. H. E. Esq. *R.N.* Brompton, Kent
Mann, Jas. Esq. Norwich
Mann, John Esq. 173, Aldersgate-street
Mann, M. Esq. Church-st. Manchester
Mann, Robt. Esq. Great Bridgewater-street, Manchester
Manning, Edward B. Esq. Lynn, Norfolk
Manning, John, Esq. 2, Dyer's-bldgs. Holborn
Manning, W. M. Esq. 11, King's-bench-walk, Temple
Manning, Wm. Esq. 7, One Stone, Mile-end-rd.
Manningford, Jno. Esq. Bristol
Mansell, Captain, *R.N.*
Mansell, Capt. Thos. *R.N.* Guernsey
Mansfield Subscription Library
Manson, Dr. Alex. *F.R.S.* Nottingham
Manton, Edward, Esq. Cheltenham
MANVERS, Rt. Hon. the Earl of
March, Joseph Ogden, Esq. Water-lane, Leeds
Marchant, Mrs. Eliz. Gray's-place, Fulham-rd.
Marcus, H. J. Esq. Leeds
Mares, John, Esq. Mayor of Maidstone
Markham, Rev. D. F. Canon of Windsor
Markham, William, Esq. Col. 2d West York Militia, Becca Hall
Markland, Capt. John Duff, *R.N.* Handley House, Woodcots, Dorset
Marks, Mr. John, King's Cross, Gray's-inn-rd.
Markwell, Mr. John, Long's Hotel, Bond-st.
Marlborough Book Society
Marmont, J. Esq. Horfield, Bristol
Marples, Messrs. D. and Co. 65, Lord-street, Liverpool
Marr, Jas. Esq. Surgeon, Saville-place, North Shields
Marr, John Marshall, Esq. 43, Portland-place
Marriott, J. C. Esq. Narborough, Norfolk
Marriott, Mrs. Horsham, Sussex
Marriott, Rev. W. M. S. Horsemanden, Kent
Marryat, Mrs. Wimbledon House, Wimbledon
Marsh, G. H. Esq. St. John's Coll. Cambridge
Marsh, Mr. Bookseller, York. 2 Copies
Marsh, Mr. Thos. Bookseller, York
Marshall, Benjamin A. Esq. St. Peter's Coll. Cambridge
Marshall, Sir Chapman, Knt. Alderman of London
Marshall, H. C. Esq. *M.C.* Cheltenham
Marshall, Captain, J. *R.N.* Upnor, Kent
Marshall, J. Esq. Water-lane, Leeds
Marshall, J. jun. Esq. Water-lane, Leeds
Marshall, J. G. Esq. Water-lane, Leeds
Marshall, J. S. Esq. 11, New Brown-st. Manchester
Marshall, John, Esq. Elm, Cambridge
Marshall, Lady, 43, Russell-square
Marshall, Mr. M. H. 121, Princes-st. Edinburgh
Marshall, P. Esq. Surgeon, Shepton Mallett
Marshall, Mr. R. Alton, Hants
Marshall, Thos. Esq. Fenny, Huddersfield
Marshall, Capt. W. 20, Circus, Greenwich
Marshall, Mr. Wm. 11, Green-ter. New River Head
Marshall, Wm. Esq. Ely, Cambridge
MARSHAM, Right Hon. Lord Viscount
Marsham, Rev. G. Allington, Kent
Marsham, Joseph, Esq. Fig-court, Temple
Marsland, Henry, Esq. *M.P.* Stockport
Marsland, Thomas, Esq. *M.P.* Stockport
Marten, William, Esq. Bradford, Yorkshire
M'Arthur, D. Esq. Park street, Bristol
Martin, Dr A. Chatham
Martin, Chas. Esq. 81, Rue Aux Ours, Rouen
Martin, Adml. Sir G. *G.C.B.* 51, Berkeley-sq.
Martin, Rev. George, Chancellor of the Diocese of Exeter

Martin, J. A. Esq. Sidbrook, near Taunton
Martin, R. Esq. 13, Bank Parade, Manchester
Martin, Simon, Esq. Norwich
Martin, Sir Roger, Bart. Burnham, Norfolk
Martin, Adml. Sir Thomas Byam, *G.C.B.K.S.* Wimpole-street
Martin, W. Esq. Norwich
Martyn, Rev. Thos. W. Lifton Rectory, Devon
Martyr, James, Esq. Union Dk.-yd. Limehouse
Marx, G. Esq. 81, Eaton-square
Maskell, J. Esq. 34, Fore-street
Mason, Hon. Mrs. Eastland Villa, Ryde, Isle of Wight
Massey, Edward, Esq. Norwich
Massingbend, Mrs. Beckingham, nr. Gainsboro'
Masson, Jno. Esq. 5 Lime-street-square
Master, Lieut. Col. W. E. Knowle Park, near Bristol
Mather, Capt. R. Clayton-street, Liverpool
Mather, Dr. 112, Irongate, Glasgow
Mather, Mr. 99, Glassford-st. Glasgow
Mathew, Dan. Byam, Esq. St. Christopher's
Mathew, Nathaniel, Esq. Ixworth, Suffolk
Matley, Richd. Esq. High-street, Manchester
Matthews, J. Esq. Gravesend
Matthews, Saml. Esq. 46, Cheapside
Matthewson, Wm. Esq. 31, Rose-st. Glasgow
Manchant, Mrs. Elizabeth, 4, Gray's-place
Maude, Edmund, Esq. 4, Harcourt-buildings, Temple. 2 Copies
Maude, Hon. Capt. J. Ashley, *R.N. C.B.* 22, Arundel-st. Strand
Maude, James, Esq. Kirkgate, Leeds
Maude, J. M. Esq. 32, Gt. Winchester-street
Maude, Captain William, *R.N.* 30, Abingdon-street, Westminster
Maudslay & Co. Messrs. Westminster-road
Maughan, Capt. W. Cheltenham
Maul, G. Esq. University College, Oxford
Maunsell, T. P. Esq. Thorpe Malsor, Northamptonshire
Maus, J. jun. Esq. Huddersfield
Maw, R. Stovin, Esq. *R.N.* Horton Lodge, Colnbrook, Bucks
Maxwell, Rev. Geo. Ower Moigne, Dorset
Maxwell, Marmaduke Constable, Esq. Terregles, near Dumfries
Maxwell, Mrs. Kirkconnel, near Dumfries
Maxwell, Peter, Esq. Beckford, Gloucestershire
Maxwell, Robert, Esq. Charleville
Maxwell, Sir W. Bart. Monreith, Wigton
May, Mr. Thos. 49. Conduit-st. Bond-street
May, Mr. W. 8, Prospect Cottage, Islington
Maynard, —. Esq. 32, Sackville-street
MAYNARD, Rt. Hon. Lady, Easton Lodge
Mayne, Capt. Charles Otway, *R.N.* 19, Hanover-terrace
Mayne, Col. J. *C.B.* 31, Melville-st. Edinburgh
Mayne, R. Esq. 42, Melville-st. Edinburgh
Mayor, George, Esq. 2, Little Distaff-lane
Mayor, Henry, Esq. 115, Upper-st. Islington
Maze, Peter, Esq. Rownham Lodge, Bristol
Maze, Peter, jun. Esq. Sheriff of Bristol
M'Bean, Mr. Duncan, 187, Athol-pl. Glasgow
M'Carthy, Alex. Esq. 4, Mountjoy-square East Dublin
M'Clure, Mr. Jno. Peel-st. Manchester
M'Coll, Dongald, Esq. St. Christopher's
M'Culloch, A. Esq. Dumfries
M'Culloch, J. Esq. Pierre Percée, Guernsey
M'Culloch, Walter, Esq. 139, George-st. Edin
M'Diarmid, Mr. J. Courier Office, Dumfries. 8 Copies
M'Donald, Mr. James, 164, Hope-st. Glasgow
M'Donald, Capt. John, *R.N.* Lewisham
M'Donald, Mr. Wm. 43, Miller-st. Glasgow
M'Donnell, Capt. T. 8, Dorset-pl. Dorset-sq.
M'Donnll, Col. Robert, *C.B.* Stranraer, N.B.
M'Dongald, Colonel, St. Christopher's
M'Gregor, Alex. Esq. St. Christopher's
Meadows, Dan. R. Esq. Burghersh House, Witnisham, Suffolk
Mears, Thomas, Esq. Whitechapel
Mears, Rev. Thos. Southampton
Meares, George G. Esq. Cornwallis House, Clifton
Mecham, Capt. Rodwell, Weymouth, Dorset
Medcalf, Wm. Esq. 17, Hanging Ditch, Manchester
Medd, John, Esq. Stockport
MEDWYN, Rt. Hon. Lord, Edinburgh
Meek, James, Esq. Comptroller of Victualling
Meeking, Charles, Esq. 62, Holborn-hill
Meeson, Richd. Jas. Esq. Stratford
Meeson, W. Esq. Stone, Staffordshire
Meggs, Capt. G. Hyde Vale, Greenwich
Meheux, John, Esq. 52, Hans-pl. Sloane-st.
Meiklam, W. Esq. Corpus Christi College, Oxford
Meikleham, Wm. Esq. 6, Maxwelton-place, Glasgow
Mein, Mr. Alex. 42, Miller-st. Glasgow
Meir, Mr. Henry, Bugle Inn, Newport, Isle of Wight
Melander, F. Commander *R.S.N.* Carlskrona
Mellborn, George, Esq. 13, Milman-street, Bedford-row
Mellor, Edwin, Esq. Ashton
Mellor, John, Esq. Ashton
Mellor, J. Esq. 2, Hilton-street, Manchester
Melmoth, J. P. Esq. Sherborne, Dorse
Melvil, Robt. A. Esq. 110, Fenchurch-street
MELVILLE, Rt. Hon. Lord Viscount
Mendelsohn, J. Esq. Berlin
Menzies, J. Esq. of Pitfodles, 24, York-place, Edinburgh
Menzies, Sir Niel, Bart. Castle Menzies, Edinburgh
Mercer, John, Esq. Maidstone
Mercer, John, jun. Esq. Ramsgate
Mercier, Francis, Esq. Stock Exchange
Mercer, John, jun. Esq. Ramsgate
Meredith, James B. Esq. 1, Heathcote-street, Mecklenburgh-square
Meriweather, Sam. Esq. Corn-street, Bristol
Merivale, J. H. Esq. 15, Woburn-place
Merridew, Mr. H. Library, Coventry
Merridew, Mr. J. Bookslr. Warwick. 10 Copies
Mestayer, Mrs. Reading, Berks
Mester, C. H. Esq. St. John's Coll. Cambridge
Metcalfe, William, Esq. Jesus Coll. Cambridge
Metevier, C. Esq. 2, Richmond-hill, Clifton
METTERNICH, His Highness the Prince
Meux, Sir H. Bart. 19, Great Russell-street
Mew, Mr. Henry, Newport, Isle of Wight
Meyrick, Wm. Esq. Merthyr Tydvil
M'Farlane, John, Esq. George-st. Manchester
M'Gillivray, S. Esq. Hudson's Bay Company
M'Gregor, Alex. Esq. Oxford-st. Liverpool
M'Grigor, Sir J. Bart. *M.D. F.R.S.* 5, Berkeley-street
Micklethwait, J. R. Esq. Rotherham, Yorksh.
Mickleburgh, James, and Son, Messrs. Thanet House, Margate
Miehan, Mr. A. J. 51, Quadrant
Michel, Rev. James, Sturminster Newton, Dorset
Michell, Capt. J. Fred. *R.N.* Totness, Devon
Michell, Edward, Esq. Truro
MIDDLETON, Rt. Hon. Lord
Middleton, Charles, Esq. Crawley
Middleton, J. Esq. 6, Gloucester-row, Clifton
Middleton, Mr. Wm. 168, George-st. Glasgow
Miers, Capel, Esq. Neath
Mildmay, Paulet St. John, Esq. *M.P.* East Gate House, Winchester
Miles, Miss Eliza, Clifton, Gloucestershire
Miles, Hy. Esq. 2, Middle Temple-lane
Miles, Philip John, Esq. *M.P.* Leigh Court, Bristol
Miles, Roger, Esq. Leicester
Miles, Wm. Esq. *M.P.* 7, Hamilton-place
Miles, Wm. Esq. 10, Dix's Field, Exeter
Milward, George, Esq. Manor House, Lechlade, Gloucester
Milford, Samuel, Esq. Truro
Mill, Sir Charles, Bart. Bury, Southampton
Mill, J. Esq. Lloyd's Coffee-house
Millar, Robt. Esq. Cowgate
Miller and Co. Messrs. 4, Broad-st. Bloomsb.
Miller, Gorrell House, Barnstaple
Miller, Horatio, Esq. Market-st. Manchester
Miller, Mr. John, jun. Library, Portsmouth
Miller, John, Esq. *F.L.Z.* and *H.S.* Nursery Villa, Clifton
Miller, John, Esq. Furnival's-inn
Miller, Jos. Esq. 6, Brunswick-ter. Commercial-road
Miller and Son, Messrs. Yarmouth, Norfolk
Miller, Mr. Robt. George Inn, Southampton
Miller, W. H. Commander of H. M. Revenue Cutter Active, Falmouth
Millett, Chas. Esq. Bramdean House, Alresford
Millett, John, N. R. Esq. Penzance
Millett, Richard, Esq. Penzance
Milliken, Messrs. Andrew & Son, Booksellers, Dublin. 34 Copies
Millner, Mr. Gainsborough
Mills, W. Esq. Cross-street, Manchester
Mills, John, Esq. 12, Park-st. Grosvenor-sq.
Mills, John, Esq. 14, Euston-square
Mills, Lieut.-Col. Willington, near Durham
Mills, Markham, Esq. Christ Church College, Oxford, and 36, Pulteney-street, Bath
Mills, M. Thomas, Esq. Taunton
Milne, H. C. Esq. Harcourt-buildings
Milner, H. Esq. 3, Hysley Cross
Milnes, Mr. Edward, Bradford, Yorkshire
Milthorp Book Society
MILLTOWN, Right Hon. the Earl of
Milward, Geo. Esq. Manor House, Lechlade, Gloucestershire
Minet, Capt. Lewis, Delvidere, Frant, Sussex
M'Innes, G. E. Esq. 4, Water-lane, Tower-st.
MINTO, Right Hon. the Earl of
M'Intosh, David, Esq 39, Bloomsbury-square
M'Intyre, John, Esq. Brown-st. Manchester
Mirehouse, John, Esq. Common Serjeant of London
Missing, Richard, Esq. Tichfield, Hants
Mitchel, Mr. John, Bookseller, 33, Old Bond-street. 4 Copies
Mitchell, Mrs. J. Tusmore House, near Brackley
Mitchell, Mr. Richard, Leicester
Mitchell, Mr. Thomas, Bradford, Yorkshire
Mitford, Robt. Esq. 34, Russell-square
Mittis, Thomas, Esq. King's-road, Chelsea
M'Iver, D. Esq. 53, Water-street, Liverpool
M'Kenzie, Miss C. 1, Castle-st. Edinburgh
M'Laren, Mr. Hamilton, 20, Miller-st. Glasgow
M'Leod, James, Esq. 75, Argyle-st. Glasgow
M'Millan, Dr. Quinton, Milford

M'Millan, Mr. T. 7, Stegman's-row, Islington
M'Murdo, Colonel Bryce, Dumfries
M'Murdo, Chas. Esq. High-street, Liverpool
M'Murdo, D. Esq. Provan-place, Glasgow
M'Naghten, Capt. *R.N.* 10, Bedford-row
M'Namara, Hon. Mrs. Richmond, Surrey
Moad, John, Esq. Grange, Wareham
Moat, Thos. Esq. 1, Hamilton-pl. New-road
Mocatta, Moses, Esq. Russell-square
Moffat, Corn. Esq. Merton College, Oxford
Moffat, John, Esq. Settle, Yorkshire
Mogg, John Jenner, Esq. West Park, Bristol
Mohr, Mr. J. C. B. Bookseller, Heidelberg
Moises, Hugh, Esq. Amble House, Alnwick
Molesworth, T. P. Esq. St. Austin's, Lymington
Moline, R. Esq. 42, Lime-street
Molineaux, Ths. Esq. Ancoats-cr. Manchester
Molineux, C. Esq. Wolverhampton
Molini, Mr. C. F. Bookseller, 14, Paternoster-row. 3 Copies
Molini, Mr. Jos. Florence
Molloy, James Scott, Esq. Dublin
Molyneux, Edmund, Esq. Newsham House, Liverpool
MONCRIEFF, Rt. Hon. Lord, Edinburgh
Moncrieff, Hugh, Esq. Exchange-ct. Glasgow
Moneypenny, Capt. T. Frezingham House, Kent
Monins, R. E. Esq. St. John's Coll. Cambridge
Monkhouse, Cyril J. Esq. 3, Craven-street
MONSON, Rt. Hon. Lord
Montagu, H. S. Esq. Somerset House
Montefiore, H. J. Esq. Stock Exchange
Monteith, C. G. Stewart, Esq. Abercromby-place, Edinburgh
Monteith, Capt. Wm. Liverpool
Monteith, Wm. Esq. 15, Hutchinson-st. Port Glasgow, N. B.
Montgomery, Robert, Esq. Dublin
Montgomery, William, Esq. Annick Lodge, Ayrshire
Moody, Miss, Newmarket
Moon, J. Esq. Cromford-court, Manchester
Moor, Lieut. Philip, *R.N.* Cullumpton, Devon
Moore, John, Esq. Mayor of Plymouth
Moore, —, Esq. Queen's College, Cambridge
Moore, Ambrose, Esq. Milk-street
Moore, Capt. Chas. *R.N.* Aldburgh, Suffolk
Moore, Charles, Esq. Yarmouth, Norfolk
Moore, Rev. Charles, Penzance
Moore, Jas. Esq. Bridge-street, Manchester
Moore, Wm. Esq. Grimeshill, Westmorland
Moore, James, Esq. Montague House, Bristol
Moore, Mr. Jno. jun. Leicester
Moore, Lieut. J. *R.N.* Swanage
Moore, Mr. Robt. Castle-street, Cambridge
Moore, Rev. R. St. Giles's, Woodyates, Dorset
Moore, Richard, Esq. Marine Parade Hotel
Moore, Mr. Wm. Agent to the Londonderry Steam Packet Company
Moore, Rev. William, Truro
Moore, W. Esq. Wychnon Lodge, Staffordshire
Moorhouse and Brown, Messrs. Hull
Morcom, Wm. Esq. Redruth
Mordan, Mr. J. S. 22½, City-road
Mordaunt, Mr. A. Southampton
More, Richard, Esq. Norwich
Morgan, Chas. Esq. Ruperra, near Newport, Monmouth
Morgan, David, Esq. Stratford Green, Essex
Morgan, G. J. Esq. Ashford, Kent
Morgan, H. M. Esq. Houghton Lodge, Hants
Morgan, Richard, Esq. Old Market-st. Bristol
Morgan, Thos. Esq. 1, Upper Seymour-street
Morgan, Wm. Esq. 38, Princes-st. Bristol
Morice, John, Esq. *F.S.A.* Upper Gower-st.
Morland, W. A. Esq. Lamberhurst, Kent
MORLEY, Rt. Hon. the Earl of
Morley, Francis, Esq. Huddersfield
MORPETH, Rt. Hon. Lord Viscount, *M.P.*
Morphew, William, Esq. Sevenoaks, Kent
Morrice, Wm. Esq. Eling, near Southampton
Morris, Dr. Trevor-square, Chepstow
Morris and Goulding, Messrs. Princes-street, Manchester
Morris, Joseph, Esq. Bradford, Yorkshire
Morris, James, Esq. 10, Portman-square
Morris, Lady, Thames Bank, Great Marlow
Morris, S. C. Esq. Burton-on-Trent
Morris, T. Esq. Collector of Customs, Bristol
Morris, V. Esq. Retreat, Battersea
Morrison, Rev. A. *A.M.* Romsey, Hants
Morrison, Mr. Duncan, 95, Hutchison-st. Glasgow
Morrison, John, Esq. 76, Cheapside
Morrison, J. W. Esq. *F.R.S.* Royal Mint
Morrison, Capt. R. Liverpool
Mortimer, Wm. Esq. Richmond-ter. Clifton
Mortlock, Wm. Esq. Cambridge
Morton, Colonel J. W. Ryde, Isle of Wight
Morton, J. Esq. 23, Deansgate, Manchester
Morton, John, Esq. Worcester Coll. Oxford
Morton, Thos. Esq. Morton-pl. Kilmarnock
Mosedale, Mr. Richard, Wrexham. 6 Copies
Mosley, Charles, Esq. 63, Mount-pleasant, Liverpool
Mosley, Elias Jos. Esq. 5, Lord-st. Liverpool
Mosley, Lewin, Esq. 62, Mount-pleasant, Liverpool
Mosley, Richard, Esq. Piccadilly
Mosman, Adam, Esq. 7, Prince Edwin-st. Liverpool
Moss, John, Esq. Derby.
Moss, George, Esq. St. Katharine's
Mossop, Rev. Isaac. Smarden, Kent
Mostyn, Sir Edw. Bart. Talacre, Flintshire
Mott, Wm. Esq. Christ Church Coll. Oxford
Mottershead, Mr. John, 8, Nile-st. Liverpool
Mouh, Thos. Esq. Bowker Bank, Manchester
Mount, T. Esq. Saltwood, Kent
Mountcastle, W. Esq. Market-st. Manchester
MOUNT EDGECUMBE, Right Hon. the Earl of
Mountford, Rich. Esq. Park House, Shiffnal
Mountfort, Henry, Esq. Beamhurst Hall
Mountain, Wm. Esq. Saracen's Head Inn, Skinner-street
Mower, Geo. Esq. Woodseats, nr. Chesterfield
Mowle, J. Esq. Earl of Roden Steamer, Liverpool
Moyse, Walter, Esq. Lynn, Norfolk
M'Queen, Mr. W. H. 184, Tottenham-ct.-rd.
M'Taggart, J. Esq. *M.P.* 22, Manchester-sq.
M'Tear, Thos. Esq. 55, Falconer-st. Liverpool
Muckleston, Mr. J. 41, Piccadilly
Muir, Wm. Esq. Leith
Muirdie, Mr. Robt. 13, Montrose-st. Glasgow
Muirl, Thomas, Esq. Ingram-st. Glasgow
Mule, Mr. Secretary to the King of Denmark
Muller, C. H. Esq. Norwich
Muller, Mrs. E. Tarras, near Wimborne, Dorset
Mundy, Mr. R. Rochester
Munday, Admiral George, Grosvenor-place
Mundell, A. Esq. 37, George-st. Westminster
Munro, Mrs. Robert, 14, Bridge-st. Blackfrs.
Munt, Mr. R. P. 36, Wood-street
Murdock, Thos. Esq. *F.R.* and *A.S.* 8, Portland-place
Murdock, Wm. Esq. Port Dundas, Glasgow
Murgatroyd, Mr. William, Bradford, Yorkshire
Muriel, C. Esq. Wellington-street, Southwark
Muriel, John, Esq. Ely, Cambridge
Murly, G. B. Esq. Langport, Somersetshire
Murphy, Wm. Esq. Cork
Murray, J. Esq. jun. Ancot's-lane, Manchester
Murray, James A. Esq. 13, Mecklenburg-sq.
Murray, P. A. Esq. Virginia-street, Glasgow
Murray, Robert, Esq. Port Glasgow, N. B.
Musgrave, Thos. jun. Esq. Monkgate, York
Musgrove, Miss Jane, Library, Manchester
Muskett, Henry, Esq. Clippesby, Norfolk
M'Vicar, John, Esq. Mosley-st. Manchester
M'William, Robt. Esq. 12, Torrington-square
Mylius, Henry, Esq. 3, Token-house-yard

N.

Nadin, J. jun. Esq. St. John's-st. Manchester
Nairne, Rev. C. Great Chart, Kent
Naish, H. B. Esq. Glastonbury
Nall, Mr. George, Bookseller, Leek
Napier, Professor Macvey, 39. Castle-st. Edin.
Nares, Rev. Dr. Biddenden, Kent
Nash, Dr. Worcester
Nash, Mr. James, Cow-cross, West Smithfield
Nash, Mrs. Slade, Worcester
Nash & Son, Messrs. Booksellers, Tunbridge Wells. 11 Copies
Nason, Mr. Nuneaton
Nattriss, Mr. Thomas, Wine-street, Bristol
Naylor, George P. Esq. Sheffield
Naysmith, Mr. Alex. 47. York-place, Edinb.
Neale, F. J. Esq. Trinity College, Cambridge
Neale, J. P. Esq. 26. Norfolk-street, Strand
Neale, Mrs. Stoke, near Guildford
Neale, T. T. M. Esq. *LL.B.* Ipswich
Neave, John, Esq. Dix's-fields, Exeter
Neave, Mr. J. Fordingbridge, near Southampton
Need, Mr. George, Nottingham
Needham, C. jun. Esq. Milk-st. Manchester
Needham, John, Esq. Milk-st. Manchester
Needham, John, Esq. George-st. Manchester
Neill, Mr. John, 25, Queen-street, Glasgow
Nell, Wm. Esq. Bank Top, Manchester
Nelthorp, J. T. Esq. Nuthurst Lodge, Sussex
Nevill, Hon. and Rev. W. Birling, Kent
Neville, Wm. Henry, Esq. Esher, Surrey
New, Rev. Francis Thomas, Shepton Mallett
Newall, —, jun. Market-st. Manchester
Newall, Captain David Rae, *H.E.I.C.S.* 84 Gloucester-place, Portman-square
Newall, Walter, Esq. Seagate
Newark Clinton Arms Book Society
—— Stock Library
Newbould, Henry, Esq. Sheffield
Newcastle-under-Lyne and Pottery Permanent Library
Newcastle-upon-Tyne Literary and Philosophical Society
—————— Religious Book Club
—————— Trinity House of
Newcombe, Capt. *R.N.* 12, Queen-Charlotte road, New-road
Newcombe, Mrs. Bloomsbury-square 2 Copies
Newdigate, F. Esq. Blackheath
Newell, G. W. Esq. Holyport Green, near Maidenhead
Newenham, R. C. O. Esq. Dundanion House, Cork. 13 Copies
Newhouse, J. Esq. Brunswick House, Huddrsfld
Newington, S. Esq. Worcester Coll. Oxford

Newman, Henry Wenman, Esq. Thornbury-park, Gloucestershire
Newman, Robert W. Esq. Mamhead, Devon
Newman, Wm. Esq. Darley-hall, near Barnsley, Yorkshire
Newman, W. L. Esq. Guildhall
Newman, and Co. Messrs. Booksellers, 32, Leadenhall-street. 2 Copies
Newmarsh, George B. Esq. Hull
Newnham, H. Esq. Farnham, Surrey
Newton, Edmund, Esq. Norwich
Newton, J. P. Esq. Stagwood-hill, Huddersfield
Newton, James, Esq. Stockport
Newton, John, Esq. South Lambeth
Newton, W. Esq. 13, Chester-ter. Regent's-pk.
Niccolls, R. Esq. Crumpwell, Oswestry
Nicholas, Francis, Esq. Ealing, Middlesex
Nicholl, J. jun. Esq. *L. L. D.* Doctors'-commns
Nicholls, Rev. R. Dimland House, Cowbridge
Nicholls, N. Esq. 30, Harleyford-place, Kennington
Nicholson, J. C. Esq. 1, Catharine-st. Liverpl.
Nicholson, Robert, Esq. Bradford, Yorkshire
Nicolle, P. C. Esq. Southampton
Nielson, A. Esq. Port Glasgow, N. B.
Nightingale, J. Esq. Rochester
Nightingale, Miss, Bryan House, Blackheath,
Nightingale, Peter, Esq. Upper Brook-street Manchester
Nisbet, Mr. J. W. 39, Wigmore-street, Cavendish-square
Nixon, Capt. Edgerton-road, Blackheath
Nixon, J. Lyons, Esq. Lieut.-Governor of St. Christopher's
Nixon, H. Esq. 6, Watling-street, Manchester
Nixon, John, Esq. Trinity-square, Tower-hill
Noad, G. F. Esq. Worcester College, Oxford
Noble, Thomas, Esq. 24, Park-row, Leeds
Noel, C. H. Esq. Wellingore Hall, Lincolnshire
Noel, Hon. and Rev. F. J. Teston, Kent
Nooth, Major Henry, Stonehouse, Devon
Norcliffe, Major N. York
NORDENSKIOLD, Baron, Captain Royal Swedish Navy
Nordenskiold, Rear-Adm. O. G. Swedish Navy
NORFOLK, His Grace the Duke of
Norfolk and Norwich Literary Institution
Norman, George, Esq. 1, Circus, Bath
Norreys, R. J. Esq. Dawg Holme, Cheshire
Norrie, J. W. Esq. Albany-st. Regent's-park
Norris & Son, Messrs. Booksellers, Uttoxeter. 6 Copies
North, Frederick, Esq. *M.P.* Hastings
NORTHAMPTON, Most Noble the Marchioness of
Northcote, Sir H. Stafford, Bart. Pynes, near Exeter
Northey, Colonel, Cheltenham
Northey, E. R. Esq. Epsom, Surrey
Northey, Captain, W. B. Hawkhurst, Kent
Norton, Charles, Esq. 30, Mecklenburg-sq.
Norton, J. E. Esq. Saville Cottage, Clifton
Norton, Mr. Joseph, Wolverhampton
Norton, S. Esq. Town Malling, Kent
Norton, W. J. Esq. New-street, Bishopsgate
Norwich Book Society
——— Public Library
Norwood, Rev. G. Willesborough, Kent
Norwood, Weller, Esq. Charing, Kent
Nott, Thomas, Esq. Bere Regis, Dorset
Nottidge, George, jun. Esq. Bocking, Essex
Nottingham Subscription Library
Novelli, J. Esq. Cheetham-hill, Manchester
Novelli, Lewis, Esq. 21, York-st. Manchester
Novossilzoff, —, President of the Imperial Council, St. Petersburg
Nowell, Alex. Esq. Underley-park, Westmorlnd
Nugent, Sir Charles Edmund, *K.G.H.* Admiral of the Fleet
Nugent, Dr. Cork, Ireland
Nun, Mrs. St. Margaret's, Ireland
Nunn, Roger, Esq. Colchester
Nurse, W. Esq. Trinity College, Cambridge
Nuttall, —. Esq. Newport-place, Bolton
Nuttall, Rob. Esq. Kempsey House, Worcestrs.

O.

Oakey, Jno. Esq. London-wall
Oakley, Mr. John, Finsbury, Kent
Oakley, Mr. North Parade, Derby
Oakes, O. R. Esq. Newton Cottage
Oakes, Rev. Charles, Tastock
Observer Sunday Newspaper
Occleshaw, Wm. Esq. Piccadilly, Manchester
Occleston, Mrs. 81, Fountain-st. Manchester
O'Connell, Daniel, Esq. *M.P.* 5, Park-street, Westminster
Odling, George, Esq. 159, High-street, Boro'
Ody, R. S. Esq. 292, Strand
Officers of the Chatham Division of Royal Marines
Ogden, Robert, Esq. London-rd. Manchester
Ogden, Thos. Esq. Brook-street, Manchester
Ogle, Sir Charles, Bart. 4, Belgrave-square
Oldershaw, R. Esq. Mansion-house, Islington
Oldfield, B. Esq. White Bear Inn, Manchester
Oliphant, Capt. W. K. Ship Mary Catherine, Liverpool
Olivant, Thomas, Esq. Polygon, Manchester
Oliver, Alex. Esq. St. James's-sq. Manchester
Oliver & Boyd, Messrs. Booksrs. Edinburgh
Oliver, Major, Potterne, near Devizes
Oliver, Capt. Robert, *R.N.* H.M.S. Phœnix
Oliver, Vice-Admiral R.D. Fitzwilliam-square, Dublin
Oliver, Samuel, Esq. 83, Hatton-garden
Oliver, Thomas, Esq. Spring-gardens
Oliver, Wm. Esq. St. Peter's Coll. Cambridge
Ollerenshaw, E. Esq. Mason-st. Manchester
Olpherts, Robt. Esq. St. Christopher's
Ommaney, Rear-Admiral John, A. *C.B.* Warblington, Hampshire
OMPTEDA, His Excellency, the Baron, Minister of State for Hanover
O'Nally, Mr. Patrick, Skylark Revenue Cruiser, Milford Station
O'Neil, Mr. C. Newman-street, Oxford-street
Onley, C. Saville, Esq. Stisted Hall, Essex
Onslow, T. Esq. Bradford Rectory, Dorset
Orchardson, Col. Maxwell, Terregles, near Dumfries
Ord, George, Esq. 62, Gt. Clyde-st. Glasgow
Ord, George, Esq. Poolfold, Manchester
O'Reilly, P. L. Esq. *R.N.* Falmouth
Ormond, J. Esq. Chambers Hall, Manchester
Ormston, Miss, Saville-pl. Newcastle-on-Tyne
Orton, Thomas, Esq. March, Cambridge
Osborn, Mr. W. 26, Up. North-pl. Gray's-inn-rd.
Osborne, George, Esq. Old Brentford
Osborne, Hon. G. Godolphin, 31, Eaton-pl.
Osborne, J. P. Esq. Colchester
Osborne, M. R. Esq. St. Ives, Huntingdon
Oswald, H. R. Douglas, Isle of Man
Oswald, James, Esq. *M.P.* Glasgow
Oswald, Rich. Alex. Esq. *M.P.* Esher, Surrey
Oswald, William, Esq. Lewisham
Oughton, S. H. Esq. High-st. Manchester
Ouseley, Sir Gore, Bart. *F.R.S.A.* 49, Upper Grosvenor-street
Overbury, Nathaniel, Esq. 8, King's-arms-yard
Overend, Wilson, Esq. Sheffield
Owen, Mr. G. D. Oswestry
Owen, J. Esq. Princess-street, Manchester
Owen, Mr. John, City-road, Finsbury-square
Owen, Joseph, Esq. Copenhagen
Owen, O. T. Esq. 146, Holborn-bars
Owen, Richard, Esq. College of Surgeons
Owen, T. B. Esq. Tedsmore Hall, Oswestry
Owen, Wm. Esq. Woodhouse
Oxford, Brazen Nose College Library
——— Exeter College Library
——— Jesus College Library
——— New College Library
——— Oriel College Library
——— Queen's College Library
——— St. John's College Library
——— The Radcliffe Library
——— Book Club

P.

Padbury, Mr. J. Speenhamland, Berks
Paddison, Mr. John, Louth
Paffard, J. H. Esq. Portsea
Page, Vice-Admiral B. W. Ipswich
Page, Rev. Dr. Gillingham, Kent
Page, Miss Maria, Welwyn, Herts
Page, Thos. Esq. Ely, Cambridge
Paget, John S. Esq. Newcastle-upon-Tyne
Paine, John, Esq. 57, High-street, Borough
Pallant, Thos. Esq. Redgrave, Suffolk
Pallet, Robt. Esq. Wimblington
Palmer, Rev. Chas. Lighthorne, Warwickshire
Palmer, Geo. Esq. 12, Upper Woburn-place
Palmer, George, Esq. Newcastle-upon-Tyne
PALMERSTON, Rt. Hon. Lord Viscount
Palmquist, Adm. Magnus, Royal Swedish Navy
Panter, John R. Esq. Houlton-street, Bristol
Papillon, T. Esq. Acrise-place, Kent
Paquiro, Mr. Rue de Grenelle, St Honoré, à Paris
Parbury & Allen, Messrs. Booksellers, Leadenhall-street. 12 Copies
Pareja, Le Chevalier de, Consul General d'Espagne
Park, Adam, Esq. Gravesend
Park, Mr. J. John O'Gaunt steamer, Liverpool
Parker, Capt. C. L. *R.N.* Alphington
Parker, Chas. Esq. 39, Bedford-row
Parker, Lieut. C. *R.N.* Parknook, Whitehaven
Parker, D. J. Esq. Canterbury
Parker, Mr. Hy. 53, Broad-street, Bloomsbury
Parker, Mr. Henry, Bookseller, Oxford
Parker, J. H. Esq. Wells, Norfolk
Parker, Mr. John, Hereford
Parker, Montague E. N. Esq. *M.P.* Whiteway, near Chudleigh
Parker, Sam. W. Esq. Scott's House, Durham
Parker, Mr. T. J. 68, Threadneedle-st.
Parker, T. N. Esq. Sweeney Hall, Oswestry
Parker, W. Esq. Grantham
Parker, Mr. W. Owersby, near Rasen, Lincolnshire
Parkerson, Burrell, Esq. Dereham, Norfolk
Parkinson & Frodsham, Messrs. Chronometer-makers, 'Change-alley. 3 Copies
Parkinson, E. Esq. 10, Old Steyne, Brighton
Parkinson, Robert, Esq. Basinghall-st. Leeds
Parkinson, Mr. Thos. 79, Oxford-street
Parr, Lt. T. *R.N.* Haslar Hospital, Portsmouth

Parr, Saml. Esq. Knowle Cottage, Devon
Parrott, G. L. Esq. *R.N.* Poole, Dorset
Parry, Dr. Charles, Sion Hill, Bath
Parry, G. F. Esq. Twysden, Lamberhurst, Kent
Parry, Mr. C. H. Bookseller, 16, Nelson-pl. Old Kent-road. 2 Copies
Parsons, Mr. H. W. Marine Library, Brighton
Parsons, Mr. Newport, Shropshire
Parsons, Sam. Esq. Nottingham
Partridge, Mr. Alderman, Colchester
Passingham, Francis, Esq. Truro
Patchett, T. Esq. 10, Shude Hill, Manchester
Paternester, Mr. C. Bookseller, Hitching
Paterson, John, Esq. 8, Mincing-lane
Paton, John, Esq. Cornbrook, Manchester
Paton, Wm. H. Esq. Virginia-bldgs. Glasgow
Patrickson, Lt.-Colonel W. G. Union Club
Pattenden, Mr. Robt. Maidstone
Pattenson, Mrs. J. Melmerby Hall, Cumbrlnd.
Patterson, C. T. Esq. Biddenden, Kent
Patteson, S. Esq. Oxford-street, Manchester
Pattison, Rob. Esq. Wrackleford House, Dorset
Paul, Capt. G. Norfolk Lodge, Brighton
Paul, John, Esq. Trevarth, Cornwall
Paul, Rev. John, 13, George-sq. Edinburgh
Paul, Joseph, Esq. Norwich
Paul, Mr. Peter, sen. 38, Broad-st. Golden-sq.
Paul, William, Esq. Truro
Pawley, Mr. Wm. Bromley, Kent
Pawme, Thos. Esq. Wellgate
Pawson, William, Esq. Greek-street, Leeds
Paxon, George, Esq. Hampstead
Payant, Jas. Esq. Tibb-street, Manchester
Payne, Chas. Esq. Freeman House, Clifton
Payne, Chas. Jas. Esq. 6, Adam-st. Adelphi
Payne, J. Esq. Milverton
Payne, Wm. Esq. Hand-court, Holborn
Payne, William, Esq. Teignmouth
Paynter, W. Esq. 4, Cornwall ter. Regent's-park
Peacock, B. Esq. Harcourt-buildings, Temple
Peacock, Rev. Edw. Fifehead House, Dorset
Peacock, Rev. Geo. *M.A.* Trinity College, Cambridge
Peacock, H. B. Esq. St. Ann's-sq. Manchester
Peacock, J. H. Esq. City of London Tavern
Peacock, Stephen, Esq. 18, Salisbury-square, Fleet-street
Peacock, W. Affleck, Esq. Corpus Christi College, Cambridge
Peake, John, Esq. Atherstone, Warwick
Pearce, Edward, Esq. Bodmin
Pearce, Jas. Esq. Chatham
Pearce, John, Esq. 9, Cockspur-st. Piccadilly
Pearson, Rev. H. Sheffield
Pearson, Mrs. Taunton
Pearson, W. H. Esq. Christ Church, Oxford
Peat, Jno. Esq. *B.A.* Sevenoaks, Kent
Peat, Captain, 12, River-street, Middleton-sq. Pentonville
Peche, Mr. M. A. Academy, Dover
Pechell, Rev. Hor. R. Bix, Henley-on-Thames
Peckham, R. Esq. Beaksbourne, Kent
Peckover, Mr. Algernon, Wisbeach, Norfolk
Peede, Ambrose, Esq. 15, Lamb'sconduit-street
Peel, Geo. Esq. Pollard-street, Manchester
Peel, Jos. Esq. Pollard-street, Manchester
Peel, Mr. Alexander, Mayor of Liverpool
Peet, Thos. Esq. St. James's-sq. Manchester
Peill, Rev. John Newton, *M.A.* Queen's College, Cambridge
Peirce, John Jas. Esq. Canterbury
Pelham, Hon. C. A. *M.P.*
Pelham, Cresett, Esq. *M.P.* Warren's Hotel

Pendarves, E. W. W. Esq. *M.P. F.R.S.* 36, Eaton-place
Pendlebury, G. Esq. Salford, Lancashire
Pendlebury, Rich. Esq. New Brown-street, Manchester
Penfold, M. P. Esq. Farnham, Hants
Penfold, Thos. Edw. Esq. 6, Harpur-street, Redlion-square
Pengilley, C. Esq. Commander *R.N.* Truro
Penn, Mr. J. Leeds Steamer, Liverpool
Penney, Joshua, Esq. Watling-street
Pennington, Col. G. *C.B.* Malshangar House, Hants
Penny, Mr. W. S. Bookseller, Sherborne, Dorset. 2 Copies
Penny, Wm. Webb, Esq. Sherborne, Dorset
Penrose, E. W. Esq. Grange Erin, Cork
Penrose, Mr. T. H. 281, High Holborn
Penrudocke, Capt. Wyngton, Ringwood, Hants
Pensam, Mr. James, Middle-row, Holborn
Penson, T. Esq. Oswestry
Penton, Mr. Edw. Basingstoke
Perceval, Hon. Capt. *R.N.* Burgh, Surrey
Percy, Henry, Esq. Nottingham
Pereira, J. Esq. *F.L.S.* Aldersgate-street
Perez, Sixto, Esq. 76, Great Portland-street
Perinton, Thos. Esq. Montague-street
Perkins, Fred. Esq. *F.L.G.* & *A.S.* Chipstead-place, Kent
Perkins, Fred. O. Esq. Park-street, Borough
Perkins, Mr. Wm. Bookseller, Haverfordwest. 2 Copies
Perrin, Right Hon. A. Lord Mayor of Dublin
Perrot, Sam. Esq. Clevehill
Perrott, E. T. Esq. Fladbury, Worcestershire
Perrott, Mrs. Chantry, near Worcester
Perrott, Robt. Esq. Bronhyddon
Perrott, W. S. Esq. Queen's College, Oxford
Perry, Miss C. Bkslr. 9, Lit. Bell-al. 2 Copies
Perry, Saml. Esq. 27, Water-street, Liverpool
Peterborough New Book Society
———— Public Library
Pettigrew, Thos. J. Esq *F.R.S.&A.S.* Saville-row
Petty, John, Esq. Acton-place, Salford
Petty, Samuel, jun. Esq. Pottery, Leeds
Phelps, Rev. W. W. Harrow
Philip, Dr. A. P. W. *F.R.S.* Cavendish-sq.
Philips, H. Leigh, Esq. Stone Fort Estate, St. Christopher's
Philips, Mr. Bookseller, Belfont
Philipps, Col. J. P. L. L. Mabus, Aberystwith
Phillimore, J. Esq. *LL.D.* Doctors'-commons
Phillip, S. Esq. Barton Hall, Manchester
Phillips, Chas. Esq. Mosley-st. Manchester
Phillips, Mr. E. jun. 19, King-st. Cheapside
Phillips, Rev. G. *M.A.* Queen's Coll. Camb.
Phillips, H. Esq. 1, Paragon, New Kent-road
Phillips, James, Esq. 9, King's-arms-yard
Phillips, John Edw. Esq. Stock Exchange
Phillips, W. Esq. 5, Brunswick-sq. Bristol
Phillips, Wm. Esq. Belle Vue House, Clifton
Phillott, Rev. Chas. Dawlish, Devon
Philpot, John, sen. Esq. 3, Southampton-st. Bloomsbury
Philpot, T. C. Esq. Monmouth
Phipps, Arthur C. Esq. Shepton Mallett
Pickard, Rev. Geo. Warmwell, Dorsetshire
Pickering, Sam. Esq. 33, Great St. Helen's
Pickering, Wm. Esq. *R.N.* 4, Richmond Hill, Clifton
Pickering, Mr. Wm. Bookslr. 57, Chancery-la.
Pickersgill, Mr. Richard, Bookseller, Clapton
Pickup, Jas. Esq. Four Yards, Manchester
Pierce, R. Esq. 41, Ludgate-hill

Pierpoint, R. W. Esq. St. John's Coll. Camb.
Pierrepont, Hon. Philip Sidney, Evenly Hall, near Brackley
Piers, John, Esq. Liverpool
Piers, Rev. O. Preston, Weymouth, Dorset
Pigot, John Hugh Smith, Esq. *F.S.A.* Brockley Hall, Somerset
Pigott, B. Esq. St. Peter's Coll. Cambridge
Pigott, Mr. J. W. Lawrence-lane
Pike, Ebenezer, Esq. Black Rock, Ireland
Pike, Mr. Derby
Pilcher, Jerh. Esq. 46, Russell-square
Pilcher, Jno. G. Esq. Morgan's-la. Southwark
Pinchard, John, Esq. Taunton
Pinney, Chas. Esq. Camp House, Clifton
Pinney, John Frederick, Esq. Somerton
Piper, Thos. Esq. Denmark-hill, Surrey
Pippet, George, Esq. Cornetrowe House, near Taunton
Pirie, John, Alderman of London
Pitcher, Wm. Esq. Grove, Blackheath
Pitman, G. J. Esq. 29, Gower-st. Bedford-sq.
Pitt, W. Moreton, Esq. Kingston House, near Dorchester
Plane, John, Esq. Maidstone
Plater, Rev. E. C. Whitstable, Kent
Platt, Geo. Esq. Denne Park, Horsham
Platt, James, Esq. New Boswell-court
Platt, Thos. J. Esq. 39, Tavistock-square
Platt, Thos. Esq. 26, Brunswick-square
Platts, H. Esq. Southampton-st. Chancery-la.
Player, John, Esq. Saffron Walden
Playfair, W. H. Esq. 17, Gt. Stewart-st. Edinbh.
Plint, Thos. Esq. Oxford-row, Leeds
Plowden, Mrs. Henry Chicheley, Newtown Grove, near Lymington
Plumer, J. Julius, Esq. Baliol College, Oxford
Plummer, Jos. G. Esq. King-street House, Great Yarmouth
Plummer, Robt. Esq. Newcastle-upon-Tyne
Plymouth Institution, Athenæum
Plymouth Public Library
Pocklington, Jos. Esq. West Smithfield
Pocock, Sir G. Bart. Brandsgrove House, Hants
Pocock, Mr. Walter, Cow-cross, West Smithfield
Podmore, Geo. Esq. Keppel-st. Russell-sq.
Pointer, Miss, Alphington, Exeter
Pointer, Henry, Esq. Cheltenham
Poland, Sir W. H. Winchester Hall, Highgate
Pole, Sir J. W. Bart. Shute House, Devon
Polesica, —, Esq. St. Petersburg
Polhill, H. W. O. Esq. University Coll. Oxford
Polhill, Capt. John, Rushton, near Taunton
Pollit, Jas. Esq. Cannon-st. Manchester
Pomfret, Virgil, Esq. Tenterden, Kent
Ponsonby, Hon. F. Trinity College, Cambridge
Poole & Boult, Messrs. Booksellers, Chester. 10 Copies
Pooley, John, Esq. Corn Brook, Manchester
Pooly, Mr. Joseph, Maidstone
Poore, Rev. Jno. *D.D.* Murston, Kent
Pope, Geo. Esq. 12, Gray's-inn-square
Popham, C. W. Esq. Trevarno, Helston
Poplar Book Society, Limehouse
Porch, Mr. J. 43, Lime-street
Porch, T. P. Esq. the Abbey, Glastonbury
Porcher, Chas. Esq. Normanston, Lowestoft
Porter & Wright, Messrs. Booksellers, Pall-mall. 30 Copies
Porter, Dr. Wm. Ogilvie, Portland-sq. Bristol
Porter, W. F. Esq. Commerce-ct. Lord-street, Liverpool
Porthouse, Mr. Thos. 10, Northampton-square, Goswell-street

Portsmouth Royal Marine Library
Potter, Wm. Esq. Aldgate
Potter, Michael, Esq. King-street, Manchester
Potter, Mrs. Baile Hill, Manchester
Potter, Richard, Esq. *M.P.* Broughton House, Manchester
Potter, Sydney, Esq. Peel-street, Manchester
Potter, Thos. Esq. Cannon-street, Manchester
Potterne Book Society
Potts, Radford, Esq. Park-row, Leeds
Potts, Mr. W. Bookseller, Banbury
Poulden, A. Esq. Portsea
Poulter, J. Esq. 24, Queen's-row, Manchester
Pounsett, W. Esq. Woodside, Esher. 2 Copies
Pountney, J. D. Esq. Fresford Villa, Clifton
Pountney, John, Esq. Norris Hill, near Ashby-de-la-Zouch
Povey, John, Esq. The Derwin, Oswestry
Powell, Chas. Esq. Ashfield
Powell, D. Esq. 28, Cow Cross-street
Powell, J. Esq. Dawlish, Devon
Powell, J. P. Esq. Quex Park, Kent
Powell, J. T. Esq. Wells, Somerset
Powell, Rich. Esq. Bath-street, Bristol
Powell, T. J. Esq. Madras Army, Horsham
Powell, Thos. Esq. Stock Exchange
Powell, Thos. Esq. 6, Charlotte-st. Bristol
Powell, Mr. Wm. Caerleon, Monmouth
Powis, W. H. Esq. 6, Wilmington-square
Pownall, H. Esq.
Poynder, T. jun. Esq. Christ's Hospital
Poynton, Wm. Esq. 2, Bread-street
Prall, R. Esq. Rochester
Prat, Richard Periam, Esq. Glastonbury
Pratt, Chas. Esq. Totton, near Southampton
Pratt, James, W. Esq. 29, Little Newport-st.
Pratt, Mr. John, Bradford, Yorkshire
Preedy, W. P. Esq. Offenham, Worcestershire
Prentis, Henry, Esq. Rochester
Prentis, Geo. Esq. Maidstone
Prescot, Rev. Charles K. Rector of Stockport
Preston, B. Esq. 99, Sydney-place, Bath
Preston, Chas. Abbot, Esq. 32, Walbrook
Preston, Mr. Grant, 108, Minories
Preston, Henry, Esq. Moreby Hall, Yorkshire
Price, Benj. Esq. 3, Woodland-place, Bath
Price, Edw. Esq. Bromley, Kent
Price, Downes, Esq. Hendre-rhys-gethyn, Carnarvonshire
Price, J. Esq. Cadnant, Anglesea
Price, Jos. Esq. Monmouth
Price, Miss H. 23, Harleyford-pl. Kennington
Price, Mrs. Rhiwlas, Bala
Price, Rev. R. Lyminge, Kent
Price, Mr. W. Bookseller, Oswestry. 36 Copies
Prince, Mr. Richard, Newmarket
Prince, Sam. Esq. St. Peter's-sq. Manchester
Pringle, John, Esq. Milford
Pringle, M. Esq. Cowfold, Sussex
Prior, J. W. Esq. 67, Newington Causeway
Prior, Samuel, Esq. Blackheath
Pritchard, B. Esq. Plasmadoc, near Rhuabon
Pritchard, Mr. Edward, Milford Haven, Pembrokeshire. 12 Copies
Pritchard, Thos. Esq. 20, West Smithfield
Probyn, Captain George, *H.C.S.*
Proctor, Mrs. Ann, Kennington-oval
Proctor, Rev. George, *D.D.* Chichester House, Kemp Town
Proctor, Rev. Jas. *A.M.* 30, Brunswick-square, Brighton
Proctor, Mr. John, Ship New Harriet of Dundee
Proctor, Mr. John, Market Drayton
Proctor, Thos. Esq. Rye, Sussex
Prodgers, Rev. E. Clarence Lodge, Dulwich
Prosser, Rev. J. C. Vicarage, Devauden, near Chepstow
Protheroe, F. Esq. 16, Park-place, Clifton
Protheroe, George, Esq. 30, Park-st. Clifton
Provis, W. A. Esq. Newport, Shropshire
Prudy, Wm. Fred. Esq. Worcester
Pryce, J. Esq. New College, Oxford
Pryce, S. V. Esq. Redruth
Pryer, J. Esq. Denmark-row, Camberwell
Pryor, John, Esq. Camberwell
Pryse, J. B. Esq. Bryn Tanant
Puckle, J. Esq. Brasennose College, Oxford
Puget, J. Hy. Esq. Brunswick-sq. Brighton
Pugh, Saml. Esq. Rue d'Elbœuf, 51, Faubourg St. Sever, Rouen
Pughton, S. H. Esq. High-st. Manchester
Puke, Capt. Swedish Royal Navy, Carlskrona
Puleine, James, Esq. 1, King's-bench-walk, Temple
Pullen, J. T. Esq. 21, Wilmington-square
Pulley, Henry, Esq. Norwich
Pulling, J. Esq. Corpus Christi Coll. Camb.
Purchas, Capt. W. J. *R.N.* Cambridge
Purday, Mr. Thos. Sandgate, Kent
Purlervent, Wm. Esq. Shepton Mallett
Purnell, Wm. Esq. Belle Vue, Clifton
Puthes & Besser, Messrs. Bkslrs. Hamburgh
Putnam, James, Esq. John-street, Portland-pl.
Pyne, Rev. William, Langport
Pyper, Wm. Esq. High School

Q.

Quekett, E. Esq. Langport, Somersetshire
Quicke, J. Esq. Newton St. Cyres, near Exeter
Quiddington, Mr. V. 24, George-st. Glasgow
Quinton, Hy. C. Esq. Queen-square

R.

Radcliffe, —, Exeter College, Oxford
Radford, S. R. Esq. Derby
Radford, Thos. Esq. Mosley-street, Manchester
Radford, Thos. Edw. Esq. Dock-office, Hull
Radley, James, Esq. Adelphi Hotel, Liverpool
Raikes, Thos. Esq. Welton, Hull
Raleigh, Jos. Esq. Tibb-street, Manchester
Ralfe, Mr. Wm. Bookseller, Tunbridge Wells
Ramage, John, Esq. Aberdeen
Ramsden, J. C. Esq. *M.P.* 6, Upper Brook-st.
Ramsden, Colonel Thomas, Heath, Halifax
Ramshaw, Captain
Ramshay, W. Esq. 6, Crown-office-row, Temple
Randall, W. Esq. Corpus Christi Coll. Oxford
Randall, R. Esq. Southampton
Randell, Hy. Esq. New-square, Lincoln's-inn
Rangeley, Rev. Mr. Queen's Coll. Cambridge
Ranger, Mr. J. H. Portsmouth
Rankin, Jonathan, Esq. 65, Ingram-st. Glasg.
Ransom, John, Esq. Holt, Norfolk
Ransom, Wm. Esq. Stowmarket, Suffolk
Ransome, J. A. Esq. St. Peter's-sq. Manchr.
Raper, Col. P. V. Richmond, Surrey
Rasenberg, Mr. C. 1, Warnford-ct. Throgm.-st.
Rashleigh, Rev. Peter, Southfleet, Kent
Ratcliff Amicable Reading Society
Ratcliff, Mr. S. Faversham
Rathbone, Capt. John, Ship Nashville of New Orleans, Liverpool
Rathbone, W. Esq. Salt House Dock, Liverp.
Raupp, Albert, Esq. Boulevard Cavchoise, 53, Rouen
Ravenscroft, W. R. Esq. Norfolk-st. Manchr.
RAVENSWORTH, Right Hon. Lord
Rawe, Mr. Thos. East-street, Southampton
Rawe, Mr. Wm. Cheapside
Rawes, Captain Richard, Stratford
Rawes, W. F. Esq. Caius College, Cambridge
Rawes, W. T. Esq. Bromley, Kent
Rawle, R. Esq. Trinity College, Cambridge
Rawlins, John Hart, Esq. St. Christopher's
Rawson, Chas. Esq. Gledholt, Huddersfield
Rawson, Mr. James, Leicester
Rawson, W. Esq. Brown-street, Manchester
Rawsthorne, J. Esq. 4, Greenwood-st. Manchr.
Raymond, J. H. Esq. 5, New-sq. Lincoln's-inn
Rayner, Capt. Thos. 1, Park-pl. Regent's-pk.
Rayner, Wm. Esq. Ely, Cambridge
Read, Mr. Richard, Werting, Basingstoke
Read, Thos. Esq. 6, Lansdown-pl. West, Bath
Reade, Compton, Esq. Shipton-ct. Oxfordsh.
Reade, Sir Thomas, Tunis
Reader, Mr. S. Reading
Reddall, J. Esq. Dallington House, Northamp.
Readdy, Messrs. J. & Son, Church-la. Spitalfds.
Redenhalgh, G. L. Esq. Polefield House
Redenhalgh, Mrs. Poole Bank, Manchester
Redhead, Lawrence, Esq. Kennington-green
Redmond, Mrs. E. Summer Hill, Wexford
Redmond, Mrs. Bettyville, Wexford
Redruth Public Library
Reed, Alfred, Esq. Canterbury
Reed, C. Esq. Waterfield House, Worthing
Reed, Rev. C. Tynemouth, Northumberland
Reed, Edw. jun. Esq. 44, Wimpole-street
Reed, Francis, Esq. Ipswich, and Grove House, Teignmouth, Devon
Reed, John, Esq. Prestwick Lodge, Northumb.
Reed, Tho. Wm. Esq. Trevissome, nr. Penryn
Reed & Son, Messrs. Sunderland
Rees, John, Esq. Gt. Surrey-st. Blackfriars
Rees, Thos. Esq. 8, King's Parade, Clifton
Rees, Mr. W. Bookseller, Llandovery
Rees, Rev. W. North Walsham, Norfolk
Reeve, Chas. Esq. 3, Chatham-place
Reeve, J. C. Esq. 11, Gt. Cumberland-place
Reeves, William, Esq. Kennington-green
Reid, Wm. Esq. Lignorpond-street
Reid, Mr. Andrew, Bkslr. Berwick. 3 Copies
Reid, George, Esq. 8, Broad-street-buildings
Reid, Sir John Rae, Bart. *M.P.* 8, Broad-st.-buildings
Reid, J. Esq. 26, Aldersgate-street
Reid, Mr. John, 94, Miller-st. Glasgow
Reid, Samuel J. Esq. Rochester
Reid, Walter, Esq. Navy Pay Office, Devonpt.
Reise, J. Esq. Booth-street, Manchester
Reiss, James, Esq. Mosley-road, Manchester
Reitzel, Mr. C. A. Bookseller, Copenhagen. 7 Copies
Remmett, R. Esq. St. John's Col. Cambridge
Remnant & Edmonds, Messrs. Lovell's-court, Paternoster-row 29 Copies
Rendell, Robert, Esq. Wadebridge, Cornwall
Reneau, Mr. H. 3, Park-terrace, Camden-town
Renkin, Wm. Esq. Kilmarnock
Renner, Capt. Ralph, Royal Saxon, Liverpool
Rennie, G. jun. Esq. 1, Chesham-pl. Belg-sq.
Rennie, Sir J. *F.R.S.* 15, Whitehall-place
Repington, C. E. Esq. Tamworth
Resley, J. H. Esq. New College, Oxford
Reveley, W. Aust. Esq. 8, South-sq. Gray's-inn
Reville, Rev. Mr. Sheffield
Reynard, E. H. Esq. Sunderlandwick, Driffield
Reynolds, A. F. Esq. Welton Grange, Hull

Reynolds, Capt. *R.N.* Penair, near Truro
Reynolds, Edw. Esq. Fordlands, Devon
Reynolds, Rev. H. *M.A.* Jesus Coll. Oxford
Reynolds, Jos. Esq. St. Michael's Hill, Bristol
Reynolds, Miss, Gray's Green, Bewdley
Reynolds, Mr. Pat. Fair Trader Steamer, Livpl.
Reynolds, S. V. Esq. Canon's Grove, near Taunton
Rhodes, Abram. Esq. Roundhay, near Leeds
Rhodes, G. F. Esq. Belfair, near Exeter
Rhodes, J. Esq. 54, Judd-st. Brunswick sq.
Rhys, Capt. 19, Portland-place, Bath
Ricardo, Francis, Esq. Stock Exchange
Ricardo, Mrs. Warleigh, near Bath
Rice, —, Esq. Fairy Hall, Mottingham, Kent
Rice, Mr. C. Booksr. 123, Mount-st. 3 Copies
Rice, Mrs. Dover
Rice, Rev. Edward, Christ's Hospital
Rich, Capt. E. L. *R. N.* Exmouth, Devon
Rich, Mr. O. Bookseller, Redlion-square, Holborn. 6 Copies
Richards, G. C. Esq. Gravesend
Richards, George, Esq. Cross-st. Manchester
Richards, John, Esq. Kirkland Westmorland
Richards, Richard, Esq. Penzance
Richards, S. Esq. 2, Tavistock-square.
Richards, Capt. W. Moreton House, Redruth
Richards, Wm. Rd. Esq. *M.P.* Cadogan-place, Sloane-street
Richardson, Christopher, jun. Esq. Limehouse
Richardson, Colonel, 95, Sydney-place, Bath
Richardson, H. F. Esq. 7, Ironmonger-lane
Richardson, Capt. J. Ship Otterspool, Liverpool
Richardson, Mr. J. M. 23, Cornhill. 75 Copies
Richardson, Mr. J. R. 50, Queen-st. Glasgow
Richardson, Mr. James, 28, Miller-st. Glasgow
Richardson, Jos. Esq. 13, Charlotte-st. Bristol
Richardson, Mr. Pelham, Bookseller, Royal Exchange. 10 Copies
Richardson, Randall W. Esq. Corpus Christi College, Cambridge
Richardson, Rob. Esq. Commercolly, Bengal
Richardson, T. Esq. 9, Bethel-pl. Camberwell
Richardson, Thos. Esq. 1, Gray's-inn-square
Richardson, Sir W. H. Upper Harley-street
Richardson, Rev. Thomas, York
Richmond Book Society
Richmond, Mrs. Ravensworth Castle, Durham
Richmond, W. Esq. Dockray-sq. Tynemouth
Rickards, Charles, Esq. Piccadilly
Rickards George H. Esq. Piccadilly
Rickards, Rev. George, Worthy, near Leeds
Rickards, Mrs. Taunton
Rickards, Samuel, Esq. Piccadilly
Ricketts, Carew, Esq. Winchester
Ricketts, Fred. Esq. Stapleton, Bristol
Ricketts, H. Esq. The Grove, Brislington, Bristol
Ricketts, M. Esq. Lake House, Cheltenham
Ricketts, W. H. Esq. Hill-court, Worcestersh.
Ricord, Vice-Admiral, St. Petersburg
Riddle, George, Esq. Meadow-place, Lambeth
Riddle, Sir Jas. Miller, Bart. 33, Moray-place, Edinburgh
Riddlesden, Lieut.-Col. Rocester, Staffordshire
Rideout, Rev. J. Rector of Woodmancote, Sussex
Rider, Rt. Esq. 6, Walton's-bldgs. Manchester
Ridge, Mr. G. Booksr. Sheffield. 5 Copies
Ridge, Messrs. Samuel & Charles, Booksellers, Newark. 4 Copies
Ridge, Mr. Sam. Bksllr. Grantham. 4 Copies
Ridge, Samuel, Esq. Stock Exchange
Ridgeway, John W. Esq. Norfolk-st. Manchester
Ridgeway, Messrs. James and Sons, Booksellers, 169, Piccadilly
Ridley, Mr. E. 6, St. James's-pl. Clerkenwell
Ridsdale, J. H. Esq. 5, Albion-street, Leeds
Ridyard, Wm. Esq. Brunswick-st. Liverpool
Riel, P. R. Esq. 26, Buchanan-st. Glasgow
Rigby, Ed. Esq. 29, York-bldgs. Manchester
Riley, Lieut. J. W. Commander of H. M. Packet L'Espoir, Falmouth
Rintoul, Jas. Esq. 15, Queen-street, Edinburgh
Rio de Janeiro British Subscription Society
Ripley, Richard, Esq. Mill Garth, Leeds
Ripley, W. H. Esq. University Coll. Oxford
RIPON, Right Hon. the Earl of
Rippon, Cuthbert, Esq. *M.P.* Manchest.-bldgs.
Risley, T. H. Esq. New College, Oxford
Rivers, Mr. E. Southampton
Rivers, Sir H. Bart. Martyr Worthy, Winchester
Rivington & Co. Messrs. Waterloo-pl. 6 Copies
Robartes, T. J. Agar, Esq. Lanhydrock, near Bodmin
Robarts, A. W. Esq. *M.P.* Hill-st. Berkeley-sq.
Robbins, Mr. M. G. Wisbeach, Norfolk
Robbins, Lieut. Col. Sir Wm. Castle Malwood, near Stony Cross, Herts
Roberts, Lieut.-Col. H. Milford, nr. Lymington
Roberts, Major C. Everton, Lymington
Roberts, Miss H. Oswestry
Roberts, Rev. Henry, Stourbridge, Worcester
Roberts, J. Esq. 34, Oxford-terrace
Roberts, John, Esq. 13, St. James's-pl. Bristol
Roberts, John, Esq. Bangor
Roberts, Rev. N. Cefn, near Wrexham
Roberts, T. Esq. West End Lodge, Esher
Roberts, T. Esq. Royal Dock-yard, Devonport
Roberts, Mr. Wm. Milford
Roberts, Mr. Bookseller, Chesterfield
Robertson, Archd. Esq. 5, Kent-sq. Liverpool
Robertson, Dr. A. Northampton
Robertson, B. Esq. 5, Brompton-square
Robertson, Duncan, Esq. St. Christopher's
Robertson, Mr. J. Hampden, Bucks
Robertson, Jas. Esq. Exchange-bgs. Liverpool
Robertson, Mr. John, 24, Miller-st. Glasgow
Robertson, Mr. John, 74, Buchanan-st. Glasgow
Robertson, Mr. John, Bookseller, 25, Lower Sackville-street, Dublin
Robertson, W. Esq. 16, Clapham-road-place
Robeson, Wm. Henry, Esq. Bromsgrove
Robin, Jas. Esq. Jersey
Robins & Son, Messrs. Booksllrs. Tooley-st.
Robins, Rev. S. Up. Gloucester-st. Dorset-sq.
Robins, Thomas, Esq. Liskeard, Cornwall
Robinson, Charles, Esq. York
Robinson, C. S. Esq. Caversham
Robinson, Chas. Shackleford, Esq. Caversham House, Reading
Robinson, Dr. Doncaster
Robinson, Rev. Francis, *M.A.* Rector of Stonesfield, Oxon
Robinson, G. Esq. 22, Swan-st. Manchester
Robinson, George, Esq. Doncaster
Robinson, Messrs. G. & J. Liverpool. 11 Copies
Robinson, H. jun. Esq. 5, Henrietta-st. Cov-gn
Robinson, Mr. John, Bookseller, Putney
Robinson, Jas. Esq. Huddersfield
Robinson, John E. Esq. Cambridge
Robinson, John, Esq. Eccleshill Hall, near Bradford
Robinson, Lieut. L. A. *R.N.* H.M. Packet Viper, Falmouth
Robinson, Matt. A. Esq. 25, Cumberland-terrace, Regent's-park
Robinson, Capt. M. 3, Upper Newington, Livpl.
Robinson, Miss Mary, Leeds. 2 Copies
Robinson, R. Esq. Richmond Cottage, Clifton
Robinson, Robert, Esq. Hoddesdon
Robley, Rev. I. Islington, Salford
Robson, Thos. Esq. Aylesford, Kent
Roch, Nicholas, Esq. Alderman of Bristol
ROCHESTER, Right Rev. the Lord Bishop of
Rodd, Rev. C. Northill Parsonage, Cornwall
Rodd, Francis Hearle, Esq. Trebartha Hall, Northill, Cornwall
Rodd, Richard, Esq. Devonport
Rodgers, R. W. J. Esq. 5, Burton-street
Rodwell, Christ. B. Esq. 33, North Bank, Regent's-park
Rodwell, Henry, Esq. 41, Finsbury-square
Rodwell, Mr. J. Bookseller, 4, New Bond-st. 3 Copies
Roe, George, Esq. Dublin
Roe, Major John, Launceston
Roe, Miss L. Springfield, Liverpool
Roe, Mr. W. Bookseller, Newbury. 4 Copies
Roger, James D. Esq. Tortola
Rogers, Arthur, Esq. 29, Leazes-terrace, Newcastle-on-Tyne
Rogers, Rev. J. Canon Residentiary of Exeter
Rogers, John, Esq. Jesus College, Cambridge
Rogers, Mr. Rt. Bksllr. Newmarket. 4 Copies
Rogers, Thomas, Esq. Helston, Cornwall
Roget, Dr. P. M. *Sec. R.S.* 39, Bernard-street
Roke & Varty, Messrs. Booksllrs. 31, Strand
Rolandi, Mr. P. Bookseller, 20, Berners-st.
Rolfe, G. Esq. Thornbury, Gloucestershire
Rolfes, W. G. Esq. Walcot-place, Lambeth
ROLLE, Right Hon. Lady
Rolles, Vice-Admiral Robert, Brighton
Rolls, John E. W. Esq. The Hendre, near Monmouth
Romsey Reading Society
Rooke, Capt. L. C. *R N.* 28, Royal Crescent, Bath
Rooke, Rev. G. Yardley Hastings, Northampt.
Rooke, Jno. Esq. York-st. Cheetham, Lancash.
Rooke, Jos. Esq. York-st. Cheetham, Lancash.
Room, James, Esq. Queen's-square, Bristol
Roome, Col. Henry, 23, Sloane-street
Rose, Right Hon. Sir G. H. 7, Old Palace-yd.
Rose, H. John, Esq. *B.D.* Fellow of St. John's College, Cambridge
Rose, Jos. F. Esq. 11, Great Surrey-street
ROSEBERRY, Right Hon. the Earl of
Ross, Alexander, Esq. Inspector General, Custom-house, Liverpool
Ross, Chas. Esq. Inverleith-row, Edinburgh
Ross, Capt. Charles, *R.N.* Superintendent Royal Dock-yard, Devonport
Ross, Dan. Esq. Perth-road, Dundee
Ross, Edward, Esq. Dublin
Ross, F. W. L. Esq. Broadway House, Topsham
Ross, G. Esq. 20, Chapel-st. Grosvenor-pl.
Ross, Major G. 20, Alexander-sq. Brompton
Ross, Capt. Horatio, *M.P.* 112, Sloane-street
Ross, Colonel Sir Hew Dalrymple, *K.C.B. K.T.S.* 129, Park-street
Ross, Mr. John, 8, John-street, Glasgow
Ross, Mr. John, jun. 22, Ingram-st. Glasgow
Ross, Miss, St. Cuthbert's Lodge, Kirkcudbright
Ross, Thos. B. Esq. St. Clement's, Ipswich
Ross, Thomas, Esq. Wakefield
Ross, Major Wm. 23d Royal Welch Fusiliers
Ross, W. Esq. Belmont House, Bishop's Waltham, Hants
Ross, Wm. Esq. Cannon-street, Manchester
Ross, Wm. Esq. 12, Lambridge, Bath
Rossiter, James, Esq. 4, Kennington-terrace
Rossi, R. Esq. 22, Harp-lane, Tower-street

Rosson, J. Esq. 5, Bouverie-st. Fleet-st.
Rosson, J. Esq. 11, King's-bench-wlk. Temple
Rostron, John, Esq. Eaglesfield, Southampton
Rostron, L. Esq. Sussex-street, Manchester
Rotch, B. Esq. *M.P.* Lowland's, Harrow-on-the-Hill
Rothery, Wm. Esq. Doctors-commons
Rothwell, P. Esq. Bolton, Lancashire
Rothwell, Peter, Esq. Sunning Hill
Rougemont, Francis, Esq. Broad-st.-buildings
Roughsedge, Hornby, Esq. Bentham House, near Settle, Yorkshire
Roughton, Miss, Belvoir-street, Leicester
Rourman & Schweigerd, Messrs. Booksellers, Vienna. 7 Copies
Rouse, B. Esq. Wellington-street, Borough
Rouse, Rolla, Esq. Woodbridge, Suffolk
Rouse, Mr. Wm. jun. Bradford, Yorkshire
Routh, William, Esq.
Routledge, Rt. Esq. 13, Hamilton-pl. New-road
Rowand, Michael, Esq. Glasgow
Rowden, J. Esq. Heytesbury, Wilts
Rowden, Mr. Heytesbury, Wilts
Rowe, Mr. F. Bookseller, Plymouth
Rowell, John, Esq. 5, Peel-st. Manchester
Rowland, Messrs. A. & Son, 20, Hatton-grdn.
Rowland, Capt. C. Harbour Master, Greenwich
Rowland, Dan. Esq. Saxonbury, Frant, Sussex
Rowland, J. Esq. *B.A.* Queen's Col. Cambr.
Rowlands, D. Esq. Chatham Dock-yard
Rowles, Byron George, Esq.
Rowlett, W. Esq. White Bayes, Burton, Dorset
Rowley, Alex. Esq. Burlington-st. Manchester
Rowley, Vice-Admiral Sir Charles, *K.C.B. K.M.T.* Fern Cottage, Winkfield
Rowley, R. C. Esq. Holbecks, Suffolk
Rowley, Mr. Thomas, 37, Liquorpond-street
Roxbourg, Adam, Esq. Tibb-st. Manchester
ROXBURGHE, His Grace the Duke of
Roxby, R. B. Esq. 46, Lime-street
Roy, Richard, Esq. Fulham Lodge
Roy, Rev. Robert, Burlington House, Fulham
Roy, Rev. William, *D.D.* Skirbeck
Roy, Wm. Esq. 8, Church-lane, Liverpool
Royal Exchange Assurance Company
Roylance, P. Esq. 35, Hanging Ditch, Manchr.
Ruck, Benj. Esq. Maidstone
Rudderforth, Mr. T. 52, Newington Causeway
Rudge, Mr. A. J. 29, St. Martin's-le-Grand
Rudge, Edw. Esq. *F.R.S. F.S.A. F.L.S.* & *F.H.S.* 44, Wimpole-street
Rudkin, John, Esq. Peasenhall, Suffolk
Rumley, Lieut. Gen. C. Sidmouth
Rump, Robert, Esq. Wells, Norfolk
Rumsey, N. Esq. Beaconsfield
Rushbridger, G. Esq. Stone, Staffordshire
Rushbrooke, Col. *M. P.* Rushbrooke Park
Rusher, Messrs. J. & Co. Booksellers, Reading. 10 Copies
Rusher, Mr. J. G. Banbury
Rushout, Hon. Ann, Wanstead Grove, Essex
Rushton, Jos. Esq. Albion-bldgs. Manchester
Ruskin, J. J. Esq. Herne Hill
Russel, John, Esq. Heriot-place, Edinburgh
Russell, A. Esq. Dartford, Kent
Russell, C. Esq. Queen's Coll. Cambridge
Russell, Mr. Edward, Maidstone
Russell, George, Esq. Merthyr Tidvil
Russell Institution, Great Coram street
Russell, J. Esq. Goulden-terrace, Islington
Russell, Wm. Congreve, Esq. *M.P.* King's Heath, Birmingham
RUSSIA, Scientific Committee of the Imperial Navy
Russia, Imperial Academy of Sciences
Rust, J. Edgar, Esq. Abbot's Hall, Stowmrkt.
RUTLAND, His Grace the Duke of
Rutter, Dr. Liverpool
Rutter, J. C. Esq. 4, Ely-place
Ryan, Major Thos. 50th Regiment, Chatham
Ryde, Isle of Wight, Marine Library of
Ryder, Mr. James, Jersey
Ryle, J. Esq. *M.P.* Park House, Macclesfield
Ryle, J. C. Esq. Christ Church Coll. Oxford

S.

Sabb, John, Esq. Epsom, Surrey
Sabine, H. S. Esq. Bradford Peverell, Dorset
Sabine, J. S. Esq. Muckleford House, Dorset
Sack, F. Esq. 4, Foukes-buildings, Tower-st.
Sackin, Benj. Esq. Frederick-street, Bishop Wearmouth
Sadleir, Rev. Dr. Fellow of Trin. Col. Dublin
Sadler, Mr. Francis, 1, Fore-st. Cripplegate
Saffron, Hy. Esq. Huddersfield
Sainsbury, Miss, 40, York-place, Portman-sq.
SALISBURY, Rt. Rev. the Lord Bishop of
Salisbury and Wiltshire Library and Reading Society
Salomons, D. Esq. Throgmorton-street
Salomons, P. J. Esq. 2, Magdalen-row, Goodman's-fields
Salt, Thos. Esq. Weeping Cross, Stafford
Salte, Wm. Geary, Esq. Artillery-pl. London
Salvin, A. Esq. *F.S.A.* Somerset-st. Portm.-sq.
Salvin, Bryan J. Esq. Burn Hall, near Durham
Salvin, W. T. Esq. Croxdale Hall, nr. Durham
Salwey, Miss Elizabeth, The Lodge, Ludlow
Sampson, Benj. Esq. Tullimaar, near Truro
Sampson, Edward, Esq. Henbury
Sampson, Mr. George, Ipswich
Sams, Miss H. Bookseller, Hoddesdon
Sams, Mr. Booksllr. St. James's-st. 4 Copies
Sams, Wm. Hy. Esq. Ixworth, Suffolk
Samson, Miss, 48, Hunter-st. Brunswick-sq.
Samson, S. Esq. Smeeth, Kent
Samuel, D. M. Esq. 17, Hanover-terrace
Samuel, Mr. Lewis, Lord-street, Liverpool
Samuels, John, jun. Esq. Tibb-st. Manchester
Samwell, W. L. W. Esq. Upton Hall, Northamp.
Sandbach, Dan. Esq. Lloyd-st. Manchester
Sandell, John, Esq. 87, Hatton-garden
Sandeman, D. G. Esq. Melville-st. Edinburgh
Sanders, J. Esq. Whitstable, Canterbury
Sanders, E. Lloyd, Esq. Stoke Hill House, near Exeter
Sanders, G. Esq. Clifton-hill House, Bristol
Sanders, H. Esq. 36, Lower Crescent, Clifton
Sanders, John Naish, Esq. 3, Beaufort-buildings, Clifton, Bristol
Sanders, T. R. Esq. Ridgeway Villa, Bristol
Sanderson, Jabez, Esq. Newmarket-buildings, Manchester
Sandilands, Hon. John, Calder House, Mid Calder, near Edinburgh
Sandle, Mr. Bardfield, Essex
SANDON, Lord Viscount, *M.P.*
Sandon, Mr. Charles, Newcastle Wharf, New North-road, Hoxton
Sands, Mr. Alex. Reepham Library, Norfolk
Sandwich Book Society
Sandwith, Colonel, Oriental Club, Hanover-sq.
Sandys, Rev. John, 8, Canonbury-pl. Islington
Sandys, Chas. Esq. Canterbury
Sanford, E. A. Esq. *M.P.* 4, Richmond-terrace
Sankey, R. Esq. Canterbury
Sankey, Mr. R. Ludlow. 7 Copies
Sanxay, Mrs. Epsom, Surrey
Sargon, Mr. G. 65, Gt. Queen-st. Lincoln's-inn-fields
Sartoris, Ed. T. Esq. Trinity Coll. Cambridge
Saull, W. D. Esq. 15, Aldersgate-street
Saumarez, Lieut.-General Sir Thos. Guernsey
Saunders, Mr. B. Booksr. Nassau-st. Dublin
Saunders, John, Esq. 57, Cannon-street
Saunders, R. Esq. H.M. Customs, St. Christopher's
Saunders and Ottley, Messrs. Booksellers, 50, Conduit-street. 11 Copies
Saunders, T. B. Esq. 19, Lincoln's-inn-fields
Saunders, T. Esq. *F.S.A.* 34, York-terrace, Regent's-park
Saunderson, Mr. Robt. Bala, Wales. 2 Copies
Savage, F. Esq. Springfield, Westbury, Bristol
Savage, John, Esq. Alderman of Bristol
Savage, Col. Sir John B. *K.G.H.* 6, Torrington-square
Savage, Thos. Esq. Cloisters, Temple
Savery, Frederick, Esq. 6, John-street, Adelphi
Savile, Hon. C. S. Queen's Coll. Cambridge
Sawbridge, S. E. Esq. Olantigh, Kent
Sayer, Robt. Esq. Sibton Park, Suffolk
Scale, Hy. Esq. Penydarron, Merthyr Tydvil
SCARBOROUGH, Rt. Hon. the D. Countess of
Scarborough Agricultural Library
————, General Library of
Scard, Mr. B. Eling, Southampton
SCARSDALE, Right Hon. Lord
Scarth, T. Esq. Barnard Castle
Scarth, W. Gilyard & Sons, Messrs. Mill Garth, Leeds
Schaumburg & Co. Messrs. Booksllrs. Vienna 4 Copies
Schenk'scheBuchhandlung, Brunswick. 2 copies
Schevez, George, Esq. 20, Brandon-pl. Glasgow
Schofield, G. & I. Esqrs. Haistuck, Yorkshire
Scholefield, Rev. James, Every-st. Manchester
Scholefield, Rich. B. Esq. St. John's Coll. Cam.
Scholes, Jos. Esq. 10, Broken Bank, Salford
Scholey, George, Esq. Alderman of London
Scholey, J. B. Esq. 21, Grove hill-ter. Cambwl.
Schoolbred and Cook, Messrs. Tottenham-court-road
Schreiber, J. N. Esq. Melton, Suffolk
Schubothe, Mr. G. H. Bookseller, Copenhagen
Schünemann, Mr. C. Bookseller, Bremen
Schwabe, Martin, Esq. Cooper-st. Manchester
Schwann, Fred. Esq. Huddersfield
Scole, Suffolk, Book Club
Scoresby, Rev. Wm. *B.D F.R.S.* & Mem. Inst. of France, Exeter
Scott, Andrew, Esq. 39, London-st. Edinburgh
Scott, David, Esq. Cannon-street, Manchester
Scott, Right Rev. Dr. 34, Gt. Ayer-st. Glasgow
Scott, Major-General Edw. 8, Sion-hill, Bath
Scott, Francis Caterch, Esq. 59, Charlotte-st. Edinburgh
Scott, Mr. Hudson, Booksllr. Carlisle. 4 Copies
Scott, J. Esq. Dartford, Kent
Scott, J. Esq. Winfrith, Dorset
Scott, Jeremiah, Esq. Waterloo-street, Leeds
Scott, John, Esq. Calls, Leeds
Scott, John, Esq. Bishop Wearmouth
Scott, J. W. Esq. *M.P.* Rotherfield Park, Alton
Scott, Mr. John, Mosley-street, Manchester
Scott, Jos. Esq. Halfmoon-st. Manchester
Scott, Page Nicol, Esq. Norwich
Scott, William, Esq. Hall-place
Scott, Wm. Esq. St. Christopher's
Scovell, Mr. Chas. Southampton

Scovell, Mr. George, 29, Clerkenwell-close
Scudamore, G. A. Esq. Back King-st. Manchester
Scurlock, J. Trevor, Esq. Doctors'-commons
Scurr, Rev. R. W. Vicarage, Aldburgh, Suffolk
Seacombe, Mr. J. Bookllr. Chester. 2 Copies
Seager, James, Esq. Poole, Dorset
Seagrim, Chas. Esq. Winchester
Seale, Lieut. Col. *M.P.* 102, Gloucester-place
Searle, Thos. Esq. 56, Gower-st. Bedford-sq.
Seddon, Peter, Esq. Broughton, Manchester
Seddon, Wm. Esq. Ardwick-st. Manchester
Sedgwick, Miss, Homerton, Middlesex
Sedgwick, Mr. Wm. 9, Regent-street
Seeley, Mr. B. Bookseller, Kingston, Surrey
Seeley & Sons, Messrs. Booksellers, Fleet-st.
SEGRAVE, Right Hon. Lord
Selby, Hy. Coll. Esq. Swainsfield
Selby, Jas. Esq. Otford, Kent
Semper, Hugh Ryley, Esq. St. Christopher's
Sencombe, Mr. I. Bookseller, Chester
Senior, Jas. Esq. Lascellas Hall, Huddersfield
Senior, Jos. Esq. Dalton Lodge, Huddersfield
Serrell, Rev. S. Langton Matravers, Dorset
Seton, Robert, Esq. 72, Upper Norton-street
Sewell & Cross, Messrs. Reading-room at
Sewell, G. D. Esq. Frith-street, Soho
Sewell, John, Esq. 28, Upper Thames-street
Sewell, Mr. Jos. Newcastle & Carlisle Steamer, Liverpool
Sewell, Rev. Wm. *A.M.* Exeter Coll. Oxford
Seymer, Rev. G. A. Iwerne Courtney, alias Shroton, near Blandford, Dorset
Seymer, H. Esq. Knoyle, Wilts
Seymer, H. K. Esq. Handford, Dorset
Seymour, Hon. Capt. Sir Geo. 17, Whitehall-pl.
Seymour, Fred. Esq. Kemp Town, Brighton
Seymour, Wm. Esq. 27, Brunswick-square
Shackell, Wm. Esq. Hammersmith
Shackleford, Jas. Shuckburgh, Esq. Lutterworth, Leicestershire
Shafto, S. D. Esq. University Coll. Oxford
Shand, Wm. Jno. Esq. 28, Miller-st. Glasgow
Shann, Thomas, Esq. Leeds
Sharp, Jos. Esq. 16, Bread-street
Sharp, James, Esq. 13, Hatton-garden
Sharp, R. C. Esq. 50, Mosley-st. Manchester
Sharpe, J. Esq. 60, Hutchinson-st. Glasgow
Sharpe, Mr. Richard, Maidstone
Sharpe, W. C. Esq. St John's Coll. Cambridge
Shaw, Mr. Fred. Bookseller, Dundee. 2 Copies
Shaw, David, Esq. Huddersfield
Shaw, George, Esq. Holloway Villa, Bath
Shaw, George, Esq. Swan-st. Briggate, Leeds
Shaw, Mr. J. C. City of Dublin Company's Works, Clarence Dock
Shaw, Mrs. J. F. Bookseller, 18, Southampton-row, Russel square
Shaw, Sir James, Bart. Chamberlain of London
Shaw, Lieut. Col. 10, Widcombe-crescent, Bath
Shawe, Robt. Newton, Esq. Kesgrave Hall, Woodbridge, Suffolk
Shearcroft, Mr. J. F. Bookseller, Braintree, Essex. 6 Copies
Shears, D. T. Esq. Lawn, South Lambeth
Sheerness Book Society
Sheffield, Jos. James, Esq. Wellington-pl. Commercial-road
Sheldon & Sons, Messrs. Mason-st. Manchstr.
Shelley, J. N. Esq. Epsom, Surrey
Shelmerdine, H. Esq. King-st. Manchester
Shelton, Thomas, Esq. Edinburgh
Shepheard, J. Esq. Charmarle, Dorset
Shepherd, J. Esq. Yeardon House, near Leeds
Shepherd, Capt. John, *R.N.* 37, Dorset-square
Sheppard, Captain, Granby-street, Leicester
Sheppard, Rev. John, *M.A.* Blackheath
Sheppard, Jos. Fran. Esq. Clevedon, Somerset
Shepherd, Mr. R. A. Bookseller, Newman-street, Oxford-street
SHERBORNE, Right Hon. Lord
Sherbrooke, Mrs. Oxton Hall, Southwell, Notts
Sherer, J. W. Esq. Leamington Priors
Sheridan, Mr. Gloster Hotel, Ryde
Sherratt, Thos. Esq. Salford
Sherwin, Frank, Esq. 9, Burton-street
Sherwood and Co. Messrs. Booksellers, Paternoster-row. 7 Copies
Sherwood, Col. 10, Great Cumberland-street
Sherwood, Richard, Esq. Chaddleworth, Berks
Sherwood, Thos. Esq. 4, Mecklenburg-square
Shewell, John, Esq. Stock Exchange
Shilleto, Wm. Esq. Langbourn Chambers, Fenchurch-street
Shirley, Rear-Admiral G. J. 35, Gay-st. Bath
Shirley, Rev. W. A. Shirley-vicarage, nr. Ashbourne
Shirley, W. P. Esq. Debtling, near Maidstone
Shone, Mr. W. Bookseller, Bangor. 7 Copies
Shore, J. Esq. 23, Guildford-street
Short, Mr. E. W. Booksr. Nuneaton. 2 Copies
Shortland, Rev. H. V. *A.M.* Tilehurst, Berks
Shuiber, Mr. John, Rotherhithe
Shotter, Jas. Esq. Farnham, Hants
Shrewsbury Subscription Library
Shuckard, Mr. L. Old Ship Hotel, Brighton
Shute, Arthur W. Esq. Gloucester
Shuttleworth, G. E. Esq. Poultry
Shuttleworth, J. Esq. Bishop's Tawton, Devon
Sidebotham, J. Esq. Church-st. Manchester
Sidebottom, Mrs. Ann, St. Mary's Manchester
Sidebottom, Henry, Esq. 52, Spring-gardens, Manchester
Sidebottom, W. Esq. Cleveland-bldgs. Manchr.
Sedgwick, Mr. James, Skipton
SIDMOUTH, Rt. Hon. Lord Viscount
Siely, B. C. Esq. Beech Grove, North Walsham
Sikes, Capt. *R.N.* Arundel-street, Strand
Silvertop, Colonel, 55, Lower Grosvenor-street
Silvester, Mr. H. P. Bookseller, Newport, Salop. 3 Copies
Silvester, Mr. S. Bookseller, Market Drayton. 3 Copies
Sim, Rev. Henry, Longford, near Ashbourn
Sim, Robt. Esq. Murray Gate
Simkin, Edw. Esq. 2, New Cavendish-street, Portland-place
Simms, Mr. G. Booksr. Manchester. 40 Copies
Simmons, Wm. Esq. 10, King's-bench-walk, Temple
Simpkin & Marshall, Messrs. Stationers'-court. 90 Copies
Simpson, Edwin, Esq. Albion-street, Leeds
Simpson, R. H. Esq. 12, Camden-place, Bath
Simpson, John, Esq.
Simpson, John, Esq. Alderman of York
Simpson, Joseph, Esq. Woodhouse-la. Leeds
Simpson, Joseph, Esq. St. Petersburg
Simpson, Mrs. Herne hill
Simpson, R. W. Esq. Commercial-street, Leeds
Simpson, Mr. Thos. Bksellr. Wolverhampton. 12 Copies
Simpson, Wm. W. Esq. 8, Montague-place, Russell-square
Simpson, Dr. York
Sims, James, Esq. Chasewater, near Truro
Sims, Robt. Esq. 36, Compton-street
Sims, Mr. William, 51, Great Queen-street
Simson, Mr. G. Bookseller, Hertford. 3 Copies
Simson, Capt. Thos. Brig Rapier, Liverpool
Sinclair, Mr. J. Dumfries
Singleton, Cuthbert, Esq. 1, Newman
Singleton, John, Esq. Pitsmoor, Sheffield
Singleton, Jonathan, Esq. Briggate, Leeds
Singleton, W. Esq. Dock-street, Leeds
Skelton, John, Esq. Calls, Leeds
Skinner, Samuel, Esq. 23, Portland-place
Skurry, Rev. Benj. Hornington, Wiltshire
Slade, Hy. Esq. Frome, Somerset
Slade, Lieut. Gen. Sir John, Bart. Mansell House, North Petherton
Slade, Robt. Esq. Poole, Dorset
Slade, T. jun. Esq. Poole, Dorset
Sladen, Jos. Esq. jun. 2, Grove-end-road, Regent's-park
Sladen, John, Esq. Fennell-st. Manchester
Slater, A. B. Esq. 10, Sackville-street
Slater, Francis, Esq. 1, Montague-place, Clapham-road
Slater, Mrs. Spa, Gloucester
Slater, Wm. Esq. Princess-st. Manchester
Slatter, Mr. H. Bookseller, Oxford. 2 Copies
Slatter, Rev. Wm. Iffley, near Oxford
Sleigh, Lieut. J. *R.N.* Folkestone, Kent
Sleigh, Captain Wm. Niagara Cottage, Stapleford, near Nottingham
Sleight, Rob. P. Esq. Lougate, Hull
Slingsby, Rev. H. Stour Provost, Dorset
Sloane, James, Esq. 113, Brunswick street, Glasgow
Slocock, Chas. Esq. Donnington, Berks
Slocock, E. Esq. West Mills, Newbury, Berks
Sly, Mr. James, Ship Forfield, Liverpool
Smail, Lieut. W. A. *R. N.* 18, Dublin-street, Edinburgh
Smalley, C. Esq. St. John's Coll. Cambridge
Smallpiece, John, Esq. Guildford
Smallpiece, Mark, Esq. Guildford
Smallwood, Mr. J. J. Northampton
Smart, John, Esq. Highbury-park
Smerdon, Chas. Esq. 4, Portland-pl. Clifton
Smith, A. Bridges, Esq. Abbey Villa, Bath
Smith, A. H. Esq. Queen's Coll. Cambridge
Smith, Abel, Esq. *M.P.* 39, Berkeley-square
Smith, Anwick, Esq. Langley Grove, near Durham
Smith, Archd. Esq. 204, St. Vincent-st. Glsgw
Smith, Mrs. Asheton, Vaenol, near Bangor
Smith, C. Esq. East Malling, Kent
Smith, Charles, Esq. 12, Paper-buildings
Smith, C. J. Esq. 2, King's-arms-yard
Smith, Chas. Esq. High street, Manchester
Smith, Rev. C. Lessingham, Cheltenham
Smith, E. T. Esq. 3, Alfred-pl. North Brixton
Smith, Edwin, Esq. 4, Gray's-inn-square
Smith, Elder and Co. Messrs. Booksellers, Cornhill. 16 Copies
Smith, Gustavus, Esq. Salbury Castle, Devon
Smith, Capt. H. John of Newfoundland, Liverpool
Smith, Henry, Esq. Fell-street, Wood-street
Smith, J. Esq. Pitt Press, Cambridge
Smith, J. G. Esq. Ashley Down
Smith, Jas. Esq. Mount Pleasant-sq. Manchr.
Smith, Captain John, Fan Lodge, Falmouth
Smith, John, Esq. Ashbourne-road, Derby
Smith, John, Esq. High-street, Manchester
Smith, John, Esq. 22, Grosvenor-square
Smith, John, Esq. Claremont-pl. Brixton-rd.
Smith, Mr. J. Bookslr. Maidstone. 2 Copies
Smith, Mr. John, Clarence Dock, Liverpool
Smith, Rev. Dr. John Pye, Homerton
Smith, Rev. J. J. *M.A.* Caius Coll. Cambridge
Smith, Milton, Esq. High-st. Manchester

Smith, Miss, Bookseller, Staines. 3 Copies
Smith, M. E. Esq. 1 King's Bench-wk. Temple
Smith, Mr. M. Alnwick
Smith, Mrs. Ashby-de-la-Zouch
Smith, N. B. Esq. Brockenhurst, Hants
Smith, P. J. Esq. Wood-st. Cheapside
Smith, P. P. Esq. St. John's Coll. Cambridge
Smith, Mr. R. English Hotel, Rue Ramassé, Rouen
Smith, Robt. Esq. Critchill-place
Smith & Son, Messrs. Bkrs. Glasgow, 22 Copies
Smith, Stephen, Esq. Peel-street, Manchester
Smith, T. Hogan, Esq. Forberry-grove, near Newbury
Smith, Thos. Esq. Church-st. Manchester
Smith, Thos. Esq. Old Brentford
Smith, Thos. B. Esq. St. Mary Cray
Smith, Thos. Esq. South Hill, Liverpool
Smith, Messrs. Wm. & Co. Marsden-square, Manchester
Smith, Mr. William, Stockport, Cheshire
Smith, W. Masters, Esq. Camer, Gravesend
Smith, W. Esq. Exchange-st. West, Liverpool
Smith, Wm. Esq. Whitborne-court
Smith, Wm. Esq. of Carbeth, 112, Hope-st. Glasgow
Smith, Wm. Esq. Hemel Hempstead
Smith, Wm. Esq. Reddish House, Stockport
Smith, William, Esq. Leeds
Smithson, Robert, Esq. York
Smyth, Edmund, Esq. Hersham
Smyth, Sir John, Bart. Ashton-court, Bristol
Smyth, W. T. Esq. Little Houghton, Northamp
Smyth, Miss, Innage House, Shiffnal
Smythe, Rev. E.
Snell, John, Esq. Edmonton
Snell, Wm. Esq. 20, Ingram-street, Glasgow
Snoad, Mr. E. H. Ashford, Kent
Snoulton, O. jun. Esq. Canterbury
Snow, P. Duveluz, Esq. Queen's Coll. Camb.
Snowden, T. H. G. Esq. Ramsgate
Soames, Mrs. Mary, Pinner Lodge, Middlesex
Sole, Wm. Esq. St. Neot's, Huntingdon
Solly, R. H. Esq. 48, Gt. Ormond-st. Bloomsbury
Solly, Joseph, Esq. Dyer's-ct. Aldermanbury
SOMERSET, His Grace the Duke of
Somerset, Rev. P. H. Villiers, Rector of Honiton
Somerville, Henry, Esq. Stafford
Somerville, Jas. Somerville, Esq. Dinder House, near Wells, Somerset
Somerville, John, Esq. 63, Candleriggs, Glasg.
Somes, Mrs. S. Stratford
Soot, Jas. Esq. Seagate
Soper, Richd. Esq. Mayor of Totness, Devon
Sorby, James, Esq. Sheffield
Sotheby, Mr. E. S. 13, Lower Grosvenor-st.
Sotheby, Rev. T. H. North Mymms, Herts
Sotheran, Mr. Henry, Bookseller, York
Sotheron, Admiral Frank, 58, Grosvenor-street
South, Sir James, Astronomer Royal, Observatory, Kensington
South, John F. Esq. 7, Upper Stamford-street
South, Lancelot, Esq. 9, Cunningham-place, St. John's Wood
SOUTHAMPTON, Right Hon. Lord
Southby, Miss, Chieveley
Southcomb, Lewis, Esq. South Molton, Devon
Southerne, E. V. Esq. Woodhouse-lane, Leeds
Southgate, F. Esq. Gravesend
Southwark Book Society of Friends
——— Literary Society
SOUTHWELL, Right Hon. Lord Viscount
Sowerby, Jas. Esq. 2, Albion-bldgs. Manchstr.

Soy, Mr. J. Britannia Steamer, Liverpool
Spankie, Mr. Sergeant, *M.P.* Russell-square
Sparkes, Henry, Esq. Pensylvania, Exeter
Sparkes, Joseph, Esq. Exeter
Sparkes, Thomas, Esq. Exeter
Sparrow, J. E. Esq. Ipswich
Sparrow, N. Esq. Feversham
Spence, Capt. Henry Hume, *R.N.* 25, Devonshire-street, Portland-place
Spence, W. Esq. 32, Alfred-place, Bedford-sq.
SPENCER, Right Hon. the Earl
Spencer, Mr. R. R. Maidstone
Spencer, Robt. Esq. Holyhead
Spencer, T. Esq. 53, St. John-street-road
Spens, Colonel, Mussleburgh, N.B.
Sperling, J. M. Esq. Halstead, Essex
Spicer, David, Esq. Portsea
Spicer, J. Esq. Somerford Grange, Dorset
Spicer, J. W. Esq. Esher place, Surrey
Spicer, W. J. Esq. Royal College, Chelsea
Spiers, B. Esq. New Brown-street, Manchester
Spode, Mrs. the Mount, Newcastle-under-Lyne
Spooner, Ralph, Esq. Bolton, Lancashire
Spooner, Mr. Thos. Ely, Cambridge
Spragg, Chas. H. Esq. Exeter College, Oxford
Springett, R. Esq. Finchcocks, Goudhurst
Spry, J. H. Esq. 5, Charter-house-square
Spurdens, Rev. W. T. North Walsham, Norf.
Spurgeon, C. Wm. Esq. Lynn Regis, Norfolk
Spurgin, Thos. Esq. Saffron Walden
Spurrell, Charles, Esq.
Spurway, Lieut. John, *R.N.* Milverton
Spyers, Mr. Thos. 6, Main-street, Glasgow
Stables, H. Esq. Crossland Mills, Huddersfield
Stacy, Mr. John, Norwich
Stafford, Mr. C. Bookseller, Shefford, Bedfordshire. 2 Copies
Stafford, Mrs. M. Marine Library, Worthing. 3 Copies
Stainbank, Jas. Esq. 58, Marsden street, Manchester
Stainton, Henry, Esq. Carron-wharf, Upper Thames-street
STAIR, Right Hon. the Earl of
ST. ALBAN'S, Her Grace the Duchess of
Stamp, Capt. T. *R.N.* Bowness, Westmorland
St. André, Mr. Durant, Consul General de France, 44, Montague-square
Stanfield, Clarkson, Esq. *A.R.A.* 36, Mornington-crescent, Hampstead-road
Stanfield, Mr. J. Bookseller, Wakefield, Yorkshire. 21 Copies
Stanfield, Mr. John, Bookseller, Bradford, Yorkshire. 8 Copies
Stanger, Joshua, Esq. Wandsworth
Stanforth, Samuel, Esq. Liverpool
STANLEY, Rt. Hon. Lord, *M.P.*
Stanning, Mr. Oxford
Stanser, Mr. Cob-hill Cottage, Fulham
Stansfield, Thos. W. Esq. Burley Wood, Leeds
Stanton, Joseph, Esq. Brighton
Starie, Wm. Esq. 11, Dorset-place, North, Clapham-road
Stark, Mr. A. Booksr. Gainsborough. 4 Copies
Starkey, J. Esq. Spy Park, near Devizes
Starling, Alfred, Esq. Yarmouth, Norfolk
Starling, John, Esq. Lynn Regis, Norfolk
Starr, Thos. Esq. Canterbury
St. Christopher's, Private Subscription Rooms, at
St. Clair, Capt. D. L. *R.N.* Staverton Court, Gloucestershire
Steadman, Mrs. —, Enfield
Steavenson, A. T. Esq. 14, Great Carter-lane, Doctors'-commons

Steddy, Lieut. Jno. *R.N.* Charing, Kent
Stedman, —, Esq. Eltham
Stedman, F. Esq.
Stedman, Mr. R. Bksllr. Godalming. 6 Copies
Steel, W. S. Esq. York-street, Manchester
Steere, C. Esq. Southampton, Hants
Steet, G. Esq. 35, Gt. Ormond-st. Bloomsbury
Steggall, Dr. John, Ely-place
Stein, J. Esq. Chalmington House, Dorchester
Steinsthal, L. Esq. 74, Bloomsbury, Manchester
Stennett, Mrs. Islington-crescent, Wem
Stephen, Mr. Alex. 60, Great Russell-street
Stephens, Capt. E. L. *R.N.* Basingstoke
Stephens, Edw. Esq. Berkeley-square, Bristol
Stephens, H. W. Esq. Bishopsteignton, Devon
Stephens, Capt. John, Heavitree, Exeter
Stephens, John, Esq. Spring Hall, Waterford
Stephens, Nathaniel C. Esq. Truro
Stephens, Rev. Wm. W. Southfield, Tunbridge Wells
Stephenson, Gen. B. C. 16, Hertford-street, May-Fair
Stephenson, R. L. Esq. St. John's Coll. Camb.
Stephenson, R. L. Esq. St. John's Col. Camb.
Stephenson, Mr. Rochester
Stephenson, Mr. Wm. Bksllr. Hull. 2 Copies
Stephenson, Wm. Esq. Huddersfield
Stepney Book Society
Sterling, Chas. Esq. 62, Miller-st. Glasgow
Sterling, Geo. Esq. John-street, Glasgow
Sterling, Major-Gen. Mussleburgh, N. B.
Stevens, Rev. Dr. R. Dean of Rochester
Stevens, Adam. Esq. St. Christopher's
Stevens, Jas. Esq. Merthyr Tydvil
Stevens, Wm. Esq. St. Christopher's. 2 Copies
Stevenson, Seth Wm. Esq. Norwich
Stevenson, Mr. Thos. Bookseller, Cambridge 2 Copies
Steward, A. H. Esq. Stock Park, Ipswich
Steward, Henry, Esq. Cambridge
Steward, Lieut.-Colonel, Nottington, Dorset
Steward, Timothy, Esq. Norwich
Steward, Wm. Esq. Great Yarmouth
Stewart, A. Campbell, Esq. of Castle Stewart, and St. Fort, Dundee
Stewart, A. R. Esq. Dublin
Stewart, Alex. Esq. Belvne Crescent, Edinb.
Stewart, Capt. *R.N.* Mussleburgh, N.B.
Stewart, Chas. Alex. Esq. Aldburgh, Suffolk
Stewart, D. Esq. Pool-ct. Pool-la. Liverpool
Stewart, F. B. Esq. *R.N.* Blackhetah Park
Stewart, Edward, Esq. *M.P.* Bryanston-square
Stewart, J. Shaw, Esq. 12, Shadwick-pl. Edin.
Stewart, John, Esq. 5, Mersey Chambers, Liverpool
Stewart, Mr. James, 11, Old Broad-street
Stewart, R. Esq. Old Post-office-ct. Glasgow
St. George, A. F. Esq. Dublin
Stirling, J. F. Esq. *R.N.* Woburn Farm, Chertsey
Stiven, John, Esq. 63, Miller-street, Glasgow
Stiven, Robt. Esq. 49, Miller-street, Glasgow
Stock, Thos. Esq. Henbury-crescent
Stocken, Fred. Esq. 28, Little Queen-street
Stockley, Mr. G. Bookseller, 44, Holywell-street, Strand
STOCKMAR, Baron, Claremont, Surrey
Stocks, B. & Sons, Messrs. Trinity-st. Leeds
Stocks, Saml. Esq. Mosley-street, Manchester
Stodart, R. Esq. 20, Athole-crescent, Edinb.
Stoddart, E. Esq. Ashford, Kent
Stoker, Robt. Esq. Holt, Norfolk
Stokes, A. J. Esq. St. Botolph's, near Milford
Stokes, Chas. Scott, Esq. Cateaton-street
Stokes, Hy. Esq. Fakenham, Norfolk

Stokes, J. Esq. Oakover, near Ashborne
Stoltesforth, Dr. Sigismund, Dover
Stone, Edw. Esq. Pall-mall East
Stone, George, jun. Esq. Lombard-street
Stone, Henry, Esq. Lombard-street
Stone, Miss, Dartmouth-row, Blackheath
Stone, Mrs. Beccles, Suffolk
Stone, Webb, Esq. Deputy-Lieut. Trull, near Taunton
Stopford, Capt. *R.N.* 45, Gloucester-place
Storer, C. Esq. St. John's Coll. Cambridge
Storks, T. T. Esq. Jesus College, Cambridge
Storr, Mr. R. Bookseller, Grantham. 3 Copies
Stott, J. Esq. Bank-street, Leeds
Stow, Mr. David, 85, Buchanan-st. Glasgow
Stow, W. F. Esq. Hanover-square, Leeds
Stowell, Rev. Hugh, Salford, Lancashire
St. Paul, Horace, Esq. Ewart Park, Wooler, Northumberland
St. Petersburg, Naval Academy of
Straford, J. C. Esq. Cheltenham
Strange, Thos. Esq. 65, Houndsditch
STRATHALLAN, Right Hon. Lord Viscount
Strather, Wm. Esq. Alnwick
Stratton Literary Institution
Stretton, W. B. Esq. Dan-y-Park, Crickhowell, Brecon
Stride, Messrs. and Co. Redbridge, near Southampton
Stringer, Miles, Esq. 30, Russell-square
Strong, Mr. William, Bristol
Strother, Thomas, Esq. Briggate, Leeds
Struthers, Jas. Esq. 40, Guildford-st. Glasgow
Struthers, Robt. Esq. Grun Head, Glasgow
Strutt, Josh. Esq. St. Peter's-street, Derby
Strutt, Miss, St. Helen's House, Derby
Stuart, Daniel, Esq. Upper Harley-street
Stuart, Jas. Esq. Jersey Villa, Cheltenham
Stuart, Hon. Major-General P. Commander-in-chief, Edinburgh
Stuart, R. Esq. 26, Pall-mall, Manchester
Stuart, Rear-Admiral, 52, Upper Brook-street
Stuart, Robt. Esq. 26, Pall-mall, Manchester
Stubbs, Mr. John, 5, Ann's-sq. Manchester
Stuckey, J. Esq. Hill House, Langport
Stuckey, Mrs. George, M. ditto
Stuckey, Vincent, Esq. ditto
Sturgeon, J. Kemp, Esq. Dorking
Sturmy, Herbert, Esq. 8, Wellington-st. Boro'
Stylman, H.L.S. Esq. Christ Church, Oxford
Styles, Mr. Frederick, Market, Cambridge
Sudlow, John, Esq. Princess-st. Manchester
Suett, John, Esq. Doncaster
SUFFIELD, Right Hon. Dowager Lady
Sugden, J. Esq. Woodsome Lees, Huddersfield
Sullivan, Capt. Sir Chas. Bart. *R.N.* Thames Ditton
Sully, Dr. Henry, Taunton
Summers, James, Esq. Haverfordwest
Sumpton, Capt. P. Ship Cœur-de-Lion, Livpl.
Surmon, Mr. H. Red Lion-yard, Aldersgate-st.
Surplice, S. H. Esq. Nottingham
SUTHERLAND, His Grace the Duke of
Sutherland, Dr. A. R. *F.R.S. F.G.S.* 1, Parliament-street
Sutherland, J. Esq. *A.M.* Southwold, Suffolk
Sutherland, Jas. Esq. 5, Pen-ct. Fenchurch-st.
Sutherland, Robert, Esq. His Majesty's Consul, Maracaybo
Sutton, Capt. H. F. Brig Sisters, Liverpool
Sutton, R. Manners, Esq. Trinity Coll. Camb.
Sutton, Jas. Esq. Shardlow Hall, near Derby
Sutton, James, Esq. Stock Exchange
Sutton, Miss, Regent-street, Cambridge
Sutton, Robt. Esq. Stock Exchange
Sutton, Rev. S. Northfleet
Sutton, Rev. T. Manners, Great Chart, Kent
Swaffham Book Club
Swain, Chas. Esq. Fennel-st. Manchester
Swaisland, C. Esq. Crayford, Kent
Swallow, Luke, Esq. Huddersfield
Swallow, Thos. Esq. Fennell-st. Manchester
Swan, Alex. Esq. Hythe, Kent
Swan, John, Esq. Burwall House, Kent
Swann, George, Esq. York
Swann, William, Esq. Works, near Sheffield
Swanston, Thos. Esq. *M.D.* St. Christopher's
Swanston, Wm. Esq. St. Christopher's
Sweet, S. W. Esq. Dorset-square
Sweetland, John, Esq. Teignmouth, Devon
Sweetland, Wm. Esq. Star Cross, Devon
Swete, J. Beaumont, Esq. Oxton House, Exeter
Swift, Mr. C. H. 78, Fleet-street
Swindell, Mr. John, Aldburgh, Suffolk
Swiney, Dr. Arlington-street, Camden-town
Swinnerton, Mr. Jas. Bookseller, Macclesfield. 5 Copies
Sword, Jas. jun. Esq. 43, Hutchinson-st. Glasg.
Swyer, Mr. R. York Hotel, Manchester
Sykes, Capt. *R.N.* 11, Royal Crescent, Bath
Sykes, John, Esq. Beech Grove, Leeds
Sykes, John, Esq. Sheffield
Sykes, Lieut.-Col. W. H. *F.R.S.* 47, Albion-street, Hyde-park
Sykes, Rev. W. Vicar of Cullumpton, Devon
Sylvester, Mr. John, 85, Great Russell-street
Syms, Fredk. George, Esq. 29, Craven-street
Symes, Wm. Esq. 3, Tavistock-square
Symins, George, Esq. Murray Gate
Symonds, Capt. *R.N.* East End Cottage, Lymington
Symonds, Major, H. W. Chaddlewood, Devon
Symons, Samuel, Esq. Gouvens, near Wadebridge, Cornwall
Sympson, Rev. Chas. J. Peversal, Notts
Synnot, R. W. Esq. Clapham-common

T.

Tabor, John, Esq. 25, Finsbury-square
Tadman, William, Esq. Norwich
Tagg, Mr. William, Bookseller, Maidenhead. 5 Copies
Tahourdin, G. Esq. Carlton Chambers, Regent-street
Tait, Capt. J. H. 6, Bellevue-crescent, Edinb.
TALBOT, Right Hon. Earl
Talbot, C. R. M. Esq. *M.P.* 63, St. James's-street
Talbot, Hon. & Rev. Gustavus, Ingistrie
Talbot, John, H. Esq. *M.P.* Bettyville, Wexford
TALLEYRAND, His Excellency le Prince de
Tandy, Capt. Danl. *R.N.* Topsham, Devon
Tanner, Hy. Esq. Wearmouth Walk, Bishop Wearmouth
Tanner, Wm. Esq. Devizes, Wilts
Tanqueray, Edw. Esq. Vine-st. Bloomsbury
Tapp, Benjamin, Esq. Longate, Hull
Taprell, W. Esq. 8, Caroline-pl. Mecklenburg-square
Tapson, John, Esq. 1, Little Love-la. Wood-st.
Tarleton, Dr. Penley Hall, near Ellesmere
Tarrence, G. M. Mikee, Esq. 29, George-st. Edinburgh
Tasker, Mr. Jno. Bookseller, Skipton. 7 Copies
Tassell, Robt. Esq. Maidstone
Tassell, Thos. jun, Esq. Maidstone

H

Tasswell, G. M. Esq. Canterbury
Tastet, Fermin de, Esq. Bishopsgate-church-yard. 2 Copies
Tate, Rev. F. B. Charing, Kent
Tate, Wm. Esq. St. Ann's-street, Manchester
Tatem, Jas. George, Esq. High Wycombe
Tattersall, Mrs. Church-hill, Doddington, Sittingbourne
Tattershall, E. B. Esq. 9, Great James-street, Bedford-row
Tatton, T. W. Esq. Christ Church, Oxford
Taunton and Somerset Institution, Taunton
Tawes, Andrew, Esq. 11, Royal-ter. Edinburgh
Tayler, George, Esq. Fleathar
Tayler, Captain, J. N. *R.N. C.B.* Belle Vue House, Devizes, Wilts
Tayler, Mrs. Wimbourne, Dorset
Tayler, Thomas, R. Esq. Portsea
Tayleur, W. Esq. *M.P.* 22, Mount-street
Tayleur, W. H. Esq. Seel-street, Liverpool
Tayleur, Dr. W. E. Teignmouth, Devon
Taylor, Admiral, Maize-hill, Greenwich
Taylor, Beaumont, Esq. Huddersfield
Taylor, Chas. Esq. Christ Church, Oxford
Taylor, David, Esq. 148, Gallowgate, Glasgow
Taylor, Mr. David, Bookseller, Rye
Taylor, Rev. Dr. Dedham, Essex
Taylor, Ed. Joseph, Esq. Water-lane, Leeds
Taylor, Dr. Geo. Weymouth, Dorset
Taylor, George, Esq. Adelphi-st. Salford
Taylor, Guth. J. Esq. Assistant Surgeon, *R.N.* Sea Gull Packet, Falmouth
Taylor, Lieut.-Gen. Sir Herbert, *K.G.H.* St. James's Palace
Taylor, J. Esq. 6, Berkeley-square, Bristol
Taylor, J. A. Esq. Worcester College, Oxford
Taylor, Jas. Esq. 82, Hutchinson-st. Glasgow
Taylor, James, Esq. 15, Furnival's-inn
Taylor, John, Esq. Bridge-street, Manchester
Taylor, John, Esq. Mosley-st. Manchester
Taylor, John, Esq. Newsome, Huddersfield
Taylor, Mr. J. Bookseller, Upper Gower-st.
Taylor, Mr. John, Leicester
Taylor, P. A. Esq. 5, Euston-square
Taylor, Richd. Esq. Perran-wharf, near Truro
Taylor, Saml. Esq. 30, Cooper-st. Manchester
Taylor, Mr. Thomas, Cranbrook
Taylor, Thos. L. Esq. Diss, Norfolk
Taylor, William H. Esq. Great Yarmouth
Taylor, Wm. Esq. Huddersfield
Taylor, Wm. Esq. Ashbourne-road, Derby
Teal, Henry, Esq. Albion-street, Leeds
Teale, Edward, Esq. Leeds
Teale, T. P. Esq. Leeds
Tebbutt, J. R. Esq. Deansgate, Manchester
Tebbutt, John, Esq. Pall-mall, Manchester
Telford, Thos. Esq. *F.R.S.* Abingdon-street
Tempest, Miss M. C. Broughton Hall, Yorksh.
Temple Book Club
Temple, G. Esq. Heytesbury, Wilts
Temple, Inner, the Hon. Society of
Templeman, J. Esq. 33, Pulteney-street, Bath
Templeman, Rev. N. Cranbourne, Dorset
Templer, Henry, Esq.
Templer, J. Esq. 23, Great Tower-street
Tenby Reading Society
Tennant, Alex. Esq. 46, Miller-st. Glasgow
Tennant, C. J. Esq. Cochrane-st. Glasgow
Tennant, John, Esq. St. Rollox-street, Glasgow
Tennant, Thos. Esq. Little Woodhouse, Leeds
Tennant, W. Esq. Kemp-town, Brighton
Tennent, J. E. Esq. *M.P.* The Lodge, Belfast
Tennent, Lieut.-Col. H. 10, Russell-place, Fitzroy-square

Tennent, Mr. John Robert, Dunchatten
TENTERDEN, Right Hon. Lord
Tetlow, John, Esq. Cannon-st. Manchester
Thackery, Rev. Geo. *D.D.* Provost of King's College, Cambridge
THANET, Right Hon. the Earl of
Thelwell, Richd. Esq. St. Ann's-square, Manchester
Thesiger, Frederick, Esq. 9, Montague-place, Bedford-square
Thick, Mr. Charles James, 3, Copthall-bdgs.
Thirkill, F. Esq.
Thiselton, Mr. J. Faversham
Thistlethwayte, Thos. Esq. Connaught-place
Thomas, Capt. White Ladies, Worcester
Thomas, Mr. C. J. Bungay, Suffolk
Thomas, Mr. David, R. Union-street, Dundee
Thomas, George, Esq. Truro
Thomas, J. C. Esq. Redcliff-street, Bristol
Thomas, John, Esq. 48, Upper, Harley-street
Thomas, R. G. Esq. 21, Lombard-street
Thomason, W. Esq. 15, Church-st. Manchester
Thompson, C. J. Esq. 9, Upper Phillimore-place, Kensington
Thompson, Chas. Esq. Huddersfield
Thompson, Fredk. Esq. 5, Brick-court, Temple
Thompson, Mr. George, Bookseller, Bury St. Edmund's. 15 Copies
Thompson, James, Esq. 22, George-street Hanover-square. 2 Copies
Thompson, Jas. Esq. 9, George-st. Minories
Thompson, John T. Esq. Paul's-wharf, Upper Thames-street
Thompson, Jonathan, Esq. 29, Church-street, Manchester
Thompson, P. B. Esq. *M.P.* 29, Berkeley, sq.
Thompson, Rev. Wm. 5, Canonbury-place, Islington
Thompson, Thos. Esq. Fawcet House, Bishop Wearmouth
Thompson, Mr. W. 14, Old Burlington-street
Thompson, W. Esq. *M.P.* Alderman of London
Thomson, Jas. T. Esq. Ravensdale, Isle of Man
Thomson, John, Esq. 33, Back King-street, Manchester
Thomson, Dr. John, *F.L.S.* Hermitage-place, St. John's-street-road
Thomson, Edmund, Esq. 92, Cannon-street, Manchester
Thomson, J. R. Esq. Clarence Club
Thomson, Robert, Esq. Edinburgh
Thorman, J. Esq. 8, Lawrence-pountney-hill
Thornborough, Captain, *R.N.* Clifton
Thornton, H. Esq. Lastington, Barnard Castle
Thornton, Robert, T. Esq. Barbadoes
Thornton, R. Esq. Beccles, Suffolk
Thornton, R. Esq. Old Swan, London-bridge
Thorold, H. Esq. Cuxwold, Lincolnshire
Thorowgood, W. Esq. Acre-lane, Brixton
Thorp, Rev. Mr. *A.M.* Topsham, Devon
Thorp, Saml. Esq. Cannon-street, Manchester
Thorp, Rev. Thos. *M.A.* Trinity College, Cambridge
Thorp, George, Esq. 10, Pinners' Hall
Threlfall, John, Esq. 6, New Market-street Manchester
Thring, John, Esq. Warminster
Thrower, S. Esq. Cambridge
Thurling, Mr. C. Bookseller, Carlisle
Thurnall, A. W. Esq. Cambridge
Thurnam, Mr. C. Bookseller, Carlisle. 2 Copies
Thurston, Simon, Esq. 9, Southampton-street, Bloomsbury-square
Thwaites, Henry, Esq. 39, Euston-square
Thwaites, Jos. Esq. Staples
Tice, W. Esq. Sopley, nr. Christchurch, Hants
Tichborne, Sir H. J. Bart. Tichborne Park, Hants
Tickner, Edward, Esq. Bride-lane, Fleet-street
Tielans, J. E. Esq. 147, Fenchurch-street
Tillard, R. H. Esq. St. John's College, Cambridge
Tillett, Mr. Alexander, York-terrace, York-road
Tilley, T. Harry, Esq. Falmouth
Tilson, Thomas. sen. Esq. Brixton-hill
Tilson, Tho. jun. Esq. 12, Finsbury-pl. South
Times Newspaper
Timothy, Mr. D. 31, Barbican
Tims, Mr. R. Moore, 85, Grafton-st. Dublin
Tinley, J. Esq. Dockray-square, Tynemouth
Tinling, Rear-Admiral Charles, Southampton
Tippet, Edward, Esq. Cambourne, Cornwall
Tippet, John, Esq. Pydar-street, Truro
Titley, Anthony, Esq. Leeds
Titley, Mr. Edward, Fountain-st. Manchester
Tobin, Capt. Geo. *R.N.* Teignmouth, Devon
Tobin, Sir John, Oak Hill, Liverpool
Tobin, Thomas, Esq. Bold-street, Liverpool
Tobin, Thos. Esq. Ballincollig, county Cork
Tod, Colonel, 16, Sussex-place, Regent's-pk.
Todd, A. Esq. Barnard Castle
Todd, Mr. Christopher, Bookslr. Scarborough
Todd, John, Esq. Wright-street, Hull
Todd, Lieut.-Col. 18, Sussex-pl. Regent's-pk.
Todd, Mr. York
Todd, Messrs. and Co. Cork
Todd, T. Esq. Twickenham Park, Middlesex
Todd, Mr. William, 11, Miller-street, Glasgow
Todd, W. Esq. Leeds
Toke, N. R. Esq. Godington Park, Kent
Toke, Nicolas, Esq. Dunmow, Essex
Tollemache, Vice-Admiral, J. R. D. 148, Piccadilly
Tolley, Mr. Wm. Tiverton
Tolson, J. S. Esq. Dalton, Yorkshire
Tomkins, B. Esq. 42, Upper Thames-street
Tomlin, James, Esq.
Tomlins, Jas. Thos. Esq. Hatton-garden
Tomlins, P. N. Esq. Painters' Hall, Queenhithe
Tomlinson, William, Esq. St. Helen's-place
Tomson, Richard, jun. Esq. Elms, Ramsgate
Tooke, Wm. Esq. *M.P. F.R.S. V.P.* Soc. Arts, &c. 12, Russell-square
Toone, W. S. Esq. 34, King-street, Holborn
Tootal & Gunthorpe, Messrs. Wakefield
Tootal, Thos. Esq. Oxford-road, Manchester
Topping, Chas. Esq. Maidstone
Torrens, Colonel, *M.P.* Woolwich
Tothill, Rich. Esq. Heavitree, near Exeter
Tothill, Wm. Esq. Redland, Bristol
Tottie, Charles, Esq. Gt St. Helens. 10 Copies
Tottie, Thos. Wm. Esq. Leeds
Tower, C. Esq. St. John's College, Cambridge
Towers, S. Esq. Angel Hotel, Dale-st. Liverpool
Towgood, Fredk. Esq. St. Neot's, Huntingdon
Towle, B. Esq. Borrowash House, near Derby
Towle, J. Esq. Borrowash Mill, near Derby
Town, John, Esq. Trinity-street, Leeds
Town, Joseph, Esq. Trinity-street, Leeds
Towncad, C. Esq. 6, Mosley-bdgs. Manchester
Townend, Robt. Esq. Fountain-st. Manchester
Townend, T. Esq. The Polygon, Manchester
Townend, Wm. Esq. Hightown, Huddersfield
Townend, William, Esq. Aldred-place, Salford, Lancashire
Townsend and Co. Messrs. Hull
Townsend, John, Esq. Nottingham
Townsend, Jos. Esq. Alveston, Stratford-on-Avon
Townsend, R. Esq. Speenhamland, Berks
Townsend, R. E. Esq. Doctors'-commons
Townsend, Mrs. Thomas, Penzance
Townsend, W. Esq. 9, Clarence-ter. Regent's-pk.
Townsend, Wm. Esq. Bread-st. Manchester
TOWNSHEND, Lord Charles
TRADE, Honourable the Board of
Trafford, Leigh, Esq. Manchester
Trafford, Thos. Jos. Esq. Trafford Park, near Manchester
Trapp, B. Esq. Clare Hall, Cambridge
Travers, Geo. F. Esq. Fairfield Lodge, near Exeter
Travis, Wm. H. Esq. East Bergholt, Suffolk
Trecothick, James, Esq. Broadstairs
Tregaskis, R. Esq. Perran-wharf, near Truro
Tregonwell, S. B. Esq. Bourne, Christchurch, Hants
Treherne, C. H. Esq. 134, Leadenhall-street
Treloar, Thomas, Esq. Truro
Tremlow, T. F. Esq. Christ Church, Oxford
Trentham, W. H. Esq. St. John's College, Cambridge
Trevenen, Miss Emily, Helston, Cornwall
Treuttel and Wurtz, Messrs. Paris
Tribe, Edward, Esq. 86, Great Russell-street
TRINITY HOUSE, Corporation of
TRINITY HOUSE; The Merchant Elder Brethren of, viz.
Capt. John Henry Pelly, Deputy Master
Capt. Abel Chapman
Capt. Sir John Woolmore, *K.C.H.*
Capt. Aaron Chapman, *M.P.*
Capt. Thomas Brown
Capt. Isaac Robinson
Capt. Andrew Timbrell
Capt. Daniel Stephenson
Capt. Edward Chapman Bradford
Capt. James Young
Capt. Robert Welbank
Capt. John Hayman
Capt. William Stanley Clarke
Capt. Richard Drew
Capt. John Rees
Capt. Henry Nelson
Capt. John Locke
Capt. Alexander Weynton
Capt. Charles Weller
Capt. Philip Ripley
Triscott, Commr. R. S. *R.N.* Dunstanville-terrace, Falmouth
Trotter, Alex. Esq. 17, Orchard-street
Trotter, Chas. Esq. Holmfirth, Huddersfield
Trotter, Sir Coutts, Bart. Grosvenor-square
Trotter, Capt. H. D. *R.N.* 17, Orchard-st.
Trotter, Miss, Epsom, Surrey
Troughton, Mr. Edward, 136, Fleet-street
Trowbridge Book Society
Trowell, Mrs. Thorn Hill, Derby
Trower, George, Esq. 13, Russell-square
Trueman, Michael, Esq. Hanging Ditch, Manchester
Trye, H. N. Esq. Leckhampton-ct. Gloucestershire
Tubbs, Robt. Esq. 14, George-st. Portman-sq.
Tuck, Rev. G. R. *M.A.* Emanuel College, Cambridge
Tucker, Chas. Esq. 28, Gloucester-place
Tucker, Capt. M. Gloucester-pl. Portman-sq.
Tucker, Rev. Chas. Baring-crescent, Heavitree, Exeter
Tucker, Wm. Esq. Ducie-place, Manchester

Tudor, E. E. Esq. St. Christopher's
Tudor, William, Esq. 6, Queen's-parade, Bath
Tuffell, Mr. J. Rochester
Tugwell, G. H. Esq. Crow Hall, Bath
TULLAMORE, Lord Viscount, *M.P.*
Tullet, Mr. J. T. 3, Palace-row, New-road
Tullock, Benj. Esq. Newcastle
Tupper, C. C. Esq. Isle of Man
Tupper, Mr. George, Hemel Hempstead
Tupper, John, C. Esq. Sands, Isle of Man
Turley, E. A. Esq. Worcester
Turnbull, Dr. A. 48, Russell-square
Turnbull, Mr. James, 60, Ingram-st. Glasgow
Turnbull, Wm. Esq. Hodson-sq. Manchester
Turner, Alfred, Esq. 32, Redlion-square
Turner, Charles, Esq. Norwich
Turner, Mr. Chas. Sun Hotel, Southampton
Turner, Col. *H.E.I.C.* Royal-ter. Edinburgh
Turner, Edwin, Esq. Stockport
Turner, Edw. Esq. Polgwynne, near Truro
Turner, Edwin, Esq. Hunslet-lane, Leeds
Turner, Dr. G. Stockport
Turner, Rev. Geo. Spelsbury, Oxon
Turner, Mr. H. Sevenoaks, Kent
Turner, J. Aspinale, Esq. Cross-st. Manchester
Turner, Mr. Matthew, Beverley. 3 Copies
Turner, Mr. Beverley
Turner, Ralph, Esq. Peel-street, Manchester
Turner, Samuel, Esq. Gray's-inn
Turner, Thos. Esq. St. Christopher's
Turner, Thos. Esq. Mosley-street, Manchester
Turner, W. Meryweather, Esq. 2, Brick-court, Temple
Turton, Sir Thos. Bart. 8, Lower Grosvenor-pl.
Tweedie, N. Esq. 37, Glassford-st. Glasgow
Tweedy, Robert, Esq. Redruth
Tweedy, W. M. Esq. Truro
Tweedy, William, Esq. Truro
Twells, John, Esq. 5, Highbury-pl. Islington
Twiss, George, J. Esq. Cambridge
Twiss, Travers, Esq. *M.A.* University College, Oxford
Twopenny, Edward, Esq. Rochester
Tyler, Adml. Sir Chas. *G.C.B.* Cottrell, Cardiff
Tyndall, Thomas, Esq. Fort, Bristol
Tynte, Colonel, *M.P. F.R.S.* Haswell House, Bridgewater
Tyrell, Edward, Esq. City Remembrancer, Guildhall
Tyrrell, Mr. Gerrard, Bookseller, 11, Lower Sackville-street, Dublin. 2 Copies
Tyrrell, J. Esq. Carlton Chambers, 8, Regent-st.
Tyrrell, John, Esq. Exeter
Tysoe, C. Esq. 9, New Cannon-st. Manchester
Tyssen, Saml. Esq. Narborough, Norfolk
Tytler, Col. Sam. 11, Melville-st. Edinburgh

U.

Uhthoff, Rev. Henry, Huntingfield, Suffolk
Underwood, C. Esq. 4, St. Michael's-terrace
Ungless, Mr. W. H. Eye
United Service Club (Junior), Charles-street, Regent-street
Unthank, Hugh, Esq. Market-st. Manchester
Unwin, Rev. Edw. Park-fields, near Derby
Upcher, A. Esq. Trinity College, Cambridge
Upfill, T. Esq. Birmingham
Uppleby, J. G. Esq. Park-lane, Leeds
Upton, Edmund, Esq. 39, Chapel-street, Grosvenor-place
Upton, George, Esq. Queen-street, Cheapside
Upward, Henry, Esq. 2, Great St. Helen's
Usill, Abraham, Esq. Wisbeach, Norfolk
Uttoxeter Permanent Library

V.

Vail, Aaron, Esq. 13, Old Cavendish-street
Vale, John, Esq. 7, Hertford-st. Mayfair
Valpy, Capt. A. B. *R.N.* Streatley, Berks
Van Baerle, Capt. at Messrs. Greenwood & Co.
Vandeleur, Major R. Weymouth, Dorset
Vandercom, J. F. Esq. 10, Mecklenburg-sq.
Van Zandt, Mrs. Netherday House, nr. Taunton
Van Zeller, F. J. Esq. 15, St. Helen's-place
Van Zeller, John, Esq. Liverpool
Varty, Mr. T. 4, Little Ormond-st. Queen-sq.
Varty, W. Esq. Bishopsgate-street
Vassall, Capt. Spencer, *R.N.* H.M.S. Harrier
Vattemare, Monsieur Alexandre, chez Mons. Rollin, Changeur au Palais Royal, 115, à Paris
Vaudry, John C. Esq. Stockport
Vaughan, Edw. T. Esq. Christ's Coll. Camb.
Vaughan, George. Esq. 10, Cumberland-ter.
Vaughan, Hugh, Esq. Crete Hill, Bristol
Vaughan, Rev. J. Gotham, Nottingham
Vaughan, Mrs. Eliz. 10, Cumberland-terrace
Venables, Chas. Esq. Woburn, nr. Gt. Marlow
Venables, William, Esq. Alderman of London
Vernon, Hon. Geo. J. *M.P.* 25, Walton-crescent
Vernon, Mrs. 15, Hereford-st. Oxford-street
Vicars, C. G. Esq. St. John's Coll. Cambridge
Vice, Mr. W. Bank-street, Leicester
Vice, William, Esq. Truro
Vickers, Jos. Esq. Clapham Park
Vidall, Robt. Studley, Esq. *F.S.A.* Cornboro' House, Devon
Vidler, Finch, Esq. Merrow, & 13, Millbank-row, Westminster
Vienna, Fürst Rasumowsky
Vienna, Royal Imperial Library of
Vieweg, Mr. F. Bookseller, Brunswick
Vignoles, Dr. Charles, Dublin Castle
Vigor, Wm. Esq. Basingstoke
VILLIERS, Lord Viscount, *M.P.*
Vincent, Capt. A. A. *R.N. K.H.* Walmer
Vincent, C. F. Esq. Albany-chamb. Piccadilly
Vincent, Geo. Giles, Esq. Sanctuary, Westminster Abbey
Vincent, Robt. Esq. 73, Basinghall-street
Vining, John, Esq. 3, Richmond Hill, Clifton
Vipan, Wm. Esq. Mepal, Cambridge
Virtue, Mr. G. Bookseller, 26, Ivy-lane, Paternoster-row
Vise, Joseph, Esq. Stilton
Vivian, Capt. *R.N.* Maidstone
Vivian, J. Ennis, Esq. *M.P.* Truro
Voight, Mr. Huddersfield
Vooght, Geo. Esq. Crimplesham, Norfolk
Vyse, Mr. Thos. Cripplegate-buildings

W.

Wackerbarth, Franz Diedrick, Esq. *B.A.* Corpus Christi College, Cambridge
Wade, Mr. James, Bradford, Yorkshire
Wade, Jos. Esq. 3, Rownham-place, Bristol
Wade, Mr. Joseph, Bradford, Yorkshire
Wadison, Robert, Esq. Austin Friars
Wadkin, Henry, Esq. 7, Short-st. Manchester
Waghorn, Lieut. T. *R.N.* Snodland, Kent
Wagstaff, J. Esq. Stalybridge
Wainwright, F. Arnold, Esq. Sidmouth
Wait, Charles, Esq. 3, Albion-place, Bristol
Wait, Emanuel, Esq. Gas-light Office, Bristol
Waite, Captain B. L. Packet Ship Pacific, Liverpool
Waite, William, Esq. Leeds
Waithman, J. Esq. 104, Fleet-street
Wakefield, F. Esq. 70, Old Broad-street
Wakefield New Book Society
——— Gentlemen's New Book Society
——— Subscription Library
Wakeling, H. W. 5, St. John's-sq. Clerkenwell
Wakeman, Sir Offley, Bart. Perdiswell Hall, Worcestershire
Walenn, Mr. William, 36, Great Portland-st.
Wales, John C. Esq. High-st. Manchester
Wales, Robert James, Esq. Wisbeach, Norfolk
Walford, A. Esq. Albion-bldgs. Manchester
Walker, Benjamin, Esq. Leeds
Walker, C. A. Esq. *M.P.* Belmont, Wexford
Walker, Chas. Esq. Ashford Court, Salop
Walker, Chas. Ludlow, Esq. Mayor of Bristol
Walker, Henry, Esq. Wakefield
Walker, J. F. Esq. Montagu-place, Poplar
Walker, Mr. James, 34, Glassford-st. Glasgow
Walker, John, Esq. Princess-st. Manchester
Walker, Miss, Granby-street, Leicester
Walker, Mrs. Berry Hill, Mansfield, Notts
Walker, Mrs. Peckham Grove, Worcester
Walker, P. Esq. Bungay, Suffolk
Walker, Rev. Thos. *M.A.* Christ Coll. Camb.
Walker, Thos. Esq. New Bailey-st. Manchstr.
Walker, Mr. Wm. Bookseller, 196, Strand. 8 Copies
Wall, Mr. F. H. Bookseller, Richmond, Surrey. 7 Copies
Wall, Col. Saml. Worthy Park, Winton, Hants
Waller, John, Esq. Stock Exchange
Waller, John, Esq. 21, Lincoln's-inn-fields
Wallis, Chas. E. Esq. 44, Gt. Marlborough-st
Wallis, John, Esq. Mayes-st. Manchester
Wallis, John, Esq. St. Petroc, Bodmin
Walmsley, Thomas, Esq. Mayor of Stockport
Walmsley, T. Esq. 30, Pall-mall, Manchester. 2 Copies
Walsh, Major-Gen. Anthony, 51, Cadogan-pl.
Walsh, Sir John, Bart. *M.P.* 28, Berkeley-sq.
Walsh, Percival, jun. Esq. Oxford
Walshman, Dr. Thomas, Kennington-common
Walter, George, Esq. 36, Cornhill
Walter, John, Esq. *M.P.* Bearwood, Berks
Walther, Mr. D. Bksellr. 42, Piccadilly. 2 Copies
Walton, B. Esq. Tettenhall, Wolverhampton
Walton, Mr. John, Bookseller, Shrewsbury
Walton, Mr. J. 20, Little Britain
Walton, Mr. W. 20, Little Britain
Wanchope, J. Esq. Trinity College, Cambridge
Warburton, Hugh, Esq. Swan-st. Manchester
Warcup & Sons, Messrs. Booksllrs. Deptford
Warcup, W. M. Esq. Dereham, Norfolk
Ward & Fisher, Messrs. Norwich
Ward, J. Esq. Holwood House, near Bromley
Ward, Saml. N. Esq. Hayes, near Bromley
Ward, T. E. Esq. The Lodge, Oswestry
Wardle, H. M. Esq. Priestlands, near Lymington
Ware Reading Society
Ware, Samuel, Esq. *F.S.A.* 34, Portland-place
Waring, Samuel, Esq. Stoke Bishop, Bristol
Warminster Book Society
Warneford, Rich. Esq. Field-court, Gray's-inn
Warner, Abraham, Esq. St. Christopher's
Warner, Mrs. Colonel, 46, Brompton-row
Warre, Thomas, Esq. 13, Cumberland-terrace
Warren, Augustus, Esq. 57, Great Russell-st.
Warren, Capt. C.B. Superintendent of His Majesty's Dock-yard, Woolwich

Warren, Mr. J. Bookseller, Royston.
Warren, Dr. P. *F.R.S.* 31, Lower Brook-st.
Warren, R. P. Esq. Trinity College, Cambridge
Warrington, W. H. Esq. Columbine House, Jersey
Warry, E. T. Esq. Lyndhurst, Hants
Warry, George, Esq. Sherborne, Dorset
Warwick Library
Warwick, W. S. Esq. 24, Russell-square
Washburn & Co. Messrs. Booksellers, Salisbury-square
Wason, Rigby, Esq. *M.P.* 2, Queen-square, Westminster
Wastell, William, Esq. 59, Burton-crescent
Waterfield, Richard, Esq. *B.D.* Fellow of Emanuel College, Cambridge
Waters, James, Esq. 1, Arthur-street, West, London-bridge
Waters, W. Esq. 1, Arthur-st. West,' London-bridge
Watford, Alex. Esq. Cambridge
Watkin, J. Esq. St. Ann's-sq. Manchester
Watkins, George, Esq. 22, Lincoln's-inn-fields
Watkins, O. V. Esq. Cannon-st. Manchester
Watkins, Mr. Thomas, 17, Cork-st. Bond-st.
Watkinstone, Mr. John, Rye-lane, Peckham
Watson, Miss Arabella, 3, Upper George-street
Watson, Dr. 63, St. Vincent-street, Glasgow
Watson, Sir F. B.
Watson, Hewitt Cotterell, Esq. Ditton-marsh, Surrey
Watson, Joseph, Esq. Wakefield
Watson, Mr. J. G. 21, South Hanover-street, Glasgow
Watson, Mr. Robert, Swinhar
Watson, R. L. Esq. 5, Saville-pl. Newcastle-on-Tyne
Watson, Thomas, Esq. 7, Aldermanbury
Watson, J. H. Esq. Silver-street, Hull
Watson, William, Esq. Ashley-place, Bristol
Wattley, George, Esq. St. Christopher's
Wattley, John, W. Esq. St. Christopher's
Watts, Jas. Esq. New Brown-st. Manchester
Watts, John, Esq. New Brown-st. Manchester
Watts, T. C. Esq. Cranbrook, Kent
Waude, Mr. John, Kent-road
Wayte, Samuel, Esq. 24, King's-sq. Bristol
Wayte, Mr. Thomas, Bookseller, Ashby-de-la-Zouch. 9 Copies
Webb, Mr. J. Fountain Inn, West Cowes
Webb, Miss, 13, Bedford-st. Bedford-sq.
Webb, Miss Susan, Clifton Down
Webb, Mr. Thomas, Bookseller, 43, Lower Sackville-street, Dublin. 3 Copies
Webb, Thomas, Esq. Dublin
Webbe, Joseph, Esq. Huddersfield
Webber, W. C. F. Esq. Oxford
Webster, Mr. Thomas, Lowgate, Hull
Webster, R. M. Esq. 149, Aldersgate-street
Webster, Rev. G. Mountjoy, Codford St. Mary Rectory, near Salisbury
Wedd, Richard, Esq. Maidstone
Weddon, William, Esq. Sheffield
Weeding, Thomas, Esq. 41, Mecklenburg-sq.
Weeks, H. Esq. 12, Cook's-ct. Lincoln's-inn
Weidmannsche, —, Buchhandlung, Leipzig
Welby, Sir W. E. Bart. Denton Hall, Lincsh.
Welch, Geo. Esq. 8, Canonbury-sq. Islington
Welch, George K. Esq. Christchurch, Hants
Welch, Dr. J. G. Maidstone
Welch, Joseph James, Esq. 7, Farringdon-st.
Weld, J. Esq. Lulworth Castle, Lymington
Weld, Humph. Esq. Chidcock House, Dorset
Weld, Samuel, Esq. 44, Welbeck-street

Welkin, Geo. Esq. Trinity Hall, Cambridge
Weller, George, Esq. 5, New-inn
WELLESLEY, Most Noble the Marquis
Wellesley, Hon. & Rev. Gerald Valerian, Prebendary of Durham
WELLINGTON, His Grace the Duke of
Wells, John, Esq. 2, Peel-st. Manchester
Wells, Reading Society of
Welsan, Andrew, Esq. 12, Forth-street, Leith
Welsh, David, Esq. 7, Northumb.-st. Edinb.
Welsh, J. H. Esq. 9, Gray's-inn-square
Welsh, John, Esq. 3, Maryland-st. Liverpool
Welshman, J. W. Esq. Mosley-st. Manchester
WENLOCK, Right Hon. Lord
Wentworth, W. Fitzwilliam, sen. Esq. *R.N.* Leith
Were, T. B. Esq. Richmond-terrace, Bristol
Werninck, H. Esq. Camberwell
West, J. W. Esq. 5, St. John's-street
West, T. Esq. Union Bank, Brighton
Westeley, Mr. F. C. Bookseller, 165, Strand
Western Literary and Scientific Institution, Leicester-square
Westhead, Edward, Esq. High-st. Manchester
Westhorp, Rev. S. M. Sibton Vicarage, Suffolk
Weston, H. Esq. Borough Bank, Southwark
Weston, James, Esq. Fenchurch-street
Weston, L. W. Esq. 24, Cross-st. Manchester
Weston, Mr. New Walk, Leicester
Weston, Warwick, Esq.
Wetenhall, Edwd. Esq. Glastonbury
Wetmore, W. Esq. Thornbury, Gloucestershire
Wetton, Mr. C. C. Library, Egham. 5 Copies
Wetton, Mr. R. Bookseller, Chertsey. 2 Copies
WEYMOUTH, Right Hon. Lord Viscount
Whaley, Rev. J. G. Witnesham, Suffolk
Whalley, John, jun. Esq. Swinegate, Leeds
Wharton, J. C. Esq. Christ's Coll. Cambridge
Wharton, Mr. Jas. Bugle-st. Southampton
Whately & Booth, Messrs. Booksellers, Halifax. 2 Copies
Whatman, Jas. Esq. Vinters, near Maidstone
Wheble, Jas. Esq. Woodley Lodge, Berks
Wheeler, Rev. Allen, Worcester
Wheeler, C. Esq. 28, Leadenhall-street
Wheeler, Jas. Esq. New Cannon-st. Manchstr.
Wheelhouse, W. Esq. Norwich
Wheelwright, G. Esq. Merton Coll. Oxford
Wheldon, G. Esq. Hurton Hill, near Hartlepool
Wheler, Sir T. Bart. Cross House, Torrington
Whichcord, John, Esq. Maidstone, Kent
Whinyates, Lieut.-Col. E. C. Royal Artillery, Woolwich
Whiskin, J. Esq. Ashby-st. Northampton-sq.
Whiston, R. Esq. *M.A. F.T.C. Camb.* Rochester
Whitacre, John, Esq. Woodhouse, Yorkshire
Whitbread, Lady Elizabeth, Grove House, Kensington Gore
Whitby, Major, Worcester
Whitby, Mrs. Newlands, near Lymington
White, Andrew, Esq. Bishop Wearmouth
White, Charles, Esq. 10, Lime-street
White, Mr. C. Bookslr. Doncaster. 18 Copies
White, Henry, Esq. Porters, Shenley
White, H. C. Esq. Hemel Hempstead
White, J. Esq. 39, Old Broad-street
White, Mr. Jas. South Frederick-st. Glasgow
White, John F. Esq. 13, South-sq. Gray's-inn
White, John, Esq. Doncaster
White, Mr. Joseph, East Cowes
White, Mr. P. Green Isle Steamer, Liverpool
White, Miss, Chevington, Suffolk
White, Richd. Esq. Fawcet-st. Bp. Wearmouth

White, Mr. T. Metis Dock, West Cowes
White, W. Esq. 153, St. Vincent-st. Glasgow
White, William, Esq. Blackfriars-road
White, William, Esq. Canterbury
Whitehead, John, Esq. Greek-street, Leeds
Whitehead, R. Esq. West Farleigh, Kent
Whitehead, Rev. Robert, Dock-yard, Chatham
Whitehouse, Richd. Esq. Castle-st. Holborn
Whitelock, John, Esq. 70, Aldermanbury
Whiting, Charles, Esq. Beaufort House, Strand. 2 Copies
Whiting, J. Esq. The Grove, Carshalton, Surrey
Whitling, H. Esq. 27, New Broad-street
Whitlow, J. Esq. 20, Market-pl. Manchester
Whitlow, Thos. Esq. 24, Ridgefield, Manchstr.
Whitmore, Aug. Esq. 11, Furnival's-inn
Whitmore, Frederick, Esq. 24, Lombard-street
Whitmore, W. L. Esq. 11, Bedford-row
Whitmore, H. Esq. Coldbath-square
Whitoff, Rev. Henry, Huntingfield, Suffolk
Whitrong, Thos Esq. St. Christopher's
Whitshed, Adml. Sir J. H. *G.C.B.* Holbrook Farm, Sussex
Whittaker & Co. Messrs. Ave-Maria-lane. 32 Copies
Whittuck, Saml. Esq. Hanham Hall, Gloucest.
Whitworth, John, Esq. St. James's-square, Manchester
Whowell, T. Esq. Mount Fort House, Barnsbury Park
Wickes, William, Esq. Aylsham, Norfolk
Wickham, Edw. Esq. Chatham, Kent
Wickham, H. Esq. Frinsbury, Kent
Wigan, A. Esq. Clave House, East Malling, Kent
Wiggett, Mr. James, 138, Drury-lane
Wight, Lieut. A. S. *R.N.* Dover
Wightwick, Mr. John, Tenterden, Kent
Wigley, Miss M. M. Shakenhurst, nr. Bewdley
Wigney, Isaac Newton, Esq. *M.P.* Brighton
Wilcocks, Jas. Esq. 4, Barnard's-inn, Holborn
Wilde, Mr. George, Neptune Hotel, Liverpool
Wilde, Mrs. Thomas, 69, Guildford-street
Wilder, T. B. S. Esq. Seven Oaks, Kent
Wilkie, D. Esq. *R.A.* 7, Terrace, Kensington
Wilkin & Fletcher, Messrs. Bksllrs. Norwich. 2 Copies
Wilkins, C. Esq. 18, York-crescent, Clifton
Wilkins & Son, Messrs. Booksellers, Derby
Wilkinson, Anthy. Esq. Coxhoe Hall, near Durham 2 Copies
Wilkinson, Edw. Esq. Blackheath
Wilkinson, H. Esq. 6, Euston Grove. 2 Copies
Wilkinson, Jas. Esq. Heaton-lane, Manchester
Wilkinson, John, Esq. East Parade, Leeds
Wilkinson, John, Esq. 50, Burton-crescent
Wilkinson, Lieut.-General, Durham
Wilkinson, Rev. M. Redgrave, Suffolk
Wilkinson, Rev. Mr. Rodwell, Weymouth
Wilkinson, Rev. T. Carlisle
Wilkinson, William, Esq. George's-court, Briggate, Leeds
Wilkinson, William, Esq. 53, Old Broad-st.
Wilkinson, William, Esq. Grove House, Sheffield
Wilks, John, Esq. *M.P.* Finsbury-square
Willans, P. & John, Esqrs. Leeds
Willcox, B. M. Esq. 46, Lime-street
Willert, P. F. Esq. 9, Police-st. Manchester
Willett, Henry, Esq. Norwich
Willett, W. J. Esq. 18, Essex-street, Strand
Williams, Adm. Sir T. Portsmouth Dock-yard
Williams, B. jun. Esq. Broughton Mill, Manchester

Williams, C. Esq. St. John's Coll. Cambridge
Williams, Charles, Esq. 19, Ely-place
Williams, Rev. Dr. College, Winchester
Williams, Edw. A. Esq. Bromley
Williams, Commander Edw. (R.) Twickenham
Williams, Mr. E. W. 3, Gerrard-street, Soho
Williams, George Arthur, Esq.
Williams, Mr. George, Bookseller, Stourport. 3 Copies
Williams, Mr. G. A. Bookseller, Cheltenham. 21 Copies
Williams, Colonel Henry, Falmouth
Williams, Henry, Esq. 37, Back, Bristol
Williams, Hyde, Esq. 110, Fenchurch-street
Williams, Isaac, Esq. Cottage-crescent, Bath
Williams, John, Esq. Cannon-st. Manchester
Williams, J. jun. Esq. Magdalen Coll. Camb.
Williams, J. Esq. London-rd. Mill, Manchstr.
Williams, John, Esq. Burncoose, near Truro
Williams, John, Esq. Pitmarston, Worcestersh.
Williams, John, Esq. Stock Exchange
Williams, Mr. J. Hibernia Steamer, Liverpool
Williams, L. W. Esq. Old Bailey, Ludgate-hill
Williams, Michael, Esq. Trevince, near Truro
Williams, Miss, Duffryn
Williams, Mr. Bookseller, Brecon
Williams, P. U. Esq. *M.P.* Haunch Wood House, Nuneaton
Williams, Philip, Esq. 15, Upper Bedford-pl.
Williams, R. Esq. *M.P.* 36, Grosvenor-square
Williams, R. D. Esq. Widcombe Villa, Clifton
Williams, R. E. Esq. Weston Grove, Thames-Ditton
Williams, Richard, Esq. Mayor of Penryn
Williams, Stephen T. Esq. Truro
Williams, Thos. Esq. Lyncombe House, Bath
Williams, Wm. Esq. Tregullow, Cornwall
Williams, Wm. Paul, Esq. Penryn
Williamson, H. H. Esq. Greenway Bank, High Sheriff of Staffordshire
Williamson, John, Esq. 3, Raymond-bldgs.
Williamson, Joshua, Esq. 5, Nicholas-lane
Williamson, Walter, Esq. St. Christopher's
Willis, —, Esq. Vicar's Hill Cottage, Lymington
Willis, George, Esq. 18, St. James's-street
Willis, Messrs. James & William, Thatched House, St. James's-street
Willmore, Mr. J. T 23, Polygon, Somers Town
WILLOUGHBY DE ERESBY, Right Hon. Lord
Willoughby, Mr. Francis, Midshipman, H.M.S. Caledonia
Willoughby, Mr. James, Midshipman, H.M.S. Magicienne
Willoughby, Capt. Sir N. *R.N.*
Willoughby, Jos. Esq. Cheetwood, Manchester
Willmott, J. A. Esq. Rochester
Willyams, Humphrey, Esq. Truro
Wilman, Hon. Mrs. Pounsford Park, Somerset
Wilmot, Sir Robert, Bart. Brighton
Wilne Society, near Derby
Wilson, Mr. Adam, Aston-street, Glasgow
Wilson, Sir Alexander, 45, Pulteney-st. Bath
Wilson & Co. Messrs. Booksellers, Halifax 2 Copies
Wilson, Rev. Daniel, Islington
Wilson, Rev. Dr. Southampton
Wilson, Lieut. Gen. Alexander, St. Petersburg
Wilson, G. Esq. 3, Pall-mall, Manchester
Wilson, G. St. V. Esq. Redgrave Hall, Suffolk
Wilson, George, Esq. Monmouth
Wilson, Sir Giffin, *F.R.S.* 2, Stratford-place
Wilson, Mr. E. Bookseller, Royal Exchange. 2 Copies
Wilson, Henry, Esq. Stowlangtoft Hall, near Bury, Suffolk
Wilson, Henry, Esq. 66, Guildford-street
Wilson, Mr. J. Hawkhurst, Kent
Wilson, Mr. Isaac, Bookseller, Hull. 5 Copies
Wilson, J. Esq. 53, St. John's-st. Clerkenwell
Wilson, J. A. Esq. 13, Coventry-street
Wilson, Mr. James W. Louth
Wilson, John, Esq. Sheffield
Wilson, John J. Esq. 25, Northampton-square
Wilson, John B. Esq. Southborough, Tunbridge Wells
Wilson, John, Esq. Hunslet-lane, Leeds
Wilson, Josiah, Esq. Stamford-hill
Wilson, Miss, Belmont, Leeds
Wilson, Mrs. Highfield, near Sheffield
Wilson, R. H. Esq. 61, King's-st. Manchester
Wilson, Rev. Robert, Ashwelsthorpe
Wilson, Rev. R. Otway, St. Paul's, Poole, Dorsetshire
Wilson, Robt. Esq. Albion Hotel, Manchester
Wilson, Samuel, Esq. Alderman of London
Wilson, Mr. Thos. Trentham-street, Liverpool
Wilson, Sir T. M. Bart. Charlton, Kent
Wilson, T. Esq. Edgerton Lodge, Huddersfield
Wilson, Thos. Esq. Dulwich-place, Dulwich
Wilson, Wm. Jas. Esq. Mosley-st. Manchester
Wilson, W. W. Carus, Esq. Casterton Hall, Westmorland
WILTON, Right Hon. the Earl of
Winby, Mr. William, 16, Price-st. Liverpool
WINCHESTER, Right Rev. Lord Bishop of
Windey, Nathan, Esq. 24, Park-street, Bristol
Windham, J. S. Esq. 26, Brunswick-terrace, Brighton
Windlesham Book Society
Windsor, John, Esq. Piccadilly, Manchester
Windus, J. Esq. 8, Heathcote-street, Mecklenburg-square
Wing, Charles, Esq. 22, Aberdeen-place, Maida-hill
Wingate, Mr. A. Royal Exchange-sq. Glasgow
Wingate, Mr. Andrew, Queen-street, Glasgow
Wingrove, Col. G.P. *R.M.* Unity-pl. Woolwich
Winnington, Sir T. E. Bart. *M.P.* Stanford-court, Worcestershire
Winnys, Jas. Esq. Leith
Winstanley, Jas. jun. Esq. 1, George-street, Newcastle-on-Tyne
Wintelar, G. Esq. 6, Broad-street-buildings
Winter, C. Esq. Watt's House, near Taunton
Winter, T. W. Esq. 24, Cannon-pl. Brighton
Winterborn, Benj. Esq. Cambridge
Winterbottom, John Kenyon, Esq. Stockport
Wintle, J. Esq. 14, Lansdown-crescent, Bath
Wintle, Thomas, Esq. Clare-street, Bristol
Wintle, Rev. Thos. *B.D.* St. John's Coll. Oxfd.
Winwood, John, Esq. Clifton, Bristol
Wire, David, Esq. 30, St. Swithin's-lane
Wisbeach Literary Society
Wise, Bulinglield, Esq. Thornham, Kent
Witham, Henry, T. Main, Esq. Lartington, near Barnard's Castle
Wither, Rev. H. J. Bigg, Worting Rectory, Basingstoke
Withers, W. Esq. Church House, Holt
Withington, Jas. Esq. Pendleton, Manchester
Withnall, J. Esq. 23, Cannon-st. Manchester
Wix, William, Esq. *F.R.S.* Tunbridge Wells
Wolff, A. J. Esq. Greenhays, Manchester
Wolff, Mr. James, Southampton
Wolrige, Capt. Wm. *R.N.* Lympston, Devon
Wolstenholme, J. H. Esq. Huddersfield
Wolverhampton Library
Wombwell, G. Esq. 15, George-st. Hanover-sq
Wood, C. Esq. Brazennose-street, Mancheser.
Wood, C. Esq. *M.P.* 3, Richmond-terrace, Whitehall
Wood, Cornelius, Esq. King-st. Manchester
Wood, David, Esq. Dinham, Ludlow
Wood, Mrs. Elizabeth, Canterbury
Wood, Geo. Esq. Wood Lodge, Hockering, Norfolk
Wood, George, Esq. High-st. Manchester
Wood, Hy. Orme, Esq. St. John's Coll. Camb.
Wood, Hamilton, Esq. Fountain-st. Manchsr.
Wood, Rev. Dr. J. Master of St. John's Coll. Cambridge
Wood, Mr. J. Bookseller, Market Harborough. 5 Copies
Wood, J. N. Esq. 59, Faulkner-st. Liverpool
Wood, J. Esq. Falcon-street, Aldersgate
Wood, J. Esq. St. Bartholomew's Hospital
Wood, John, jun. Esq. Woodbridge, Suffolk
Wood, J. F. Esq. Caan Park, near Edinburgh
Wood, James, Esq. High-street, Manchester
Wood, Jno. Esq. Meltham Mills, Huddersfield
Wood, John, Esq. Dalton, Yorkshire
Wood, John, Esq. Friday-street, Manchester
Wood, Johnson, Esq. Aldersgate-street
Wood, Mrs. Chestham, Sussex
Wood, Messrs. P. & C. Leith
Wood N. Esq. Pebor, Carmarthenshire
Wood, R. Esq. Heartly-place, Old Kent-road
Wood, Rev. Thos. Ashford, Kent
Wood, Thomas, Esq. Lowestoff, Suffolk
Wood, Thomas F. Esq. Stowmarket, Suffolk
Wood, Rev. William, Staple Grove, Taunton
Woodall, George, Esq. York
Woodbridge, Jas. Esq. Wateringbury, Kent
Woodburn, A. Esq. 57, Mill-street, Glasgow
Woodburn, Allen, Esq. 112, St. Martin's-lane
Woodburn, Mrs. Hendon, Middlesex
Woodburn, Samuel, Esq. 112, St. Martin's-la.
Woodburn, Wm. Esq. Terregles Banks, Dumfries
Woodcock, Henry, Esq. St. Christopher's
Woodcock, Miss, Barburne House, Worcestersh.
Woodcroft, Rupert, Esq. New Cannon-street, Manchester
Woodhead, Geoffery, Esq. Cateaton-st. Mnchstr.
Woodhouse, Thomas Theakstone, Esq. 26, Wood-street, Cheapside
Woodhouse, John, Esq. Ashby-de-la-Zouch
Woodhouse, Capt. Thos. 13, Goree Piazzas, Liverpool
Woodhouse, W. H. Esq. Ashby-de-la-Zouch
Woodlark and Adamson, Messrs. Leith
Woodriffe, Captain, *R.N.* Greenwich Hospital
Woodruffe, J. Esq. Ashton-under-Lyne
Woods, Mrs. Balladoole, Isle of Man
Woods, P. Esq. 24, Lord-street, Liverpool
Woods, William, Esq. Furnival's-inn Hotel
Woodthorpe, Henry, Esq. *LL.D. F.S.A.* Town Clerk of London
Woolbright, John, Esq. Bold-street, Liverpool
Woolcombe, Hy. Esq. Recorder of Plymouth
Woollaston, Miss Kath. Hyde, Eltham
Wooller, William, Esq. Stockport
Woolley, J. Esq. Denmark-hill, Camberwell
Woolley, Rear-Adml. I. 11, Camden-pl. Bath
Woolley, William, Esq. Stock Exchange
Woolterton, J. Esq. 7, Euston-place, New-rd.
Woolwich Division of Royal Marines.
WORCESTER, Right Rev. Lord Bishop of. 2 Copies
Wordsworth, Joshua, Esq. Leeds
Workman, M. Esq. Basingstoke

Wormald, Mr. R. 6, Broad-street buildings
Wormald, Thomas, Esq. 42, Bedford-row
Worms, S. B. Esq. Stock Exchange
Worrall, George, Esq. Frenchay
Worsley, Charles C. Esq. Winster, Derby
Worsley, Rev. H. *LL.D.* Field House, Newport
Worsley, Rear-Adml. R. Stainton, Woodhouse
Wotton, Mr. Richard, King's Langley
Wrangham, W. Esq. Epsom, Surrey
Wren, Major James, Raleigh, Devon
Wrexham Book Society
Wright, Colonel, Lympston, Devon
Wright, Mr. C. N. Bookseller, Nottingham. 10 Copies
Wright, Rev. C. L. Newington, near Sittingbourne
Wright, E. Esq. Oriel College, Oxford
Wright, Mr. Edgar, at Mr. Neron's, Bapaume, Rouen
Wright, Rev. G. Bilham House, near Doncaster
Wright, Griffith, Esq. Mayor of Leeds
Wright, Henry, C. Esq. 40, Tavistock-street, Covent-garden
Wright, J. Esq. 225, St. Vincent-st. Glasgow
Wright, J. Smith, Esq. Rempstone Hall, Notts
Wright, John, Esq. Itchen Ferry, Southampton
Wright, John, Esq. Lenton House, Nottingham
Wright, Mr. John, 106, Crawford-street
Wright, Marcus, Esq. Trinity Coll. Cambridge
Wright & Sons, Messrs. Royal Colonnade, Brighton
Wright, Miss, Frogmore
Wright, Mr. Richard, High-street, Leicester
Wright, Wm. Esq. 109, Cannon-st. Manchester
Wright, William, Esq. Stockport
Wrightson and Webb, Messrs. Booksellers, Birmingham. 15 Copies
Wyatt, Edward, Esq. Lichfield
Wyatt, Rev. C. F. Broughton, near Banbury
Wycombe Literary Society
Wycombe, Mrs. Phœbe, Bookseller, Maidstone
Wyld, J. H. Esq. 83, Redcliff-street, Bristol
Wyld, W. H. Esq. 83, Redcliff-street, Bristol
Wyld, C. E. Esq. Magdalen Coll. Cambridge
Wyllie, R. C. Esq. 4, Hertford-st. May Fair
Wyndham, Rev. Dr. Hinton, near Christchurch, Hants
Wynham, Chas. Esq. Donhead Hall, Wilts
Wynn, Sir Watkin W. Bart. *M.P.* 2 Copies
Wynne, Colonel, Carthwyn, Denbighshire
Wynne, Wm. Esq.
Wynter, Rev. Dr. President of St. John's College, Oxford
Wythe, John, Esq. Eye, Suffolk

Y.

YARBOROUGH, Right Hon. Lord, 2 Copies
Yard, A. C. Esq. Harcourt-buildings, Temple
Yard, G. B. Esq. Trinity College, Cambridge
Yarde, G. H. Esq. Topsham, Devon
Yarmouth Book Club
Yarrow, Mr. N. 42, King-street, Snow-hill
Yates, Chas. Esq. 103, St. John-street
Yates, E. Esq. Fairlawn, near Seven Oaks
Yates, T. L. Esq. Lime-street-square
Yates, James, Esq. Byrom-street, Manchester
Yates, Mr. J. Bookseller, 118, Grafton-street, Dublin. 2 Copies
Yates, Mrs. Mary, Star Hotel, Manchester
Yates, Richd. Esq. Bread-street, Manchester
Yates, R. V. Esq. Brunswick-st. Liverpool
Yates, S. Esq. 16, Bury-street, St. Mary-axe
Yates, Dr. Thomas, Brig
Yates, Wm. Esq. Hoole Hall, Chester
Yeates, Rev. Wm. Collumpton, Devon
Yeatman, Rev. H. F. Stock House, Dorset
Yeats, Dr. G. D. Tunbridge Wells
Yeats, Jno. Esq. 26, St. Ann's-st. Manchester
Yelverton, Honourable W. H.
Yewens, Wm. Esq. 6, Pinners' Hall, Broad-st.
Yonge, Dr. James, Plymouth
Yonge, Rev. C. Swaffham, Norfolk
YORK, The Rev. the Dean of
York, Simon, Esq. Erthig, Denbighshire
—— Philosophical Institution
—— Select Library
——, The Recorder of
Youell, Edw. Esq. Great Yarmouth
Young, Archd. Esq. Bank-court, Glasgow
Young, Edw. Esq. Hawkhurst, Kent
Young, F. Esq. 13, Bedford-place
Young, G. A. Esq. 2, Upper Portland-place
Young, G. W. Esq. 2, Canonbury-sq. Islington
Young, Geo. Fred. Esq. *M.P.* Limehouse
Young, George, Esq. 27, Mark-lane
Young, Mr. George, Queen's-street, Glasgow
Young, John, Esq. St. Thomas-st. Winchester
Young, Thomas, Esq. Northumberland-square, Tynemouth
Younge, Mr. George R. 163, Ingram-st. Glasgow
Younger, R. B. Esq. Woodlands, Guernsey
Yuile, Mr. David, 40, Miller-street, Glasgow
Yule, Major Wm. 31, Regent-ter. Edinburgh
Zachary, M. M. Esq. 5, Royal Adelphi-terrace
Zeitter, Mr. J. F. 5, New Cavendish-street
Zuoler, Frederick, Esq. Consul for Belgium

WHITING, BEAUFORT HOUSE, STRAND.

OMISSIONS.

Adderley, C. B. Esq. Christ's College, Oxford
Barwise, Captain John, Whitehaven
Bellas, Rev. S. *A.M.* Queen's College, Oxford
Butterworth, Joseph, Esq. Cross-street, Manchester
Dilke, Charles Wentworth, Esq. 9, Lower Grosvenor-place
Eastwick, E. Esq. Merton College, Oxford
Elwes, D. Esq. Barton, Lincolnshire
Grimes, E. Esq. Oriel College, Oxford
Hall, John, Esq. Breezer's-hill, Ratcliff
Lister, Miss, Shibden Hall, near Halifax
Luscombe, E. K. Esq. Christ's College, Oxford
Rose, Rev. Mr. Kirk-colm, Wigtonshire
SELKIRK, Right Hon. the Earl of. 2 Copies
Scott, J. jun. Esq. 80, Old Broad-street
WALDEGRAVE, Right Hon. the Earl

ERRATA.

Ainslie, John, Esq. Waverton	*read* Ainslie, John, Esq. Wavertree
Baker, H. Shenstone, Esq.	— Baker, H. Sherstone, Esq.
Benham, Mr. W. A. 65, Strand	— Benham, Mr. W. A. 52, Lamb's Conduit-street
Beresford, T. B. Esq.	— Beresford, J. B. Esq.
Blackbourne, E. Esq.	— Blackmore, E. Esq.
Butterworth, J. A. Esq.	— Butterworth, S. A. Esq.
Colson, Rev. W. Piddlehinton	— Colson, Rev. J. M. Piddle Hinton
Copeland, Thomas, Esq. *M.P.*	— Copeland, W. T. Esq. *M.P.* Lord Mayor of London. 57 Copies
Courteney, Charles Leslie, Esq.	— Courtenay, Charles Leslie, Esq.
D'Urban, Captain, W.D. *R.N.* Warminster	— D'Urban, Captain W. *R.N. L.L.D. F.R.A.S.* Warminster
Gouldsborough, John, Esq.	— Gouldesborough, John, Esq.
Hargreaves, W. Esq. Woodhouse-lane, Leeds	— Brunswick-place, Leeds
Hewsworth, Henry H. Esq.	— Hemsworth, Henry W. Esq.
Humphreys, J. Esq.	— Humphries, J. Esq.
Kershaw, Mrs. Leeds	— Kirshaw, Mrs. Leeds.
Patrickson, Lieut. Col. W. G.	— Patrickson, Lieut. Col. W. E.
Pole, Sir J. W. Bart.	— Pole, Sir T. W. Bart.
Pountney, J. D. Esq. Fresford Villa	— Freshford Villa
Trafford, Thomas Joseph, Esq.	— Trafford, Thomas James, Esq.
Wheler, Sir T. Bart.	— Wheeler, Sir Trevor, Bart.

Zeitfracht Medien GmbH
Ferdinand-Jühlke-Straße 7
99095 Erfurt, Deutschland
produktsicherheit@kolibri360.de